T4-AEC-130

DATE DUE			
5/17/01			
12/10/12			

Demco No. 62-0549

F. Scott Fitzgerald
Critical Assessments

Fitzgerald in 1921. Photograph from a private collection.

F. SCOTT FITZGERALD
Critical Assessments

◆

Edited by
Henry Claridge

VOLUME II
Early Writings, *This Side of Paradise*,
The Beautiful and Damned, *The Vegetable*,
and *The Great Gatsby*

HELM INFORMATION

Selection and editorial matter
© 1991 Helm Information Ltd
Helm Information Ltd
The Banks, Mountfield,
Near Robertsbridge, East Sussex TN32 5JY

ISBN 1-873403-02-X

A CIP catalogue record for this book
is available from the British Library.

All rights reserved: No reproduction, copy
or transmission of this publication may be
made without written permission.

No paragraph of this publication may be
reproduced, copied or transmitted save
with written permission or in accordance
with the provisions of the Copyright Act
1956 (as amended), or under the terms of
any licence permitting limited copying
issued by the Copyright Licensing Agency,
7 Ridgmount Street, London WC1E 7AE.

Any person who does any unauthorised act
in relation to this publication may be liable
to criminal prosecution and civil claims for
damages.

Frontispiece: Fitzgerald in 1921. Photograph
from a private collection.

Typeset by Leaper & Gard Ltd, Bristol, England
Printed and bound by Hartnolls, Bodmin

Contents

VOLUME II:
Early Writings, *This Side of Paradise*, *The Beautiful and Damned*, *The Vegetable* and *The Great Gatsby*

Early Writings

39	ALAN MARGOLIES, Introduction to *F. Scott Fitzgerald's St Paul Plays, 1911–1914*, Princeton, 1978	1
40	JOHN KUEHL, Introduction to *The Apprentice Fiction of F. Scott Fitzgerald*, New Brunswick, New Jersey, 1965	8
41	DONALD A. YATES, 'The Road to *Paradise*: Fitzgerald's Literary Apprenticeship', *Modern Fiction Studies*, Spring 1961	19
42	MARIUS BEWLEY, 'Scott Fitzgerald: The Apprentice Fiction', *Masks and Mirrors*, London, 1970	32

This Side of Paradise (1920)

43	HEYWOOD BROUN, 'Paradise and Princeton', *New York Tribune*, 11 April 1920	39
44	ANONYMOUS REVIEW, 'A Remarkable Young American Writer', *New York Evening Post*, 17 April 1920	41
45	ROBERT C. BENCHLEY, 'Books and Other Things', *New York Morning World*, 21 April 1920	43
46	MARGARET EMERSON BAILEY, 'A Chronicle of Youth by Youth', *The Bookman*, June 1920	46
47	H.L. MENCKEN, 'Books More or Less Amusing', *Smart Set*, August 1920	48
48	FRANCES NEWMAN, 'Carnegie Library Notes', *Atlanta Constitution*, 13 February 1921	49
49	SY KAHN, '*This Side of Paradise*: The Pageantry of Disillusion', *Midwest Quarterly*, January 1966	52

50 JAMES W. TUTTLETON, 'The Presence of Poe in *This Side of Paradise*', *English Language Notes*, June 1966   64

The Beautiful and Damned (1922)

51 HENRY SEIDEL CANBY, 'The Flapper's Tragedy', *Literary Review of the New York Evening Post*, 4 March 1922   71
52 JOHN PEALE BISHOP, 'Mr. Fitzgerald Sees the Flapper Through', *New York Herald*, 5 March 1922   74
53 VIVIAN SHAW (GILBERT SELDES), 'This Side of Innocence', *The Dial*, April 1922   78
54 H.L. MENCKEN, 'Fitzgerald and Others', *Smart Set*, April 1922   81
55 ZELDA SAYRE (ZELDA FITZGERALD), 'Friend Husband's Latest', *New York Tribune*, 2 April 1922   83
56 MARY M. COLUM, 'Certificated, Mostly', *The Freeman*, 26 April 1922   86
57 SERGIO PEROSA, '*The Beautiful and Damned*', *The Art of F. Scott Fitzgerald*, Ann Arbor, 1965   88
58 RICHARD ASTRO, '*Vandover and the Brute* and *The Beautiful and Damned*: A Search for Thematic and Stylistic Reinterpretations', *Modern Fiction Studies*, Winter 1968   97
59 ROBERT ROULSTON, '*The Beautiful and Damned*: The Alcoholic's Revenge', *Literature and Psychology*, 1977   113
60 WAYNE C. WESTBROOK, *Wall Street in the American Novel*, New York, 1980   122

The Vegetable; or From President to Postman (1923)

61 JOHN F. CARTER JR., 'Scott Fitzgerald's Play', *Literary Review of the New York Evening Post*, 23 June 1923   129
62 ANONYMOUS REVIEW, 'New Comedy at Shore', *Philadelphia Evening Bulletin*, 20 November 1923   131
63 HENRY DAN PIPER, from *F. Scott Fitzgerald: A Critical Portrait*, London, 1965   132
64 CHARLES SCRIBNER III, Introduction to *The Vegetable*, New York, 1976   137

The Great Gatsby (1925)

65 F. SCOTT FITZGERALD, Introduction to *The Great Gatsby*, New York, 1934   147
66 MAXWELL PERKINS, 'Letter to F. Scott Fitzgerald' (20 November 1924), *Editor to Author: The Letters of Maxwell Perkins*, New York, 1950   150

67	LAURENCE STALLINGS, 'The First Reader—Great Scott', *New York World*, 22 April 1925	153
68	H.L. MENCKEN, 'As H.L.M. Sees It', *Baltimore Evening Sun*, 2 May 1925	156
69	WALTER YUST, 'Jazz Parties on Long Island—But F. Scott Fitzgerald is Growing Up', *New York Evening Post Literary Review*, 2 May 1925	160
70	WILLIAM ROSE BENÉT, 'An Admirable Novel', *Saturday Review of Literature*, 9 May 1925	163
71	CARL VAN VECHTEN, 'Fitzgerald on the March', *The Nation*, 20 May 1925	166
72	EDITH WHARTON, 'Letter to F. Scott Fitzgerald' (8 June 1925), *The Letters of Edith Wharton*, New York, 1988	168
73	GILBERT SELDES, 'Spring Flight', *The Dial*, August 1925	170
74	T.S. ELIOT, 'Letter to F. Scott Fitzgerald' (31 December 1925), New York, 1945	173
75	GILBERT SELDES, 'New York Chronicle', *New Criterion*, January 1926	174
76	ANONYMOUS REVIEW, 'New Novels—*The Great Gatsby*', *Times Literary Supplement*, 18 February 1926	176
77	L.P. HARTLEY, 'New Fiction', *Saturday Review*, 20 February 1926	178
78	CONRAD AIKEN, '*The Great Gatsby*', *New Criterion*, October 1926	179
79	PETER QUENNELL, '*The Great Gatsby*', *New Statesman and Nation*, 1 February 1941	180
80	G. THOMAS TANSELLE AND JACKSON R. BRYER, '*The Great Gatsby*: A Study in Literary Reputation', *New Mexico Quarterly*, Winter 1963	181
81	BRUCE HARKNESS, 'Bibliography and the Novelistic Fallacy', *Studies in Bibliography*, 1958	195
82	DOUGLAS TAYLOR, '*The Great Gatsby*: Style and Myth', *University of Kansas City Review*, Autumn 1953	209
83	R.W. STALLMAN, 'Gatsby and the Hole in Time', *Modern Fiction Studies*, November 1955	220
84	ROBERT ORNSTEIN, 'Scott Fitzgerald's Fable of East and West', *College English*, December 1956	240
85	W.J. HARVEY, 'Theme and Texture in *The Great Gatsby*', *English Studies*, February 1957	247
86	JOHN HENRY RALEIGH, 'F. Scott Fitzgerald's *The Great Gatsby*: Legendary Bases and Allegorical Significances', *University of Kansas City Review*, October 1957	256
87	RICHARD CHASE, '*The Great Gatsby*', *The American Novel and Its Tradition*, New York, 1957	261

88	J.S. WESTBROOK, 'Nature and Optics in *The Great Gatsby*', *American Literature*, March 1960	265
89	A.E. DYSON, '*The Great Gatsby*: Thirty-Six Years After', *Modern Fiction Studies*, Spring 1961	270
90	PAUL LAUTER, 'Plato's Stepchildren, Gatsby and Cohn', *Modern Fiction Studies*, Winter 1963	282
91	KENNETH E. EBLE, 'The Craft of Revision: *The Great Gatsby*', *American Literature*, November 1964	290
92	LEO MARX, from *The Machine in the Garden: Technology and the Pastoral Ideal in America*, New York, 1964	300
93	E. FRED CARLISLE, 'The Triple Vision of Nick Carraway', *Modern Fiction Studies*, Winter 1965	307
94	VICTOR A. DOYNO, 'Patterns in *The Great Gatsby*', *Modern Fiction Studies*, Winter 1966	316
95	JOHN W. ALDRIDGE, 'The Life of Gatsby', *Time to Murder and Create*, New York, 1966	327
96	DAVID L. MINTER, 'Dream, Design, and Interpretation in *The Great Gatsby*', *Twentieth Century Interpretations of "The Great Gatsby": A Collection of Critical Essays*, Englewood Cliffs, New Jersey, 1968	343
97	BRIAN M. BARBOUR, '*The Great Gatsby* and the American Past', *Southern Review*, Winter 1973	350
98	RON NEUHAUS, '*Gatsby* and the Failure of the Omniscient "I"', *Denver Quarterly*, Spring 1977	359
99	ARNOLD WEINSTEIN, 'Fiction as Greatness: The Case of *Gatsby*', *Novel*, Fall 1985	369
100	GEOF COX, 'Literary Pragmatics: A New Discipline. The Example of Fitzgerald's *The Great Gatsby*', *Literature and History*, Spring 1986	387
101	DAN McCALL, '"The Self-Same Song that Found a Path": Keats and *The Great Gatsby*', *American Literature*, November 1970	406
102	NORMAN FRIEDMAN, 'Versions of Form in Fiction—*Great Expectations* and *The Great Gatsby*', *Accent*, Autumn 1954	415
103	EDWARD VASTA, '*Great Expectations* and *The Great Gatsby*', *The Dickensian*, September 1964	432
104	ROBERT ROULSTON, 'Traces of *Tono-Bungay* in *The Great Gatsby*', *Journal of Narrative Technique*, Winter 1980	439
105	R.W. STALLMAN, 'Conrad and *The Great Gatsby*', *Twentieth Century Literature*, April 1955	447
106	ROBERT EMMET LONG, '*The Great Gatsby* and the Tradition of Joseph Conrad: Part I', *Texas Studies in Literature and Language*, Summer 1966	456

107 ROBERT EMMET LONG, '*The Great Gatsby* and the Tradition of Joseph Conrad: Part II', *Texas Studies in Literature and Language*, Fall 1966   474
108 GARY SCRIMGEOUR, 'Against *The Great Gatsby*', *Criticism*, Winter 1966   489

Early Writings

39
Introduction to
F. Scott Fitzgerald's St Paul Plays, 1911–1914

◆

ALAN MARGOLIES

ON AUGUST 8 and 9, 1911, in St. Paul, Minnesota, at the St. Paul Academy, then on Dale Street and Portland Avenue, a group of young friends who lived in the Summit Avenue area presented a theatrical performance for the benefit of the city's Protestant Orphan Asylum. A brief curtain raiser, *A Pair of Lunatics*, starring two of the youngsters, Dorothy Greene and Scott Fitzgerald (who would celebrate his fifteenth birthday the next month), was followed by magic tricks performed by a third youngster, Gustave Schurmeier. This, in turn, was followed by the major attraction, John Madison Morton's *A Regular Fix*, a comedy with a cast of ten including Fitzgerald in a minor role.

The group quickly grew to some forty members and soon was the Elizabethan Dramatic Club, named—according to a news clipping in Fitzgerald's scrapbook in Princeton University Library—for its "directress," Elizabeth Clay Rogers Magoffin, who had just turned twenty that previous March. Attorney Samuel McAfee Magoffin, her father, claimed two governors of Kentucky as ancestors, and her mother, Elizabeth Moran Rogers Magoffin, could boast of such distinguished forebears as Thomas Dudley, first governor of Massachusetts, Henry Clay, and George Rogers Clark. The Magoffin home, at 540 Summit, was less than two blocks from the Academy and not much further in a slightly different direction from Holly Avenue where the Fitzgeralds lived from 1909 to 1914. When the novelist's family finally moved to Summit Avenue, first to 593 in 1914 and then to 599 in 1918 ("In a house below the average / Of a street above the average," he was to write),[1] they were just a block or so away from the Magoffins. But Fitzgerald's association in the drama club with Elizabeth

SOURCE *F. Scott Fitzgerald's St Paul Plays, 1911–1914*, Princeton University Library, 1978, pp. 3–10.

Clay Rogers Magoffin was, so far as is known, the only major link between the two families.

It was in the Magoffin home in August, 1911, that the Elizabethan Dramatic Club, during its organizational meeting, performed *The Girl from Lazy J*, Fitzgerald's first effort for the group. The play was brief and extremely flawed. Yet, the performance signalled an important event for the young playwright who had also appeared in the leading role. "I begin to get my head turned," he wrote in his scrapbook between the programs for *A Regular Fix* and this latest production. And, undoubtedly, Elizabeth Magoffin further contributed to these feelings of pride when she gave him a photograph that year inscribed "To Scott 'He had that Spark—Magnetic Mark—' With the best love of the one who thinks so," as well as a poem including a line explaining that "the Spark is a gift, and a part of our God."[2]

During each of the following three summers, an Elizabethan Dramatic Club production of a Fitzgerald play was performed for charity. While each was a great improvement over Fitzgerald's first effort, and while the last two, especially, were applauded in newspaper accounts of the group's activities, none was a polished, mature work. The reader should not expect anything like the novelist's professional efforts. In these plays, however, one will find the talent and enthusiasm of the boy who would grow up to become one of America's greatest writers.

Though born in St. Paul in 1896, Fitzgerald had spent much of the first twelve years of his life in New York State, his family first having moved to Buffalo in 1898, then to Syracuse in 1901, and then back to Buffalo in 1903. Finally, in 1908, after his father Edward Fitzgerald was dismissed from Procter and Gamble, the firm for whom he had worked during this period, the Fitzgeralds returned to St. Paul.

Fitzgerald's *Ledger*, the outline chart of his life probably first begun in 1919 or 1920, records some of his early flirtations with the stage. "He remembers the attic where he had a red sash with which he acted Paul Revere," a note for his seventh year states.[3] Another note, this time for September, 1906, when he was ten, tells us "He made up shows in Dugham's attic, all based on The American Revolution and a red sash and three cornered hat." Four months later, his family was taking advantage of his exhibitionistic streak. Of this time he wrote, "His mother got the idea he could sing so he performed 'Way down in colon town' and 'Don't get married any more' for all visitors." Meanwhile, during the years 1906 through 1908, he was attending many of the stock company performances in Buffalo with his friend Hamilton Wende, and according to Andrew Turnbull, re-enacting a good number of these performances for the neighborhood children. Then, after his family returned to St. Paul, he attended many of the vaudeville shows at the Orpheum Theatre, again re-enacting what he had seen.[4] Further, he continued to write plays. In 1909, he constructed a half hour drama titled *Arsène Lupin*, based on the adventures of the popular detective character of the day, hand lettered cards of admission referring to himself as "stageman," and presented the play in the living room of his friend Teddy Ames.[5] And a *Ledger* note for the following year tells of a "Play in Cecil's attic." In addition, at the St. Paul Academy between 1909 and 1911 he participated in debates, recitations, and dramatic exercises. One news article in his scrapbook, for example, tells of a "literary meeting" at the school on May 12 of his final year during which he and Teddy Ames imitated stage personalities Montgomery and Stone singing "Travel, Travel Little Star."

Of course, to emphasize Fitzgerald's interest in theatre too much during these early years is to create a distortion. As the notes for the *Ledger* testify, his youthful literary zeal manifested itself in many areas. A note for January, 1907, for example, states: "He began a history of the U.S. and also a detective story about a necklace that was hidden in a trap door under the carpet. Wrote celebrated essay on George Washington & St. Ignatius." Another, this time for June, 1909, states: "Wrote The Mystery of the Raymond Mortgage. Also 'Elavo' (or was that in Buffalo) and a complicated story of some knights." He summed up this activity in a note for January, 1911, referring to himself as an "inveterate author." During the 1909–10 and 1910–11 school years, while he was attending St. Paul Academy, four of his short stories, "The Mystery of the Raymond Mortgage," "Reade, Substitute Right Half," "A Debt of Honor," and "The Room With the Green Blinds," as well as a news article, appeared in *Now and Then*, the St. Paul Academy magazine. During the following two school years, while he was attending the Newman School in Hackensack, New Jersey, three more stories, "A Luckless Santa Claus," "Pain and the Scientist," and "The Trail of the Duke," as well as "Football," a poem, and at least two news articles in addition were published in the *Newman News*.

But at the St. Paul Academy, Fitzgerald's theatre activity had impressed one of his teachers most of all. "I imagined he would become an actor of the variety type," wrote C.N.B. Wheeler years later.[6] Further, Fitzgerald's literary activity during the summers between 1911 and 1914 seems to have been devoted mainly to his work with the Elizabethan Dramatic Club. After that first year at the Newman School, during which he attended many shows in New York (*The Little Millionaire, The Quaker Girl, Over the River,* and *The Private Secretary* are mentioned in is *Ledger*), he returned to St. Paul with his next play—"wrote it on a train," he said in the *Ledger—The Captured Shadow*.

"ENTER SUCCESS!," he wrote in his scrapbook next to the clippings for *The Captured Shadow*. One again he played the leading role, this time that of a gentleman burglar. The play was performed before a paying audience on August 23, 1912, at the Oak Hall school for girls on Holly Street, only a short walk from Fitzgerald's home, and there were many rewards. The show had raised sixty dollars for the Baby Welfare Association. For the cast there was dinner the preceding evening at the Schurmeier home, then a theatre party, a hayrack party, and dinner at the Town and Country Club during the afternoon and evening following the performance. And for Fitzgerald and his friends there was much favorable publicity. As was the custom for such charity activities, especially when some of the youngsters were the children of prominent St. Paul residents, most of the notices appeared in the society section of the local newspapers. A reviewer stated, "Much comment was elicited by the young author's cleverness as well as by the remarkable amateur work accompanied by the others in the cast."[7]

The following year, on April 28, at the Trinity Lyceum in Hackensack, the Newman School Comedy Club presented a double bill, *The Power of Music* and David Garrick's version of *The Taming of the Shrew*. In the opener, Fitzgerald had the role of a king whose son eventually succeeds as concert violinist despite the opposition of the court. Next to the program in his scrapbook, Fitzgerald wrote, "the young king à la Donald Bryan," an allusion to the popular musical comedy star. Then four months later, his third Elizabethan Dramatic Club play, *Coward*, a Civil War tale, received even more newspaper acclaim than *The Captured Shadow*. (A few of these accounts, some advertisements, and the *Ledger* for July, 1913, refer to it as *The Coward*.) In his scrapbook, Fitzgerald wrote, "—THE GREAT EVENT—." Not only was he the author again, but now he had *two* parts, one as brother of the heroine, the other, a minor role as a Union soldier who attempts to steal her necklace; in addition, he was now listed in the program as "Stage Manager." Finally, because of the turnout at the performance on August 29, 1913, at the downtown Y.W.C.A. auditorium—"a large and fashionable audience," according to as reviewer—and because of the $150 raised for the Baby Welfare Association, it was accorded a second showing on September 2 at the White Bear Yacht Club in Dellwood, some twelve miles away. Here, after being treated to dinner, the cast performed to an audience of 300 more.[8]

Fitzgerald entered Princeton that fall and he soon became active in the Triangle Club. He submitted lyrics for the 1913–14 show, and, when they were not accepted, he helped out at rehearsals. In addition, he began working on the show for the following year, *Fie! Fie! Fi-Fi!*, for which he was eventually to receive credit for writing the lyrics and claimed, in addition, to have written the book. Then, at the end of the school year, he returned home this time for his final Elizabethan Dramatic Club play, *Assorted Spirits*.

Once again Fitzgerald was applauded in the local newspapers for his work. "Scott Fitzgerald, the 17-year-old playwright ... turned out a roaring farce and is clever throughout," wrote one reviewer. And once again Fitzgerald not only had a major role, this time that of Peter Wetherby, the owner of the house that is haunted by the "assorted spirits," but he also again was listed as "Stage Manager." The first performance, on August 8, 1914, at the Y.W.C.A. auditorium raised $300 for the Baby Welfare Association and another performance the following night at the White Bear Yacht Club garnered another $200. It was during the first act of this second performance before a crowd of 200 that the light fuses blew, explosions were heard, and the house was plunged into darkness. All of this happened just as one of the actors costumed as a devil had made his entrance, and this apparently only added to the fears of the more impressionable in the audience. Fitzgerald averted panic when he "proved equal to the situation, however, and leaping to the edge of the stage," according to a newspaper article, "quieted the audience with an improvised monologue."[9]

After the demise of the Elizabethan Dramatic Club, Fitzgerald, of course, continued to remain active in theatre at Princeton, where he wrote the lyrics for two more Triangle productions, *The Evil Eye* (1915–16) and *Safety First* (1916–17). In addition, he contributed two short plays to the *Nassau Literary Magazine*, "Shadow Laurels," published in April, 1915, and "The Debutante," January, 1917. But he was also writing short stories, humorous articles and sketches, poems, and jokes for the *Nassau Literary Magazine* and the *Princeton Tiger*, and while still at Princeton began the first version of the novel that eventually would be *This Side of Paradise*. Only once again would he devote any extended length of time to the theatre, and that to his political satire, *The Vegetable*, that closed after a brief tryout in Atlantic City in 1923. His papers at Princeton University Library contain hints of later attempts at writing other full length plays, but none was ever completed.

But the early theatre experience was always an important influence on Fitzgerald as a writer of fiction. From his two early novels, *This Side of Paradise* and *The Beautiful and Damned*, with their scenes in play form, to *The Great Gatsby*, a dramatic novel with dramatic scenes, limited point of view, and a time scheme superimposed upon a dramatic curve, to his unfinished final novel, *The Last Tycoon*, planned to fit a five-act formula, Fitzgerald never forgot what he had learned as a playwright. Further, he used some of the events from this early experience in a number of stories, most specifically in the 1928 Basil Duke Lee tale, "The Captured Shadow." Here he blended a number of events from 1911 to 1914 to create a story that gives the reader a sense of Fitzgerald's capacity in the Elizabethan Dramatic Club. In many ways, the almost sixteen-year-old playwright Basil Duke Lee is the young Fitzgerald and Riply Buckner is the young Gustave Schurmeier, his friend. Basil's methods in writing his play may be a clue to help us understand Fitzgerald's early methods. For humor Basil relies heavily on a collection of joke books and a "Treasury of Wit and Humor." Plots are based vaguely on New York shows. "This had been a season of 'crook comedies' in New York," Fitzgerald wrote of Basil's desire to write a play, "and the feel, the swing, the exact and vivid image of the two he had seen, were in the foreground of his mind. At the time they had been enormously suggestive, opening out into a world much larger and more brilliant than themselves that existed outside their windows and beyond their doors, and it was this suggested world rather than any conscious effort to imitate 'Officer 666,' that had inspired the effort before him."[10]

And if Miss Halliburton in this short story is modelled upon Elizabeth

Magoffin, then the latter's function in the Elizabethan Dramatic Club, especially after the first year, may not have been too large. "I'll be the business manager and you'll direct the play, just like we said," Riply advises Basil, "but it would be good to have her there for prompter and to keep order at rehearsals. The girls' mothers'll like it."[11] Both Arthur Mizener and Andrew Turnbull, Fitzgerald's biographers, agree with this view of Elizabeth Magoffin, Turnbull in particular referring to the young Fitzgerald as the "mainspring" of the drama group.[12]

On May 22, 1914, some three months before the final Elizabethan Dramatic Club production, Elizabeth Magoffin directed a cast of Camp Fire Girls and Y.M.C.A. boys at the St. Paul Y.W.C.A. in a pageant depicting the past, present, and future of St. Paul. The text was her 520-line poem "Saint Paul, Minnesota," a nondescript work privately published later that year.[13] A local newspaper referred politely to the pageant, giving it little of the praise bestowed on the Fitzgerald plays.[14] During the following years, Miss Magoffin continued her interests in drama and in 1929 and 1930 participated in the formation of one of the very early little theatre groups in the area, the St. Paul Players. After her marriage to Peter Garnett in 1935, she eventually left St. Paul, and then, after the death of her husband, she moved in the early 1940s to Lexington, Kentucky, where she resided until her death in 1951. Throughout this period she retained her transcriptions of the four Fitzgerald plays—in all probability the promptbooks used during the performances—as well as Fitzgerald's holograph manuscript of *The Girl from Lazy J* and the few leaves in his hand from *Coward*. A friend remembers Elizabeth Magoffin Garnett, during the latter part of her life, proudly recalling her association with the young Fitzgerald, referring to his early brilliance, and reading aloud from the plays.[15] In 1952, Princeton University Library obtained these materials from members of Elizabeth Magoffin Garnett's family.

Notes

1. Fitzgerald to Alida Bigelow, September 22, 1919, in *The Letters of F. Scott Fitzgerald*, ed. Andrew Turnbull (New York: Scribners, 1963), p. 456.
2. The photograph and poem are in Fitzgerald's scrapbook at Princeton University Library.
3. All Ledger citations are from *F. Scott Fitzgerald's Ledger: A Facsimile* (Washington, D.C.: Bruccoli Clark/Microcard Editions, 1972).
4. Andrew Turnbull, *Scott Fitzgerald* (New York: Scribners, 1962), pp. 12 and 25.
5. Fitzgerald's scrapbook.
6. Turnbull, *Scott Fitzgerald*, p. 20.
7. The clippings are in Fitzgerald's scrapbook.
8. Ibid.
9. Ibid.
10. F. Scott Fitzgerald, *Taps at Reveille* (New York: Scribners, 1960), p. 72.
11. Ibid., p. 74.
12. Arthur Mizener, *The Far Side of Paradise*, rev. ed. (Boston: Houghton Mifflin, 1965), p. 47, and Turnbull, *Scott Fitzgerald*, p. 43.

13. A copy of the privately printed poem as well as a carbon typescript, both with corrections in Elizabeth Magoffin's hand, are in the Minnesota Historical Society, St. Paul, Minnesota.

14. *St. Paul Pioneer Press*, May 23, 1914, p. 11.

15. Members of the Magoffin family, including Chester Seims of Darien, Connecticut, and Ralph Magoffin of Columbia, South Carolina, provided me with some of the information about Elizabeth Magoffin's background. Mrs. Jean Merritt of Lexington, Kentucky, recalled the event described above.

40
Introduction to *The Apprentice Fiction of F. Scott Fitzgerald*

◆

JOHN KUEHL

An unpublished autobiography marked "Outline Chart of My Life," but commonly called "Ledger" (The F. Scott Fitzgerald Papers, Princeton University Library), shows Scott Fitzgerald to have been an actor from the age of seven: "He remembers the attic where he had a red sash with which he acted Paul Revere" (September, 1903); "He made up shows in Ingham's attic, all based on the American Revolution and a red sash and three cornered hat. He did tricks and mysteriously vanished a dime" (September, 1906); "His mother got the idea he could sing so he performed 'Way down in colon town' and 'Don't get married anymore' for all visitors" (January, 1907). Besides writing four plays between the summer of 1911 and the summer of 1914 for the local Elizabethan Dramatic Club, he played the lead in two and important parts in both of the others.

If, like Dick Diver (*Tender Is the Night*, New York, 1934), Scott Fitzgerald felt compelled to perform, like Jay Gatsby (*The Great Gatsby*, New York, 1925), he also undertook proprietary roles. For instance, his childhood diary, "Thoughtbook" (The F. Scott Fitzgerald Papers), contains a section dated February 24, 1911, and entitled "The gooserah and other clubs," which informs us that the author originated "the gooserah club" and helped to originate "the white handkerchief club." "Thoughtbook," itself, would serve as the source of Basil Duke Lee's "Book of Scandal," just as the title of one of the Basil Duke Lee stories, "The Scandal Detectives" (*Taps at Reveille*, New York, 1935) would recall an actual organization of this name founded—probably by Fitzgerald—in March, 1911.

Most important, however, like Monroe Stahr (*The Last Tycoon*, New York, 1941), who would guide motion pictures "way up past the range and power

SOURCE *The Apprentice Fiction of F. Scott Fitzgerald*, New Brunswick, NJ, 1965, pp. 3–16.

of the theatre," Fitzgerald entertained in the role of creative artist. Scott Fitzgerald was a born storyteller. One early piece states, "It is because of Skiggs that this story was written," and another, "It is unfortunately one of those stories which must start at the beginning, and the beginning consists merely of a few details." We do not require his frequent consciousness of himself as a writer, though, to realize that he thoroughly enjoyed entertaining his readers. In his apprentice fiction Fitzgerald employed dramatic beginnings, surprise endings, and lively scenes. He chose exciting subjects: solving a murder mystery; winning a football game single-handedly; an act of physical courage in the Civil War; avenging the murder of a son after the Civil War; giving away money on Christmas Eve; doing unto a Christian Scientist what he has done unto you; searching futilely for a nobleman; rediscovering a father; overcoming doubt before joining the Jesuits; the debut of a *femme fatale*; regret at having flunked out of college; Shakespeare raping Lucrece's "real-life" model, then composing a poem about it; a boy's attempt to kiss a fickle girl; demoralization and death during World War I; a man finally winning an old flame only to lose his writing ability.

He presented these subjects with considerable narrative sense, as a brief summary of one story's action will indicate. "The Pierian Springs and the Last Straw" contains two parts. The opening section of the long first part elaborates the statement, "My Uncle George assumed, during my childhood, almost legendary proportions"; he drank heavily and was a "mesogamist" who "had been engaged seven times" and "had written a series of novels" about bad or not quite good women. The closing section takes the narrator—now a twenty-year-old easterner—to "the prosperous Western city that still supported the roots of our family tree," where, in the Iroquois Club, his uncle explains why his life stopped "at sixteen minutes after ten" one October evening. For an entire decade he has put up with the ridicule of the woman responsible, but on the present occasion she grows unbearably sarcastic. When she says she often talked her dead husband out of horsewhipping him, George stamps her wedding ring into "a beaten button of gold." Then Part I ends and the nephew departs. A couple of short paragraphs, Part II describes the uncle's fate while implying the nephew's relation to it. We learn that the older man and the widow soon eloped, with the result that he "never drank again, nor did he ever write or in fact do anything except play a middling amount of golf and get comfortably bored with his wife." The nephew's awareness of storytelling is illustrated by such comments as "The story ought to end here" and "Unfortunately the play continues into an inartistic sixth act." His last assertions refer facetiously to "my new book on *Theories of Genius*," so we feel that he may become the family author, and if he does, will probably continue to exploit Scott Fitzgerald's own budding gift for irony.

II

The "Thoughtbook," whose dated entries extend from August, 1910, to February 24, 1911, shows that Fitzgerald was a born storyteller even in the keeping of a diary. That at the age of fourteen he had already developed the raconteur's sense of time is indicated through his juxtaposing the definite past, the indefinite past, and the present. That he dramatized factual events is shown by many episodes that focus on a memorable day and that contain stretches of direct dialogue.

> "Jim was so confident the other night that you had a crush on him."
> "Well Jim gets another think"
> "Shall I let him know you dont like him."
> "No: but you can let him know that he isn't first."
> "I'll do that"
> "Now if you had thought that it might be different."
> "Good" said I
> "Good" repeated she and then the convestion [sic] lagged.

"Thoughtbook" also reveals that Fitzgerald was a born psychologist. He characterized two of his friends thus: Paul Ballion "was awfully funny, strong as an ox; cool in the face of danger polite and at times very interesting." Margaret Armstrong "is not pretty but I think she is very attractive looking. She is extremly graceful and a very good dancer and the most interesting talker I have ever seen or heard." He recorded other people's reactions to him: "Violets' opinean of my character was that I was polite and had a nice disposition and that I thought I was the whole push and that I got mad too easily." And his reaction to other people: "Bob Clark is interesting to talk to because he lets me do a lot of talking"; "Now I dont dislike him [Paul Ballion]. I have simply out grown him"; "I think it is charming to hear her [Margaret Armstrong] say, 'Give it to me as a compliment' when I tell her I have a trade."

C. N. B. Wheeler, English teacher and athletic coach, has described the Scott Fitzgerald of St. Paul (Minnesota) Academy days (1908–1911) as a psychologist as well as an entertainer: "a sunny light-haired boy full of enthusiasm who fully foresaw his course in life even in his schoolboy days.... I helped him by encouraging his urge to write adventures. It was his best work, he did not shine in his other subjects. He was inventive in all playlets we had and marked his course by his pieces for delivery before the school.... He wasn't popular with his schoolmates. He saw through them too much and wrote about it.... I imagined he would become an actor of the variety type, but he didn't.... It was his pride in his literary work that put him in his real bent." (Andrew Turnbull, *Scott Fitzgerald*, New York, 1962, p. 20)

Fitzgerald's precocity as an observer of human character is foreshadowed in the four stories written for the St. Paul Academy *Now and Then*. The main figures of the first two, both of whom are handicapped, act heroically but under rather conventional circumstances: the "pretty light" substitute halfback, Reade, and the "wounded" Confederate private, Jack Sanderson, vanquish their respective football and battlefield foes and earn cheers from their comrades.

In the other two *Now and Then* stories, the characters are either passive or active. A mystery confronts two pairs of men, but while the observers, Chief Egan and Robert Calvin Raymond, record, the observed, John Syrel and Governor Carmatle, act. This passage implies Chief Egan's envy of John Syrel: "He was not a tall man, but thanks to the erectness of his posture, and the suppleness of his movement, it would take no athlete to tell that he was of fine build. He was twenty-three years old when I first saw him, and was already a reporter on the News. He was not a handsome man: his face was clean-shaven, and his chin showed him to be of strong character."

The protagonists of all three stories Scott Fitzgerald published during his residence at the Newman School of Hackensack, New Jersey (1911–1913), combine both active and passive traits. But the author's assessment of the protagonists' experience in two early Princeton pieces, "Shadow Laurels" and "The Ordeal," is even more complex. Although they overcome their difficulties, they do so less successfully than the protagonists of the three Newman School stories.

In "Shadow Laurels" Jacques Chandelle, whose "eyes are clear and penetrating," whose chin "is sharp and decisive," and whose manner "is that of a man accustomed only to success," feels the need after a separation of twenty-eight years to "sense" his father again. This he does, thanks to some of the deceased's old Parisian cronies. Discovering through them that Chandelle senior was a magnificent failure, Jacques begins to metamorphose into him: "His face is a little red and his hand unsteady. He appears infinitely more gallic than when he entered the wine shop." As the son departs, the old crony shouts the father's name, "Jean, Jean, don't go—don't." The young man of "The Ordeal," to whom "pleasure, travel, the law, the diplomatic service" are open, is, nevertheless, about to take religious vows. Yet the very day he must file toward the altar with the other novices, he finds himself "pitted against an infinity of temptation."

The protagonists of "Shadow Laurels" and "The Ordeal" triumph only ostensibly. Jacques Chandelle and the young man accomplish what they set out to do, the former managing to rediscover his father and the latter managing to go through with his religious vows, but both contain the seeds of failure. "Shadow Laurels" implies that Jacques Chandelle is more like his reprobate father than he imagines, and "The Ordeal" shows that the young man's faith has been preserved only through an external force—"the stained window of St. Francis Xavier." These two 1915 stories represent, then, an interim stage in the development of the author's hero.

In "The Spire and the Gargoyle," which was written two years later, the hero flunks an *actual* test. No previous Fitzgerald protagonist had failed completely. In this case, the boy has to a very large extent brought his failure about himself: "Fifty cut recitations in his first wild term had made necessary the extra course of which he had just taken the examination. Winter muses, unacademic and cloistered by Forty-second Street and Broadway, had stolen hours from the dreary stretches of February and March. Later, time had crept insidiously through the lazy April afternoons and seemed so intangible in the long Spring twilights. So June found him unprepared."

Total failure on the part of the main figures of subsequent Princeton pieces had been prefigured as early as the *Now and Then* stories, where the heroes were handicapped or fragmented into actors and passive observers. Inevitably, Scott Fitzgerald's juvenile protagonist, through personal weakness or some external force or both, would become the *homme manqué*, a term Fitzgerald himself would use to describe Dick Diver.

The evolution involved sex. In "The Ordeal," the young man's worldly temptation is epitomized by a female, "waiting, ever waiting": "He saw struggles and wars, banners waving somewhere, voices giving hail to a king—and looking at him through it all were the sweet sad eyes of the girl who was now a woman." In "Sentiment—and the Use of Rouge," Clay Syneforth, twenty-two years old and "champion of sentiment," comes home after two years of war to find the girls' heavily painted faces expressing "half enthusiasm and half recklessness." Just before Syneforth and his dead brother's fiancée sleep together, "He put his arm around her, never once taking his eyes from her face, and suddenly the whole strength of her appeal burst upon him.... He knew what was wrong, but he knew also that he wanted this woman, this warm creature of silk and life who crept so close to him. There were reasons why he oughtn't to have her."

Speaking of *la belle dame sans merci*, Mario Praz has written: "*Salammbô* is a picture in the manner of Delacroix, except that instead of the beautiful female slaves agonizing under the ferocious eye of Sardanapalus, we have the beautiful male slave suffering unspeakable tortures under the eye of his goddess-like beloved; for with Flaubert we have entered the dominion of the Fatal Woman, and sadism appears under the passive aspect which is usually called masochism (as though the active and passive aspects were not usually both present in sadism, and a mere change of proportions really justified a change of name)." (*The Romantic Agony*, New York, 1956, pp. 153–4)

After the *homme manqué*, the *femme fatale*, Fitzgerald's vampiric destroyer, is the most vital character he ever created. She pervades the later fiction. For instance, Jonquil of "The Sensible Thing," Judy of "Winter Dreams," and Josephine of the five Josephine stories surround themselves with devoted males whom they seem to delight in torturing with uncertainty. Josephine "had driven mature men to a state of disequilibrium" (*Taps at Reveille*, p. 178) and Judy was destined to "bring no end of misery to a great number of men." (*All the Sad Young Men*, New York, 1926, p. 59) Another young lady, Ailie Calhoun of "The Last of the Belles," was proud of the fact that a man may have committed suicide over her. (*Taps at Reveille*, p. 260) But more pertinently, the *femme fatale* pervades the apprentice fiction too. From the heroine of "A Luckless Santa Claus" (Christmas, 1912) to the heroine of "The Pierian Springs and the Last Straw" (October, 1917), she acts as the most persistent and powerful barrier to the protagonist's success. The *femme fatale* is no mere foil, however. Her development into an independently significant figure represents one of the major achievements of these early writings, whose author told his secretary, "I am half feminine—at least my mind is.... Even my feminine characters are feminine Scott Fitzgeralds." (*Scott Fitzgerald*, p. 259)

That Fitzgerald's conception of the *femme fatale* was intimately bound up with personal experience seems clear from statements like this to his daughter: "When I was your age I lived with a great dream. The dream grew and I learned how to speak of it and make people listen. Then the dream divided one day when I decided to marry your mother after all, even though I knew she was spoiled and meant no good to me. I was sorry immediately I had married her but, being patient in those days, made the best of it and got to love her in another way. You came along and for a long time we made quite a lot of happiness out of our lives. But I was a man divided—she wanted me to work too much for *her* and not enough for my dream." (Andrew Turnbull [ed.], *The Letters of F. Scott Fitzgerald*, New York, 1963, p. 32) Actually, Fitzgerald had been associated with strong-willed females before marrying Zelda Sayre.

His mother, Mary McQuillan, was the daughter of an Irish immigrant who had prospered in St. Paul as a wholesale grocer. There were many things he resented about her, among them that she had taste neither in dress nor in books and that she was overindulgent. In an article called "Author's House" (*Esquire*, July, 1936), Fitzgerald indicates that her overindulgence was responsible for his choosing the passive life of an artist rather than a more active, more "heroic" life. He conducts an anonymous visitor to his cellar, where there is "all the complicated dark mixture of my youth and infancy that made me a fiction writer instead of a fireman or a soldier," and, pointing to the darkest corner, he says: "Three months before I was born my mother lost her other two children and I think that came first of all though I don't know how it worked exactly. I think I started then to be a writer." All his life Fitzgerald felt that his mother had made him soft rather than strong, had kept him from becoming the "hero" his fantasy wished him to be.

Regardless of whether or not Mary McQuillan should bear the ultimate responsibility for her son's preoccupation with the *femme fatale*, there is no denying that from childhood through marriage this kind of female fascinated him. At eleven, he found Kitty Williams irresistible: "I dont remember who was first but I know that Earl was second and as I was already quite over come by her charms I then and there resolved that I would gain first place ... We talked and talked and finally she asked me if I was going to Robin's party and it was there my eventful day was. We played postoffice, pillow, clapp in and clapp out and other foolish but interesting games. It was impossible to count the number of times I kissed Kitty that afternoon. At any rate when we went home I had secured the coveted 1st place. I held this until dancing school stopped in the spring and then relinquished it to Johnny Gowns a rival. On valentines day that year Kitty received no less than eighty four valentines."

"Thoughtbook" records another childish affair immediately succeeding this one, the new *belle dame sans merci* being Violet Stockton: "She was very pretty with dark brown hair and eyes big and soft. She spoke with a soft southern accent leaving out the r's. She was a year older than I but together with most of the other boys liked her very much. I met her through Jack Mitchell who lived next door to her. He himself was very attached as was Art Foley.... Finally Violet had a party which was very nice and it was the day after this that we had the quarrel. She had some sort of book called flirting by sighns and Jack and I got it away from Violet and showed it too all the boys. Violet got very mad and therefor *I* went home.... *I just hate Violet*.... Not much has happened since Violet went away. The day she went away was my birthday and she gave me a box of candy. Her latest fancy is Arthur Foley. He has her ring She wrote him a letter to ask him for his picture"

Fitzgerald's "Ledger" records his college romance with Ginevra King in a series of short statements whose very matter-of-factness lends them poignancy: January, 1915: "Met Ginevra"; June: "Ritz, Nobody Home and Midnight Folie with Ginevra.... Deering: I'm going to take Ginevra home in my electric": August: "No news from Ginevra"; October: "Dinner with Ginevra in Waterbury"; November: "Letters to G.K."; February, 1916: "Long letters to Ginevra"; March: "Ginevra fired from school"; April: "Ginevra & Living on the train. A facinating story"; August: "Lake Forrest. Peg Carry. Petting Party. Ginevra. Party"; November: "Ginevra and Margaret Cary to Yale game"; January, 1917: "Final break with Ginevra"; June: "Ginevra engaged?"; September: "Oh Ginevra"; July, 1918: "Zelda.... Ginevra married."

When Scott Fitzgerald met her, Ginevra King was sixteen, a junior at Westover, and already popular with the Ivy League boys. Arthur Mizener has summed up their relationship: "For Ginevra, he became for a time the most important of her many conquests. As she said herself many years later, '... at this time I was definitely out for quantity not quality in beaux, and, although Scotty was top man, I still wasn't serious enough not to want plenty of other attention!' ... To the end of his life he kept every letter she ever wrote him (he had them typed up and bound; they run to 227 pages). Born and brought up in the best circumstances in Chicago and Lake Forest, Ginevra moved for him in a golden haze." (*The Far Side of Paradise*, Boston, 1951, pp. 48–9) The duration and depth of Fitzgerald's feeling toward the girl are shown by a remark from a letter of November 9, 1938, to Frances

Turnbull: "In *This Side of Paradise* I wrote about a love affair that was still bleeding as fresh as the skin wound on a haemophile." (*The Letters of F. Scott Fitzgerald*, p. 578)

Between his infatuation with Kitty Williams, Violet Stockton, and other childhood sweethearts and his unrequited love for Ginevra King, he contributed two stories to the *Newman News* which introduced the *femme fatale*. Though both heroes of these stories are humiliated, neither is destroyed.

"A Luckless Santa Claus" begins: "Miss Harmon was responsible for the whole thing. If it had not been for her foolish whim, Talbot would not have made a fool of himself, and—but I am getting ahead of my story." What is "her foolish whim"? A challenge to wealthy, indolent, "faultlessly dressed" Harry Talbot to give away twenty-five dollars, two dollars at a time, in an hour and a half period one Christmas Eve, a challenge these words explain: "Why you can't even spend money, much less earn it!" And how does her fiancé make "a fool of himself"? By accosting people who greet his generosity with a mistrust and contempt, which reach their climax when he gets badly mauled and must return "hatless, coatless, collarless, tieless." But Talbot is merely humiliated, not destroyed, for he soon deserts Miss Harmon for his maulers.

Technically, "The Trail of the Duke" closely resembles "A Luckless Santa Claus." We are given another aimless rich boy as victim and another silly girl friend as victimizer. Compared to Harry Talbot's experience, however, Dodson Garland's seems trivial since it hinges upon a simple misunderstanding instead of treating an ironic, thematically important circumstance. Mirabel Walmsley asks Dodson to find a missing duke. Thinking she means the Duke of Matterlane, he searches for him in the streets and in bars like Sherry's, Delmonico's, and Martin's, while he overimbibes ginger ale. When Dodson returns "crestfallen and broken-hearted," Mirabel, after revealing that the missing duke was a dog, invites him to meet the real duke the next day. He refuses and goes home, a reaction reminiscent of Harry Talbot's desertion of Miss Harmon.

The *femme fatale* plays a crucial role in four Princeton pieces published in 1917 by *The Nassau Literary Magazine* between January, the month Fitzgerald and Miss King made their final break, and October, the month before Fitzgerald was commissioned a second lieutenant in the regular army.

Both Isabelle of "Babes in the Woods" and Helen of "The Debutante" are based on Ginevra King. They differ from the girls who set the foolish quests, to the extent that calculation differs from capriciousness. Having played off another young man against him, Isabelle becomes Kenneth Powers' dinner partner. After achieving her purpose of attracting Kenneth's full attention, she abandons the first young man who has been "fascinated and totally unconscious that this was being done not for him but for the black eyes that glistened under the shining carefully watered hair a little to her left."

Although the young men in these stories are not destroyed, they suffer more than the humiliation to which their earlier counterparts were subjected. Throughout "The Debutante," a "huge pierglass" constantly reminds us of the narcissism of the heroine, the typical debutante soon to metamorphose into flapper or vamp. She coldly and clearly analyzes her fickleness and then heartlessly dismisses her most recent beau. Before he departs emotionally shattered, he has been brought to the verge of tears.

The most extreme instance of suffering at the hands of a woman occurs in "Sentiment—and the Use of Rouge," which deals with a slightly older set. In this story the hero's seduction by the *femme fatale* makes him a participant in the "new materialistic world" which he fears and despises. Through his actions he betrays not only the memory of his dead brother but also his own deepest convictions.

III

To one extent or another, the protagonists of *This Side of Paradise* (New York, 1920), *The Beautiful and Damned* (New York, 1922), *Tender is the Night*, and *The Last Tycoon* combine a particular flaw *of* with general superiority *to* their society. Invariably, the flaw involves the *femme fatale*. Amory Blaine, though scarred, manages to survive three women, while Anthony Patch succumbs to one. Dick Diver is destroyed by his wife and Monroe Stahr sinks into a state of "emotional bankruptcy" partly because of the dead Minna.

The protagonists of *This Side of Paradise* and *The Beautiful and Damned* begin life with every advantage, the first being the son of wealthy, cultured midwesterners, and the second the grandson of a multimillionaire. Yet Amory loses his money, goes overseas, and must work in an advertising agency, and Anthony becomes insane after he has inherited his grandfather's fortune.

The protagonists of *Tender Is the Night* and *The Last Tycoon* fare no better. Dick degenerates from the serious, brilliant professional, whose learned articles have been standard in their line, to a "quack," a "shell." Monroe experiences Dick's same "lesion of vitality," but he perishes physically as well as deteriorating morally.

The points of similarity between the apprentice and mature fiction are scattered rather than clustered; no one juvenile work shares themes, characters, and techniques with any single work written during maturity. The only exception to this rule happens to be Fitzgerald's final college story, "The Pierian Springs and the Last Straw." It is also his best early story, despite the curious fact that he never placed it in *The Smart Set*, H. L. Mencken's chic *avant-garde* monthly, in which four of Fitzgerald's other college pieces were published. Perhaps Mencken never saw "The Pierian Springs" because Fitzgerald deliberately set the story aside, planning eventually to rework it. Whether that in fact happened cannot be determined, but, though qualitatively worlds apart, "The Pierian Springs" and *The Great Gatsby* bear so many and such striking similarities that the undergraduate story seems a kind of crude template for the masterwork that Fitzgerald was to publish seven and a half years later.

There are a number of resemblances between the story's protagonist, Uncle George, and the novel's antagonist, Tom Buchanan: both drink heavily, act promiscuously, and injure a finger of the woman they love. More crucial, however, are the resemblances between Uncle George and Jay Gatsby, Fitzgerald's best known male victim. About thirty years old and purveyors of disreputable merchandise, each assumes mythical stature. Gatsby is variously represented as Trimalchio and as a relative of Kaiser Wilhelm or Von Hindenburg, a German spy or a murderer. The nephew refers to his Uncle George as Romeo, Byron, Don Juan, Bernard Shaw, Havelock Ellis, "the Thomas Hardy of America," "the Balzac of his century." Jay Gatsby's personality is "an unbroken series of successful gestures" and Uncle George's is "a series of perfectly artificial mental tricks, ... gestures." Jay Gatsby tells his story to Nick Carraway and Uncle George tells his to the nephew. Like Gatsby, who "took Daisy one still October night" and "felt married to her," George believes "life stopped at twenty-one one night in October at sixteen minutes after ten." Like Gatsby, who "knew women early" and "became contemptuous of them," George becomes a misogynist. And like Gatsby, who also collected "presentable" trophies, George was inspired by a young lady "to do something for her, to get something to show her." Each is destroyed—Gatsby actually and George figuratively—because each allows abstract ideals to become incarnated in an unworthy woman and because each thinks he can repeat a past, which both story and novel frequently juxtapose to the present.

The resemblances between Myra Fulham of "The Pierian Springs" and Daisy Buchanan of *The Great Gatsby* are also remarkable. Uncle George applies adjectives to the former that apply equally well to the latter: "unprincipled," "selfish," "conceited," "uncontrolled." He claims, "When she wanted a boy there was no preliminary scouting among other girls for information, no sending out of tentative approaches meant to be retailed to him. There was the most direct attack by every faculty and gift that she possessed. She had no divergence of method—she just made you conscious to the highest degree that she was a girl." This sexuality expresses itself in Myra's "eternal mouth" and in Daisy's voice "full of money." Uncle George is betrayed first with a man "from another college" and then with "a crooked broker"—"the damn thief that robbed me of everything in this hellish world." Daisy betrays Gatsby with Tom.

The apprentice fiction of Scott Fitzgerald—stories composed between the ages of thirteen and twenty-one and submitted with unqualified success to school and college publications—discloses his amazing progress from the boy who wrote "The Mystery of the Raymond Mortgage" to the incipient artist who wrote "The Pierian Springs and the Last Straw." That the author's essential self emerges here is proved, among other evidence, by their containing his prototypal hero, the *homme manqué*, and heroine, the *femme fatale*.

41

The Road to *Paradise*: Fitzgerald's Literary Apprenticeship

◆

DONALD A. YATES

If there are no such persons as "born writers," F. Scott Fitzgerald was the next best thing. He was a "born observer." To this quality he brought a youthful self-confidence and an unwavering conviction that he could produce out of his own head stories as entertaining as any he had read. He preserved this egotism, almost intact, up to the time when he published *This Side of Paradise*. Between 1909, the date of his first published work, and 1920, the date of *Paradise*, he was not consciously preparing himself for a career as a novelist; but the surprisingly large amount of writing he did during the years leading up to his first popular success nonetheless contributed toward that end. The individual pieces which he composed during his early years—stories, plays, poetry, satire, and even song lyrics—run close to one hundred in number. It is evident, therefore, that the sudden success of his first novel was only to a small degree ascribable to chance. Fitzgerald had actually had an extensive apprenticeship.

Why did the young boy from St. Paul write? In the beginning it was to please himself. Later, he wrote to please others with the inventions of his imagination. At Princeton, for a while, writing for publication was, as he saw it, the thing to do. Finally, in his last fifteen months at school, following a severe set-back to his youthful ambitions, and as a result of the influence of several "literary" classmates, he found in writing not only something to believe in, but something eminently worth *living for*. The author's pre-1920 writings tell this story.

EARLY WRITINGS

I

Fitzgerald's first published work, "The Mystery of the Raymond Mortgage," appeared in the September 1909 issue of the *Now and Then*. This was the school publication of the St. Paul Academy, a local country day school he was then attending. He had written other things before—a play at the age of seven and a story of knighthood at the age of ten, among other pieces—but these are lost now. However, we have no reason to suppose that they were unlike "The Raymond Mortgage" with respect to its marked degree of imitation of other models. The style of Conan Doyle and touches of LeBlanc pervade this story about a double murder and the theft of a "valuable mortgage." There is the bumbling chief of police and the bright newspaperman who solves the case. There is a butler (who is killed) and clues (footprints and spent bullets) and complications too elaborate for the story to support. There are implausibilities: a dead woman is left at the scene of the crime for four days while the investigation proceeds. (At this early stage, the young writer found it necessary to evoke a new day for each new development.) Yet, despite its extravagant weaknesses and flaws, the story has undeniable color and a good sense of movement. Since it is the most complex of Fitzgerald's early stories, perhaps more than anything else it reveals the young writer's serious concern over *plot*. This is an interesting point; for if Fitzgerald's subsequent *Post* stories suffer from one consistent fault, this fault is overplotting.

Between 1910 and 1911, Fitzgerald wrote three more stories for the *Now and Then*. One was a simple football anecdote entitled "Reade, Substitute Right Half," in which a "light haired stripling" strongly resembling the would-be football hero, Fitzgerald, saves the day with a brilliant run. The other two stories, "A Debt of Honor" and "The Room with the Green Blinds," are Civil War tales that turn on rather dramatic surprise endings.

Most of these reflect the *imitative* side of the young writer. They suggest to us the type of books he was reading and the sort of stories he was hearing from his father, who was fond of recounting tales of the Civil War. These were adventures fashioned by the same Scott who invented games for the neighborhood children to play. Characteristically, these pieces had little to do with life as he was observing it. At the same time, however, he was keeping a personal record of his observations—prose jottings that came closer than any of these fictions to expressing his intimate feelings. This record, which Fitzgerald called his "Thoughtbook," foreshadows some of his best pages.

The "Thoughtbook," kept between 1910 and 1911, was a sort of adolescent's diary, in which were recorded the random and baffling shiftings of favor that describe the eternal drama churned up between youthful members of the opposing sexes. Fitzgerald was a very shrewd observer of these trends. Because popularity meant so much to him, and possibly because he was fascinated by its fickle nature, he proved to be a considerably gifted teen-aged sociologist in these matters. The "Thoughtbook," which he divided into chapters, contains lists of favorite boys and girls. (At one point, he enters the proviso: "This list changes continually. Only authentic at date of chapter.") It also contains descriptions of specific incidents involving his young friends. A good illustration of Fitzgerald's natural style and dramatic insight is given in Chapter IX, dated August, 1910.

> Kitty Williams is much plainer to my memory. I met her first at dancing school and as Mr. Van Arnum (our dancing teacher) chose me to lead the march I asked her to be my pardner. The next day she told Marie Louty and Marie repeated it to Dorothy Knox who in turn passed it on to Earl that I was third in her affections. I don't remember who was first but I know that Earl was second and as I was already quite overcome by her charms I then and there resolved that I would gain first place. As in the case of Nancy there was one day which was preeminent in my memory. I went in Honey Childenton's yard one morning where the kids usually congregated and beheld Kitty. We talked and talked and finally she asked me if I was going to Robin's party and it was there that my eventful day was. We played postoffice, pillow, clapp in and clapp out and other foolish but interesting games. It was impossible to count the number of times I kissed Kitty that afternoon. At any rate when we went home I had secured the coveted 1st place. I held this until dancing school stopped in the spring and then relinquished it to Johnny Gowns a rival. On valentine's day that year Kitty received no less than eighty four valentines. She sent me one which I have now as [and] also one which Nancy gave me. Along in a box with them is the lock of hair—but wait I'll come to that. That Christmas I bought a five pound box of candy and took it around to her house. What was my surprise when Kitty opened the door. I nearly fell down with embarrassment but I finally stammered "Give this to Kitty," and ran home.

This excerpt from the "Thoughtbook" represents what Fitzgerald, even at an early age, could do well: observe people and their interrelationships, project himself into their midst, and capture the essence of his experiences in objective and dramatic terms. His obsession with popularity and his attention to the relative ranking of his friends, to be sure, is a facet of the personality of the young egotist. But it is also true that this preoccupation with the standards and procedures of society carries through to the best of the novels and stories he was to write in the two decades that lay ahead of him.

If the passage dedicated to Kitty Williams seems laced with ambition and self-assurance, it should readily be accepted as characteristic of the boy. It appears that Fitzgerald was a kind of neighborhood Belasco, an irrepressible entertainer. He was always dreaming up things for others to do. In view of this, it seems apparent that his early writings were not produced out of a desire for publication and fame. It is likely that what he wrote during this period was strictly for his own pleasure—be it the pleasure of accomplishment or that pleasure he received indirectly from observing that his fictions were amusing his young friends and, in some cases, grownups as well.

One of the adults who were most dazzled by the young Fitzgerald was

Miss Elizabeth Magoffin of St. Paul, under whose patronage he wrote, in August of 1911, a short play entitled *The Girl from the Lazy J*.[1] This was the first in a series of four plays that Fitzgerald wrote for production by the Elizabethan Dramatic Club, which was headed by Miss Magoffin.

The Girl from the Lazy J is a western. It has a cast of five characters, a number of rather awkward soliloquies, and a minimum of motivated plot action. The plot centers on the drama inherent in concealed identities (a theme Fitzgerald was to exploit in subsequent plays). The manuscript carries Miss Magoffin's superficial corrections; but it is apparent that she was but lightly critical with her "young genius."

That fall, the boy's parents, with the financial help of an aunt, sent him to the Newman School at Hackensack, New Jersey. He had not proved himself either a popular fellow (he was considered too "fresh") or a diligent student at the Academy, and his enrollment at Newman was intended to be a means to get him straightened out and studying. But at Newman, too, his brightness and freshness soon made him a marked man among his classmates. Nor did he turn over a new leaf academically. He continued to write secretly and sought his chief stimulation outside the classroom, in the New York theaters where he saw and was greatly impressed by his first Broadway shows. The only record that remains of the writing he did during his first year at Newman is the thirty-six line poem entitled "Football," which was published in the *Newman News*.[2]

The shows he attended on Broadway ultimately had their effect. In the spring of 1912, on his way back home to St. Paul on the train, Fitzgerald wrote a new play which he entitled *The Captured Shadow*.

II

The Captured Shadow was presented by the Elizabethan Dramatic Club in August of 1912. To judge from a reading of the manuscript as we have it in young Fitzgerald's own hand, it must indeed have been a successful play. It is undoubtedly the best piece of dramatic writing that he had done up to this time. The play flows along very well; there is a particularly good opening and development in the first act; there are smooth entrances and exits; and there is a considerable amount of movement and action. The humor of the opening scene (arising from the extraction of juicy bits of information from an eavesdropping domestic by the "indignant" mistress who had surprised the servant in the act) must have amused the audience. The scene obviously amused Fitzgerald. Moreover, it suggests that he had learned something important about dramatic technique: that the audience takes delight in being given a conversation from which, through insights lent by the author, it can extract more meaning than is apparent on the surface.

The story is essentially an imitation of the type of melodrama that had so impressed the young author in the plays he saw in New York. The hero might have sprung full-blown straight out of *Alias Jimmy Valentine*. The sense of the gallant roguery of Arsène Lupin (one of Fitzgerald's early heroes) is manifest throughout the play. However, together with the influences of his models the young playwright mixed in some of his own favored brand of entertainment. There is interpolated a whole series of timeless childhood jokes and vaudeville gags that "keeps the show loose," so to speak. Some examples: a character stammers. "But-but-but-" and is cut off with the inane quip, "You talk like a goat!" (which probably drew a laugh anyway); someone comments that a certain loud suit looks cheap and the wearer promptly replies, "Why it's all covered over with checks!"

The mystery play is not fair in the placing and follow-up of clues, but it would seem that no one took note of the fact. There is a pleasant little romance woven into the drama which is resolved with a good final line (a Fitzgerald trademark) when the "Captured Shadow," revealed as a celebrated society figure in disguise, admits that he has succumbed to the heroine's charms and now is indeed a truly "captured" Shadow.[3]

Fitzgerald returned to Newman that fall with an apparent dedication to try to get the things he wrote into print. Now on the editorial staff of the *Newman News*, he made a total of five contributions to the magazine during 1912–1913, which was his last year at the school. Two of these pieces, "Election Night" and "School Dance," are merely brief observations that serve only to indicate Fitzgerald's interest in the social functions of the school. The remaining three items are short stories. Of these, "Pain and the Scientist" is a simple anecdote with a meager amount of trimming. It deals with a man who has become angered at the attitude of his Christian Scientist neighbor who tries to convince him that there is no such thing as pain. The story ends with the neighbor's "comeuppance": after lecturing the protagonist on his childish attitude toward pain, he has an accident and is obliged to beg his "pupil" to release him from his discomfort. It is a slight little tale.

The two other stories represent an important step forward both in the writer's development and in his search for the "right" material. "A Luckless Santa Claus" deals with a wealthy young man who takes up his fiancée's bet that he cannot *give away* twenty-five dollars on Christmas Eve. To his dismay, he finds he cannot do it. "On the Trail of the Duke" is also a "plotted" story that concerns a young beau who is sent by his girl friend to search for a missing duke who has wandered away from her house. The fellow has heard that a French duke had been visiting and assumed that this was whom he was to look for. He returns many hours later empty-handed, only to find that the "Duke" was his girl's missing poodle, which has since returned. These two stories, executed in similar style, are remarkably well carried off. They offer proof that Fitzgerald was learning some things about the art of writing prose.

But perhaps more significant than the lively descriptions, the charming and convincing dialogue, the increasing sensitivity towards his characters—all of which are evident here—is the fact that Fitzgerald had discovered material for which he had a definite feeling: he had chosen to deal with comfortably wealthy young people of his own time. He was, as we know, exceptionally well equipped to explore in this area of society. Seven years later he would publish a first novel that is peopled with young men and women of similar social and economic status.

In these *Newman News* stories published during the year preceding his arrival at Princeton we already glimpse clear flashes of the future moralistic writer of fables about the young and the rich. Consider, from "A Luckless Santa Claus," the following:

> In the parlor of a house situated on a dimly lighted residential street somewhere east of Broadway, sat the lady who ... started the whole business. She was holding a conversation half frivolous, half sentimental, with a faultlessly dressed young man who sat with her on the sofa. All this was quite right and proper, however, for they were engaged to be married in June.

And this paragraph from "On the Trail of the Duke":

> In his house on upper Fifth Avenue, young Dodson Garland lay on a divan in the billiard room and consumed oceans of mint juleps, as he grumbled at the polo that had kept him in town, the cigarettes, the butler, and occasionally breaking the Second Commandment. The butler ran back and forth with large consignments of juleps and soda and finally, on one of his dramatic entrances, Garland turned towards him and for the first time that evening perceived that the butler was a human being, not a living bottle-tray.

The importance of Fitzgerald's discovery of the charms of writing about his own time and about his own "generation" is demonstrated by the fact that henceforth, until the publication of *This Side of Paradise*, he would write only two stories that did not have contemporary backgrounds. And after *Paradise* his fame as a short-story writer was based on the portraits of his own "creations"—the flapper and her beaux.

In St. Paul, in the late summer of 1913, just a month before he appeared on the Princeton campus, his third play written for the Elizabethan Dramatic Club was presented. The title was *Coward*, and Fitzgerald returned to the Civil War period for his scene. It is the most ambitious of his juvenile plays. The cast contains seventeen characters who are deployed over two acts (with an interim time lapse of three years) with an undeniable dramatic sense. Once again the opening is effective, and once more the exits and entrances are smoothly managed. The plot is developed around the occupation of a Virginia home by Yankee soldiers. (The author's bias favors the South.) A Southerner who in the first act demonstrates himself a coward is redeemed by curtaindrop in the second. The resolution of a long-pending romance provides the curtain line, as it did in *The Captured Shadow*. Playing on the title of the drama, Fitzgerald was the hero Holworthy confess to having been—three years before—a "coward" in romance as well as in battle.

For all of its implausibilities and youthful excesses, the play appears to have been a success. A subsequent "command" performance was given on September 12 at the nearby White Bear Yacht Club at Dellwood, Minnesota; and for the second time in five days the young Fitzgerald received the enthusiastic approval of his audience and of the local press. This glory must have seemed sufficient to last for a while, for there is no record of Fitzgerald's having written anything for publication or performance during the next year—until the presentation in September of 1914 of his last play for the Elizabethan Dramatic Club. While at Newman, he had learned about a theatrical group at Princeton called the Triangle Club which staged original operettas. We have his own words to the effect that he chose Princeton primarily in order to play on the Tiger football team and, secondly, in order to be able to write for Triangle. He failed on his first day out to make the Princeton freshman football team, and therefore likely poured all his energies into work on the 1914–1915 Triangle show. To this single-minded dedication we must attribute the silence from September 1913 to September of the following year.

III

Fitzgerald's attendance at Princeton between fall of 1913 and November of 1917 is properly divided into two distinct periods. He attended steadily from September of 1913 through November of 1915 when he left school owing to a combination of health and academic problems. He returned in September of 1916 as a junior and as a member of the Class of '18. He had fallen a year behind his original class. This setback had a lasting effect on him. What he wrote before and after this reversal should properly be considered as belonging to two distinct phases of his development as a writer.

During his first year at Princeton Fitzgerald worked a great deal on the book and lyrics for the Triangle show, *Fie! Fie!, Fi-Fi!* At the same time he was beginning to associate with several literarily inclined young men from whom he felt he could learn many things about this exciting thing called the English language. He now spent time with young poets and dedicated intellectuals such as John Peale Bishop and Edmund Wilson. His classes were of less importance to him than his new friends; they and the Triangle lyrics kept him away from many of his lectures. Consequently, his freshman year was not an unqualified academic success, and he was obliged to report to Princeton early in the fall of 1914 to make up several class deficiencies. He still found time, however, to write and polish up his fourth and final drama for the Elizabethan Dramatic Club—a two-act farce entitled *Assorted Spirits*. It appears in the reading to be the least successful of the St. Paul plays. As before, he had found himself a common enough plot (a house is made to seem haunted in order to reduce its sale price) and he once again inserted a simple little romance; but the play seems to lack the exuberant spirit of the earlier pieces. Perhaps he had temporarily lost interest in the dramatic form, perhaps he turned out the play merely because it was expected of him. Whatever the reason, we cannot doubt that his imagination was racing ahead to the fall in anticipation of the work remaining to be completed on the Triangle show.

In September he passed off his conditions and was accepted as a sophomore, although he was not allowed to take part officially in Triangle activities. His ultimate contribution to *Fie! Fie!, Fi-Fi!* consisted of seventeen song lyrics. Taken as a group, they strike one as being competently executed; but one sees little of Fitzgerald in them and much of W. S. Gilbert. Now barred from full participation in the Triangle presentation, he decided to go home for the holidays while the show went on tour. In St. Paul, as it happened, he had a more significant experience than he likely could ever have had traveling with the Triangle group. Near the end of the vacation he met and fell desperately in love with a girl from Westover by the name of Ginevra King. She would serve as the model for the emancipated, desirable but elusive young heroine in much that Fitzgerald wrote up until the time of the publication of *This Side of Paradise*. She gave substance to the vague, faceless "society girl" that he had already begun to describe.

By the following spring Fitzgerald had adjusted himself well enough to the Princeton environment to be able to get down to some serious writing. In the April 1915 issue of the *Nassau Lit*, the school literary magazine, he published a story written in dramatic form called "Shadow Laurels." It showed that he had absorbed quite a bit from his friends, if not from his teachers, concerning the business of writing. The scene of the story is a wine shop in Paris. A trio of neighborhood *habitués* are approached by a stranger who is inquiring into the facts surrounding the death of his father who, many years before, had died in that part of Paris. The young man had always believed that his father had been a failure and that his death must have occurred under sordid circumstances. The three local customers immediately recall the father and assure the son that his parent had not been a worthless fellow, that, on the contrary, he had been an educated man, a poet and a musician who had brought beauty and wonder into their lives. He had been fond of drinking, yes, but he had died as an artist. In the end, the three men drink a toast with the grateful son to the memory of the father.

The play has two important features. It is written with a poetic sensitivity that Fitzgerald had probably acquired from reading François Villon and others of the decadent romantics. The discovery that a poetic tone can be used to refine and heighten the effect of prose was the single most important step in the development of Fitzgerald's narrative art during the first stage of his career at Princeton. Also significant is the likelihood that the source for the story came from deep within the author himself. Fitzgerald had always considered his father a failure, which, by objective standards, he was. But he had taught his son to read and write and had told him many fantastic and wonderful stories that had stimulated the boy's imagination.

In "Shadow Laurels" Fitzgerald seems to be reaching down into his private feelings for the first time to grasp a subject for his prose. Since we know he was being exposed to the traditionally enlightening college experience of having old ideas and faiths brought into doubt, it seems probable that he used the story as a means of reevaluating the degree of his indebtedness to his father.

The June 1915 issue of the *Nassau Lit* carried his next story, "The Ordeal." This is an account of the mystical occurrence experienced by a young man at the moment he takes his vows for priesthood. The story is strangely vague and inconclusive. It would seem to reflect Fitzgerald's unsettled feeling regarding his Catholicism. Since Newman days, he had been greatly influenced by his friend and advisor, Sigourney Fay. In fact, Father Fay and Shane Leslie together "had induced Fitzgerald to believe he was the future Catholic novelist for the United States."[4] While this ambition was not realized, Fitzgerald nonetheless was able to deal more meaningfully with the theme of religious experience in subsequent stories—of which "Absolution" is perhaps the best example.

"The Ordeal" is the last significant prose piece published by Fitzgerald for nearly a year and a half. His grades during his sophomore year were not good, and he found himself obliged once again to submit to reexamination in the fall. The deficiencies were not satisfactorily made up. So it was that in November of 1915, now in poor health, he withdrew from school. That year's Triangle show, *The Evil Eye*, with book written by Edmund Wilson, again carried seventeen lyrics by Fitzgerald. But the bitterly disappointed student had been forcibly removed from what he always felt was his rightful place in the spotlight. The experience of marking time while his class moved ahead was one that affected him deeply. When he returned to Princeton in September of 1916 he was, in many ways, a different person.

IV

The 1916–1917 Triangle show was called *Safety First*, and for it Fitzgerald produced twenty-one lyrics. This was the third operetta for which he had provided the songs, and one observes that he had now developed and perfected his natural facility for versifying to a point where some of his best lyrics possessed genuine wit and polish. Included in the *Safety First* score is the following bright verse about Charlotte Corday:

Back where Robespiere [sic] ruled
In frivolous fickle France
That's when someone was fooled

And fooled in a bold way
Fooled in the old way
Young Miss Charlotte Corday
Of the "Follies of Ninety Three"
Asked old Marat to buy her a hat
Oh mercy on me!
So Marat he had it sent
And to her flat he went. Oh:
Chorus: Charlotte Corday, Charlotte Corday,
You had them all on the string.
Gee they were mean to guillotine
A sweet little innocent thing!
Got the hat when you wanted it,
Tried it on but it didn't fit.
Then you joined the wrath club,
Stabbed him in the bathtub.
Served him just right, he was a fright,
You were impetuous through life.
Many a dame does just the same,
But stabs with her eyes, not a knife.
Still, we've thought upon it
And we wear your bonnet,
Charlotte Corday, Charlotte Corday,
You were some girl in your day!

    It was a more sober young man, however, who wrote these songs. After January of 1917, the amount of humorous material that Fitzgerald published gradually declined. (He had been in earlier years a frequent contributor to the Princeton humor magazine, *The Tiger*; but his *Tiger* pieces had always been slight and—he must have realized this—inconsequential.) It appears that it was during his period of readjustment at Princeton that Fitzgerald's humor was transformed into the irony that pervades so much of his subsequent work.

    With the frivolity and gaiety of the Triangle show behind him, it was the *Nassau Lit* that then assumed greatest importance as a means for making his creative talents known. Between January and October of 1917, the magazine published six of his short stories and five poems. Included in this production are the best prose pieces that he wrote prior to the publication of *This Side of Paradise*. This is explained in part by the fact that by late fall his romance with Ginevra King had come to a moment of crisis. When the new year began, Fitzgerald had to face the painful truth that their relationship was for all purposes ended. In the manner of "Shadow Laurels," he now used his stories as means of coming to grips with and attempting to understand his past experience. "The Debutante," published in the January 1917 issue, is an episode in play form that depicts a bored, fickle, pseudo-sophisticated young society girl in the process of driving one of her ardent beaux to despair. It is a brief little sketch, but Fitzgerald fully understood the impression he wanted to convey and he conveyed it effectively. In the February issue appeared his story "The Spire and the Gargoyle." He had written it originally in the midst of his depression, while he was waiting to return to school. It concerns a boy who has collected fifty cuts in his spring term and finds himself obliged to take an exam that will determine whether he will be able to return in the fall as a sophomore. The "spire" is the romantic symbol of university existence (which ideally has no imposed disciplines); the "gargoyle" represents the instructor who grades the boy's paper and mercilessly fails him. The second half of the story expresses Fitzgerald's sense of despair over the injustice of a dull, plodding pedagogue (who subsequently takes a job teaching in a high school) having in his hands the power to destroy the plans of a bright, ambitious, gifted young man. It remains a moving and eloquent expression of Fitzgerald's disillusionment at that time.

The April issue carried his "plotted" story "Tarquin of Cheapside," which is structurally similar to his St. Paul Academy piece, "The Room with the Green Blinds." Both stories build to a melodramatic surprise ending. "Tarquin," however, is a far superior narrative in that Fitzgerald's cultivation of poetry had enabled him to produce a carefully controlled poetic prose that is actually the story's outstanding feature. In May, having reconsidered his experience with Ginevra King, he published "Babes in the Woods," a story about two young people feeling each other out in the early stages of their romance. It is a more effective story than "The Debutante," partly because it probes deeper into the author's feelings for its emotional tension. Fitzgerald now understood his two young people (Isabelle and Kenneth) quite well. These two stories, in revised form, figure in *This Side of Paradise*. Isabelle, incidentally, remains as the name of the book's early heroine, and Kenneth becomes Amory. Both stories were sold in 1919 to the *Smart Set* before *Paradise* was accepted for publication.

In June the *Lit* published Fitzgerald's "Sentiment—and the Use of Rouge," a war-time story set in England, full of literary allusions and "big" questions. It is the least successful story of this late period for it clearly reveals Fitzgerald to be, in philosophical matters, a decidedly immature thinker. (However, readers of his first two novels will perceive that he was not one to give up without a fight.) The last story Fitzgerald published in the *Lit* was "The Pierian Spring and the Last Straw," which appeared in the October issue. In it the narrator's uncle tells of a sad love affair which we recognize as a new version of the Ginevra King experience. Time has now separated the author from his days of apprehension and ultimate sorrow, and we observe "Fitzgerald the writer" reviewing an incident from the life of "Fitzgerald the boy from St. Paul" and molding the fundamental emotions into a well-fashioned literary creation.

The twenty-one-year-old Princeton student had now acquired all of the individual writer's tools that he would use in his first novel. His material had been determined, his style had been set, his artistic sensitivities had been awakened and sharpened. Most significantly, he had begun to live *actively*, conscious of his time. He would borrow other ideas and he would adapt other styles; but henceforth all of these would be measured against his acquired sense of what was esthetically correct and desirable.

V

In November of 1917, the month after the publication of "The Pierian Spring," the young writer left Princeton to accept a commission in the U.S. Army as a second lieutenant. Fitzgerald's life as a student had come to an end. However, before he left Princeton, he brought to Dean Christian Gauss, his friend, the manuscript of a novel on which he had been working—in the hope that Gauss would recommend it to a publisher. He had titled it *The Romantic Egoist* and had filled its pages with his personal experiences and his youthful philosophy. This was the first draft of the novel that would eventually form part of *This Side of Paradise*. Dean Gauss found it to be unmarketable and advised Fitzgerald to do more work on it. The writer believed in the book and took it with him when he left Princeton to report for duty. What happened to him and his manuscript in the next two years properly belongs to the study of his first novel. In reality, of course, the break between these two early stages of Fitzgerald's life was not distinct or abrupt. In a sense, the "school" and the "young novelist" periods merge into and reflect one another. Fitzgerald came to be in the "outside world" the image of what he had been during his school years, but magnified because of society's larger perspective. In his writing, too, the close interrelationship is implicit. It is true, as many have pointed out, that *This Side of Paradise*, being so unmistakably autobiographical, clearly depicts the life of the young writer. But it is also true that, when considered in detail, Fitzgerald's early writings explain and illuminate the novel called *This Side of Paradise*.

Notes

1. This play and those written for production in the summers of 1913 and 1914 have been believed lost. But copies of *The Girl from the Lazy J*, *Coward*, and *Assorted Spirits*—copied out in Miss Magoffin's hand—are now located among the Fitzgerald papers at the Firestone Library in Princeton.
2. Fitzgerald's football "obsession," which makes itself evident early in his life, often found expression in what he wrote. His dream of football glory was a persistent illusion, one which he cherished for another twenty-five years. For an examination of this facet of the author's personality, see the present writer's "Fitzgerald and Football," *Michigan Alumnus Quarterly Review*, Fall, 1957.

3. A fairly close account of the 1912 production of this play is given in Fitzgerald's story "The Captured Shadow," which appeared in the December 29, 1928 *Post*. The story is included in *Taps at Reveille* and in Malcolm Cowley's selection of Fitzgerald's stories (*The Stories of F. Scott Fitzgerald*: Scribners, 1951).

4. Shane Leslie, "Scott Fitzgerald's First Novel": *The Times Literary Supplement*, November 6, 1959, p. 643.

42

Scott Fitzgerald: The Apprentice Fiction

MARIUS BEWLEY

Although nearly all critics recognize today the quality of Scott Fitzgerald's best fiction, from time to time one still hears a violent dissenting opinion. The case against Fitzgerald was succinctly stated in a 1951 essay by Leslie Fiedler: "And so a fictionist with a 'second-rate sensitive mind' ... and a weak gift for construction is pushed into the very first rank of American novelists, where it becomes hard to tell his failures from his successes. Who cares as long as the confetti flies and the bands keep playing!" It is a little difficult to know in the context what Fiedler means by a "second-rate mind." But a novelist who discovers and is possessed by an important subject, one which is centrally significant in the experience of his country and time, and who gives that subject vivid and effective embodiment in his work, hardly deserves such an epithet, however intended. Fiedler knows perfectly well that Fitzgerald has a subject, but he doesn't like it. As he tells us in his book on the American novel published in 1960: "There is only one story that Fitzgerald knows how to tell.... The penniless knight ... goes out to seek his fortune and unhappily finds it.... He finds in his bed not the white bride but the Dark Destroyer." Apart from the fact that one is sick to death of categories like these, the interpretation is likely to seem prejudiced and less than honest to anyone who disagrees with Fiedler's bright but falsifying description of Fitzgerald as the "laureate" of "the American institution of *coitus interruptus.*"

Fitzgerald's discovery of his subject was a progressive one, and he moves into a fuller consciousness and control of it until the end. Although Mr. Fiedler's intention is not complimentary, he comes close to an exact formulation when he describes Gatsby, Fitzgerald's most representative hero, as "the naif out of the West destined ... to die of a love for which there is no worthy object." In writers who are, in a sense, born with an innate subject to write about, their early work can be peculiarly revealing, both as to subject

SOURCE *Masks and Mirrors*, London, 1970, pp. 154–159.

matter and tone, and this is true of Fitzgerald.

In *The Apprentice Fiction of F. Scott Fitzgerald,* John Kuehl has collected the early stories written between 1909 and 1917—the earliest written while he was at St. Paul's Academy, three while he was at Newman School in Hackensack, and the remainder while he was an undergraduate at Princeton. While these stories are clearly "apprentice fiction," several of them are remarkably good, and collectively they indicate that Fitzgerald had already found his subject, although there are few intimations that he was yet aware of the moral dimensions of it which he would exploit so wonderfully in *The Great Gatsby.*

Kuehl has provided a series of excellent critical commentaries on the stories, which relate them to Fitzgerald's later development. Recognizing that nearly all of them deal with frustration of moral defeat, however disguised, he writes in his introduction: "Inevitably, Scott Fitzgerald's juvenile protagonist, through personal weakness or some external force or both, would become the *homme manqué,* a term Fitzgerald himself would use to describe Dick Diver." And in a later comment on one of the Princeton stories he says: "All the plots he thought of 'had a touch of disaster in them.' He anticipated that lovely girls would go to ruin, that wealth would disintegrate, that millionaires would be 'beautiful and damned.'"

A glance at his subjects will indicate how early the characteristic temper of his sensibility asserted itself. In "Shadow Laurels," which is written in dialogue, an eminently successful man returns to his native city, seeking information about his father, whom he had never known. He discovers not only that his father was a drunkard and wastrel, but there are intimations to the eyes of the other characters that the successful man is very much the son of his father. In "The Spire and the Gargoyle," part of which he incorporated in *This Side of Paradise,* an undergraduate flunks out of Princeton and is haunted by a sense of defeat and nostalgia ever afterward. In "The Ordeal," a Jesuit novice about to take his vows is sorely tempted to refuse them. He overcomes the temptation, but in a way that disturbingly suggests the victory has been mechanical and external only. In what is perhaps the best of the stories, "The Pierian Springs and the Last Straw," a writer who somewhat resembles the novelist Fitzgerald was to become, after many years marries the girl he had loved in his youth, and finds that it destroys his talent. In these stories it is not only subject matter and a propensity towards disaster that anticipate the mature writer: their romantic alignment is particularly insistent.

All during Fitzgerald's life, Keats was his favorite poet. "For awhile after you quit Keats all other poetry seems to be only whistling or humming," he wrote to his daughter; and he has several times remarked on the frequency with which he read Keats when he was very young. In the year of his death he wrote that he still could not read "Ode to a Nightingale" "without tears in my eyes." Keats's strong verbal influence in the more poetic passages of

Fitzgerald's prose is obvious—perhaps in *The Great Gatsby* most of all. But one guesses that essentially it was Keats's attitude to experience that seized and dominated his imagination, and may have exerted some influence on Fitzgerald's choice of themes and subject matter.

Throughout Keats's poetry there is a sense of transience and loss, at times an almost unbearably poignant sense of passage and dissolution. The origin of this is understandable in terms of Keats's biography; but there is a somewhat similar sense of transience in Fitzgerald's writing. In the latter case it is a little difficult to guess its cause, but it is pervasive. His second novel, *The Beautiful and Damned*, has a good many passages like these:

> Beautiful things grow to a certain height and then they fail and fade off, breathing out memories as they decay. And just as any period decays in our minds, the things of that period should decay too, and in that way they're preserved for a while in the few hearts like mine that react to them.
>
> There's no beauty without poignancy, and there's no poignancy without the feeling that it's going, men, names, books, houses—bound for dust—mortal—

This sense of loss soon grew sharper and more bitter. It is of the essence of Gatsby's ordeal that he believed the past could be repeated, almost as Keats had written to Benjamin Bailey, "We shall enjoy ourselves here after by having what we called happiness on earth repeated in a finer tone...." But Fitzgerald is not to be identified with Gatsby. He understands, as his heroes do not, the element of irrevocable, tragic loss in which his vision is grounded. "Winter Dreams," one of his better short stories, concludes with a statement which makes its own comment on Gatsby's private dream:

> "Long ago," he said, "long ago, there was something in me, but now that thing is gone. Now that thing is gone. I cannot cry. I cannot care. That thing will come back no more."

Fitzgerald never learned to triumph over this theme of loss and defeat in his fiction as Keats does in his poetry. In Fitzgerald's case it moves from the elegiac to the tragic but never to victory, as it does, for example, in the great speech from "Hyperion" in which Oceanus, the vanquished Titan, accepts the infinite loss entailed in a fall from divinity:

> *As Heaven and Earth are fairer, fairer far*
> *Than Chaos and blank Darkness, though once chiefs;*
> *And as we show beyond that Heaven and Earth*
> *In form and shape compact and beautiful,*
> *In will, in action free, companionship,*
> *And thousand other signs of purer life;*
> *So on our heels a fresh perfection treads,*
> *A power more strong in beauty, born of us*
> *And fated to excel us, as we pass*
> *In glory that old Darkness.*

In this superb vision of an endless evolution into beauty and perfection, forever canceling out the stages past, the redemptive factor for Keats is of course the power of his genius and splendor of his poetry. But although Fitzgerald's sense of loss is in many ways strangely Keatsian, a resolution similar to Keats's is beyond him—and not merely because he has not Keats's astounding genius. Fitzgerald's ultimate subject is the character of the American Dream in which, in their respective ways, his principal heroes are all trapped. If the American Dream seems delusively to carry a suggestion of infinite possibilities, it tolerates no fresh perfections beyond its own material boundaries. If it engenders heroic desires in the hearts of its advocates, it can only offer unheroic fulfillments. For this reason Fitzgerald's novels, and *Gatsby* above all, are tragedies. The heart of the tragedy is that these heroes must die of a love for which there is no worthy object. Fiedler was quite right about that, but hopelessly wrong in seeing this theme as trivial. An abiding faith in the paradox that infinite satisfactions can be had in the devout pursuit of success, money, and romantic love has always been the corrupting element in American society. To have invented a series of fables dramatizing this central truth and its consequences for America is not indicative of a "second-rate mind."

In Kuehl's well-edited collection of Fitzgerald's apprentice fiction we encounter this kind of hero in whom the seeds of defeat and tragedy are suggested, even in the flush of success, in perhaps a majority of the stories. Not until *The Great Gatsby* would Fitzgerald gain full control of the subject, and transform it into an effective instrument for probing the nature of the American experience, but partly for this very reason these early attempts are illuminating. The Romantic tone, the tragic bias, the critical irony, have all already been established.

This Side of Paradise

1920

43
Paradise and Princeton

◆

HEYWOOD BROUN

We have just read F. Scott Fitzgerald's *This Side of Paradise* and it makes us feel very old. According to the announcement of his publishers, Mr. Fitzgerald is only twenty-three, but there were times during our progress through the book when we suspected that this was an overstatement. Daisy Ashford is hardly more naïve. There is a certain confusion arising from the fact that in spite of the generally callow quality of the author's point of view he is intent on putting himself over as a cynical and searching philosopher. The resulting strain is sometimes terrific.

Of course, Mr. Fitzgerald is nearer to college memories than we are and, moreover, we have no intimate knowledge of Princeton, and yet we remain unconvinced as to the authenticity of the atmosphere which he creates. It seems to us inconceivable that the attitude toward life of a Princeton undergraduate, even a freshman, should be so curiously similar to that of a sophomore at Miss Spence's.

"Ever read any Oscar Wilde?" inquires d'Invilliers, the young poet, of Amory Blaine, our hero, who has been presented as a youngster of a somewhat literary turn. "No. Who wrote it?" answers Amory, and we refuse to believe that young Mr. Fitzgerald is not pulling our leg. Then, too, in spite of the bleak and jaded way in which the author sums up the content of college life, it is evident that he is by no means unimpressed with the sprightliness of conduct and conversation which he assigns to his undergraduate characters, though it is silly conversation and sillier conduct.

It is probably true that in some respects Fitzgerald has painted a faithful portrayal of the type of young man who may be described as the male flapper, but our objection lies in the fact that to our mind the type is not interesting. After all, the reviewer who has been through several seasons of tales about sub-debs cannot view with anything but horror the prospect of being treated to exhaustive studies of her brother and first cousins.

In making himself responsible for the descriptions of college pranks and larks the author has undertaken a task of enormous difficulty. Things done

SOURCE *New York Tribune*, 11 April 1920, p. 9.

in a spirit of alcoholic exuberation must of necessity sound flat and unprofitable to the mature and cold, sober reader. When Fitzgerald writes, "The donor of the party having remained sober, Kerry and Amory accidentally dropped him down two flights of stairs, and called, shamefaced and penitent, at the infirmary all the following week," he does scant justice to Kerry and Amory. After all, in the mood and at the moment it can hardly have seemed such a silly trick as it must appear to the reader in Fitzgerald's laconic statement.

The thing that puzzled us most was the author's description of the violent effect of the sex urge upon some of his young folk. On page 122, for instance, a chorus girl named Axia laid her blond head on Amory's shoulder and the youth immediately rushed away in a frenzy of terror and suffered from hallucinations for forty-eight hours. The explanation was hidden from us. It did not sound altogether characteristic of Princeton.

There are occasional thrusts of shrewd observation and a few well turned sentences and phrases in *This Side of Paradise*. It is only fair to add that the book has received enthusiastic praise from most American reviewers. Fitzgerald has been hailed as among the most promising of our own authors. And it may be so, but we dissent. We think he will go no great distance until he has grown much simpler in expression. It seems to us that his is a style larded with fine writing. When we read, "It was like weakness in a good woman, or blood on satin: one of those terrible incongruities that shake little things in the back of the brain," we cannot but feel that we are not yet grown out of the self-conscious stage which makes writing nothing more than a stunt.

44
A Remarkable Young American Writer

◆

ANONYMOUS REVIEW

By whatever number of years and books the arrival of F. Scott Fitzgerald on the skyline of eminent authorship may be distant, on the immediate landscape he has "arrived" in a manner not to be overlooked. His first novel, published in his twenty-fourth year, manifests striking talent. As to equipment, he has had special opportunities to observe American life through the last few years in the new and significant aspects of which we have all been aware, but which age or circumstances have debarred our older interpreters from penetrating.

Through him our youngest adult generation of the class socially preferred and our educational system's most recent output of the class endowed with brains and temperament give us self portraits done with a critical eye and a sure hand. Mr. Fitzgerald's subject, Amory Blaine, is a member of both these classes. While writing piecemeal the record of Amory's progress, compiling a kind of loose scrapbook of the history of the case, he affords us much inside knowledge of the atmosphere that surrounds a luxurious twentieth century childhood in the Middle West, a very high-caste "prep" school in the East, the corresponding caste among the students of a leading university, and at least one "younger set" of that hard, competitive, conspicuous element of present-day society in New York which rules itself altogether by the gold standard.

But quickly, lest the foregoing seem to indicate a dreary novel by a topheavy young sociological realist, let it be added that *This Side of Paradise* is a very enlivening book indeed, a book really brilliant and glamorous, making as agreeable reading as could be asked. It has a profusion of incidental appetizing features. In the Princeton part, for example, Mr. Fitzgerald quite casually does big college life better than any of a hundred writers, attempting it with might and main, have succeeded in doing it since "Philosophy Four." And in the Eleanor episode, one of Amory's numerous love affairs ("Young

SOURCE *New York Evening Post*, 17 April 1920, book review section, p. 2.

Irony" is the title of that chapter), he achieves a romantic idyl of real distinction.

For reviewing purposes *This Side of Paradise* is an easy book to say things about, a hard one to characterize or even to inventory. It begins with Amory in small boyhood, a superficially spoiled but fundamentally undamaged boyhood (that, at least, is Amory's own valuation later on) passed under the wing of a spoiled, emotional mother. It ends with Amory, back from the war and penniless, engaged in a conscious sublimation of his natural egotism. We leave him at the start of an ascetic career of effort to better the state of mankind, to "give people a sense of security," apparently by way of militant Socialism. The idea appears to have been a demonstration of the processes of experience in a sensitive and expressive temperament whereby this change is prepared and brought about.

It seems to the present reviewer that some of the most important processes concerned, while indicated, are outside the consciousness of both Amory and his biographer. It isn't as an accomplished demonstration of all the deeper facts of Amory that the book is so triumphantly interesting. That was not to be expected of any author of Mr. Fitzgerald's age, getting psychological material, as he must, by introspection.

But if Amory is not a mature study, he is a tempting subject for one and will delight the analysts. They will note that for all his dalliances and love affairs he remains not only corporeally virginal but fiercely chaste of soul. The girls he falls in love with he idealizes desperately, without sentimental illusion. Crude sexual opportunity revolts him in a mystical way, and with this inhibition is mixed up the influence on his character of association with Mgr. Darcy, the fine prelate between whom and Amory, since the latter's sixteenth year, there has existed a devotion of the paternal-filial nature. At the end we have Amory identifying "the problem of sex" with "the problem of evil," while he is and all along has been, without religion.

There are clever things, keen and searching things, amusingly young and mistaken things, beautiful things and pretty things—these last named including some pleasant poems—and truly inspired and elevated things, an astonishing abundance of each, in *This Side of Paradise*. You could call it the youthful Byronism that is normal in a man of the author's type, working out through a well-furnished intellect of unusual critical force. Better, perhaps, you would call it the resultant of a struggle between that sort of romantic rebellion and an intellectual purpose to emulate the H.G. Wells of—say, *The Research Magnificent.*

The real import of whatever you chose to call it would be that Mr. Fitzgerald had not completely found himself as yet. For your own part, having found him, you would be unlikely to lose sight of any of his future work.

45
Books and Other Things

ROBERT C. BENCHLEY

One of the troubles with writing book reviews is that one has so little time for reading. I never seem to be able to catch up with the new books. For weeks and weeks people have been writing and talking about young Mr. F. Scott Fitzgerald's *This Side of Paradise*, and I have been intending to read it, so that the young man might not have to wait too long before finding out what I thought about his first book. I really owed it to Mr. Fitzgerald, it seemed to me. So I read it and liked it.

As an account of the career of a boy through preparatory school, Princeton, love and life, *This Side of Paradise* may not be a great book. Frankly, I don't know a great book when I see one. I have to wait and find out what other people think about it. But in spite of its immaturity, its ingenuousness and its many false notes, it is something *new*, and for this alone Mr. Fitzgerald deserves a crown of something very expensive.

He tells a story in a new way, without regard to rules or convention, and it is an interesting story. In these days when any one can (and does) turn out a book which has been done hundreds of times before and bids fair to be done hundreds of times again, simply by following Stevenson's advice and playing "the sedulous ape" to successful predecessors, I should be inclined to hail as a genius any twenty-three-year-old author who can think up something new and say it in a new way so that it will be interesting to a great many people.

Mr. Fitzgerald's characters are very clever most of the time. Especially when they are making love. I may have been particularly gauche about my own love-making, but as I remember it (and I am corroborated in this by the only other witness) the affair did not go off anywhere near so smoothly or cleverly as that of Mr. Fitzgerald's Amory (aged twenty-three) and Rosalind (aged nineteen). It was Mr. Fitzgerald's whim to write this scene in the manner of a play.

>   He—You and I are somewhat alike—except that I'm years older in experience.
>   She—How old are you?

SOURCE *New York Morning World*, 21 April 1920, p. 10.

He—Almost twenty-three. You?
She—Nineteen—just.
He—I suppose you're the product of a fashionable school.
She—No, I'm fairly raw material. I was expelled from Spence—I've forgotten why.
He—What's your general trend?
She—Oh, I'm bright, quite selfish, emotional when aroused, fond of admiration—
He (suddenly)—I don't want to fall in love with you—
She (raising her eyebrows)—Nobody asked you to.
He (continuing coldly)—But I probably will. I love your mouth.
She—Hush! Please don't fall in love with my mouth—hair, eyes, shoulders, slippers—but not my mouth. Everybody falls in love with my mouth.
He—It's quite beautiful.
She—It's too small.
He—No, it isn't—let's see.
(He kisses her again with the same thoroughness.)
She (rather moved)—Say something sweet.
He (frightened)—Lord help me!
She (drawing away)—Well, don't, if it's so hard.
He—Shall we pretend? So soon?
She—We haven't the same standards of time as other people.
He—Already it's—other people.
She—Let's pretend.
He—No, I can't; it's sentiment.
She—You're not sentimental?
He—No, I'm romantic—a sentimental person thinks things will last—a romantic person hopes against hope that they won't. Sentiment is emotional.

Pretty subtle stuff for a twenty-three-year-old to hand out extemporaneously to a nineteen-year-old, and equally deep return shots on the part of the nineteen-year-old. There may be courses in that at Princeton and Miss Spence's, however. They teach so many things nowadays.

But the queer part of it is that within a fortnight the two young people had lost all of their cleverness and were just a couple of poor, bleating things like the rest of us. In the following scene we find none of the epigrammatic sparkle, none of the cynical observations on life and love, which marked the dialogue two weeks earlier. Simply the sound of good old-fashioned Vermont maple syrup such as can be overheard by any one anywhere during the months of April, May and June. Incidentally, I would call the attention of Miss Spence's English department to the opening line of its ex-pupil. Maybe she was expelled for a similar breach.

'Sit like we do,' she whispered. 'I knew you'd come to-night,' she said softly, 'like summer, just when I needed you most—darling, darling!'
His lips moved lazily over her face.
'You taste so good,' he sighed.
'How do you mean, lover?'
'Oh, just sweet, just sweet.' He held her closer.
'Amory,' she whispered, 'when you're ready for me I'll marry you.'
'We won't have much at first.'

'Don't' she cried. 'It hurts when you reproach yourself for what you cannot give me. I've got your precious self—and that's enough for me.'
'Tell me'—
'You know, don't you? Oh, you know.'
'Yes, but I want to hear you say it.'

Etc.

Either Mr. Fitzgerald got tired or Amory and Rosalind had just a little good stuff worked up in advance and used it all at their first meeting. Two weeks is a short time for a couple of high-class conversationalists to go bad in. Maybe they were really in love.

46
A Chronicle of Youth by Youth

MARGARET EMERSON BAILEY

"Just as the boiling pot gives off heat, so through youth and adolescence we give off calories of virtue." Since this, as Mr. Fitzgerald sees it, is the process of molten youth as it takes shape and hardens, his novel is less a history of its assumption of form than of its loss of radiance. Were this all, *This Side of Paradise* would contain little new. More tolerantly, certainly more humorously, the same process has been set forth by a score of English novelists. But though referred to still as "the younger group," they show by their very tolerance and humor that they have passed on, that their experiences have already become recollections. They are reviewing youth with a memory—not a sensation—of its joy and bitterness, and are looking back to its problems with a wistful patronage. Mr. Fitzgerald, in contrast, gives the impression of being still in the thick of the fight, and of having the fierceness of combat. The dust of conflict is still in his eyes and he does not even see very clearly. At times he cannot distinguish youth's friend from its foe or perceive where it has met with defeat and where conquered. The battle is on and the besetting forces loom very large. They take shape allegorically; it is their exaggeration and the very solemnity with which they are viewed that give the book value, for they make it a record at the very moment of the encounter.

Amory Blaine, the hero of this tale, starts life with a handicap. "From his mother he inherits every trait except the inexpressible few which make him worth while." An exotic she may no longer be called, for in novels her species has become indigenous to the Middle West and is constantly culled there whenever costly and poisonous beauty is needed to color the page. Unfortunately for her son, whose coming she had looked upon as a burden, she finds him a source of diversion and takes delight in the precocity developed by her companionship. Had it not been for his heritage from his father, the calories of his virtue must have been multitudinous to have held out. As it is, the

SOURCE *The Bookman* LI, June 1920, pp. 471–472.

worst that she does for him is to cut him off from his kind and from a normal boy's "roughing it," to make him acutely conscious of his good looks, and to give him a snobbish belief in himself as a personage reserved for special adventure. But once she has worked what havoc she may, she drops him with a swiftness amazing even in a person of her fleeting interest, and he is left to the leveling process of school and college. From both as well as from the war, he emerges with mind awakened and consequently with a lessened conceit, save where it is concerned in the *amourettes* which lead up to the tragedy, so splendidly black, of the lost Rosalind. It is in relation to these that the author sets himself the task of the social historian, presenting society in its mad reaction to war. For the hero does not need to go to the underworld in his quest for excitement. The débutante of old days, the Victorian "virginal doll," has been transformed to the "baby vamp," who if she is too hard-headed to follow in morals the Queens of the Movies, has at least adopted their manners. Against her, Amory hasn't a chance. And when to disillusionment is added the loss of money and of his friends who are pushed out of the story in a way to which no vigorous characters would submit, he goes down like Brian de Bois Guilbert, "the victim of contending passions." One would think in such a moment that it would be small comfort to "know one's self," though it is with that triumphant if unconvincing protestation that the book closes.

Such a summary is undoubtedly too hard on the book, for it overstresses its failure to arouse sympathy. It also fails to take into account passages, sometimes whole chapters, of brilliant cleverness—those for example where the author takes a fling at modern literary movements or satirizes the already jaded débutante as she makes her curtsy to the world. Little, moreover, does Mr. Fitzgerald care for the conventions of form; and there is something very taking in the nonchalance with which he passes from straight narrative to letters, poems, or dramatic episodes. Quite as wilful is his style. But in all its affectations, its cleverness, its occasional beauty, even its sometimes intentioned vulgarity and ensuing timidity, it so unites with the matter as to make the book a convincing chronicle of youth by youth.

47
Books More or Less Amusing

◆

H.L. MENCKEN

The best American novel that I have seen of late is also the product of a neophyte, to wit, F. Scott Fitzgerald. This Fitzgerald has taken part in The *Smart Set*'s display of literary fireworks more than once, and so you are probably familiar with his method. In *This Side of Paradise* he offers a truly amazing first novel—original in structure, extremely sophisticated in manner, and adorned with a brilliancy that is as rare in American writing as honesty is in American statecraft. The young American novelist usually reveals himself as a naïve, sentimental and somewhat disgusting ignoramus—a believer in Great Causes, a snuffler and eye-roller, a spouter of stale philosophies out of Kensington drawing-rooms, the doggeries of French hack-drivers, and the lower floor of the Munich Hofbräuhaus. Nine times out of ten one finds him shocked by the discovery that women are not the complete angels that they pretend to be, and full of the theory that all of the miners in West Virginia would become instantly non-luetic, intelligent and happy if Congress would only pass half a dozen simple laws. In brief, a fellow viewing human existence through a knot-hole in the floor of a Socialist local. Fitzgerald is nothing of the sort. On the contrary, he is a highly civilized and rather waggish fellow—a youngster not without sentiment, and one even cursed with a touch of two of pretty sentimentality, but still one who is many cuts above the general of the land. More, an artist—an apt and delicate weaver of words, a clever hand, a sound workman. The first half of the story is far better than the second half. It is not that Fitzgerald's manner runs thin, but that his hero begins to elude him. What, after such a youth, is to be done with the fellow? The author's solution is anything but felicitous. He simply drops his Amory Blaine as Mark Twain dropped Huckleberry Finn, but for a less cogent reason. But down to and including the episode of the love affair with Rosalind the thing is capital, especially the first chapters. Not since Frank Norris's day has there been a more adept slapping in of preliminaries.

SOURCE *Smart Set* LXII, August 1920, p. 140.

48
Carnegie Library Notes

◆

FRANCES NEWMAN

It is not, of course necessary that all American reviewers—critic is a rather lofty word—should have read *Sinister Street* once a month or so during the six years that one has been privileged to do so, and peraps one official skimming might have been dimmed by the intervention of a fairly prolonged war. But an equally casual skimming of the reviews of *This Side of Paradise* has revealed in only the *New Republic* a glance at Mr. Fitzgerald's "acquisitive eye on 'Sinister Street.'" And as the next line continued "without its obesity," one gathers that this R.V.A.S. has no very tender regard for Michael Fane. But if *Sinister Street* was until very lately the apple of one's eye and if even the discovery of a new apple has not caused one to love it less, the perusal of *This Side of Paradise* becomes nothing less than agony.

Now, naturally, one knows no more of Mr. Fitzgerald's literary affections than he has seen fit to reveal in print, but it rather seems that his memory is much more highly developed than his imagination and that he has no idea how good a memory he really has. As some forgotten writer said when *Queed* was first delighting the world, Mr. Harrison might have imitated Robert Chambers, but he had instead risen to the altitude of imitating the author of *Septimus*, and so one might take it kindly that young Mr. Fitzgerald has hitched is wagon to Mr. Mackenzie rather than to Ralph Barbour, and so, if it were only Mr. Walpole or Mr. Cannan or even Aldous Huxley, one could. But the vulgarizing of one's perfect book is more than can be endured in silence.

Mr. Fitzgerald certainly did not sit down with the desire to write a story of youth and after casting about for a model, say to himself that he would write an American parody of *Sinister Street*. No one in his senses would do that. So it must follow that he has been betrayed by his too retentive memory. The suffering of witnessing the desecration of an idol has made the reading of every one of his words impossible, so it is quite possible that one has missed the most distressing of the affinities between the career of Amory Blaine and Michael Fane—one had not, until the moment of writing them, realized that

SOURCE *Atlanta Constitution*, 13 February 1921, p. 2.

the names rhyme—and one may also have missed some of Mr. Fitzgerald's felicities, even all of them. This sincere flattery begins at the very beginning, by a caricature of Mrs. Fane, that vague and charming woman, which after being united with some of the less pleasing frailties of Michael's nurse, is called the sophisticated mother of Amory. Mr. Fitzgerald has even provided a dignitary of the Catholic church for Amory to discuss his divergences from other boys with—quite as Michael had his Mr. Viner for the same high use. And just, also, as Michael had his Wilmot to introduce him to Oscar Wilde and Walter Pater and Mademoiselle de Maupin, even to the decadents of another age—Petronius and Apuleius and Suetonius, Amory had his D'Invilliers to discover to him the glories of *Dorian Gray* and Swinburne and Pater, of Gautier, and Huysmans, of "the racier sections of Rabelais, Boccaccio, Petronius and Suetonius." And Michael was called Narcissus by this Wilmot; Mr. Fitzgerald has provided a section entitled "Narcissus on Duty." The first book of *Sinister Street* is called "Dreaming Spires," and most properly since Matthew Arnold gave the phrase to Oxford; the entry of Amory into Princeton is heralded by the title "Spires and Gargoyles." Michael was teased by his governess because his sympathies were the sympathies of the late G.A. Henty, even to the point of sympathizing with the American colonists against his own British forbears; Amory had all the "Henty biasses," even to the point of sympathizing with the southern confederacy. Michael was rigid about dividing Oxford into "good eggs and bad men"; Amory's world was divided into "slickers and big-men." And there are endless phrases and incidents that have risen from poor Mr. Fitzgerald's subconscious mind rather than from his observation.

Such a comparison is undoubtedly vain and frivolous, but this young man, in the phrase of his period, has positively "asked for it." To one who cherishes *Sinister Street* and one who cherishes some hope for the American novel, it is impossible to read *This Side of Paradise* without having one's blood-pressure mount to a dangerous degree and without one's temperature becoming unendurable. And it would not be so very annoying if any number of critics for whom one had high regard had not taken it so very seriously. Such panegyrics as might have greeted the plays of Euripides or the Divine Comedy—but which certainly did not—have flowed from the most respectable sources; the book has had both the success of esteem and the success of popularity.

As for the ways in which *This Side of Paradise* differs from *Sinister Street*, except for a few essentially trivial ones, a comparison would be rather like one between "Irene" and "Tristan and Isolde." There is, however, the fundamental one that Michael Fane, in spite of some eccentricities of ancestry, was a gentleman. And there is also the difference that Mr. Fitzgerald's youths serve Athena and Aphrodite quite interchangeably.... But both of these books end with a crisis of youth and a cry in the dark—rather significantly, the darkness of Rome and the darkness of New Jersey.

Of course, Mr. Fitzgerald is young—so young that he thinks eight years passed between the eighteenth amendment and the day when the Fifth Avenue traffic lights were still a subject of conversation—and Dr. Johnson might charitably decide that one should be surprised to find it done at all. But if one must have youth, let us have Daisy Ashford's youth and let us not be confronted with a choice between Mr. Fitzgerald's youthful patchwork and Miss Opal Whiteley's childish labor.

But the crowning glory of *This Side of Paradise* may be regarded as the fact that about his twenty-third year this Amory Blaine "was where Goethe was when he began 'Faust'; he was where Conrad was when he wrote 'Almayer's Folly.'" Now, quite apart from the difficulty of conceiving that Goethe and Conrad were at the same place, one grieves for the loss it is to American letters that this gifted Amory should be only the creation of Mr. Fitzgerald's brain.

49
This Side of Paradise: The Pageantry of Disillusion

◆

SY KAHN

In his first novel, *This Side of Paradise*, published in 1920 when the author was twenty-three years old, F. Scott Fitzgerald announced the major themes of his total work. The novel reveals that Fitzgerald had an early grasp of his essential material although he had not yet learned to exploit it expertly. In some ways his first novel is the most instructive of his four completed novels; here he nakedly and naïvely exposed his themes before his increased sophistication shaped his insights into the more impressive configurations of *The Great Gatsby* (1925) and *Tender is the Night* (1934). In Amory Blaine, hero of *This Side of Paradise*, we can see the child who is father to the later men, and in his dilemmas we find the compelling themes of Fitzgerald's work.

All of Fitzgerald's heroes, his "brothers" as he called them, from Amory Blaine to Dick Diver, were men concerned with fashioning a code or sustaining a belief, and, most important, all feel the restraints of the American Puritan heritage. Like Nick Carraway, the narrator in *The Great Gatsby*, they are men full of "interior rules" whose sources lie in the moral codes of American life previous to World War I. Despite the impact of the first World War on sexual mores and drinking, and the fact that, according to Amory, "four men have discovered Paris to one that discovered God," he remains a conscience- and guilt-ridden character. Fitzgerald said of himself that his was a New England conscience raised in Minnesota; Midwest-born, Minnesota-raised Amory is Fitzgerald's fictional counterpart. "Now a confession will have to be made," wrote Fitzgerald early in *This Side of Paradise*, "Amory had rather a Puritan conscience. Not that he yielded to it—later in life he nearly completely slew it—but at fifteen it made him consider himself a great deal worse than other boys...." The important word here is "nearly," both for Amory and for Fitzgerald himself. There is no evidence in the novel that Amory triumphed over, much less slew, his Puritan conscience. Indeed, it is that very conscience that shapes his imagination and his vision of reality

SOURCE *Midwest Quarterly* VII, January 1966, pp. 171–194.

and prepares him for a series of disillusionments.

As its title suggests, *This Side of Paradise* is something of an allegory in which American Youth is caught between the forces of Good and Evil. Among Americans, and especially among the young, "morality" and "sex" are interchangeable terms. Frequently the judgment of "right" and "wrong" behavior rests almost exclusively on sexual behavior. Evil is identified with sex: there the devil wields his greatest powers. If Dante were a young American, Francesca and Paolo might sit at the right hand of Satan. On a number of occasions Amory finds himself caught between his Puritan distrust of sex and the body and the relaxed social and sexual rituals of his time. Like many of his readers, Amory idealized women but found it difficult to maintain his ennobled feelings when they were tested by flesh and blood, the frequent dilemma of the Puritan conscience and a theme much employed in American literature ever since Hawthorne explored it. Amory's ambivalence is dramatized early in the novel when he goes to a party and finds himself alone with Myra and on the verge of his first kiss.

> Sudden revulsion seized Amory, disgust, loathing for the whole incident. He desired frantically to be away, never to see Myra again, never to kiss anyone; he became conscious of his face and hers, of their clinging hands, and he wanted to creep out of his body and hide somewhere safe out of sight, up in the corner of his mind.
> "Kiss me again." Her voice came out of a great void.
> "I don't want to," he heard himself saying. There was another pause.
> "I don't want to!" he repeated passionately.

Many critics have noted that *This Side of Paradise* seems odd to us now as a novel of "flaming youth," and that its scenes of moral laxness and dissipation are today's innocent conventions. It may never have been the revelation of youthful manners, however, that accounted for the book's popularity; it may well have been Fitzgerald's manipulation of the puritanical Amory Blaine that wrenched the conscience of his readers and dramatized their own youthful dilemmas in much the same way as Salinger's Holden Caulfield speaks for the questing youth of the 1950's and 60's.

Amory's early skirmishes with girls anticipate his later engagement with women and the full battle of the sexes. During his Princeton days he carries on a romantic and sentimental correspondence with Isabelle Borgé. During a weekend at Isabelle's home, however, Amory discovers that it is not the girl but his egoistic image of himself as conquering lover that has enchanted him, and the romance is punctured as easily as he bruises her neck with his shirt stud when he embraces her. Her simple and fleshly "ouch" punctuates the college romance, and the spat that follows makes Amory aware that "he had not an ounce of real affection for Isabelle." This comic interlude further dramatizes the difference between woman as romantic illusion and woman as reality, but the theme is lightly touched here. Isabelle was never flesh or woman enough to impel the deeper dilemmas of Amory Blaine.

Not long before the conclusion of his college romance a more instructive incident occurs in Amory's life which announces a theme that Fitzgerald will combine with the themes of sex and evil to complicate the vision of his hero. Returning to Princeton by car, Amory and his friends discover that another carload of students has overturned and killed Dick Humbird, one of the promising men of Princeton. The sudden shock of Humbird's death unnerves and penetrates Amory deeper than he can know. Here is the first victim of many scenes of violence and death in Fitzgerald's novels, bizarre and surrealistic scenes which he depicted with unusual skill and which always carry a heavy burden of meaning. Humbird's death is announced by a spectral "old crone" whose cracked, hollow voice and flapping kimono complete the image of a night-riding harpy. Oracularly she points to the corpse lying under a roadside arc-light, face down in a widening circle of blood. The night wind stirs a broken fender "to a plaintive tinny sound." In this novel, set in the years during and immediately after World War I, Fitzgerald calls the roll of Amory's dead classmates, beginning with Humbird, just as he continued to count the dead of his generation all his life. The event marks a transition in Amory; it breaks his illusion that youth is permanent and indestructible.

Some weeks after Humbird's death, Amory and his college friend Fred Sloan escort two chorus girls during an evening in New York. The events of this evening lay open for us the tortured heart and mind of the youngest of Fitzgerald's "brothers." Now Amory must face the full reality of women as sexual creatures, neither glamorized nor sentimentalized. The two couples go to a cafe where Amory is aware of being watched by a middle-aged, faintly smiling man in a brown sack suit. Then, Amory and the others go to upper Manhattan where the girls have an apartment among the "tall, white-stone buildings, dotted with dark windows" that stretch endlessly, "flooded with bright moonlight that gave them a calcium pallor." From the moment that the mysterious, pale-faced man has scrutinized Amory, the party develops a sensual and evil atmosphere. The white buildings and the moonlight recall the arc-light which spotlighted Humbird's death and anticipate the spectral appearance of the ominous man in the apartment. While Amory sat on the sofa with Axia, "There was a minute while temptation crept over him like a warm wind, and his imagination turned to fire...." At that instant he is astonished to discover the man who had been in the cafe: "There the man sat, half leaned against a pile of pillows in the corner of the divan. His face was cast in the same yellow wax as in the cafe, neither the dull, pasty color of a dead man—rather a sort of virile pallor—nor unhealthy...."

This image of the devil is the symbol of shock, born of the impact of sensuality upon Puritan morality, conscience, and Catholic sense of sin. The most shocking detail about the man is his feet, which are encased in moccasins, "pointed, though, like the shoes they wore in the fourteenth century, and with the little ends curling up." It is "unutterably terrible" that the toes seem to fill them to the end. First Amory is transfixed by this vision of evil; then he bolts. Fitzgerald continues to build Amory's terror by carefully patterning the images of pale light throughout the successive scenes, images that connect these events with Humbird's death scene. Down the long streets of New York shines the moonlight, palely reflected from the white buildings. He is horrified to realize that he is not fleeing the strange footsteps but following them, setting, as it were, his own foot on the path to hell:

> ... he turned off the street and darted into an alley, narrow and dark and smelling of old rottenness. He twisted down a long, sinuous blackness, where the moonlight was shut away except for the tiny glints and patches ... then suddenly sank panting into a corner by a fence, exhausted.

Thus Amory escapes, in fact, his sexual encounter with Axia, haunted as he is by a man whose face is a pallid mask reminiscent of Humbird and of the devil himself. But his flight down moon-drenched streets leads him to an alley whose sexual symbolism makes him psychologically experience what he has physically avoided.

No Goodman Brown ever emerged from his bewitched forest more haunted and guilt-ridden than young Amory from the stone jungle of twentieth-century New York. On the streets of the city he seems caught up in an interior morality play that obliterates his surroundings. As he walks, praying for someone "stupid" and "good" to save him, he hears something clang "like a low gong struck at a distance," and again, by this device, we are reminded of the torn fender of Humbird's death car banging in the wind. Then before Amory's eyes: "a face flashed over the two feet, a face pale and distorted with a sort of infinite evil that twisted it like a flame in the wind; *but he knew, for the half instant that the gong twanged and hummed, that it was the face of Dick Humbird* [Fitzgerald's italics]." By means of the device of light and sound imagery, Fitzgerald associates the devil with the face of the dead classmate and creates a vision in which the major themes of sex, evil, and death meet to shape the face and figure of the devil.

For the rest of this momentous weekend Amory reverberates to his encounter with temptation and evil. The painted faces of Broadway make him ill, and he rails at Sloan that New York is "ghastly" and "filthy" while Sloan wonders what would have happened if Amory had "gone through with our little party." He abandons Sloan for a purgative "head massage" in a barber shop, but "the smell of the powders and tonics brought back Axia's sidelong, suggestive smile, and he left hurriedly." On the train for Princeton a "painted woman" brings on a new wave of nausea and he changes cars, until finally, back at Princeton, on a wild and windy night, he joins his friend Tom. As the young men settle down to try to study, and the "wet branches moved and clawed with their fingernails on the window pane," both of them are suddenly electrified by a sense of the presence of evil. Tom thinks he sees the flash of a face at the window. "Something was looking at you," he tells Amory, and Amory, unnerved, replies, "I've had one hell of an experience. I think I've seen the devil or—something like him."

If the white buildings of New York, blanched by the moon, are the symbols of evil, the gothic spires of Princeton are the architecture of sanity and safety. Early in the novel Fitzgerald establishes this contrast when he tells us that through the shell of Amory's undergraduate consciousness "had broken a deep and reverent devotion to the gray walls and Gothic peaks and all they symbolized as warehouses of dead ages." Consequently, when Amory returns to the college after his encounter with "the devil" in New York, "he nearly cried aloud with joy when the towers of Princeton loomed up beside him and the yellow squares of light filtered through the blue rain." Here there is no phallic thrust of dark-windowed, pale buildings, but rather the steady lights, green spaces, and chaste spires of sanctuary. For Amory Blaine, transplanted from Minnesota to Princeton, the University is his stronghold, the monastic fortress for his Catholic-Puritan conscience this side of Paradise.

During the last years of his college life, Amory's encounter with sensuality provides a "sombre background ... that filled his nights with a dreary terror and made him unable to pray." An indifferent Catholic, he is, nevertheless, almost as much disturbed by the "ghost of a code," this "gaudy, ritualistic, paradoxical Catholicism," as he is by the specters born of his puritanical conscience. In America, Leslie Fiedler has pointed out, "The sensibility of the Catholic ... becomes like everything else puritan." Amory illustrates the point early in the novel when he derides the easy kiss, the hip flask, the petting interlude in parked cars even though he tries to play the role of the alert and conforming adolescent of his time. Following his encounter with death and the devil, in the interlude before his graduation and participation in the war, Amory does find in Clara Page, a distant cousin, a woman he can idealize. Monsignor Thayer Darcy, family friend and confidant, urges Amory to seek her out in Philadelphia. He discovers in Clara a woman in whom sex has been translated into intelligence and vitality. She is blonde and saintly, husbandless but with babies to care for; in short, she is the Madonna figure that permits the man haunted by puritanical notions of sexual evil to release his ardor in pure and exalted feeling. Clara is Beatrice to his incipient Dante. Images of light accumulate about her blonde head, haloed and hallowed as she is by young Amory's romantic idealism. "She was immemorial," we are told immediately about her, and too good for any man. Gradually he falls in love with her, or, more rightly, with his own ideal of what women should be, creatures of light, as her name suggests, intelligence and charm, but essentially untouchable. He is entranced with her at church when "she knelt and bent her golden hair into the stained-glass light." Spontaneously and to their mutual embarrassment he calls "St. Cecilia" and confesses that "if I lost faith in you I'd lose faith in God." She reveals to him that she has never been in love, which, of course, brightens the halo about her: "she seemed suddenly a daughter of light alone." Clara remains unsullied and sanctified. Amory realizes she could have been a "devil" if God had bent her soul a little the other way. As Fitzgerald's novels reveal, Madonnas with "bent souls" are the inevitable partners for Fitzgerald's tormented brethren, his "spoiled priests."

After Amory graduates he goes to France to fight, but Fitzgerald telescopes the years 1917 and 1918 by the device of quoting several letters. He misses the opportunity here of deepening the history of Amory's disillusion because he could not construct incidents for Amory from a world he himself did not know. Indeed Fitzgerald served in the army, but he was never sent abroad. The metaphor of war was not natural to him, not a part of his vision or disillusioning experience as it was for his contemporary, Ernest Hemingway. Consequently, when next we truly confront Amory, it is in post-war New York, and with no sense that he is a veteran, and the clear notion that he is still a virgin. It is in the battle of the sexes rather than in the trenches that Amory receives his sudden and lasting wounds.

In his engagement to Rosalind Connage, the post-war debutante-flapper, Amory suffers painful disillusionment. The trauma of her eventual rejection of him is the first expression of a situation that haunts Fitzgerald's total work with nightmarish regularity. It is probable that the source of Fitzgerald's obsessive concern with losing the girl one loves was in his fear of losing his fiancée Zelda Sayre because he had neither the position nor money to support her. In Amory Blaine's loss of Rosalind, for these very reasons he plays out a drama that might have been his own. In his work there are many variations on the nightmare: Gatsby and Daisy, Diver and Nicole, to state the most obvious examples. The wealthy Rosalind breaks her engagement with Amory because his meager job in an advertising agency cannot hope to support her in any style. "You'd hate me in a narrow atmosphere. I'd make you hate me," she tells him. It is the recognition of this hard, economic fact that eventually turns Amory toward socialism at the end of the novel. "I'm sick of a system," he says then, "where the richest man gets the most beautiful girl if he wants her...." Fitzgerald never underestimated the fact that love and economics are intertwined in human affairs, and that when the forces of love and wealth are pitted against each other, wealth often strips love of its sentimentalities and illusions. There is not a single hero in his novels who is not, one way or another, undone by the power and strategies of wealth. Amory is the first of Fitzgerald's innocent Adams disemboweled by savage Eves.

In the despair of his disillusion he discovers that New York, which once gave him a vision of the devil, now offers him a variety of dissipations: drunkenness, half-remembered encounters in night clubs, and finally a severe beating. In Fitzgerald's novels his heroes take beatings at those points when they are emotionally bankrupt. These manifest the psychic wounding that has taken place and symbolize as well the desire for punishment for having lost one's moral grip. One remembers Anthony Patch of *The Beautiful and Damned* beaten up on a New York street, and Dick Diver mauled by taxi drivers after his sexual capitulation to Rosemary in Rome, both men at the nadir of their disillusionment and at their lowest emotional ebb. As for Jay Gatsby, he is shot to death and thus saved at the last moment from complete disillusionment about Daisy, as if only death could keep a Fitzgerald man from the inevitable knowledge of the failed female.

Having painfully learned that attractiveness and intelligence are not adequate substitutes for wealth, Amory retreats to Washington to visit Thayer Darcy, but missing connections, he decides to recuperate with an ancient uncle in Maryland. In the fields of Ramilly County he meets nineteen-year-old Eleanor Savage, whom he finds one stormy night perched atop a haystack reciting Verlaine while rain pours and lightning cracks. Her last name, the lightning flashes, as when Tom saw the devil looking at Amory, and Amory's opening address to her inform us that the young man is about to encounter evil again. "Who the devil is there in Ramilly County ... who would deliver Verlaine in an extemporaneous tune to a soaking haystack?" he asks. When she inquires who he is, he replies "I'm Don Juan," and the new romance commences. The wild landscape of Maryland, "the half-sensual, half-neurotic quality of this autumn with Eleanor," insure that Amory is about to pass another season in hell. To Maryland both bring small histories of youthful disillusionment. If Amory has seen Rosalind unmask the face of love to reveal the tight-lipped face of wealth, Eleanor has discovered that the romantic mask hides the leering face of sex. For three weeks they take various poses with each other, until one moonlit night when they seemed "dim phantasmal shapes, expressing eternal beauty in curious elfin moods," they symbolically turn out of the moonlight into the "trellised darkness of a vine-hung pagoda," and he catches her in his arms. In a euphemistic passage, Fitzgerald suggests that Amory has at last been sexually initiated, but the "novel of flaming youth" is not so graphic or direct as to make this certain: "'you are mine—you know you're mine!' he cried wildly ... the moonlight twisted in through the vines and listened ... the fireflies hung upon their whispers as if to win his glance from the glory of their eyes."

Following this ambiguous encounter, on this last night of Amory's vacation in Maryland, they take their horses for a "farewell trot by the cold moonlight." Angry at the world which forces her to subordinate her intelligence to less clever men in order to attract them, angry at a world that will not sustain romantic illusions, angry at moons that turn cold and clear, she rails, "Oh, just one person in fifty has any glimmer of what sex is. I'm hipped on Freud and all that, but it's rotten that every bit of real love in the world is ninety-nine percent passion and one little soupçon of jealousy." Amory is quick to agree that sex is "a rather unpleasant overpowering force that's part of the machinery under everything. It's like an actor that lets you see his mechanics!"

Now Amory comes fully to grips with the idea that torments him and abuses his idealism, and in the following passage speaks for his postwar generation poised on the edge of the decade that is to reveal many changes in American attitudes:

> You see everyone's got to have some cloak to throw around it. The mediocre intellects, Plato's second class, use the remnants of romantic chivalry diluted with Victorian sentiment—and we who consider ourselves the intellectuals cover it by pretending that it's another side of us, has nothing to do with our shining brains; we pretend that the fact that we realize it is really absolving us from being a prey to it. But the truth is that sex is right in the middle of our purest abstractions, so close that it obscures vision.

Whatever images of romantic love they had attempted to create together lie shattered about them; the touch of flesh explodes their illusions. Relentlessly Amory advances his argument: there is no protection against sex, neither intellect nor conversation; nor the Catholic church, counters Eleanor, which shakes him:

> Thousands of scowling priests keeping the degenerate Italians and illiterate Irish repentant with gabble-gabble about the sixth and ninth commandments. It's just all cloaks, sentiment and spiritual rouge and panaceas. I tell you there *is* no God, not even a definite abstract goodness; so it's all got to be worked out for the individual by the individual here in the high white foreheads like mine, and you're too much the prig to admit it.

To Amory this is blasphemy, an evil he cannot reconcile with some hard, inner core of values, perhaps his Irish-American puritanism. Eleanor, in a paroxysm of outrage at her discovery of the endless masquerades of sex, turns her horse toward a dark cliff in a suicide attempt. At the last moment she throws herself off the horse while it goes whinnying over the edge. Neither of these babes in the wood is old enough to sustain feeling for the other without romantic illusion, though they are able, some years later, to exchange melancholy poems. In retrospect he realizes that under that high-riding "evil moon" they could "see the devil in each other," and the old puritanical notion that beauty is often the mask for evil fixes itself in his soul.

There remain several more crucial incidents in the novel to complete the pageantry of Amory Blaine's disillusion. Alone in Atlantic City he meets Alec Connage, Rosalind's brother, accompanied by two women, and Amory becomes involved in Alec's sexual intrigue. They catch him up in a distressed moment when he is recalling the gaiety of Princeton escapades, innocent and boisterous, on these same boardwalks and beaches, and now, a few years later, so many of his classmates are already dead. His youth seems vanished and he vaguely longs for death; his listlessness and disillusion are deepened by the thought that women can only hold men by appealing to the worst in them, the "thesis of most of his bad nights."

Agreeing to occupy a hotel room connecting with Alec's, to substitute for a friend of Alec's who needed to leave, Amory goes to the room, mourning the lost Rosalind, and falls asleep while an ominous moon sears the sky. He is awakened by a house detective pounding on Alec's door and the frightened voices of Alec and Jill, a "gaudy, vermillion-lipped blonde," coming from the connecting bathroom. In a terrified moment Alec explains that he cannot lie that Jill is his wife since the house detective knows her, and that he will be liable under the Mann Act; meanwhile the miserable Jill retreats to Amory's bed. At this point Fitzgerald again lifts this scene by the device of surrealistic detail to a level that clearly exposes the themes of the novel:

> Amory realized there were other things in the room besides people ... over and around the figure crouched in the bed, there hung an aura, gossamer as a moonbeam, tainted as a stale, weak wine, yet a horror, diffusively brooding already over the three of them ... and over by the window among the stirring curtains stood something else, featureless and indistinguishable, yet strangely familiar.

Caught between these two evil presences in his room, he swiftly decides to take responsibility for Jill, to take the blame off Alec, and at that instant the specters near the bed and window vanish. In that listening, suspended moment evil forms the spectral shapes of sex and death. For shortly after this incident, in a short scene at the police station, Amory learns that Monsignor Darcy has died, and he knows that it was his ghost that stirred the curtains of the hotel bedroom.

Later, back in New York, in a dreary, rainy autumn, Amory continues to mourn the lost Rosalind. She has disillusioned him about love, and her brother has completed the emotional carnage by the tawdry escapade in Atlantic City. Once again he is sensitized to "the fetid sensuousness of stale powder on women" as he walks the streets and recoils from the poor of New York whose poverty seems more vile than it is when sex drives the penniless men and women together; "it was an atmosphere wherein birth and marriage and death were loathsome, secret things." The fact that he is jobless and that his mother has made bad investments, destroying his private income, makes him all the more fearful and scornful of the poor as one might shun the worst image of oneself. Better to be corrupt and rich than innocent and poor, he thinks; it is essentially cleaner. In the convent of his mind he reviews the names of his dead loves as a monk might tell the beads of his rosary: Isabelle, Clara, Rosalind, Eleanor.

Amory's romantic imagination and persistent idealism, rooted in his Irish-Catholic, Puritan-Midwestern-American background save him from complete despair. If on the one hand his puritanical sensibilities operate to prepare him for outrage, frustration, and disillusionment, especially in his encounters with women, on the other hand they provide him with a certain armor against *amour*. The ambiguity is, perhaps, suggested by his name. Fitzgerald implies as well that Amory's romanticism and idealism are mystical legacies passed on to him by the death of Monsignor Darcy. Amory's sacrifice of reputation for Alec, and his realization that Alec will eventually hate him for it bring him "the full realization of his disillusion, but of Monsignor's funeral was born the romantic elf that was to enter the labyrinth with him." In the later novels, particularly *The Great Gatsby* and *Tender is the Night*, the romantic idealism of his heroes, elves in the labyrinth, at once insures their inevitable defeat in a world where the labyrinth is more torturous and dangerous, and the emotional and monetary stakes higher. Fitzgerald recognized that real minotaurs make short work of chivalrous and charming elves.

After various shocking disillusionments have knocked Amory's idealism off-balance, he reacts for a time by imagining himself deteriorating in the sweet acid of sensual abandon, a sort of evil heaven where disillusioned Puritans go:

> Port Said, Shanghai, parts of Turkestan, Constantinople, the South Seas—all lands of sad, haunting music and many odors, where lust could be a mode and expression of life, where the shades of night skies and sunsets would seem to reflect only moods of passion: the color of lips and poppies.

He would like to "let himself go to the devil," and "to sink safely and sensuously out of sight." But these thoughts also give rise to a sense of panic and guilt as he wonders if merely thinking such thoughts does not create an evil aura around him that may infect the innocent. He fears he has lost the ability to "scent evil," to ferret out instinctively "the deeper evils in pride and sensuality." The Puritan need to identify and judge evil sobers and steadies him and dispels the colorful specters of sensuality.

> The pageantry of his disillusion took shape in a world-old procession of Prophets, Athenians, Martyrs, Saints, Scientists, Don Juans, Jesuits, Puritans, Fausts, Poets, Pacifists; like costumed alumni at a college reunion they streamed before him as their dreams, personalities, and creeds had in turn thrown colored lights on his soul.

Women had not proved adequate to his imagination; philosophers and political leaders canceled out each other's thoughts; few were the men who were not emotional or intellectual or spiritual cripples. Yet he feels that he has "escaped from a small enclosure into a great labyrinth," and that he will undertake its mysteries, starting all inquiries with himself, chastened by self-reproach, loneliness, and disillusion.

In this mixed mood of regeneration and disillusion, Amory sets off, like a pilgrim in a more apparent allegory, to walk to Princeton. On a cool, gray day, "that least fleshly of all weathers; a day of dreams and far hopes and clear visions," his sense of the real begins to clarify. "The problem of evil had solidified for Amory into the problem of sex," which comes as no surprise if we have followed his history, and his thought leads him to link evil with beauty. Each time he has reached out for beauty, "it had leered out at him with the grotesque face of evil. Beauty of great art, beauty of all joy, most of all the beauty of women." To his mind beauty has too many associations with license and indulgence and weakness, and weak things are never good. Before he reaches Princeton, he stops at twilight in an old graveyard, a scene symbolically appropriate to a purging of the past and to these phoenix-like moments of transition. If certain illusions are to be buried there, certain revelations have given him new strength. The graves do not convince him that life is vain; "Somehow he could find nothing hopeless in having lived."

After midnight Amory arrives at Princeton and once again finds in the towers and spires and late-burning lights the fit symbols of his hopes. No ominous white buildings here, no evil moon. The novitiates must learn to bear the shock of exploding illusions, must grow up to find "all Gods dead, all wars fought, all faiths in man shaken." He feels sorry for them but not for himself; he is safe and free now, to "accept what was acceptable, roam, grow, rebel." Thus at the end of the novel, in a gesture more richly ambiguous of both acceptance and crucifixion than perhaps Fitzgerald could know at twenty-three, Amory "stretched out his arms to the crystalline, radiant sky" and announces, "I know myself... but that is all."

Fitzgerald's first novel reveals a number of observations that were to become persistent themes in his later work. The young Amory wants above all else to have popularity and power. Later he discovers that it is not admiration he wants, or even love, "but to be necessary to people, to be indispensable," and to give them "a sense of security." These "immense desires" are also manifest in Gatsby and even more dramatically revealed in Dick Diver. Furthermore, Fitzgerald's description of Rosalind announces a catalog of ideas thematically developed in his subsequent work. "Her fresh enthusiasm, her will to grow and learn, her endless faith in the inexhaustibility of romance, her courage and her fundamental honesty—these things were not spoiled." Spoiled, however, they are doomed to be, and it is in the loss of these qualities in his characters that we sense the pathos of their defeat. Fitzgerald called evil the forces that brought about these failures. When Monsignor Darcy writes of Amory that he has "that half-miraculous sixth sense" by which he detects evil, "the half-realized fear of God" in his heart, the lines reveal the author as tellingly as they do Amory Blaine. Taken as a whole, Fitzgerald's fiction testifies to his talent for identifying the corruption and moral failure masked by the surface glitter and carnival antics of the 1920's. His concern with evil, as he understood it, is everywhere apparent in his work, and his desire to reveal it prompted him to write in *This Side of Paradise*: "Every author ought to write every book as if he were going to be beheaded the day he finished it."

Under the edict of this urgent credo, Fitzgerald created heroes who were clearly projections of himself, and these "brothers" must confront the disillusionments that instruct them and sometimes break and kill them. They are brothers in another sense, too, in that they are related to each other by thematic blood lines. His heroes are variously undone by an idealism bravely asserted but doomed. Amory, it is true, unlike his elder "brothers," survives his disillusioning experiences by virtue of his resilient youth and his sense of flexing and stretching a new, marvelous self, but one cannot help imagining, especially in the light of the novels that followed, that his judgments concerning sex and beauty will doom him, will drive him into a corner, much as Dick Diver fades away into Upper New York after his fall in Italy and France. The final image of Amory, opening his arms to receive the limitless universe, becomes, from another angle of vision, the dead Gatsby floating in his pool, or a broken Dick Diver making an ironic sign of the cross over the beach on the Riviera. Yet Amory Blaine, Jay Gatsby, and Dick Diver are meant to win our sympathy because they cling to a romantic, Platonic image of themselves in spite of their disillusioning pilgrimages. There is no doubt that Fitzgerald intended these heroes to be nobler and more humane in their defeat than the people and forces that undo them. The elder heroes hang crucified upon the crosses of their idealism, defeated yet elevated above the men and women who have nailed them there. They have walked a terrain where certain events disarm and disillusion them, but Fitzgerald's craft insures that his heroes remain the brightest points in the landscape.

50

The Presence of Poe in *This Side of Paradise*

◆

JAMES W. TUTTLETON

The four women of Amory Blaine's life—Isabelle, Clara, Rosalind, and Eleanor—lead him to a disillusioned perception that "Inseparably linked with evil was beauty—beauty, still a constant rising tumult; soft in Eleanor's voice, in an old song at night, rioting deliriously through life like superimposed waterfalls, half rhythm, half darkness. Amory knew," Fitzgerald wrote, "that every time he had reached toward it longingly it had leered out at him with the grotesque face of evil. Beauty of great art, beauty of all joy, most of all the beauty of women."[1] This is hardly an original observation about the lure of beauty for young men or how the problem of evil may solidify into the problem of sex. But what is remarkable about Blaine's disillusionment is how Fitzgerald uses references to Edgar Allan Poe and his work to define the sense in which beauty becomes in Blaine's mind inseparably linked with evil.[2]

After breaking off with Rosalind, Amory Blaine goes on a three-week bender. This episode, "one of the most vivid ... in *This Side of Paradise*," grew out of Zelda's rejection of Fitzgerald during their early courtship and his subsequent alcoholic binge.[3] His own, or Blaine's, inebriation seems to have suggested to Fitzgerald a number of useful connections with the poems, stories, and biography of another romantic who had turned to alcohol—Edgar Allan Poe. After he sobers up, Blaine goes to Maryland and spends some time in the country. He walks through the corn-fields "reciting 'Ulalume' and congratulating Poe for drinking himself to death in that atmosphere of smiling complacency" (223).[4] During a violent thunderstorm, Blaine hears a woman quoting Verlaine's "Chanson d'Automne." This poem, appropriately heavy with a Poesque "langueur / Monotone," was written by a poet who, like many of the other French symbolists, greatly admired and imitated Poe.[5] When Amory climbs up into the haystack where Eleanor Savage has hidden herself from the storm, she admits that she recog-

SOURCE *English Language Notes* III, June 1966, pp. 284–289.

nizes him as "the blond boy that likes 'Ulalume' ..." (225). She reveals that she has heard him reciting the poem as he walked through the countryside. She says "recite 'Ulalume' and I'll be Psyche, your soul" (226).

Their meeting is developed in part through other Poe allusions—allusions perhaps less explicit than these. Blaine, for example, thinks to himself: "Suppose, only suppose, she was mad." "I'm not," she says. "Not what?" he asks. "Not mad. I didn't think you were mad when I first saw you, so it isn't fair that you should think so of me." His response is "How on earth—" (226). Eleanor's uncanny ability to "read Amory's mind" strikes me as perhaps a conscious recollection on Fitzgerald's part of that "peculiar analytic ability" of C. Auguste Dupin of Poe's Parisian tales of ratiocination. In "The Murders in the Rue Morgue," for example, the narrator is astonished one evening, as they walk through the Palais Royal, at Dupin's reading his very thoughts, although "neither of us had spoken a syllable for fifteen minutes at least."[6] The subject of their particular silent meditation on that evening was the inappropriateness of Chantilly to play the role of Xerxes in Crébillon's tragedy of that name. The devious avenues by which Dupin followed the narrator's silent free associations to this conclusion are too complicated to detail here, but the narrator's generalizations perhaps deserve remark in view of their similarity to a passage in *This Side of Paradise*: "There are few persons who have not, at some period in their lives, amused themselves in retracing the steps by which particular conclusions of their own minds have been attained. The occupation is often full of interest; and he who attempts it for the first time is astonished by the apparently illimitable distance and incoherence between the starting-point and the goal. What, then, must have been my amazement when I heard the Frenchman speak what he had just spoken, and when I could not help acknowledging that he had spoken the truth" (145). Amory Blaine's astonishment at Eleanor's ability to "read his mind" is similar, and like Poe's narrator of "The Murders in the Rue Morgue," Fitzgerald remarks: "As long as they knew each other Eleanor and Amory could be 'on a subject' and stop talking with the definite thought of it in their heads, yet ten minutes later speak aloud and find that their minds had followed the same channels and led them each to a parallel idea, an idea that others would have found absolutely unconnected with the first" (226).

As Fitzgerald develops the character of Eleanor, it is clear that he intends her to have much in common with Poe's Ligeia. Just as Poe's narrator gives a highly detailed physical description of Ligeia—particularly her face (of which the eyes are extraordinarily prominent), so Fitzgerald similarly preoccupies himself with the face of Eleanor. As the lightning flashes during the eerie thunderstorm in which they meet, Amory sees the face of Eleanor: "Suddenly the lightning flashed in with a heap of overreaching light and he saw Eleanor, and looked for the first time into those eyes of hers. Oh, she was magnificent—pale skin, the color of marble in starlight, slender brows, and eyes that glittered green as emeralds in the blinding glare. She was a witch

..." (227). Eleanor describes herself as having a delicate, aquiline nose, an uncanny temperament. In Poe's narrative Ligeia too has an aquiline nose, pale skin the color of marble, but her eyes are black. "The expression of the eyes of Ligeia! How for long hours have I pondered upon it! How have I, through the whole of a midsummer night, struggled to fathom it!" (83). Eleanor remarks to Blaine: "I've got beautiful eyes, though, haven't I. I don't care what you say, I have beautiful eyes" (227). Although Eleanor and Ligeia are not exact doubles, the resemblances between them are striking. Just as Poe's narrator was possessed of a passion to discover what secret more profound than the well of Democritus lay hidden in the expression of Ligeia's eyes, so Amory afterward sought to discover whether it was "the infinite sadness of [Eleanor's] eyes that drew him or the mirror of himself that he found in the gorgeous clarity of her mind" (222).

Ligeia is an extraordinarily intelligent woman, although Poe would never have called her clarity of mind "gorgeous." Her learning, Poe's narrator remarks, "was immense—such as I have never known, in woman." Indeed, he continues, "where breathes the man who has traversed, and successfully, *all* the wide areas of moral, physical, and mathematical science?" (84). Similarly, Eleanor is an immensely intelligent woman, as she remarks to Amory: "'Rotten, rotten old world,' broke out Eleanor suddenly, 'and the wretchedest thing of all is me—oh, *why* am I a girl? Why am I not a stupid—? Look at you; you're stupider than I am, not much, but some, and you can lope about and get bored and then lope somewhere else, and you can play around with girls without being involved in meshes of sentiment, and you can do anything and be justified—and here I am with the brains to do everything, yet tied to the sinking ship of future matrimony. If I were born a hundred years from now, well and good, but now what's in store for me—I have to marry, and that goes without saying. Who? I'm too bright for most men, and yet I have to descend to their level and let them patronize my intellect in order to get their attention'" (237). Just as she is perhaps more intelligent than Amory, so Ligeia is more intelligent than her husband, who concedes: "I saw not then what I now clearly perceive, that the acquisitions of Ligeia were gigantic, were astounding; yet I was sufficiently aware of her infinite supremacy to resign myself with a child-like confidence, to her guidance through the chaotic world of metaphysical investigation at which I was most busily occupied during the earlier years of our marriage" (84).

Like Ligeia, Eleanor is preoccupied with metaphysical questions. When Amory first meets her on the haystack amidst the storm, she has just made what she calls a "great decision"—she has concluded that she does not believe in immortality. Ligeia does. The power of the human will to overcome the power of death is, in fact, the center of Poe's short story: Ligeia thoroughly believes the doctrine, attributed to Glanvill, that "Man doth not yield himself to the angels, nor unto death utterly, save only through the weakness of his feeble will" (80). Her apparent reincarnation in the body of

Lady Rowena Trevanion of Tremaine is a dramatic demonstration of that belief.

The morbid peculiarity of Ligeia's intelligence is matched in Eleanor Savage's mental disturbance. Her relationship to Blaine, which is "half-sensual, half-neurotic" (233), is destroyed suddenly when Eleanor tries to commit suicide in his presence: " 'I've got a crazy streak,' she faltered, 'twice before I've done things like that. When I was eleven my mother went—went mad—stark raving crazy. We were in Vienna—' " (240). Perhaps his swift perception of Eleanor's insanity is what led Blaine—for no apparent reason—to call her "Madeline" on that first night in the haystack. No other explanation seems consistent with Blaine's evident knowledge of Poe's work and with the pattern of Poe allusions Fitzgerald is here developing. For Madeline, the sister of Roderick in Poe's "The Fall of the House of Usher,"[7] suffers from some "constitutional and ... family evil" which baffles the skill of her physicians, "transient affections of a partially cataleptical character ..." (100–101). Similarly, a constitutional and family disease of the mind nearly destroys Eleanor.

But though she is not Madeline, Eleanor's name of course calls up a host of associations with Poe's heroine Lenore of the poems "The Raven" and "Lenore." Poe's narrator asked the Raven whether he should, after death, clasp Lenore within the distant Aidenn, that is, in Paradise. Amory Blaine and Eleanor Savage, however, wanted never to meet again: "But Eleanor— did Amory dream her? Afterward their ghosts played, yet both of them hoped from their souls never to meet" (222). Theirs was truly a relationship this side of Paradise.

Did Amory dream Eleanor? This question suggests that Blaine and Eleanor Savage may enact an experience comparable to that of the narrator and Psyche in "Ulalume" and that in some sense Eleanor may be taken, if not as Blaine's psyche, at least as a mirror image of one aspect of Blaine's mind during his progressive disillusionment. These echoes of Poe—from "Ulalume," *The Murders in the Rue Morgue*, "Ligeia," *The Fall of the House of Usher*, "The Raven," and "Lenore"—in their union of terror and beauty, reinforce Fitzgerald's underlying purpose: to dramatize, in Blaine's relationship to Eleanor Savage, the fourth and final woman who disillusioned him, "the last time that evil crept close to Amory under the mask of beauty, the last weird mystery that held him with wild fascination and pounded his soul to flakes" (222).

Notes

1. F. Scott Fitzgerald, *This Side of Paradise* (New York, 1960), p. 280. Hereafter, quotation from this work, a Scribner reset of the 1920 edition, will be followed by page numbers in parenthesis in the text.

2. The literary relationship between Fitzgerald and Poe has not been extensively examined, nor has Poe's influence on this novel been noted. It is a markedly derivative novel: Fitzgerald once called *This Side of Paradise* "'a Romance and a Reading List,' and confessed in 1936 that 'the number of subheads I used ... was one of the few consciously original things' about it." (John Kuehl, "Scott Fitzgerald's Reading," *Princeton University Library Chronicle*, XXII [Winter, 1961], 70.) But despite the reading lists it contains, only apprenticeship novels like Joyce's *A Portrait of the Artist as a Young Man*, Wilde's *The Portrait of Dorian Gray*, Compton MacKenzie's *Sinister Street*, and H. G. Wells's *Tono-Bungay* and *The New Machiavelli* have been established as influences on it. Fitzgerald's father is known to have read him Poe's "The Raven" and "The Bells" (Andrew Turnbull, *Scott Fitzgerald* [New York, 1962], p. 15). From his study of Fitzgerald's library, Kuehl lists "The Fall of the House of Usher," "Ulalume," "The Raven" and "The Bells" as works Fitzgerald "probably read." As for any direct influence, Kuehl remarks only that "Poe probably influenced the language and the tone of earlier stories like 'The Mystery of the Raymond Mortgage' (1909) and 'The Room with the Green Blinds' (1911)" (p. 84, footnote 69).

3. Turnbull, p. 96. On the same page Turnbull relates Fitzgerald's horror of poverty to Poe's remark "that he wouldn't put the hero of 'The Raven' in poor surroundings because 'poverty is commonplace and contrary to the idea of Beauty.'" But Turnbull makes no connection here between Fitzgerald's drinking and Poe's. Elsewhere, however, in connection with Fitzgerald's crack-up, Turnbull observes that Fitzgerald "drank the way Baudelaire describes Poe drinking— not as an epicure 'but barbarously, with a speed and dispatch altogether American, as if he were performing a homicidal function, as if he had to kill something inside himself, a worm that would not die.' There was a terrible deliberateness about the way Fitzgerald dosed himself with gin" (Turnbull, p. 187).

4. The association in Fitzgerald's mind between Baltimore, Poe, and alcoholism was probably suggested by Griswold's biography. Although the Griswold charges against Poe have now been largely rejected, the claim that Poe was an alcoholic was generally accepted at the time Fitzgerald was writing *This Side of Paradise*. Even as late as September 23, 1935, as his remarks to his secretary Laura Guthrie suggest, Fitzgerald still associated Baltimore with Poe's alcoholism. Thus in a letter from the Hotel Stafford in Baltimore Fitzgerald wrote: "I have stopped all connections with M. Barleycorn. Baltimore is warm but pleasant ... I love it more than I thought—it is so rich with memories—it is nice to look up the street and see the statue of my great uncle [an approximate identification of Francis Scott Key] and to know that Poe is buried here and that many ancestors of mine have walked in the old town by the day" (Alexander Turnbull, ed. *The Letters of F. Scott Fitzgerald* [New York, 1964], p. 531.) Since *This Side of Paradise* reflects through Amory Blaine the young Fitzgerald's mental state during his Princeton years, the name Poe may be significant in another connection. Apparently the death of one of his classmates seriously unsettled Fitzgerald's mind. Thus in an article entitled "Princeton" Fitzgerald observed that "the death of Johnny Poe with the Black Watch in Flanders starts the cymbals crashing for me, plucks the strings of nervous violins as no adventure of the mind that Princeton ever offered" (*College Humor*, December, 1927, p. 28; Arthur Mizener, *The Far Side of Paradise* [Boston, 1949], p. 38). Perhaps in some extraordinary way, the memories of the poet Poe "dead of alcoholism" and of the classmate Poe dead in battle fused and were transformed in the alembic of Fitzgerald's imagination to be expressed as Blaine's alcoholic despondency over the death of love. One additional coincidence: Fitzgerald's Baltimore lawyer in the late thirties was named Edgar Poe.

5. See, for example, Célestin P. Cambiaire, *The Influence of Edgar Allan Poe in France*. (New York, 1927), pp. 135–149; Haldeen Braddy, *Glorious Incense: The Fulfillment of Edgar Allan Poe* (Washington, 1953), pp. 100, 109.

6. *Selected Writings of Edgar Allan Poe*, ed. Edward H. Davidson (Boston, 1956), p. 144. Hereafter, quotations from this Riverside Edition will be followed by page numbers in parenthesis in the text.

7. Besides "Ulalume," "The Fall of the House of Usher" is the only other Poe title mentioned in *This Side of Paradise*. It is only one of many titles on Amory Blaine's reading list during his student days (p. 17).

The Beautiful and Damned
1922

51
The Flapper's Tragedy

HENRY SEIDEL CANBY

This is a pathetic story. It is the bitter cry of the children who have grown up in their pleasant vices and found them no longer pleasant, but only expensive habits. Mr. Fitzgerald's flapper has grown harder as she has grown older. The paint that was so piquant begins to fleck off, the pursuit of pleasure grows feverish. His college dilettantes come to the crossroads and, finding that the only lesson to be learned from life is that there is no lesson to be learned from life, chuck what ideals they had, cut their unsuccessful friends, and go after material success. Or they become still more dilettantish and end in perfect futility. Getting drunk on Saturday nights becomes a necessity. Without money the world is unendurable. Gloria, the beautiful girl, loses her only spiritual virtue, the clean instinct for splendid physical living. Anthony, the would-be connoisseur, becomes an alcoholic. His brilliant group of friends find their own particular damnations.

In other words, Scott Fitzgerald, rather surprisingly, has written a tragedy, an almost uncompromising tragedy, which is more than their critics have led us to expect from one of the younger generation. He has felt the implications of a rudderless society steering gayly for nowhere and has followed them down the rapids to final catastrophe. Not, of course, in any Puritan fashion nor with an Ibsen view of the sins of the race, but simply because his story led him that way; and defiantly scoffing at lessons, joyously dwelling upon the life that leads his friends to perdition, he follows. I admire him for it; and if *This Side of Paradise* showed in certain passages and in the essential energy of the whole that he had glimpses of a genius for sheer writing, this book proves that he has the artist's conscience and enough intellect to learn how to control the life that fascinates him.

He has not yet learned that lesson, a lesson which even those who believe, as he pretends to believe, that life is meaningless, must learn. He has chosen to wallow in naturalism, to be a romantic unrestrained, and he must pay the price. The scenes of debauchery in this book will be very much censured, by some on moral grounds, by others (more justly, I think) on artistic; his

SOURCE *Literary Review of the New York Evening Post*, 4 March 1922, p. 463.

verbose excursions into philosophy and literary criticism will be mentioned without favor. And it will be his own fault. Following what he believes to be popular taste, he has decided to gratify curiosity as to what they do on Broadway after midnight with the fullest detail, and to supply scenes at riotous country-house week-ends regardless of taste and proportion. Following his own desire, he has reported his own reactions to life and its problems in general with a fulness only justifiable in a young man's diary. Like a reporter with a moving-picture camera, he has squirmed into hallways and hid behind café tables until the result is an endless film of racy pictures, relieved by aesthetic vaporings. "Give 'em all the truth," has been his motto, and therefore from one point of view *The Beautiful and Damned* is not so much a novel as an irresponsible social document, veracious, in its way, as photographs are always veracious in their way, but often untruthful, as photographs are often untruthful, and with about the same relation to the scope and significance of life that is possessed by a society drama in the films.

Thanks to these excesses, Mr. Fitzgerald will miss his due meed of praise for some very outstanding accomplishments, and his book will be talked about for what is least valuable in it. Readers who spend their time counting the number of cocktails drunk in each chapter are not in the proper mood to appreciate subtler claims upon their attention. They will miss in their pursuit of sensationalism the evidences of great and growing artistic power which this book undoubtedly displays. No finer study of the relations between boy husband and girl wife has been given us in American fiction. If Anthony Patch, the hero, is a nullity, scarcely worth following after the graceful sketch of is first steps in connoisseurship, Gloria is an original creature, frightening in her truth. And when he is not showing off in pseudo-wit, or trying to shock the bourgeoisie, or discovering profound truths of philosophy which get muddled before he can grasp them, how this novelist can write!

Of course, like Mr. Hergesheimer's *Cytherea*, this novel is another picture of a society upset by modernism. And like Mr. Hergesheimer, Mr. Fitzgerald is too much in the whirl, too much in love with its abandoned irresponsibility, to understand it, and to be detached while still sympathetic. But if *The Beautiful and Damned* is a less competent book than *Cytherea*, and if its author is far more deeply involved in the life he tries to see as from without, nevertheless the mute witness of the story to tragedy is more impressive simply because it is the youngest generation, yesterday's children, who are dancing and suffering there. Of course, it is only the flapper fringe of them that he depicts, but in that margin are involved the more sensitive spirits, those richer in life as well as in gayety, the feelers and some of the thinkers, young men and young women who visibly embody the charm and the inspiration of youth. Fitzgerald has written of them as a man would write who watches a cabaret dance through rosy films of exhilaration, but his knowledge of their hearts is nevertheless poignant, and he is never too intoxicated with the excitement of living to miss the tragedy waiting behind. It is a pathetic story, which seems to say, "Here we are, we youngsters, and this is how we can drink and suffer and wonder and pretend to have no hope. What do you make of us?"

The answer is that we are a little disgusted, a little touched, and profoundly interested. When Mr. Fitzgerald himself grows up, in art as well as in philosophy, he may tell us more, and more wisely. He will write better novels, but he will probably never give us better documents of distraught and abandoned but intensely living youth.

52
Mr. Fitzgerald Sees the Flapper Through

◆

JOHN PEALE BISHOP

However barren may have been the wise and their old wisdoms, Scott Fitzgerald, at the time when he was writing *This Side of Paradise*, found ample comfort in the doings of feckless and brave hearted young. Amory Blaine, like another Playboy, went romancing through a foolish world, kissing innumerable girls between 9 o'clock and midnight, drinking wittily with his fellows from midnight until the milkman brought up the dawn, discarding old loves and dead beliefs like a brisk young snake, who every month might slough off his dry shell for a new, shining green skin. Even the breaking of his heart was a sound to be listened to and enjoyed like the rest. Mr. Fitzgerald has in the meanwhile lost none of his alertness in observing the manners and speech of his contemporaries, but he no longer finds any great pleasure in the American scene. Life it seems is now meaningless; the beautiful are damned; the glamour he once saw was only a gauze curtain lowered before the stage to conceal the fact that those twilight nymphs were, after all, only middle aged chorus ladies.

Anthony Patch, who succeeds Amory Blaine as a figure through whom Mr. Fitzgerald may write of himself, is when *The Beautiful and Damned* opens 25, and it is already two years "since irony, the Holy Ghost of this later day," has, theoretically at least, descended upon him. Irony was the final polish of the shoe, the ultimate dab of the clothes brush, a sort of intellectual 'There!'—yet at the brink of this story he has as yet gone no further than the conscious stage.

Since the younger generation, as they are commonly called, began finding publishers and appearing on lecture platforms, this word irony has been heard with such frequency that I have begun to wonder just what these young men mean by it. Mr. Fitzgerald invokes it, and Stephen Vincent Benét inscribes it on all his gay banners, and even Donald Ogden Stewart is frequently heard to murmur it between whacks with his buffoon's bladder. And I am a little confused, for clearly they do not mean that faculty which

SOURCE *New York Herald*, 5 March 1922, section 8, p. 1.

allows one to smile appreciatively when Tragedy enters wearing a propitious mask and speaking equivocal phrases. Their irony is not that good counsellor of Anatole France, who, in smiling, renders life a thing to be loved the more, who rails neither at love nor beauty, who teaches us to mock liars and fools, which we should, without her, be feeble enough to hate. As I say, I am a little uncertain just what these young men mean when they hold themselves to speak ironically. For they have not that superb detachment which would allow them to expose the littleness of their characters without ever seeming themselves to rush in with a measuring rod, their mockery is not dispassionately gay, they cannot allow circumstances to slaughter their heroes without applying a dagger or two with their own hands.

II

With Mr. Fitzgerald, if one is to judge by his latest book, he means to say that Anthony has found out that life is purposeless, beauty in no way allied with the truth, all effort, even of the intellect, unreasonable. Anthony is, when he is presented to us, a man "aware that there could be no honor and yet had honor, who knew the sophistry of courage and yet was brave." Later, it is true, he turns out to be an arrant coward on occasion and disports himself most dishonorably. Of irony he never either in the beginning nor at the end achieves more than a passing glimpse.

As a matter of fact, Anthony Comstock Patch is a rather futile young man with a pallid skin and dark polished hair, shy enough in his extreme youth to have spent his time among many books without deriving from them either erudition or richness of mind. It is his inherent laziness rather than a fine skepticism which prevents him from ever accomplishing more than a single precious essay toward his volume on the Renaissance Popes. It is his uxoriousness which makes of him a pathetic adjunct to the more vivid Gloria, the thinness of his zest for life which makes him turn, more and more thirstily, toward alcohol. Sophisticated, he is constantly under the illusion that he is rather superior in intellect and character to the persons about him; disillusioned, he is at the mercy of circumstances.

In 1913 he is living in an apartment in the Fifties of New York trying to prove that an American can live idly and gracefully on seven thousand a year. He is awakened each morning by a frayed English servant with the exquisitely appropriate name of Bounds; he arises to bathe in his mirrored and crimson carpeted bathroom; he arranges his impeccable toilet and saunters forth to savor life effortlessly. He pays hasty and unwilling visits to his grandfather, Adam J. Patch, once known as a financier who had risen by none too creditable means, now as a reformer employing a retinue of paid moralists. He loafs and invites his soul with two friends—Maury Noble, imperturbably feline, self-consciously superior, animated by an undisguised boredom, and Richard Caramel, a bulgy young novelist, with one brown and one topaz eye, who is destined before he is 30 to have written a number of utterly silly novels which he will believe to be wise.

Comes then into his life one Gloria—as Mr. Fitzgerald with a recently acquired fondness for the D.W. Griffith order of words might well say—"Coast to Coast Gloria," she of the bobbed hair and the many sounding kisses, with lips carmined and sweetly profane, with an enduring taste for gumdrops and swiftly passing fancies for attractive young men. She is Rosalind of *This Side of Paradise* seen through slightly older and less romantic eyes; she is the girl of the Off Shore Pirate portrayed at full length with a more careful treatment of light and shade and more conscious accumulation of detail. Born in Kansas City, Mo., of a Bilphist mother and father engaged in the celluloid business, she has been brought to her twenty-third year in surroundings of inescapable vulgarity. She has the wit to perceive that there is something tawdry in her prettiness; she has not the innate perception of form which would have allowed her to become beautiful. It has obviously been within Mr. Fitzgerald's intention to give her a touch of that immemorial loveliness which is in Donna Rita despite her peasant origin, a suggestion of that power to drive young men wild which was Zuleika Dobson's for all her rococo vulgarity. He has allowed her a sensitiveness to sensuous impressions, a more delicate perception than might be expected from a flapper with a past so monotonous in its promiscuity. Gloria has the hard and solitary will of a child and a child's petulance and vanity. Spoiled, contemptuous, willful, she feels pathetically that somewhere her beauty might have had its due; here she must take whatever adulation comes her way, nor as if the admirer be second rate or worse. The book belongs to her as the earlier volume belonged to Amory Blaine. Not because she is the more vivid character than Anthony but because she is more vividly imagined, more consistently presented. There is something about him that suggests that he has been made out of too many and too discordant bits of observation, like the philosophy of William Blake, which, as T.S. Eliot says, was made out of the odds and ends he happened to find in his pocket.

At their first contact Anthony is stirred from his carefully composed calm and for a while Mr. Fitzgerald returns to his earlier moods to manage their meetings with romance:

> Oh, for him there was no doubt. He had arisen and paced the floor in sheer ecstasy. That such a girl should be; should poise curled in a corner of the couch like a swallow newly landed from a clean, swift flight, watching him with inscrutable eyes. He would stop his pacing and, half shy each time at first, drop his arm around her and find her kiss.
>
> She was fascinating, he told her. He had never met any one like her before. He besought her jauntily but earnestly to send him away; he didn't want to fall in love. He wasn't coming to see her any more—already she had haunted too many of his ways.
>
> What delicious romance! His true reaction was neither fear nor sorrow—

only this deep delight in being with her that colored the banality of his words and made the mawkish seem sad and the posturing seem wise.

III

They marry and Mr. Fitzgerald takes up his theme in earnest. He is prepared to show that this disintegration of a young man who, for all his lack of illusion, cannot bear the contact with life, of a girl who for all her hardness of heart cannot gracefully survive the passing of her first youth.

The middle portions of the book are at once too long and too hurried. That is, incidents are presented diverting in themselves which have no bearing on the theme. And in those places where the material presented is essential to the story, the deductions made are too violent, the transitions too abrupt. One is hardly prepared that Anthony should, even under the influence of Gloria, his own idleness and a diminishing income, turn so quickly from his pleasant nonchalance to so consistent a dipsomania. Gloria's beauty fades out and her nerves wear thin at a strangely early age.

Yet, taken as a whole, it seems to me that the book represents both in plan and execution an advance on *This Side of Paradise*. If, stylistically speaking, it is not so well written, neither is it so carelessly written. The minor characters are admirably foreshortened; the criticism applied to them seems at times unfortunately Menckenian, the art through which they are shown often comes too close to burlesque. The alcoholic interludes are, if frequent, agreeably heady. The humor with which the quarrels of Gloria and Anthony are touched, the satiric description of army life in a Southern conscript camp, Anthony's adventures in bond selling are excellently done, with skill and a fine zest and whips adroitly applied.

In order to arrive at those qualities in Scott Fitzgerald which are valuable it may not be unprofitable to compare him with an Englishman like Aldous Huxley. Both are of an age and both have a gift of wit and phantasy, an eye for the absurdities of their contemporaries. Huxley has erudition, a rich knowledge of contemporary literature, taste even when dealing with the indecencies of life, the attitude of the philosopher even in contemplating a sow and her litter of pigs. But he is exceedingly weary, his grace is that of a man well bred but tired. Whereas Fitzgerald is at the moment of announcing the meaninglessness of life magnificently alive. His ideas are too often treated like paper crackers, things to make a gay and pretty noise with and then be cast aside; he is frequently at the mercy of words with which he has only a nodding acquaintance; his aesthetics are faulty; his literary taste is at times extremely bad. The chapter labeled "Symposium," pictorially good, does not seem clearly thought out or burdened with wisdom. The episode entitled "Flash Back in Paradise" might, except for its wit, have been conceived in the mind of a scenario writer. But these are flaws of vulgarity in one who is awkward with his own vigor.

53
This Side of Innocence

♦

VIVIAN SHAW (GILBERT SELDES)

The impression Mr Fitzgerald's work makes on his elders is so intense that one is grateful for the omission of the name of the Deity from his new title. To his contemporaries, "interested only in ourselves and Art," his revelations are of quite secondary importance and he has neither the critical intelligence nor the profound vision which might make him an imposing figure. His elders, naturally, do not require these things of him, since they have other sources of supply, and they are the best judges of his immediate significance. To them he presents a picture of the world which is no longer theirs, and even when they doubt his supreme truthfulness they can safely go behind the book to the author and say that this is what the younger generation would like us to think.

It cannot, of course, continue indefinitely, because even about so bright and cheerful a talent as Mr Fitzgerald's the shadows of the prison house are bound to close. Especially since he has been considered as a revealer and an artist he has had to grow quickly, and he can say (I speak not of his private life with which I am unacquainted, but of his fiction) "my grief lies onward and my joy behind." The golden lads and girls of *This Side of Paradise* are in the new novel, but they are far more than Amory Blaine and Rosalind aware of their kinship in the dust with the world's chimney-sweepers. It is not only because of the tragedy into which Gloria and Anthony Patch are somewhat hastily precipitated. Tragedy, and particularly in our own time a rather meaningless tragedy, are quite the natural thing for young people to deal in; it was surprising and creditable to him that Mr Fitzgerald's first book held so steadily to a gay worldliness. Nor is it Mr Fitzgerald's increasingly detailed naturalism which marks the change in him. The new thing is his overburden of sentiment and his really alarming seriousness. Sentiment, to be sure, has been surreptitiously conveyed, and so made more poignant and, when it doesn't come off, more objectionable, by being presented always with scepticism. (This is, I believe, the real nature of the author's noted irony.) It is very strange that Mr Fitzgerald should render emotion directly, that is without

SOURCE *The Dial* LXXII, April 1922, pp. 419–421.

sentimentality, so that the early love of Anthony and Gloria has the credible, somewhat incomprehensible atmosphere of any love affair to any outsider; so, too, the quite successful episode of Anthony and Geraldine, the attractive although virginal usher. It is whenever he approaches either the mind or the soul of his characters that Mr Fitzgerald becomes romantic. The first state culminates in the testament of Maury Noble, which reads like a *résumé* of *The Education of Henry Adams* filtered through a particularly thick page of *The Smart Set*. The second stage sets in heavily when the author finds his catastrophe approaching far too rapidly and tries to conceal his failure to foreshorten by forcing the dramatic pace over into melodrama.

I do not know whether this change in Mr Fitzgerald is due to alien influence; nor, when I mention the most impressive of his teachers, do I wish to suggest that he is in any sense plagiarizing. The pellmell of ideas, or rather of the names of ideas, in the book is startling, and more startling is the incipient philosophy of the author; but the book is important not for these. It is important because it presents a definite American *milieu* and because it has pretentions as a work of art; the degree of success (the degree, that is, of importance) comes out in comparison with the work of another American novelist: Mrs Edith Wharton. It is not essential for my purpose to know whether Mr Fitzgerald has read *The House of Mirth* and *The Custom of the Country*, since I wish to make a comparison, not an accusation.

Lily Bart's tragedy and that of Anthony Patch are similar in direction and Undine Spragg is an older sister of Gloria Gilbert. Lily dies undefiled, to be sure, and Anthony lives ignominiously; that difference is beyond criticism. But where the comparison injures Mr Fitzgerald is in the treatment of the gradual disintegration of the physical lives of the two characters, for Mrs Wharton, with a fraction of the detail, has given the effect of the lapse of time, has kept Lily's character active and growing before us, and has given us, all the while, the results of Lily's poverty upon her; Mr Fitzgerald has clearly intended us to see that as the strain of life grew more tense, Anthony became incapable of that devotion to abstractions which made him so entertaining before, but as Anthony had somehow ceased to exist long before he got to camp, the remaining scenes are impotent. As for Gloria and Undine, the methods used are singularly alike and the younger writer comes out of the comparison rather well. His half-chapter of preparing the stage for Gloria's entrance is remarkable; he gives her general effect circuitously so that when she appears it matters very little whether he can stop to describe her, which he actually never does, adding touches to the created character as his story proceeds. The Gilberts are not in the same country as the Spraggs; literally, since Apex City, or wherever it was for the Spraggs, came effectively on the scene, while the background of the Gilberts is pure conversation. But the careful treatment of Gloria in the beginning brings its own reward to the author; as Anthony recedes, Gloria becomes more and more vivid. She is, at first, a presence; Undine (Mrs Wharton understands irony) has a soul. In the second half of the book Gloria slowly acquires being. If Mr Fitzgerald had followed his subject to the bitter end, instead of to an end which is merely bitter, the triumph of Gloria would have been inevitable.

The failure to carry Gloria through, his seeing her as a flapper and not as a woman, marks the precise point at which Mr Fitzgerald now rests—this side of innocence, considerably this side of the mad and innocent truth. He is this side too, of a full respect for the medium he works in; his irrelevance destroys his design. I have nothing against his sudden descents into the dialogue of the printed play, if that is the most effective way of presenting his scene, although I wish he did not do this whenever he has a crowd to handle and something in itself insignificant to tell. His interludes are usually trivial and never contribute to the one thing they can create, his atmosphere. But I do wish that Mr Fitzgerald would stop incorporating into his novels his wingéd words and his unrelated episodes as they are published from time to time. It indicates a carelessness about structure and effect which one who has so much to gain from the novel ought to find displeasing.

54
Fitzgerald and Others

◆

H.L. MENCKEN

F. Scott Fitzgerald's *The Beautiful and the* [sic] *Damned* is an *adagio* following the *scherzo* of *This Side of Paradise*. It starts off ingratiatingly and disarmingly, with brilliant variations upon the theme of the *scherzo*, but pretty soon a more sombre tune is heard in the bullfiddles, and toward the end there is very solemn music, indeed—music that will probably give a shock to all the fluffier and more flapperish Fitzgeraldistas. In brief, a disconcerting peep into the future of a pair of the amiable children dealt with in *This Side of Paradise*. Here we have Gloria Gilbert, the prom angel, graduating into a star of hotel dances in New York, and then into a wife, and then into the scared spectator of her husband's disintegration, and then, at the end, into a pathetic trembler on the brink of middle age. And here we have Anthony Patch, the gallant young Harvard man, sliding hopelessly down the hill of idleness, incompetence, extravegence and drunkenness. It is, in the main, Anthony's story, not Gloria's. His reactions to her, of course—to her somewhat florid charm, her acrid feminine cynicism, her love of hollow show and hollower gayety, her fear of inconvenient facts—are integral parts of the intricate machinery of his decay, but one feels that he would have decayed quite as rapidly without her, whatever may be said for the notion that a wife of another sort might have saved him. There is little that is vicious about Anthony; he is simply silly—the fearful end-product of ill-assorted marriages, a quite typical American of the third generation from shirt-sleeves. The forthright competence of his old grandfather, Adam J. Patch, the millionaire moralist, has been bred out of the strain. Into it have come dilutions from a New England blue-stocking and worse. He is hopeless from birth.

The waters into which this essentially serious and even tragic story bring Fitzgerald seemed quite beyond the ken of the author of *This Side of Paradise*. It is thus not surprising to find him navigating, at times, rather cautiously and ineptly. The vast plausibility that Dreiser got into the similar chronicle of Hurstwood is not there; one often encounters shakiness, both in the

SOURCE *Smart Set* LXVII, April 1922, pp. 140–141.

imagining and the telling. Worse, the thing is botched at the end by the introduction of a god from the machine: Anthony is saved from the inexorable logic of his life by a court decision which gives him, most unexpectedly and improbably, his grandfather's millions. But allowing for all that, it must be said for Fitzgerald that he discharges his unaccustomed and difficult business with ingenuity and dignity. Opportunity beckoned him toward very facile jobs; he might have gone on rewriting the charming romance of *This Side of Paradise* for ten or fifteen years, and made a lot of money out of it, and got a great deal of uncritical praise for it. Instead, he tried something much more difficult, and if the result is not a complete success, it is nevertheless near enough to success to be worthy of respect. There is fine observation in it, and much penetrating detail, and the writing is solid and sound. After *This Side of Paradise* the future of Fitzgerald seemed extremely uncertain. There was an air about that book which suggested a fortunate accident. The shabby stuff collected in *Flappers and Philosophers* converted uncertainty into something worse. But *The Beautiful and the* [sic] *Damned* delivers the author from all those doubts. There are a hundred signs in it of serious purpose and unquestionable skill. Even in its defects there is proof of hard striving. Fitzgerald ceases to be a *Wunderkind*, and begins to come into his maturity.

55
Friend Husband's Latest

ZELDA SAYRE (ZELDA FITZGERALD)

I note on the table beside my bed this morning a new book with an orange jacket entitled *The Beautiful and Damned*. It is a strange book, which has for me an uncanny fascination. It has been lying on that table for two years. I have been asked to analyze it carefully in the light of my brilliant critical insight, my tremendous erudition and my vast impressive partiality. Here I go! ...

... Now, as to the other advantages of the book—its value as a manual of etiquette is incalculable. Where could you get a better example how not to behave than from the adventures of Gloria? ... And as a handy cocktail mixer nothing better has been said or written since John Roach Straton's last sermon.

It is a wonderful book to have around in case of emergency. No one should ever set out in pursuit of unholy excitement without a special vest pocket edition dangling from a string around his neck.

For this book tells exactly, and with compelling lucidity, just what to do when cast off by a grandfather or when sitting around a station platform at 4 a.m., or when spilling champagne in a fashionable restaurant, or when told that one is too old for the movies. Any of these things might come into any one's life at any minute.

Just turn the pages of the book slowly at any of the above-mentioned trying times until your own case strikes your eye and proceed according to directions. Then for the ladies of the family there are such helpful lines as: "I like gray because then you have to wear a lot of paint." Also what to do with your husband's old shoes—Gloria takes Anthony's shoes to bed with her and finds it a very satisfactory way of disposing of them. The dietary suggestion, "tomato sandwiches and lemonade for breakfast" will be found an excellent cure for obesity.

Now, let us turn to the interior decorating department of the book. Therein can be observed complete directions for remodeling your bathroom along modern and more interesting lines, with plans for a bookrack by the

SOURCE *New York Tribune*, 2 April 1922, section 5, p. 11 (edited version).

tub, and a detailed description of what pictures have been found suitable for bathroom walls after years of careful research by Mr. Fitzgerald.

The book itself, with its plain green back, is admirably constructed for being read in a tub—wetting will not spoil the pages; in fact, if one finds it growing dry simply dip the book briskly in warm water. The bright yellow jacket is particularly adapted to being carried on Fifth Avenue while wearing a blue or henna colored suit, and the size is adaptable to being read in hotel lobbies while waiting to keep dates for luncheon.

It seems to me that on one page I recognized a portion of an old diary of mine which mysteriously disappeared shortly after my marriage, and also scraps of letters which, though considerably edited, sound to me vaguely familiar. In fact, Mr. Fitzgerald—I believe that is how he spells his name—seems to believe that plagiarism begins at home.

I find myself completely fascinated by the character of the heroine. She is a girl approximately ten years older than I am, for she seems to have been born about 1890—though I regret to remark that on finishing the book I feel no confidence as to her age, since her birthday is in one place given as occurring in February and in another place May and in the third place in September. But there is a certain inconsistency in this quite in accord with the lady's character.

What I was about to remark is that I would like to meet the lady. There seems to have been a certain rouge she used which had a quite remarkable effect. And the strange variations in the color of her hair from cover to cover range entirely through the spectrum—I find myself doubting that all the changes were of human origin; also the name of the unguent used in the last chapter is not given. I find these æsthetic deficiencies very trying. But don't let that deter you from buying the book. In every other way the book is absolutely perfect.

The other things I didn't like in the book—I mean the unimportant things—were the literary references and the attempt to convey a profound air of erudition. It reminds me in its more soggy moments of the essays I used to get up in school at the last minute by looking up strange names in the Encyclopædia Britannica.

I think the heroine is most amusing. I have an intense distaste for the melancholy aroused in the masculine mind by such characters as Jenny Gerhardt, Antonia and Tess (of the D'Urbervilles). Their tragedies, redolent of the soil, leave me unmoved. If they were capable of dramatizing themselves they would no longer be symbolic, and if they weren't—and they aren't—they would be dull, stupid and boring, as they inevitably are in life.

The book ends on a tragic note; in fact a note which will fill any woman with horror, or, for that matter, will fill any furrier with horror, for Gloria, with thirty million to spend, buys a sable coat instead of a kolinsky coat. This is a tragedy unequaled in the entire work of Hardy. Thus the book closes on a note of tremendous depression and Mr. Fitzgerald's subtle manner of having Gloria's deterioration turn on her taste in coats has scarcely been equaled by Henry James.

56
Certificated, Mostly

♦

MARY M. COLUM

Mr. Scott Fitzgerald could never utter the names of Mr. H. G. Wells and Edward Fitzgerald in the same breath: none of his young heroes could ever come up to seek his fortune in Chicago armed with one treasured book, that book being a Wells—at least he could not do it with the approval of the author. Mr. Fitzgerald's heroes would probably bring a Swinburne, and the poems that they would know by heart would be "The Hounds of Spring" and "Dolores." They would, perhaps, be a little more commonplace than Mr. Floyd Dell's young hero but how intelligent they would be, and how well they would compare with young gentlemen of the same denomination in other countries! This is one of Mr. Fitzgerald's real merits: his chief merit, however, is that with him there has stepped into the ranks of the young novelists a satirist; so rare an apparition in this—indeed, in any—country, that he ought to be rocked and dandled and nursed into maturity, or given any treatment whatever that will ensure his free development. He uses his weapon so stumblingly yet that it is hard to know how strong or how finely-tempered it may be. For instance, when he causes his hero to be called "Anthony Comstock Patch" at the request of a reforming, uplifting grandfather, he is indulging in a sort of buffoonery that is not above the level of the popularly called satire of the afternoon columnists: if Thackeray had so dealt with one of his characters, he would have made it seem as if the gods from all time had decided upon this piece of mockery. Again, when he satirizes the hypocrisies of people during the war, he is simply flogging a dead horse, besides taking up what is now a popular occupation. A genuine satirist would never berate unpopular things; and, of all unpopular things, war-behaviour is now the most unpopular.

The story of this book deals with the married life of two young people, of that class which in Europe is called the middle class, but which in America is nearly always called the upper. These two have grown up without any of the discipline which is the training for life invented by the aristocracy, or the prudent worldly-wisdom which is the substitute invented by the *petite*

SOURCE *The Freeman* V, 26 April 1922, pp. 162–164.

bourgeoisie: they are peculiarly the product of a commercial civilization. The book deals with a life in America which has had few serious interpreters, and Mr. Fitzgerald has done it with impressive ability. The story of these two young people and their life in various places, including their amazing existence in that uncivilized form of shelter peculiar to New York, the two-room-and-bath apartment, is told with real conviction. They have no occupation and no responsibilities, and tragedy overtakes them—in so far as tragedy can overtake the tender-minded and the undisciplined; for tragedy, like happiness, is the privilege of the strong. Mr. Fitzgerald's character-drawing is, in the main, somewhat amateurish, and he uses his people indifferently to express opinions quite unrelated to their characters. A certain easy grasp of conventional technique is his, especially in showing the interplay of the characters on each others' lives. His best and most consistent piece of character-drawing is that of Bloeckman, whose evolution is indicated with great subtlety. A novelist, and particularly a novelist who is a satirist, has to be on the outside as well as on the inside of his characters, and Mr. Fitzgerald has not the faculty of standing away from his principal characters: with Bloeckman he has done this, and also with the gentleman who appears for a moment to teach salesmanship. Everything in this salesmanship episode is done excellently and the satirist's touch is revealed in all of it. *The Beautiful and Damned* is indeed an achievement for so young a writer. It is one which, however, would seem less striking in England where they have had the highly intelligent commonplace for so long, or in France where they are the greatest masters of the highly intelligent commonplace in the world. Mr. Fitzgerald is yet young enough to achieve the feat of stepping down the peaks of his intelligence into that region where the great adventurers among the arts sought for "roots of relish sweet, and honey wild, and manna-dew"; though I must own that one does not find too many signs of it.

57
The Beautiful and Damned

◆

SERGIO PEROSA

The theme of *The Beautiful and Damned*—published serially in *The Metropolitan Magazine* (September 1921–March 1922) before being issued in book form—is the dissipation and deterioration of the inner self. Two people, husband and wife, are equally guilty of an excessive indulgence in illusions and dreams. This idea of a motivated failure of the protagonists was in the author's mind since the very first conception of the new novel, even if he was thinking at the time of giving a new portrait of the young aesthete:

> My new novel [he had written in 1920] called *The Flight of the Rocket*, concerns the life of one Anthony Patch between his 25th and 33d years (1913–1921). He is one of those many with the tastes and weaknesses of an artist but with no actual creative inspiration. How he and his beautiful young wife are wrecked on the shoals of dissipation is told in the story. (*Letters*, Turnbull, ed., [New York, 1963], p. 145.)

If ties with the "young artist" that Amory had been are still visible, we cannot say that the new novel was to continue his story, because Anthony Patch is bound from the start to become a failure, and his story is to be seen in close interdependence with the story of his wife. The interdependence of the two characters was emphasized in the title of the manuscript, which was called "The Beautiful Lady Without Mercy" and had furthermore an epigraph taken from Keats's "La Belle Dame Sans Merci."[1] This epigraph disappeared in the published version of the novel—the new title clearly indicating that both Anthony and Gloria were victims of a romantic conception of the world. But the main theme of the dissipation of the two characters remained as it had been conceived originally, all the more painful because their ruin is the result of an apparent, but deceptive material victory. Anthony and Gloria struggle against philistinism and hypocritical morality so as to be able to prolong their dissipation, but their victory, reached when it is too late, only serves to make the feeling of incurable defeat the more terrible. "The victor belongs to the spoils," reads the new epigraph: and there was never a more bitter and hollow victory than this one, which leaves the

SOURCE *The Art of F. Scott Fitzgerald*, Ann Arbor, 1965, pp. 36–46.

two characters among the spoils and remnants of their struggle and of their existence. It is a pathetic struggle, too weakly and too selfishly fought to become tragic, which reveals the flaws of decay and deterioration under the golden appearance of success. As with Amory in the earlier novel, the story of the two characters, so "beautiful and damned," is developed as a moral parable, linearly unfolded, though with a better feeling for the general structure. And the parable is precisely that of the youthful dreams and illusions that gradually become a lethargy and then a nightmare and are involved in an inevitable ruin.

The novel is divided into three books,[2] each in turn divided into three chapters. Each book represents a distinct moment in the development of the story, while the chapters themselves mark the progressive unfolding of the parable. From a complete abandonment to dreams at the beginning, the two protagonists fall to tasting the lees of an illusory happiness and find that the dreams have become nightmares. Just as in *This Side of Paradise*, a "portrait" of Anthony is given at the very beginning: he is a sophisticated and blasé aesthete, who lives in a comfortable ivory tower in a New York apartment. More mature than Amory and lacking his sentimental obsession with socialism, Anthony has the advantage of a certain culture (he reads Flaubert's *Education Sentimentale* ...), is independent and rich and has his future assured by the prospect of a big inheritance. He is more refined than his predecessor and enjoys the close friendship of a small set of people, through whom he makes hesitant and timid approaches to the world. His real desire is to perpetuate his pleasant life; he is content to contemplate his own image (there is a touch of Narcissus in him, too) in the golden mirrors and polished surfaces of his house. His favorite retreat is the bathtub, and there he weaves immaterial dreams, castles in the air, reveries of himself contemplating sensual beauties, or playing imaginary violins:

> He felt that if he had a love he would have hung her picture just facing the tub so that, lost in the soothing steamings of the hot water, he might lie and look up at her and muse warmly and sensuously on her beauty.... (*BD*, pp. 11–12.)
>
> He raised his voice to compete with the flood of water pouring into the tub, and as he looked at the picture of Hazel Dawn upon the wall he put an imaginary violin to his shoulder and softly caressed it with a phantom bow. (*BD*, p. 17.)

All his social and cultural attempts dissolve in that dreamy atmosphere. He feels compelled to do something, and he can think of nothing better than writing a history of the Middle Ages. He feels that he should allow himself some diversions, and he finds a girl, Geraldine, who offers him a new mirror in which to gaze at himself. She is held at a distance and kept for certain hours, because "she was company, familiar, and faintly intimate and restful. Further than that he did not care to experiment—not from any moral compunction, but from a dread of allowing any entanglement to disturb what he felt was the growing serenity of his life."

A "Flash-Back in Paradise," however, marking the birth of the "beautiful" Gloria, is sufficient to put the serenity of his life in jeopardy. Gloria is a new, more dangerous incarnation of the "debutante" or flapper, both careless and fascinating. She, too, is possessed by an illusory dream, the dream of a beauty to whom all is due, who accepts no responsibility and subordinates every other aspect of life to an aesthetic principle. To Gloria, "who took all things of life for hers to choose from and apportion, as though she were continually picking out presents for herself from an inexhaustible counter," it is enough for people to "fit into the picture." She does not mind "if they don't do anything." "I don't see why they should—in fact it almost astonishes me when anybody does anything."

Her meeting with Anthony is therefore perfectly logical and unavoidable. And yet, if the aesthete gives up his dream of detachment from the world, of aloofness and isolation, it is only to replace it with a new dream—the dream of eternal love. He knows very well that he is not "a realist," that Gloria requites his love because he is "clean," but greatly interested as he is by every girl "who made a living directly on her prettiness," there is no possible escape for him. It can be either "white" or "black magic," but Gloria fills him with dissatisfaction, then panic, and finally brings him to the altar.

Anthony and Gloria throw their illusions together, but the dream of one cannot but suffer in contact with that of the other. The illusion of love as an absorbing way of life collides with the ideal that sees marriage as a means of satisfying one's vanity:

> Marriage was created not to be a background but to need one—says Gloria—. Mine is going to be outstanding. It can't, shan't be the setting—it's going to be the performance, the live, lovely, glamorous performance, and the world shall be the scenery. (*BD*, p. 147.)

After the precarious "radiant hour" (that opens the second book), Anthony finds his serenity compromised, while Gloria finds herself without the much-coveted security. Her "tremendous nervous tension" contrasts with his utter cowardice. A new dream, that of an expected inheritance, keeps them together. But Adam Patch is not so eager to die, and he disapproves of their fast spending and reckless living. He keeps a close watch on them, while they are unconsciously preparing their ruin. Anthony tries in vain to go on with his book and has a short and fruitless working experience; Gloria plays with the idea of becoming a film actress, but her husband objects to it. His further attempt to write commercial short stories is also a failure.

Their dream becomes gradually an inexcusable form of lethargy, and after their refusal to have a child, this lethargy kills even the illusion of eternal love. "Gloria has lulled Anthony's mind to sleep ... [she] realized that Anthony had become capable of utter indifference toward her, a temporary indifference, more than half lethargic...." Only a childish vision of future happiness and security stirs them at times from their lethargy:

That spring, that summer, they had speculated upon future happiness—how they were to travel from summer land to summer land, returning eventually to a gorgeous estate and possible idyllic children, then entering diplomacy or politics, to accomplish, for a while, beautiful and important things, until finally as a white-haired (beautifully, silkily, white-haired) couple they were to loll about in serene glory, worshipped by the bourgeoisie of the land.... These times were to begin "when we get our money"; it was on such dreams rather than on any satisfaction with their increasingly irregular, increasingly dissipated life that their hope rested. (*BD*, p. 277.)

Their expectation could not rest on weaker foundations. In a highly dramatic scene, Adam Patch, the old millionaire, who is a prohibitionist and a supporter of a Victorian moral code, visits them at the climax of a drunken party. The blow proves fatal for him and for the hopes of Anthony and Gloria as well, because they are disinherited.

Then lethargy turns into a nightmare. Even Anthony realizes that he "had been futile in longing to drift and dream; no one drifted except to maelstroms, no one dreamed without his dreams becoming fantastic nightmares of indecision and regret." This realization, however, is only temporary, and the two react by attaching themselves desperately to the hope of winning back the inheritance. They have now to contest the will, but their struggle (related in the third book) is really on two fronts, because their inner tensions break the remaining ties of love and destroy all their serenity. Anthony welcomes the diversion offered by the war and enlists to escape, as it were, his own self and his contradictions, but even this illusion is wrecked by the ruthless impact of reality.

Stationed in a southern military camp, Anthony ends by getting himself entangled in a sordid love affair, which is represented as "an inevitable result of his increasing carelessness about himself.... He merely slid into the matter through his inability to make definite judgments." This same inability is responsible for his breaking bounds to go and see his new girl, with the inevitable result of being stripped of his rank. Thus, even his respectability and self-respect are ruined, and he plunges again into a nightmare of helpless impotence and dissatisfaction. Meanwhile, Gloria, who has recognized the failure of their love ("That she had not been happy with Anthony for over a year mattered little"), falls back on the obstinate dream of her beauty. She flirts with old friends and new acquaintances, makes a new attempt to go into the movies, which results in bitter failure, and is unable to come to terms with reality. Not understanding that circumstances and people change, she reverts to childhood, dreaming of being a child again, of being protected, expecting "to wake in some high, fresh-scented room, alone, and statuesque within and without, as in her virginal and colorful past."

But the present intrudes; it offers only the pale image of an Anthony who, back from the military camp, spends his time in the house turning his back on every human or worldly contact. The aesthetic recluse has become the melancholy hermit of indigence and helplessness. Anthony spends his time wearily reading newspapers in the midst of disorder and filth, and now more than ever he has recourse to the deceptive relief of drinking. He too reverts to the dream of his past youth, and he too discovers that he is unfit for the present. Even his drinking aims at recreating an equivocal atmosphere of dreamy sentimentalism and decadent aestheticism:

> There was a kindliness about intoxication—there was that indescribable gloss and glamor it gave, like the memories of ephemeral and faded evenings. After a few high-balls there was magic in the tall glowing Arabian night of the Bush Terminal Building....
> ... the fruit of youth or of the grape, the transitory magic of the brief passage from darkness to darkness—the old illusion that truth and beauty were in some way entwined. (*BD*, p. 417.)

Anthony comes to realize that it *is* an illusion, but it is a devastating realization. His psychological balance is broken, and he resorts to pointless violence. He provokes Bloeckman, his former rival, to a fight, and when Dorothy, the southern girl, comes to see him in New York, he suffers a nervous collapse. It is at this point that the news reaches him that he has finally won his suit against the will and that he owns thirty million dollars.

Their dream is realized, but only when it is too late. The slow and inexorable passing of time has made this victory *in extremis* a hollow one. With a touch of dramatic irony, the reversal of fortune overtakes the two characters only when their initial situation has been reversed. Anthony, sophisticated and blasé at the beginning, is now an empty shell who goes to Europe with a doctor at his side. Sparkling Gloria, who used to divide people into clean and unclean, now herself appears "sort of dyed and *unclean.*"

If we read the story in this way—disentangling its meaning from the mass of obtrusive material and subsidiary aspects—it becomes clear enough that it is a parable on the deceptiveness of dreams, on the impossibility of evading reality through illusions, and on the painful destructiveness of time. The very evil that wears away the life of the flapper who refuses to grow up, and the life of the "philosopher" who cannot come to grips with reality and experience, is hidden in their youthful dreams, in their careless attitude of defiance toward the world, in their refusal to evaluate and accept the effects of time. Far from being the mouthpiece or the singer of the jazz age, Fitzgerald was its lucid accuser. He was well aware of its equivocal dangers, of its irresponsible attitudes, and he pitilessly exposed its disastrous consequences—even admitting that his denunciation was achieved almost in spite of his own intentions and was brought to light in the novel almost unconsciously.

If the meaning of the story told in *The Beautiful and Damned* must be identified with the gradual denunciation of Anthony's and Gloria's irresponsible progress of deterioration, and with an exposition of their guilty behavior toward themselves and the world, one cannot deny that in many passages Fitzgerald reveals a tendency to bestow on Anthony, if not on Gloria, a kind of moral greatness that contradicts the *objective* development of his adventure.

At times Fitzgerald seemed to falter between a desire to show the "heroic" side of Anthony and a willingness to criticize his pointless endeavors. The story itself admits of no other possibility than a bitter denunciation of Anthony and Gloria, because their actions speak for themselves, and there is little doubt as to their purport. But at the very end of the book Anthony is represented in an ambiguous light and almost praised for his refusal "to give in, to submit to mediocrity, to go to work":

> Anthony Patch, sitting near the rail and looking out at the sea, was not thinking of his money [!], for he had seldom in his life been really preoccupied with material vainglory.... No—he was concerned with a series of reminiscences, much as a general might look back upon a successful campaign and analyze his victories. He was thinking of the hardships, the insufferable tribulations he had gone through. They had tried to penalize him for the mistakes of his youth....
> Only a few months before people had been urging him to give in, to submit to mediocrity, to go to work. But he had known that he was justified in his way of life—and he had stuck it out staunchly....
> "I showed them," he was saying. "It was a hard fight, but I didn't give up and I came through!" (*BD*, pp. 448–49.)

His last words are words of self-satisfaction and defiance, and his long struggle is here represented in a sympathetic light. This final reversal of the moral judgment is even more apparent in the magazine version of the novel, in which Fitzgerald not only defended the grandeur of Anthony's and Gloria's desperate attempt, but went so far as to exalt the validity of its motivation—"the freshness and fulness of their desire." "Their fault was not that they had doubted but that they had believed," Fitzgerald had written. Their only "disastrous extremes" were identified with "the exquisite perfection of their boredom, the delicacy of their inattention, the inexhaustibility of their discontent," and their figures acquired a halo of romantic suffering and purity. It is worthwhile quoting the whole final passage of the magazine version, which justifies, among other things, the title of the last chapter ("Together with the Sparrows") which was retained in the book:

> That exquisite heavenly irony which had tabulated the demise of many generations of sparrows seems to us to be content with the moral judgments of man upon fellow man. If there is a subtle and yet more nebulous ethic somewhere in the mind, one might believe that beneath the sordid dress and near the bruised heart of this transaction there was a motive which was not weak but only futile and sad. In the search for happiness, which search is the greatest and possibly the only crime of which we in our petty misery are capable, these two people were marked as guilty chiefly by the freshness and fulness of their desire. Their illusion was always a comparative thing—they had sought glamor and color through their respective worlds with steadfast loyalty—sought it and it alone in kisses and in wine, sought it with the same ingenuousness in the wanton moonlight as under the cold sun of inviolate chastity. Their fault was not that they had doubted but that they had believed.
> The exquisite perfection of their boredom, the delicacy of their inattention, the inexhaustibility of their discontent—were disastrous extremes—that was all.

> And if, before Gloria yielded up her gift of beauty, she shed one bright feather of light so that someone, gazing up from the grey earth, might say, "Look" There is an angel's wing!" perhaps she had given more than enough for her tinsel joys.[3]

The logical development of the story is here given a deliberate twist; and it is perhaps significant that this idea of a moral comment on his characters that would justify their struggle and explain its motivations came to Fitzgerald, it seems, at the last moment and in a sudden flash, since in the manuscript version of the novel the story closed simply with the return of Gloria to her Paradise:

> The stars greeted her intimately as they went by and the winds made a soft welcoming flurry in the air. Sighing, she began a conversation with a voice that was in the white wind.
> "Back again," the voice whispered.
> "Yes."
> "After fifteen years."
> "Yes."
> The voice hesitated.
> "How remote you are," it said, "Unstirred.... You seem to have no heart. How about the little girl? The glory of her eyes is gone—"
> But Beauty had forgotten long ago.

Such a conclusion probably belonged to an early conception of the novel, when Gloria (*la belle dame sans merci*) was to be represented as the main cause of Anthony's deterioration and ruin. But it makes it clear that Fitzgerald had not completely mastered his material when he published the novel and that his final rehabilitation of Anthony was due to a sudden impulse which reflected, somehow, a basic uncertainty as to his real stature and accomplishments. Traces of this wavering attitude toward Anthony can in fact be found in other passages of the book as well, and they must be acknowledged, even if it means recognizing that *The Beautiful and Damned* does not present a story as straightforward as one would like to have it.

Consider, for instance, the nature of Anthony's relationship with his few friends, especially at the beginning. It is clear that he enjoys an unquestionable superiority over Maury Noble and Richard Caramel, but even after his "downfall" Fitzgerald represents him as superior to both Noble and Caramel. It is true that Noble, in spite of his nihilistic tirade in the middle of the book (at the end of the chapter entitled "Symposium"), succumbs to a respectable, middle-class marriage, and that Caramel undertakes a brilliant career as a commercial novelist—a career which gives him fame and fortune, but does not redeem him from the limitations of his talent and the meanness of his compromises. Still, Anthony does not do any better than they: but by using these two figures, Fitzgerald apparently wished to set off in relief the purity, "the exquisite perfection" and the inaccessibility of Anthony, who remains true to his initial ideals without ever descending to a vulgar compromise. This is made quite clear in an episode toward the end, when poor

Caramel is violently abused by Anthony, and Fitzgerald seems to watch the performance with great gusto.

The same might be said, with different qualifications, of Gloria, whose fascinating personality predominates in many episodes of the book and whose charm is felt both by Fitzgerald and the reader. But even if Fitzgerald's intent—conscious or unconscious—was to extol the "beauty" of his two characters by contrasting them with the mediocrity of middle-class life and ideals, we must still say that the remedy proposed is worse than the evil indicated and that this alternative to reality denies its own reasons, because the two protagonists are "damned" without hope by their actions and attitudes, as they are developed and made apparent in the story. And they are damned not only in the eyes of the world, or for moralistic considerations on the part of the readers, but because their story *is* a story of self-destruction, which naturally results in inner and outer ruin.

All this must be taken into consideration to understand the exact nature and quality of the book and its deeper meaning, in spite of the many misleading suggestions that we have to confront. *The Beautiful and Damned* is not "a distressing tragedy which should be, also, one hundred percent meaningless," as Edmund Wilson claimed, if we see beyond the surface into its *objective* line of development. And it is not a mere "muddle" in the presentation of the two characters, as Arthur Mizener maintained,[4] if we see their true natures behind the screen of their self-complacency. The book has a meaning and a significance, even if its theme is not rigorously focused and consistently developed to its logical conclusion.

The reason for this incongruity lies perhaps in the fact that Fitzgerald's attempt was too ambitious. Soon after his autobiographical *This Side of Paradise*, he was facing a new and complex theme which required a considerable amount of objective treatment. Amory had been a direct projection of the writer himself. To Anthony and Gloria he gave many characteristics, traits, and apprehensions of his own and of his wife, but he imagined his characters' experience as a possibility, rather than representing his own private experience. It was not simply a question of evoking or recreating a personal reality—it was rather a question of bringing to life an imaginary situation, which he had contemplated as a possibility, with no immediate connection with his own life, and which was to be represented in its objective development.[5] In this ambitious attempt Fitzgerald proved himself unequal to the exacting task of controlling the objective development of his characters according to a rigorous thematic principle. He tried to detach himself from his characters, to stand aside and unfold their story in all its implications, going so far as to pass a moral judgment on them. On the other hand, he sympathized with his characters and shared some of their illusions and not a few of their attitudes, with the result that he felt like justifying, incongruously, the greatness of their attempt. He had, in other words, to expose and denounce two characters who appealed to him, or to justify their beauty in spite of their damnation. He wanted to do both things, and the thematic unity of the book was seriously compromised. The double choice offered in the title is reflected in the lack of a consistent resolution of its conflicting motives. The objective and inescapable result of the action is that Anthony and Gloria are "damned": and they cannot be, therefore, as "beautiful" as the author tries to make them.

This is why we have to conclude that *The Beautiful and Damned* is a transitional novel. It lies half-way between a youthful success and the achievement of maturity. But if it is a novel of transition, it is so because some of the limitations of *This Side of Paradise* were transcended. Flappers and philosophers celebrate no triumphs in this novel. If they do seem to gain a victory, it is soon shown to be illusory and deceptive, a subtle form of irredeemable defeat, the snare of moral misery. Although sympathizing with the defiant attitude of his heroes, Fitzgerald feels the need to pass a moral judgment on them, and even in their glamorous and careless way of life he reveals the hidden flaw of failure and defeat. In spite of his enthusiasms, in *The Beautiful and Damned* Fitzgerald is concerned with exposing the inner meaning of life, not with reproducing its brilliant surface alone; he is concerned with suffering and the bitter aspects of experience, not with its playful manifestations. "I guess I am too much of a moralist at heart"—he was to write in his notes—"and really want to preach at people in some acceptable form, rather than to entertain them."[6] This inclination—if not yet this intention—is already present in his second novel.

Notes

1. In the MS there is also an epigraph from Samuel Butler: "Life is a long process of getting tired," which was not used in the printed text.

2. In the MS the three books bear these titles: "The Pleasant Absurdity of Things," "The Romantic Bitterness of Things," and "The Ironic Tragedy of Things."

3. In *The Metropolitan Magazine*, LV (March 1922), p. 113; see also *Letters*, p. 152.

4. Cf. Mizener, *The Far Side of Paradise*, p. 140. Wilson's essay "S.F." had appeared in *The Bookman*, March 1922. See also William Troy, "Scott Fitzgerald—The Authority of Failure" (1945), and J. F. Powers, "Dealers in Diamonds and Rhinestones," both in A. Kazin (ed.) *F. Scott Fitzgerald*.

5. "Gloria [he wrote his daughter years later] was a more trivial and vulgar person that your mother. I can't really say there was any resemblance except in the beauty and certain terms of expression she used, and also I naturally used many circumstantial events of our early married life. However the emphases were entirely different. We had a much better time than Anthony and Gloria did." As quoted in *The Far Side of Paradise*, pp. 124–25. This did not prevent reviewers from interpreting the novel as autobiography.

6. *The Crack-Up*, p. 305 and *Letters*, p. 63; on the subject of Fitzgerald's moralism, cf. also *The Far Side of Paradise*, pp. 3–4, 16, and 18, among others.

# 58
Vandover and the Brute and *The Beautiful and Damned*: A Search for Thematic and Stylistic Reinterpretations

♦

RICHARD ASTRO

Most students of literature would be willing to argue that a valid source study can be highly useful in shedding new light on certain thematic devices and stylistic techniques which might appear in any given literary work. Moreover, because many critics often neglect or condemn a given work on the grounds that it represents a deviation from the author's generally established thematic or stylistic pattern, source studies are beneficial in that they often provide a new framework against which the work under consideration may be judged.

This is certainly the case with F. Scott Fitzgerald's *The Beautiful and Damned*, a work that even Fitzgerald's most reputable critics have condemned as immature, unrealistic, trivial, and generally unsuccessful when viewed in comparison with the vast thematic and technical successes of *The Great Gatsby*.[1] However, the value of this type of criticism seems somewhat dubious in that it judges *The Beautiful and Damned* only in relation to Fitzgerald's achievement in *The Great Gatsby*. In other words, it seems hardly fair to assume that Fitzgerald embraced the same motives in all of his works, and it is thus indeed a mistake to condemn any one of his novels for failing to achieve the ends realized in any other work without considering the possibility that Fitzgerald's motives in the two works might have been entirely different. In short, then, most critics have failed to realize that Fitzgerald's literary objectives in *The Beautiful and Damned* are wholly different from those in any of his other novels, for in this work Fitzgerald's writing assumes new and, for Fitzgerald, unique directions, and thus the novel must be re-

SOURCE *Modern Fiction Studies* XIV, Winter 1968, pp. 397–413.

evaluated in terms of the author's successes and failures in achieving these directions.

The most practicable manner in which to understand and appraise the motivating forces in *The Beautiful and Damned* is through a study of Fitzgerald's literary sources in this novel, and it is the contention of this study that *The Beautiful and Damned*, while embodying many of the typically refreshing stylistic qualities found in all of Fitzgerald's works, is patterned largely after Frank Norris' second novel, *Vandover and the Brute*. Thus, by defining the parallels which exist between *The Beautiful and Damned* and *Vandover and the Brute*, fresh insight may be shed on Fitzgerald's work, insight which enables the novel's value to be measured in terms of a new and more satisfying perspective.

In any source study, it is very helpful to know an author's opinion of the person and writings of his alleged source. While there are only a few recorded remarks concerning Fitzgerald's attitude towards Norris, they conclusively support the thesis that not only did Fitzgerald regard the California novelist as a highly gifted craftsman but that he openly confessed to a desire to utilize Norris' literary ideas and attitudes in his own fiction.

In a letter to Maxwell Perkins written just a year before the first serialized publication of *The Beautiful and Damned*, Fitzgerald admits: "I've fallen lately under the influence of an author who's quite changed my point of view. He's a chestnut to you, no doubt, but I've just discovered him—Frank Norris. I think *McTeague* and *Vandover* are both excellent. I told you last November that I'd read *Salt* by his brother Charles and was quite enthusiastic about it. Odd! There are things in *Paradise* that might have been written by Norris—those drunken scenes, for instance—in fact, all the realism. I wish I'd stuck to it throughout."[2]

Similarly, in Fitzgerald's highly autobiographical novel, *This Side of Paradise*, the novelist notes that Amory Blaine (whose basic intellectual development parallels that of Fitzgerald) is most definitely aware of *Vandover and the Brute*: "[Amory was] rather surprised by his discovery through a critic named Mencken of several excellent American novels: *Vandover and the Brute*, *The Damnation of Theron Ware*, and *Jennie Gerhardt*."[3]

In another letter written a few months after the one to Perkins, Fitzgerald told James Branch Cabell that Norris had a direct influence on the writing of *The Beautiful and Damned*: "I have just finished an extraordinary novel called *The Beautiful Lady* [afterwards *The Beautiful and Damned*] which shows touches of your influence, much of Mencken, and not a little of Frank Norris."[4] Henry Piper's brief article, "Frank Norris and Scott Fitzgerald," which is generally unsuccessful because of its failure to provide a meaningful analysis of the parallels between Norris' and Fitzgerald's works, is valuable, however, in pointing out that the influence of Frank Norris, the man, on Scott Fitzgerald, the man, was for Fitzgerald "a shock of recognition."[5] Piper notes that Fitzgerald must have been impressed with Norris who like himself was a western writer and who had started writing in college.[6] Further, Piper notes that in the first draft of *The Beautiful and Damned*, Fitzgerald had written that Richard Caramel, a writer and one of the novel's chief supporting characters, regarded himself as "the great American novelist—the only authentic realist since Frank Norris."[7]

Turning now to *Vandover and the Brute* and its influence on *The Beautiful and Damned*, it is of the utmost importance to fully understand Norris' thematic design in his novel. It is often wrongly assumed that all of Norris' novels are pure naturalistic fiction in the Zola tradition; that all of Norris' central characters are doomed to drift through life, totally unable to control or determine either their temporal or their ultimate destiny. Although the influence of Zola and the naturalistic tradition is manifest in varying degrees in most of Norris' fiction (notably in *McTeague*), it would certainly be a gross error to suggest that Norris unhesitatingly adheres to naturalistic doctrines in all of his writings.

This is certainly the case with *Vandover and the Brute* which is far less a naturalistic novel than a moralizing tract against self-indulgence which identifies a static condition (Vandover's) with evil and dynamism with goodness. Vandover's dissipation does not result from his impotent attempts to act in opposition to a determined fate; rather his destruction results from his own apathy. Vandover degenerates not because his struggles are in vain, but because he doesn't struggle at all.

From the novel's outset, Vandover's main character trait is his destructive self-indulgence. Norris reports that upon returning to San Francisco after four years at Harvard, years which were unprofitable in terms of substantial academic achievement, "Vandover found that he could be contented in almost any environment, the weakness, the certain pliability of his character easily fitting itself into new grooves, reshaping itself to suit new circumstances."[8] Norris defines Vandover's self-indulgence as a pre-occupation with sensual pleasures combined with a lethargic attitude toward all situations and problems which pose even the slightest degree of tension and anxiety: "Vandover was self-indulgent—he loved these sensuous pleasures, he loved to eat good things, he loved to be warm, he loved to sleep. He hated to be bored and worried—he liked to have a good time" (p. 27).

Vandover tries to dismiss crucial events in his life, treating them as evils to be avoided if at all possible, and thus, if it can be said with any certainty that Vandover acts at all, his actions consist solely in continued efforts to avoid a confrontation with displeasing situations. Hence, even after his father's death, an event which Vandover attributes in part to his own failure to achieve the success his father had intended for him and which, therefore, makes a heavier impact on him than any previous encounter in his life (though he was also momentarily affected by the suicide of Ida Wade, a girl whom he had made pregnant), Vandover's grief soon subsides as he quickly accommodates himself to a more self-indulgent existence. Norris thus asserts that, at this point, Vandover's rapid process of deterioration is well underway: "But it was not long before Vandover had become accustomed to his father's death, and had rearranged himself to suit the new environment which it had occasioned. He wondered at himself because of the quickness with which he had recovered from his grief, just as before he had marvelled at the ease with which he had forgotten Ida's death. Could it be true, then, that nothing affected him very deeply?" (pp. 138–139).

Forced to manage his father's fiscal affairs, Vandover regards the task of handling routine business matters as an endless boredom, and prefers to enjoy his idle, sensuous pleasures:

> By the end of three weeks Vandover had sickened of the whole thing. The novelty was gone, and business affairs no longer amused him. Besides this, he was anxious to settle down in comfortable rooms....
>
> Little by little Vandover turned over the supervision and management of his affairs and his property to Adams and Brunt, declaring that he could not afford to be bothered with them any longer. This course was much more expensive and by no means so satisfactory from a business point of view, but Vandover felt as though the loss in money was more than offset by his freedom from annoyance and responsibility. (pp. 147–148)

Norris goes on to state that after his father's death, "a new life now began for Vandover, a life of luxury and aimlessness which he found charming. He had no duties, no cares, no responsibilities" (p. 157). Once a promising artist, Vandover, in his pre-occupation with idle pleasures, neglects his painting: "As rapidly as ever, his pliable character adapted itself to the new environment; he had nothing to do; there was lacking both the desire and necessity to keep him at the easel; he neglected his painting utterly" (p. 157).

Norris presents the process of self-destruction as a rapid continuum, and thus it is not long before Vandover's total existence consists in the enjoyment of the idle pleasures afforded him by the comfortable furnishings of his San Francisco apartment:

> Now that there was nothing to worry him, and little to occupy his mind, Vandover gave himself over considerably to those animal pleasures which he enjoyed so much. He lay abed late in the morning, dozing between the warm sheets; he overfed himself at table, and drank too much wine; he ate between meals, having filled his sideboard with pates, potted birds, and devilled meats; while upon the bamboo table stood a tin box of chocolates out of which he ate whole handfulls at a time. He would take this box into the bathroom with him and eat while he lay in the hot water until he was overcome by the enervating warmth and by the steam and would then drop off to sleep. (pp. 160–161)

Vandover's lethargy results in the end of his love affair with the society belle, Turner Ravis. Turner terminates her relationship with Vandover because she "could only be in love by being loved" (p. 190), and the self-indulgent Vandover loves nothing besides his own pleasures. It is thus natural that Vandover, though momentarily stunned by his forfeiture of Turner, soon regards this loss as of no greater magnitude than his loss of interest in art and his boredom with financial affairs:

> But little by little as he frequented the society of such girls as Ida Wade, Grace Irving, and Flossie, his affection for Turner faded. As the habits of passionate and unhealthy excitement grew upon him he lost first the taste and then the very capacity for a calm, pure feeling. His affection for her he frittered away with fast girls and abandoned women, strangled it in the foul, musk-laden air of disreputable houses, dragged and defiled it in the wine-list of the Imperial. In the end he had quite destroyed it, wilfully, wantonly killed it. (p. 190)

Even when he is threatened with financial disaster, Vandover refuses to expend any creative energy in his own behalf. Hence, when he is being swindled out of eight thousand dollars by his former college friend, Charlie Geary, Vandover prefers to forfeit the money than to make even the slightest attempt to defend his rights. Thus he tells Geary: "Can't we settle the whole matter today? Right here—now. I'm sick of it, sick of everything. Let's get it done with" (p. 233). In short, Vandover does get "it done with," but at a cost of eight thousand dollars.

Vandover's self-indulgent lethargy reaches its greatest extreme when he comes bored with the same sensual pleasures that were formerly his greatest source of satisfaction. It is at this point, states Norris, that Vandover has degenerated to "a state of absolute indifference": "But though nothing could amuse him, on the other hand, nothing could worry him; in the end the very riot of his nerves ceased even to annoy him.... He had no pleasures, no cares, no ambitions, no regrets, no hopes. It was mere passive existence, an inert, plantlike vegetation, the moment's pause before the final decay, the last inevitable rot" (p. 244). What is more important, Vandover fully understands the progress and ramifications of is own dissipation, but is simply too lazy to check its course. Thus, near the novel's conclusion, Vandover tells Dolly Haight, his other college friend: "It's too late for me now, and I'm not even sorry that it *is* too late. Dolly, I don't *want* to pull up. You can't imagine a man fallen as low as that, can you? Dolly, *I can get used to almost anything.* Nothing makes much difference to me nowadays ..." (p. 268).

Vandover's degeneration is thus the result of his own self-indulgence, of his continued apathy and refusal to provide and sustain a meaningful foundation for his own existence. Vandover is not pre-destined to a senseless state of lethargic indifference in which he is powerless to act; rather he carries out his self-destruction by means of his own design, a design which is doomed to failure in a society which insists that true human happiness can result only from creative human action.

Just as Vandover's self-indulgence is the basis of the thematic direction in *Vandover and the Brute*, Anthony's and Gloria's apathetic willingness to idly glide through life is the central theme in Fitzgerald's *The Beautiful and Damned*. Moreover, it is this strain of self-indulgence that eventually destroys the central characters in both novels.

In a letter to Charles Scribner, Fitzgerald stated that *The Beautiful and Damned* is the story of Anthony Patch, "one of those many with the tastes and weaknesses of an artist but with no actual creative inspiration. How he and his beautiful young wife are wrecked on the shoals of dissipation is told in the story."[9] Anthony, like Vandover, has the potential to become an accomplished artist (in Anthony's case, a medieval scholar), but, also like Vandover, he refuses to convert his native ability into creative action. Anthony simply prefers to drift through life, enjoying only those sensual pleasures which afford him neither pain nor anxiety, while awaiting a large inheritance which he plans to receive upon the death of his wealthy grandfather.

Like Vandover, one of Anthony's greatest sources of pleasure consists in the comforts afforded him by the regal furnishings of his apartment. It is in his apartment, Fitzgerald affirms, that for Anthony, "all life began." Fitzgerald's unique skill as a novelist is apparent in this scene in which he vividly sketches the lavish manner in which Anthony has furnished his bathroom:

> His bathroom, in contrast to the rather portentous character of his bedroom, was gay, bright, extremely habitable and even faintly facetious....
> The bathtub, equipped with an ingenious bookholder, was low and large. Beside it a wall wardrobe bulged with sufficient linen for three men and with a generation of neckties. There was no skimpy glorified towel of a carpet—instead, a rich rug, like the one in his bedroom a miracle of softness that seemed almost to massage the wet foot emerging from the tub....
> All in all a room to conjure with—it was easy to see that Anthony dressed there, arranged his immaculate hair there, in fact did everything but sleep and eat there. It was his pride, this bathroom.[10]

Until he meets Gloria, Anthony revels in the joyful surroundings of his apartment and dedicates his life to a detachment from what he regards as the mundane existence of involved human relationships, a detachment characterized less by Anthony's accomplished dedication to any sort of definable aesthetic ideal, than to his mere love of idleness (in this regard it is interesting that he vaguely plans to write a history of the Middle Ages, for as Perosa suggests, what could be more remote from the modern world than medieval studies).[11]

Anthony's meeting with Gloria, however, changes the direction of his life, for Anthony's dedication to a life of solitary detachment is immediately replaced by a dream of eternal but self-oriented love with a woman whose self-indulgent nature surpasses even his own. Moreover, Anthony and Gloria base their relationship on the illusion that love and not work can and will sustain them, that nothing else matters as long as love remains. Early in their relationship, Anthony spells out his credo of idleness to Gloria: "'I want to know just why it's impossible for an American to be gracefully idle'—his words gathered conviction—'it astonishes me. It—it—I don't understand why people think that every young man ought to go down-town and work ten hours a day for the best twenty years of his life at dull, unimaginative work, certainly not altruistic work'" (p. 65). Far from being alarmed by the realization that her husband-to-be has no intentions of ever working, the self-indulgent Gloria passively confesses that she does not care whether or not people actually do anything: "'I just think of people,' she continued, 'whether they seem right and fit into a picture. I don't mind if they don't do anything. I don't see why they should; in fact it always astonishes me when anybody does anything'" (p. 66). Gloria tells Anthony that life for her means only the enjoyment of idle pleasures and, more important, an avoidance of all painful or threatening events and situations: "'I want to just be lazy and I want some of the people around me doing things, because that makes me feel comfortable and safe ... and I want some of them to be doing nothing at all, because they can be graceful and companionable to me. But I never want to change people or get excited over them'" (p. 66).

It is thus Anthony's and Gloria's self-indulgence, their joint adherence to a pleasure-seeking and pain-avoidance philosophy of life which is the basis of their marriage. Thus, on the last page of her diary, which ends soon before their marriage, Gloria significantly notes with overtones which foretell her eventual disaster, that her life with Anthony will be a continuous existence of "blowing bubbles—that's what we're doing, Anthony and me. And we blew such beautiful ones to-day, and they'll explode and then we'll blow more and more, I guess—bubbles just as big and just as beautiful, until all the soap and water is used up" (p. 147).

The inadequate basis of Anthony's and Gloria's marriage implies the inevitability of its failure, and thus their dream slowly becomes a form of inexcusable lethargy which destroys their illusion of eternal love and results in a total nightmare. The story of Anthony's and Gloria's marriage is a study in the falseness of their self-indulgent attitude towards life and is a striking testimony of Fitzgerald's attitude, like Norris' in *Vandover and the Brute*, that it is impossible for any man or woman to permanently avoid a full confrontation with reality.

There are further parallels between the two novels in that the final stages of the deterioration of the leading characters are marked by similar events and attitudes. Vandover turns to gambling as an escape mechanism by which he attempts to shield himself from his dissipated condition. Thus, Norris states: "here at last was the new pleasure for which he had longed, the fresh violent excitement that alone could arouse his jaded nerves, the one thing that could amuse him" (p. 252). Similarly, Anthony demands an escape device, and thus Fitzgerald, who was certainly more familiar with alcohol than with gambling, conveniently makes Anthony an alcoholic. Hence, throughout the later sections of *The Beautiful and Damned*, Fitzgerald artfully portrays Anthony's increasing satisfaction with being continually drunk:

> But he hated to be sober. It made him conscious of the people around him, of that air of struggle, of greedy ambition, of hope more sordid than despair, of incessant passage up or down, which in every metropolis is most in evidence through the unstable middle class....
>
> There was a kindliness about intoxication—there was that indescribable gloss and glamour it gave, like the memories of ephemeral and faded evenings. (p. 417)

In the end, like Vandover, Anthony is no longer pleased by the sensuous pleasures which he once so thoroughly enjoyed. Fitzgerald reports that for Anthony, "there was nothing, it seemed, that grew stale so soon as pleasure" (p. 418). Again, like Vandover, Anthony's and Gloria's miserable life of idle self-indulgence strips them not only of their self-integrity, but also of their public image. Once a most exquisite couple in an age of radiance, Anthony and Gloria soon appear in a different light: "Within another year, Anthony and Gloria had become like players who had lost their costumes, lacking the pride to continue on the note of tragedy—so that when Mrs. and Miss Hulme of Kansas City cut them dead in the Plaza one evening, it was only that Mrs. and Miss Hulme, like most people, abominated mirrors of their atavistic selves" (p. 405). One only has to recall the final scenes in *Vandover and the Brute* in which Vandover is shunned by a family of self-righteous common laborers to note the parallel themes of physical degeneration in the two novels. And while Anthony and Gloria never descend to the point of actually wearing rags (perhaps nobody wore rags during the Jazz Age) the symbolic resemblance between them and Vandover is nevertheless evident.

Mizener objects to Fitzgerald's creation of Anthony and Gloria on the grounds that they are not convincing as intelligent and sensitive characters; that they are not more sinned against than sinning and thus there is no adequate cause for their suffering, nor adequate grounds in their characters for the importance Fitzgerald gives it.[12] What Mizener apparently fails to realize in his appraisal of Anthony and Gloria is that Fitzgerald never intended them to be more sinned against than sinning, nor did he intend to endow them with the lofty character traits that Mizener seems to desire. In other words, Anthony and Gloria are not tragic figures (in either the traditional or modern sense of the word) because Fitzgerald never intended them to be tragic. In short, *The Beautiful and Damned* is a successfully conceived moralistic tract against self-indulgence, not an imperfectly drawn tragedy of the twentieth-century intellectual.

It is quite true that Fitzgerald often sympathizes with Anthony and Gloria, a sympathy which overtly detracts from the novel's effectiveness. On the other hand, the question arises as to what can be expected from a novelist whose own fears about his and Zelda's life so closely paralleled the fictional lives of Anthony and Gloria? In a letter to his daughter, Fitzgerald once explained his great dream and Zelda's self-indulgent destruction of that dream: "When I was your age I lived with a great dream. The dream grew and I learned how to speak of it and make people listen to it. Then the dream divided one day when I decided to marry your mother after all, even though I know she was spoiled and meant no good to me.... She realized too late that work was dignity, and tried to atone for it by working herself, but it was too late and she broke and is broken forever."[13] In a similar vein, Fitzgerald tells Scottie later in the same letter: "I never wanted to see again in this world women who were brought up as idlers. And one of my chief desires in life was to keep you from being that kind of person, one who brings ruin to themselves and others.... I think that idlers seem to be a special class for whom nothing can be planned, plead as one will with them ... their only contribution to the human family is to warm a seat at the common table."[14]

It is thus evident that Fitzgerald believed that his life with Zelda dangerously approached that of Anthony and Gloria. Hence, when one understands the similarity between Fitzgerald's conception of his own and his wife's life with the attitudes of the leading characters in *The Beautiful and Damned*, it is readily apparent why Fitzgerald found it very difficult to condemn the imperfections in characters whom he really loved. And while it is true, as mentioned above, that this tendency to sympathize with Anthony and Gloria compromises the novel's thematic unity, it is similarly true that Fitzgerald's deep emotional identification with his characters supplies an added dimension of importance to his moralizing in the novel.

It has been sufficiently noted that self-indulgence and its destructive force on human life is the central theme of *Vandover and the Brute* and *The Beautiful and Damned*. But the parallels hardly end here, for there are a myriad of other similarities between the two novels. In addition to their love of idleness, their pre-occupation with sensuous pleasures, and their devotion to types of escape mechanisms, Vandover and Anthony share many other qualities.

As Piper points out in his extensive study of Fitzgerald's work, *F. Scott Fitzgerald, a Critical Portrait*, both men are products of wealth and culture.[15] Both attended Harvard, accumulating only mediocre academic records. Vandover is the son of a respected San Francisco businessman who has made a substantial amount of money in real estate speculation, and Anthony is the grandson of Adam Patch, a former capitalist tycoon turned philanthropist, whose estate amounts to the fantastic sum of thirty million dollars.

Vandover and Anthony require vast sums of money to sustain their self-indulgent ways of life, and both receive their inheritance too late to help them. While Richard Lehan suggests that their resulting failures are occasioned by their scorn for the business world,[16] it actually seems less scorn than sheer apathy which destroys Vandover and Anthony. When Vandover collects his father's estate (which has dwindled somewhat due to the decline in San Francisco real estate values), he is already too apathetic to muster the initiative to apply his father's money to good purpose. Norris thus states that because Vandover's interest in money is like all his other ambitions, "nothing made much difference, after all. His money had come too late" (p. 246).

Similarly, when Anthony finally receives his fortune, he has already become a mentally incompetent individual for whom money has no value. Thus, Fitzgerald, as well as Norris, imposes a touch of irony on his character's demise by making his dissipation all the more meaningless.

As Piper and Lehan note,[17] Vandover and Anthony have extended affairs with lower class women, affairs in which neither has any genuine feelings for the girl he seduces, but only for the self-indulgent pleasure afforded by such a liaison. Vandover's intrigue with Ida Wade means no more to him than an opportunity to satisfy a momentary impulse for sexual gratification. Similarly, Anthony's lengthy war-time affair with Dorothy Raycroft is conceived by Anthony purely in terms of self-indulgent sexual delight. On the other hand, and Piper and Lehan neglect this point, Ida and Dorothy fall in love with their disinterested lovers, and both threaten suicide when they fear they are being abandoned, though only the despondent Ida actually goes through with it.

At the same time, as Piper suggests, Vandover and Anthony forfeit the love and respect of the genuine women in their lives.[18] At the end of *The Beautiful and Damned*, it is apparent that Gloria, though dissipated herself, has fallen out of love and has lost her respect for Anthony in the same manner in which Turner Ravis' feelings for Vandover change when she tells him she wants no more to do with him.

The final stages of Vandover's self-destruction as well as Anthony's dissipation are marked by futile attempts to borrow money from former friends. Vandover, in need of money with which to gamble, approaches Charlie Geary in hopes of securing a fifty dollar loan, but is violently cursed by Geary and ejected by force. Anthony, who, like Vandover, needs money to support his "habit," attempts to borrow ten dollars from the newly-rich Maury Noble, but is so hopelessly humiliated by Noble that he cannot even find the words to voice his request.

Finally, there are instances in the last pages of both novels in which Vandover and Anthony are completely crushed in physical brawls, scenes which add an element of physical impotence to their already complete emotional dissipation. Vandover is mauled by a fellow gambler whom he has falsely accused of cheating. In reporting this incident, Norris notes that Vandover emerges from the beating drunk, alone, and totally dissipated:

> Toedy kicked him in the stomach and made him abominably sick. Then they went away and left Vandover alone in the little dirty room, racked with nausea, very drunk, fallen forward upon a table and crying into his folded arms.... His hands and his coat sleeves, the table all about him, were foul beyond words, but he slept on in the midst of it all, inert, stupefied, a great swarm of flies buzzing about his head and face. (p. 297)

Similarly, Anthony receives a literal "kick in the teeth" from Joseph Bloeckman when he wrongly accuses Bloeckman of attempting to seduce Gloria:

> Anthony cracked up against the staircase, recovered himself and made a wild drunken swing at his opponent, but Bloeckman, who took exercise every day and knew something of sparring, blocked it with ease and struck him twice in the face with two swift smashing jabs. Anthony gave a little grunt and toppled over onto the plush green carpet, finding, as he fell, that his mouth was full of blood and seemed oddly loose in front. (p. 437)

Anthony's physical beating ends with his being thrown out of a cab in front of his apartment. Fitzgerald states that Anthony crashed down "against the stone steps of the apartment house," where, like Vandover, "he lay without movement, while the tall buildings rocked to and fro above him" (p. 441). It is interesting to note that both beatings result from false accusations by Vandover and Anthony. It thus seems, that when faced with the final reality of total self-annihilation, Vandover and Anthony make single but feeble attempts to justify themselves, attempts which are as mis-directed and therefore as futile as has been the course of their entire lives.

In addition to the thematic parallels and the similar character traits and actions of Vandover and Anthony, the two novels exhibit further similarities in regard to their supporting characters, structure, and style, similarities which suggest that Fitzgerald admired and utilized many more of Norris' fictional techniques than has generally been conceded. In creating the society in which Vandover moves, Norris provides his leading character with two close friends who not only serve a thematic purpose of their own, but who also serve as foils against which Vandover's actions (or inaction) and attitudes may be measured.

First, there is Charlie Geary, Vandover's deceitful college associate, a ruthless materialist who unmercifully tramples and desecrates anything and everything which obstructs his path to financial success. Geary's attitude towards life consists of no more than an avowed acceptance of the struggle for survival in which the strong survive and the weak perish, and Charlie is determined to be among the strong. Early in the novel, he explains his materialistic, self-oriented philosophy of life to Vandover in a tone which suggests a dreaded portent of future events and which makes Vandover's later deception by the damnable Geary all the more pathetic: "'A man's got to rustle if he's going to make a success at law. *I'm* going to make it go, by George, or I'll know the reason why. I'll make my way in this town and my pile. There's money to be made here and *I* might just as well make it as the next man. Every man for himself, that's what *I* say; that's the way to get along. It may be selfish, but you've got to do it'" (p. 82).

Vandover's other friend is the significantly named Dolly Haight, a hypersensitive individual who is as destined to be among the perishable weak as Charlie Geary is determined to be among the surviving strong. Unlike Vandover who has the native ability to act in his own behalf but is too lethargic to do so, Dolly is incapable of meaningful action despite the strength of his efforts. (Indeed, the pure naturalism which does exist in the novel is manifest in the characters of the submissive Dolly Haight and the interior-driven Charlie Geary). Norris epitomizes Dolly's fated destiny in the episode in which, after finally summoning the courage to have illicit relations with a woman of low estate, Haight catches an incurable venereal disease. In short, Dolly Haight cannot act, and thus the only action he ever really completes kills him.

Norris has no love for society's Charlie Gearys or Dolly Haights. To be sure, the materialistic Geary succeeds in achieving the object of his desires, but Norris makes it quite clear that these goals are hardly worth the effort required to achieve them. Similarly, the fragile Dolly Haights in the world cannot and do not deserve to survive. Vandover has the potential to fashion a meaningful existence for himself; Charlie and Dolly are each doomed to their own particular type of damnation by the innate structures of their constitutions. Hence, one gets the distinct impression that, despite his many weaknesses and self-delusions, Vandover appeals to Norris far more than either Charlie Geary or Dolly Haight.

In almost an identical fashion, Fitzgerald provides Anthony with two friends, Maury Noble and Richard Caramel. At the novel's outset, Maury is a self-ordained sceptic, but eventually he becomes a ruthless materialist who, like Geary, disdains to help his dissipated friend. Maury remains highly cynical throughout the novel, and Fitzgerald seems to suggest that it is Maury's pathetic cynicism which leads him to compromise with his once humanistic ideals and to show an increasing contempt for his fellow man. As the novel progresses, Maury's life becomes totally devoid of thought or content, and Fitzgerald seems to imply that Maury is more damnable than Anthony, for Anthony, unlike Maury, retains his fine creative mind although he refuses to use it: "He [Maury] was sorry for no one now—on Monday morning there would be his business, and later there would be a girl of another class whose whole life he was; these were the things nearest his heart. In the strangeness of the brightening day it seemed presumptuous that with this feeble, broken instrument of his mind he had ever tried to think" (p. 260).

Dick Caramel, Anthony's other close friend, differs from Norris' Dolly in that he is a writer who manages to produce a worthwhile novel (on the other hand, Fitzgerald wanted to put some of himself in the character of Caramel; Caramel's novel is significantly named *The Demon Lover*, a title which was once intended for *The Beautiful and Damned*). But Dick resembles Dolly in that he remains Anthony's friend even in the latter's ultimate stages of degeneration just as Dolly maintains his friendship with Vandover long after the rest of Vandover's friends have forsaken him. Further, the names Dolly and Caramel similarly imply an aura of feebleness, a feeling of plasticity and lack of direction. Moreover, just as Dolly is less admirable than Vandover, Dick is less worthy of praise than Anthony. While Anthony realizes the cause and significance of his own dissipation, Caramel is too stupid to know that by writing inferior novels, he is compromising with his own standards, or to see the success he has won by compromising it not worth having. Late in *The Beautiful and Damned*, Dick proudly tells Anthony: "My publishers, you know, have been advertising me as the Thackeray of America" (p. 423), and Anthony suddenly realizes the full magnitude of Caramel's self-delusion:

> Anthony tried to remember what he had read lately of Richard Caramel's. There was "A Shave-tail in France," a novel called "The Land of Strong Men," and several dozen short stories, which were even worse. It had become the custom among young and clever reviewers to mention Richard Caramel with a smile of scorn. "Mr." Richard Caramel they called him. His corpse was dragged obscenely through every literary supplement. He was accused of making a great fortune by writing trash for the movies. As the fashion in books shifted he was becoming almost a byword of contempt. (pp. 421–422)

Anthony never compromises with himself in the sense that Maury and Richard compromise with their ideals, and it is evident that Fitzgerald, while he despises a great deal about Anthony, admires his constancy. Thus, despite his shortcomings, Anthony does emerge a more self-knowledgeable and, therefore, a more satisfying character than either of his friends. Hence, Norris and Fitzgerald provide a pair of contrasting figures who serve as corrupted norms against which their leading characters may be judged, and it is readily apparent that both authors have a higher regard for their main figures than for any of the other prominent figures in their novels.

Turning to the question of style, it is noteworthy that Fitzgerald employs three devices in *The Beautiful and Damned* which he uses very sparingly, if at all, in his other works, and which are therefore significant in relation to this study due to the fact that they similarly appear in *Vandover and the Brute*.

First, Fitzgerald relies more heavily on the direct narrative in *The Beautiful and Damned* than in any of his later novels, a technique which severely hampers the novelist's usually unique manner of presentation. While it is a matter of sheer speculation as to why Fitzgerald decided to make such extensive use of the direct narrative, it is noteworthy that the style of the narrative in *Vandover and the Brute* bears a strong resemblance to that in *The Beautiful and Damned*.

Second, like Norris in *Vandover and the Brute*, Fitzgerald employs a rather extensive amount of documentation in *The Beautiful and Damned* in what appears to be an attempt to lend authenticity to the tone of the narrative. This is particularly apparent in the section of the novel in which Fitzgerald discusses Gloria's diary, and the ineffectiveness of this documentation in the sense of its inability to serve much of a thematic purpose, suggests that Fitzgerald was toying with a new stylistic idea, one which is used in many of Norris' novels and which reaches its perfection in Fitzgerald's fiction in the discussion of Nicole's letters in *Tender is the Night*.

Finally, Fitzgerald concludes *The Beautiful and Damned* with an unusual and highly effective technical device in which Anthony and Gloria are seen for the last time, not through their own or through the author's eyes, but as they appear to two totally disinterested spectators. As Gloria comes into view, one of the disinterested viewers remarks to her companion: "I can't stand her, you know. She seems sort of—sort of dyed and *unclean*, if you know what I mean. Some people just have that look about them whether they are or not" (p. 448).

Similarly *Vandover and the Brute* concludes with Vandover being critically surveyed by a group of detached observers whose only interest in Vandover concerns his ability to clean their dirty house. In both novels, the device of ending the story with a depreciatory comment on the leading characters by detached observers accentuates the reality of the depths to which these dissipated characters have plunged. In short, the reader feels that this final glimpse of Vandover and the last portraits of Anthony and Gloria are authentic; that this is the way they really end up.

It would be impossible to discuss at length all of the lesser parallels between *Vandover and the Brute* and *The Beautiful and Damned*. But in order to escape the charge of missing any pertinent information which seems relevant to a discussion of Norris' influence on Fitzgerald, it seems advisable to briefly enumerate several other ideas and techniques which are common to both novels.

1. *The Beautiful and Damned* and *Vandover and the Brute* are not entirely restricted to appraisals of individual characters. Both novels express their author's criticism of American social and economic norms as a whole, and throughout both books one may readily note persuasive commentary on and evaluations of the American way of life which are very similar in their tone and point of view. One only has to compare Norris' description of the events and situations centering around the San Francisco football crowd in *Vandover and the Brute* with Fitzgerald's critical portraits of life in New York City throughout *The Beautiful and Damned* to note the distinctive parallels between the two novelists' point of view.

2. Vandover and Anthony sparingly, but nevertheless definitely, exhibit anti-semitic prejudices. Anthony always regards Joseph Bloeckman with an air of contempt partly because Bloeckman is a Jew, though, of course, there are many other reasons for his distaste for Bloeckman. Anthony's anti-semitism, which travels below the surface throughout most of the story, comes to the surface near the novel's conclusion when he calls Bloeckman a "Goddam Jew," after the latter refuses to lend him money. What it is important to note in this regard is that Anthony's charge is not merely the result of any momentary frustration, but is rather a capsule view of his basic feelings towards Bloeckman which have been built up and sustained during the course of the novel.

Similarly in *Vandover and the Brute*, when a diamond merchant drowns after the ship that he and Vandover are on capsizes, Vandover's regrets about the drowning are tempered by the fact that, after all, the salesman was a Jew.

3. While it is indeed a minor point, it is interesting to note that Vandover's hyper-sensitive friend, Dolly, in *Vandover and the Brute* and the lawyer who handles Anthony's inheritance lawsuit in *The Beautiful and Damned* bear the same last name. While it would be unfair to unequivocally assert that Fitzgerald borrowed the name from Norris, the very fact that "Haight" is by no means a common name seems to validate the nature of the inquiry as to its origin in Fitzgerald's novel.

By means of an extensive investigation of many aspects of *Vandover and the Brute* and *The Beautiful and Damned*, it is apparent that Fitzgerald's basic themes, many of his character studies, and several of his stylistic techniques in his novel distinctly parallel many of the themes, character portraits, and stylistic devices of *Vandover and the Brute*. And, accepting this, it logically follows that Fitzgerald's basic purpose in *The Beautiful and Damned* is thus very similar to Norris' in *Vandover and the Brute*. In short, to repeat what has been said earlier but which needs reiteration, *The Beautiful and Damned* is not, as has often been assumed, a futile attempt to describe the glorified illusion of human dreams; it is rather a didactic tract against self-indulgence. Further, the lack of the tragic element concerning Anthony's and Gloria's dissipation does not make them failures as characters, for Fitzgerald never intended them to be tragic. To be sure, as has been pointed out, the novelist sympathizes with Anthony and Gloria, but there is no evidence anywhere in the novel that he wants to extoll their tragic dignity. Finally, while Fitzgerald's use of the direct narrative and documentation in *The Beautiful and Damned* is by no means totally effective, it must be remembered that the novelist was conducting a pre-determined stylistic experiment, not merely writing in a haphazard fashion. Hence, when these stylistic devices are viewed in this perspective, they seem to achieve an added degree of respectability and lend added importance to Fitzgerald's motives in the novel as a whole.

It would be foolish to insist the *The Beautiful and Damned* is Fitzgerald's best work, for when this work is viewed in relation to *The Great Gatsby*, its merits are overshadowed by the excellence of the later novel. Nevertheless, *The Beautiful and Damned* has its merits as a successful attempt to probe new fictional depths, and as such it must be regarded as a unique achievement in the catalogue of Fitzgerald's fiction.

Notes

1. For criticism which contends that *The Beautiful and Damned* is not a successful novel see Arthur Mizener, *The Far Side of Paradise*, Sentry edition (New York, 1965), pp. 151–159. Also see Kenneth E. Eble, *F. Scott Fitzgerald*, Twayne's United States Authors Series (New Haven, 1963), pp. 68–75.

2. *The Letters of F. Scott Fitzgerald*, ed. Andrew Turnbull, Delta Book edition (New York, 1965), pp. 143–144.

3. F. Scott Fitzgerald, *This Side of Paradise* (New York, 1920), p. 209.
4. *Letters*, p. 464.
5. Henry Dan Piper, "Frank Norris and Scott Fitzgerald," *Huntington Library Quarterly*, XIX (August, 1956), 393–400.
6. Piper, p. 394.
7. Piper, p. 396.
8. Frank Norris, *Vandover and the Brute*, from *The Complete Works of Frank Norris* (New York, 1928), Vol. V. p. 23. All citations from this work refer to this edition and hereafter will be cited by page number only.
9. *Letters*, p. 145.
10. F. Scott Fitzgerald, *The Beautiful and Damned* (New York, 1922), p. 11. All citations from this work refer to this edition and hereafter will be cited by page number only.
11. Sergio Perosa, *The Art of F. Scott Fitzgerald*, trans. Charles Matz and the author (Ann Arbor, 1965), p. 37.
12. Mizener, p. 156.
13. *Letters*, p. 32.
14. *Letters*, p. 33.
15. Henry Dan Piper, *F. Scott Fitzgerald, a Critical Portrait* (New York, 1965), p. 90.
16. Richard D. Lehan, *F. Scott Fitzgerald and the Craft of Fiction* (Carbondale, 1966), p. 22.
17. Piper, *F. Scott Fitzgerald*, p. 90, and Lehan, p. 22.
18. Piper, *F. Scott Fitzgerald*, p. 90.

59
The Beautiful and Damned: The Alcoholic's Revenge

◆

ROBERT ROULSTON

Probably the least loved of F. Scott Fitzgerald's novels, *The Beautiful and Damned* has been castigated for its content no less than for its deficient artistry.[1] The criticisms are not unmerited. Most of the book's "ideas" are shallow, some are vicious, and few are sustained with much consistency by the narrative line. Furthermore, Fitzgerald's evident inability to decide whether to admire or despise the protagonist has led to a damaging disunity of tone.

Yet despite its defects *The Beautiful and Damned* is an engrossing and at times moving work. Much of its power comes from the vigor of Fitzgerald's writing. But at least as much results from what undoubtedly caused many of the blemishes of this highly autobiographical novel—the intensity of Fitzgerald's involvement with Anthony Patch's follies and ordeals. As an exercise in self-exploration, it is often no less illuminating and no less compelling than *The Crack-Up*, which is also marred by lapses in judgment. But, whereas in *The Crack-Up* Fitzgerald achieves his most telling effects through bold, quotable, and disquieting epigrams, in *The Beautiful and Damned*—where the authorial comments often seem unwitting parodies of Wilde, Shaw, Samuel Butler and H. L. Mencken—he strikes his deepest resonances within us through the interplay between incidents and imagery.

It is not surprising that the work makes its profoundest impact in those regions of creativity where the selection of specifics was least likely to be affected by Fitzgerald's abstract formulations about his own travails or about the society he held to be at least partly responsible for his woes. Throughout 1920 and 1921, when he wrote most of *The Beautiful and Damned*, he was experiencing a psychological crisis of a sort likely to confound the most disciplined intellect. By comparison, his troubles in the mid-1930's, which impelled him to write *The Crack-Up*, were easy to comprehend, albeit no less difficult to resolve. After all, any perceptive man whose health is failing,

SOURCE *Literature and Psychology* 27, Part 4, 1977, pp. 156–163.

whose wife has gone insane, and whose income is plunging should be able to define the sources of his misery. But in the early 1920's Fitzgerald acquired the things he had most fervently desired—success and a beautiful glamorous wife. Instead of finding satisfaction, however, he was awash in marital and professional tribulations which were exacerbated by his growing dependence upon alcohol.

Whatever else *The Beautiful and Damned* may or may not do, it records in fictional form the progress of Fitzgerald's malady. True, by 1921 he had not sunk to the bestial level reached by Anthony Patch in the novel's final chapter. Nevertheless, most of Anthony's drunken outrages are all too similar to incidents in Fitzgerald's life. But like all true artists, Fitzgerald was not content merely to report. He needed to probe, to explain. In this instance, though, he was caught in the coils of a psychological problem which a psychiatrist was to declare to be "as inscrutable as the mystery of his writing talent."[2]

But even though Fitzgerald could not ferret out *the* cause of his spiritual malaise of which his drinking was the most visible symptom, *The Beautiful and Damned* indicates that he sensed in his own development a process akin to the one Karl A. Menninger was later to discern as characteristic of alcoholic patients. "Such individuals," according to Menninger, "as children, have endured bitter disappointment, *unforgettable* disappointment, *unforgivable* disappointment. They feel, with justification, that their entire subsequent life is a prolonged, disguised reaction to this feeling."[3]

That Fitzgerald carried from childhood such a sense of betrayal should be self-evident to anyone who has read much of his fiction where a recurring theme is that of the young romantic disillusioned—a pattern that prevailed throughout his own youth from at least as early as his sixth birthday when none of the guests appeared for the party which he had anticipated so eagerly.[4] Similar betrayals were to befall him in school, in love, and even in war when his desire to fight overseas was frustrated by the advent of the Armistice. But by the time he wrote *The Beautiful and Damned*, the most recent such disappointment—the disillusionment he felt in the wake of his ardently sought rise to fame and his no less intensely desired marriage to Zelda Sayre—must have seemed to epitomize all such previous experiences. At no point in *The Beautiful and Damned* does Anthony seem to speak more clearly for his creator than when he says: "Things are sweeter when they're lost. I know—because I once wanted something and got it.... And when I got it it turned to dust in my hands."[5]

Such pain pervades the book. Its least effective manifestations are Fitzgerald's sophomoric asides to the reader and the "philosophical" pronouncements of Anthony, Gloria, and Maury. But even these excrescences are consonant with the prevailing bitterness of the work. What gives *The Beautiful and Damned* its peculiar rancor is that alone of Fitzgerald's major writings it offers an across the board, all-out assault upon his boyhood years, the two decades preceding World War I, and obliquely upon values embodied by his own parents—in fact, upon those forces which had shaped his character and aroused expectations which recent events had shattered.

Thus, in vain might we search through *The Beautiful and Damned* for something that so often glimmers throughout the pages of Fitzgerald's other works—nostalgia for pre-war America. In his first and even more overtly autobiographical first novel, *This Side of Paradise*, the hero and his friends cast fond glances backward, regretting the way the conflict had "ruined the old backgrounds" and "killed the individualism" out of their generation; and they pitied a new breed of young people grown up to find "all the gods dead, all wars fought, all faiths in men shaken."[6] A decade later in "Babylon Revisited" Fitzgerald would extol this earlier era by exclaiming of the story's protagonist: "He wanted to jump back a whole generation and trust in character again as the eternally valuable element."[7] Even in *The Great Gatsby*, published a mere three years after *The Beautiful and Damned*, Fitzgerald has his narrator reject frenzied "modern" New York in favor of the Midwest with its old-fashioned virtues.

In *The Beautiful and Damned*, however, Fitzgerald, by making Anthony Patch ten years older than Fitzgerald himself was, defiles his own adolescent years by imposing upon them many of his most recent and still rankling tribulations. Moreover, as Robert Sklar has perceptively noted, although the action of the book transpires mostly during the second decade of this century, the novel's "mood and themes belong to a decade even earlier."[8] The impetus for this double leap backward in time may have been, as Sklar suggests, the impact of Dreiser and Norris upon Fitzgerald. But the consequence was that he was able to taint the past which had given him his illusions with recent events which had disillusioned him.

Of perhaps even greater significance is the fact that in *The Beautiful and Damned* Fitzgerald demolished his own childhood and adolescence. Whereas he incorporated experiences from at least the latter phase of his youth into *This Side of Paradise*, in his second novel he concocted for Anthony Patch's formative years a past which bears almost no resemblance to Fitzgerald's own. Gone are the Mid-western background, the Catholic upbringing, the gaucheries at Newman school, and the failures at Princeton. Gone too are the genteel ineffectual father and the dowdy doting mother. But before Fitzgerald kills them off in a few sentences near the beginning of the first chapter, he invests them with an effete glamor, while simultaneously tarnishing them with sarcasm, making the father "an inveterate joiner of clubs, connoisseur of good form, and a driver of tandems" (p. 5) and the mother a Boston Society Contralto—the last role anyone would have envisioned for poor Mollie McQuillan Fitzgerald with her untidy appearance and ungainly manners.

Yet, as Fitzgerald's favorite poet, John Keats, observed, "the fancy cannot cheat so well." And so this stratagem for evading his complex, often hostile attitude toward his parents could not succeed in a work otherwise so autobiographical. The very act of excising them so completely is, in itself, a kind of literary parricide. (And it should not be forgotten that his fourth novel was to be about matricide before he abandoned the project in favor of what was to evolve into *Tender Is the Night*.) But even after having been murdered with a stroke or two of the pen, Fitzgerald's real parents continue to haunt the pages of this book about a young man's descent into alcoholism just as they indubitably haunted the labyrinths of its creator's psyche.

The greatest bitterness in *The Beautiful and Damned* is focused upon forces Fitzgerald would inevitably have associated with his mother. One need not give total assent to the theories of Freud in order to concur with the aforementioned psychiatrist when he states that Fitzgerald's mother may "have been responsible for his vanity and high expectations of himself"[9]—traits that presumably predisposed him toward alcoholism.

The emasculating mother has become, of course, a cliché of popular fiction and cinema. But clichés often express reality; and in Fitzgerald's case his mother did pamper him. She also treated him almost as a human doll, lavishing upon his appearance all the attention she did not bestow upon her own frumpish person. To be sure, since Fitzgerald disposes of his mother a mere five pages into the novel, we see few instances of her unmanning her offspring. But it is a truism that a man's attitudes toward women are molded by his perception of his mother. And Fitzgerald perceived his mother as "a neurotic, half insane with pathological nervous worry," and as someone with whom he "never had anything in common except a restless stubborn quality"—he also once described her as a "funny old wraith" who emitted a "suggestion of the Witch's Cave."[10]

Throughout *The Beautiful and Damned* Fitzgerald evokes a feminine ideal antithetical to the image he held of Mollie—an ideal which the women in Anthony's life betray just as Zelda with her mad antics, her pouting, and her demands upon his time was betraying Fitzgerald's expectations. Not only is Anthony's "Golden Girl," Gloria, unlike Mollie in that she is beautiful, but she is described as "cool" and above all as "clean" (pp. 102, 131). Indeed, Gloria is obsessed with cleanliness both in herself and in others. It is one of the qualities she most admires in Anthony before they marry and a quality that makes her overlook the faults of her Jewish friend, Rachael. But in one of her discourses on the subject she makes it clear that she associates a lack of physical cleanliness with moral contamination: "Women soil easily ... far more easily than men. Unless a girl's very young and brave it's almost impossible for her to go down hill without a certain hysterical animality, the cunning dirty sort of animality" (p. 235).

Now, of course, Mollie McQuillan hardly went "down hill" with a "dirty sort of animality." Her morals, if not her grooming, seem to have been beyond reproach. Nevertheless, her son's inclination to equate immorality with untidiness hardly betokens a high degree of filial esteem for her habits.

And surely when he implanted throughout *The Beautiful and Damned* passages identifying women with decay, decline, and ruin, he was guided by recollections of his mother's having pampered him as he was by resentment against Zelda for distracting him from his work. In fact, the two sets of resentments would only have reinforced each other because a doting overanxious "witch" and a narcissistic temptress can have a similarly destructive effect upon the men on whom they work their wiles. Thus, however much Gloria Patch may chide Anthony for being idle, she contributes to his inertia. Half siren, half Calypso, she saps him of his will. When he wants to escape from his debilitating ennui by going to Europe as a war correspondent, her arms, "sweet and strangling ... around him," deter him (p. 209). And the effect of her "melancholy tears" is once again "a triumph of lethargy" (p. 215). Anthony's love for Gloria, indeed, often seems, no less than his craving for alcohol, an addiction which saps his will as it intoxicates him.

Fitzgerald, however, does not confine such motifs in *The Beautiful and Damned* to Gloria; he bestows upon even minor female characters a similar propensity for betraying the expectations they arouse. There is, for example, the girl in a red negligé whom Anthony observes through the window of his apartment. Instead of being the vision of loveliness he first takes her to be, she turns out to be "fat, full thirty-five, utterly undistinguished" (p. 19). On another occasion, after his bridal dinner he lies in bed listening to the city's sounds "promising that, in a little while, life would be beautiful" when amidst the noises from the streets comes a woman's laughter which grows increasingly strident. Finally it evokes in him "his old aversion and horror toward all the business of life" (p. 150). And life itself, he concludes, is that "ghastly reiterated female sound" (p. 150). A kindred misogyny affects Fitzgerald's portrayal of the beautiful Rachael Jerryl who flirts with Anthony at a party and who, during the war, is unfaithful to her husband (pp. 269, 366). Geraldine Burke, Anthony's plebian girlfriend, may be "moral at heart," but she too will be caught by "an inevitable wave ... that would wash her off the sands of respectability" (p. 88). Even in his fantasies, Anthony envisions women as enticers and betrayers. In his story of the Chevalier O'Keefe, the medieval hero withdraws to a monastery to be "forever free from sex" only to be tempted as he stands upon "the very top of the Tower of Chastity" by a peasant girl whose beauty as she adjusts her garter so arouses him that he falls out "bound for the hard earth and eternal damnation" (p. 91). Lest the point of all these barbs against women and their erotic appeal be forgotten, Fitzgerald revives it with allusions to Keats's *La Belle Dame sans Merci* and with frequent references to the title of a novel by Anthony's friend, Dick Caramel, *The Demon Lover*—a title, incidentally, Fitzgerald once considered using for *The Beautiful and Damned*.

The supreme temptress in the book, though, is Dorothy Raycroft with whom Anthony has an affair during the war when he is stationed in South Carolina. Of course, Dorothy no less than Gloria is a projection of Zelda whom Fitzgerald had met in Alabama while he was in the army. But, whereas Zelda belonged to a socially prominent family, Dorothy is thoroughly plebian and is thus, by Anthony's patrician code, a more legitimate object for his non-connubial lusts. Dorothy may be vulgar and she may have a bad reputation, but like Gloria she is "clean" (p. 325). But clean or not, she causes Anthony to be demoted and confined to the guard house. Her refusal to give him up drives him to his most desperate act in the novel when, in the final chapter, he attempts to murder her.

In a study of this scope we cannot possibly cite all the passages in *The Beautiful and Damned* in which Fitzgerald links the South with sex, violence, and decadence. But such passages abound, and the fact that they do reflects no less upon his own father than they do upon Zelda. Edward Fitzgerald, we must recall, had been born in Montgomery County, Maryland, where during the Civil War his family had been staunchly pro-Confederate; in fact, his cousin had been the brother-in-law of Mary Suratt who had been executed for being an accessory to the murder of Lincoln. The Minnesota-born Scott Fitzgerald understandably identified his father with the South. Later he would also associate him with "that certain series of reticences and obligations that go under the poor old shattered word 'breeding'."[11] In *The Great Gatsby* Fitzgerald has Nick Carraway acquire from his father "a sense of fundamental decencies,"[12] and in *Tender Is the Night* he implies that Dick Diver's moral decline is more than a little attributable to a falling away from the values embodied by Dick's clergyman father, a native of Westmoreland County, Virginia, which is only a few miles away from Edward Fitzgerald's birthplace in Maryland.

In *The Beautiful and Damned*, however, the South stands for voluptuousness and corruption. When Anthony strolls with Dorothy through her Carolina town in "a sleepy dream," the place seems to him "more of Algiers than of Italy, with faded aspirations pointing back over innumerable generations to some warm, primitive Nirvana, without hope or care" (p. 377). There Negro music turns a dance hall "into an enchanted jungle of barbaric rhythms" (p. 317). Once, by one of those juxtapositions of which he was fond, Fitzgerald associates his father's part of the South—the region around Washington, D.C.—with somnolence, reaction, self-righteousness, and, incongruously, the puritan ethic. When Anthony and Gloria visit Robert E. Lee's home across the Potomac River from the capital, Gloria, who feels that "trying to preserve a century by keeping its relics up to date is like keeping a dying man alive with stimulants," compares the place to a graveyard in Tarrytown, New York, and then comments: "Sleepy Hollow's gone. Washington Irving's dead and his books are rotting in our estimation year by year" (p. 166). But, if Tarrytown was the home of Washington Irving and, as such, has resonances of Rip Van Winkle as well as of the Headless Horseman, it is in *The Beautiful and Damned* also the home of Anthony's ogre of a grandfather, Adam Patch.

Adam seems less a father surrogate than an amalgam of attributes that Fitzgerald identified with his mother and her family and of qualities he associated with his father and the Fitzgerald clan. Like Edward Fitzgerald, Adam represents traditional values. But in *The Beautiful and Damned* those values take the form not of "reticences and obligations" or of a "sense of fundamental decencies" but of the worst kind of self-righteous, bigoted moralism. A man without taste, culture, or even intelligence, Adam uses his vast fortune to deliver "body blows at liquor, literature, vice, art, patent medicine, and Sunday theatre" (p. 4). But, for all his inadequacies, Adam possesses a trait his grandson conspicuously lacks—a capacity for hard work. Now, one of the major sources of confusion in *The Beautiful and Damned* is over Fitzgerald's failure to indicate clearly whether he regarded Anthony's idleness as an aristocratic disdain for vulgar toil or mere sloth. Richard Astro argues that the novel is a moralistic tract modelled on Norris's *Vandover and the Brute* and as such "identifies a static condition ... with evil and dynamism with goodness."[13] The design of the book supports such an interpretation. But, if Fitzgerald's main purpose was to deride indolence and extol effort, he undermined that purpose by making his active characters as unappealing as his passive ones. Dick Caramel, the hard-working author, becomes a hack; the formerly languid Maury Noble turns into a cynical money grubber. As for Adam Patch, the self-made millionaire, he has nothing except industriousness to commend him. It would be going too far to equate Anthony's odious grandfather with Fitzgerald's own, Philip Francis McQuillan, who amassed a substantial fortune, a portion of which kept the Fitzgeralds in comfort after Edward Fitzgerald lost his job as a salesman for Proctor and Gamble. Yet the fact remains that Fitzgerald did associate the McQuillans with "new" money, and certainly his mother's lack of grace and charm could only have heightened his inclination to look upon them as lacking those patrician adornments he identified with his elegant if unsuccessful father. Surely, too, some of the rancor toward climbers in *The Beautiful and Damned*—be they Anglo-Saxon like Gloria's vulgar friend, Muriel Kane, Black like the insufficiently deferential elevator operator in Anthony's apartment building, or Jewish like the motion picture magnate, Joseph Bloeckman—owes something to Fitzgerald's sense of having been a "parvenu" because of the social liabilities imposed upon him by what he termed the "black Irish half" of his family. Those liabilities, in fact, were a major obstacle between Fitzgerald and something he wanted throughout his youth perhaps more than anything else—acceptance by those he admired and envied.

When Fitzgerald came to write his last two novels he would find much to admire in both sides of his heritage. Thus, in *Tender Is the Night*, he would make Dick Diver most attractive when struggling to develop his talents as a physician. And, in *The Last Tycoon*, he would make another Jewish movie producer, Monroe Stahr, seem positively titanic as he strives against the ravages of ill health to uphold artistic standards at his studio. But, if these later protagonists have some of the drive of his mother's father, they are at their most attractive whenever they exhibit a poise and dignity that reflect the finest standards of the Tidewater aristocracy which had produced Edward Fitzgerald.

But, whereas by the 1930's Fitzgerald—beset by new woes but fortified by a wisdom born of years of suffering—could be just to his parents and their respective milieus, in 1920 and 1921 the demons he had identified with Edward and Mollie Fitzgerald drove him to excoriate in *The Beautiful and Damned* everything he could connect with his father and mother. Since these two people—so dissimilar in their backgrounds, personal demeanors, and temperaments—typified so many different facets of American life, few aspects of pre-war America remain unscathed in the novel. H. L. Mencken's iconoclasm and Dreiser's and Norris's pessimism may have been catalysts for the book's unrelieved negativism. But surely the bitterness, the unrelenting misogyny, the want of *joie de vivre*, and the almost equal contempt for those who strive and those who repine owe more to Fitzgerald's own state of mind than to literary or philosophical models. In *The Beautiful and Damned*, Fitzgerald damns a past he cannot exorcise much as a tippler in a tavern might rail at a well-meaning but impolitic meddler. The invective may be intemperate, the charges excessive. Yet a detached observer need not find the spectacle distasteful if the drunkard is articulate and the meddler too self-satisfied. As parents go, Edward and Mollie Fitzgerald were not especially bad. And as American decades go, the two at the beginning of our century were hardly among the worst. Yet the very existence of the neurosis which was making Fitzgerald ever more dependent upon alcohol indicates that he had legitimate complaints against his parents, just as conditions in the United States during the Prohibition era suggest that he and his contemporaries had valid complaints against pre-war America for having engendered those conditions. These complaints resound through the interstices of *The Beautiful and Damned* much as a cry of drunken rage might echo through the alleys of a city at night.

Notes

1. Writers of scholarly articles have shown little enthusiasm for the work if the number of articles in print is an accurate indication: the MLA annual bibliographies list fewer items dealing explicitly with *The Beautiful and Damned* than with any other novel by Fitzgerald. As for book-length critical studies of Fitzgerald, although they generally note that *The Beautiful and Damned* is an advance over *This Side of Paradise* in terms of structure, they nearly all object to the book on either aesthetic or thematic grounds. Thus Robert Sklar, in *F. Scott Fitzgerald: The Last Laocoon* (New York: Oxford Univ. Press, 1967), pp. 95, 172, finds the novel a product "of careless haste and intellectual confusion" and "the nadir of Fitzgerald's capacity to comprehend and control his material." K. G. W. Cross dismisses the book's ideas as "both trite and repugnant" in *Scott Fitzgerald* (New York: Barnes & Noble: 1964), p. 38. In *F. Scott Fitzgerald and the Craft of Fiction*

(Carbondale: Univ. of Southern Illinois Press, 1966), pp. 82–83, Richard D. Lehan calls it a "novel of unassimilated idea" and contends that it is "thematically unclear." James E. Miller, Jr., in *The Fictional Technique of Scott Fitzgerald* (The Hague: Martinus Nijhoff, 1957), pp. 54–58, claims that its themes clash, that it contains "an ugly note of racism," and that Fitzgerald was "too close to his material to see it clearly." Although kinder to the books than most critics, Sergio Perosa, in *The Art of F. Scott Fitzgerald*, tr. Charles Matz and the author (Ann Harbor: Univ. of Michigan Press, 1965), p. 46, complains of the Dreiserian style and notes that there "is little selectivity in these pages." Henry Dan Piper, in *F. Scott Fitzgerald: A Critical Portrait* (New York: Holt, 1965), pp. 92, 98, maintains that Fitzgerald was "too close to actual experience" and that he tried to make the story "serve too many purposes."

2. Donald W. Goodwin, MD., "The Alcoholism of F. Scott Fitzgerald," *Journal of the American Medical Association*, 212 (April 6, 1970), 90. Goodwin does not discuss *The Beautiful and Damned*.

3. *Man Against Himself* (New York: Harcourt, Brace, 1938), p. 169.

4. Andrew Turnbull, *Scott Fitzgerald* (New York: Scribner's, 1962), p. 11. Unless there are indications to the contrary, statements in this article about Fitzgerald's life are substantiated either by Turnbull or by Arthur Mizener in *The Far Side of Paradise: A Biography of F. Scott Fitzgerald* (Boston: Houghton, Mifflin, 1951).

5. *The Beautiful and Damned* (New York: Scribner's, 1922). p. 341. Subsequent references to the novel will be to this edition with page numbers cited in parentheses in the text.

6. *This Side of Paradise* (New York: Scribner's, 1920), pp. 228, 304.

7. In *Babylon Revisited and Other Stories* (New York: Scribner's, 1960), p. 214.

8. Sklar, p. 93.

9. Goodwin, p. 89.

10. *The Letters of F. Scott Fitzgerald*, ed. Andrew Turnbull (New York: Dell, 1966), pp. 437, 556.

11. *Ibid.*, p. 522.

12. *The Great Gatsby* (New York: Scribner's, 1925), p. 2.

13. "*Vandover and the Brute* and *The Beautiful and Damned*: A Search for Thematic and Stylistic Reinterpretations," *Modern Fiction Studies*, 14 (Winter 1968–69), 399.

60
From *Wall Street in the American Novel*

♦

WAYNE W. WESTBROOK

Money and prosperity were the substance of the American Dream that F. Scott Fitzgerald knew to be futile and empty. The dream falls into dissolution in Fitzgerald's fiction and ends up as meaningless as the story in "Babylon Revisited," about a man who found his life filled to the full, then drained to the dregs by the stock market Crash of 1929. The dream is as illusory and unbelievable as the anecdote in *The Beautiful and Damned* about an assistant secretary in a brokerage office who invested all his savings in Bethlehem Steel, hung on patiently, and built a triumphal palace in California. Anthony Patch, in that novel, although lured and victimized by this dream, saw through its golden aura, viewing it as a "fruitless circumambient striving toward an incomprehensible goal, tangibly evidenced only by the rival mansions of Mr. Frick and Mr. Carnegie on Fifth Avenue." The only time it did seem romantic was when he was under the kindliness of intoxication, "And Wall Street, the crass, the banal—again it was the triumph of gold, a gorgeous sentient spectacle; it was where the great kings kept the money for their wars." The dream of Jay Gatsby in *The Great Gatsby* was as bright and shining as the many suns mirrored in the window of his automobile, as sad and lonely as his Long Island mansion.

Like a moth by a candle, Scott Fitzgerald was dazzled by wealth. The "era of extravagance" was still very much apparent in New York and Newport in the teens and twenties, as the heirs of the great nineteenth-century fortunes—the William Astors, the Vanderbilts, the Hydes, the Whitneys, the Ryans, the Guggenheims, the Schiffs, the Goulds, the Rockefellers, and the Morgans—lived like feudal lords. The newly rich could only imitate this type of royalty, predicating taste on money, manners on social position, and breeding on success in giving dinners and parties. Fitzgerald himself worshiped wealth, old or new, half wondering if those who had it didn't live off somewhere in a country as unreal as fairyland. Yet he privately disliked

SOURCE *Wall Street in the American Novel*, New York, 1980, pp. 145–148.

the rich, that leisure class which spent its time squandering money rather than earning it. Even though money did save them from selling their souls in the financial or commercial marketplace, the rich in Fitzgerald's fiction are damned anyway. They may have avoided the system, but they didn't dodge the devil.

Although he resented the rich, Scott Fitzgerald also understood their tragedy, as well as the tragedy of a capitalist society in which money, like nothing else, could produce such individual ruin and failure. But, portray failure though he did, Fitzgerald never offered an alternative to the money dream as London and Sinclair had. Those socialistic ideas preached by Amory Blaine in *This Side of Paradise*, for example, were not the novelist's. His own "political conscience had scarcely existed," nor had he ever done much "thinking save within the problems of his craft," as he frankly admitted in several self-dissecting articles toward the end of his life.

The portrait of the three generations of Patches in *The Beautiful and Damned* is a portrait of the newly rich class, the American plutocracy. In the genteel financial novels of Robert Grant and Edith Wharton, this new social species is identified strictly with Wall Street and capitalism. Where the old established aristocratic class is broken down and slowly replaced by the new in Grant and Wharton, the new moneyed class represented by the Patch family in Fitzgerald's fiction is doomed to extinction for lack of depth and roots. Each generation of Patches—grandfather, son, and grandson—is corrupted and weakened, not strengthened by money. Bequests, trusts, legacies, and Christmas gifts neither hold this family (or class) intact nor perpetuate it. Anthony Patch, in fact, is able to draw "as much consciousness of social security from being the grandson of Adam J. Patch as he would have had from tracing his line over the sea to the crusaders. This is inevitable; Virginians and Bostonians to the contrary notwithstanding, an aristocracy founded sheerly on money postulates wealth in the particular."[1]

Founder of the family fortune, Adam Patch is a personification of the vanishing nineteenth-century robber baron. At the conclusion of the Civil War he came home a major, "charged into Wall Street, and amid much fuss, fume, applause, and ill will he gathered to himself some seventy-five million dollars." Years later, basking in a moment of past glory, Old Adam boastfully recollects how he sent "three members of the firm of Wrenn and Hunt to the poorhouse." A vast store of Wall Street money, however, brings the Patch patriarch neither sweetness nor light, producing instead a deterioration of body, spirit, and mind. A stroke at age fifty-seven leaves Adam prematurely senescent. Suddenly, he turns remorseful about his past and grows obsessed with the hereafter. Aware of the selfishness of his misspent years and fearful that he must atone for their wickedness, the Wall Street millionaire, like a Mephistopheles converted to inscrutable good, consecrates "the remainder of his life to the moral regeneration of the world." Still another obsession takes hold in the shape of a strange idée fixe about reform, which prompts him to adopt a hypocritical moral righteousness completely without forbearance and a shallow philanthropy devoid of love and generosity. Patch is an Adam whose sins are never absolved. A fallen financier, he keeps reappearing unexpectedly in the novel like some dark avenging angel, an awful reminder of the damnation of money and a symbol of death. Actually the money lust has reduced him to a skeleton and toothless death's head, with all traces of life drawn out:

> It had sucked in the cheeks and the chest and the girth of arm and leg. It had tyrannously demanded his teeth, one by one, suspended his small eyes in dark-bluish sacks, tweaked out his hairs, changed him from gray to white in some places, from pink to yellow in others....[2]

Patch resembles old Hargus in Frank Norris's *The Pit*, or old Henry Grimes in Upton Sinclair's *The Metropolis*, money and death figures who appear years beyond their actual age after a life of sin in high finance.

Adam Ulysses Patch, Anthony's father, did not live long enough to squander the Patch millions, although he managed to make a small dent in them and then compose a dull and smug set of memoirs entitled "New York Society as I have Seen It."[3] He passed his gaudy and dandyish habits on to his son, who, like Chauncey Chippendale, went to Harvard and made the Pudding. Expectations of a multi-million-dollar inheritance significantly weaken Anthony, as they did his own father, and strand him without character, purpose, or moral fiber. When the anticipated windfall fails to come, however, Patch, like young Chippendale and Lily Bart, resorts to the stock market in a symbolic revolt against the tyrannical money figure in the family. Chauncey, who had already turned to speculation before his uncle's will was invalidated, was in fact rebelling against his father's financial conservatism and authority. Lily made "investments" on Wall Street to free herself from her Aunt Peniston's financial control as well as to show defiance and independence when she was disinherited. Anthony Patch, when Old Cross Patch changes his will, is so dangerously becalmed in a sea of debt while still under full financial sail that he, too, turns to the stock market, but only to sell off bonds his grandfather had earlier set aside for him. Oddly enough, the Fall for these financial innocents occurs not when the family fortune is originally accumulated, but when they, the second or third generation, are deprived of their inheritance of it. Ironically, the "golden day" finally does arrive for Anthony Patch, when the court decision that took his $30 million away is reversed. The money comes too late, though. Headed at long last with Gloria for Italy aboard *The Berengaria*, but confined to a wheelchair as a result of his mental breakdown, Anthony's incapacitation is a haunting reminder of Old Adam's senility after he himself had become rich.

Notes

1. F. Scott Fitzgerald, *The Beautiful and Damned* (1922; reprinted New York: Charles Scribner's Sons, 1950), p. 4.
2. Ibid., p. 14.
3. Fitzgerald modeled Adam Ulysses Patch after real-life New York socialite Ward McAllister. McAllister was court chamberlain for Mrs. William Backhouse Astor, grande dame of Manhattan society in the 1870s and 1880s. A fop and dilettante, he wrote his memoirs, entitled *Society as I Have Found It* (1890). McAllister is most remembered for inventing the term "the Four Hundred," often used in reference to the elite of New York Society. A fuller discussion of this source can be found in the *Fitzgerald/Hemingway Annual* (1979), "Portrait of a Dandy in *The Beautiful and Damned*," by Wayne W. Westbrook.

The Vegetable; or From President to Postman

1923

61
Scott Fitzgerald's Play

◆

JOHN F. CARTER JR.

I have no quarrel with the theatrical managers who rejected this play; as drama and as literature it is thoroughly and ostentatiously vulgar.

When I accuse Mr. Fitzgerald of vulgarity in *The Vegetable* I do not mean merely that it is written about vulgar people and that their language and idiom and environment are vulgar. I mean that the conception, treatment, and technique are distinctly cheap. I mean that the play is devoid of ideas and beauty; that it lacks sincerity, simplicity, and intellectual ruggedness.

Mr. Fitzgerald's literary career has been a disappointment. His sensational *This Side of Paradise* reminded one of Compton Mackenzie's *Sinister Street* both in subject and style. But it possessed a poignancy, a youthful passion, that caused us to hope that Mr. Fitzgerald might produce some vivid and original literature. Since then he has gracefully slipped along the pages of the popular magazines to a portentous psychological novel, *The Beautiful and Damned*, until he seems to have come to a dead stop with *The Vegetable*, his first published play.

This play is laboriously and glibly ironic. It is based on the idea of mental limitations. It is the story of Jerry Frost, a railway clerk of zero mentality, whose boyhood dream was to be a postman and who had vague desires to be the President of the United States. He drinks some synthetic gin purveyed to him, with threadbare buffoonery, by a bootlegger named Snooks. (In passing it may be said that Snooks is the only character sufficiently convincing to persuade one that he was drawn from the life.) Then Jerry has a nagging wife named Charlotte. Her nagging is obviously only introduced for dramatic effect, and as a character she is infinitely inferior to Sinclair Lewis's study of Zilla Riesling in a similar role in *Babbitt*. Charlotte's younger sister, Doris, and her fiancé, Fish, a young undertaker from Dubuque, Ia., together with Jerry's valetudinarian father, Dada, complete the cast. Jerry drinks the gin and falls asleep.

In the second act he dreams that he is President, and presumably conveys Mr. Fitzgerald's idea of the naïve mental conceptions of a $3,000 a year

SOURCE *Literary Review of the New York Evening Post*, 23 June 1923, p. 782.

railway clerk as to what the life of the President is like. At the White House everything is white—trees, clothes, even cigars. Barrie did that sort of thing charmingly and well in *A Kiss for Cinderella*. Fitzgerald lays it on as thick as possible, with burlesque Senators, Judge Fossile of the Supreme Court, and a cheap parody army officer named General Pushing. It is possible that the burlesque of the Government and the White House may shock the public's sense of *lèse-majesté* enough to make this act a drawing card. In print it is worse than tedious.

In the last act Jerry, who disappeared on the night of the gin drinking, returns in the role of postman, thus satisfying his boyhood desire, as the dream satisfied the Presidency complex! Mr. Fitzgerald blandly omits to give any explanation as to how, when, where, or why Jerry Frost became a postman. However, his wife, who has really worried over his disappearance, looks forward to a reunited life with "the best postman in the world."

The prose of *The Vegetable* is a fair imitation of Ring Lardner, the spirit an obvious act of deference to Mencken's virulent contempt for the American people. In consequence it is trashy and betrays a smugness of viewpoint that shows that one more of our bright young men has succumbed to the glamour of the self-advertising business.

62
New Comedy at Shore

ANONYMOUS REVIEW

F. Scott Fitzgerald made his debut as a playwright at the Apollo Theatre here last evening with *The Vegetable*, a comedy based on his book of that name. The apostle of the flappers has abandoned his theme of the deadly young female species and turned his satirical realism to X-raying the great American home of a humble white collar worker, with little gray matter above the white.

In the first act, with the artful aid of Ernest Truex at his best and funniest, he skilfully shows, or rather, shows up, the more or less happy, more or less turbulent, home of Jerry Frost, railroad clerk, and his nagging wife, Charlotte. Nothing much happens, except that Jerry, after a deal of verbal buffeting from his spouse and her sister, is visited by his tough but genial bootlegger, and on the wings of synthetic gin soars far above the cares of family life.

The second act, supposed to show Jerry's gin-fizzled dream of himself in the White House as President, does little else than demonstrate that Mr. Fitzgerald would better stick to his modernist realism and leave fantasy to those of lighter touch and whim.

The third act comes back to that horror of amateur interior decorating which to Jerry is home, and his sitting room. It develops that Jerry, after his bad dreams of realizing his boyhood ambition to become President, has fled from his home to bring to actual realization his later ambition, always stifled by his wife, to be a postman. He comes back after two weeks to a wife reduced to tearful contrition for her past nagging, and a happy ending is achieved but not until Mr. Fitzgerald has revealed that he is as little at home with tender and old-fashioned sentiment as he is with fantasy.

However the comedy has many bright moments of keen mockery of our foibles and inanities. Minna Gombel, as the wife; Ruth Hammond, as Doris, the one lone Fitzgerald flapper of the piece and Malcolm Williams as Snooks, the irresistible bootlegger, all do their best to emphasize Mr. Fitzgerald's strong points, though they can't quite lift that second act out of the bog.

SOURCE *Philadelphia Evening Bulletin*, 20 November 1923, p. 10. A review of the first performance of *The Vegetable*.

63
From *F. Scott Fitzgerald: A Critical Portrait*

♦

HENRY DAN PIPER

Fitzgerald began writing *The Vegetable*, his only full-length published play, as we have already noted, in November, 1921, immediately after sending back his half-hearted corrections of the proofs of *The Beautiful and Damned*. As soon as it was finished the following March he took it to New York to have it read by George Jean Nathan, then one of the country's most influential drama critics, and Edmund Wilson. Considering its limitations as drama as well as its subsequent unhappy stage history, one wonders why these friends didn't advise him to put it aside and go back to writing novels. But both admired the frothy vaudeville skits he had published in *Smart Set* several years earlier and encouraged his ambitions to become a successful Broadway playwright. Discussing his friend in a recent book, Nathan wrote:

> I hope that young F. Scott Fitzgerald will turn from the one-act form to the three-act form one of these days: I feel that he will confect a genuinely diverting comedy. He has a good sense of character, a sharp eye, a gracious humor, and an aptitude for setting down adolescent dialogue that Tarkington has rarely matched.

Nathan was eager to do all that he could to help get the script produced. And Wilson wrote its author: "So far as I am concerned, I think it is one of the best things you ever wrote ... marvelous—no doubt the best American comedy ever written.... I think you have a gift for comic dialogue even though you can never resist a stupid gag—and should go on writing plays." *The best American comedy ever written!* This was heady praise indeed. Whether Wilson meant it seriously or not, Fitzgerald assumed that he did, and quoted Wilson's opinion proudly in a letter to Max Perkins. But unfortunately Nathan's and Wilson's opinions regarding Fitzgerald's dramatic talent were not universally shared. One producer after another—Gilbert Miller, Arthur Hopkins, George Selwyn, Jed Harris—turned down the script as did Frank Craven the actor, whom Fitzgerald had hoped would take the leading role.

SOURCE *F. Scott Fitzgerald: A Critical Portrait*, London, 1965, pp. 94–99.

Everyone had ideas for improving it, and, after spending almost a year tinkering with it, Fitzgerald's efforts were rewarded when Sam Harris agreed to put it on with Ernest Truex as the star. An Atlantic City tryout was scheduled for early November, 1923, to be followed by a premiere on Broadway.

Fitzgerald devoted the summer and fall of 1923 to revising the script for Harris and Truex, and he persuaded himself that he had a great success on his hands. "Harris wants the play because he thinks it will be *the* flapper play," he wrote Ober not long before it opened. "... I feel that Acts I and III are probably the best pieces of dramatic comedy in English in the last five years." But the first night audience in Atlantic City thought otherwise, and the production folded a few performances later.

The idea of *The Vegetable*, a spoof on Washington politics, was an excellent one. The story centers on a henpecked little man, Jerry Frost, who is married to a shrew named Charlotte. Most of the time Charlotte sits around the house eating chocolates and reading popular magazines, notably *The Saturday Evening Post.* She is unhappy because Jerry hasn't risen in the world and become rich and successful like the heroes in her favorite magazine stories. Recently, Jerry has taken a genteel white-collar job as a clerk in a railroad office because Charlotte wants him in a respectable position. But he is bored by the tedious routine and dislikes being cooped up inside all day. What Jerry would like to be more than anything else is a postman. He wants to work outside and likes the idea of bringing people good news. If Charlotte would let him take a postman's job, he would try to be "the best postman in the world."

But to Charlotte Frost, her husband is a hopeless failure, a vegetable. The play's title comes from a passage which Fitzgerald, on his title page, credited as having come "From a Current Magazine."

> Any man who doesn't want to get on in the world, to make a million dollars, and maybe even park his toothbrush in the White House, hasn't got as much to him as a good dog has—he's nothing more or less than a vegetable.

The first act of the play takes place on that fateful night in 1920 when Senator Warren G. Harding of Ohio was selected by the Republican Party as its candidate for President of the United States. While Jerry is sitting at home drinking bootleg gin and waiting for news of the convention's choice, he falls asleep and dreams that he himself has been elected President. The second act is a comic nightmare purporting to show what happens when a well-intentioned incompetent like Jerry is put in the White House. Everyone takes advantage of him—not least, his closest friends and relatives. Washington is honeycombed with corruption, and Jerry is finally impeached and convicted. On waking, he is so upset by this dream that he quits the railway clerk's job he has always disliked and runs away. Before long, we get news that he has become a postman and is happy doing the job that he likes best. The third act ends happily with a tearful, lonely Charlotte ready at last to take Jerry back on his own terms.

Perhaps if *The Vegetable* had appeared on the scene a year or so later, it might have found a more responsive audience. When it opened in the autumn of 1923 President Harding had been dead only a few months. Teapot Dome had not yet assumed the proportions of a national scandal, and the average theater-goer was not ready to ridicule the White House. John Farrar expressed the Babbitt-like complacency of the era when, reviewing *The Vegetable* in the influential *Bookman* magazine, he called it "impudent" and "more of a commentary on Fitzgerald's generation than upon American life."

The remarkable thing was that Fitzgerald, with his chronic lack of interest in political matters, had guessed so well what was really going on in Washington. If impudence and a lack of respect for the tribal gods were the play's only faults, then it would be ripe for revival today. But it had other shortcomings. A decade later Kaufman and Ryskind's *Of Thee I Sing* showed what could be done with first-rate political satire. Fitzgerald once claimed that *Of Thee I Sing* had been plagiarized from *The Vegetable* and thought seriously of bringing suit. Luckily, he did not. Comparison of the two shows that the musical owed little if anything to *The Vegetable*.

In spite of his teen-age triumphs as an impresario, and his later Triangle successes, Fitzgerald did not know enough about the professional stage to write successful full-length plays. For all the cleverness of its theme and dialogue, *The Vegetable* lacked the one thing that is essential—unified progression toward a climax. A lot is said, but nothing ever happens. This sense of the theater was the one important talent that George Jean Nathan had omitted from his list of Fitzgerald's qualifications as a dramatist. But not to possess it was fatal; without it Fitzgerald's comic sense and his ear for dialogue counted for very little.

Indeed, Fitzgerald is an excellent example of the novelist whose sense of drama can be conveyed only by means of the written page. *The Vegetable* was dramatic only in a literary sense. It relied entirely on words and failed to exploit those non-verbal elements which are as important to a play as language. The result was something that read much better than it acted. One wonders if Edmund Wilson's and George Jean Nathan's failure to take account of this shortcoming was the result of their thinking of the play in literary rather than theatrical terms.

Another fault of the play was its half-baked fantasy. The dream sequence in the second act was intended to contrast with the comic realism of the first and third acts. It should have been the most striking and original feature of the play. To do justice to the stupidity and corruption of Washington at that time, Fitzgerald needed the merciless satire of a Swift or the absurd surrealism of a Bosch or a Kafka. Instead, in his second act nightmare, he fell back on the gentle whimsy and spoofing of *Trial by Jury* and *Alice in Wonderland*. The result was the arch nonsense and coy fantasy that shows up in some of his poorer magazine stories.

Here again the advice of Nathan and Wilson was not especially helpful. Nathan, as co-editor of *Smart Set*, had not only encouraged Fitzgerald to write such trivial dramatic skits as "Mr. Icky" and "Porcelain and Pink," but he had gone out of his way to praise them in his essays. Wilson in his occasional essays and reviews seems to have regarded Fitzgerald more as an accomplished author of librettos and vaudeville skits than as a serious moralist—a kind of Noel Coward or Cole Porter. In his 1922 *Bookman* review of *Tales of the Jazz Age*, Wilson ignored the only two first-rate stories in the collection and gave his attention to such smart-aleck nonsense as "Mr. Icky" and "Jemina." Overlooking the larger human problems raised by such excellent pieces as "May Day" and "The Jelly-Bean," Wilson said that the stories in *Tales of the Jazz Age* were "the most charming of ballets—something like the Greenwich Village Follies with overtones of unearthly music." When he reached out for other authors with whom to compare Fitzgerald, those who came to mind were Lewis Carroll, W.S. Gilbert, and Edward Lear.

Like *The Beautiful and Damned*, *The Vegetable* also suffered from the effort to make it serve too many different purposes. Fitzgerald began by wanting to make this play a protest against the contemporary dream of success from which he himself had only recently awakened. Jerry Frost wants only to do the job for which he is best qualified. But in order to satisfy his producer, Fitzgerald was obliged to reshape his play to amuse the same audiences that read his magazine stories. Among Fitzgerald's papers are a number of scenes that he wrote for the stage version that opened in Atlantic City. In his attempt to obtain all the laughs that he could for Sam Harris, he had drifted away from his original idea, cluttering his script with jokes about everything of topical interest he could think of—flappers, bootleggers, politicians, Washington, morticians, marriage.

Max Perkins, with his unusual insight, had been particularly disturbed about what had happened to Fitzgerald's original idea. The shrewd analysis Perkins wrote in pencil on the back of one of Fitzgerald's letters to him (a comment Fitzgerald may never have seen) is the best account that has been written about what Fitzgerald had initially intended to say:

> The underlying idea [is that] ... God meant Jerry to be a good egg and a postman; but having been created, in a democratic age, Free and Equal, he was persuaded that he ought to want to rise in the world.... He is therefore very unhappy, and so is his wife, who holds the same democratic doctrine.
>
> Your story shows, or should, that this doctrine is sentimental bunk; and to do this is worthwhile because the doctrine is almost universal: Jerry and his wife are products of a theory of democracy which you reduce to the absurd....
>
> But when you come to the second act, which is the critical point of the play, and so in the expression of your idea, you seem to lose sense of your true motive. Partly, this is because you have three motives here, the main motive of Jerry's story and its meaning, and two subordinate motives—(1) of conveying through the fantastic visions and incidents which are the stuff of a dream caused

by a 1923 prohibition brew *the sense of a comic nightmare*, and (2) of satirizing the general phenomena of our national scene. You have, I think, simply got more or less lost in the maze of these three motives by a failure to follow the green line of the chief one—Jerry's actual story, or that stage of it which shows him that he doesn't want to be President. Satirize as much as you can, the government, the army, and everything else, and be as fantastic as you please, but keep one eye always on your chief motive. Throughout the entire wild second act there should still be a kind of *wild logic*.

In spite of its limitations as a stage play, *The Vegetable* is an authentic document of the Jazz Age. A year before the lid blew off Teapot Dome and exposed the corruption of the Harding administration, Fitzgerald had already sensed the absurdity of electing someone like Harding to the Presidency. He had seen, too, the connection between such a phenomenon and the American dream of success that he himself had once accepted so unquestioningly. Yet, not only did his contemporaries miss the drift of *The Vegetable*, but readers since then have continued to do so. In a recent essay, Maxwell Geismar, a critic who is usually at his best in dealing with the social implications of literature, dismisses Fitzgerald's play as a trivial satire "of the moneyed elite [written] for the bourgeois makers of money." "Fitzgerald," Geismar continues, "is not at all concerned, as Dos Passos, with the human implications of our cultural patterns." But frail as it is as a play, *The Vegetable* is more than a "trivial satire." It fails because of its dramatic ineptitudes, not because it deals trivially with a trivial problem.

64

Introduction to *The Vegetable*

◆

CHARLES SCRIBNER III

Among the published works of Scott Fitzgerald, *The Vegetable* stands out as something of a curiosity. As the author's only published full-length play, it represents his one attempt to establish himself as a successful playwright. It also represents Fitzgerald's brief excursion into the realm of political satire. In *The Vegetable* an ordinary railroad clerk, Jerry Frost, gets drunk on the eve of Warren Harding's nomination and suddenly finds himself and his entire family in the White House. The consequences are, of course, disastrous, but fortunately Jerry is able to escape them by simply waking up. Much relieved, he can finally fulfill his true calling: to be a postman. Although the play was a failure and Fitzgerald quickly returned to writing short stories and novels, this little-known work deserves to be made available to Fitzgerald's public. Because of its possible interest to students, the publishers have also decided to add appendices, which include scenes cut from the manuscript during the author's many revisions as well as final "corrections and addenda" for the acting script. If, on the one hand, these documents suggest some of Fitzgerald's difficulty and uncertainty in writing for the stage, on the other they clearly reflect the amount of care and craftsmanship that went into this venture.

As a boy, Fitzgerald had a special love for the theater and enjoyed a precocious success as a playwright and impresario. At fourteen, he presented *The Girl from "Lazy J"* at an organizational meeting of the Elizabethan Dramatic Club of St. Paul, Minnesota. As he wrote in his scrapbook, his "head was turned," and the next year the club produced his second drama, *The Captured Shadow*, as a benefit performance for the Baby Welfare Association. Fitzgerald himself played the "Shadow," and later in his scrapbook he wrote, "Enter Success!" This was followed the next summer by a two-act melodrama, *The Coward*, about a reluctant Confederate soldier. According to one reviewer, it, too, was a "decided success." This was just before

SOURCE *The Vegetable*, New York, 1976, pp. v–xx.

Fitzgerald's departure for Princeton, but it was not his final production for the club. The summer following his freshman year, he returned to St. Paul and wrote a comedy, *Assorted Spirits*, in which he also acted and served as stage manager. His final performance was unexpectedly memorable, for at one point during the show a fuse blew and there followed an explosion and sudden darkness. But the seasoned actor seized his cue and proceeded to calm the audience with an improvised monologue.

During the academic year, Fitzgerald had become active in the Princeton Triangle Club, which annually produced an original musical comedy. The 1914–15 show, *Fie! Fie! Fi-Fi!*, owed its plot and lyrics to Fitzgerald. In fact, the very notion of a sustained plot tying together the musical numbers was considered a real innovation and the *Louisville Post* proclaimed that Fitzgerald "could take his place right now with the brightest writers of witty lyrics in America." And, to be sure, he continued to write the lyrics for the next two Triangle productions: *The Evil Eye* (1915–16) and *Safety First* (1916–17). In addition, he published in the *Nassau Literary Magazine* a one-act play, *The Débutante*, which would eventually become a chapter in his first novel, *This Side of Paradise*. Though one critic felt that it was "somewhat far-fetched" (an understandable tendency in a Triangle writer), it was praised as "a devastating skit on the foibles of young femininity."

How was Fitzgerald rated by his college contemporaries? In the graduating class poll, he received six votes as their favorite dramatist (Shakespeare received sixty-one and Shaw twenty-nine)—not a bad start. But after Princeton his theatrical career gave way to the ambition of becoming a serious and successful novelist. Yet, his love for scriptwriting was never wholly suppressed, for in his first two novels—*This Side of Paradise* and *The Beautiful and Damned*—several episodes were set as dramatic dialogues complete with stage directions. And two "short stories" for The *Smart Set* magazine were conceived and published as one-act plays: "Porcelain and Pink" and "Mr. Icky" (in *Tales of the Jazz Age*, 1922).

Finally, having published a novel and a collection of short stories (*Flappers and Philosophers*, 1920), Fitzgerald turned his eyes toward Broadway and in the late fall of 1921 wrote to his agent, Harold Ober, "I am conceiving a play which is to make my fortune," adding in a subsequent letter that it "is the funniest ever written." Then, with no less self-confidence, he wrote to his editor at Scribners, Maxwell Perkins, that he was at work on "an awfully funny play that's going to make me rich forever." From the very start, Fitzgerald viewed the play as something to guarantee his fortune, if not fame as well. On the day before publication of *The Beautiful and Damned*, he wrote to Ober that he was sending him the first draft of the play (which had as yet no title) to be placed with a producer. His opinion of it was still high, but he clearly foresaw the revisions that lay ahead: "I should not, I suppose I should say now, want to collaborate with anyone else in a revision of this. I'm willing to revise it myself with advice from whomsoever they should designate—but

I feel that Acts I and III are probably the best pieces of dramatic comedy written in English in the last 5 years and I wouldn't let them go entirely out of my possession nor permit the addition of another name to the authorship of the play."

That was in March. By May he had revised the script, and his former college companion Edmund Wilson was trying to place it with the Theatre Guild. In a long and very revealing letter of 26 May 1922, Wilson offered much praise and suggested structural changes (see Appendix I):

> So far as I am concerned, I think it is one of the best things you ever wrote. I have read only the first version—I didn't take time to read the second because the Theater Guild insisted that they were in a great hurry about it—so won't criticize it now at length. I thought the millionaire episode—except the first scene—a little weak and the last act too palpably padded. As for the battle scene, it was fine and you made a great mistake to have allowed them to kid you into removing it. The Guild thinks so too and have expressed disappointment that it isn't in the revised version—so, if they decide to take it, I think you ought to put it back. I should suggest that you make the White House and Battle the second act and the millionaire and postman the third: this would do away with the necessity of stalling along at the beginning of the postman scene simply in order to make it into a whole act.—As I say, I think that the play as a whole is marvellous—no doubt, the best American comedy ever written. I think you have a much better grasp on your subject than you usually have—you know what end and point you are working for, as isn't always the case with you.... I think you have a great gift for comic dialogue—even though you never can resist a stupid gag—and should go on writing plays.... By the way, the great question is, have you read James Joyce's *Ulysses?* Because if you haven't, the resemblances between the drunken visions scene in it and your scene in the White House must take its place as one of the great coincidences of literature.

(It was, in fact, a coincidence.) Soon afterwards, the Guild turned down the play, but Wilson told Fitzgerald that he ought to have it published even before it was accepted for production.

Fitzgerald then set out to revise a second time and in July wrote to Perkins, "At present I'm working on my play—the same one.... Bunny Wilson says that it's without a doubt the best American comedy to date (that's just between you and me)." By August, it had finally been given a title, *Gabriel's Trombone*, an allusion to a scene, later cut from the script (Appendix I), in which the imminent Apocalypse is predicted by Jerry's senile father, a Last Judgment heralded in tones familiar to the Jazz Age.

> *Dada:* The world is coming to an end. The last judgment is at hand. Gabriel's Trump will blow one week from today just at this hour.
> *Fish:* What's a trump?
> *Doris:* It's something like a trombone, only not so good.

Fitzgerald asked Perkins if *Scribner's Magazine* would be interested in serializing it, "that is, of course, on condition that it is to be produced this fall." Perkins replied that he was "mightily interested," adding that "it would be most unusual if we should publish a play in *Scribner's*, but we have no rule against it and would like to consider the possibility." In the mean time, no producer was found and Fitzgerald continued to revise. By December, the manuscript was in Perkins's hands, now reworked for the third time, and it bore a new, far simpler title: *Frost*. Perkins wrote a lengthy and extremely perceptive critique, which not only articulated the central theme of the satire but also suggested further revisions:

COMMENT ON "FROST"

(To save space I've omitted most of the "I thinks," "It seems to mes," and "I may be wrong buts": they should, however, be understood)

I've read your play three times and I think more highly of its possibilities on the third reading than ever before;—but I am also more strongly convinced that these possibilities are far from being realized on account of the handling of the story in the second act. The reader feels, at the end, confused and unsatisfied:— the underlying motive of the play has not been sent home. And yet this motive, or idea, has been sufficiently perceived to prevent the play from being a sheer burlesque, like a comic opera. In the second act it seems to me that you yourself have almost thought it *was* that.

The underlying idea, a mighty good one, is expressed, or should be, in the story of Jerry Frost.

God meant Jerry to be a good egg and a postman; but having been created, in a democratic age, Free and Equal, he was persuaded that he ought to want to rise in the world and so had become a railroad clerk against his taste and capacity, and thought he ought to want to become President. He is therefore very unhappy, and so is his wife, who holds the same democratic doctrine.

Your story shows, or should, that this doctrine is sentimental bunk; and to do this is worthwhile because the doctrine is almost universal: Jerry and his wife are products of a theory of democracy which you reduce to the absurd. The idea is so good that if you hold to it and continuously develop it, your play, however successful simply as fun, will be deeply significant as well.

Moreover, the means you have selected to develop the idea are superb—the bootlegger, the super-jag his concoction induces, Jerry thereby becoming President, etc. (and dreams have a real validity nowadays on account of Freud). In fact all your machinery for expressing the idea is exactly in the tune of the time and inherently funny and satirical.

But when you come to the second act, which is the critical point in the play, and so in the expression of your idea, you seem to lose sense of your true motive. Partly, this is because you have three motives here, the main motive of Jerry's story and its meaning, and two subordinate motives—(1) of conveying through the fantastic visions and incidents which are the stuff of a dream caused by a 1923 prohibition brew, *the sense of a comic nightmare*, and (2) of satirizing the general phenomena of our national scene. You have, I think, simply got more or less lost in the maze of these three motives by a failure to follow the green line of the chief one—Jerry's actual story, or that stage of it which shows him that he *doesn't* want to be President. Satirize as much as you can, the government, the army, and everything else, and be as fantastic as you please, but keep one eye always on your chief motive. Throughout the entire wild second act there should still be a kind of *wild logic*.

Aside then from imparting in this act the sense of a dream, you are using the difficult weapon of double edged satire—you are satirizing the conception held by Jerry and his like of the High Offices of President, Secretary of the Treasury, etc., and you are at the same time satirizing those high offices themselves. You begin excellently by making all the appurtenances of the Presidency, like the house, white; and the behavior or Jerry's wife and sister-in-law are all within the scope of your purpose. The conduct of Dada as Secretary of the Treasury seems as though it ought to be a fine piece of two edged satire cutting both against the popular idea of the business of that official and against the official himself as he usually is, but the psychology of it is not made quite comprehensible; and the best instance of double satire is seen when General Pushing appears with fifer and drummer and medals—that is just the right note. Why couldn't you do the same for bankers, and senators, etc.?

Maybe I can better express what I mean by examples. The selection of so obscure a man as Jerry for President is itself the stuff of satire in view of present political methods, and much could be made of it. The coffin episode as you use it results as things do in a dream from Jerry's talk with Fish etc. and so it helps to give the sense of a dream, and that is all it does. But suppose coffins were being cornered by "The He-Americans Bloodred Preparedness League" as a preparedness measure, and that this was tied up with General Pushing's feeling that a war was needed:—that would be a hit at extravagant patriotism and militarism as well as having its present value as part of a dream. Suppose the deal over the Buzzard Isles resulted in the Impeachment of Jerry—what a chance that would give to treat the Senate as you have the general and the Army, and also to bring Jerry's affairs to a climax. You could have Jerry *convicted*, and then (as a hit at a senatorial filibuster) you could have his party place the Stutz-Mozart Ourangatang Band outside the Capitol (it would have appeared for the wedding of Fish), and every time the Justices of the Supreme Court began in chorus to pronounce the sentence, Stutz-Mozart would strike up the National Anthem in syncopated time and everyone would have to stand to attention. At present, the narrative of the second act lacks all logic; the significance of the approaching end of the world eludes me,—except as a dreamer's way of getting release from a desperate situation.

I've now used a great many words to make this single point:—each part of the second act should do three things—add to the quality of a fantastic dream, satirize Jerry and his family as representing a large class of Americans, and satirize the government or army or whatever institution is at the moment in use. And my only excuse for all this verbiage is, that so good in conception is your motive, so true your characters, so splendidly imaginative your invention, and so altogether above the mere literary the whole scheme, that no one could help but greatly desire to see it all equalled in execution. If it were a comparative trifle, like many a short story, it wouldn't much matter.

Fitzgerald was obviously intrigued by the idea of using a President's impeachment as the climax of Act II. In fact, this new development led to the highlight of the entire play: President Frost's oration in his own defense, a perfect piece of impassioned rhetoric that says absolutely nothing. It is also a virtuoso performance in mixing metaphors:

JERRY [nervously]. Gentlemen, before you take this step into your hands I want to put my best foot forward. Let us consider a few aspects. For instance, for the first aspect let us take, for example, the War of the Revolution. There was ancient Rome, for example. Let us not only live so that our children who live after us, but also that our ancestors who preceded us fought to make this country what it is!

General applause.
And now, gentlemen, a boy to-day is a man to-morrow—or, rather, in a few years. Consider the winning of the West—Daniel Boone and Kit Carson, and in our own time Buffalo Bill and—Jesse James!
Prolonged applause.
Finally, in closing, I want to tell you about a vision of mine that I seem to see. I seem to see Columbia—Columbia—ah—blindfolded—ah—covered with scales—driving the ship of state over the battle-fields of the republic into the heart of the golden West and the cotton-fields of the sunny South.
Great applause. Mr. Jones, with his customary thoughtfulness, serves a round of cocktails.

But if Fitzgerald exploited this scene to satirize political speeches he also found an opportunity to carry the satire a step further by injecting some real history into his fantasy. The subsequent declaration of impeachment by Chief Justice Fossile, for all its absurdity, was no mere play of the author's imagination. Rather, he had turned to his history books and had lifted almost verbatim the opening speech of Congressman George Boutwell of Massachusetts at President Andrew Johnson's impeachment hearings: "In the Southern Heavens, near the Southern Cross, there is a vast space which the uneducated call a hole in the sky, where the eye of man, with the aid of the powers of the telescope, has been unable to discover nebulae, or asteroid, or comet, or planet, or star or sun. In that dreary, dark, cold region of space ... the Great Author of the celestial mechanism has left the chaos which was in the beginning. If the earth was capable of the sentiments and emotions of justice and virtue ... it would heave and throw ... and project this enemy of two races of men into that vast region, there forever to exist in a solitude eternal as life...." Paradoxically, if we compare this quotation with Fitzgerald's version (pages 109–10) we discover that the caricatured Chief Justice is actually *less verbose* than his historical counterpart. The author must have thoroughly enjoyed this delicious bit of irony.

In January of 1923, Fitzgerald sent Perkins a list of ideas for the play. He wanted John Held, Jr., the originator of the cartoon "flapper," to design the jacket cover with "little figure—Dada, Jerry, Doris, Charlotte, Fish, Snooks and Gen Pershing [*sic*] scattered over it." The popular cartoonist followed the author's wishes and brilliantly captured the spirit of the play. This is one book that can be judged fairly by its cover, and so that original design has been kept for this present edition. Fitzgerald also requested that it "be advertised, it seems to me rather as a book of humor ... than like a play—because of course it is written to be read." This remark contained an unfortunate truth, as the eventual performance would demonstrate. For all its revisions, *The Vegetable* remained a novelist's, not a dramatist's, play, in which the lengthy stage directions often provide the most entertaining moments. Fitzgerald also suggested writing a preface and inserting "the subtitle 'or from President to postman' (note small p.)."

He never wrote the preface, but when the book went to press its title had been changed once again, to *The Vegetable*, and was accompanied by a quotation "from a current magazine" on the title page:

> Any man who doesn't want to get on in the world, to make a million dollars, and maybe even park his toothbrush in the White House, hasn't got as much to him as a good dog has—he's nothing more or less than a vegetable.

It has been suggested that Fitzgerald got his idea for the final title from a passage in H. L. Mencken's essay "On Being an American": "Here is a country in which it is an axiom that a businessman shall be a member of the Chamber of Commerce, an admirer of Charles M. Schwab, a reader of *The Saturday Evening Post*, a golfer—in brief, a vegetable." If so, Fitzgerald obviously reversed the meaning of Mencken's epithet with a kind of deadpan irony, which was later enriched by having Charlotte discover the quotation in her *Saturday Evening Post* (see Appendix II). But Fitzgerald's dramatic satire is never as severe as Mencken's, whatever his debt to the essayist may have been. It owed at least as much to his college days in the Triangle Club. The result is rather a mixture of satire and slapstick. One senses a basic indecisiveness beneath the banter, as though he were a composer who had forgotten his key and had begun a seemingly endless series of modulations. This was not the material for success in performance, no matter how entertaining it might be for the reader.

This book received mixed reviews, some enthusiastic in their praise. Although late in life Edmund Wilson claimed that he had never approved of the published version, that Fitzgerald had taken "too much advice" and had "ruined the whole thing," nevertheless he was perhaps the most laudatory. In his review for *Vanity Fair* Wilson wrote that Fitzgerald's play "is, in some ways, one of the best things he has done. In it he has a better idea than he usually has of what theme he wants to develop, and it does not, as his novels sometimes have, carry him into regions beyond his powers of flight. It is a fantastic and satiric comedy carried off with exhilarating humor. One has always felt that Mr. Fitzgerald ought to write dialogue for the stage and this comedy would seem to prove it. I do not know of any dialogue by an American which is lighter, more graceful or more witty. His spontaneity makes his many bad jokes go and adds a glamor to his really good ones."

Another reviewer found that "Fitzgerald's first act is Sinclair Lewis, his last act is James M. Barrie—and his middle act is nightmare." And still another called the play "a caricature of a caricature." Many saw only nonsensical riot; others, genuine satire. One critic even considered it "the most moral book in years," the moral being simply that "what the country needs is more good postmen and fewer bad Presidents." For a brief moment it even made the best-seller list.

Encouraged, Fitzgerald placed the script with Sam Harris, who scheduled it for a fall production. During the summer Fitzgerald commuted to New York from Long Island to attend rehearsals and make still more changes for the acting script (see Appendix II). The play finally opened on Monday, November 19, 1923, at Nixon's Apollo Theatre in Atlantic City. Ernest Truex played the title role—"the best postman in the world," as Fitzgerald inscribed the play to him. It was a disaster or, in the author's own wry words, a "colossal Frost." It closed almost immediately. Fitzgerald's hopes for fortune in the theater evaporated, and he was forced to turn out a spate of short stories to improve his financial situation. His *literary* "recovery" was to take another two years and a new novel, *The Great Gatsby* (1925). After his first disappointment, Fitzgerald never really regained interest in the play. Later there were to be a few revivals, mostly by amateur groups, and even some talk of selling movie rights. But except for a momentary worry in 1932 that Ryskind and Kaufman had plagiarized *The Vegetable* in *Of Thee I Sing*, he gave his play little further thought. In his opinion, the whole venture had simply been a wasted year and a half.

But was it? The constant revising, the special demands imposed by a play—a short, carefully constructed work—coming after the sprawling *Beautiful and Damned* proved an ideal exercise for a young writer. Though the final piece was flawed, Fitzgrerald had nevertheless gained valuable experience in literary craftsmanship. In an indirect way, *The Vegetable* prepared him for writing *The Great Gatsby*. And it may be more than pure coincidence that shortly after its publication *Gatsby* was adapted for the stage by Owen Davis and was a success on Broadway. Unfortunately Fitzgerald was abroad and was unable to attend its happy opening night.

Possibly *The Vegetable* was, above all, a victim of bad timing. The audience at Atlantic City in 1923 was still unaware of most of the scandals surrounding their deceased President. It was not until a year later that the lid blew off Teapot Dome. Fitzgerald's political fantasy contained far more truth than the audience was prepared to take in. But a half-century later, after one near-impeachment and with much useful hindsight, this not-so-fantastic spoof can be experienced afresh. Interestingly enough, it has already enjoyed several successful revivals abroad: in the Netherlands, France, Czechoslovakia, and England. Evidently, Fitzgerald's caricature of the American dream and its political system is more entertaining on the foreign stage. Whatever its appeal for those still on the home front, *The Vegetable* at the very least presents a new facet of Fitzgerald's life and work. As his daughter recently pointed out, "It was one of his few efforts, until much later in his life, to write about the country outside of its country clubs."

The Great Gatsby

1925

65
Introduction to *The Great Gatsby*

◆

F. SCOTT FITZGERALD

To one who has spent his professional life in the world of fiction the request to "write an introduction" offers many facets of temptation. The present writer succumbs to one of them; with as much equanimity as he can muster, he will discuss the critics among us, trying to revolve as centripetally as possible about the novel which comes hereafter in this volume.

To begin with, I must say that I have no cause to grumble about the "press" of any book of mine. If Jack (who liked my last book) didn't like this one—well then John (who despised my last book) *did* like it; so it all mounts up to the same total. But I think the writers of my time were spoiled in that regard, living in generous days when there was plenty of space on the page for endless ratiocination about fiction—a space largely created by Mencken because of his disgust for what passed as criticism before he arrived and made his public. They were encouraged by his bravery and his tremendous and profound love of letters. In his case, the jackals are already tearing at what they imprudently regard as a moribund lion, but I don't think many men of my age can regard him without reverence, nor fail to regret that he got off the train. To any new effort by a new man he brought an attitude; he made many mistakes—such as his early undervaluation of Hemingway—but he came equipped; he never had to go back for his tools.

And now that he has abandoned American fiction to its own devices, there is no one to take his place. If the present writer had seriously to attend some of the efforts of political diehards to tell him the values of a métier he has practised since boyhood—well, then, babies, you can take this number out and shoot him at dawn.

But all that is less discouraging, in the past few years, than the growing cowardice of the reviewers. Underpaid and overworked, they seem not to care for books, and it has been saddening recently to see young talents in

SOURCE *The Great Gatsby*, New York, 1934, pp. vii–x. This is Fitzgerald's introduction to the Modern Library edition of his novel.

147

fiction expire from sheer lack of a stage to act on: West, McHugh and many others.

I'm circling closer to my theme song, which is: that I'd like to communicate to such of them who read this novel a healthy cynicism toward contemporary reviews. Without undue vanity one can permit oneself a suit of chain mail in any profession. Your pride is all you have, and if you let it be tampered with by a man who has a dozen prides to tamper with before lunch, you are promising yourself a lot of disappointments that a hard-boiled professional has learned to spare himself.

This novel is a case in point. Because the pages weren't loaded with big names of big things and the subject not concerned with farmers (who were the heroes of the moment), there was easy judgment exercised that had nothing to do with criticism but was simply an attempt on the part of men who had few chances of self-expression to express themselves. How anyone could take up the responsibility of being a novelist without a sharp and concise attitude about life is a puzzle to me. How a critic could assume a point of view which included twelve variant aspects of the social scene in a few hours seems something too dinosaurean to loom over the awful loneliness of a young author.

To circle nearer to this book, one woman, who could hardly have written a coherent letter in English, described it as a book that one read only as one goes to the movies around the corner. That type of criticism is what a lot of young writers are being greeted with, instead of any appreciation of the world of imagination in which they (the writers) have been trying, with greater or lesser success, to live—the world that Mencken made stable in the days when he was watching over us.

Now that this book is being reissued, the author would like to say that never before did one try to keep his artistic conscience as pure as during the ten months put into doing it. Reading it over one can see how it could have been improved—yet without feeling guilty of any discrepancy from the truth, as far as I saw it; truth or rather the *equivalent* of the truth, the attempt at honesty of imagination. I had just re-read Conrad's preface to *The Nigger*, and I had recently been kidded half haywire by critics who felt that my material was such as to preclude all dealing with mature persons in a mature world. But, by God! it was my material, and it was all I had to deal with. What I cut out of it both physically and emotionally would make another novel!

I think it is an honest book, that is to say, that one used none of one's virtuosity to get an effect, and, to boast again, one soft-pedalled the emotional side to avoid the tears leaking from the socket of the left eye, or the large false face peering around the corner of a character's head.

If there is a clear conscience, a book can survive—at least in one's feelings about it. On the contrary, if one has a guilty conscience, one reads what one wants to hear out of reviews. In addition, if one is young and willing to learn, almost all reviews have a value, even the ones that seem unfair.

The present writer has always been a "natural" for his profession, in so much that he can think of nothing he could have done as efficiently as to have lived deeply in the world of imagination. There are plenty other people constituted as he is, for giving expression to intimate explorations, the:

—Look—this is here!

—I saw this under my eyes.

—*This* is the way it was!

—No, it was like this.

"Look! Here is that drop of blood I told you about."

—"Stop everything! Here is the flash of that girl's eyes, here is the reflection that will always come back to me from the memory of her eyes.

—"If one chooses to find that face again in the non-refracting surface of a washbowl, if one chooses to make the image more obscure with a little sweat, it should be the business of the critic to recognize the intention.

—"No one felt like this before—says the young writer—but *I* felt like this; I have a pride akin to a soldier going into battle; without knowing whether there will be anybody there, to distribute medals or even to record it."

But remember, also, young man: you are not the first person who has ever been alone and alone.

66
Letter to F. Scott Fitzgerald (20 November 1924)

MAXWELL PERKINS

Dear Scott:

I think you have every kind of right to be proud of this book.[1] It is an extraordinary book, suggestive of all sorts of thoughts and moods. You adopted exactly the right method of telling it, that of employing a narrator who is more of a spectator than an actor: this puts the reader upon a point of observation on a higher level than that on which the characters stand and at a distance that gives perspective. In no other way could your irony have been so immensely effective, nor the reader have been enabled so strongly to feel at times the strangeness of human circumstance in a vast heedless universe. In the eyes of Dr. Eckleburg various readers will see different significances; but their presence gives a superb touch to the whole thing: great unblinking eyes, expressionless, looking down upon the human scene. It's magnificent!

I could go on praising the book and speculating on its various elements, and means, but points of criticism are more important now. I think you are right in feeling a certain slight sagging in chapters six and seven, and I don't know how to suggest a remedy. I hardly doubt that you will find one and I am only writing to say that I think it does need something to hold up here to the pace set, and ensuing. I have only two actual criticisms:

One is that among a set of characters marvelously palpable and vital—I would know Tom Buchanan if I met him on the street and would avoid him—Gatsby is somewhat vague. The reader's eyes can never quite focus upon him, his outlines are dim. Now everything about Gatsby is more or less a mystery, i.e. more or less vague, and this may be somewhat of an artistic intention, but I think it is mistaken. Couldn't *he* be physically described as distinctly as the others, and couldn't you add one or two characteristics like the use of that phrase "old sport"—not verbal, but physical ones, perhaps. I think that for some reason or other a reader—this was true of Mr. Scribner[2]

SOURCE *Editor to Author: The Letters of Maxwell Perkins*, ed. John Hall Wheelock, New York, 1950), pp. 38–41.

150

and of Louise[3]—gets an idea that Gatsby is a much older man than he is, although you have the writer say that he is little older than himself. But this would be avoided if on his first appearance he was seen as vividly as Daisy and Tom are, for instance—and I do not think your scheme would be impaired if you made him so.

The other point is also about Gatsby: his career must remain mysterious, of course. But in the end you make it pretty clear that his wealth came through his connection with Wolfsheim. You also suggest this much earlier. Now almost all readers numerically are going to be puzzled by his having all this wealth and are going to feel entitled to an explanation. To give a distinct and definite one would be, of course, utterly absurd. It did occur to me, though, that you might here and there interpolate some phrases, and possibly incidents, little touches of various kinds, that would suggest that he was in some active way mysteriously engaged. You do have him called on the telephone, but couldn't he be seen once or twice consulting at his parties with people of some sort of mysterious significance, from the political, the gambling, the sporting world, or whatever it may be. I know I am floundering, but that fact may help you to see what I mean. The *total* lack of an explanation through so large a part of the story does seem to me a defect—or not of an explanation, but of the suggestion of an explanation. I wish you were here so I could talk about it to you, for then I know I could at least make you understand what I mean. What Gatsby did ought never to be definitely imparted, even if it could be. Whether he was an innocent tool in the hands of somebody else, or to what degree he was this, ought not to be explained. But if some sort of business activity of his were simply adumbrated, it would lend further probability to that part of the story.

There is one other point: in giving deliberately Gatsby's biography, when he gives it to the narrator, you do depart from the method of the narrative in some degree, for otherwise almost everything is told, and beautifully told, in the regular flow of it, in the succession of events or in accompaniment with them. But you can't avoid the biography altogether. I thought you might find ways to let the truth of some of his claims like "Oxford" and his army career come out, bit by bit, in the course of actual narrative. I mention the point anyway, for consideration in this interval before I send the proofs.

The general brilliant quality of the book makes me ashamed to make even these criticisms. The amount of meaning you get into a sentence, the dimensions and intensity of the impression you make a paragraph carry, are most extraordinary. The manuscript is full of phrases which make a scene blaze with life. If one enjoyed a rapid railroad journey I would compare the number and vividness of pictures your living words suggest, to the living scenes disclosed in that way. It seems, in reading, a much shorter book than it is, but it carries the mind through a series of experiences that one would think would require a book of three times its length.

The presentation of Tom, his place, Daisy and Jordan, and the unfolding of their characters is unequaled so far as I know. The description of the valley of ashes adjacent to the lovely country, the conversation and the action in Myrtle's apartment, the marvelous catalogue of those who came to Gatsby's house—these are such things as make a man famous. And all these things, the whole pathetic episode, you have given a place in time and space, for with the help of T. J. Eckleburg and by an occasional glance at the sky, or the sea, or the city, you have imparted a sort of sense of eternity. You once told me you were not a *natural writer*—my God! You have plainly mastered the craft, of course; but you needed far more than craftsmanship for this.

As ever,

Notes

1. *The Great Gatsby*, Charles Scribner's Sons, 1925.
2. Charles Scribner, Senior (1854–1930), president of Charles Scribner's Sons.
3. Mrs. Maxwell E. Perkins.

67
The First Reader
—Great Scott

♦

LAURENCE STALLINGS

The Great Gatsby is F. Scott Fitzgerald's latest. It is the tale of a curious and shady fellow who conducts a large and lusty country house for a miscellany of random guests in the vicinity of Westhampton, L.I. It is published by Charles Scribner's Sons.

Fitzgerald introduced the gin-and-petting novel of college life, wrote some excellent short stories, tried his hand at another novel—a study of flapper marriage—and topped it with some indifferent work spelled out for the sake of the easy money.

In this new book he is another fellow altogether. *The Great Gatsby* evidences an interest in the color and sweep of prose, in the design and integrity of the novel, in the development of character, like nothing else he has attempted. If you are interested in the American novel this is a book for your list.

Even the staid fellows who shrugged at Fitzgerald's stuff when he first brutally rang the bell of notoriety in *This Side of Paradise* must have known, and fearsomely too, that the child would some day be father to the novelist.

He was, in writing, something like the prodigals of his fiction: bursting with a gorgeous zest of life, interesting, highly diverting, above all possessed of a streak of talent as broad as it was erratic.

The Great Gatsby is no spontaneous burst of erratic divertissement proffered with an insolent grace. It is a novel written with pace and fine attention. Above all, handling the most exaggerated social scheme in the new world, it never once overdoes the thing.

The talent is here aplenty; the erratic streak is curbed, the impudence takes on the civilized urbanity of the man at ease in art.... You will not find, in others of Fitzgerald's works, such a paragraph as this one on his married heroine:

SOURCE *New York World*, 22 April 1925, p. 13.

> For Daisy was young and her artificial world was redolent of orchids and pleasant, cheerful snobbery and orchestras which set the rhythm of the year, summing up the sadness and suggestiveness of life in new tunes. All night the saxophones wailed the hopeless comment of the "Beale Street Blues" while a hundred pairs of golden and silver slippers shuffled the shining dust. At the gray tea hour there were always rooms that throbbed incessantly with this low, sweet fever, while fresh faces drifted here and there like rose petals blown by sad horns around the floor.

Now, the novelist who wrote that is not the Bacchic young man who leered over the minor amorous artifices of our younger fellows.

Fitzgerald, writing of his hero Gatsby and his unquenchable love for a woman several aeons above him in point of sophistication, writes in the first person and by some unaccountable paradox achieves impersonality in theme and treatment. Gatsby, darkling adventurer with a fortune made in bootlegging, in swindling, by other devious trades and bargains, lives in this fiction. Lives in his palace of country life—an establishment which Lewis Mumford has rightly analyzed as the Utopia of modern escape from the urban canyons—and lives against a background of all Fitzgerald's world.

Gatsby, come to the village of West Egg mysteriously to rear his shining palace on the sand and fill it with any who ever has painted a bad picture, written a bad novel, or made a million dollars, has come for love of the woman Daisy.

"There was something gorgeous about him," says the novelist, "some heightened sensitivity to promises of life." Fitzgerald, making him grow, would be as tender about his bootlegger-magnate as Keats was about Endymion. The man does grow, and through an honest process, for Fitzgerald unburdens all Gatsby's past before his reader, even hewing desperately to the truth of his fall.

I do not think for one moment in reading this book that "here is a great novel" or even, that "here is a fine book." The novelist has not brought it off in grand style; has, in fact, supplied little more than a sheaf of notes on a gorgeous plan for a novel on the topside life about us.

But in this, even though it not be God's plenty, there is more worth than in all his other work. One reading it knows that the fair-haired boy of American fiction will not sink gracefully into the sort of middle-aged precocity who once rang the bell. There is a sincerity of feeling for Gatsby, put forward with a delicacy of irony pointed with occasional lapses into brutality, which is distinguished, and worth many better matured novels.

Gatsby himself lingers after the book is done. That is the real criticism of the novel, for his lingering is due to the lack of breadth in the portrait. Miss Cather's *A Lost Lady* was identical in its effect, and from this fault. Only the full maturation of the fiction was in question. The maturity of viewpoint in *The Great Gatsby* no more than in *A Lost Lady* could be questioned.

Also, it is the first authentic book, from the civilized point of view, upon the scene it surveys. The earlier Fitzgerald was barbarous; those who have followed him have aped his barbarity. I think that this book leaves all this far behind. I should like to read a review of it by Thomas Beer, author of *Sandoval,* and peer of all our young men.

68
As H.L.M. Sees It

H.L. MENCKEN

Scott Fitzgerald's new novel, *The Great Gatsby*, is in form no more than a glorified anecdote, and not too probable at that. The scene is the Long Island that hangs precariously on the edges of the New York city ash dumps—the Long Island of gaudy villas and bawdy house parties. The theme is the old one of a romantic and preposterous love—the ancient *fidelis ad urrum* motif reduced to a *macabre* humor. The principal personage is a bounder typical of those parts—a fellow who seems to know everyone and yet remains unknown to all—a young man with a great deal of mysterious money, the tastes of a movie actor and, under it all, the simple sentimentality of a somewhat sclerotic fat woman.

This clown Fitzgerald rushes to his death in nine short chapters. The other performers in the Totentanz are of a like, or even worse quality. One of them is a rich man who carries on a grotesque intrigue with the wife of a garage keeper. Another is a woman golfer who wins championships by cheating. A third, a sort of chorus to the tragic farce, is a bond salesman—symbol of the New America! Fitzgerald clears them all off at last by a triple butchery. The garage keeper's wife, rushing out upon the road to escape her husband's third degree, is run down and killed by the wife of her lover. The garage keeper, misled by the lover, kills the lover of the lover's wife—the Great Gatsby himself. Another bullet, and the garage keeper is also reduced to offal. Choragus fades away. The crooked lady golfer departs. The lover of the garage keeper's wife goes back to his own consort. The immense house of the Great Gatsby stands idle, its bedrooms given over to the bat and the owl, its cocktail shakers dry. The curtain lurches down.

II

This story is obviously unimportant, and though, as I shall show, it has its place in the Fitzgerald canon, it is certainly not to be put on the same shelf

SOURCE *Baltimore Evenuing Sun*, 2 May 1925, p. 9.

with, say, *This Side of Paradise*. What ails it, fundamentally, is the plain fact that it is simply a story—that Fitzgerald seems to be far more interested in maintaining its suspense than in getting under the skins of its people. It is not that they are false; it is that they are taken too much for granted. Only Gatsby himself genuinely lives and breathes. The rest are mere marionettes—often astonishingly lifelike, but nevertheless not quite alive.

What gives the story distinction is something quite different from the management of the action or the handling of the characters; it is the charm and beauty of the writing. In Fitzgerald's first days it seemed almost unimaginable that he would ever show such qualities. His writing, then, was extraordinarily slipshod—at times almost illiterate. He seemed to be devoid of any feeling for the color and savor of words. He could see people clearly and he could devise capital situations, but as writer qua writer he was apparently litle more than a bright college boy. The critics of the Republic were not slow to discern the fact. They praised *This Side of Paradise* as a story, as a social document, but they were almost unanimous in denouncing it as a piece of writing.

It is vastly to Fitzgerald's credit that he appears to have taken their caveats seriously and pondered them to good effect. In *The Great Gatsby* the highly agreeable fruits of that pondering are visible. The story, for all its basic triviality, has a fine texture, a careful and brilliant finish. The obvious phrase is simply not in it. The sentences roll along smoothly, sparkingly, variously. There is evidence in every line of hard and intelligent effort. It is a quite new Fitzgerald who emerges from this little book and the qualities that he shows are dignified and solid. *This Side of Paradise*, after all, might have been merely a lucky accident. But *The Great Gatsby*, a far inferior story at bottom, is plainly the product of a sound and stable talent, conjured into being by hard work.

III

I make much of this improvement because it is of an order not often witnessed in American writers, and seldom indeed in those who start off with a popular success. The usual progression, indeed, is in the opposite direction. Every year first books of great promise are published—and every year a great deal of stale drivel is printed by the promising authors of a year before last. The rewards of literary success in this country are so vast that, when they come early, they are not unnaturally somewhat demoralizing. The average author yields to them readily. Having struck the bull's eye once, he is too proud to learn new tricks. Above all, he is too proud to tackle hard work. The result is a gradual degeneration of whatever talent he had at the beginning. He begins to imitate himself. He peters out.

There is certainly no sign of petering out in Fitzgerald. After his first experimenting he plainly sat himself down calmly to consider his deficiencies. They were many and serious. He was, first of all, too facile. He could write entertainingly without giving thought to form and organization. He was, secondly, somewhat amateurish. The materials and methods of his craft, I venture, rather puzzled him. He used them ineptly. His books showed brilliancy in conception, but they were crude and even ignorant in detail. They suggested, only too often, the improvisations of a pianist playing furiously by ear but unable to read notes.

These are the defects that he has now got rid of. *The Great Gatsby*, I seem to recall, was announced a long while ago. It was probably several years on the stocks. It shows on every page the results of that laborious effort. Writing it, I take it, was painful. The author wrote, tore up, rewrote, tore up again. There are pages so artfully contrived that one can no more imagine improvising a fugue. They are full of little delicacies, charming turns of phrase, penetrating second thoughts. In other words, they are easy and excellent reading—which is what always comes out of hard writing.

IV

Thus Fitzgerald, the stylist, arises to challenge Fitzgerald, the social historian, but I doubt that the latter ever quite succumbs to the former. The thing that chiefly interests the basic Fitzgerald is still the florid show of modern American life—and especially the devil's dance that goes on at the top. He is unconcerned about the sweatings and sufferings of the nether herd; what engrosses him is the high carnival of those who have too much money to spend and too much time for the spending of it. Their idiotic pursuit of sensation, their almost incredible stupidity and triviality, their glittering swinishness—these are the things that go into his notebook.

In *The Great Gatsby*, though he does not go below the surface, he depicts this rattle and hullabaloo with great gusto and, I believe, with sharp accuracy. The Long Island he sets before us is no fanciful Alsatia; it actually exists. More, it is worth any social historian's study, for its influence upon the rest of the country is immense and profound. What is vogue among the profiteers of Manhattan and their harlots today is imitated by the flappers of the Bible Belt country clubs week after next. The whole tone of American society, once so highly formalized and so suspicious of change, is now taken largely from frail ladies who were slinging hash a year ago.

Fitzgerald showed the end products of the new dispensation in *This Side of Paradise*. In *The Beautiful and the* [sic] *Damned* he comes near the bottom. Social leader and jail bird, grand lady and kept woman, are here almost indistinguishable. We are in an atmosphere grown increasingly levantine. The Paris of the Second Empire pales to a sort of snobbish chautauqua; the

New York of Ward McAllister becomes the scene of a convention of Gold Star Mothers. To find a parallel for the grossness and debauchery that now reign in New York one must go back to the Constantinople of Basil I.

69
Jazz Parties on Long Island —But F. Scott Fitzgerald is Growing Up

◆

WALTER YUST

It has been said that Robert Frost is the poet of gray New England gone or going to seed. I read this novel with a parallel notion that F. Scott is the poet of that portion of society which crashes madly enough along the border line between culture that money brings and vulgarity that money scarcely ever either conceals or dissipates—a portion of society that embodies disillusion and practices, out of caprice and indifference, a harshness in camaraderie cheaply tragic. This portion of society may be entirely fictitious. That is, there may be on the whole of Long Island no one like any of the personalities of this story. But it doesn't matter. The dissolution, the tawdry tragedy of much of life, as revealed in these pages, is bitterly true.

The Great Gatsby is, for me, Mr. Fitzgerald's most carefully devised story; his always assured, and sometimes prodigal, pen—but he, of all artists, must use the typewriter—is here more often restrained; from the opening page to the last, he has held successfully to one tone, to one vision—that of a group of people whom he perhaps sees in the composite figure of a clown, half-crazed by his own fripperies, laughing, blatant, weak, pitiable. He has admirably laid beneath livid colors the torture of horror.

The Great Gatsby is the story of a man who is gratuitously called great—a young man who grasps desperately after his especial brand of beauty, a tatterdemalion of romantic graces....

Irony tinctures the story, as alcohol tinctures the personalities in it. Here in pungent solution are the ideals, the hopes and the pleasures of people. Once Mr. Fitzgerald's flappers and jellybeans, they are flappers and jellybeans no longer, they are less innocent, less naive, a little older and wiser—if wisdom be the name for disillusion. Alcohol—bootleg—in a manner symbol-

SOURCE *New York Evening Post Literary Review*, 2 May 1925, p. 3.

izes their decay, not that they are all of them drunkards, but that they use liquor, and imitation liquor to boot, when less vivid persons prime themselves in conventional fashion with the comfortable unbottled illusion of a quiet home, hard work, dreams for the future, the consciousness of purpose in life.

Gatsby, mounting by questionable Wallingford practices the ladder to the social heights of East Egg, seems, of all the represented characters of the story, to be the only one with fixed aim, with a clear and distinct notion that he can do something and that there *is* something for men and women to do, with life. His friends are surface lights and darknesses; their interminable jamborees, their nervous, spasmodic enthusiasms, their exaggerated and violent expressions of a well-being they neither feel nor especially desire—beyond these he describes a beauty, whole, clear-cut, three-dimensioned. A frightful accident, the ironic gesture of indifferent fate, snuffs him and his ideal out. F. Scott appears at this point a little willful, and indeed sentimental—but he casts his calculated glamour. Gatsby is actually as incapable of tragedy as Daisy is, or Tom, or Myrtle, all of whom meet irritations and pain with bad liquor, hectic parties, cynicisms. Tragedy would annihilate them. They couldn't bear up under it. And Gatsby is better wilfully dead.

The novel is one that refuses to be igored. I finished it in an evening, and had to. Its spirited tempo, the motley of its figures, the suppressed, undersurface tension of its dramatic moments, held me to the page. The stark vulgarity of Myrtle's friends, the unhealthy sinister excitements of Gatsby's, invited as intense and as impersonal an interest as the panic of crawling things under a suddenly lifted moss-grown stone. It is not a book which might, under any interpretation, fall into the category of those doomed to investigation by a vice commission, and yet it is a shocking book—one that reveals incredible grossness, thoughtlessness, polite corruption, without leaving with the reader a sense of depression, without being insidiously provocative.

It is an extraordinary book in more ways than one—none more extraordinary than in its power to throw a spell over the reader. I think of the novel now with increasing surprise. The impression grows that while there is no incredible personality in the book, there is no memorable one. The figures fit the pattern of the story easily; they have been cut out for it. But there seems to be no one of them that remains, not even Gatsby himself, to convince me that I have followed his movements with some excitement for weeks and weeks. Four hours I knew them all; watched them with complete absorption. But now the book is ended, they are quite gone—vanished.

It was not my intention in the beginning to make any comparison between Frost and Fitzgerald. Since the names have been placed side by side, however, they might serve to indicate a distinction. Mr. Frost expresses his New England locality and tragedy through richly drawn personality. Mr. Fitzgerald expresses another kind of decay, not through individuals so much as through crowds. The party in Myrtle's apartment is as raw and vulgar and pulsing and unforgettable as life itself and the hectic assemblies on Gatsby's lawns are. Groups of persons live in the pages of Mr. Fitzgerald's book as no one person ever does. A poet of discords, he gives us starkly the asymmetry, the motley, the cacophony of crowds—whether they are crowds of three or of a hundred and three.

70
An Admirable Novel

♦

WILLIAM ROSE BENÉT

The book finished, we find again, at the top of page three, the introductory remark:

> No—Gatsby turned out all right at the end; it was what preyed on Gatsby, what foul dust floated in the wake of his dreams that temporarily closed out my interest in the abortive sorrows and short-winded elations of men.

Scott Fitzgerald's new novel is a remarkable analysis of this "foul dust." And his analysis leads him, at the end of the book, to the conclusion that all of us "beat on, boats against the current, borne back ceaselessly into the past." There is depth of philosophy in this.

The writer—for the story is told in the first person, but in a first person who is not exactly the author, but rather one of the number of personalities that compose the actual author,—the hypothecated chronicler of Gatsby is one in whose tolerance all sorts and conditions of men confided. So he came to Gatsby, and the history of Gatsby, obscured by the "foul dust" aforementioned, "fair sickened" him of human nature.

The Great Gatsby is a disillusioned novel, and a mature novel. It is a novel with pace, from the first word to the last, and also a novel of admirable "control." Scott Fitzgerald started his literary career with enormous facility. His high spirits were infectious. The queer charm, color, wonder, and drama of a young and reckless world beat constantly upon his senses, stimulated a young and intensely romantic mind to a mixture of realism and extravaganza shaken up like a cocktail. Some people are born with a knack, whether for cutting figure eights, curving an in-sheet, picking out tunes on the piano, or revealing some peculiar charm of their intelligence on the typewritten page. Scott Fitzgerald was born with a knack for writing. What they call "a natural gift." And another gift of the fairies at his christening was a reckless confidence in himself. And he was quite intoxicated with the joy of life and rather engagingly savage toward an elder world. He was out "to get the world by the neck" and put words on paper in the patterns his exuberant fancy

SOURCE *Saturday Review of Literature* I, 9 May 1925, pp. 739–740.

suggested. He didn't worry much about what had gone before Fitzgerald in literature. He dreamed gorgeously of what there was in Fitzgerald to "tell the world."

And all these elements contributed to the amazing performance of *This Side of Paradise*, amazing in its excitement and gusto, amazing in phrase and epithet, amazing no less for all sorts of thoroughly bad writing pitched in with the good, for preposterous carelessness, and amazing as well as for the sheer pace of the narrative and the fresh quality of its oddly pervasive poetry. Short stories of flappers and philosophers displayed the same vitality and flourished much the same faults. *Tales of the Jazz Age* inhabited the same glamour. *The Beautiful and Damned*, while still in the mirage, furnished a more valuable document concerning the younger generation of the first quarter of the Twentieth Century. But brilliant, irrefutably brilliant as were certain passages of the novels and tales of which the "boy wonder" of our time was so lavish, arresting as were certain gleams of insight, intensely promising as were certain observed facilities, there remained in general, glamour, glamour everywhere, and, after the glamour faded, little for the mind to hold except an impression of this kinetic glamour.

There ensued a play, in which the present writer found the first act (as read) excellent and the rest as satire somehow stricken with palsy, granted the cleverness of the original idea. There ensued a magazine phase in which, as was perfectly natural, most of the stories were negligible, though a few showed flashes. But one could discern the demands of the "market" blunting and dulling the blade of that bright sword wildly whirled. One began to believe that Fitzgerald was coming into line with the purveyors of the staple product. And suddenly one wanted him back in the phase when he was writing so well and, at the same time, writing so very badly. Today he was writing, for the most part, on an even level of magazine acceptability, and on an even level of what seemed perilously like absolute staleness of mind toward anything really creative.

But *The Great Gatsby* comes suddenly to knock all that surmise into a cocked hat. *The Great Gatsby* reveals thoroughly matured craftsmanship. It has structure. It has high occasions of felicitous, almost magic, phrase. And most of all, it is out of the mirage. For the first time Fitzgerald surveys the Babylonian captivity of this era unblinded by the bright lights. He gives you the bright lights in full measure, the affluence, the waste, but also the nakedness of the scaffolding that scrawls skeletons upon the sky when the gold and blue and red and green have faded, the ugly passion, the spiritual meagreness, the empty shell of luxury, the old irony of "fair-weather friends."

Gatsby remains. The mystery of Gatsby is a mystery saliently characteristic of this age in America. And Gatsby is only another modern instance of the eternal "fortunate youth." His actual age does not matter, in either sense. For all the cleverness of his hinted nefarious proceedings, he is the coney caught. For he is a man with a dream at the mercy of the foul dust that sometimes seems only to exist in order to swarm against the dream, whose midge-dance blots it from the sky. It is a strange dream. Gatsby's,—but he was a man who had hope. He was a child. He believed in a childish thing.

It is because Fitzgerald makes so acid on your tongue the taste of the defeat of Gatsby's childishness that his book, in our opinion, "acquires merit." And there are parts of the book, notably the second chapter, that, in our opinion, could not have been better written. There are astonishing feats that no one but Fitzgerald could have brought off, notably the catalogue of guests in Chapter IV. And Tom Buchanan, the "great, big hulking specimen," is an American university product of almost unbearable reality.

Yet one feels that, though irony has entered into Fitzgerald's soul, the sense of mere wonder is still stronger. And, of course, there is plenty of entertainment in the story. It arises in part from the almost photographic reproduction of the actions, gestures, speech of the types Fitzgerald has chosen in their moments of stress. Picayune souls for the most part, and Gatsby heroic among them only because he is partly a crazy man with a dream. But what does all that matter with the actual narration so vivid and graphic? As for the drama of the accident and Gatsby's end, it is the kind of thing newspapers carry every day, except that here is a novelist who has gone behind the curt paragraphs and made the real people live and breathe in all their sordidness. They are actual, rich and poor, cultivated and uncultivated, seen for a moment or two only or followed throughout the story. They are memorable individuals of today—not types.

Perhaps you have gathered that we like the book! We do. It has some miscues, but they seem to us negligible. It is written with concision and precision and mastery of material.

71
Fitzgerald on the March

CARL VAN VECHTEN

What will be the future of F. Scott Fitzgerald? This query has been futilely repeated whenever a new book from his pen has appeared, since the initial interrogation which greeted the publication of that sophomoric masterpiece, *This Side of Paradise*. It will be asked more earnestly than before by prescient readers of *The Great Gatsby*, who will recognize therein a quality which has only recently made its debut in the writings of this brilliant young author, the quality vaguely referred to as mysticism. Moreover this is a fine yarn, exhilaratingly spun.

Mr. Fitzgerald is a born story-teller; his words, phrases, and sentences carry the eye easily through to the end of his books. Further, his work is imbued with that rare and beneficient essence we hail as charm. He is by no means lacking in power, as several passages in the current opus abundantly testify, and he commands a quite uncanny gift for hitting off character or presenting a concept in a striking and memorable manner. The writer he most resembles, curiously enough, despite the dissimilarity in their choice of material and point of attack, is Booth Tarkington, but there exists at present in the work of Mr. Fitzgerald a potential brutality, a stark sense of reality, set off in his case by an ironic polish, that suggests a comparison with the Frank Norris of *Vandover and the Brute*, or *McTeague*.

Up to date, Mr. Fitzgerald has occupied himself almost exclusively with the aspects and operations of the coeval flapper and cake-eater. No one else, perhaps, has delineated these mundane creatures quite as skilfully as he, and his achievement in this direction has been awarded authoritative recognition. He controls, moreover, the necessary magic to make his most vapid and rotterish characters interesting and even, on occasion, charming, in spite of (or possibly because of) the fact that they are almost invariably presented in advanced stages of intoxication. More cocktails and champagne are consumed in the novels of Scott Fitzgerald than a toper like Paul Verlaine could drink in a lifetime. *The Beautiful and Damned*, indeed, is an epic of inebriation beside which *L'Assommoir* fades into Victorian insipidity.

SOURCE *The Nation* CXX, 20 May 1925, pp. 575–576.

In *The Great Gatsby* there are several of Mr. Fitzgerald's typical flappers who behave in the manner he has conceived as typical of contemporary flapperdom. There is again a gargantuan drinking-party, conceived in a rowdy, hilarious, and highly titillating spirit. There is also, in this novel, as I have indicated above, something else. There is the character of Jay Gatsby.

This character, and the theme of the book in general, would have appealed to Henry James. In fact, it did appeal to Henry James. In one way or another this motif is woven into the tapestry of a score or more of his stories. In Daisy Miller you may find it complete. It is the theme of a soiled or rather cheap personality transfigured and rendered pathetically appealing through the possession of a passionate idealism. Although the comparison may be still further stressed, owing to the fact that Mr. Fitzgerald has chosen, as James so frequently chose, to see his story through the eyes of a spectator, it will be readily apparent that what he has done he has done in his own way, and that seems to me, in this instance, to be a particularly good way. The figures of Jay Gatsby, who invented an entirely fictitious career for himself out of material derived from inferior romances, emerges life-sized and life-like. His doglike fidelity not only to his ideal but to his fictions, his incredibly cheap and curiously imitative imagination, awaken for him not only our interest and suffrage, but also a certain liking, as they awaken it in the narrator, Nick Carraway.

When I read Absolution in the *American Mercury* I realized that there were many potential qualities inherent in Scott Fitzgerald which hitherto had not been too apparent. *The Great Gatsby* confirms this earlier impression. What Mr. Fitzgerald may do in the future, therefore, I am convinced, depends to an embarrassing extent on the nature of his own ambitions.

72
Letter to F. Scott Fitzgerald (8 June 1925)

◆

EDITH WHARTON

Pavillon Colombe
St. Brice-Sous-Forêt (S&O)
Gare: Sarcelles

June 8, 1925

Dear Mr. Fitzgerald,

    I have been wandering for the last weeks and found your novel—with its friendly dedication—awaiting me here on my arrival, a few days ago.

    I am touched at your sending me a copy, for I feel that to your generation, which has taken such a flying leap into the future, I must represent the literary equivalent of tufted furniture & gas chandeliers. So you will understand that it is in a spirit of sincere deprecation that I shall venture, in a few days, to offer you in return the last product of my manufactory.

    Meanwhile, let me say at once how much I like Gatsby, or rather His Book & how great a leap I think you have taken this time—in advance upon your previous work. My present quarrel with you is only this: that to make Gatsby really Great, you ought to have given us his early career (not from the cradle—but from his visit to the yacht, if not before) instead of a short résumé of it. That would have situated him, & made his final tragedy a tragedy instead of a "fait divers" for the morning papers.

    But you'll tell me that's the old way, & consequently not *your* way; & meanwhile, it's enough to make this reader happy to have met your *perfect* Jew, & the limp Wilson, & assisted at that seedy orgy in the Buchanan flat, with the dazed puppy looking on. Every bit of that is masterly—but the lunch with Hildesheim,[1] and his every appearance afterward, make me augur still greater things!—Thank you again.

Yrs. Sincerely
Edith Wharton

SOURCE *The Letters of Edith Wharton*, ed. R.W.B. Lewis and Nancy Lewis, New York, 1988, pp. 481–482.

THE GREAT GATSBY

Note

1. The name should be Wolfsheim. Hildesheim was misspelled Hildeshiem in the first edition of *The Great Gatsby*.

73

Spring Flight

◆

GILBERT SELDES

There has never been any question of the talents of F. Scott Fitzgerald; there has been, justifiably until the publication of *The Great Gatsby*, a grave question as to what he was going to do with his gifts. The question has been answered in one of the finest of contemporary novels. Fitzgerald has more than matured; he has mastered his talents and gone soaring in a beautiful flight, leaving behind him everything dubious and tricky in his earlier work, and leaving even farther behind all the men of his own generation and most of his elders.

In all justice, let it be said that the talents are still his. The book is even more interesting, superficially, than his others; it has an intense life, it must be read, the first time, breathlessly; it is vivid and glittering and entertaining. Scenes of incredible difficulty are rendered with what seems an effortless precision and crowds and conversation and action and retrospects—everything comes naturally and persuasively. The minor people and events are threads of colour and strength, holding the principal things together. The technical virtuosity is extraordinary.

All this was true of Fitzgerald's first two novels, and even of those deplorable short stories which one feared were going to ruin him. *The Great Gatsby* adds many things, and two above all: the novel is composed as an artistic structure, and it exposes, again for the first time, an interesting temperament. "The vast juvenile intrigue" of *This Side of Paradise* is just as good subject-matter as the intensely private intrigue of *The Great Gatsby*; but Fitzgerald racing over the country, jotting down whatever was current in college circles, is not nearly as significant as Fitzgerald regarding a tiny section of life and reporting it with irony and pity and a consuming passion. *The Great Gatsby* is passionate as *Some Do Not* is passionate, with such an abundance of feeling for the characters (feeling their integral reality, not hating or loving them objectively) that the most trivial of the actors in the drama are endowed with vitality. The concentration of the book is so intense that the principal characters exist almost as essences, as biting acids that find

SOURCE *The Dial* LXXIX, August 1925, pp. 162–164.

themselves in the same golden cup and have no choice but to act upon each other. And the *milieux* which are brought into such violent contact with each other are as full of character, and as immitigably compelled to struggle and to debase one another.

The book is written as a series of scenes, the method which Fitzgerald derived from Henry James through Mrs. Wharton, and these scenes are reported by a narrator who was obviously intended to be much more significant than he is. The author's appetite for life is so violent that he found the personality of the narrator an obstacle, and simply ignored it once his actual people were in motion, but the narrator helps to give the feeling of an intense unit which the various characters around Gatsby form. Gatsby himself remains a mystery; you know him, but not by knowing about him, and even at the end you can guess, if you like, that he was a forger or a dealer in stolen bonds, or a rather mean type of bootlegger. He had dedicated himself to the accomplishment of a supreme object, to restore to himself an illusion he had lost; he set about it, in a pathetic American way, by becoming incredibly rich and spending his wealth in incredible ways, so that he might win back the girl he loved; and a "foul dust floated in the wake of his dreams." Adultery and drunkenness and thievery and murder make up this dust, but Gatsby's story remains poignant and beautiful.

This means that Fitzgerald has ceased to content himself with a satiric report on the outside of American life and has with considerable irony attacked the spirit underneath, and so has begun to report on life in its most general terms. His tactile apprehension remains so fine that his people and his settings are specifically of Long Island; but now he meditates upon their fate, and they become universal also. He has now something of extreme importance to say; and it is good fortune for us that he knows how to say it.

The scenes are austere in their composition. There is one, the tawdry afternoon of the satyr, Tom Buchanan, and his cheap and "vital" mistress, which is alive by the strength of the lapses of time; another, the meeting between Gatsby and his love, takes place literally behind closed doors, the narrator telling us only the beginning and the end. The variety of treatment, the intermingling of dialogue and narrative, the use of a snatch of significant detail instead of a big scene, make the whole a superb impressionistic painting, vivid in colour, and sparkling with meaning. And the major composition is as just as the treatment of detail. There is a brief curve before Gatsby himself enters; a longer one in which he begins his movement toward Daisy; then a succession of carefully spaced shorter and longer movements until the climax is reached. The plot works out not like a puzzle with odd bits falling into place, but like a tragedy, with every part functioning in the completed organism.

Even now, with *The Great Gatsby* before me, I cannot find in the earlier Fitzgerald the artistic integrity and the passionate feeling which this book possesses. And perhaps analysing the one and praising the other, both fail to convey the sense of elation which one has in reading his new novel. Would it be better to say that even *The Great Gatsby* is full of faults, and that that doesn't matter in the slightest degree? The cadences borrowed from Conrad, the occasional smartness, the frequently startling, but ineffective adjective— at last they do not signify. Because for the most part you know that Fitzgerald has consciously put these bad and half-bad things behind him, that he trusts them no more to make him the white-headed boy of *The Saturday Evening Post,* and that he has recognized both his capacities and his obligations as a novelist.

74
Letter to F. Scott Fitzgerald (31 December 1925)

T.S. ELIOT

FROM T.S. ELIOT
FABER AND GWYER LTD.
Publishers

24 Russell Square,
London, W.C.1
31st December, 1925

F. Scott Fitzgerald, Esqre.,
c/o Charles Scribners & Sons,
New York City.

Dear Mr. Scott Fitzgerald,

The Great Gatsby with your charming and overpowering inscription arrived the very morning that I was leaving in some haste for a sea voyage advised by my doctor. I therefore left it behind and only read it on my return a few days ago. I have, however, now read it three times. I am not in the least influenced by your remark about myself when I say that it has interested and excited me more than any new novel I have seen, either English or American, for a number of years.

When I have time I should like to write to you more fully and tell you exactly why it seems to me such a remarkable book. In fact it seems to me to be the first step that American fiction has taken since Henry James....

By the way, if you ever have any short stories which you think would be suitable for the *Criterion* I wish you would let me see them.

With many thanks, I am,
Yours very truly,
T.S. Eliot

P.S. By a concidence Gilbert Seldes in his New York Chronicle in the *Criterion* for January 14th has chosen your book for particular mention.

SOURCE *F. Scott Fitzgerald: The Crack-Up*, ed. Edmund Wilson, New York, 1945, p. 310.

75
New York Chronicle

◆

GILBERT SELDES

The Great Gatsby, by F. Scott Fitzgerald, has given me an extraordinary pleasure; even if Sinclair Lewis' *Arrowsmith* and Mrs. Wharton's *The Mother's Recompense* are as good as their admirers believe them to be, I should still feel that Fitzgerald's novel is more important. Lewis and Mrs. Wharton are known quantities and one can predict their line of development; Fitzgerald is much younger, his talent is only beginning to mature; and, until now, it has appeared to be the most abundant talent, most casually wasted, in American fiction. For Fitzgerald's person I have long had an affectionate regard, and it annoyed me not to find wholly admirable his first two novels, *This Side of Paradise* and *The Beautiful and Damned*. The first was an American step-child of *Sinister Street*, the collegiate portions, with traces of H. G. Wells; the second, a much better work, influenced by Mrs. Wharton and Joseph Conrad, had, although I was too obtuse to discover it for myself, a strong satiric strain, and this appeared again in *The Diamond as Big as the Ritz*, one of Fitzgerald's few good shorter pieces, and in *The Vegetable*, a play with a central episode like that of *Beggar on Horseback*, which it anticipated, but without success on the stage. The first novel had a fabulous success; Fitzgerald had just left Princeton and must have been about twenty-one at the time. It was treated as an *exposé* of love-making at our colleges; and, because of it, the word 'petting', soon to be displaced by 'necking', supplanted its almost-synonym, flirting, in our vocabulary. The second novel, too, was successful, and Fitzgerald began to write endlessly for the popular magazines, stories and travel-sketches and even an aritcle on 'How to Live on $30,000 a Year'. It was after this last had been written, after the experience for it had been gained at the price named, that Fitzgerald took his enchanting household and the unfinished manuscript of *The Great Gatsby* to the south of France.

I mention these small details because they are the normal circumstances of American authorship, only multiplied a hundred times. They are the prelude, usually, to extremely bad novels; and they form the prelude, in this

SOURCE *New Criterion* IV, January 1926, pp. 170–171.

case, to an extremely good one. *The Great Gatsby* is a brilliant work, and it is also a sound one; it is carefully written, and vivid; it has structure, and it has life. To all the talents, discipline has been added. The form is again derived from James through Mrs. Wharton, and there are cadences direct from the pages of Conrad; but I feel that Fitzgerald has at last made his borrowings his own, and that they nowhere diminish the vitality of his work. The subject, too, ought to be of interest outside America; it is a drama of an intense passion played on Long Island, the summer home of wealth, and even, in spots, of Society, near New York. Fitzgerald has no feeling for Main Street; his satire is not that of reformer; and he has certainly the best chance, at this moment, of becoming our finest artist in fiction. The press has not been too enthusiastic about *The Great Gatsby*; Mencken has notably discovered its virtues, but so intense is our preoccupation with the drab as subject, that this story of a Long Island Trimalchio has been compared to the preposterous stories of high-life written by Robert W. Chambers. At the moment of writing, *The Constant Nymph* is the best-seller, and, in addition, is receiving unlimited critical praise. I am not concerned with Fitzgerald's royalties; but he stands at this time desperately in need of critical encouragement, and temporarily I shall agitate for an outrageous import tax on English novels.

76
New Novels
— *The Great Gatsby*

ANONYMOUS REVIEW

F. Scott Fitzgerald, author of *The Great Gatsby*, is a young American novelist whose work has not hitherto reached England. We understand that with his previous novels, one of which had a university setting, he has won a large amount of popularity in his own country, and that the present novel, his latest, is an effort in a rather different direction from that of ordinary American popular fiction. However this may be, *The Great Gatsby* is undoubtedly a work of art and of great promise. Mr. Fitzgerald has grasped the economical construction of a story, and his power of telling conciseness enables him, without being obscure, to compass a great deal in a short space. He uses words like living things, instead of like dead counters.

Gatz, or Gatsby, is a Conradian hero—one of those beings, like Almayer or the hero of *Heart of Darkness*, who are lifted above all the evil that they do or seek, above all the dirty trails that shoddy souls leave over the world, and above all the tragedy or destruction in which they finally sink, by some great elemental loyalty to a dream that, in a different world, would have been beautiful. Mr. Fitzgerald has imagined a son of broken-down and shiftless farm folk who, in his youth, found a platonic conception of himself and "invented just the sort of Jay Gatsby that a seventeen-year-old boy would be likely to invent, and to this conception he was faithful to the end." His dream universe of "ineffable gaudiness," realized partially by five years of secretaryship to a dissolute old millionaire, is enriched by an experience of love when, as a young officer, he had had a month of Daisy Buchanan and known an almost superhuman ecstasy. Daisy, then unmarried, belonged to his dream universe of beauty, money, and ease; penniless Gatsby, having illicitly entered it in the disguise of uniform, comes back after brilliant service in the war to find himself still outside it and Daisy married. By the mouth of Mr. Carraway, who is related to Daisy and visits her home on Long Island, there is told what Gatsby did in order to enter into his dream again. All passes in

SOURCE *Times Literary Supplement*, 18 February 1926, p. 116.

one summer. Gatsby, wealthy through lending himself to nameless corruptions, keeps open house upon the shore of West Egg, because the green light of the Buchanans' dock, on the opposite shore of East Egg, twinkles to him in the darkness. All the lavish show of drunken vulgarity is simply kept up to bring that green light nearer. Through Carraway Gatsby meets Daisy again—the weak, shallow creature who loves only by moments—and their meeting, which culminates in Daisy's weeping over Gatsby's exhibition of multitudinous shirts in his wardrobe, is an admirable piece of writing. And so Gatsby, steadfast in all his corruption, becomes involved in the life of Daisy Buchanan and her sensual savage of a husband Tom, whose typical outing with his mistress, the wife of a seedy garage keeper, throws a queer light on the manners of New York. Tragedy is not long in coming, for Tom suspects Gatsby, and on the amazing afternoon when Gatsby tells him to his face that Daisy no longer loves him, it is Daisy's tawdriness that brings the dream to the ground with a crash. Daisy, having shattered Gatsby's life, can do no more than wrap him finally in death and dishonor. Mr. Fitzgerald finally maintains, besides his hard, sardonic realism, the necessary emotional intensity, but we must admit that it needs perhaps an excess of intensity to buoy up the really very unpleasant characters of this story.

77
New Fiction

◆

L.P. HARTLEY

Mr. Scott Fitzgerald deserves a good shaking. Here is an unmistakable talent unashamed of making itself a motley to the view. *The Great Gatsby* is an absurd story, whether considered as romance, melodrama, or plain record of New York high life. An adventurer of shady antecedents builds a palace at a New York seaside resort, entertains on a scale which Lucullus would have marvelled at but could not have approved, and spends untold sums of money, all to catch the eye of his one time sweetheart, who lives on an island opposite, unhappily but very successfully married. At last, after superhuman feats of ostentation and display, the fly walks into the web. A train of disasters follows, comparable in quantity and quality with the scale of the Great Gatsby's prodigies of hospitality. Coincidence leaps to the helm and throws a mistress under a motor-car. The car does not stop, which, all things considered, is the most natural thing that happens in the book. An injured husband finds the Great Gatsby in suicidal mood sitting on a raft in his artificial lake and (apparently) forestalls him; anyhow they are both discovered dead. The elder Gatsby is unearthed and gives a pathetic account of his son's early years. All the characters behave as if they were entitled to grieve over a great sorrow, and the book closes with the airs of tragedy. Mr. Fitzgerald seems to have lost sight of O. Henry and hitched his wagon to Mr. Arlen's star. It is a great pity, for even in this book, in the dialogue, in many descriptive passages, there are flashes of wit and insight, felicities of phrase and a sense of beauty. His imagination is febrile and his emotion overstrained; but how good, of its kind, is his description of Gatsby's smile, which:

> faced—or seemed to face—the whole eternal world for an instant, and then concentrated on *you* with an irresistible prejudice in your favour. It understood you just as far as you wanted to be understood, believed in you as you would like to believe in yourself, and assured you that it had precisely the impression of you that, at your best, you hoped to convey.

The Great Gatsby is evidently not a satire; but one would like to think that Mr. Fitzgerald's heart is not in it, that it is a piece of mere naughtiness.

SOURCE *Saturday Review* CXLI, 20 February 1926, pp. 234–235. This is an edited version.

78
The Great Gatsby

◆

CONRAD AIKEN

In *The Great Gatsby* Mr. Fitzgerald has written a highly colored and brilliant little novel which, by grace of one cardinal virtue, quite escapes the company of most contemporary American fiction—it has excellence of form. It is not great, it is not large, it is not strikingly subtle; but it is well imagined and shaped, it moves swiftly and neatly, its scene is admirably seized and admirably matched with the theme, and its hard bright tone is entirely original. Technically, it appears to owe much to the influence of the cinema; and perhaps also something to Henry James—a peculiar conjunction, but not so peculiar if one reflects on the flash-backs and close-ups and paralleled themes of that "little experiment in the style of Gyp," *The Awkward Age*. Mr. Fitzgerald's publishers call *The Great Gatsby* a satire. This is deceptive. It is only incidentally a satire, it is only in the *setting* that it is satirical, and in the tone provided by the minor characters. The story itself, and the main figure, are tragic, and it is precisely the fantastic vulgarity of the scene which gives to the excellence of Gatsby's soul its finest bouquet, and to his tragic fate its sharpest edge. All of Mr. Fitzgerald's people are real—but Gatsby comes close to being superb. He is betrayed to us slowly and skillfully, and with a keen tenderness which in the end makes his tragedy a deeply moving one. By so much, therefore, *The Great Gatsby* is better than a mere satire of manners, and better than Mr. Fitzgerald's usual sort of superficial cleverness. If only he can refrain altogether in future from the sham romanticism and sham sophistication which the magazines demand of him, and give another turn of the screw to the care with which he writes, he may well become a first-rate novelist.

SOURCE *New Criterion* IV, October 1926, pp. 773–776.

79
The Great Gatsby

◆

PETER QUENNELL

It would be doing Scott Fitzgerald a grave injustice to suggest that his novel was merely an essay in social satire, with special reference to the abuses of the capitalist system. His strictures on the worlds he describes are implied, not stated. *The Great Gatsby* is one of the most typical and also one of the most brilliant products of that exciting, disappointing period which witnessed the birth and extinction of so many hopes and crashed at last into the doldrums of a vast depression. It is a period piece with an unusual degree of permanent value, having the sadness and the remote jauntiness of a Gershwin tune, the same touches of slightly bogus romanticism—"the stiff tinny drip of the banjoes on the lawn"; the headlights of departing cars which wheel like long golden antennae across the obscurity of the "soft black morning"—the same nostalgic appeal to be taken seriously, a plea that in Scott Fitzgerald's case has, I think, succeeded. A large number of American mannerisms start with Scott Fitzgerald (who somehow never repeated that early triumph, though many of his long short stories are well worth reading) and not a few modern novelists are his unconscious imitators. Today when the Bum is a best-selling hero—the Share-Cropper, the vagrant Okie, the landless Poor White—it is refreshing to read this romantic tract on the sorrows of Dives.

SOURCE *New Statesman and Nation* XXI, 1 February 1941, p. 112.

80
The Great Gatsby: A Study in Literary Reputation

♦

G. THOMAS TANSELLE AND
JACKSON R. BRYER

When the reviewer for the Boston *Transcript* commented on *The Great Gatsby* in the issue of May 23, 1925, he said that "no critic will attempt, even in the distant future, to estimate Mr. Fitzgerald's work without taking *The Great Gatsby* into account, even though its author should create many more books." The statement is true: Fitzgerald did create many more books and we do think of *Gatsby* as Fitzgerald's central achievement. But this is not exactly what the reviewer had in mind. He was not advancing any extravagant claims for the excellence of the novel; by saying "*even* in the future," he was merely implying that *Gatsby* represents such an important development in Fitzgerald's career that it will remain historically and biographically important despite the later (and presumably greater) works that will be the full flowering of his talent. At first glance, the statement is one which, read in the light of present-day opinion, may seem farsighted and perspicacious, but which, if read in context and without the hindsight gained from years of Fitzgerald idolatry, is a typical reviewer's comment. The reviewer saw some merit in the book, to be sure, but there is no indication that his remark is anything more (or very much more) than a polite compliment, or that he had singled the book out as one which might possibly be ranked some day among the greatest works of literary art.

The fact is, of course, that it is difficult for a contemporary commentator to detect a future masterpiece—particularly when the work later comes to be thought of as a masterpiece *representative* of its times. The reviewer is likely either to dismiss the work as trivial or to say that no such people as it depicts ever existed. Fitzgerald, now regarded as the historian of the Jazz Age, was frequently criticized during his lifetime for writing about unreal characters or unbelievable situations. A book like *The Great Gatsby*, when it was praised at

SOURCE *New Mexico Quarterly* XXXIII, Winter 1963, pp. 409–425.

all, was praised for its style or its insight into American society; it was not given the kind of serious analysis it has received in the last twenty years, with emphasis on its symbolic and mythic elements. The novel may have been compared to works by Edith Wharton, Henry James, and Joseph Conrad, but it was not felt necessary to draw in Goethe, Milton, and Shakespeare, as Lionel Trilling has done. The fact that *The Great Gatsby* has been elevated to such heights serves to emphasize the mildness of the praise (and the vehemence of the criticism) with which it was received. The vicissitudes of the book's reputation form an instructive illustration of the problems involved in literary judgment. Since the book is today read in such a different way from the approach used by the contemporary reviewers (indeed in a way impossible for them), must one conclude that time is a prerequisite for the perspective needed in critical judgments? That a contemporary can never see as much in a work as a later generation can? That it is necessary to get far enough away from the period so that questions of realism in external details do not intrude?

There have been—it goes without saying—admirers of the novel from the beginning. Gertrude Stein wrote to Fitzgerald of the "genuine pleasure" of the book brought her; she called it a "good book" and said he was "creating the contemporary world as much as Thackeray did his." T. S. Eliot, after referring to the novel as "charming," "overpowering," and "remarkable," declared it to be "the first step that American fiction has taken since Henry James." Edith Wharton wrote, "let me say at once how much I like Gatsby"; she praised the advance in Fitzgerald's technique and used the word "masterly." And Maxwell Perkins' adjectives were "extraordinary," "magnificent," "brilliant," "unequaled"; he believed Fitzgerald had "every kind of right to be proud of this book" full of "such things as make a man famous" and said to him, "You have plainly mastered the craft."

But the reviewers were not generally so enthusiastic, and several were quite hostile. In the years following the book's publication, there were a few critics who spoke highly of the book from time to time, but the comments on *Gatsby* between 1925 and 1945 can almost be counted on one's fingers, and certainly the significant discussions require no more than the fingers of one hand. Between 1927 and the appearance of *Tender Is the Night* in 1934, there were fewer than ten articles on Fitzgerald, and in these only three important (though very brief) comments on *The Great Gatsby*; between 1934 and Fitzgerald's death in 1940 there were only seven articles, containing a few brief allusions to *Gatsby*, and one discussion in a book; in 1942 and 1943 there was one discussion each year. In 1945, however, with the publication of essays by William Troy and Lionel Trilling, Fitzgerald's stock was beginning to rise, and the Fitzgerald "revival" may be said to have started. It continued at such an accelerated pace that in 1951 John Abbott Clark wrote in the Chicago *Tribune*, "It would seem that all Fitzgerald had broken loose." The story of the changing critical attitudes toward *The Great Gatsby* is a study in the patterns of twentieth-century critical fashions (since the mythic significance of the book was discovered at the same time that the New Criticism was taking over) as well as of the (perhaps) inevitable course of events in literary decisions. It is the success story of how "an inferior work" with an "absurd" and "obviously unimportant" plot became a book that "will be read as long as English literature is read anywhere."

I

When Scribner's published *The Great Gatsby* on April 10, 1925, Fitzgerald was an author with a considerable reputation, for *This Side of Paradise* had aroused a great deal of comment five years before and four other books had come from him since. *Gatsby* therefore, was given prominent reviews in many of the important newspapers and journals. If it can be said in general that the most distinguished periodicals praised the book and that the attacks came from the lesser ones, it can also be said that those attacks were quite vehement and reached a large audience.

For example, *Gatsby* was introduced to New Yorkers (just two days after its publication, on April 12) by the *World*, which headed its review, in large letters, "F. Scott Fitzgerald's Latest a Dud." The reviewer considered the novel "another one of the thousands of modern novels which must be approached with the point of view of the average tired person toward the movie-around-the-corner, a deadened intellect, a thankful resigning of the attention, and an aftermath of wonder that such things are produced." After discovering "no important development of ... character" in the book, he dismissed it quickly—"with the telling of the plot *The Great Gatsby* is, in newspaper parlance, covered."

Six days later, Ruth Hale, in the Brooklyn *Eagle*, carried the attack even farther when she wrote that she could not find "one chemical trace of magic, life, irony, romance or mysticism in all of *The Great Gatsby*" and that Fitzgerald, whom she called "the boy,"

> is simply puttering around. It is all right as a diversion for him, probably. He does, obviously, like to use hifalutin words and hifalutiner notions to concoct these tales. There may be those who like to read him. But why he should be called an author, or why any of us should behave as if he were, has never been explained satisfactorily to me.

America went on in the same vein the next month with a very brief comment on *Gatsby* in a review of several new books: "an inferior novel, considered from any angle whatsoever ... feeble in theme, in portraiture and even in expression." And the Springfield *Republican* (July 5, 1925) found the book "a little slack, a little soft, more than a little artificial" because "the characters ... are blurred and incomprehensible. The 'Great Gatsby' himself ... is unconvincing at best. Jordan ... is the only person who stands out at all from the faintly melodramatic plot. It is a half-hearted novel that might have been composed and might better be read during a hot wave." In other words, *Gatsby* "falls into the class of negligible novels."

Other periodicals were more charitable, if rather hesitant. The *Independent* (May 2, 1925) admitted that *Gatsby* was good (better than any of Fitzgerald's earlier work except *This Side of Paradise*, which contained "all he knew") and that Fitzgerald was now "over the awkward age" so that he might be able to write effectively "outside the field of sophisticated juveniles"; but his attempt at tragedy in *Gatsby* "somehow has the flavor of skimmed milk." Similarly Walter Yust, in a review published in the New York *Evening Post* on the same day as the *Independent's* comments, found decided weaknesses as well as strengths in the book. Although it was a novel that "refuses to be ignored," it was at the same time "one that reveals incredible grossness, thoughtlessness, polite corruption, without leaving the reader with a sense of depression, without being insidiously provocative."

May 2 also saw the publication of another long and balanced review, that of H. L. Mencken. He criticized the plot ("in form no more than a glorified anecdote"):

> The story is obviously unimportant, and though, as I shall show, it has its place in the Fitzgerald canon, it is certainly not to be put on the same shelf with, say, *This Side of Paradise*. What ails it, fundamentally, is the plain fact that it is simply a story—that Fitzgerald seems to be far more interested in maintaining its suspense than in getting under the skins of its people.

That is, except for Gatsby himself, the characters are "mere marionettes—often astonishingly lifelike, but nevertheless not quite alive." But the book is redeemed by "the charm and beauty of the writing," and the story, "for all its basic triviality, has a fine texture, a careful and brilliant finish. The obvious phrase is simply not in it.... There is evidence in every line of hard and intelligent effort." Fitzgerald has taken to heart the stylistic criticisms of his earlier novels, so that now one can find pages "full of little delicacies, charming turns of phrase, penetrating second thoughts," "pages so artfully contrived that one can no more imagine improvising them than one can imagine improvising a fugue." Mencken sees Fitzgerald the stylist challenging Fitzgerald the social historian, but he surmises that the latter is Fitzgerald's chosen role—although Fitzgerald "does not go below the surface," he is very accurate in his depiction of it ("The Long Island he sets before us ... actually exists"). When Mencken turned his attention to *Gatsby* again several weeks later for his *American Mercury* column (July 1925), he was still stressing the book's style, its "evidences of hard, sober toil." Fitzgerald's "whole attitude," he believed, "has changed from that of a brilliant improvisateur to that of a painstaking and conscientious artist," and, while *Gatsby* may be "in part too well-made," it is "sound and laudable work."

At least two other reviewers were in agreement with Mencken. On April

19, Isabel Paterson had declared (in the New York *Herald Tribune*) that the novel contained "not one accidental phrase ... nor yet one obvious or blatant line" but that Fitzgerald was not able to go beneath "the glittering surface," and that the characters "remain types." Her ambivalent conclusion was that *Gatsby* "is the first convincing testimony that Fitzgerald is ... an artist" and at the same time that it is "a book of the season only"—but "so peculiarly of the season, that it is in its small way unique." And on May 5 the New York *Post* made the same sort of distinction between the book's style and its content: Fitzgerald demonstrates "an admirable mastery of his medium," but the "plot and its developments work out too geometrically and too perfectly for *The Great Gatsby* to be a great novel."

When this *Post* reviewer said that Fitgerald, with *Gatsby*, "definitely deserts his earlier fiction which brought him a lot of money and a certain kind of renown and enters into the group of American writers who are producing the best serious fiction," he was giving voice to the sort of observation that constantly reappears in these reviews—the place *Gatsby* occupies in Fitzgerald's career. Thus Llewellyn Jones, in one of the earliest reviews, believed that

> F. Scott Fitzgerald has got his second wind, and the people who were dolefully shaking their heads over him some time ago are going to be fooled. *The Great Gatsby* is written with all the brilliancy and beauty that we associate with youth and with a sense of spiritual values that is sincere and mature. (Chicago *Evening Post*, April 17)

Similarly, the following day, Fanny Butcher commented in the Chicago *Tribune* on the implications of the new novel ("as different from the other two as experience is from innocence") for Fitzgerald's development: "*The Great Gatsby* proves that Scott Fitzgerald is going to be a writer, and not just a man of one book. It is bizarre. It is melodramatic. It is, at moments, dime novelish. But it is, despite its faults, a book which is not negligible as any one's work, and vastly important as Scott Fitzgerald's work." Edwin Clark, in the New York *Times* the next day, felt that the novel took "a deeper look at life" than any of Fitzgerald's earlier work and showed that his sense of form "is becoming perfected." The *Literary Digest* for May found in this "graceful, finished tale" with "a kind of delicate unreality" a Fitzgerald who exhibits "a new awareness of values" and who is "no longer the impudent youngster," who is "still gay and as extravagant as ever" though "not quite as tolerant, and no longer indifferent" since he displays a new emotion, for him—pity. Carl Van Vechten, too, saw a new element in Fitzgerald in this "fine yarn, exhilaratingly spun": "a quality which has only recently made its debut in the writings of this brilliant young author, the quality vaguely referred to as mysticism" (*Nation*, May 20). The *New Yorker* (May 23) declared that the novel "has Fitzgerald's extravagance but a new maturity, as well as any amount of flash and go.... The young man is not petering out." And Louis Bromfield (in the August *Bookman*) believed that Fitzgerald was now "freed of the excesses of youth," since the "gaudy world" of his earlier books "has been left behind somewhere in the middle distance."

The favorable reviews not only tried to ascertain the position of *Gatsby* in Fitzgerald's career but also compared it with the work of other writers. Edwin Clark, in his *Times* review, detected a resemblance to *The Turn of the Screw*, for evil in both cases is suggested, he said, rather than made explicit. The *Bookman* (for June) compared the novel (a story of "a modern Cagliostro") with another one under review, Edith Wharton's *The Mother's Recompense*, and concluded that one "cannot deny its vitality. ... It is Fitzgerald writing with his old gusto, with driving imagination, and with a sense of the futility of life...." The *Outlook* proceeded, in July, to compare Fitzgerald's satiric catalogue of guests at Gatsby's party with Eugene Field's listing of the first families of Kentucky in his poem "The Peter-Bird" and decided (presumably on other grounds) that Fitzgerald "has serious intentions as a novelist." Early in 1926 Gilbert Seldes noted that Fitzgerald's "form is ... derived from James through Mrs. Wharton, and there are cadences direct from the pages of Conrad"; yet Fitzgerald "has at last made his borrowings his own, and ... they nowhere diminish the vitality of his work" (*New Criterion*, January).

This review of Seldes', with its statement that Fitzgerald "has certainly the best chance, at this moment, of becoming our finest artist in fiction," represents the opposite pole from the reaction of the *World*, which had labeled the book a "dud." Seldes' comments are a restatement of the highly favorable opinion he had expressed in the *Dial* several months earlier (August 1925), when he called *Gatsby* "one of the finest of contemporary novels." Fitzgerald, he believed, was no longer concerned only with the exterior of American life (or the "dubious tricks" of his earlier work) but has now "attacked the spirit underneath, and so has begun to report on life in its most general terms," recognizing "both his capacities and his obligations as a novelist." Conrad Aiken, reviewing the English edition in October 1926 for the *New Criterion* (where one of Seldes' reviews had appeared earlier), considered the book not "great" nor "large" nor "strikingly subtle" but nevertheless "well imagined and shaped," with a setting "admirably seized and admirably matched with the theme" and a "hard bright tone" that is "entirely original." He thought of the novel as not merely a satire, but a tragedy: Gatsby himself "comes close to being superb" as Fitzgerald reveals him to us with a "keen tenderness" that "makes his tragedy a deeply moving one."

At this pole of enthusiastic praise come also the reviews of William Rose Benét and Thomas Caldecot Chubb. Benét, in the *Saturday Review of Literature* (May 9, 1925), described *Gatsby* as "disillusioned" and "mature," with "pace" and "admirable 'control.'" Chaper Two "could not have been better written," while the catalogue of guests in Chapter Four could have been brought off by no one but Fitzgerald. Contrary to the opinions of Mencken and Isabel Paterson, Benét felt that the author has "made the real people live and breathe in all their sordidness.... They are memorable people of today—not types."

But it is Chubb, writing in the *Forum* (in August 1925), who probably came closer than any other reviewer to expressing the present-day attitude toward the book. Fitzgerald's "most attractive book" is "a fable in the form of a realistic novel," "at once a tragedy and an extraordinarily convincing love tale and an extravaganza...." While the publishers claimed that Gatsby "would only be possibly in this age and generation," Chubb felt "that he would be possible in any age and generation and impossible in all of them.... there is something of Jay Gatsby in every man, woman, or child that ever existed." Referring to Fitzgerald's brilliance (he "has every bit of the brilliance that we associate with hard surfaces"), Chubb asserts, "To recommend this book on the ground of technical excellence is of course superfluous. I recommend it as a study of ... sentimentalists by one whose heart does not ever beat erratically."

The British reaction to the book in 1926 was not markedly different from the American. That is, there were those who felt, with the *Times Literary Supplement* (February 18), that it was "undoubtedly a work of art and of great promise" and those who thought the story hardly "worth the telling," an example of "[u]ndoubted talent ... wasted on the poor material of the melodramatic corruptions of America's over-rich 'smart set' in post-war times" (*Dublin Magazine*, July– September 1926). Edward Shanks found himself on the side of the *Times*, with L. P. Hartley in the opposing camp, while the *New Statesman* (March 27) was rather noncommittal about this "satirist with a pretty thick velvet glove." Shanks, in the April *London Mercury*, said that *Gatsby* leaves "no doubt as to Mr. Fitzgerald's talents" and shows him handling "his grotesque material with an artist's discretion and ... moderation": "Where he might well be flamboyant, he is dry; where he might be ragingly sentimental, he is full of commonsense." Hartley, on the other hand, saw in *Gatsby* only "an absurd story, whether considered as romance, melodrama, or plain record of New York high life," the work of a man whose "imagination is febrile" and whose emotion is "over-strained"; and he hoped "that Mr. Fitzgerald's heart is not in it, that it is a piece of mere naughtiness" (*Saturday Review*, February 20).

It would be a mistake to emphasize such unfavorable reviews and to say that *Gatsby* was not recognized as an excellent novel upon its appearance. The most striking characteristic of the reviews as a whole is not that they failed to praise the novel (for most of them did find something to admire in it) but that they praised it for the wrong reasons—or at least different reasons from those we now give. It was a good novel, they said, because 1) it reminded one of Conrad or James; 2) it showed an advance in Fitzgerald's artistry; 3) it had an admirable style, if not much could be said for the story; 4) it was a fine story, regardless of what one thought of the style. It was a good novel, in other words, but not extraordinary or great. Only one reviewer placed it among "the finest of contemporary novels," and only one thought of it as a "fable" and a "tragedy"; none discussed its symbolism nor its function as myth. And all their reactions perhaps serve to support Trilling's statement that "the book grows in weight of significance with the years."

II

As those years passed, *The Great Gatsby* gradually began to receive more attention, but it was not until 1945, fully twenty years after the novel's publication, that any considerable amount of serious discussion was directed toward it. In 1934 John Chamberlain was able to say (in the New York *Times* on September 20) that "many critics have been extremely discerning and loyal about *The Great Gatsby*," but his comment could have been based (and one must remember that the book had been out nine years) only on a handful of brief discussions (probably three) in addition to the reviews. Rebecca West, in the January 1929 *Bookman*, had called it "surely a remarkable novel" (which had "not been superseded in the common mind by better books"). Two years later Gorham Munson had remarked (October 1931 *Bookman*), almost parenthetically, "There is more art in *The Great Gatsby* than there is in the whole shelf of Mr. Dreiser's works." And Lawrence Leighton, in his 1932 *Hound and Horn* survey of the state of the American novel, had turned to *Gatsby* with "complete admiration" for Fitzgerald's "technical skill" and had found the book "worth the whole of a Dos Passos novel in its exposition of the dreariness of American life." James Gray, in two reviews of other Fitzgerald books for the St. Paul *Dispatch*, had also praised *Gatsby*—in 1926 as "a beautiful literary accomplishment" and in 1933 as "a skillful, wise and affecting book."

When Gray then wrote in 1940, "Perhaps some day it [*Gatsby*] will be rediscovered," he may have been a harbinger of what was to happen later in the decade, but he was speaking from the midst of a long period of neglect of the book—between Chamberlain's remark in 1934 and the beginning of the revival in 1945, there were no more than five or six articles that could be thought of in any way as contributing to a study of *Gatsby* (only one of them exclusively on that novel) and two or three comments in books. There had been a significant brief mention of the work in a *London Mercury* article by Harry T. Moore in March 1935, referring to *Gatsby* as "almost a great novel" and "one of the few books of the 1920's that can still stand on its feet," and Harlan Hatcher's description in the same year, in his book on modern American fiction, of the "pace and drive," "proportion and firmness of structure" of Fitzgerald's "best piece of work." James Gray had written two articles, in 1937 and 1940, the first (*Saturday Review of Literature*, June 12) pronouncing *Gatsby* Fitzgerald's "finest work" and the second (St. Paul

Dispatch, December 24) describing it as "one of those small masterpieces which inevitably misses tremendous popular success because its implications are more subtle than the casual public cares to disentangle from a melodramatic story." There had been a few comments on *Gatsby* in the rash of articles that appeared upon Fitzgerald's death in 1940: John Dos Passos in the *New Republic* (February 17, 1941) labeling it "one of the few classic American novels," *Esquire* (for March 1941) asserting that it "will undoubtedly be read and studied a century hence," Margaret Marshall (*Nation*, February 8, 1941) believing that it "will continue to be relevant" because it "caught and crystallized the underlying 'values' of a period." And, finally, there had been Peter Quennell's study, in the *New Statesman* (February 1, 1941), of one of the book's "many virtues" ("its delineation of two rich men during the American boom"), which concluded that it is "a period piece with an unusual degree of permanent value."

As for critical books in the early forties, Oscar Cargill, in *Intellectual America* (1941), pointed out two weaknesses in what was "one of the swiftest moving of modern novels"; Alfred Kazin, in *On Native Grounds* (1943), found it "very skillful, often superb technically, and yet curiously hollow at times." The publication of *The Last Tycoon* in 1941 even caused some critics to waver in assigning first place to *Gatsby*. Clifton Fadiman (in the *New Yorker*, November 15, 1941) called the new novel "an advance over *The Great Gatsby*"; J. Donald Adams (New York *Times*, November 9) saw in it a "detachment" lacking in *Gatsby*, previously Fitzgerald's greatest work; and James Thurber (*New Republic*, February 9, 1942) thought that, if finished, it would rank with *Gatsby*. By 1944 (during which year virtually the only remark about *Gatsby* was J. Donald Adams'—in *The Shape of Books to Come*— that it "will be read when most of the novels of the Twenties are entirely forgotten") there was still no general agreement about Fitzgerald, even though he was beginning to be discussed in more academic journals. If Charles Weir could then view the major works (in the *Virginia Quarterly Review*) as attempts at tragedy (generally unsuccessful because Fitzgerald failed "to make the reader contemplate the problem in its larger implications"), Leo and Miriam Gurko (*College English*) could rate him "a minor writer."

All this changed abruptly, however, in 1945. In the fall of that year the publication of *The Crack-Up* was the occasion for a general reassessment, in which, even if Isidor Schneider (writing for the *New Masses*, December 4) thought *Gatsby* not fully successful, J. Donald Adams (in the September *American Mercury*) reiterated his belief that it was "one of the few American novels of the period between the wars that has some lien on posterity" and that Fitzgerald was "Hemingway's born superior." But it was in two essays by Lionel Trilling and one by William Troy that the beginnings of the revival could most clearly be seen. On August 25, Trilling reviewed *The Crack-Up* for the *Nation*, discussing Fitzgerald in relation to practically all the important writers of the past: "I am aware," he said, "that I have involved Fitzgerald with a great many great names," but he declared that the "disproportion" would not seem large to readers of "the mature work." This mature work included *Gatsby*, which New Directions reissued with an introduction by Trilling that enumerated the excellences of the book: its form, its poetic style, its grasp of "a moment of history as a great moral fact," and, above all, its hero, who "may be taken not only as an individual character but also as a symbolic or even allegorical character ... to be thought of as standing for America itself." Troy took a similar approach in the autumn issue of *Accent*, where he termed Gatsby "one of the few truly mythological creations in our recent literature" and analyzed Fitzgerald's preoccupation with failure and his "exasperation with the multiplicity of modern human existence." Even in a brief English survey of American literature (Marcus Cunliffe's Penguin history), *Gatsby* became "a brilliant little novel ... with a moving elegiac quality"; and for Sterling North, reviewing the *Portable Fitzgerald* in the Chicago *Sun* (October 7), the novel "dates not at all." Almost the only dissenting voice was that of Charles Poore, who judged that *Gatsby* "did not have the insight" of *This Side of Paradise* (New York *Times*, September 27).

Between 1945 and the zenith of 1951–53, commentary on the book appeared steadily, if not exactly in large quantity. In 1946 John Berryman wrote in the *Kenyon Review* that *Gatsby*, "a masterpiece," was "better than any other American work of fiction since *The Golden Bowl*"; James Gray, in his *On Second Thought*, referred to *Gatsby* as Fitzgerald's "best book"; and Arthur Mizener, in the *Sewanee Review*, published his first attempt at Fitzgerald biography-criticism (although, in looking at the *Portable* in the *Kenyon Review* that spring, he considered *Tender Is the Night* to be "surely Fitzgerald's most important novel"). The rest of the forties found only specialized or peripheral articles, such as Milton Hindus' discussion of anti-Semitism in Fitzgerald's portrayal of Wolfsheim (which stirred up some letters about *Gatsby* from the readers of *Commentary* in 1947), Alan Ross's analysis (in the December 1948 *Horizon*) of the relation between the man and his work (*Gatsby* being "the one novel" in which Fitzgerald "exactly and beautifully canalized the various strands of his own temperament"), Martin Kallich's 1949 study in the *University of Kansas City Review* of Fitzgerald's attitude toward wealth, D. S. Savage's general chronicle (*World Review*, August 1949) of Fitzgerald's work (in which *Gatsby* is "superlative," "a masterpiece of sympathetic understanding"), Frederick J. Hoffman's comparison (in the 1949 *English Institute Essays*) of Edith Wharton and Fitzgerald (who had "an inadequate sense of the past"), Paul L. MacKendrick's comparison of the *Satyricon* and *Gatsby* in the *Classical Journal* (both contributing to the "literature of protest"), Michael F. Moloney's critique of "half-faiths" and "social awareness" in Fitzgerald (*Catholic World*, 1950), and the January 20, 1950, *Times Literary Supplement's* survey of Fitzgerald (with *Gatsby* seen as "extraordinarily successful in blending reflection and movement").

When 1951 came, however, there was no doubt that the revival was in full swing. That year saw the production of more than thirty articles about Fitzgerald in addition to two books about him, reviews of those books, and commentary on him in still others. The most important sign of Fitzgerald's new stature was, of course, the biography by Arthur Mizener, *The Far Side of Paradise*, in which Gatsby, a "romantic," is discussed as an "embodiment of the American dream as a whole," with this dream being "the book's only positive good." Reviewers of the Mizener work also gave special mention at times to *Gatsby*. To the *TLS* (November 23, 1951), Fitzgerald "is now very generally recognized as having written in *The Great Gatsby* (1925), one of the best—if not the best—American novels of the past 50 years"; John Chamberlain in the *Freeman* (February 12) thought that *Gatsby* and *Tender Is the Night* "will be read as long as English literature is read anywhere"; and Orville Prescott in the *Times* (January 29) declared that "only a few in each generation write novels as good" as *Gatsby*, "a mature and integrated work of art." The extent of the enthusiasm is shown by the reviewer for the *Listener* (December 13): "Today, it does not seem so certain that Fitzgerald was right in thinking Hemingway the greater writer." The other book of 1951 was the collection of articles and reviews about Fitzgerald edited by Alfred Kazin, *F. Scott Fitzgerald: The Man and His Work*, which contained a number of reprinted pieces on *Gatsby* by Mencken, T. S. Eliot, and Maxwell Perkins.

Several other books that year discussed *Gatsby* as an important work of art, notably John W. Aldridge's *After the Lost Generation* (the theme of wealth), Riley Hughes in Harold C. Gardiner's *Fifty Years of the American Novel* (*Gatsby* will last because in it there is "disjunction between the author and the objects of his compassion"), Frederick J. Hoffman's *The Modern Novel in America*, and Heinrich Straumann's *American Literature in the Twentieth Century* (*Gatsby* has "an extraordinary unity of purpose in theme, plot, characterization and atmosphere"). But in general it can be said that the shorter discussions of *Gatsby* during 1951 fall into two groups: comments on *Gatsby's* relation to the man Fitzgerald, and disparaging remarks from those who disagreed with the new high valuation of Fitzgerald. Into the first category fall articles like Malcolm Cowley's "Fitzgerald: The Double Man" (*Saturday Review of Literature*, February 24), Leslie Fielder's *New Leader* article entitled "Notes on F. Scott Fitzgerald" (which agrees that *Gatsby* is Fitzgerald's "best book"), Henry Dan Piper's analysis in Princeton's library journal of the father-image in Fitzgerald, and D. S. Savage's psychoanalytical study (in *Envoy*) of wealth and the "incest motive" in *Gatsby* and *Tender Is the Night*. The other group, the camp of the dissenters, includes Edward Dahlberg (with his caustic indictment, in the November 5 *Freeman*, of Fitzgerald's "sloven writing" and of *Gatsby*, a "novel without ideas" and an example of Fitzgerald's "peopleless realism"), Baird W. Whitlock (who wrote to the *TLS* that the "peak" of twentieth-century American literature must be "a good deal higher" than *Gatsby*), several writers of letters to the *Saturday Review of Literature*, and Ben

Ray Redman (who, in the same issue of that magazine, believed "that praise of [Fitzgerald's] work now outruns discretion").

Anyone familiar with academic criticism could predict the rest of the story. Given the facts so far—the "discovery" and elevation of a formerly underrated twentieth-century novel—the kinds of articles to follow, swept along in the giant wave of enthusiasm, conform to a pattern. There is no point in doing more than very briefly tracing this pattern since 1952. The spring of that year saw discussions of the "social thinking" in *Gatsby* (Richard Greenleaf in *Science & Society*) and of its "concern for the archetypal and essential forms of the American character and experience" (Charles Holmes in the *Pacific Spectator*); in the summer it was again studied as a "social document" (William Van O'Connor in *American Quarterly*); in the fall its symbolism and themes were treated in *College English* (by Tom Burnam); and before the end of the year its themes were scrutinized two more times, by Edwin Fussell (in *ELH*) and Henry Wechsler (in the Washington and Jefferson *Wall*). Through 1953, 1954, and 1955 many important critics turned their attention to the book, discussing it in terms of its commentary on money (Malcolm Cowley in the *Western Review*, 1953), its mythology (Douglas Taylor in the *University of Kansas City Review*, 1953), its criticism of America (Marius Bewley in the *Sewanee Review*, 1954), its theme of "time confused and disordered" (Robert Wooster Stallman in *Modern Fiction Studies*, 1955), even its telephone symbolism (B. B. Cohen in the Indiana *Folio*, 1954), bringing in comparisons with Benjamin Franklin (Floyd Watkins in the *New England Quarterly* and Hugh Maclean in *College English*, 1954), Dickens (Norman Friedman in *Accent*, 1954), T. S. Eliot (John Bicknell in the *Virginia Quarterly Review*, 1954), Conrad (Robert Stallman in *Twentieth Century Literature*, 1955), and Sophocles' *Oedipus* (Hans Meyerhoff's *Time in Literature*). Frederick J. Hoffman, who felt *Gatsby* was "a sentimental novel," also believed that its "details are presented with brilliantly accurate insight, greater than any other found in modern American literature" (*The Twenties*, 1955); R. F. Richards, in a 1955 "dictionary" of American literature, discerned in it "one of the most perfect structures in literature"; Robert Spiller, in his *Cycle of American Literature* (1955), thought it Fitzgerald's "most finished novel"; and Louis Untemeyer (in his Fitzgerald chapter of *Makers of the Modern World*) talked of its "unforgettable" scenes and "universal" implications.

In the late fifties there was no slackening of the pace. The comparisons continued—with Hemingway (Arthur Mizener in the fifteenth *Perspectives U.S.A.*), Conrad again (Jerome Thale in *Twentieth Century Literature*, 1957), and Dreiser (Eric Solomon in *Modern Language Notes*, 1958)—and there were studies focused on the narrator, Nick Carraway (Thomas Hanzo in *Modern Fiction Studies*, 1957), the theme of the "unending quest of the romantic dream" (Robert Ornstein in *College English*, 1956), and of reality versus imagination (Don Wahlquist in *Inland*, 1957), its use of legends and myth (John Henry Raleigh in the *University of Kansas City Review*, June and

October 1957, and Richard Chase in his *American Novel and Its Tradition*), its blending of "the abstract, the ideal, and the mythical" with a "realistic treatment of our culture" (J. R. Kuehl in *Texas Studies*, 1959), its pattern and structure (John W. Aldridge in Charles Shapiro's collection of *Twelve Original Essays on Great American Novels*), and the symbolism of Dr. Eckleberg's eyes (Milton Hindus in *Boston University Studies in English*, 1957) and of noses (John C. Weston in *Fitzgerald Newsletter*, 1959). By 1958 Matthew J. Bruccoli was able to say (in the *Newsletter*) that Fitzgerald "is still the most consistently underrated American writer," even though, the year before, James E. Miller had published a full-length monograph on Fitzgerald's technique (including a detailed discussion of *Gatsby*) and that year the Bodley Head in London began reprinting Fitzgerald's work (with an introduction by J. B. Priestley). Also in 1958 some uncollected material was gathered together as *Afternoon of an Author*, which provoked from the London *Times* (on October 9) the obiter dictum that *Gatsby* "has a significance that can be accorded to few American books written between the wars." In 1959 Peter Munro Jack gave *Gatsby* a place in the "James Branch Cabell period" (in Malcolm Cowley's collection, *After the Genteel Tradition*); Frederick E. Faverty (in *Your Literary Heritage*) praised the book's realism, its technique, and its "arresting" symbolism; and Mizener, in a new paperback edition of his biography, compared *Gatsby* to Stendhal's *Le Rouge et le Noir*.

By 1960 *Gatsby* was without doubt thought of as a classic, so that no one was surprised to find it discussed in works with such broad titles as J. B. Priestley's *Literature and Western Man* or Leon Howard's *Literature and the American Tradition*, and Arthur Mizener found it in order to survey in the New York *Times* (April 24) some of the earlier criticism (concluding that only recently had "the obvious values" of the novel "been reasonably established"). From J. S. Westbrook's explication of the novel in *American Literature* in 1960, through Richard C. Carpenter's in the *Explicator* in 1961, Charles E. Shain's 1961 pamphlet in the Minnesota series, and the entire issue of *Modern Fiction Studies* (Spring 1961) devoted to Fitzgerald (with two articles on *Gatsby*), down to Andrew Turnbull's biography and the whole volume of material about *Gatsby* edited by Frederick J. Hoffman in 1962 (including Henry Dan Piper's discussion of the religious background of the novel), academic criticism has shown no sign of declining. Within the last year alone there have been detailed treatments of the novel in books about Fitzgerald (Kenneth Eble takes up its structure and "romantic vision," William Goldhurst its relation to the work of Mencken, Hemingway, Lardner, and Edmund Wilson) and articles on its "statement and technique" (Michael Millgate in *Modern Language Review*), its "imagery and meaning" (Guy Owen in *Stetson Studies*), its use of the grotesque (Howard Babb in *Criticism*), of "the artifact in imagery" (M. Bettina in *Twentieth Century Literature*), and of Platonic thought (Paul Lauter in *Modern Fiction Studies*). When one looks back over the seventy-five or more articles and chapters that have, since 1950, been wholly or partialy devoted to *Gatsby*, one has no difficulty in agreeing with Charles Shain's statement that *Gatsby* "has been discussed and admired as much as any twentieth-century American novel." And when, on top of that, one looks at the dozen or so doctoral dissertations that discuss the book and the articles and books in French, Italian, German, Dutch, and Swedish, one is likely—if not totally overwhelmed—to have some disquieting thoughts.

Of course, doubts about the "revival" did go along with the enthusiasm—there is always the minority report. If Martin Schockley's decision in his 1954 *Arizona Quarterly* article that it was time to "place upon Fitzgerald's brow the small and wilted laurel that is his" seems too harsh, Albert J. Lubell made the same point more temperately the next year in the *South Atlantic Quarterly* when he asserted that the "recent criticism of [Fitzgerald], attempting to correct the wrong of his undue neglect, itself needs a corrective." And P. K. Elkin, in the *Australian Quarterly* of June 1957, praised *Gatsby* very highly, but not until he had pointed out how a great deal of the revival had "obscured" Fitzgerald's "more substantial attributes." But the dissenters are a part of the general enthusiasm, and it goes without saying that any such revival of interest in a work of literature is not based entirely on cool and balanced judgment. In 1961 (for a summer reading issue of the New York *Herald Tribune's* book review) Jerome Weidman listed *Gatsby* as one of his seven favorite books because "it catches better than anything I have ever read, heard, or can remember, the extraordinary time during which I grew up and, to return to its meticulously written pages strewn with incandescent images that grow brighter with the years, is to be again a part of that time." His statement perhaps explains the revival as well as anything does.

More is involved here than the question of whether contemporaries can accurately judge a work of art—or, indeed, whether we are still (only two generations after *Gatsby* appeared) too close to have perspective. There is more involved than the question of how accurate *Gatsby* is in portraying a particular period. It is rather a matter of the way we look back at that period and of the values we place on certain kinds of criticism. How often do our sentimental and nostalgic feelings determine our critical reactions? How often is a literary judgment self-perpetuating? An examination of the reputation of *The Great Gatsby* may serve as an index to the critical taste of the last forty years; but, beyond that, it is a case study in the workings of literary evaluation—of the critical snowballing process by which a work becomes established as a classic. Such an inquiry is disturbing, not in the sense that every subjective value judgment leaves room for doubts, but because one begins to feel that this process follows a pattern, that it has become mechanical, that a great deal of energy may have been misdirected. This is not to say that *Gatsby* does not deserve the attention it has received. It is merely a way of saying that *Gatsby* has provided us with more than one fable—that the story of its reception is itself a parable showing up what is best and what is worst in recent criticism.

81
Bibliography and the Novelistic Fallacy

◆

BRUCE HARKNESS

It is a truth universally acknowledged, that a critic intent upon analysis and interpretation, must be in want of a good text.[1] It is also universally acknowledged that we live in an age of criticism, indeed of "new criticism"—which means that we as critics are dedicated to a very close reading of the text. Sometimes, it is true, that critical principle leads to abuses. The symbol-hunting, the ambiguity-spinning become wonders to behold. As one objector has put it, "nose to nose, the critic confronts writer and, astonished, discovers himself."[2] Nonetheless, the principle of close reading is held central by us all. Immediately that one contemplates novel criticism, however, an oddity appears: the last thing we find in a discussion by a new critic is some analysis of the actual text.

The modern critic is apt to be entirely indifferent to the textual problems of a novel. He is all too prone to examine rigorously a faulty text. As Gordon Ray and others have pointed out, even the Great Cham of British Criticism errs in this respect. F. R. Leavis defends the early Henry James in *The Great Tradition*: "Let me insist, then, at once, ... that his [James's] 'first attempt at a novel,' *Roderick Hudson* (1874), in spite of its reputation, is a very distinguished book that deserves permanent currency—much more so than many novels passing as classics." Professor Ray adds that "Mr. Leavis goes on to quote three long paragraphs to illustrate the novel's 'sustained maturity of theme and treatment....' These remarks are amply warranted by the passage that Mr. Leavis cites. But unhappily he has quoted, not the text of the first edition of 1877 [while carefully dating it from the time of composition to make it appear all the more precocious], which is simple enough, but that of the New York edition of 1907, revised in James's intricate later manner. This leaves him," concludes Leavis's critic, "in the position of having proved at length what nobody would think of denying, that James's writing at the age of sixty-four has all the characteristics of maturity."[3]

SOURCE *Studies in Bibliography* XII, 1958, pp. 59–73.

Unhappily, few of us can afford to laugh at the poor new critic. We all know the truth that we must have a good text, but most of us do not act upon it. A commonplace? Yes, and unfortunately, I have only that commonplace to urge; but I claim good company. Jane Austen, with whom I started, recognized that *Pride and Prejudice* had no profoundly new meaning. She ironically developed upon commonplaces: don't act on first impressions; don't interfere in your best friend's love affair; don't ignore your younger daughters. My point is that, ironically, everyone ignores the bibliographical study of the novel. People who would consider it terribly bad form to slight the textual study of a play or poem—or even doggerel—commit bibliographical nonsense when handed a novel. It seems that the novel just doesn't count. A key error in many studies of the novel is simply this, that the novel is unconsciously considered a different order of thing from poetry—a poem's text must be approached seriously. I shall illustrate by mentioning the sins of editors, reprinters, publishers, scholars, and, alas, bibliographers. Then, after discussing a few of the many reasons for this bibliographical heresy, I shall turn to my main illustration of the need for textual bibliography, *The Great Gatsby*.

II

A list of representative errors, by no means exhaustive, by sound men whom I admire in all other respects will make clear how faulty the texts of novels are, and how little we care. A good editor has put *The Nigger of the "Narcissus"* in *The Portable Conrad*, an excellent volume the introductions to which contain some of the best Conrad criticism. But what, one may wonder, is the copy-text for *The Nigger*? A search through the book discloses two references, the less vague of which reads as follows: "It is from the editions published and copyrighted by the latter [Doubleday and Company] that the texts reproduced in this volume have been drawn" (p. 758).

After a spot of searching the reader can discover for himself that the copy-text for *The Nigger of the "Narcissus"* is not the collected English edition, which as is well known was Conrad's major concern. The copy-text was an early American publication, which Conrad habitually did not supervize. The new critic immediately asks, does it make any difference?

The collected English edition was, as one might suspect with an author who was constantly revising, changed in many ways. This final version cuts down Conrad's intrusive "philosophizing," and corrects Donkin's cockney accent, among other shifts.[4] I yield to no man in my admiration for Conrad, but if he has a fault, it lies in that adjectival "philosophy" which is admired by some, charitably overlooked by others, and condemned by a few as pipe-sucking old seadog-talk. Surely the following, from the early part of Chapter Four, is inappropriate in the mouth of the sailor-narrator: "Through the perfect wisdom of its grace [the sea's] they [seamen] are not permitted to meditate at ease upon the complicated and acrid savour of existence, lest they should remember and, perchance, regret the reward of a cup of inspiring bitterness, tasted so often, and so often withdrawn before their stiffening but reluctant lips. They must without pause justify their life...." Most of this passage, and much similar sententiousness, were cut by Conrad from the collected English text; but they all stand in *The Portable Conrad.*

As for the class of books known loosely as "reprints," I suppose that no one expects a good text for twenty-five or thirty-five cents. These books I am not concerned with, but the more serious paperbacks, obviously intended for use in colleges, are sometimes faulty. For example, Rinehart Editions' copy of *Pride and Prejudice* reprints Chapman's excellent text—but suppresses the indication of three volume construction by numbering the chapters serially throughout.[5] Though three volumes are mentioned in the introduction, this misprinting of such a tightly constructed novel can only be regretted, for the effect on the college reader must be odd.

What of the publisher of more expensive novels? It can easily be seen that errors are not limited to the paperback field. Consider, for example, the one-volume Scribner edition of James's *The Wings of the Dove,* dated 1945 or 1946. Here is no scrimping for paperback costs, but the book is not what one would think. It is not a reprint of the famous New York edition; it is another, unacknowledged impression of the 1902 first American edition, dressed up with a new-set New York preface—an odd procedure the reason for which is not apparent. The publisher nowhere tells the reader that this is like some wines—an old text with a new preface. Yet one line of print would have made the matter clear. It is only by his own efforts of collation of the preface and the text itself that the reader knows where he is.[6]

To turn to the errors of scholarship, take F. O. Matthiessen's lengthy appreciation of Melville's phrase "soiled fish of the sea" in *White Jacket.* Melville's narrator says of himself, after he had fallen into the sea, "I wondered whether I was yet dead or still dying. But all of a sudden some fashionless form brushed my side—some inert, soiled fish of the sea; the thrill of being alive again tingled...." This section Matthiessen acclaims as being imagery of the "sort that was to become peculiarly Melville's ... hardly anyone but Melville could have created the shudder that results from calling this frightening vagueness some '*soiled* fish of the sea'!" Then follows a discussion of the metaphysical conceit and its moral and psychological implications.

As has been pointed out, the genius in this shuddering case of imagery is not Melville, who wrote *coiled* fish, not *soiled* fish. "Coiled fish" stands in the first editions of *White Jacket,* and to an unknown Constable printer should go the laurels for soiling the page with a typographical error.[7]

Matthiessen's error does not concern me now, but it does concern me that the scholar who first caught the mistake has a strange but perhaps understandable attitude toward textual matters. Recognizing that such an error "in the proper context" might have promulgated a "false conception," the scholar feels that the slip does not actually matter in Melville's case. Furthermore, he feels that Matthiessen's position is essentially sound—he was merely the victim of "an unlucky error." While sympathiszing with common sense and professional etiquette, one may still wonder, however, how many such slips in illustration are allowable. Could the critic, if challenged, produce as many sound illustrations as one would like? Does not Matthiessen, in his categorizing of conceits, virtually admit that this particular kind is rare in *White Jacket*?

When we look at the texts of novels from the other way, how many good editions of novelists do we have? How do they compare with the poets? We know a good bit about the bibliographies of Scott, Trollope, Meredith, but those of Dickens, Thackeray, Conrad, Hawthorne, and many more are completely out of date.[8] How many collected editions can be put on the same shelf with Chapman's 1923 Jane Austen? "We have virtually no edited texts of Victorian novelists," says Mrs. Tillotson in the introduction of *Novels of the Eighteen-Forties* (1954). How slowly we move, if at all.

Take Hardy for example. In 1946 Carl Weber said that "many scholars have apparently made no attempt to gain access to Hardy's definitive texts." In March, 1957, a scholar can complain that "As late as November 1956, sixty full years after the publication of the book, the only edition of *Jude* printed in the United States took no account of either of the two revisions which Hardy gave the novel.... The New Harper's Modern Classics edition ... [however] is *almost* identical with that of the definitive 1912 'Wessex Edition.'"[9] One is hardly surprised that Professor Weber is the editor.

Sixty years is a long time, but American literature is no better off. *Moby-Dick*, our greatest novel, presents no problem of copy-text. Yet more than 100 years went by after publication before we had what a recent scholar called the "first serious reprint," by Hendricks House. Before that, the careful reader did not even know, for example, the punctuation of the famous "Know ye, now, Bulkington?" passage. But how good is this reprint? The same scholar—not the editor—asks us to consider it a definitive edition. His reasons? It contains only 108 compositor's errors and twenty silent emendations.[10] Would anyone make such a claim for a volume of poems?

So much for editors, publishers, scholars. The sins of the bibliographer are mainly those of omission. For well-known reasons he tends to slight 19th- and 20th-century books in general, and in consequence most novels.[11]

The critic therefore needs convincing that novels should be approached bibliographically. The critic appreciates the sullied-solid-sallied argument about Shakespeare, but not that of 108 typos for *Moby-Dick*. A false word in a sonnet may change a fifth of its meaning; the punctuation at the end of the "Ode on a Grecian Urn" can be considered crucial to the meaning of the whole poem; but who, the critic argues from bulk, can stand the prospect of collating 700 pages of Dickens to find a few dozen misplaced commas? Like the "soiled fish" reading of *White Jacket*, a few mistakes seriously damage neither novel nor criticism. They are swallowed up in the vast bulk of the novel, which by and large (and excepting a few well-known oddities such as *Tender is the Night* in which case one must be sure which text one is attacking) is decently printed and generally trustworthy. The critic feels that a mistake here or there in the text is immaterial. "It doesn't *really* alter my interpretation," is the standard phrase.

This attitude has long since been defeated by bibliographers for all genres except the novel. One wonders indeed, if the critic would be willing to make his plea more logical. Could not the attitude be extended to some formula for trustworthiness versus error? It ought not to be difficult to arrive at a proportion expressing the number of errors per page, exceeding which a novel could be condemned as poorly printed.

Amid bad reasoning, there is some truth to the critic's defence against bibliography. The argument can be shifted from the ground of a novel's size and a reader's energy to the aesthetic nature of the novel. The critic is certainly right in maintaining that novels are more loosely constructed, even the best of them, than poems or short stories. The effects of a novel are built through countless small touches, and the loss of one or two—whether by error in text or inattention in reading—is immaterial. Putting aside the counter claim that this truth is damaging to the critical and crucial premise of close reading, surely all is a matter of degree. And what is more, the theory applies mainly to character portrayal. If we fail to recognize Collins as a fawning ass on one page, we will certainly see him aright on another.

That much must be granted the critic. In other concerns, however, the novel may not be repetitive. To give just one illustration: F.Scott Fitzgerald's *Last Tycoon* as published in unfinished form contains a boy whom the reader should compare to the "villain" of the piece, Brady (or Bradogue as he was called in an earlier draft). In Fitzgerald's directions to himself left in his MSS, he says "Dan [the boy] bears, in some form of speech, a faint resemblance to Bradogue. This must be subtly done and not look too much like a parable or moral lesson, still the impression must be conveyed, but be careful to convey it *once* and not rub it in. If the reader misses it, let it go—don't repeat."[12]

My last and painful reason why virtually no one is concerned with the texts of novels is this: most bibliographers are also university teachers and many of them suffer from schizophrenia. I do not refer to that familiar disease which makes us scholars by day and diaper washers by night, but that split in the man between Graduate Seminar number 520 in Bibliography and Freshman "Intro. to Fic.," 109. How many of us make bibliographical truths part of our daily lives or attempt to inspire our graduate students so to do? In this respect many bibliographers are like socialists and Christians: walking arguments for the weakness of the cause.

Let me give one or two illustrations from experience. Not very long ago I sat in a staff meeting while we worried over a sentence of Conrad's introduction to *Victory* in the Modern Library edition. The sentence contained the odd phrase "adaptable cloth," used about mankind. It made no sense until it was finally pointed out that "adap-table" was divided at the end of the line in both American collected edition and reprint—a domestically minded compositor was talking about a table cloth, while Conrad was saying that Man is "wonderfully adaptable both by his power of endurance and in his capacity for detachment." And our silly discussion had gone on despite long teaching, and one's natural suspicion of the cheaper reprints that perforce must be used in college classes.

More seriously, consider Dickens' *Great Expectations*, taught to freshmen at many universities, by staffs composed of men nearly all of whom have been required to "take" bibliography. Yet how many of these teachers have turned to the facts of serial publicaton to explain the figure of Orlick, extremely puzzling by critical standards alone? One immediately sees that Orlick's attack on Mrs. Joe, which ultimately causes her death, is used by Dickens to pep up a three instalment sequence the main purpose of which is simply to let Pip age. This sequence would have been too dull, too insistent on domestic scenes round the hearth while Pip gradually withdraws from Joe, were it not for the Orlick subplot.[13] The novel apparently had to have thirty-six weekly units, and Dickens therefore could not simply skip this period of Pip's life. The figure of Orlick may not be critically acceptable, but he is at least understandable when one views him in the light of publishing history.

I am also indicting myself for not understanding this point; for it was not many months ago that I looked up the weekly issues of *All the Year Round* and now have far more detail than, as the saying goes, "the short space of this article will permit the discussion of." I was derelict in my duty partly because life is short and bibliography is long, but also partly because I unconsciously resented the editor of my paperback *Great Expectations* whose job I was having to do.

For I am more familiar with the schizophrenia than most people, though mine takes a different form. With critics I am apt to claim to be a bibliographer; among bibliographers, I proclaim myself a critic.

The critic, one must recognize, can argue on aesthetic grounds against working on the texts of novels. He can produce the *tu quoque* argument. And he can say that the bibliographer neglects *what* he is working on. Of 244 articles on textual bibliography in the *Studies in Bibliography* list for 1954, only three were related to novels.[14] "What has the bibliographer been doing?" asks the new critic.

It may be that under the aspect of eternity George Sandys' *Ovid* is more important than Conrad's *Nostromo* or Melville's *Moby-Dick*, but it would be hard to convince the novel critic of that.

III

For these reasons I have chosen F. Scott Fitzgerald's *The Great Gatsby* as my main illustration. It brings out nearly all my points: inconsistent editing, an unknown or unidentified text, a publisher who is good but vague, important errors in an important book, schizophrenia in the bibliographer-teacher. Not only is *Gatsby* a fine novel, but it is taught so often because it contains many of the basic themes of American literature: West versus East; the search for value; the American dream; crime and society; and in young Jim Gatz's "General Resolves," it even reaches back to Ben Franklin and Poor Richard.

How many know, however, what they have been teaching?

The Great Gatsby exists in print in three main versions: the first edition, beginning in April, 1925; a new edition in the volume with *The Last Tycoon* and certain stories, beginning in 1941; and a sub-edition of the latter text in the Modern Standard Authors series (*Three Novels*) together with *Tender is the Night* and *The Last Tycoon*, beginning in 1953.[15] Though *Gatsby* in the *Three Novels* version is another impression of *The Last Tycoon* plates I call it a sub-edition because *Gatsby's* position is different, coming first in the volume, and there are many changes in the text.[16]

So far as I know, the only available information about the text of *Gatsby* is buried in the notes to Arthur Mizener's *The Far Side of Paradise*. Mizener says that Fitzgerald found a misprint in the first edition: the future Nick Carraway speaks of at the end of the novel should be "orgiastic," not "orgastic".[17]

> It was one of the few proof errors in the book [adds Mizener], perhaps because Scribner's worked harder over *Gatsby* than over Fitzgerald's earlier books, perhaps because [Ring] Lardner read the final proofs. The only other proof error Fitzgerald found was the reading of "eternal" for "external" on p. 58 [of the first edition]. ... Edmund Wilson's reprint in his edition of *The Last Tycoon* corrects all it could without access to Fitzgerald's personally corrected copy.[18]

Let us couple these comments with Matthew Bruccoli's interesting article on Fitzgerald's *This Side of Paradise*. Bruccoli is surprised that thirty-one errors are corrected in later impressions of the novel. He concludes that "the first printing was an inexcusably sloppy job," although Fitzgerald was himself in part responsible for the difficulty. We might infer two things, therefore: far fewer errors in *Gatsby's* first edition, and a correction of the world "eternal," in *The Last Tycoon*.

Not so. The correction to "external" is not made in the second impression of the first edition, nor in any impression of *Last Tycoon* (202.2, TN 38.2). Though there are only four changes from the first to second impression of the first edition, there are no less than twenty-seven changes between *First* and *Last Tycoon*. Between *First* and the 1953 *Three Novels*, there are more than 125 changes. Of these changes about fifty are quite meaningless. They change "to-morrow" with a hyphen to "tomorrow," for example. Or they change "Beale Street Blues" to *Beale Street Blues*. This class of change will not be commented upon nor included in statistics, except to add that the publisher was not at all consistent in making such alterations.[19]

There are, in other words, 75 changes of moment between the first edition and *Three Novels*—forty-four more than in *This Side of Paradise*. Many of them are more important. Of the changes the August, 1925, first edition brought, the most important was the substitution of the word "echolalia" for "chatter" in the phrase "the chatter of the garden" (*First* 60 line 16).[20]

But we must remember that *Last Tycoon* and *Three Novels* are both posthumous, and that of the twenty-seven changes from *First* to LT, twelve are clearly errors, seven are dubious improvements, and only eight are clearly better readings. Of them all, the word "orgiastic," apparently, alone has the author's authority. What's more, the sub-edition *Three Novels* retains all but two of these bad changes. An example of an error begun in LT and 132.8 of TN). The sentence of Nick's, "It just shows you," is dropped from the text, thereby making the punctuation wrong and leading the reader to confuse speakers.

Between *First* and *Three Novels* the changes are of several kinds. In addition to the fifty or so "meaningless" changes, there are (a) fifteen changes of spelling, including six that change the meaning of a word and others that affect dialect; (b) seventeen changes in punctuation, including quotation marks, paragraph indication, and so on: (c) six incorrect omissions of a word or sentence or other details: (d) six proper deletions of a word or more; (e) thirty-one substantive changes—the substitution of a word or the addition of a phrase or sentence. For instance, Gatsby is transferred from the Sixteenth to the Seventh Infantry during the war. (See *First* 57.17, LT 201.12, TN 37.12.)

For when we turn to *Three Novels* we must move out of the camp of strict bibliography into the field of its important ally, publishing history. Fitzgerald's own copy of the first impression, with pencilled notes in the margins, is now located at the Princeton University Library and was used to make the sub-edition.

Of the seventy-five changes between *First* and TN, thirty-eight are with Fitzgerald's sanction and thirty-seven are without. Most of the thirty-seven changes not recommended by Fitzgerald are "corrections" made by a publisher's staff editor or by Malcolm Cowley, who supervized the sub-edition. However, some of this group are clearly errors, many of them having crept into the text by way of the *Last Tycoon* version. The noteworthy thing is that no reader knows the authority for *any* of the changes. The sub-edition itself does not even announce that it takes into account Fitzgerald's marginal comments—which, one would have supposed, would have been good business as well as good scholarship.

Furthermore, some of the thirty-eight "sanctioned" changes were only queried by Fitzgerald: no actual rewording was directed. An example is the phrase "lyric again in." Fitzgerald questioned "again" and the editor dropped it. But in five instances of Fitzgerald's questioning a word, no change was made—as, for example, Fitzgerald expressly asked for a change that was not made. At *First*, 50.1, Fitzgerald corrected "an amusement park" to "amusement parks," but the later version does not record the request (TN 32.32).

On the whole, one can say this, therefore: that about sixty of the changes from *First* to *Three Novels* are proper. That is, they either have the author's authority or are stylistic or grammatical improvements or are immaterial. I speak just now as a devil's advocate—a critic with a jaundiced eye toward bibliography. He would call the deletion of a comma from a short compound sentence "immaterial," though it was not done by the author.[22] I am trying, in other words, to make the text sound as good as I can. Problems arise, however, from the fact that awkward readings sometimes come from purely typographical errors, sometimes from editor's decision, and sometimes from Fitzgerald's own notes. Everyone would accept such changes as "an Adam study" for "an Adam's study." (*First* 110.26, LT 233.20, TN 69.30); but by the same token few critics will be pleased by a Fitzgerald marginal correction reading "common knowledge to the turgid sub or suppressed journalism of 1902," instead of "common property of the turgid journalism of 1902" (*First* 120.11, TN 76.5).

We are left then with fifteen or sixteen errors begun or continued in *Three Novels*, errors which I trust even the newest of new critics would accept as having some degree of importance. That degree of course varies. The dedication "Once again, to Zelda," is left off, for example. Dialetical words are falsely made standard English, or half-doctored-up, as in this sentence where the word in *First* was "appendicitus": "You'd of thought she had my appendicitis out" (*First* 37.4, LT 188.37, TN 24.37). Sentences start without a capital[23] or end without a period[24] or are dropped altogether.[25] Quotation marks appear or disappear[26] and awkward readings come from nowhere. To illustrate that last: on page 149.10 of *First* Nick says that "the giant eyes of Doctor T. J. Eckleburg kept their vigil, but I perceived, after a moment, that other eyes were regarding us with peculiar intensity from less than twenty feet away." The eyes are Myrtle Wilson's but in *Three Novels* 95.1 (and LT 259.1) the sentence is confused when "the" is added without any reference and "from" and "with peculiar intensity" are dropped: "the giant eyes of Doctor T. J. Eckleburg kept their vigil, but I perceived, after a moment that *the* other eyes were regarding us less than twenty feet away" (italics added). Another dubious change is this: a joking slip or drunken mistake by Daisy is corrected—"Biloxi, Tennessee" becomes academically placed in its proper governmental locality.[27] One hardly needs to add that none of these changes have Fitzgerald's sanction.

The biggest errors, critically speaking, are ones that also occur in *Last Tycoon*. The principle of order in *The Great Gatsby* is a simple one: Nick

Carraway, the narrator, tells his story wildly out of chronological order, but *in* the order that he learned it—with one exception.[28] The first half of the book is concerned with the development of the outsiders' illusions about Jay Gatsby—he is "nephew to Von Hindenburg," and so on (TN 47). The second half is a penetration in depth of Gatsby's illusion itself. The shift in the theme of the book is marked by the one major sequence which Nick gives the reader out of the order in which he himself learned it. I refer to the Dan Cody episode from Gatsby's early days.[29]

Now the most important structural unit in the book below the chapter is the intra-chapter break signified by a white space left on the page.[30] In *Last Tycoon* and *Three Novels* four of these important indications of structure are suppressed.[31] Oddly enough, it is the one following the Dan Cody story that is the first one missing. The detail that divides the book into its two structural elements is botched.

In the *Three Novels* version of *Gatsby*, then, we have a book quite well printed—surprisingly so when we look at the galley proofs. They are filled with changes—with page after page added in long hand, with whole galleys deleted or rearranged. (I would estimate that one-fifth of the book was written after the galley stage.) And we have a book that tries to take into account the author's latest stylistic revisions. Unfortunately, it is also a book that has far too many errors.

Perhaps this is the place to mention the third Scribner edition of *Gatsby*, the paperback Student's Edition, which uses TN as copy text. Have matters been improved? Some have, but more errors have been added. There are twelve changes from TN to SE: it makes two distinct improvements, including the replacement of the dedication; but it adds three places in which intra-chapter breaks are suppressed.[32] The other changes are "immaterial" typographical errors such as "turned to be," instead of "turned to me" (SE 71.17 and TN 54.20) and "*police*," instead of "pol*ice*" (SE 27.27 and TN 22.19).

I hope it is clear, then, that *Three Novels* represents the best present text of *Gatsby*. No doubt it and the Student's Edition will be the ones most used in colleges for some time. It should also be clear that in *Three Novels*, we have this kind of book:

1. A book which nowhere gives the reader the authority for seventy-five changes, all of them posthumously printed.

2. One which fails to make use of all of Fitzgerald's corrections.

3. One which contains thirty-seven changes which Fitzgerald did not authorize—some of which are of most dubious value.

4. A book which contains at least fifteen quite bad readings, one of which is of the highest structural importance.

So, armed with this mixed blessing, or with the worse one of *Last Tycoon*, or worst of all, with a reprint by another publisher which has none of Fitzgerald's corrections and additions, many students unwittingly face the next semester with their prairie squints. Only a nonexistent, eclectic text, combining the best of the August, 1925 first edition and the *Three Novels* text of *The Great Gatsby* would be proper.[33]

Could we not as critics pay more attention to Bibliography, and we as Bibliographers to criticism? Can not we somehow insist that editing actually be done—instead of the practice of putting a fancy introduction on a poor text? Can not we have sound texts reproduced and publisher's history started by the editor? Can not we know *what it is* we have in our hands? For it is simply a fallacy that the novel does not count.

Notes

1. This article represents an expanded form of a paper read at the Bibliography Section of the 1957 Modern Language Association meetings.

2. Marvin Mudrick, "Conrad and the Terms of Modern Criticism," *Hudson Review*, VI (1954), 421.

3. Gordon N. Ray, "The Importance of Original Editions," in *Nineteenth-Century English Books*, by Gordon N. Ray, Carl Weber, and John Carter (1952), p. 22. See also "Henry James Reprints," *TLS*, Feb. 5, 1949, p. 96.

4. C. S. Evans of the editorial department of Heinemann wrote Conrad on 2 Sept., 1920, about Donkin's inconsistent dialect: "I have queried spelling of 'Hymposed,'" and so on. (See *Life and Letters* [London: Heinemann, 1927], II, 247–248, for the exchange with Evans.) J. D. Gordon in *Joseph Conrad: The Making of a Novelist* (1940), p. 139, et passim, discusses many of the revisions of the text.

It might be possible to defend the use of an early text for *The Nigger*, but no reason is given in *The Portable Conrad*.

5. Though I cannot pretend to have examined them all, I know of only one independently produced paperback novel with good textual apparatus. This is Rinehart Editions' *Lord Jim*, which contains a collation of the four main texts. Riverside's *Pride and Prejudice* has a good text, but again Chapman's edition lies behind it. There must be, I am sure, many more good texts beside *Lord Jim* in the higher class of paperbacks, and even in the cheaper ones. But what publishers draw them to our attention, and what publisher doesn't (apparently) feel that a properly edited paperback novel will frighten away the common reader by its appearance?

6. Furthermore, it would be difficult to defend the choice of first-edition text, as one might for *The Nigger of the "Narcissus,"* or *Roderick Hudson*, since James was writing in his intricate manner by 1902.

7. See J. W. Nichol, "Melville's 'Soiled Fish of the Sea,'" *AL*, XXI (1949), 338–339.

8. See John Carter, *op. cit.*, p. 53 et passim; reasons for the lack of bibliographical study are also discussed.

9. Robert C. Slack, "The Text of Hardy's *Jude the Obscure*," *N-CF*, XI (1957), 275. Italics added.

10. William T. Hutchinson, "A Definitive Edition of *Moby-Dick*," *AL*, XXV (1954), 472–478.

11. See Fredson Bowers, *Principles of Bibliographical Description* (1949), p. 356 ff, for a discussion of these reasons on the part of the bibliographer. One should admit, furthermore, that the non-professional bibliographers, the scholarly readers and editors, may have reasons which are indefensible, but are nevertheless *reasons*. I daresay one would be shocked to know how many trained men feel today that novels aren't really "literature"; or that modern printing is either perfect or too complicated ever to be fathomed.

12. F. Scott Fitzgerald, *The Last Tycoon*, in *Three Novels* (1953), p. 157. Italics added.

13. See instalments 8, 9, 10 (Chapters XII and XIII, XIV and XV, XVI and XVII). The Pip-Magwitch strand is early developed as much as can be without giving away the plot. Pip loves Estella early, but is apprenticed back to Joe by the beginning of chapter XIII. The glad tidings of Great Expectations don't come until instalment 11. Without Orlick, more than four chapters

would have to deal with domestic bliss and withdrawal. Orlick is introduced and attacks Mrs. Joe, all in the ninth instalment.

At the other end of the book a similar situation obtains. The reconciliation with Miss Havisham comes in instalment 30; that with Joe is brief enough not to be needed until after instalment 33. Estella is not brought in until the end. Instalments 31, 32, 33 are needed, therefore, to make the 36 weekly unit structure complete—but they cannot all contain the secret plan to get Magwitch down stream. The reader cannot go boating with Pip, Startop, and Herbert for two entire instalments before the diastrous attempt to get Magwitch out of the country; so instalment 32 is devoted to Orlick's attempt to kill Pip.

In other words, serial publication took Dickens to melodrama, but not quite in the crude form that one's unsubstantiated suspicions would indicate.

14. There are, it is encouraging to note, signs of change. In the last year or two, one has the feeling that perhaps six or eight articles appeared on the texts of 19th- or 20th-century novels. For example, see Linton Massey, "Notes on the Unrevised Galleys of Faulkner's *Sanctuary*," *SB*, VIII (1956), 195–208 or Matthew J. Bruccoli, "A Collation of F. Scott Fitzgerald's *This Side of Paradise*," *SB*, IX (1957), 263–265. The latter article is especially interesting, in pointing out changes between impressions of editions.

Having mentioned Dickens, I must add that Mrs. Tillotson has followed up her remark (*op. cit.*) that we have no Victorian texts, and "no means, short of doing the work ourselves, of discovering how (and why) the original edition differed from the text we read." I refer of course to John Butt and Kathleen Tillotson, *Dickens at Work* (1957); on the importance of part publication, it deals mainly with novels other than *Great Expectations*. While it also illustrates how long it takes for a general appreciation of the importance of bibliographical facts to culminate in a specific study, the book makes my comments on Dickens, so to speak, unspeakable.

15. The first edition has had three impressions: April, 1925, August, 1925, and August, 1942. I have collated three copies of the first impression, including Fitzgerald's personally corrected volume now located at Princeton. The August, 1942 impression I have not examined. I would like to record here my special thanks to Lawrence D. Stewart of Beverly Hills, California, for most kindly checking my collating against his copy of the rare second impression.

The second edition of *Gatsby* is that printed with *The Last Tycoon* and certain stories, as supervised by Edmund Wilson. It uses as copy-text the August, 1925 edition. I have collated three impressions, 1941, 1945, 1948.

The sub-edition of *Gatsby*, as printed with *Tender is the Night* and *The Last Tycoon*, in the *Three Novels* volume, has been collated in three impressions, 1953, 1956, 1957.

The parent company, Scribner's, has permitted several reprints, which I have not examined thoroughly. There is also a recent (1957), third edition of *Gatsby*, by Scribner's, a paperback, called "Student's Edition."

I shall refer to these editions of *Gatsby* by the short but obvious forms of *First*, *Last Tycoon* or LT, *Three Novels* or TN, Student's Edition or SE. For convenience I shall give the line in a page reference by a simple decimal; as TN 31.30, for *Three Novels*, p. 31, line 30. [Matthew J. Bruccoli, "A Further Note on the First Printing of *The Great Gatsby*," *SB*, XVI (1963), 244, supplements this information. *Editor's note*.]

16. My thanks are due to Princeton University Library for permitting me to examine both Fitzgerald's own copy of *Gatsby* and the surviving manuscripts. Doubtless I should add that since my special concern is the printed texts, I did not rigorously collate the mass of MS, TS, and galleys.

I would like also to thank Wallace O. Meyer of Scribner's, Harold Ober, Edmund Wilson, Malcolm Cowley, and Dan C. Piper for their advice and for patiently answering my queries about the changes in the texts.

17. The comment is a trifle misleading, because the reading "orgastic" stands in MS, galleys, and first edition. Perhaps this is another example of Fitzgerald's well-known weakness in matters of spelling, grammar, and so on; at any rate, it can hardly be called a "proof error."

18. Arthur Mizener, *The Far Side of Paradise* (1951), p. 336, n. 22. Mizener points up the generally sad fate of Fitzgerald's texts by mentioning that the reprints of The Modern Library, New Directions, Bantam (first version), and Grosset and Dunlap all have the word "orgastic." One therefore assumes they reprint the first edition, though at least the Modern Library reprints the second impression. The later Bantam edition and *The Portable Fitzgerald* both use the faulty *Last Tycoon* as copy-text.

19. See, for example, the word "to-day," in LT, p. 280 line 36 and TN, p. 116 line 36; but "to-day" (as in *First*, p. 184 lines 7 and 10) is kept three lines later—LT p. 281.1, TN p. 117.1. In addition to forty-two such changes, there are six more which are nearly as minor; the word "sombre" is changed to "somber"; "armistice"" to "Armistice," as examples. All these, and the change in the spelling of a name (Wolfshiem to Wolfsheim) which was usually but not always wrong in the first edition, are not included in my statistics.

20. See LT 203.4 and TN 39.4. The other changes in the August, 1925 *First* are as follows:
April, 1925 it's driver p. 165.16
August 1925 its driver
April some distance away p. 165.29
August some distance away.
April sick in tired p. 205.9 & 10
August sickantired
All four are, presumably, authorial.

21. See "lyric again in," *First* 62.17, LT 204.12. "lyric in," TN 40.12. Cf. "turbulent," *First* 20.17, LT 178.25, TN 14.25; "turbulence," *First* 7.28, LT 171.3, TN 7.3.

22. See *First*, 35.21: Her eyebrows had been plucked and then drawn on again at a more rakish angle, but the efforts of nature.... LT 188.7 and TN 24.7 remove the comma.

23. *First* 111.14 and LT 234.5 When I try ... TN 70.6 when I try ...

24. *First* 115.25 generating on the air. So LT 236.33. TN 72.33 generating on the air.

25. The sentence "It just shows you," mentioned above as an error begun in LT.

26. *First* 141.6, LT 253.38, TN 89.38. Tom Buchanan is speaking and by closing a paragraph with quote marks, LT and TN give the reader the momentary impression that the next sentence and paragraph beginning "Come outside ..." is by someone else.

First 139.26, LT 253.7, TN 89.7 represent the obverse. "The bles-sed pre-cious ... spoken by Daisy loses the quotation mark in LT and TN.

27. See *First* 153.8, LT 261.14, TN 97.14. TN alone reads "Biloxi, Mississippi." I realize that the line can be interpreted in other ways, that for example, Fitzgerald wished an obviously fictional town. But I cannot agree that Fitzgerald was so ignorant of Southern geography as to put the city in the wrong state. I am all the more certain that Fitzgerald meant it as a joke because there is other geographical wordplay in the same scene, and it is only four pages earlier that Tom snorts that Gatsby must have been an Oxford man—"Oxford, New Mexico."

28. The statement is not quite accurate: there are one or two other violations of this order, minor ones very late in the book. For example, the giving of the Michaelis's testimony, p. 124 of TN is apparently after the scene on pp. 119 ff.

29. The scene was, in the manuscript, at the place where it is referred to in the chapter now numbered VIII, pp. 112 of TN. Fitzgerald then changed it to its present position, ending at TN 76, LT 241, *First* 121—Chapter VI.

30. Since I have mentioned Conrad so often, it might not be amiss to add Conrad's name to the list of influences mentioned by Cowley in the introduction to *Three Novels*. (See Fitzgerald's introduction to the Modern Library *Gatsby* and *The Crack-Up* for his interest in Conrad.) The time scheme of *Gatsby* is, of course, Conradian, as well as the narrator. And there are quite a few passages that echo Conrad—the closing section on the old Dutch sailors' feelings in New York might be a twist on parts of "Heart of Darkness." "In the abortive sorrows and short-winded elations of men," p. 4 of TN's *Gatsby*, is just one of the verbal echoes of Conrad. More pertinently, the intra-chapter break was a device very much used by the older author. For a detailed examination of this relationship, see R. W. Stallman, "Conrad and *The Great Gatsby*," *TCL* I (1955), 5–12.

31. See *First* 121.26, LT 240 foot, TN 76 foot; *First* 163.26, LT 267 foot, TN 103 foot; *First* 192.16 LT 285 foot, TN 121 foot; *First* 214.21, LT 299.21, TN 135.21. In all but the last of these the break in the page comes at the turn-over of the page and, unfortunately, no space was left for it.

32. For the suppressed intra-chapter breaks, see TN 126.31 and SE 167.26; TN 132.24 and SE 175.19; TN 136.24 and SE 181.7. The other improvement is at TN 89.7 and SE 117.3, where SE returns to *First* to get the quotation marks of "The bles-sed ..." as spoken by Daisy, correctly once more. SE 175.1 does not restore Nick's sentence "It just shows you." but it does "correct" the quotation marks that were wrong in the preceding sentence in TN 132.9.

33. I should add that the collation of these three editions has of course not been reproduced

in full here—and there are several places in the text that call for emendation though there are no changes between editions. For example, Tom brings the car to a dusty spot under Wilson's sign. (So in *First* 147 and TN 93.23 and SE 123.7). Should it be a dusty stop?

82
The Great Gatsby: Style and Myth

◆

DOUGLAS TAYLOR

Few critics dispute the superbness of Scott Fitzgerald's achievement in *The Great Gatsby*. In precision of workmanship, elegance of prose style, and control of dramatic point of view, it represents to my mind Fitzgerald's genius at its sustained best. No other novel of the period, with the exception of *The Sun Also Rises*, can be said to have succeeded so perfectly in transforming the mind and manners of its time into something artistically worthy of the intense moral and social conditions which produced them. The features of the book which stand out most strongly in one's mind—the swirling, sideshow anonymity of Gatsby's Long Island parties, the huge, ominous eyes of the oculist's sign brooding perpetually over the hot, desolate "valley of ashes," the shrill, oppressive atmosphere of Myrtle Wilson's flat, the brutal, cowardly truculence of Tom Buchanan, the poignant dream and pathetic bad taste of Gatsby himself—concentrate a multiple image of an America that had lost its standards and its sense of the moral fitness of things, and had given itself over to a self-deceiving myth that would some day come apart like wet cardboard.

The book is so very good that one is tempted occasionally to go along with the assumption that some influence, other than his own moral growth, operated to aid his imagination in organizing and disciplining his thought and feeling as maturely as it did. Nevertheless, the use of a dramatic narrator to unify a series of swift and intensive scenes was a technique ideally adapted to a talent of Fitzgerald's kind, for, aside from the advantages of compositional compactness, such a method allowed his imagination to project in the form and subject of the novel a conception which enabled him to externalize and to exploit simultaneously from within and without both sides of a nature that was split between sentiment and self-criticism. Gatsby and Nick Carraway unquestionably are coextensive with his own feelings about

SOURCE *University of Kansas City Review* XX, Autumn 1953, pp. 30–37. Reprinted in *The Modern American Novel: Essays in Criticism*, ed. Max Westbrook, New York, 1966, pp. 59–76.

each side of this nature, and are developed within a context of insights which control their precise moral and creative meanings through a bifocal view that manipulates at once the attitudes of intimacy and detachment with a distinctness that is never blurred.

Fitzgerald's bifurcated relation to his experience, so eloquently underscored in *Gatsby*, has been commented upon frequently by his critics, but Malcolm Cowley has provided the perfect figure to concretize the opposition in Fitzgerald's temperament between the wish to belong and the fear of being unaccepted, between the impulse to participate and the tendency to observe, a man who desired to do and yet to become. "He cultivated a sort of double vision," wrote Mr. Cowley—

> It was as if all his novels described a big dance to which he had taken ... the prettiest girl ... and as if at the same time he stood outside the ballroom, a little Midwestern boy with his nose to the glass, wondering how much the tickets cost and who paid for the music.[1]

This sense of "double vision" informs both the general organization of *Gatsby* and the arrangement of its smallest thematic details, and, at one point very early in the narrative, Fitzgerald seems to have embedded in a casual reflection of Nick Carraway's an image which not only emphasizes this double view and represents what may be Fitzgerald's own evaluation of one of the major defects of his earlier novels, but offers a possible aesthetic justification for the novel's form as well. It is when Nick, having settled at West Egg and looking forward to the long, quiet days of summer, decides to revive a somewhat neglected habit of reading, doing so with the feeling that "... I was going to bring back all such things into my life and become again that most limited of all specialists, the 'well-rounded man.' This isn't just an epigram—*life is much more successfully looked at from a single window, after all.*"[2] Invariably, Nick's experience will demonstrate both an aspect of its nature and the bifocal continuity of the book itself, as when he pauses wistfully amidst the busy loneliness of the New York evening to watch a thick congestion of crowded taxicabs moving toward the theatre district, and notes how "Forms leaned together in the taxis as they waited, and voices sang, and there was laughter from unheard jokes, and lighted cigarettes made unintelligible circles inside. Imagining that I, too, was hurrying toward gayety and sharing their intimate excitement, I wished them well."[3] The fine control of language in this passage, with its precise use of detail that mingles several qualities of sensation in a swift interplay of mood, feeling, and idea, the tonal proportions of the colloquial rhythms of the first sentence that evoke and lengthen, through its strong liquid properties, the extent of Nick's longing for the warmth and attachment the experience suggests, the sudden withdrawal and running-away of the emotion expressed in the half-nostalgic, half-ironic "I wished them well," indicates the degree to which Fitzgerald's imagination had matured along with the sense of poetic artistry which could compress and modulate variations of action, character, and atmosphere in words that could feel through to the essential quality of a situation and reproduce its most accurate overtones. This flexible and lyrically differentiated kind of prose is duplicated on every page of the novel, and represents a very real development over the confused mixture of tonal and stylistic peccancies that cluttered his earlier writing, where his uncertainty and insufficiency of understanding tended to force him into the use of illegitimate rhetorical and incantatory devices of language in an attempt to communicate intensities of feeling inaccessible to his imagination.

In Nick Carraway, Fitzgerald conceived a figure who was to function as a center of moral and compositional activity which fused both the dramatic action and the values it implied. His character, though literally credible, can be regarded as a kind of choric voice, a man who embodies the moral conscience of his race, "... a guide, a pathfinder, an original settler,"[4] who "... wanted the world to be ... at a sort of moral attention forever,"[5] but never forgets that "... a sense of the fundamental decencies is parcelled out unequally at birth."[6] The very form and larger idea of the novel allows for this possibility, and throughout the narrative, such a relation to the action is suggested both by the nature of his detached moral involvement and by the pitch and timbre of a diction that compels one to have an instinctive faith in his point of view.

Furthermore, it is the position of Fitzgerald to bring out some of the most subtle and ironic proportions of his subject matter by juxtaposing Nick's feelings and the context from which they issue. In the scene, for example, where Daisy and Gatsby meet after five years, Fitzgerald has used the image of a defunct mantelpiece clock to symbolize the discontinuity of time their reunion implies. Gatsby, nervous and miserably uncomfortable, and leaning against the mantel, had almost knocked the clock to the floor —

> "I'm sorry about the clock," [Gatsby] said.
> My own face has now assumed a deep tropical burn. I couldn't muster up a single commonplace out of the thousand in my head.
> "It's an old clock," I told them idiotically.
> I think we all believed for a moment that it had smashed in pieces on the floor.
> "We haven't met for many years," said Daisy, her voice as matter-of-fact as it could ever be.
> "Five years next November."
> The automatic quality of Gatsby's answer set us all back at least another minute.[7]

The tonal and compositional elements of this passage develop with faultless imaginative detail a tension between inner feeling and outer statement which generates the most evocative kind of emotional and atmospheric irony: the awkward banality of the conversational surface which runs counter to the seriousnesss of the subject combines with Nick's. "It's an old clock" to carry the irony forward in the phrase "smashed in pieces," and, moving with appropriate figurativeness through the diminishing segments of the remembered time-sequence expressed in "many years" and "five years" to the audacious telescoping of Nick's "set us all back at least another minute," it functions to obliterate artistically the immensity of the moral and psychological distance which separates Gatsby's dream and Daisy's presence, and connects itself dramatically with the image of the defunct clock to complete and reinforce the unsensed irony. This running concentration both of intellect and emotion in Nick's central intelligence thus allowed Fitzgerald to control and intensify the internal and external proportions of his subject in modes which held its values in distinct but inter-animated states of sympathy and evaluation, a method which resulted in a dramatic effectiveness he had never before achieved.

II

Inasmuch as Nick Carraway's point of view represents the significant moral force of *Gatsby*, one is led inevitably to recognize the nature of Jay Gatsby's "incorruptible dream" through the continuous series of moral and emotional insights which reflect Nick's understanding of the importance of the values involved. In spite of the pathetically naïve assumptions which lie behind Gatsby's vision of life, Nick chooses ultimately to commit himself to the beliefs it fosters, because, seen against the callous, destructive charm of Daisy and Tom Buchanan's world, it becomes, to his mind, not the gaudy, unsplendid show-piece which attracts the vagrant and the vulgar, but a creative dream of intense magic and passion of purpose that flows from an innate fineness of heart and feeling. It is the worth and dignity of which the human will and imagination is capable traduced by a specious conviction, inarguably American in character, that the noblest intensities of existence are available if the objects with which they are ostensibly synonymous can be possessed. Such a conviction impels Gatsby to believe that his pink suits and period rooms will somehow secure his dream's right to reality, and to disregard tragically the qualitative points of difference between the self-conscious standards of a superimposed wealth and those ingrained in the certitudes of an aristocratic moneyed class. He assumes, with all the immaturity of his race, that living across the courtesy bay from Daisy entitles him to share the complicated dimensions of her world, but the distance which separates them is of a greater and less tangible kind than any narrow extension of water or the green dock-light toward which he yearns: there are all the years of Daisy's assurance and certainty and self-indulgent pride, a way of life that has made her ignorant of unsatisfied longings and of wishes that could not be had, a whole cynical hierarchy of things taken for granted, like her expensive home in Louisville that always hinted of "... bedrooms upstairs more beautiful and cool than other bedrooms ...," and seemed "... as casual a thing to her as [Gatsby's] tent out at camp was to him."[8] But enchanted by the amenity and charm of Daisy and her world, by the romantic possibilities for subtlety and graciousness of purpose its mystery and mobility promise, he commits the force of his idealizing imagination to the intense, allusive variousness of its life. His personal tragedy is his failure to understand the complex quality of the mind and motives which go into her fine-seeming world of wealth, for he is captivated by the delightful, exquisitely ordered surface without discerning the behind-the-doors ruthlessness, the years of infinite duplicity and subterfuge that a shrewd, self-preoccupied class has practiced to preserve the power and well-being such a surface implies. Only after the accident, when his vision starts to come to pieces like one of those toy clocks won at carnivals, and he has "... lost the old warm world, paid a high price for living too long with a single dream,"[9] does he probably sense how very different the very rich are. "They were careless people," Nick concludes of Tom and Daisy, "... they smashed up things and creatures and then retreated back into their money or their vast carelessness, or whatever it was that kept them together, and let other people clean up the mess they had made ...,"[10] and the most eloquent irony of the novel is generated by the subtle interplay between, on the one hand, the elegance and charm of Daisy's world as opposed to the cunningness of its inner corruption and, on the other, the gaudy elaborateness of Gatsby's efforts to emulate its surface as contrasted with the uncontaminated fineness of his heart.

In the frantic tenacity of Gatsby's belief that the conditions of both youth and love could be repeated if a way of life commensurate with their particular circumstances could be evolved, the whole complex tissue of Fitzgerald's feeling about time, money, and emotional innocence are developed along with the mixture of sympathy and insight his own divided temperament adopted toward these features of experience. Like Gatsby, Fitzgerald felt very strongly about the sadness and magic of the past and the remembrance of the youth and hope and feeling that had gone into its rush of individual moments, as he felt an intense fascination for the life of inherited wealth; but, unlike him, Fitzgerald, though committed imaginatively to both the charm and necessity of such sentiments, understood their value critically and creatively in relation to their total effect on human life and conduct. And in the themes of youth and wealth, two of the most brooding, compulsive images of the American mind, the one with all its overtones of romance, virtue, and emotional intactness, the other with its corresponding associations of happiness and a kind of millennial fulfillment—with the possible irony of corruption—Fitzgerald took hold of the essential qualities by which the American experience could be interpreted and expressed, and the last pages of the novel make explicit the significance of Gatsby as an avatar of a national consciousness that has committed the manifold vastness of its resources to the acquisition of "... the orgastic [*sic*] future that year by year recedes before us."[11] His story takes on the proportions of a mythic or archetypal idea: his dream becomes the tawdry, painted dream of a continent that has forfeited its will to the infinite, deceptive optimisms of film and advertising gauds which have the finality of excommunicatory edicts, while his parties, set in a world that is "... material without being real, where poor ghosts, breathing dreams like air, drifted fortuitously about. ...,"[12] crystalize into the whirling incoherence that stands for the obtrusive, unfeeling largeness of the American social experience itself.

III

In developing the implications of his theme, Fitzgerald seems to have further enriched their quality by uniting them—perhaps unconsciously—with a level of social-anagogic meaning that is at once actual and ironic in its dimensions. With frequent scriptural analogies which, though only general in outline, evoke echoes of the Last Supper, the Week of the Passion, and the Crucifixion, as well as numerous other Biblical accounts, Gatsby and the recurring symbols of the novel are given a quality of profane divineness which points ironically toward the idea of a land and people whose actual deification of its aggressive faith in its vision of life has become a formidable secular dogma. The statement that "... Jay Gatsby of West Egg, Long Island, sprang from his Platonic conception of himself," that "He was a son of God—a phrase which, if it means anything, means just that—and he must be about His Father's business, the service of a vast, vulgar, and meretricious beauty,"[13] confirms one's feeling that Fitzgerald had in mind the thought of the "self-formed" nation that has made "the American dream" a pageantry and "the success story" an ideal, a nation which is withdrawing progressively from the social, moral, and political reality that surrounds and affects its daily actions into a specious but comforting public image of itself which every popular feature of its cultural life has helped to create and is compelled to maintain. Thus, Gatsby, overtly identified with the figure of Christ, can be regarded as morally and poetically interchangeable with the spirit of a land that believes its destiny to transcend both natural and human limitations, and which, like Simon Magus (Acts 8: 9–24), the sorcerer of Samaria who bewitched the people into thinking he had the power of God, and with whom Fitzgerald seems to have crossed the Christ-image to reinforce the irony of his meaning, is convinced its wealth can buy the mystery of the Holy Ghost.

To realize this aspect of his theme and to engage it cogently with the national drama it signifies, Fitzgerald developed the general character of Gatsby's experience to correspond with that of the life and agony of Christ. From the moment he boards Dan Cody's yacht on Lake Superior until his burial and subsequent resurrection in the wonder of the "Dutch sailors' eyes,"[14] the movement of his life follows the triadic rhythm of both Christian and pre-Christian myth: purpose, passion, pain, or insight: Denying his parents, his symbolic rebirth aboard the yacht, coinciding with the phrase "His Father's business," parallels Christ's action at the Temple (Luke 2: 46–49), where he disclaims Joseph and Mary, saying "'I must be about My Father's business,'" while Gatsby's travel with Dan Cody, his almost genuflective feeling for Daisy, his blue, purposive parties that spin out like cotton-candy the fluff and faith of a "Universe of ineffable gaudiness"[15] suggest respectively, and by profane contrast, Christ's temptation of the Mountain (Luke 4: 4–8), when Satan let Him look on "all the kingdoms of the world in a moment of time," His passionate visionary love of man, and His itinerant dissemination of an incorruptible, unpretentious faith that offered another kind of mystery and achievement. Moreover, the rapid unfolding of crucial scenes which lead up to Gatsby's burial—the furtive, unquiet indefiniteness of his reunion with Daisy, the ridding of his house of partygoers, her deliberate words at the luncheon that betray their liaison to Tom,[16] the struggle, or *agon*, between the two men in the suite at the Plaza,[17] Daisy's cowardly, conspiratorial behavior following the accident, Tom's vicious report to Wilson which results in Gatsby's death, the trial, denial, and flight of Daisy, of Wolfsheim, of Klipspringer, of the multitude of hangers-on who lived gainfully on his dream's outer edges—have their sacred equivalents in the accounts of the Gospels of the Passion, the Last Supper, and the Crucifixion, which relate variously Christ's precariousness and distress in His final week of life, His purging of the Temple, Judas' apostasy and betrayal, His arrangement before the Pharisaic Sanhedrin and struggle with Caiaphas, the High Priest, His false accusers, the trial, denial, and flight of Peter and the disciples, and His execration and crucifixion by the mob. The scriptural analogy is made complete when Gatsby's father, like the titular Joseph, arrives to bury his son, and by the sudden appearance at the funeral of "Owl-Eyes," whose metonymic name points poetically to the grotesque omniscience of the oculist's sign—the novel's fantastic image of the commercialized desolation of the American spirit—and whose presence corporealizes the symbol of Gatsby's spiritual Father. (Appropriately, both men, each seeming to make tangible a side of Gatsby's antipodal nature—Gatz, his veneration of the vulgar and the ostentatious, "Owl-Eyes," his inner fineness and generous integrity of mind—are brought together at his grave to suggest dramatically the deathly release and return of substance and spirit to their beginnings.) In the final pages, Nick's reflective identification of Gatsby with the Dutch sailors and the American past can be viewed, in a sense, as a resurrection, for it evokes and gives a transient lyric body to the memory of a dead dream that lies "... somewhere back in that vast obscurity beyond the city, where the dark fields of the republic rolled on under the night"[18] reincarnating him in a past he tried so desperately to revive, and uniting its quality with the idea of a nation which persists wistfully and religiously in its belief in the inexhaustible fullness of its native possibilities.

If this hasty and somewhat superficial analogic reading of *Gatsby* is considered as a possible approach to its larger moral content, then Gatsby's death, as Christ's, can be understood as a symbolic enactment of the concept of the mythic Scapegoat-Hero but its dramatization in a context which runs against its positive religious implications of rejuvenescence and redemption turns its meaning into one of ironic nullification and defeat. Aside from the literal aspects of Gatsby's preparation for swimming and the manner of his death, the details which invest these final actions have a suggestiveness of tone that accommodates itself tenably to his ritualistic concept of piety and consecration: his bathing trunks, the finality and passivity of his movements, the appropriately autumnal season, his death on water and the slow, symbolic commingling of his blood with the pool's motion to describe within a revolving cluster of dead leaves "a thin red circle" on its surface[19] carry strong overtones of a primitive kind of sacrificial readiness for death which, combined with the immediate factor of natural infertility and decline, echo something of the old animistic response to affliction and unrest, the ceremonious mutilation of life for spiritual salvation and renewal through the reintegrative mystery of death and transfiguration. The circular unity of the image on the surface of the pool, however, confutes whatever expectancy of expiration one traditionally connects with the spirit of such a rite, for, in addition to spelling out the rounded, repetitive pattern of Gatsby's life—his withdrawal and rebirth by water, the foreshadowing of his rain-wet burial—, the image reverberates with an overwhelming connotation of nullity to negate and silence the opposed associations which call up not only the apocalyptic flow of blood and water from the pierced, dying body of Christ, but evoke as well the figure of earth with all its suggestions of efficacy and regeneration, and telescope ultimately into the reproductive symbol of the vaginal orifice. Furthermore, this affirmation of nullity is given substantial ironic reinforcement by the artistic fact which identifies Gatsby's death with the autumnal processes of decay (of which the circular image is but a compressed iteration) rather than with the fecund generative powers of spring, as was the case in both the ancient vegetation ceremonies and the greater ritual form of the Crucifixion, a calculated displacement of mythic stress which rounds off the archetypal dimensions of Fitzgerald's irony and points up its relation to a richer and more permanent context of human meaning.

As Yeats and Eliot and Joyce had seized on ancient dignities to gather flux into an "artifice of eternity," so Fitzgerald has used myth in *The Great Gatsby* in a less monumental fashion to alchemize the anarchy of modern life into a unity and permanence. Whatever one may think of the moral beliefs such a device assumes, the manipulation particularly of the novel's climax in ritual terms to dignify a tragic but otherwise commonplace homicide seems to me an extremely effective method for representing, by contrast with the vital social-religious solidarity of antiquity, the contemporary break-up, decline, and disappearance of that intense, imperative kind of spiritual awareness which unifies with its commonly-held hierarchy of values and attachments every layer of a social-cultural complex, and which combines conscience and imagination in the feelings and ideas it projects into the forms and ceremony of religious belief. It is the dramatic postulation of such an awareness which generates in proportion to the degree of its absence in modern American life the ironic moral interplay between the values associated with the symbolic quality of Gatsby's death and the actual remoteness or exclusion of these same values from the moral habits which the American national mind takes for granted. Lacking this awareness, and at best only popularly or unctuously attached to the traditional spiritual resources which nourished and deepened the indefatigable faith of atavistic America, its total national life is given over to a vulgar optimism of illimitableness and extravagance of achievement that ostensibly issues from the composite character of its national past, but to which it bears only the most spurious and distorted kind of relation. Not only does its outlook rest on premises which vitiate the spirit of historical America, but it also has come to acknowledge little more than a perfunctory connection with the moral values which gave a firmness and vitality of purpose to the visionary shapings of the continent by ancestral Americans.

Something of this ambiguous moral reciprocity between modern America and the quality of its national past is sounded throughout the novel in the reiterative "ghost" and its variant "ghostly," verbal motifs which function technically to modulate character and condition, but which, in addition to anticipating and advancing the literal plot element, serve also to strengthen the total aspect of the thematic design. Suggesting, as they do, through an ironic association with the Holy Ghost, the spiritual destination of a people who, like Dante's Trimmers on the circle outside the Acheron, are rejected both by Heaven and Hell, the motifs lead into the morally related idea of a land which has continued to rely for its identity on a myth of itself and its past until the social historical reality it reflects has neither the substance of a physical present nor the definiteness of the historical past, but drifts, as intangible and defunct as the dream it seeks to possess, between two modes of reality to neither of which it can ever rightly belong. In this last respect, Fitzgerald has brought into immediate focus a problem which is central to both the novel's theme and to human experience in general—the rich, equivocal reciprocity between two urgent and equally deceptive orders of being: the opposition between the levels of appearance and reality, between mind and activity, between what seems and what is. Does the past have an existential reality to which the novel's characters, as ghosts, do not belong; or is the past a ghost in which the characters, as people, unreally perform? Which reality is more valid from the point of view of moral and emotional experience, the subjective or objective past or present, historical America or its immediately modern counterpart? The problem in its more pandemic sense is one which Lionel Trilling has observed in another context to be the concern of all literature,[20] and in suggesting its nature with reference both to the overall development of his central theme and to the subtle inweaving of his parallels, Fitzgerald achieved a unity and completeness of artistic expression which, in range and depth of general import, gives an encompassing and enduring force to the multiplicity of American moral and social experience. In doing so, he revealed not a romantic limitation of insight, as Mr. Mizener seems to think, in committing Nick Carraway—and himself—to Gatsby's point of view,[21] but rather a discipline and sureness of mind which led him to sense somehow that Jay Gatsby was at once larger and more significant in the issues he dramatized than the literalness concentrated in his "capacity for wonder."

IV

In elucidating above what seemed to me to be the social-anagogic undertones of *Gatsby*, I have attempted to bring into relief a somewhat different set of relations inherent in its content without wishing either to dislocate too severely its superb coordination of thought and feeling or to give the impression of stretching it over a perverse procrustean bed of meaning. Neither has it been my object to claim for such a view an oracular exactness it cannot have, nor to suggest that the relations indicated were to any real extent a defined or consciously controlled part of Fitzgerald's intention. If, as is apparently the case, Fitzgerald was unaware of his theme's connections with religious myth, it does not inevitably mean that these same connections may not have functioned within the deeper ethical folds of his imagination as a quiet archetypal modifier of the known quality of his feelings about his subject.

Over and above this suggested archetypal mode of imagination, however, Fitzgerald, though probably having little more than conversational familiarity with the great anthropological works of his day, with Harrison or Frazer or Jung, assumedly would have had a very natural and fluent understanding of the Bible owing to the early religious training of his Irish-Catholic background, and it is this powerful imaginative influence, as well as the moral atmosphere of which it was a part, that can be said to have contributed largely to the formation of the quality of mind which, as Mr. Mizener has pointed out, makes his "... basic feeling for experience ... a religious one."[22] It is represented with greater dramatic force in the extended irony of *Gatsby*, but it is more or less present in everything he wrote. Thus, fixed, as they were, by an older and more conscionable view of experience, the scrupulous and religiously imbued attitudes which gave to everything he did the seriousness of a canonical imperative set Fitzgerald genuinely apart from the fashionable looseness of his day enabling him to disengage his moral, and hence, his creative, self from the reckless dissipations of an age to which his imprudent, romantic self was at the same time committed. And it is, I think, one of the unfortunate ironies of Fitzgerald's career that his life and art should be remembered synonymously with the adulteries and corruptions of the Jazz Age and Boom, when actually he was, like so many other serious writers of his generation, an ethical product of an older order, one which derived its sense of moral conduct from a firm belief in the importance of what he once described as "... 'good instincts,' honor, courtesy, and courage,"[23] those "... eternal necessary human values "[24] which were fundamentally opposed to the violent indecorums of the age he is popularly supposed to represent.

Notes

1. "Third Act and Epilogue," *New Yorker*, XXI (June 30, 1945), 54.
2. F. Scott Fitzgerald, *The Great Gatsby* (New York: Charles Scribner's Sons, 1925), p. 5. (Italics mine.) All references will be made to this edition unless otherwise indicated.
3. *Ibid.*, p. 70.
4. *Ibid.*, p. 4.
5. *Ibid.*, p. 2.
6. *Ibid.*, p. 2.
7. *Ibid.*, p. 109.
8. *Ibid.*, pp. 177–78.
9. *Ibid.*, p. 194.
10. *Ibid.*, p. 216.
11. *Ibid.*, p. 218.
12. *Ibid.*, p. 194.
13. *Ibid.*, p. 118.
14. *Ibid.*, p. 217.
15. *Ibid.*, p. 119.
16. *Ibid.*, p. 142.
17. *Ibid.*, p. 154–62.
18. *Ibid.*, p. 218.
19. *Ibid.*, pp. 193–95.
20. "Manners, Morals, and the Novel," *The Liberal Imagination* (New York: The Viking Press, 1950), p. 207.
21. *The Far Side of Paradise* (Boston: Houghton Miffin Co., 1951), p. 170.
22. *Ibid.*, p. 86.
23. *Tender Is the Night*, p. 266.
24. "Echoes of the Jazz Age," *The Crack-Up*, p. 22.

83
Gatsby and the Hole in Time

R. W. STALLMAN

1

In the meantime,
In between time—

What critical readings Fitzgerald's greatest novel has so far received amount to interpretations suggested in the main by Mr. William Troy's essay of 1945 with its offhand hints that *The Great Gatsby* is a criticism of the American dream, that Gatsby is a symbol of America itself, that Gatsby is one of the few truly mythological creations in our recent literature, and that the novel "takes on the pattern and the meaning of a Grail-romance—or of the initiation ritual on which it is based." Mr. Marius Bewley's "Scott Fitzgerald's Criticism of America" (*Sewanee Review*: Spring 1954) is the latest example. Now of course the novel is not, as Fitzgerald's biographer labels it, a tragic pastoral of the Jazz Age, but rather a criticism of the American dream. But to label it thus is but another oversimplification, as though *The Great Gatsby* means only that and nothing more. What the novel means can be discovered only by analyzing it. Mr. Bewley's reading oversimplifies it. "It is hardly too much to say that the whole being of Gatsby exists only in relation to what the green light symbolizes." Now the truth is that Gatsby exists in relation to everything in the novel, not solely in relation to the green light, and nothing is in the novel that does not exist in relation to everything else. If we explore it as an integrated whole, a new interpretation rewards our scrutiny.

A year before *The Great Gatsby* saw print, Fitzgerald's best friend had written him off as an irresponsible artist incapable of knowing what to do with the rare jewels that somehow fell into his lap. "I want to write something new," Fitzgerald told Maxwell Perkins, "—something extraordinary and

SOURCE: *Modern Fiction Studies* I, November 1955, pp. 2–16. Reprinted in *The Houses That James Built*, East Lansing, 1961, pp. 131–149.

beautiful and simple and intricately patterned." And new and extraordinary and beautiful and simple it is. But what transforms the novel into greatness is its intricately patterned idea. It is the idea of a myth-hero—the hero as a modern Icarus—who impersonates an Epoch while belonging to Space and Time. Gatsby belongs not exclusively to one epoch of American civilization but rather to all history inasmuch as all history repeats in cycle form what Gatsby represents—America itself. Gatsby transcends reality and time. His confused time-world results from the confused morality of the epoch he inhabits, "The Age of Confusion." Fitzgerald read Oswald Spengler's *The Decline of the West* the same summer he was writing *The Great Gatsby*, and the influence of Spengler's mixed perspectives of history is manifested in Fitzgerald's conception of a hero who confuses the past with the present and whose time-world is wrenched from the logic of time.

A "son of God" born out of his own "Platonic conception of himself," Gatsby goes "about His Father's business, the service of vast, vulgar, and meretricious beauty." The incredible Gatsby!—"liable at the whim of an impersonal government to be blown anywhere about the world." Smiling at Nick Carraway, Gatsby's smile metaphysically embraces "the whole eternal world." He resides only particularly at West Egg, for he exists simultaneously on two planes: the mythic or the impersonal *and* the human, the immaterial *and* the real. Through Nick, the narrator, the Inconceivable Gatsby is seen from the human point of view, but his universal genius is also viewed astronomically as it were from Cosmic Eyes Above. The province of his history extends from fabulous San Francisco (the city of his professed beginnings), eastward from the Golden Gate to the "clam-flats" of Lake Superior, the shores of Michigan, the peninsula of Long Island Sound, and down to the West Indies and the Barbary Coast; in Europe it extends similarly from one seaboard to the other: from England and France eastward to little Montenegro on the Adriatic. The incredible Gatsby has been three times around the continent, and he has lived in all the capitals of Europe like a rajah—"a turbaned 'character' leaking sawdust at every pore as he pursued a tiger through the Bois de Boulogne." Gatsby's world begins in the "Age of Confusion" and, crossing seas of antiquity, it romps ("like the mind of God") from the Jazz Age to the Age of Reason through the Restoration to the Dark Ages of the Holy Grail and, finally back to the Roman realms of Petronius wherein Gatsby as Trimalchio ends his career. It is no accident that Gatsby fears time; for Trimalchio (his prototype in Petronius' *Satyricon*) kept a trumpeter to annonce constantly how much of his lifetime was gone and ordered a broken urn to be carved with a horologe in its center "so that anyone looking to see the time must willy-nilly read my name."

The Unidentifiable "Mr. Nobody from Nowhere" drifts "coolly out of nowhere" to settle, across the bay from Daisy Buchanan, at West Egg, an unprecedented place which is "a world complete in itself ... second to nothing because it had no consciousness of being so." A feudal mansion of towers and Gothic library and Marie Antoinette music-rooms and Restoration salons, with vast expanses of trimmed lawns bordering upon prehistoric marshes! Gatsby's enormous house epitomizes the incomparable space-time dimensions of Gatsby himself, and Nick Carraway—staring at it as though it were the temple of some god—is compelled to ponder on time: "so I stared at it, like Kant at his church steeple, for half an hour."

2

Reach me a rose, honey, and pour me a last drop into that there crystal glass.

While Gatsby woos Daisy, Ewing Klipspringer pounds out on the keyboard the popular hits entitled "The Love Nest" and "Ain't We Got Fun?" The whole novel gets its time-theme summed up in the words of the latter: "In the meantime / In between time—." What is defined here is a hole in time. It is this empty in-between time that Fitzgerald renders in *The Great Gatsby*, that void of the corrupted present canceled out by the corrupted past—America's as well as Gatsby's. Gatsby has violated time in corrupting that in-between time of his life since he violated Daisy; and in violating Daisy, who represents the time-theme *as day*, Gatsby violated time. His repudiation of time-*now* is his sin of omission. "Just tell him the truth—that you never loved him and it's all wiped out forever." Here then is the whole conception of the novel, the idea of mending the clock—tampering with time. "'Can't repeat the past?' he cried incredulously. 'Why of course you can ... I'm going to fix everything just the way it was before,' he said, nodding determinedly. 'She'll see.'" What more colossal *hubris* can "a son of God" commit than to tinker with the temporal order of the universe! To fix time and reinstate thus the past in the present (as though the interim were unreckoned and life has passed unclocked), to wipe the slate clean and begin anew—*that* is Gatsby's illusion.

When Gatsby at Nick's house first encounters Daisy, he's leaning on the mantelpiece with his head resting "against the face of a defunct mantelpiece clock, and from this position his distraught eyes stared down at Daisy, who was sitting, frightened but graceful, on the edge of a stiff chair." They meet stiffly, nervously, on edge; he makes "an abortive attempt at a laugh. Luckily the clock took this moment to tilt dangerously at the pressure of his head, whereupon he turned and caught it with trembling fingers, and set it back in place." He apologizes: "I'm sorry about the clock," as though apologizing for arranging to meet Daisy again—an event which upsets the clock. "'It's an old clock,' I told them idiotically. I think we all believed for a moment that it had smashed in pieces on the floor." Their meeting sets the clock back, as it were, to that time when Gatsby possessed Daisy five years ago; Gatsby leaning against the clock and tilting it identifies himself thus with time. It's as though their five-year old clock is smashed to pieces; it's as though momentarily time thus stood still. That it is a scene of confusion is indicated also by the rain: "While the rain continued it had seemed like the murmur of their voices, rising and swelling a little now and then with gusts of emotion." Their moral confusion is hinted at by the confused clock and by the rainfall that spoils the day. There is happiness, however, when the rain stops and "twinkle-bells of sunshine" enter the room, Gatsby smiling "like a weather man, like an ecstatic patron of recurrent light," and repeating "the news to Daisy. 'What do you think of that? It's stopped raining.' 'I'm glad, Jay.' Her throat, full of aching, grieving beauty, told only of her unexpected joy." Daisy, as the sun shines, shines likewise. And Gatsby, "ecstatic patron of recurrent light," rejoices that the sun shines—Daisy shines as the sun because she is Day.

The Gatsby world is wrenched into confusion and disorder by Gatsby's two-way dream—into the past and into the future. "In the meantime / In between time"—what remains is the hole in time. As Gatsby cannot tell past from future, the present is the same for him as one or the other—*now* being for him the tomorrow he hopes to possess or the yesterday he hopes to recapture. It is his moral disruption that accounts for the disruption of time in the Gatsby world. In *The Great Gatsby* moral ambivalence correlates with the confused time-theme of the novel and has its corollary in Fitzgerald's Conradian technique of symbolism that is itself ambivalent.[1] The parallel to the divided selfhood of Gatsby is provided by the narrator, by the divided selfhood of the morally ambivalent Nick. Gatsby cannot distinguish time now from time past and future, nor right from wrong, whereas Nick is morally ambivalent not because he does not know right from wrong but rather because he is false to himself, a hypocrite. The Middle West is shown up for what it is by the person who best represents it, Nick Carraway.

So here is Nick back where he began, out in the West writing his bitter indictment of the East, a perplexed narrator writing backwards a dislocated chronology, confused and embittered by his own failure. His professed reason for leaving the West was to escape being "rumored into marriage," but the truth is he left the West because the East glitters with the future. "Instead of being the warm centre of the world, the Middle West now seemed like the ragged edge of the universe—so I decided to go East and learn the bond business." As a student of myth—"the shining secrets that only Midas and Morgan and Maecenas knew"—Nick studies how to gold-plate the future under the shining motto In Midas We Trust. Nick is the window of our viewpoint of Gatsby's romantic dream, the romantic being placed thus within a framework of cynical realism. Nick's character is determined thus by his function in the move. Fitzgerald's method is hinted at in Nick's remark that "life is much more sucessfully looked at from a single window, after all." But Fitzgerald has placed us before a very deceptive piece of glass, an almost opaque and certainly a very complicated frame of reference. The very events of that summer of Nick's initiation into Eastern life elude analysis because of Nick's deliberate omissions and ambiguities in rendering his account of it. His facts resist reduction to simple certitude. Whether Nick is engaged to the girl back in the West, for instance, or whether Nick possessed Jordan (as Gatsby possessed Daisy) are questions difficult to answer because the truth is camouflaged. That Nick did possess Jordan can only be inferred, but even Jordan's accusation is ambiguous in its inferences: "Nevertheless, *you did throw me over*.... I don't give a damn about you now, but it was a new experience for me, and I felt a little dizzy for a while."

In his affair with Jordan, Nick is (he admits) only "half in love with her." Gatsby tells Nick his life-history "at a time of confusion, when I had reached the point of believing everything and nothing about him." The ambivalence of Nick's divided selfhood arises from his fear of committing himself to life by more than halves, and consequently he is drawn simultaneously in two directions: towards the Jordan side of his nature and towards its opposite in Gatsby. In the scene at Myrtle's party (Chapter II) when Nick tries to leave the place and walk to the park he is drawn back every time he tries to escape; he is pulled in two directions. Looking out of the window, he sees himself as "within and without, simultaneously enchanted and repelled by the inexhaustible variety of life." The same contradiction characterizes his appraisal of Jordan, the Buchanans, Gatsby, and of the East and West worlds; each now repels and now attracts him.

3

"Sail to the West and the East will be found."—Commodore Perry to the Japanese Emperor.

It has been said that *The Great Gatsby* is a "kind of tragic pastoral, with the East the exemplar of urban sophistication and culture and corruption, and the West ... the exemplar of simple virtue."[2] Mr. Mizener tells us that Fitzgerald thought of the West as the exemplar of simple virtue, but what Fitzgerald presumably thought differs considerably from what he renders *in* his novel. What he wrote into his novel was a criticism of the West, as well as a criticism of the East. Not only is Western morality criticized in *The Great Gatsby*, but Fitzgerald presents not a single character to exemplify it. Every one of his Middle Westerners is dishonest. The only true exemplar of Christian morality is the insignificant Greek, Michaelis, and he is an Easterner. The moral rectitude of Nick is but the mask of hypocrisy. As for the Middle West, it is as narrow in outlook as Nick with his "provincial squeamishness," and it is hardened furthermore by its medieval-like "interminable inquisitions," which spare only the children and the very old. The East is not the sole exemplar of sophistication; for out West we get the pseudo-sophisticated and snobbish cliques of college youths matching their social registers: "Are you going to the Orays'? the Hersheys'? the Schultzes'?" Their holiday gayeties faintly echo the hollow celebrations of Gatsby. Nor is the West exempted from corruption. Gatsby's gangster business is carried on not only out East but also out West.

In the temporal sense as in the moral, the West is as dead as its Eastern analogy, the Eastern "wasteland" with its valley of ashes. Even the farmland characteristic by which the West is known transposes itself to the East with its valley of ashes: "a fantastic farm where ashes grow like wheat into ridges and hills and grotesque gardens; *where ashes take the form of houses* and chimneys and rising smoke and, finally, with a transcendent effort, of men who move dimly and already crumbling through the powdery air." In Gatsby's house, which vibrates only during his Neroesque parties, and in Nick Carraway's defunct castle Rackrent, West Egg is represented by dead houses—as though built by the ashes of that valley located half-way between New York City and West Egg, *where ashes take the form of houses.* But if West Egg represents the negation of life and East Egg, in the dynamic Buchanans and their equally dynamic house and lawn, represents the affirmation of vitality, distinctions between West and East Eggs become blurred on considering the fact that the East is inhabited by such lifeless characters as Wilson, Voltaire, Nick Carraway, and the lively Myrtle whose name, suggesting a graveyard vine, contradicts her presumed vitality. Like everything else in the novel, both eggs—West and East—are blunted at their contact end. They are defective, not complete wholes—"not perfect ovals—like the egg in the Columbus story, they are both crushed flat at the contact end—but their physical resemblance must be a source of perpetual wonder to the gulls that fly overhead." That's not only wit; it hints also at Fitzgerald's device of ambiguity in the presented point of view. These eggs, Nick tells us, are dissimilar in every particular except in shape and size; he does not define their dissimilarity. Now one difference between Nick's West Egg and Tom Buchanan's East Egg is indicated by the fact that what Tom deals in, financially, are stocks, whereas Nick of West Egg deals in bonds. Tom trades on stocks which fluctuate by the hour, and East Egg throbs with life—in the Buchanan house. West Egg, the deader egg comparatively, suggests the Middle West where the flux of time is defunct or fixed, not flowing in rain but frozen in snow. Mr. Gatz refuses to ship the body of his son back West because Gatsby "rose up to his position in the East." Nothing in the golden West is golden except the coaches of the Chicago, Milwaukee & St. Paul railway, and they are a murky yellow. Nobody goes West except Nick. And even when he is in the East, the rising sun "threw my shadow westward." The West, as in classical literature, figures as the land of the unliving, and that is what Nick retreats to.

They are all of them confused Middle-Western-Easterners, and the story that Nick narrates of his summer of Eastern life is a nine-reel Eastern-Western love story documenting the Decline of the West. "I see now that this has been a story of the West, after all..." And isn't it also a story about Nick, after all? The Nick story is inseparable from the Gatsby story, the one twining around the other to provide parallelisms to it. His matriculating at the Probity Trust is (as he says) like graduating backward into a second prep-school, and so Nick is put backward in time while simultaneously going forward—as a bond salesman dealing in futures. Nick thus provides analogy with Gatsby who, in his futuristic dream to repeat the past, is similarly drawn simultaneously forward and backward in time. Clocktime jumps back momentarily when Daisy asks him how long ago it was that they last met and Gatsby—reckoning by the future—answers: "'Five years *next* November.' The automatic quality of Gatsby's answer set us all back at least another minute." Gatsby has set back the clock five years in that imaginary minute, and it is this contingency that Gatsby recognizes when he admits to Nick that his scheme to meet Daisy again has been all "a terrible, terrible mistake." Gatsby's mind—"the pressure of his head"—almost upsets the temporal order of things when the "defunct mantelpiece clock" almost topples. He is again identified with time in the clock that mocks his romantic dream: "A universe of ineffable gaudiness spun itself out in his brain while the clock ticked on the wash-stand...." (VI). Again: "he was running down like an overwound clock." His so-called ancestral home at West Egg is a confused mélange of contradictory cultures and epochs, and his personal failure is symboliized by this "huge incoherent failure of a house"—the failure of Gatsby's own confused and incoherent life since five years ago when his dream possessed him. This "unprecedented place" represents his own quest to fix time, and Daisy is appalled by it because of its incoherence. Here the impossible has been achieved—time rearranged, history fixed. So Gatsby took over the house of a man who was as crazy as Gatsby about reinstating the past, a man who went into immediate decline when his unretarded neighbors obstructed his antiquarian program to have their cottages thatched with straw. It was like turning the clock back.

Nick presents himself on the first page of his story in the figure of a defunct archpriest in the confessional-box, a prig with holier-than-thou airs who has rejected all further "riotous excursions with privileged glimpses into the human heart." His summer excursion into the riotous heart of the East he now repudiates, now that he has failed at facing into life, and nettled by it he lumps his own failure with that of all the others, rationalizing that as Middle Westerners "we possessed some deficiency in common which made us subtly unadaptable to Eastern life." His initiation has ended with his retreat back home, a retreat back to the clean, hard, limited world of the West where life is conveniently regulated by the moral strait-jacket of the Simple Virtues. "When I came back from the East last autumn I felt that I wanted the world to be in uniform and at a sort of moral attention forever." So Nick on the rebound proposes to save the world by regimenting it, by policing it morally. That Nick is to be seen as the moral center of the book, as one critic proposes, that his character "can be regarded as a kind of choric voice, a man who embodies the moral conscience of his race," is a notion possible only to the duped reader who has been beguiled by the deceptive flow of Nick's words to take them at their face-value. At the center of the book what is there but a moral and temporal hole? Not Nick, but Time is the true moralist. Fitzgerald has contrived that first page of *The Great Gatsby* as a front to the whole book. Here is Nick as archprig all dressed up in a morally hard-boiled starched shirt of provincial squeamishness and boasted tolerance, the hypocrite! His boasted tolerance, as we come to see *through* his protective mask, is in fact intolerance, and his rugged morality but polished manners. His proposal to regiment the world amounts to a negation of faith in humanity and of faith in life itself, and it masks his own spiritual bankruptcy. No moral vision can radiate from Nick's closed heart. The moral uniform he would clothe the world in smothers the riotous heart; it denies life and challenges it at its very godhead. And that is what Gatsby, after all, incarnates—the life-giving force.

One thing betrays Nick, and that is his ragged lawn at Castle Rackrent; what his "irregular lawn" signifies is that Nick himself is not as morally regular as he pretends. He professes a detestation of anything messy or disorderly, yet his own lawn is never trimmed except when Gatsby has his gardener repair it. He detests careless people, yet he himself is careless; he detests bad drivers, yet he himself is a bad driver—a bad sport. And Gatsby, because his life is confused and disordered, has the same passion for order and restraint as Nick. When his parties get out of hand, Gatsby grows more correct as the hilarity mounts. Nick's morality amounts to the restraint of keeping up appearances; he is a stickler for the punctilios of correct form and decent conduct. Because "I wanted to leave things in order," Nick pays a courtesy call on Jordan before leaving for the West. His leaving things in order amounts to his shaking hands with her after having thrown her over, that being the decent thing to do!

As Myrtle is appropriately named to suit her special function on earth (*myrtle*—sacred to Venus among the ancients—is an evergreen shrub whose leaf yields spice), so too is Jordan Baker. For Jordan bears the name of the river that flows to the Dead Sea, a foul stream she is that runs between poisonous banks in a barren valley—used in Biblical times only for the brass foundries established there by Solomon. Hebrew writers did not sing her praises, and neither does Nick. While she shares the sun-attributes of Daisy in her "golden shoulder" and "autumn-leaf yellow of her hair," she belongs to the dying day and the season of the declining sun. "So we drove on toward death through the cooling twilight." Sterility characterizes the soulless Jordan. As they go over the dark bridge Nick remarks of Jordan that "unlike Daisy" she is "too wise ever to carry well-forgotten dreams from age to age," but in saying this Nick is also speaking for himself inasmuch as he, like Jordan, has no illusions. The past, though it lingers on in Jordan's aunt, who is "about a thousand years old," is dead and cannot be retrieved. Only Gatsby believes in the Wedding of the Dream. Though Nick disbelieves in it, he nevertheless arranges for the reunion of the lovers whom time has divorced, and thereby he involves himself, Honest Nick, in the adulterous affair and shares responsibility for its consequences.

Nick's duplicity is again evidenced in his half-romantic and half-cynical attachment to Jordan. He makes love to her *and* he criticizes her at the same time; indeed he is never more critical of Jordan than during his love-scenes with her. His portraits of her are unwittingly also portraits of himself, however. Her "bored haughty face" turns to the world "a cool, insolent smile" as to conceal something. Jordan is a dealer in subterfuge and "universal scepticism," and so too is Nick, though the true Nick is not to be readily guessed from the pretty portrait he paints for himself. The fact is that Nick is guilty of "basic insincerity", though it is Daisy he scorns for it. Jordan provides one more example. The Moral Nick resembles the "hard-boiled painting" of his uncle, who started the Carraways in the hardware business out West. Brass runs in the family blood. The Carraways pride themselves on their moral hardware, and Nick inherits a set of hardfast interior rules (they furnish him with "brakes on my desires"), which places him at a heightened advantage over others whose backgrounds are not so well-stocked with the polished fixtures of common decency: "as my father snobbishly suggested, and as I snobbishly repeat, a sense of the fundamental decencies is parcelled out unequally at birth." What brass! It's the hard-boiled Jordan who calls his bluff:

> "You said a bad driver was only safe until she met another bad driver? Well, I met another bad driver, didn't I? I mean it was careless of me to make such a wrong guess. I thought you were rather an honest, straightforward person. I thought it was your secret pride."
> "I'm thirty," I said. "I'm five years too old to lie to myself and call it honor."

Thus Honest Nick is identified with Crooked Jordan. They are both what they both profess to detest: bad drivers—irresponsible, careless, bad moral risks.

The cardinal virtue Nick professes—"I am one of the few honest people I have ever known"—has been stripped bare by this dissection of Fitzgerald's masked narrator, and seeing him in this light returns us to the novel to read it anew. His ambiguous honesty winks at the incurable dishonesty of Jordan, and also at his courting of her while he is writing the girl out West letters "once a week and signing them: 'Love, Nick.'" Also, while falling in love with Jordan he engages in vicarous flirtations with women picked out from strolling crowds and into whose lives he enters surreptitiously—affairs of his imagination which "no one would ever know or approve." Also, there is the short affair he has with a New Jersey office-girl who works in the *accounting* department of the Probity Trust!—an affair that Nick discreetly breaks off when it is discovered by the girl's brother, made known and disapproved. As for Nick's rumored engagement to the girl out West, he is anxious to write it off as merely "a vague understanding that had to be tactfully broken off before I was free" (free, that is, before making an offer of engagement to Jordan), but the affair out West is not yet broken off in August when he is still busy "trotting around with Jordan and trying to ingratiate myself with her senile aunt," and what is to be noticed is that in the same breath that he speaks of his rumored engagement as but a vague understanding he slips into admitting it as "that tangle back home." The truth is that the elusive Nick cannot bring himself to keep any commitments to life, and above all not a romantic one. It is this spiritual deficiency that incapacitates him for living life and that, in sum, accounts for his retreat from the East back to the West and "the thrilling returning trains of my youth."

4

>"The master's body!" roared the butler into the mouthpiece. "I'm sorry, madame, but we can't furnish it—it's far too hot to touch this noon!"

East is West, night is day, reality is unreality. Reality, substance without substance, is overwhelmed by dream and confounded by illusion. Nothing in the novel is not confused. Even geography is scrambled. The cagey Nick probes Gatsby as to what part of the West he comes from: "'What part of the Middle West?' I inquired casually." And Gatsby just as casually replies: "San Francisco." The confused identity of West and East is epitomized in the figure of Dan Cody as "the pioneer debauchee, who ... brought back to the Eastern seaboard the savage violence of the frontier brothel and saloon." Blurred or confused identity patterns everything in the book. McKee's over-enlarged portrait of Mrs. Wilson's dead mother hovers like an ectoplasm on the wall, looking like "a hen sitting on a blurred rock. Looked at from a distance, however, the hen resolved itself into a bonnet, and the countenance of a stout lady beamed down into the room."

Confused and divided selfhood, exemplified notably in Gatsby and Nick, has its counterpart motif in mistaken and crossed identity. Everyone's identity overlaps another's. Nick is misidentified as Gatsby, when Spangle mistakes him as Jay himself; Jordan is misidentified as Daisy by Myrtle; Wilson substitutes for Tom Buchanan as the murderer of Gatsby; and in the enigmatic book entitled "Simon Called Peter" self-identity is similarly repudiated. The unknown Gatsby, known only by his false name, confounds identity and, being mistaken for the "murderer" of Myrtle, he is murdered because of it. Crossed identities of persons have their parallel in the switched cars at the crack-up. The names of Gatsby's house-guests that Nick records on the margins of a defunct railroad-timetable furnish, as it were, a forest-preserve of crossed identities. With the clan of Black*buck* (the Blackbucks flip up their noses like goats at whosoever approaches them) Cecil Roe*buck*—figuratively speaking—crossbreeds, and Roebuck shares what Francis Bull has in common with the *Horn*beams. Edgar Beaver with cotton-white hair suggests not beaver but rabbit, by whom Endive (Clarence Endive) is devoured, as it were, and Beaver is pursued by Rot-Gut Ferret—*ferret* being a weasel. Dr. Civet, the surgeon who is to operate on a star (the *star* is Miss Baedeker, named after the official Baedeker guidebook for travellers, travellers through space) suggests relationship with Catlip, as *civet* translates into cat; and Catlip in turn suggests kinship with Katspaugh, Gatsby's gangster-friend. Chester Becker has the same surname as one of the gangsters who murdered Rosy Rosenthal and got the Hot Seat. The gangster Becker (who got the Hot Seat),[3] suggests relationship thus with a man named Bunsen, inasmuch as Bunsen was the inventor of the Original Burner! Nick describes Bunsen simply as a man he knew at Yale, but the connection that I detect here is not as fanciful as it may seem, for everything in the novel is punned upon, jokingly counterpointed or burlesqued, jazzed up—like Tostoff's "Jazz History of the World." Nick's timetable—outdated, outmoded, useless now—reflects the flaw in Nick's own time-sense: "an old timetable now, disintegrating in its folds, and headed 'This schedule in effect July 5th, 1922.'" Neither the timetable nor Nick is "in effect"—In the meantime / In between time.

Nick's timetable is infested with violence and disruption: Beaver had his nose shot off in the war, Muldroon strangled his wife, the Quinns are now divorced, Civet was drowned, Endive boxed a man named Etty, an automobile ran over Snell's right hand, and Palmetto killed himself "by jumping in front of a subway train in Times Square." Cannibalism, name devouring name, and violence link with confused identities: "Benny McClenahan arrived always with four girls. They were never quite the same ones in physical person, but they were so identical one with another than it inevitably seemed that they had been there before." In contrast are the innocent plant-life names of Lilly, Orchid, and Duckweed, and the Leeches, and bounding through the forest is Ewing Klipspringer, *klipspringer* being an antelope. Another daisy-chain of puns, this one not furnished by Nick's timetable, is formed by Gatsby's first name, Jay, in rime with the last names of the two women who betray him, Fay and Kaye. So too Goddard couples with Stoddard, the one interchangeable with the other.

"Almost any exhibition of complete self-sufficiency," as Nick remarks, "draws a stunned tribute from me." Nothing in the book has self-sufficiency, not even Gatsby. Every person, place or thing exists in partnership with its opposite or with its double. Everybody borrows attributes of another and/or connects with somebody else. Gatsby, the Buchanans, Klipspringer, and Nick's girl out West, and Jordan, the golf champion—they are all sportsmen, at cricket, tennis, or golf. They are all thus Dealers in Space.

The photographer McKee makes enlargements of things in space, Jordan jumps space by moving her golf-ball forward from a bad lie, and space is connoted by Miss Baedeker's name—the official guidebook for travelling about the globe. As Chester McKee fixes space, so Meyer Wolfsheim fixes time—he fixed the World Series! Fixing space and time provides thus analogy with the great Gatsby. Fitzgerald shows a marked predilection for doubling the identities of persons, places, and things; fashioning them by two or pairs. Gatsby has two fathers (Mr. Gatz and his Heavenly Father, Owl Eyes); his life divides into two parts; he is tricked by two women. Nick has two girls (one in the East and one in the West); Myrtle plans to go West with Tom, and her husband plans to go West with Myrtle. Like Miss This-or-That and the Three Mr. Mumbles, it is all rather confusing. There are two timetables, two eggs, two necklaces, and so on. Two shining eyes look blankly at McKee, Tom demanding "Two what?" McKee means his two photographs: "Two studies. One of them I call *Montauk Point—The Gulls*, and the other I call *Montauk Point—The Sea*." They have the same bewildering difference as, say, East and West Egg. Gatsby's medieval mansion is at once a houseboat and a roadhouse—"the World's Fair." "I'll be a man smoking two cigarettes," says Daisy. Jordan Baker manishly "wore her evening-dress, all her dresses, like sports clothes" (which are worn properly only in the daytime). All's confounded by mixed identity. Nothing is complete and whole as a thing in itself; nothing therefore is without imperfection. Nick reminds Daisy of an "absolute rose," but as Nick himself admits "I am not even faintly like a rose." There are no absolutes in the book. Everything resides in what is outside itself. Epochs and places share the same fate as persons. Juxtaposed upon Versailles, scenes of which are tapestried in Myrtle's love-couch, there is a blood-spattered scandal sheet, "Town Tattle." The great Voltaire sinks into Willie Voltaire, and by the same bathos the North and the South collapse into Mrs. Ulysses (Grant) *Swett* and Stonewall Jackson *Abrams*.

Everybody is maimed, physically or spiritually. Not one woman is without some physical imperfection, not even Daisy is beautiful. The physically maimed include Daisy's butler whose nose was injured from polishing too much silverware; the motion-picture director with his "blue nose"; the Becker who had his nose shot off during the war; and Wolfsheim with his "tragic nose"—"a flat-nosed Jew whistling the Rosary."

Unfinished business and frustrated or muddled and broken-off relationships characterize the maimed action of the entire novel. Characters and scenes are undeveloped; nearly every scene is broken off—not finished but disrupted ("to be continued"). The moralist Fitzgerald strikes out against the fragmented morality of his age by rendering his world thus confused and fragmentary. When Nick turns to Gatsby he finds that Gatsby has vanished, and midway in his speech Gatsby's elegant sentences halt unfinished; Wolfsheim fills in unspoken words by a wave of his hand; Daisy's voice breaks off; and Tom's gibberish ends on a dash. "'But science—.' He paused. The immediate contingency overtook him, pulled him from the edge of the theoretical abyss."

5

The Crack-up

That theoretical abyss from which Tom is pulled back materializes, so to speak, into an actual abyss—the elevator shaft down which McKee and Nick almost plunge. Gatsby nearly topples down a flight of stairs; Daisy "tumbled short" of Gatsby's sun-soaring dream; at Gatsby's parties the falling girls, swooning back into young men's arms, emit a falling laughter: it "spilled with prodigality, tipped out at a cheerful word." Figuratively speaking, everyone tumbles from some heightened promise of life and, literally, almost everyone hovers on the edge of any abyss ready for a fall.

In the opening scene where life seems overcharged with confusion and like glass ready to shatter, two women float along the ceiling suspended in air on an enormous couch that bounces about in space in denial of the laws of gravity, "buoyed up as though upon an anchored balloon." Jordan, the Balancing Girl, balances on the tip of her chin an invisible object which is quite ready to fall. (This scene is repeated in Chapter VII with the two women doing their aerial stunt as stiff "silver idols" unable to move, paralyzed as before but not now "p-paralyzed with happiness"). Wrecked cars and wrecked lives, fallen noses and fallen names pattern the motif of the fall of man and the fall of civilization itself. "Civilization's going to pieces.... Have you read 'The Rise of the Colored Empires' by this man Goddard?" Disorder confounds the time-world of *The Great Gatsby*, and the very earth, wrenched from its natural course, it theoretically about to fall into the sun. "I read somewhere that *the sun's getting hotter every year* ... *It seems that pretty soon the earth's going to fall into the sun—or wait a minute—it's just the opposite—the sun's getting colder every year.*" What Tom Buchanan here prophesies—the end of the world—occurs that very day; Gatsby's world goes to pieces with the disintegration of Wilson's world the day of the crack-up when Myrtle is killed by Gatsby's car.

Tom's combustion image embodies the central theme of the book, the theme of time confused and disordered. This key image of the earth-sun holocaust has three corollary themes or motifs imaged as (1) flights and falls, (2) confusion and the heat of the sun, and (3) the opposition of day *versus* night. This last I shall explore in the final section of this analysis. There is a contradiction in Tom's theory, and a like contradiction is at the heart of every character in the book. The earth is getting hotter *and* the sun is getting colder. The earth is falling into the sun *and* it is not falling into the sun—it's just the opposite. The main patterns of the book are epitomized in this key image, Tom's contradictory theory transposing into the human predicament. He himself is pulled in two directions, towards Myrtle and towards Daisy; Nick likewise is pulled in two directions, towards Jordan and towards Gatsby; the same contradiction fashions Gatsby's two-way dream, into the past and into the future. This earth-sun image reiterates the earth-sun attributes of Gatsby's fantastic car and the night-day attributes of Gatsby himself. Gatsby's month of love with Daisy ended on a cold autumn day, and since then the course of his life has veered away from the sun—away from Daisy, the sun he worships. So for Gatsby the sun *is* getting colder every year! In the middle of June Daisy has gone off on her wedding trip and Gatsby, not finding her in Louisville, departs on a hot day-coach with "the pale magic of her face" caught up in his own: "The track curved and now it was going away from the sun...."

As the second part of Tom's thermo-dynamics theory explains why it is so cold out in the Middle West, so the first part explains why it is so hot in the East. Summer heat and moods of confusion combine to create the dominant atmosphere of the entire book. No day in it (excepting the period subsequent to Gatsby's death-day) is without the warm sun. The day of the crack-up, though it is the last day of summer, is the hottest day of the year. The day of Gatsby's death witnesses a sharp change in the weather, night having altered the summer to autumn, and now we get the first cool day in the calendar of the novel. Gatsby resents change and he refuses to recognize it. He refuses to let the swimming-pool be drained, though autumn leaves already threaten it. Gatsby dreads autumn, the season of change and of the receding sun. That pool, unused all summer, represents the hole in time, the years unlived with Daisy—time unused. It is a pool of fixed time. "Anything I hate is to get my head stuck in a pool," says Miss Baedeker.

The Great Gatsby is clocked on fast time, and not only is time speeded up but also space. "It was nine o'clock—almost immediately afterward I looked at my watch and found it was ten." The fall of the earth into the sun is averted by Tom's injected "wait a minute," and that theoretical pause defines what is for him an impossibility, a contradiction of his dynamic forward nature. Gatsby, that "overwound clock," cannot wait even for Daisy: "I can't wait all day." No Wasting Time was one of his resolves when as a boy he plotted how to mend the clock to make the most of time, but his time-schedule ironically he recorded on the fly-leaf of *Hopalong Cassidy*! Time cannot stop Gatsby; he cannot be arrested, though a frantic policeman attempts to arrest him, only to apologize for not recognizing who the great Gatsby really is. "Excuse *me!*" The rushing-time flow of the narrative gets arrested only momentarily here and there, as when Myrtle peers out of her garage window and "one emotion after another crept into her face like objects in a slowly developing picture." And space (only in McKee's photographs is space fixed) leaps likewise its boundaries. "The lawn started at the beach and ran toward the front door for a quarter of a mile [as though the lawn were Tom himself as Yale football-end racing for the goal line], *jumping over sundials* and brick walls and burning gardens—finally when it reached the house drifting up the side in bright vines as though from the momentum of its run." So *fresh* is this grass that it climbs impertinently into Buchanan's house, and "just as things grow in fast movies," so the leaves burst hurriedly on the Buchanan trees. On the broiling afternoon of the crack-up the confused time witnesses a silver curve of moon hovering "already in the western sky." This breach in nature exemplifies the book's theme of the breach in time, and a parallel sign of nature's disorder is the premature moon shining in the afternoon sky at Gatsby's July party, a wafer of a moon. The sunset glows upon Buchanan's porch, but there are four prematurely lighted candles. "'Why candles?' objected Daisy, frowning. She snapped them out with her fingers." Daisy thereby identifies herself with Day, in opposition to Night. "I always watch for the longest day of the year and then miss it." She misses it because one season overlaps with another; summer, advancing before its appointed time, is already here (two weeks before June 21st). It is as though the stage props for Act II prematurely appeared for Act I.

Except for Wilson, McKee, and Catherine (Myrtle's sister), they are all dynamic, restless, confused, and "*advanced* people." They are advanced in the same sense as Buchanan's lawn. Buchanan's cocktails (as if self-propelled) bounce into the room: "just *in* from the pantry." The very clothes Tom wears suggest mobility: they are "riding clothes." Fitzgerald poses his characters leaning backward or leaning forward. Gatsby vibrates like "one of those intricate machines that register earthquakes ten thousand miles away." His heart pounds "in constant, turbulent riot," and even when dead he seems to vibrate. His shocked eyes protest to Nick: "Look here, old sport, you've got to get somebody for me [to come to his funeral].... I can't go through this alone." And Nick responds by addressing the dead Gatsby as if he were alive: "I'll get somebody for you, Gatsby. Don't worry."

Space and time—which formerly only the gods controlled—are conquered today by the tin chariots that hurl us at the rate of a century a minute towards the green light of the future. Our ailing machines pause in flight only long enough to get reconditioned—at garages to get repaired, at house-parties to get uplifted, or at drug-stores to get refueled: "You can buy anything at a drug-store nowadays." A garage is our temple of worship, our spiritual machines resting here for repair. Here to minister to our needs is the archpriest of commotion, an anonymity named George B. Wilson, and here—conferring in secret—is the priestess of power and pressure and combustion. She is the Jazz Age goddess not of fecundity but of dynamo-energy, a woman with "no facet or gleam of beauty," but of such panting vitality that she seems "as if the nerves of her body were continually smouldering." Out of the temple we race towards the green light, down the roadway which recedes year by year before us. It is Nick's birthday and also it is the last day of summer, this day of the crack-up. "I was thirty. Before me stretched the portentous, menacing road of a new decade."

Time as the roadway has its parallel symbol in time as the current: "So we beat on, boats against the current, borne back ceaselessly into the past."

Time-in-flux figures as rain, and time-fixed is symbolized by pools. Goddard's scientific idea (as Tom reports it) is that the white race is going to be "utterly submerged." Destiny by water conditions Gatsby's life from beginning to end. He meets death while floating in a pool, the swimming pool not before used all summer; Daisy he meets as he steps from a pool of rainwater, and as it rains then so it rains at his funeral. At every landing point in his incredible history of life juts upon water. Even his house belongs to the sea, in the persistent rumor that he lives not in a house but in a boat, "a boat that looked like a house and was moved secretly up and down the Long Island shore." "Blessed are the dead that the rain falls on"—*blessed* because the mess and refuse of their lives is washed away.

That Gatsby has connections of a supernatural order is evidenced by the yellow car he drives, that Chariot of the Sun. Bright with nickel and many layers of glass surrounding "a sort of green conservatory," it is "terraced with a labyrinth of wind-shields that mirrored a dozen suns." Thus it resembles the sun. But also—being green and terraced—it resembles the earth. As it is "swollen here and there in its monstrous length with triumphant hat-boxes and supper-boxes and tool-boxes," it bulges out into space. As tricky a contraption as any Daedalus ever conceived! A rolling hot-house as it were, Gatsby's car serves as the conservatory for his dream-flower—Daisy. (Its three-noted horn links it also with Daisy, for she wears a three-cornered hat.) Green, the color of its upholstery, symbolizes the future (as in the green light that flickers on the Buchanan dock across the bay from Gatsby); but green is also the symbol of excitements, desires unfulfilled, expectations or hopes. Nick can kiss Daisy providing he shows her his green passport: "present a green card. I'm giving out green—." Green and its analogous color yellow are grouped as complementary symbols, as in the long green railroad tickets and the murky yellow railroad cars in the Christmas scene out West (Chapter IX). Sick with disillusionment and shock at his discovery of Myrtle's infidelity, Wilson's face is *green* as Tom pulls up at Wilson's garage in Gatsby's *yellow* car (Chapter VII). Yellow becomes confused with green when Michaelis, confused about the color of the yellow death-car, reports it was a light green color. These symbols green and yellow have their counterpart in the duality of Gatsby's night-day and moon-sun selfhood.

6

In the morning,
In the evening,
    Ain't we got fun—

"The Rise of the Colored Empires"—the threat of black supremacy— means metaphorically the Rise of the Night. Daisy whispers her rejoinder to Tom's outcry: "We've got to beat them down," and she winks "ferociously toward the fervent sun." As here she is allied with the sun, her identity is revealed again in the scene at Myrtle's place, when Tom smashes Myrtle's nose. It is revealed that night by Myrtle's hysterical scream of "*Dai*sy! *Dai*sy! ... I'll say it whenever I want to! *Dai*sy! *Dai*—." Daisy as Day is threatened by the ever-rising Night. Gatsby dreads Night and loves Day. In darkness he prays with outstretched arms to the green light.

Night and day (darkness and sunlight) are juxtaposed in every section of the novel, almost in every episode excepting the terminal one which depicts sunless scenes of rain and snow and night; and as the novel ends in night, so it begins with night descending upon the setting sun. East and West, though Nick pretends to make discriminations, are alike in their dread of night. In the West an evening is "hurried from phase to phase toward its close, in a continually disappointed anticipation or else *in sheer nervous dread of the moment itself.*" Thus time now eludes them all, and night is denied.

Night is dispelled by Gatsby's day-in-night parties, artificial suns substituting for the real one. "The lights grow brighter as the earth lurches away from the sun"—the orchestra playing "yellow cocktail music," a hot jazz, hot enough to brighten up everbody amidst the darkness that everybody fears. The "spectroscopic gayety" of these fantastic parties burns up the gardens and keeps them aglow long after the immaterial guests have departed. With Gatsby's house lit up like the World's Fair, the whole corner of the peninsula seems on fire, but Gatsby has an insatiable hunger for light and proposes to Nick a visit to Coney Island, where also night is turned into day. Moonlight twines with revels and reveries, dreams that deny the logic of time—the clock on the washstand and the moon soaked with wet light his *tangled* clothes upon the floor." In that tangled time after Gatsby went away Daisy renounced the day, falling asleep at dawn to sleep all day in an evening-gown "*tangled* among dying orchids on the floor beside her bed." Gatsby's life, like Daisy's, had been "confused and disordered since then," and he longs to return to that starting place and *go over it all slowly* so as to recover "some idea of himself perhaps, that had gone into loving Daisy." But time since then has pounded on faster and faster until finally the clock he has raced against overtakes him. When the lights at his house fail to go on, the uncertain lights falling "unreal on the shrubbery" (like Gatsby's spectral dream), his house is winked into darkness and "as obscurely as it had begun, his career as Trimalchio was over."

Gatsby incarnates the power of dream and illusion, the recurrent cycles of youth's capacity for wonder by which new worlds have been conquered since the beginning of civilization—the dream of a conquest of space-and-time, the illusions which reality deflates, the power of youth and faith in hope. (As Fitzgerald puts it, there are the winged and the wingless.) Gatsby, winged upwards by his "heightened sensitivity to the promises of life," transcends "what foul dust floated in the wake of his dreams," and his sun-thoughts soar beyond the sun, beyond Daisy, "beyond everything. He had thrown himself into it with a creative passion, adding to it all the time, decking it out with every bright feather that drifted his way." Like Icarus, Gatsby soars against the tyranny of space-and-time by which we are imprisoned, only to be tragically destroyed by his own invention.

Day opposes night, and consequently throughout the novel white dominates its opposite. The futuristic green light that Gatsby prays to promises the day—Daisy. When Gatsby first knew her she drove a white roadster and wore a white dress; in the opening scene of the book she and Jordan wore white dresses; both Gatsby and Nick wear white flannels; Buchanan's red and white mansion stands amidst the white palaces of fashionable East Egg; Nick's books on banking shine in red and gold over the "white chasms of Wall Street." Out in the Middle West everything is white. Here in their homeland night is camouflaged by Christmas lights and holiday gayeties, bright snow contradicting the darkness. Nick's Middle West is represented as a long frosty dark-winter, whitened not by the sun (Daisy is out East!) but rather by the snow that keeps time frozen in.

That wintry night-world of the West—Nick's West differs from Gatsby's—is what Nick retreats to after his experience of life out East, and what he retreats from is that El Greco night-world of the East. The night-vignette Nick paints of the East as a drunken woman carried on a stretcher is an image symbolic not only of the East but also of the West, for it signifies the plight of all these Middle Western Easterners (or Eastern Middle Westerners): their isolation, their loneliness, their anonymity. Four nameles men carry the nameless woman, her hand dangling over the stretcher and sparkling "cold with jewels." Gravely the men turn in at a house—the wrong house. "But no one knows the woman's name, and no one cares." Everyone's identity overlaps with another's because everyone is without identity, isolated and anonymous and alone. "I found myself," says Nick at the end, "on Gatsby's side, and alone."[4] Gatsby's loneliness is proverbial, and Nick diagnoses what ails everyone in his confessing to that "haunting loneliness" he feels in himself and in others.

On Nick's last night in the East the moonlight discloses an obscene word some boy has chalked on the white steps of Gatsby's house, and Nick erases it. Nick performs the same service for the romantic Gatsby as the youth in *Madame Bovary* performs for that self-deluded romanticist, Emma Bovary, over whose grave a young boy kneels as in a ritual of dedication.

Notes

1. The influence of Conrad on Fitzgerald and Hemingway is spelled out in "Conrad and *The Great Gatsby*," and in the essays on *Tender Is the Night*, and *The Sun Also Rises*.

2. Arthur Mizener in *F. Scott Fitzgerald: The Man and His Work*, edited by Alfred Kazin (1951), p. 36. My reading challenges Nick Carraway's moral seriousness, his integrity. "With R. W. Stallman, W. S. Frohock finds Nick 'short on moral perspective' and Fitzgerald's style

catching the 'feeling of things' but combined with 'a romantic inability to interpret them.'" Thomas A. Hanzo in *Modern Fiction Studies*, II (Winter 1956–1957). Hanzo defends Mizener's reading. Frohock's essay, "Morals, Manners and Scott Fitzgerald," appeared in *Southwest Review*, XL (Summer 1955).

In "Scott Fitzgerald's Fable of East and West" (*College English*: December 1956), Robert Ornstein stands essentially in agreement with my interpretation (1955). He writes: "But how is one to accept, even in fable a West characterized by the dull rectitude of Minnesota villages and an East epitomized by the sophisticated dissipation of Long Island society? The answer is perhaps that Fitzgerald's dichotomy of East and West has the poetic truth of [Henry] James's antithesis of provincial American virtue and refined European-sensibility. Like *The Portrait of a Lady* and *The Ambassadors*, *Gatsby* is a short story of 'displaced persons' who have journeyed eastward in search of a larger experience of life. To James this reverse migration from the New to the Old World has in itself no special significance. To Fitzgerald, however, the lure of the East represents a profound displacement of the American dream, a turning back upon itself of the historic pilgrimage towards the frontier which had, in fact, created and sustained that dream."

3. Not before noticed is the fact that the reference here to the Becker who got the Hot Seat is Detective Charles Becker of the New York City Police Force at the time when Theodore Roosevelt was Commissioner of Police. Detevive Becker threatened to arrest Stephen Crane when Crane protested the innocence of Miss Dora Clark, arrested for street-walking. Brought into court on the charge of soliciting, she was released on the testimony of Crane: "Stephen Crane as Brave as his Hero Showed the 'Badge of Courage' in a New York Police Court"—so ran the headline in the New York *Journal* for September 17, 1896.

It is Fitzgerald's "Becker" who as Lieutenant Becker was indicted in 1912 for the murder of Herman Rosenthal, Rosenthal having been murdered in reprisal for squealing on police and gambling-house graft. Convicted twice for this murder (1912), he lost his final appeal to the higher courts and went to the electric chair in 1915. Becker was the first New York City policeman to be sentenced to death. The Becker-Rosenthal case—prolonged and sensational—swept the nation and brought about investigations into police department corruptions throughout the country.

4. Arguing that the novel can be known as an organic whole only from a perspective of its Form, Norman Friedman claims that *The Great Gatsby* has as its end "the achievement of some sort of change in the protagonist's fortune, his state of mind, or his moral character ..." (in *Accent*: Autumn 1954). He claims that Gatsby makes a "tragic self-discovery—'he must have felt that he had lost the old warm world, paid a high price for living too long with a single dream.' ..." Perhaps Gatsby did, but there is no proof of his disillusionment. What Friedman ignores is that Gatsby's so-called disillusionment is rendered from Nick's point-of-view. Nick's words cannot be taken at their face value. Friedman has lopped off Nick's expressed point-of-view. The passage he quotes begins in fact with Nick's admitted bias: "*I have an idea* that Gatsby himself didn't believe it would come [the telephone message from Daisy], and per*haps* he no longer cared. *If that was true* he must have felt that he had lost the old warm world, paid a high price for living too long with a dream." [Italics mine] It is rather Nick who is disillusioned by his experience in the East, not Gatsby.

In trying to mould the novel to a Fixed Idea of Form, Friedman misreads the substance of the hero's plight. His notion that Gatsby undergoes a change effected by the Climax of the Plot ("the disillusionment of Gatsby's faith in his ideal—a change in his state of mind") is contradicted by Gatsby's final words to Nick and his final words to the butler. To Nick he says, "I suppose Daisy'll call too," and to the butler his final words are to bring him notice if anyone telephones while he is at the swimming-pool. Nick had urged him to escape:

> "Go away *now*, old sport?"
> "Go to Atlantic City for a week, or up to Montreal."
> He wouldn't consider it. He couldn't possibly leave Daisy until he knew what she was going to do. *He was clutching at some last hope* [italics mine] and I couldn't bear to shake him free (ch. VIII).

If shaken in his faith, Gatsby nevertheless remains hopeful to the last breath. Although he dies on a Tuesday, he dies at three o'clock; although he is not exactly a Christ figure, Gatsby—a "son of God"—was waiting for a message.

Our Aristotelian critic opines that Fitzgerald's problem "was to effect a final recognition of the utter valuelessness of his ideal *in the mind of Gatsby....*" But "in the mind of Gatsby" we never get, and even from Nick's point-of-view Gatsby as Ideal remains not devoid of merit. Not even Daisy's treachery destroys Gatsby's faith—the damned fool clings to the Dream to the very end. No, he was not disillusioned. Gatsby exemplifies an ideal and remains faithful to the dream, and that is why Nick in admiration exempts him from his general condemnation.

84
Scott Fitzgerald's Fable of East and West

◆

ROBERT ORNSTEIN

> He felt then that if the pilgrimage eastward of the rare poisonous flower of his race was the end of the adventure which had started westward three hundred years ago, if the long serpent of the curiosity had turned too sharp upon itself, cramping its bowels, bursting its shining skin, at least there had been a journey; like to the satisfaction of a man coming to die—one of those human things that one can never understand unless one has made such a journey and heard the man give thanks with the husbanded breath. The frontiers were gone—there were no more barbarians. The short gallop of the last great race, the polyglot, the hated and the despised, the crass and scorned, had gone—at least it was not a meaningless extinction up an alley. (*The Crack-Up*, p. 199)

After a brief revival, the novels of Scott Fitzgerald seem destined again for obscurity, labeled this time, by their most recent critics, as darkly pessimistic studies of America's spiritual and ideological failures. *The Great Gatsby*, we are now told, is not simply a chronicle of the Jazz Age but rather a dramatization of the betrayal of the naive American dream in a corrupt society.[1] I would agree that in *Gatsby* Fitzgerald did create a myth with the imaginative sweep of America's historical adventure across an untamed continent. But his fable of East and West is little concerned with twentieth century materialism and moral anarchy, for its theme is the unending quest of the romantic dream, which is forever betrayed in fact and yet redeemed in men's minds.

From the start, Fitzgerald's personal dreams of romance contained the seeds of their own destruction. In his earliest works, his optimistic sense of the value of experience is overshadowed by a personal intuition of tragedy; his capacity for naive wonder is chastened by satiric and ironic insights which make surrender to the romantic impulse incomplete. Though able to idealize the sensuous excitement of an exclusive party or a lovely face, Fitzgerald could not ignore the speciosity inherent in the romantic stimuli of his social world—in the unhurried gracious poise that money can buy.

SOURCE *College English* XVIII, December 1956, pp. 139–143. Reprinted in *F. Scott Fitzgerald: A Collection of Criticism*, ed. Kenneth E. Eble, New York, 1973, pp. 60–66.

Invariably he studied what fascinated him so acutely that he could give at times a clinical report on the very rich, whose world seemed to hold the promise of a life devoid of the vulgar and commonplace. A literalist of his own imagination (and therefore incapable of self-deception), he peopled extravagant phantasy with superbly real "denizens of Broadway." The result in the earlier novels is not so much an uncertainty of tone as a curious alternation of satiric and romantic moments—a breathless adoration of flapper heroines whose passionate kisses are tinged with frigidity and whose daring freedom masks an adolescent desire for the reputation rather than the reality of experience.

The haunting tone of *Gatsby* is more than a skilful fusion of Fitzgerald's satiric and romantic contrarieties. Nick Carraway, simultaneously enchanted and repelled by the variety of life, attains Fitzgerald's mature realization that the protective enchantment of the romantic ideal lies in its remoteness from actuality. He knows the fascination of yellow windows high above the city streets even as he looks down from Myrtle Wilson's gaudy, smoke-filled apartment. He still remembers the initial wonder of Gatsby's parties long after he is sickened by familiarity with Gatsby's uninvited guests. In one summer Nick discovers a profoundly melancholy aesthetic truth: that romance belongs not to the present but to a past transfigured by imagined memory and to the illusory promise of an unrealizable future. Gatsby, less wise than Nick, destroys himself in an attempt to seize the green light in his own fingers.

At the same time that Fitzgerald perceived the melancholy nature of romantic illusion, his attitude towards the very rich crystalized. In *Gatsby* we see that the charming irresponsibility of the flapper has developed into the criminal amorality of Daisy Buchanan, and that the smug conceit of the Rich Boy has hardened into Tom Buchanan's arrogant cruelty. We know in retrospect that Anthony Patch's tragedy was not his "poverty," but his possession of the weakness and purposelessness of the very rich without their protective armor of wealth.

The thirst for money is a crucial motive in *Gatsby* as in Fitzgerald's other novels, and yet none of his major characters are materialists, for money is never their final goal. The rich are too accustomed to money to covet it. It is simply the badge of their "superiority" and the justification of their consuming snobberies. For those who are not very rich—for the Myrtle Wilsons as well as the Jay Gatsbys—it is the alchemic reagent that transmutes the ordinary worthlessness of life. Money is the demiurgos of Jimmy Gatz's Platonic universe, and the proof, in "Babylon Revisited," of the unreality of reality ("... the snow of twenty-nine wasn't real snow. If you didn't want it to be snow, you just paid some money"). Even before *Gatsby*, in "The Rich Boy," Fitzgerald had defined the original sin of the very rich: They do not worship material gods, but they "possess and enjoy early, and it does something to them, makes them soft where we are hard, and cynical where we are trustful...." surrounded from childhood by the artificial security of wealth, accustomed to owning rather than wanting, they lack anxiety or illusion, frustration or fulfillment. Their romantic dreams are rooted in the adolescence from which they never completely escape—in the excitement of the prom or petting party, the reputation of being fast on the college gridiron or the college weekend.

Inevitably, then, Fitzgerald saw his romantic dream threaded by a double irony. Those who possess the necessary means lack the will, motive, or capacity to pursue a dream. Those with the heightened sensitivity to the promises of life have it because they are the disinherited, forever barred from the white palace where "the king's daughter, the golden girl" awaits "safe and proud above the struggles of the poor." Amory Blaine loses his girl writing advertising copy at ninety a month. Anthony Patch loses his mind after an abortive attempt to recoup his fortune peddling bonds. Jay Gatsby loses his life even though he makes his millions because they are not the kind of safe, respectable money that echoes in Daisy's lovely voice. The successful entrepreneurs of Gatsby's age are the panderers to vulgar tastes, the high pressure salesmen, and, of course, the bootleggers. Yet once, Fitzgerald suggests, there had been opportunity commensurate with aspiration, an unexplored and unexploited frontier where great fortunes had been made or at least romantically stolen. And out of the shifting of opportunities from the West to Wall Street, he creates an American fable which redeems as well as explains romantic failure.

But how is one to accept, even in fable, a West characterized by the dull rectitude of Minnesota villages and an East epitomized by the sophisticated dissipation of Long Island society? The answer is perhaps that Fitzgerald's dichotomy of East and West has the poetic truth of James's antithesis of provincial American virtue and refined European sensibility. Like *The Portrait of a Lady* and *The Ambassadors*, *Gatsby* is a story of "displaced persons" who have journeyed eastward in search of a larger experience of life. To James this reverse migration from the New to the Old World has in itself no special significance. To Fitzgerald, however, the lure of the East represents a profound displacement of the American dream, a turning back upon itself of the historic pilgrimage towards the frontier which had, in fact, created and sustained that dream. In *Gatsby* the once limitless western horizon is circumscribed by the "bored, sprawling, swollen towns beyond the Ohio, with their interminable inquisitions which spared only the children and the very old." The virgin territories of the frontiersman have been appropriated by the immigrant families, the diligent Swedes—the unimaginative, impoverished German farmers like Henry Gatz. Thus after a restless nomadic existence, the Buchanans settle "permanently" on Long Island because Tom would be "a God damned fool to live anywhere else." Thus Nick comes to New York with a dozen volumes on finance which promise "to unfold the shining secrets that only Midas, Morgan and Maecenas knew." Gatsby's green light, of course, shines in only one direction—from the East across the Continent to Minnesota, from the East across the bay to his imitation mansion in West Egg.

Lying in the moonlight on Gatsby's deserted beach, Nick realizes at the close just how lost a pilgrimage Gatsby's had been:

> ...I became aware of the old island here that had flowered once for Dutch sailors' eyes—a fresh, green breast of the new world. Its vanished trees, the trees that had made way for Gatsby's house, had once pandered in whispers to the last and greatest of all human dreams; for a transitory moment man must have held his breath in the presence of this continent, compelled into an aesthetic contemplation he neither understood nor desired, face to face for the last time in history with something commensurate to his capacity for wonder.

Gatsby is the spiritual descendant of these Dutch sailors. Like them, he set out for gold and stumbled on a dream. But he journeys in the wrong direction in time as well as space. The transitory enchanted moment has come and gone for him and for the others, making the romantic promise of the future an illusory reflection of the past. Nick still carries with him a restlessness born of the war's excitement; Daisy silently mourns the romantic adventure of her "white" girlhood; Tom seeks the thrill of a vanished football game. Gatsby devotes his life to recapturing a love lost five years before. When the present offers nothing commensurate with man's capacity for wonder, the romantic credo is the belief—Gatsby's belief—in the ability to repeat the disembodied past. Each step towards the green light, however, shadows some part of Gatsby's grandiose achievement. With Daisy's disapproval the spectroscopic parties cease. To preserve her reputation Gatsby empties his mansion of lights and servants. And finally only darkness and ghostly memories tenant the deserted house as Gatsby relives his romantic past for Nick after the accident.

Like his romantic dream Jay Gatsby belongs to a vanished past. His career began when he met Dan Cody, a debauched relic of an earlier America who made his millions in the copper strikes. From Cody he received an education in ruthlessness which he applied when the accident of the war brought him to the beautiful house of Daisy Fay. In the tradition of Cody's frontier, he "took what he could get, ravenously and unscrupulously," but in taking Daisy he fell in love with her. "She vanished into her rich house, into her rich full life, leaving Gatsby—nothing. He felt married to her, that was all."

"He felt married to her"—here is the reaction of bourgeois conscience, not of calculating ambition. But then Gatsby is not really Cody's protégé. Jimmy Gatz inherited an attenuated version of the American dream of success, a more moral and genteel dream suited to a nation arriving at the respectability of established wealth and class. Respectability demands that avarice be masked with virtue, that personal aggrandisement pose as self-improvement. Success is no longer to the cutthroat or the ruthless but to the diligent and the industrious, to the boy who scribbles naive resolves on the flyleaf of *Hopalong Cassidy*. Fabricated of pulp fiction clichés (the impoverished materials of an extraordinary imagination), Gatsby's dream of self-improvement blossoms into a preposterous tale of ancestral wealth and culture. And his dream is incorruptible because his great enterprise is not side-street "drugstores," or stolen bonds, but himself, his fictional past, his mansion and his gaudy entertainments. Through it all he moves alone and untouched; he is the impresario, the creator, not the enjoyer of a riotous venture dedicated to an impossible goal.

It may seem ironic that Gatsby's dream of self-improvement is realized through partnership with Meyer Wolfsheim, but Wolfsheim is merely the post-war successor to Dan Cody and to the ruthlessness and greed that once exploited a virgin West. He is the fabulous manipulator of bootleg gin rather than of copper, the modern man of legendary accomplishment "who fixed the World's Series back in 1919." The racketeer, Fitzgerald suggests, is the last great folk hero, the Paul Bunyan of an age in which romantic wonder surrounds underworld "gonnegtions" instead of raw courage or physical strength. And actually Gatsby is destroyed not by Wolfsheim, or association with him, but by the provincial squeamishness which makes all the Westerners in the novel unadaptable to life in the East.

Despite her facile cynicism and claim to sophistication, Daisy is still the "nice" girl who grew up in Louisville in a beautiful house with a wicker settee on the porch. She remains "spotless," still immaculately dressed in white and capable of a hundred whimsical, vaporous enthusiasms. She has assimilated the urbane ethic of the East which allows a bored wife a casual discreet affair. But she cannot, like Gatsby's uninvited guests, wink at the illegal and the criminal. When Tom begins to unfold the sordid details of Gatsby's career, she shrinks away; she never intended to leave her husband, but now even an affair is impossible. Tom's provinciality is more boorish than genteel. He has assumed the role of Long Island country gentleman who keeps a mistress in a midtown apartment. But with Myrtle Wilson by his side he turns the role into a ludicrous travesty. By nature a libertine, by upbringing a prig, Tom shatters Gatsby's façade in order to preserve his "gentleman's" conception of womanly virtue and of the sanctity of his marriage.

Ultimately, however, Gatsby is the victim of his own small-town notions of virtue and chivalry. "He would never so much as look at a friend's wife"—or at least he would never try to steal her in her husband's house. He wants Daisy to say that she never loved Tom because only in this way can the sacrament of Gatsby's "marriage" to her in Louisville—his prior claim—be recognized. Not content merely to repeat the past, he must also eradicate the years in which his dream lost its reality. But the dream, like the vanished frontier which it almost comes to represent, is lost forever "somewhere back in that vast obscurity beyond the city, where the dark field of the republic rolled on under the night."

After Gatsby's death Nick prepares to return to his Minnesota home, a place of warmth and enduring stability, carrying with him a surrealistic night vision of the debauchery of the East. Yet his return is not a positive rediscovery of the well-springs of American life. Instead it seems a melancholy retreat from the ruined promise of the East, from the empty present to the childhood memory of the past. Indeed, it is this childhood memory, not the reality of the West which Nick cherishes. For he still thinks the East, despite its nightmarish aspect, superior to the stultifying small-town dullness from which he fled. And by the close of *Gatsby* it is unmistakably clear that the East does not symbolize contemporary decadence and the West the pristine virtues of an earlier America. Fitzgerald does not contrast Gatsby's criminality with his father's unspoiled rustic strength and dignity. He contrasts rather Henry Gatz's dull, grey, almost insentient existence, "a meaningless extinction up an alley," with Gatsby's pilgrimage Eastward, which, though hopeless and corrupting, was at least a journey of life and hope—an escape from the "vast obscurity" of the West that once spawned and then swallowed the American dream. Into this vast obscurity the Buchanans finally disappear. They are not Westerners any longer, or Easterners, but merely two of the very rich, who in the end represent nothing but themselves. They are careless people, Tom and Daisy, selfish, destructive, capable of anything except human sympathy, and yet not sophisticated enough to be really decadent. Their irresponsibility, Nick realizes, is that of pampered children, who smash up "things and creatures ... and let other people clean up the mess." They live in the eternal moral adolescence which only wealth can produce and protect.

By ignoring its context one can perhaps make much of Nick's indictment of the Buchanans. One can even say that in *The Great Gatsby* Fitzgerald adumbrated the coming tragedy of a nation grown decadent without achieving maturity—a nation that possessed and enjoyed early, and in its arrogant assumption of superiority lost sight of the dream that had created it. But is it not absurd to interpret Gatsby as a mythic Spenglerian anti-hero? Gatsby *is* great, because his dream, however naive, gaudy, and unattainable is one of the grand illusions of the race which keep men from becoming too old or too wise or too cynical of their human limitations. Scott Fitzgerald's fable of East and West does not lament the decline of American civilization. It mourns the eternal lateness of the present hour suspended between the past of romantic memory and the future of romantic promise which ever recedes before us.

Note

1. See Edwin Fussell, "Fitzgerald's Brave New World," *ELH*, XIX (Dec. 1952), 291–306; Marius Bewley, "Scott Fitzgerald's Criticism of America," *SR*, LXII (Spring 1954), 223–246; John W. Bicknell, "The Wasteland of F. Scott Fitzgerald," *VQR*, XXX (Autumn 1954). A somewhat different but equally negative interpretation is R. W. Stallman's "Gatsby and the Hole in Time," *MFS*, I (Nov. 1955), 1–15.

85
Theme and Texture in *The Great Gatsby*

♦

W.J. HARVEY

Criticism of *The Great Gatsby*, when it has not been sidetracked into biography or reminiscence of the Jazz Age, has tended to concentrate on two issues. The first of these has been concerned with the moral seriousness of the book, with what answer, if any, can be given to the hostile critic of whom John Farelly, writing in *Scrutiny*, is a good example:

> I want to suggest that there is an emptiness in his work that makes 'convincing analysis' honestly difficult, but leaves a hollow space where critics can create their own substitute Fitzgerald. And I should probe for that hollow space in what we call the *centre* of a writer's work—that around which and with reference to which he organizes his experiences; in short, his values.[1]

Closely related to this is the problem of what status we should allow Gatsby himself; in particular, we may note the attempt to see him as a mythic character and the novel as the expression of some deep-rooted and recurrent 'American Dream'.[2]

The first of these questions has been exhaustively debated and if neither side has much shaken the other's conviction, the issues are at least clearly defined; while anyone who is not an American will feel a natural diffidence about expressing any opinion on the second topic. In fact, what immediately impresses itself upon most readers—especially if they have come to *The Great Gatsby* after reading Fitzgerald's earlier novels—is not moral theme or national archetype but something much simpler, something so obvious, perhaps, that it has received remarkably little close critical skill. I mean the astonishing accession of technical power and critical attention. Less pretentious than his earlier work, *The Great Gatsby* achieves much more; in it Fitzgerald discovers not only his true subject but a completely adequate form. To say this, no doubt, is to say also that he has attained a maturity that transcends the merely aesthetic, that reveals itself also in the moral implications of the fable.

SOURCE *English Studies* XXXVIII, February 1957, pp. 12–20.

Nearly every critic of *The Great Gatsby* has stressed the tremendous structural importance of the narrator, Nick Carraway, the character through whom Fitzgerald is able to achieve that aesthetic distance from his own experience necessary for firmness of control and clarity of perception, through whom he can express that delicately poised ambiguity of moral vision, the sense of being 'within and without, simultaneously enchanted and repelled by the inexhaustible variety of life' out of which insight into the truth of things must grow. William Troy has summed it up neatly and concisely:

> In the earlier books author and hero tended to melt into one another because there was no internal principle of differentiation by which they might be separated; they respired in the same climate, emotional and moral; they were tarred with the same brush. But in *Gatsby* is achieved a dissociation, by which Fitzgerald was able to isolate one part of himself, the spectatorial or esthetic, and also the more intelligent and responsible, in the person of the ordinary but quite sensible narrator, from another part of himself, the dream-ridden romantic adolescent from St. Paul and Princeton, in the person of the legendary Jay Gatsby.[3]

Again, most critics of the novel have amply demonstrated its economy, the clarity of its narrative outline and the forceful, unbroken drive of it forward from the first page to the last, an impetus which incorporates, and even gains momentum from, the cunningly interpolated flashbacks. Many critics have expanded and expounded the significance of the major symbolic structures of the book; indeed, to insist upon its legendary nature is to insist upon these. What more, then, can be said about the mastery of Fitzgerald's technique; what aspect of it has received less than its fair share of attention?

I should like, quite simply, to discuss the language of the book. Here we find, co-existing with economy, clarity and force, an extreme density of texture. It is this which ultimately gives richness and depth to the novel, this without which the larger symbols would lose their power of reverberating in the reader's mind and the major themes of the book would seem intellectual or emotional gestures, without the pressure of felt and imaginatively experienced life behind them.

We may best begin with a fairly detailed analysis of one passage; my aim here will be to show that textural detail is not merely local in its point and effect but relates to the central themes and dominant moral attitudes expressed in the book. Analysis of prose is always liable to be cumbrous and clumsy but this very clumsiness is an oblique tribute to the dexterity and economy with which Fitzgerald achieves his effects. I take as my example a passage dealing with the end of the first of Gatsby's parties to be described in the book. The glamour and enchantment of the party, so brilliantly evoked by Fitzgerald, has here dissolved; the intoxication of night and music, champagne and youth, has vanished and the scene is closed by a dismal return to the world of sober reality, or more precisely, to the disenchanted world of the hangover. The party is over; it is time to go home. Here is the passage:

I looked around. *Most of the remaining women were now having fights with men said to be their husbands.* (1) Even Jordan's party, the quartet from East Egg, were rent asunder by dissension. *One of the men was talking with curious intensity to a young actress,* (2) and his wife, after attempting to laugh at the situation in a dignified and indifferent way, broke down entirely and resorted to flank attacks—at intervals she appeared suddenly at his side like an angry diamond, and hissed 'You promised!' into his ear.

The reluctance to go home was not confined to wayward men. *The hall was at present occupied by two deplorably sober men and their highly indignant wives.* (3) The wives were sympathizing with each other in slightly raised voices.

'Whenever he sees I'm having a good time he wants to go home.'

'Never heard anything so selfish in my life.'

'We're always the first ones to leave.'

'So are we.'

'Well, we're almost the last tonight,' said one of the men sheepishly. 'The orchestra left half an hour ago.'

In spite of the wives' agreement that such malevolence was beyond credibility, the dispute ended in a short struggle, and both wives were lifted, kicking, into the night. (4)

At first we might seem to be concerned with a piece of merely slick, glossy writing; the simile, *like an angry diamond*, is perhaps a little too smart, a little too consciously clever and contrived; it trembles on the verge of preciosity. But leaving this aside, we may see how most of the main themes are touched on tangentially in what appear to be superficial and cynical comments. I wish to concentrate on the four short passages I have, for convenient reference, italicized and numbered.

(1) This sentence, apart from the obvious implication about the sexual morality of such a society, relates as well to the rootlessness and transience of these people, the lack of any stable relationship—a point I shall discuss later. It is also one strand in the complex network of gossip, rumour and innuendo which fills the whole book.

(2) Here, the intensity is in one sense anything but curious; the relationship implied is obvious; but in another sense the intensity *is* curious in that this is a society which is flippant and cynical, gay and hedonistic, but definitely not intense in its feeling for anyone or anything; as such, it contrasts with the real intensity of the outsider who is its host, with the passion of Gatsby's dream of Daisy.

(3) Here Fitzgerald is employing a common satirical device; he is enforcing his morality by pretending to accept its opposite as the norm—sobriety becomes deplorable. Further, however, the syntactical balance of the sentence leads us to infer a causal relationship between the balanced parts—the wives are indignant because the men are sober and want, therefore, to go home. We may link this with another device Fitzgerald often uses, namely, his method of making his point by simple juxtaposition without any comment. It is a method akin to Pope's in, for example, the often-quoted line:

Puffs, powders, patches, Bibles, billets-doux

In a catalogue like this each object assumes an equal status, and the fact that a bible may be seen as sharing the importance or triviality of its context is comment enough on the society in which such an equivalence can be contemplated. So in Fitzgerald. For example, we are told that Tom and Daisy drifted around 'wherever people played polo and were rich together'. There, the juxtaposition of playing a game and being wealthy indicates the superficiality and frivolity of the rich. One finds a rather different effect achieved when Fitzgerald describes Gatsby's party: 'In his blue gardens men and girls came and went like moths among the whisperings and the champagne *and the stars*', where the phrase I have italicized illuminates by contrast the transience and evanescence of the whisperings, champagne and the moth-like men and girls.

(4) Here Fitzgerald achieves yet another effect, this time by a contrast of diction. The first half of the sentence, with its polysyllabic abstraction, approaches the inflation of mock-heroic; it is promptly deflated by the abrupt, racy description of action in the second half of the sentence.

Such analysis may seem to be breaking a butterfly upon a wheel, but the fact that it is so laboured is merely the result of trying to bring to a conscious formulation something that we respond to immediately and unconsciously in our casual reading of the novel. But it will have served its purpose if it helps to show that beneath the gaiety and wit of his prose Fitzgerald is maintaining a light but insistent moral pressure and is guiding and preparing our attitudes and responses so that we shall make a correct evaluation when the need arises. All this is done through his manipulation of the point of view afforded us by the narrator, Nick Carraway, who acts as the moral seismograph of the novel's uneasiness, premonitory quakings and final eruption into catastrophe.

We may extend this analysis by noticing how keyphrases are repeated subtly but insistently and how the work is so admirably organized, so intact as well as compact, that any one of these phrases inevitably leads to another and then to another, so that wherever the reader enters the book—whatever aspect of it he chooses to emphasize—his attention is engaged in a series of ever-widening perspectives until the whole of the novel is encompassed. Let us take, quite arbitrarily, the word *restless*; if we follow up this tiny and apparently insignificant verbal clue we shall find that it leads us swiftly and decisively to the heart of the book. Any one of a dozen other starting-points would do the same. Consider these examples:

(a) Of Nick: 'A little later I participated in that delayed Teutonic migration known as the Great War. I enjoyed the counter-raid so thoroughly that I came back restless.'

(b) Of Tom, surveying his Long Island estate: '"I've got a nice place here", he said, his eyes flashing about restlessly.' Later he is seen 'hovering restlessly about the room.'

(c) Of Jordan Baker: 'Her body asserted itself with a restless movement of her knee, and she stood up.'

These instances of our chosen key-word, all occurring within the first twenty pages of the novel, are complicated and supplemented by other phrases suggesting sudden movement, either jerky and impulsive, as of Tom:

> Wedging his tense arm imperatively under mine, Tom Buchanan compelled me from the room as though he were moving a checker to another square.

or, by contrast, of Jordan:

> She yawned and with a series of rapid, deft movements stood up into the room.

We may notice again how Fitzerald often obtains his local effects; how in the second example the unusual preposition *into* gives a peculiar force to the sentence, how, in the description of Tom, the word *imperatively* interacts with the word *compelled* so that the latter also contains the sense of *impels* and how the simile of checkers gives one the sense of manipulation, a sense which expands into the whole complex of human relationships, plots, intrigues and dreams that fills the novel.

In this context, repose is seen as a strained effort, the result of which is precarious; thus Jordan

> was extended full length at her end of the divan, completely motionless, and with her chin raised a little, as if she were balancing something on it which was likely to fall.

Even the house seems unable to stay still:

> A breeze blew through the room, blew curtains in at one end and out the other like pale flags, twisting them up toward the frosted wedding-cake of the ceiling, and then *rippled over the wine-coloured rug, making a shadow on it as a wind does on the sea.*
> The only completely stationary object in the room was an enormous couch on which two young women *were buoyed up*, as though upon an *anchored* balloon. They were both in white, and their dresses were *rippling* and fluttering as though they had just been blown back in after a short flight around the house. I must have stood for a few minutes listening to the whip and snap of the curtains and the *groan of a picture on the wall.*

In this passage one verbal trail intersects another and it is by this continual criss-cross of phrases and images that Fitzgerald achieves the effect I have already mentioned of a widening perspective. The image here, submerged beneath the surface elaboration of the prose and coming out in the phrases I have italicized is not, as one might expect, of flight but rather one of ships and the sea; a complicated image, a double exposure, so to speak, in which the whole house is seen as a ship groaning in the wind, with its flags flying, and at the same time in which the divan is a kind of ship within ship, upon the wine-coloured sea of the rug. The connecting link between the two aspects of the image is, of course, the activity and effect of the wind; both curtains and dresses ripple. There is a great deal that could be said about this kind of submerged activity in the novel to which we respond unconsciously in a casual non-analytical reading of it; for the moment, however, I am concerned only to note how the idea of restlessness is linked with the idea of the sea. We will return to this connection shortly: we may first notice how this restlessness expands and fills the opening of the book, especially the scene of the first dinner party at the Buchanans.

The dinner begins quietly enough 'with a bantering inconsequence that was never quite chatter' but the inconsequence is soon out of control; people are continually interrupting each other, changing the subject, Tom becomes vehement. Daisy is possessed by 'turbulent emotions', the air is full of whispers, implications, innuendos, people are always shifting around, the 'shrill metallic urgency' of the telephone is never absent for long. The following passage is a good example of the general atmosphere:

> Miss Baker and I exchanged a short glance consciously devoid of meaning. I was about to speak when she sat up alertly and said 'Sh!' in a warning voice. A subdued impassioned murmur was audible in the room beyond, and Miss Baker leaned forward unashamed, trying to hear. The murmur trembled on the verge of coherence, sank down, mounted excitedly and then ceased altogether.

This atmosphere is most completely expressed in Nick's feeling about Daisy:

> as though the whole evening had been a trick of some sort to exact a contributory emotion from me. I waited, and sure enough, in a moment she looked at me with a smirk on her lovely face, as if she had asserted her membership in a rather distinguished secret society to which she and Tom belonged.

Just as this passage anticipates the moments after the catastrophe when Daisy and Tom look as though they are conspiring together, so the whole scene prepares us for the picture of Tom's affair with Mrs. Wilson which by its squalor, its triviality, its commonplaceness is a preparatory contrast with the naive grandeur of Gatsby's schemes to meet Daisy once again. The atmosphere of the dinner, as I have tried to describe it, is thus established as part of the emotional and moral climate of the whole book. But it is much more than mere scene-setting; let us follow out a little further some of the implications of the restlessness motif. Ultimately this derives from the rootlessness of those people; they are strangers not only to their own country but also to their past. They live in houses that may be palaces but are certainly not homes; their intellectual ideas are shoddy and their moral attitudes to life are at best the detritus of a collapsed social framework, second-hand and conventionally assumed, so that Nick is tempted to laugh at Tom's abrupt 'transition from libertine to prig' while the most he can find to admire is the 'hardy scepticism' of Jordan Baker.

All the implications of this rootlessness radiate from another key-word, *drifting*, and we may notice how Fitzgerald, early in the book, links this idea with the idea of restlessness, when he writes of Daisy and Tom:

> Why they came back East I don't know. They had spent a year in France for no particular reason, and then drifted here and there unrestfully wherever people played polo and were rich together.

Each example of this kind of thing, when taken in isolation, may seem neutral, empty of metaphorical richness, but the interaction of these two ideas is so insistent that each tiny accretion of phrase and image builds up a powerful cumulative charge. We have already seen the image of the sea at work beneath a passage of descriptive prose, but it extends with a deceptive casualness throughout the whole book; at Gatsby's parties Nick notes 'the sea-change of faces and voices and colour' and is 'rather ill at ease among swirls and eddies of people'; at these parties Tom says one meets 'all kinds of crazy fish' and later protests that people will 'throw everything overboard'. Examples could be multiplied but we need only notice the recurrence of the metaphors of sea, drifting and voyaging in two crucial passages. The first is towards the end of Nick's prefatory comments:

> No—Gatsby turned out all right at the end; it is what preyed on Gatsby, what foul dust floated in the wake of his dreams that temporarily closed out my interest in the aborted sorrows and short-winded hopes of men.

and in the very last words of the book: 'So we beat on, boats against the current, borne back ceaselessly into the past.'

I would like to suggest that far below the surface of *The Great Gatsby*—below the particular interest of the narrative, below Fitzgerald's analysis of society, below even the allegedly 'mythic' qualities of the book—is a potent cliché, a commonplace of universal human experience to which we all respond. To say one of the bases of the novel is a cliché is not to disparage Fitzgerald—most great art is built upon similar platitudes and it is probably why the novel is alive for another age than Fitzgerald's and for non-Americans—what we should admire is the way in which he has refreshed the cliché, given it a new accession of life in his story. The cliché I refer to is easily summed up; in the words of a popular hymn it is this:

> *Time, like an ever-rolling stream,*
> *Bears all its sons away;*
> *They fly forgotten, as a dream*
> *Dies at the opening day.*

The simple truth of this fact of life is everywhere implicit in the texture of the novel, and sometimes it is more than implicit. The appropriateness of the way in which Nick records the names of all those people who went to Gatsby's house that summer has often been remarked:

> Once I wrote down on the empty spaces of a time-table the names of those who came to Gatsby's house that Summer. It is an old time-table now, dis-integrating at its folds, and headed 'This schedule in effect July 5th, 1922.'

There could be no more decorous memorial to those 'men and girls' who 'came and went like moths among the whisperings and the champagne and the stars.'

It is essential to Gatsby's tragic illusion, his belief in 'the unreality of reality; a promise that the rock of the world was founded securely on a fairy's wing,' that he should deny this fact of life and try to make the ever-rolling stream flow back up-hill.

> 'I wouldn't ask too much of her,' I ventured. 'You can't repeat the past.' 'Can't repeat the past?' he cried incredulously. 'Why of course you can!'

It is not insignificant that Nick should be so acutely aware of the passing of time, while in this context Gatsby's apology, 'I'm sorry about the clock' acquires a new level of unconscious ironic meaning. This has been stressed often enough before; the point I wish to make is that the theme, basic to *The Great Gatsby*, is not merely adumbrated, is not merely translated into terms of narrative and character, but is also expressed in the very texture of the prose, in the phrases and images, for example, which centre on words like *restless* and *drifting*. Thus the moral attitude of Nick is conveyed in precisely these terms. We may note in passing that Nick is not the fixed, static point of view some critics have supposed him; he is not the detached observer but is deeply implicated in the story he is telling and his attitude evolves and changes as the story progresses; in a sense what *The Great Gatsby* is about is what happens to Nick. At the outset he 'began to like New York, the racy adventurous feel of it at night, and the satisfaction that the constant flicker of men and women and machines gives to the restless eye'. The attractiveness and glamour of Gatsby's parties needs no stressing but Nick begins to feel oppressed and uneasy at the 'many-coloured, many-keyed commotion'. And his reaction after the catastrophe is naturally expressed in an antithesis to the terms already established.

> When I came back from the East last autumn I felt that I wanted the world to be in uniform and at a sort of moral attention forever.

Similarly, the ambiguity of Gatsby himself comes over to us in these terms. He is not the simple antithesis of Tom and Daisy; he is implicated in their kind of corruption too, and his dream is proved hollow not only by the inadequacy of the actual correlative—that is, Daisy—to the hunger of his aspiring imagination, but also by the means he uses to build up the gaudy fabric of his vision. He, too, shares in the restlessness of the actual world which will defeat his ideal, Platonic conceptions:

> This quality was continually breaking through his punctilious manner in the shape of restlessness. He was never quite still; there was always a tapping foot somewhere or the impatient opening and closing of a hand.

and a little later he tells Nick:

> 'You see, I usually find myself among strangers because I drift here and there trying to forget the sad thing that happened to me.'

This note of drifting is frequently reiterated in connection with Gatsby but it does not, as in the case of Daisy and Tom, remain unqualified; Gatsby comes out all right at the end. What we remember about him is not the restlessness or the drifting but 'an unbroken series of successful gestures', Gatsby standing in the moonlight outside the Buchanans' house, rapt in 'the sacredness of the vigil'; Gatsby in his own temple-cum-roadhouse between 'the great doors, endowing with complete isolation the figure of the host, who stood on the porch, his hand up in a formal gesture of farewell', or above all, Gatsby stretching out his arms towards the green light that is the vain promise of his future. We remember these formal poses as something theatrical or religious, but they *are* poses, moments of suspended time, something static and as such are the stylistic equivalents of Gatsby's attempt to impose his dream upon reality, his effort to make the ever-rolling stream stand still. We remember Gatsby not as drifting but as voyaging to some end and it is this sense, hinted at all the way through the book, which gives impetus to that imaginative leap whereby we encompass the ironic contrast between Gatsby and Columbus or those Dutch sailors in that moment when:

> man must have held his breath in the presence of this continent, compelled into an aesthetic contemplation he neither understood nor desired, face to face for the last time in history with something commensurate to his capacity for wonder.

Thus, starting with the idea of restlessness and going by way of its enlargement into the idea of drifting we are brought to face the largest issues that the novel propounds. This is, of course, not the only—or even the most important—strand in the textural pattern of the whole; any one of a dozen other starting points might have been taken—the contrast between East and West, for example, the subtle choreography of the terms *reality* and *unreality*, the functional role of the machine which enlarges to provide metaphors for the emotional and moral life, the religious overtones that some critics have noted, or the ideas of money and value. All of these combine and interact to give *The Great Gatsby* its satisfying depth and richness of suggestion without which the themes so often abstracted for discussion would lack both definition and reverberant power and the novel would fail to achieve that quality which Mark Schorer has described as 'language as used to create a certain texture and tone which in themselves state and define themes and meanings; or language, the counters of our ordinary speech, as forced, through conscious manipulation, into all those larger meanings which our ordinary speech almost never intends'.[4]

Notes

1. John Farelly: Scott Fitzgerald: Another View (*Scrutiny*, Vol. XVIII, No. 4, June 1952).
2. For example, Edwin S. Fussell: Fitzgerald's Brave New World (*English Literary History* Vol. 19, No. 4, December 1952).
3. William Troy: Scott Fitzgerald: The Authority of Failure (*Accent*, 1945).
4. Mark Schorer: Technique as Discovery (*Hudson Review*, Spring, 1948).

86

F. Scott Fitzgerald's *The Great Gatsby*: Legendary Bases and Allegorical Significances

◆

JOHN HENRY RALEIGH

F. Scott Fitzgerald's character Gatsby, as has often been said, represents the irony of American history and he corruption of the American dream. While this certainly is true, yet even here, with this general legend, Fitzgerald has rung in his own characteristic changes, doubling and redoubling ironies. At the center of the legend proper there is the relationship between Europe and America and the ambiguous interaction between the contradictory impulses of Europe that led to the original settling of America and its subsequent development: mercantilism and idealism. At either end of American history, and all the way through, the two impulses have a way of being both radically exclusive and mutually confusing, the one melting into the other: the human faculty of wonder, on the one hand, and the power and beauty of things, on the other.

The Great Gatsby dramatizes this continuing ambiguity directly in the life of Gatsby and retrospectively by a glance at history at the end of the novel. Especially does it do so in the two passages in the novel of what might be called the ecstatic moment, the moment when the human imagination seems to be on the verge of entering the earthly paradise. The two passages are (1) the real Gatsby looking on the real Daisy, and (2) the imaginary Dutchmen, whom Nick conjures up at the end of the novel, looking on the "green breast" of Long Island.

Here is the description of Gatsby and Daisy:

SOURCE *University of Kansas City Review* XXIV, October 1957, pp. 55–58. Reprinted in *F. Scott Fitzgerald: A Collection of Critical Essays*, ed. Arthur Mizener, Englewood Cliffs, NJ, 1963, pp. 99–103.

> Out of the corner of his eye Gatsby saw that the blocks of the sidewalks really formed a ladder and mounted to a secret place above the trees—he could climb to it, if he climbed alone, and once there he could suck on the pap of life, gulp down the incomparable milk of wonder.
>
> His heart beat faster and faster as Daisy's white face came up to his own. He knew that when he kissed this girl, and forever wed his unutterable visions to her perishable breath, his mind would never romp again like the mind of God. So he waited, listening for a moment longer to the tuning-fork that had been struck upon a star. Then he kissed her. At his lips' touch she blossomed for him like a flower and the incarnation was complete.

And below is Nick's imaginative reconstruction of the legendary Dutchman. He is sprawled on the sand at night, with Gatsby's mansion behind him and Long Island Sound in front of him:

> And as the moon rose higher the inessential houses began to melt away until gradually I became aware of the old Island that flowered once for Dutch eyes—a fresh green breast of the new world. Its vanished trees, the trees that had made way for Gatsby's house, had once pandered in whispers to the last and greatet of all human dreams; for a transitory enchanted moment man must have held his breath in the presence of this continent, compelled into an aesthetic contemplation he neither understood nor desired, face to face for the last time in history with something commensurate to his capacity for wonder.[1]

The repetition in the two passages of the words "wonder" and "flower" hardly need comment, or the sexuality, illicit in the Dutchmen's and both infantile and mature in Gatsby's—or the star-lit, moon-lit setting in both. For these are the central symbols in the book: the boundless imagination trying to transfigure under the stars the endlessly beautiful object. Now, of course, the Dutchmen and Gatsby are utterly different types of being and going in different directions. The Dutchmen are pure matter, momentarily and unwillingly raised into the realms of the spirit, while Gatsby is pure spirit coming down to earth. They pass one another, so to speak, at the moment when ideal and reality seem about to converge. Historically, the Dutch, legendarily stolid, pursued their mercantile ways and produced finally a Tom Buchanan but also, it should be remembered, a Nick Carraway. But their ecstatic moment hung on in the air, like an aroma, intoxicating prophets, sages, poets, even poor farm boys in twentieth-century Dakota. The heady insubstantiability of the dream and the heavy intractability of the reality were expressed by Van Wyck Brooks (who could well have been Fitzgerald's philosopher in these matters) in his *The Wine of the Puritans* as follows:

> You put the old wine [Europeans] into new bottles [American continent] ... and when the explosion results, one may say, the aroma passes into the air and the wine spills on the floor. The aroma or the ideal, turns into transcendentalism and the wine or the real, becomes commercialism.

No one knew better than Gatsby that nothing could finally match the splendors of his own imagination, and the novel would suggest finally that not only had the American dream been corrupted but that it was, in part anyway, necessarily corrupted, for it asked too much. Nothing of this earth, even the most beautiful of earthly objects, could be anything but a perversion of it.

The Great Gatsby, then, begins in a dramatization, as suggested, of the basic thesis of the early Van Wyck Brooks: that America had produced an idealism so impalpable that it had lost touch with reality (Gatsby) and a materialism so heavy that it was inhuman (Tom Buchanan). The novel as a whole is another turn of the screw on this legend, with the impossible idealism trying to realize itself, to its utter destruction, in the gross materiality. As Nick says of Gatsby at the end of the novel:

> ... his dream must have seemed so close that he could hardly fail to grasp it. He did not know that it was already behind him somewhere back in that vast obscurity beyond the city, where the dark fields of the republic rolled on under the night.

Yet he imagines too that Gatsby, before his moment of death, must have had his "realization" of the intractable brutishness of matter;

> ... he must have felt that he had lost the old warm world, paid a high price for living too long with a single dream. He must have looked up at an unfamiliar sky through frightening leaves and shivered as he found what a grotesque thing a rose is and how raw the sunlight was upon the scarcely created grass.

Thus Fitzgerald multiplies the ironies of the whole legend: that the mercantile Dutchmen should have been seduced into the esthetic; that Gatsby's wondrous aspirations should attach themselves to a Southern belle and that in pursuit of her he should become a gangster's lieutenant; that young Englishmen ("agonizingly aware of the easy money in the vicinity") should scramble for crumbs at Gatsby's grandiose parties (the Dutchmen once more); that idealism, beauty, power, money should get all mixed up; that history should be a kind of parody of itself, as with the case of the early Dutch and the contemporary English explorers.

Still *The Great Gatsby* would finally suggest, at a level beyond all its legends and in the realm of the properly tragic, that it is right and fitting that the Jay Gatzes of the world should ask for the impossible, even when they do so as pathetically and ludicrously as does Gatsby himself. Writing to Fitzgerald about his novel, Maxwell Perkins, after enumerating some specific virtues, said:

> ... these are such things as make a man famous. And all the things, the whole pathetic episode, you have given a place in time and space, for with the help of T. J. Eckleburg, and by an occasional glance at the sky, or the city, you have imparted a sort of sense of eternity.

A "sense of eternity"—this is indeed high praise, but I think that Perkins, as he often was, was right.

For at its highest level *The Great Gatsby* does not deal with local customs or even national and international legends but with the permanent realities of existence. On this level nothing or nobody is to blame, and people are what they are and life is what it is, just as, in Bishop Butler's words, "things are what they are." At this level, too, most people don't count; they are merely a higher form of animality living out its mundane existence: the Tom Buchanans, the Jordan Bakers, the Daisy Fays. Only Nick and Gatsby count. For Gatsby, with all his absurdities and his short, sad, pathetic life, is still valuable; in Nick's parting words to him: "You're worth the whole damn bunch put together." Nick, who in his way is as much of this world as Daisy is in hers, still sees, obscurely, the significance of Gatsby. And although he knows that the content of Gatsby's dream is corrupt, he senses that its form is pristine. For, in his own fumbling, often gross way, Gatsby was obsessed with the wonder of human life and driven by the search to make that wonder actual. It is the same urge that motivates visionaries and prophets, the urge to make the facts of life measure up to the splendors of the human imagination, but it is utterly pathetic in Gatsby's case because he is trying to do it so subjectively and so uncouthly, and with dollar bills. Still Nick's obscure instinct that Gatsby is essentially all right is sound. It often seems as if the novel is about the contrast between the two, but the bond between them reveals that they are not opposites but rather complements, opposed together, to all the other characters in the novel.

Taken together they contain most of the essential polarities that go to make up the human mind and its existence. Allegorically considered, Nick is reason, experience, waking, reality, and history, while Gatsby is imagination, innocence, sleeping, dream, and eternity. Nick is like Wordsworth listening to "the still sad music of humanity," while Gatsby is like Blake seeing hosts of angels in the sun. The one can only look at the facts and see them as tragic; the other tries to transform the facts by an act of the imagination. Nick's mind is conservative and historical, as is his lineage; Gatsby's is radical and apocalyptic—as rootless as his heritage. Nick is too much immersed in time and in reality; Gatsby is hopelessly out of it. Nick is always withdrawing, while Gatsby pursues the green light. Nick can't be hurt, but neither can he be happy. Gatsby can experience ecstasy, but his fate is necessarily tragic. They are generally two of the best types of humanity: the moralist and the radical.

One may well ask why, if their mental horizons are so lofty, is one a bond salesman and the other a gangster's lieutenant, whose whole existence is devoted to a love affair that has about it the unmistakable stamp of adolescence? The answer is, I think, that Fitzgerald did not know enough of what a philosopher or revolutionary might really be like, that at this point in his life he must have always thought of love in terms of a Princeton Prom, and that, writing in the twenties, a bond salesman and a gangster's functionary would seem more representative anyway. Van Wyck Brooks might have said, at one time, that his culture gave him nothing more to work with.

A lesser writer might have attempted to make Nick a literal sage and Gatsby a literal prophet. But it is certain that such a thought would never have entered Fitzgerald's head, as he was only dramatizing the morals and manners of the life he knew. The genius of the novel consists precisely in the fact that, while using only the stuff, one might better say the froth and flotsam of its own limited time and place, it has managed to suggest, as Perkins said, a sense of eternity.

87
The Great Gatsby

◆

RICHARD CHASE

Lionel Trilling speaks of *Gatsby* as follows: "To the world it is anomalous in America, as in the novel it is anomalous in Gatsby, that so much raw power should be haunted by envisioned romance. Yet in that anomaly lies, for good and bad, much of the truth of our national life, as, at the present moment, we think about it." The special charm of *Gatsby* rests in its odd combination of romance with a realistic picture of raw power—the raw power of the money that has made a plutocracy and the raw power the self-protective conventions of this plutocracy assume when they close in a united front against an intruder.

Gatsby gives us an unforgettable, even though rather sketchy, sense of the 1920's and what the people were like who lived in them. We know what the people were like because we are shown the publicly recognized gestures and attitudes by which they declare themselves as belonging to a certain ambiance at a certain time. Their manners (perhaps one should say their mannered lack of manners) are a clearly minted currency as readily negotiable as the money they all have such a lot of. At the same time the hero who comes to his spectacular grief is not only a man of the 1920's but a figure of legend. No one can doubt that the legend engaged the imagination of the author more deeply than the society in which the legend is played out.

Mr. Trilling attributes the continuing freshness and significance of *Gatsby* to "Fitzgerald's grasp—both in the sense of awareness and appropriation—of the traditional resources available to him." And this will apply whether we are thinking of the book as a romance or as a novel of manners. The story of Jay Gatsby is in origin an archetype of European legend and it is fascinating to observe how, in Fitzgerald's hands, this legend is modified and in some ways fundamentally changed in accordance with American ideas.

The European (perhaps universal) archetype has been memorably described, in relation to the novel, by Mr. Trilling himself. In his Introduction to *The Princess Casamassima*, Mr. Trilling refers to the legend of "The Young Man from the Provinces" which finds expression in certain great

SOURCE *The American Novel and Its Tradition*, New York, 1957, pp. 162–167.

novels, such as Stendhal's *The Red and the Black*, Dickens's *Great Expectations*, and Balzac's *Père Goriot*. The young hero of the legend is likely to come from obscure or mean beginnings. There is some mystery about his birth; perhaps he is really a foundling prince. He is "equipped with poverty, pride and intelligence" and he passes through a series of adventures which resemble the "tests" that confront the would-be knight in Arthurian legend. He has an enormous sense of his own destiny. The purpose of his quest is to "enter life", which he does by launching a campaign to conquer and subdue to his own purposes the great world that regards him as an insignificant outsider. "He is concerned to know how the political and social world are run and enjoyed," as Mr. Trilling writes; "he wants a share of power and pleasure and in consequences he takes real risks, often of his life."

At this point one begins to see how much and how little Gatsby belongs to the tradition of the Young Man from the Provinces. He has the necessary obscure beginning, born Gatz somewhere in the Middle West. He has come to the more socially advanced East and made his way to a position of wealth and influence. He is more or less a mythic figure; he seems to have sprung from "a Platonic conception of himself" rather than from any real place; he is rumored to be the nephew of the Kaiser; he pretends to be an Oxford man and to have lived like a young rajah in all the capitals of Europe; he has committed himself "to the following of a grail." A good deal of this legendary build-up is comic in tone and satiric in intent. But Arthur Mizener, Fitzgerald's biographer, is correct in saying that the ironies of *The Great Gatsby* are never allowed to destroy the credence and respect given by the author to the legend of his hero. The life and death of Gatsby inevitably call to the mind of Nick Carraway, the narrator, the ideal meaning of America itself. Gatsby somehow invokes the poetic appeal of the frontier and his pursuit of the ideal recalls once again the "transitory enchanted moment when man must first have held his breath in the presence of this continent, compelled into an aesthetic contemplation he neither understood nor desired, face to face for the last time in history with something commensurate to his capacity for wonder."

These concluding lines are so impressed and impressive, even if a little overopulent in the Conradian manner, that we feel the whole book has been driving toward this moment of ecstatic contemplation, toward this final moment of transcendence. What, at the end, has been affirmed? Apparently it is not the "power and pleasure" derived from knowing and mastering "the political and social world." At the end of *Père Goriot* what is affirmed by Eugene Rastignac's challenge to Paris *is* this "power and pleasure." And whereas it is true that Julien Sorel in *The Red and the Black* seeks an ideal transcendence, in the manner of many French heroes, from those of Racine to those of Malraux, his field of operations is social to a far greater degree than Gatsby's is ever shown to be.

Gatsby does not seek to understand and master society as an end; and we have to take it on faith that he has understood and mastered it at all—was he *really* a bootlegger and a dealer in dubious stocks? Of course he was, but neither he nor his author nor his author's narrator, himself a bond salesman, shows any interest in these activities. Nor has Gatsby's shadowy battle with the world been, as it is for his European counterparts, a process of education and disillusion. *He* does not pass from innocence to experience—if anything it is the other way around, the youth who climbed aboard the millionaire's yacht being more worldly than the man who gazes longingly at the green light across the bay. In *The Great Gatsby* society and its ways, so far as the hero knows them, are not ends but means to a transcendent ideal. Finally, as Nick Carraway thinks, the ideal is so little connected with reality that it consists merely in *having* an ideal. Ideality, the longing for transcendence, these are good in themselves. So Nick Carraway implies when he shouts across the lawn to Gatsby, "They're a rotten crowd. You're worth the whole damn bunch put together." For even though Carraway "disapproved of him from beginning to end," he is forced thus to pay tribute to Gatsby's "incorruptible dream." Nor is the abstractness of Gatsby's dream modified by the fact that it centers around Daisy Buchanan, whom he has loved and lost. He does not see her as she is; he does not seem to have a sexual passion for her. He sees her merely as beauty and innocence—a flower, indeed, growing natively on the "fresh green breast of the new world."

Fitzgerald suggests near the end of the book that Gatsby is in the legendary line of Benjamin Franklin or Poor Richard. So we see from the self-disciplinary schedule Gatsby had written down as a boy and had always kept with him:

Rise from bed	6:00	A.M.
Dumbbell exercise and wall scaling	6:15–6:30	"
Study electricity, etc.	7:15–8:15	"

and so on down to:

Study needed inventions	7:00–9:00	P.M.

But he is also of the company of Natty Bumppo, Huck Finn, and Melville's Ishmael. For although he is treated with more irony than they, as befits a later worldliness, he shares their ideal of innocence, escape, and the purely personal code of conduct. Like them he derives his values not from the way of the world but from an earlier pastoral ideal.

But Gatsby lived too late. He is made to die sordidly in his swimming pool, shot by a garage proprietor. He cannot, like Huck Finn, light out for the territory. He cannot achieve even the dubious rebirth of Ishmael in the far Pacific. He cannot die full of years, facing the setting sun and attended by the primeval prairie gods, like Natty Bumppo.

None of these earlier heroes makes an assault on a plutocracy that has settled into a position of power and prestige. That was not an option in their time and place. When Gatsby does this he becomes what his predecessors never were: a tragicomic figure in a social comedy. He does not know how to conform to the class to which Daisy belongs and to this class he seems ridiculous, with his "gorgeous pink rag of a suit," his preposterous mansion, and his chaotic parties—parties at which ordinary people seem somehow to become themselves fantastic and to assume names like Miss Claudia Hip and the Dancies (I refer here to the inspired list of names, itself a great comic achievement, at the beginning of Chapter 4—there is an only somewhat less brilliant collection of comic names in the description of the masquerade at the beginning of Cable's *Grandissimes*). In Gatsby, that is, we have a figure who is from one point of view a hero of romance but from another is related to the gulls and fops of high comedy.

No one seems to know what T. S. Eliot meant when he wrote Fitzgerald that *Gatsby* was the first step forward the American novel had made since Henry James. The statement seems meaningful, however, if we compare *Gatsby* with James's only novel of similar theme, *The American*. Christopher Newman is a more relaxed, less willful, and less self-destined figure than Gatsby, but he comes of a similarly legendary America, makes a great deal of money, and vainly pursues a woman who is the flower of a high world forever closed to him. James, however, is content with his pleasure in the old angularities of the legend of the successful American. And he sends Newman home, baffled and saddened by his rejection but not mortally hurt. It is a part of the fate of both Newman and Gatsby that they have information with which they could avenge themselves on their highly placed antagonists and that out of magnanimity they both refuse to do so.

But Fitzgerald has made more of the legend. For whereas Newman remains an odd though appealing stick of a man Gatsby has a tragic recklessness about him, an inescapably vivid and memorable destiny. He has something of that almost divine insanity we find in Hamlet or Julien Sorel or Don Quixote. Fitzgerald's great feat was to have opened out this possibility and to have made his American hero act in a drama where none had acted before. For although there had been reckless and doomed semilegendary heroes in American fiction, none had been made to play his part in a realistically presented *social* situation. Fitzgerald opened out the possibility, but scarcely more. It was not in him to emulate except for a brilliant moment the greatest art.

88
Nature and Optics in *The Great Gatsby*

J.S. WESTBROOK

In the thirties T.S. Eliot praised Djuna Barnes's *Nightwood*[1] as one of the few novels of the day that could be called "written," and explained that although her style was not designed to conceal a "vacuity of content," and was not "poetic prose," it could be fully appreciated only by "sensibilities trained on poetry." Some time ago I watched a television adaptation of *The Great Gatsby* and tried to decide why all efforts at dramatizing it had failed to suggest even remotely the values readers found in it. The best answer I could resolve upon was its "writtenness," in the very sense in which Eliot had used the word. Few novels have been made to depend so heavily upon a scheme of organization that is fundamentally linguistic; when the language is stripped away, not only the appeal but the coherency of the tale is lost.

To understand the unity of *The Great Gatsby* we must first recognize that its primary subject is the growth of an awareness. The awareness belongs to the narrator, Nick Carraway, who not only enjoys the advantage of distance in time from the events he relates, but even at the scene of their unfolding has been more of a perceiver than a participant. It is significant that his retrospections are never so concerned with what he *did* as with what he *saw*. His freedom from crucial dramatic involvement enables the internalities of poetic vision to widen and deepen the implications of the ostensibly shallow world *The Great Gatsby* deals with. Unattended by this kind of vision the purely dramatic ingredients of the novel—as the movies and television have demonstrated—merely add up to a disjointed impression of fast living in the Twenties, affording no haunting sense of the penalties levied upon an ethos by the excitements—or, more accurately, the excitations—of an era.

The lyricism, given such wide scope in the narrative, works rhetorically and visually to arrest qualities of setting, conduct, and states of mind. At the heart of the excesses, the extravagant hopes and failures of the generation portrayed, has been its refusal to countenance limitation, the consequences

SOURCE *American Literature* XXXII, March 1960, pp. 78–84.

of which are symbolized in two patterns of reference which combine to serve as the organizing principle for the poetic design of the novel. One revolves around the problem of seeing; the other around the idea of nature.

If with respect to other characters *The Great Gatsby* is a record of conduct, with respect to Carraway it is the record of an ocular initiation into the mysteries and wonders of a magical country, during which he is constantly absorbed in the process of adjusting his credulity to received visual data, and checking and rechecking to ascertain whether his eyes have played him false. The images that confront them are either blurred, or comprised of utterly improbable amalgams: the disconcerting alignment of Mrs. McKee's eyebrows; the vaguely familiar look of Meyer Wolfsheim's cufflinks, which turn out to have been constructed of human molars; the shirtless figure of Gatsby's boarder, Klipspringer, doing "liver exercises" in a silk-lined bedchamber; the "scarcely human orchid" sitting under a white plum tree at a Gatsby party who, upon closer scrutiny, turns into a "hitherto ghostly celebrity of the movies"; the whole ashen world of the dump with its ashen houses, chimneys, chimney smoke, and men; and finally the oddly frivolous corpse of Gatsby afloat on a rubber mattress in his swimming pool.

In all of these details there is a contention of elements and a striving of forms for a completion which the disparity of elements denies. Symbolically they reflect the abortive commitments of a generation whose sense of distinctions has been destroyed by the prodigious acceleration of a commercial and technical civilization. If we look at them closely, however, we find that they are bound together by another idea. In one way or another they all represent an assault upon nature, and as the tale unfolds the idea of nature insulted and abased is raised to the level of a general metaphor.

The people in *The Great Gatsby*, ironically enough, have not consciously renounced nature. They have only ceased to perceive its limits. They think continually in terms of fertility, but the forms of it that they wish upon the world are either altogether specious, or else "forced." When Carraway first arrives in West Egg, he finds "great bursts of leaves growing on the trees," but these are special leaves to go with a special place. They remind him of the way things grow "in fast movies." Whether they actually grow that way is beside the point; the atmosphere of West Egg makes them seem to. Its leaves are allied with the spirit of technology and fast money, and this sort of alliance is basic to a whole scheme of images and references that follow. So many and various are they that no convenient order of citation is possible. If the dump and the oculist's sign make up the all-encompassing symbol of the novel, it would seem unfair not to mention little touches like the wreath Myrtle Wilson wants to buy for her mother's grave, which will "last all summer." It is safe to say, however, that of all the devices whereby nature is "crossed," the most frequent involve the use of color; and in the majority of instances where colors are used it will be noted that the contexts in which they are presented deflect their primary meanings. The light on Daisy's dock is green—and electric. The "golden arms" of Jordan Baker are not simply those of a healthy girl who spends her afternoons on fairways, but of a girl whose wealth is linked with dishonesty. And the innocence of white suffers when that color is employed to describe Manhattan rising in "heaps and sugar lumps all built with a wish out of non-olfactory money." But the color which comes in for the most extensive manipulation is yellow. It figures prominently at Gatsby's parties—the "yellow cocktail music," and the stage twins in yellow dresses who do a baby act. Gatsby's cars, too, are yellow, the station wagon that transports guests to his parties and the "death car" with which Daisy runs down Myrtle Wilson. George Wilson's garage is yellow and, across the highway from it, the spectacles of Dr. T.J. Eckleburg. In general, the world of *The Great Gatsby* may be said to abound in colors, all of the brighter varieties, but the most brilliant of them attends ironically upon its unhappiest events.

Yet although we are subjected at every turn to these cheapenings, vulgarizations, and distortions of the idea of fertility, the fact that that idea is kept in the forefront of our minds from one end of the book to the other is what accounts for its pathos. If *The Great Gatsby* can be interpreted as a study of an ethos in transition, the Americans it deals with retaining a certain innocence and vitality of desire we connect with a simpler, less deceptive phase of their history, but now confused as to values, mistaking losses for gains, and committing their hopes and beliefs to symbols that are shallow and inadequate, then the continual references to violated nature deepen our sense of what they have betrayed in themselves. Significantly enough, the ineffability of their dreams and the perishability of the things upon which they are founded are evoked in repeated references to flowers. Not only is Daisy Buchanan named after a flower but her whole history has been spelled out in orchids and roses. And Gatsby, for whom, five years prior to their reunion in West Egg, Daisy has "blossomed like a flower," cannot believe that that blossoming is irreclaimable, that indeed the world cannot be made to bloom perpetually. He, even more than she, is bent upon wringing from life impossible consummations, a fact which is symbolized by the prominence of his gardens in the novel's setting, the bales of cut flowers he imports by truck to Carraway's cottage for his first meeting with Daisy, not to mention his predilection for yellow autos and pink suits. The profusion of horticultural effects becomes, at last, oppressive. There is an overripeness, an unnatural plenitude in this new Eden, and its unwholesomeness is caught in such random details as Gatsby's garden paths clogged at the end of a party with "crushed flowers and fruit rinds," the flower-laden hearse Gatsby and Carraway pass on their way into New York, and the feeling expressed by Jordan Baker on a warm afternoon in the city that "all sorts of funny fruits" are going to drop from the sky.

No wonder, then, that in everything Carraway describes there is the suggestion of hallucination, and that he finds the problem of seeing such a challenge at every turn. Nor is he entirely alone in his optical adventures. They are comically shared by a minor character named Owl Eyes, whom we first encounter exclaiming over the fact that the books in Gatsby's library contain bona fide printed matter, and who later turns up unaccountably at Gatsby's funeral and keeps wiping his glasses "inside and out." For Owl Eyes reality constitutes a phenomenon, reality is hallucination. The same, in a more tragic sense, is true of Gatsby. When he walks to his pool minutes before his demise, the world, now unyoked to his "single dream," has become fantasy. The yellow leaves overhead are "frightening," roses "grotesque," the sunlight "raw ... upon the scarcely created grass."

For the most elaborate expression of the disparity between illusion and reality, however, we must turn finally to the image of the dump presided over by the yard-high retinas of T.J. Eckleburg. It is here that we get a synthesis of the whole constellation of ironies inherent in the theme of the novel, and it is here that the idea of violated nature and that of distorted vision are brought into the most striking conjunction. Eckleburg may be thought of as a commercial deity staring out upon a waste of his own creation.[2] But the enormous eyes behind yellow spectacles are diseased, "faded," "dimmed ... by many paintless days." And the quality of dimness is carried over into the rendering of the "ash-grey men who move dimly and already crumbling through the powdery air." Their shade-like forms, along with the "small, foul river," where periodically a draw-bridge is raised to let barges through, lend the scene overtones of an inferno; but the dump is also described as a "farm where ashes grow like wheat into ridges and hills and fantastic gardens," and what is implied is that a universal myopia has apprehended fertility in "a valley of ashes," and mistaken a hell for a paradise.

The dump is introduced early in the novel, and is the scene of those ocular confusions that lead to its major dramatic climaxes. It is because Myrtle Wilson thinks the yellow car is Tom Buchanan's that she runs out to stop it. It is because George Wilson reads a portentous message in the eyes of Eckleburg ("God sees all") that he takes upon himself the role of avenger. When in the first days of the summer Gatsby's hopes of reclaiming Daisy have been at their highest, and the East has held a certain enchantment even for Carraway, it has been impossible to pass between New York and West Egg without passing the dump. And when the final event of a generally disastrous "last day" has brought all paradisiacal illusions to an end, the dump is again the setting.

Carraway's Eastern adventure, as I have tried to show, is defined largely by references to a spurious and hallucinatory order of nature, the only kind acceptable or even recognizable to the people he is thrown in with. But in fleeting intervals throughout the story we are confronted with unadulterated nature. They happen late at night when the lights of the houses have gone out. The moon survives the glow of Gatsby's parties, the stars wheel in their courses; on the night that Carraway descries Gatsby genuflecting to the light on Daisy's dock, "the bellows of the earth have blown the frogs full of life," and there is a sound of "wings beating in the trees." At such intervals the intensity of nature's own utterances is a little eerie and inexplicable, like the crashing of surf on a deserted beach. These are adumbrations of the forgotten, the "unknown" island, which can now be summoned in its fullness only in visions. Carraway's vision of it, like a buried theme in music, struggles for articulation from the early pages of the novel to the moment near its terminus, with Gatsby dead and the houses in West Egg shut up, when it emerges in the famous "ode" to a buried fertility, the "green breast of the new world" that greeted Dutch sailors' eyes. Earlier in the tale we have been told that Gatsby has felt he could climb to "a secret place above the trees [on Daisy's street] ... and once there ... suck on the pap of life, gulp down the incomparable milk of wonder." But one cannot live indefinitely on wonder, and the real fertility invoked in the vision of the old island which might have been commensurate with his "sensitivity to the promises of life" is irrecoverable.

Even when Carraway resolves upon returning to the Middle West, it will be to a part where nature has been compromised by cities, granted that sleigh bells, holly wreaths, snow, and lighted windows make for a more equable compromise than deep summer, gas pumps, and roadhouse roofs, or sunsets and the apartment houses of movie stars on the West 50's. Carraway's resolve to settle for a Midwestern city—where, unlike the palaces of East Egg and West Egg, houses "are still called through decades by a family's name"—signalizes the end of an era built on adventure and discovery, and the beginning of one built on consolidation. His reformation augurs the passing of a youthful culture into middle age, all of which accounts for the curiously affecting state of feeling communicated through the tone of his narration wherein renunciation of the Gatsby brand of sensibility is not unmixed with regrets that it has been lost to us forever.

Notes

1. Introduction to *Nightwood* (New York, 1937).
2. Fitzgerald's debt to *The Waste Land* has been generally recognized by critics, but the spirit of the poem is adapted to materials so unique that the originality of the novel is in no way impaired.

89
The Great Gatsby: Thirty-Six Years After

A.E. DYSON

In 1925 T. S. Eliot found himself as moved and interested by *The Great Gatsby* as he had been by any novel for a very long time. Since then the novel has attracted praise from a great many discriminating critics on both sides of the Atlantic, and the deep interest of first generation readers has been shared by others coming at a later time, and from different backgrounds. My own first reading of *Gatsby* is an experience I still recall vividly, and it has remained for me one of the few novels in any language (*Tender Is The Night* is another) for which the appetite regularly and pleasurably returns. Amazing enough, one reflects each time, that so short a work should contain so much, and its impact remain so fresh. Thirty-six years after its appearance I would say with confidence, then, that *Gatsby* has not only outlived its period and its author, but that it is one of the books that will endure.

Any new consideration must now, if this is so, be concerned with it as a work which belongs not only to American but to world literature; not only to the immediate soil from which it sprang (prohibition, big business, gangsters, jazz, uprootedness, and the rest) but to the tragic predicament of humanity as a whole. This is worth stating at the start, if only because an English critic might otherwise feel diffident about approaching a masterpiece which in many ways is so obviously American, and which has been cited so often in definitions of the peculiarly American experience of the twentieth century. An Englishman will miss, no doubt, many important nuances that to an American will be instantly obvious, and he will be less sure of himself in discussing ways in which Fitzgerald does, or does not, look forward to Salinger, Bellow, and other writers of our present Affluent Society. He might, however, hope to see other things (and I am relieved to find Leo Marx lending his support to this hope) which will prove no less important in a final assessment, and which might be *less* easily perceptible at home than abroad. This, at any rate, must be my excuse for venturing, in what follows, to bypass

SOURCE *Modern Fiction Studies* VII, Spring 1961, pp. 37–48.

the type of sociological interest usually and rightly displayed, and to consider *Gatsby* as something even bigger than the demythologising of the American Myth. The squalor and splendour of Gatsby's dreams belong, I shall suggest, to the story of humanity itself; as also does the irony, and judgment, of his awakening.

I

The action takes place in "the waste land" (this phrase is actually used), and is, at one level, the study of a broken society. The "valley of ashes" in which Myrtle and Wilson live symbolizes the human situation in an age of chaos. It is "a certain desolate area of land" in which "ash grey men" swarm dimly, stirring up "an impenetrable cloud, which screens their obscure operations from your sight." This devitalized limbo is presided over by the eyes of Dr. T. J. Eckleburg.

> The eyes of Dr. T.J. Eckleburg are blue and gigantic—their retinas are one yard high. They look out of no face, but instead, from a pair of enormous yellow spectacles which pass over a non-existent nose.

Dr. Eckleburg is an advertisement for spectacles, now faded and irrelevant: put there by some "wild wag of an oculist" who has himself, by this time, either sunk down "into eternal blindness, or forgot them and moved away." As a simple but haunting symbol of the *deus absconditus* who might once have set the waste land in motion Dr. Eckleburg recurs at certain crucial moments in the novel. He is the only religious reference, but his sightless gaze precludes the possibility of judging the "ash grey men" against traditional religious norms, and confers upon them the right to pity as well as to scorn. It ensures, too, that though the actual setting of the valley is American, and urban, and working-class (I intend to use the word "class" in this account again, without further apology), the relevance, as in Eliot's own *Waste Land*, is to a universal human plight.

Beneath Dr. Eckleburg's unseeing eyes the ash gray men drift. "Drift" is a word used many times, and with the exception of Gatsby himself, who at least thinks he knows where he is going, it applies to all the main characters, including Carraway, the narrator.

Tom and Daisy, the "moneyed" class, have for years "drifted here and there unrestfully wherever people played polo and were rich together." Tom's restlessness is an arrogant assertiveness seeking to evade in bluster the deep uneasiness of self-knowledge. His hypocrisy and lack of human feeling make him the most unpleasant character in the book, but he is also, when it comes to the point, one of the sanest. In the battle with Gatsby he has the nature of things on his side, so that his victory is as inevitable as it is unadmirable. The discovery that his sanity is even less worthwhile in human terms than Gatsby's self-centred fantasy is not the least of the novel's ironies.

Daisy is more complex than Tom, and far less real. Her manner has in it, as Carraway notes, all the promise of the world. Her eyes, "looking up into my face, promised that there was no-one in the world she so much wanted to see"; her voice held "a promise that she had done gay, exciting things just a while since, and that there were gay, exciting things hovering in the same hour." But this is all yesterday and tomorrow. Today, there is only emptiness. "'What'll we do with ourselves this afternoon?' cried Daisy, 'and the day after that, and the next thirty years?'"

When Gatsby arrives with his "romantic readiness," his unqualified faith in Daisy's ideal and absolute reality, he is broken against her sheer non-existence. She turns out to be literally nothing, and vanishes from the novel at the very point when, if she existed at all, she would have to start being really there. Her romantic facade, so adequate in appearance to the dreams Gatsby has built around it, is without reality. She has no belief in it herself, and so it means nothing. It is no more than an attempt to alchemize the dreariness of an unsuccessful life into some esoteric privilege of the sophisticated. The account she gives of her "cynicism" is not without genuine pain. But the pain is transmuted in the telling into a pleasure—the only genuine pleasure, one feels, of which she would be capable.

> The moment her voice broke off, ceasing to compel my attention, my belief, I felt the basic insincerity of what she had said.... I waited, and sure enough, in a moment she looked at me with an absolute smirk on her lovely face, as if she had asserted her membership in a rather distinguished secret society to which she and Tom belonged.

Behind the facade of the rich, the "rather distinguished secret society" to which they belong, is money and carelessness—the two protections upon which, in moments of crisis, they fall back, leaving those outside to sink or swim as best they can.

The social break-up at this level is paralleled in the working class. Myrtle, Tom's mistress, is the quintessence of vulgarity. Her "class" is no strong, peasant culture, but a drifting wreckage of the spiritless and defeated. Her only hope is to escape—and it is her one positive quality, her vitality, which leads her to seek happiness in a role other than that to which she is born. With Tom's prestige and money behind her she sets up a town establishment, throws parties, apes the rich, outgrows her husband ("I thought he knew something about breeding, but he wasn't fit to lick my shoe"), looks down on her own class with aloof disdain ("Myrtle raised her eyebrows at the shiftlessness of the lower orders. 'Those people! You have to keep after them all the time'"). In playing this moneyed role, she achieves most of its actual corruptions whilst adding the new ingredient of vulgarity. One minute she avoids the word "bitch" when buying a dog ("'Is it a boy or a girl?' she asked delicately"), the next takes for granted that a total stranger will want to sleep with her sister.

And yet, in a universe of ash-grey men represented by her husband and presided over by the eyes of Dr. Eckleburg, it is difficult to feel she is very obviously to blame. Fitzgerald's ironic awareness of life's perversities is symbolized in the fact that her one positive quality, her vitality, should find expression in the waste land only as vulgarity and disloyalty, and that it should become the instrument of her death. In the same way, Gatsby's great positive quality—his faith, and the loyalty to Daisy that goes with it—finds expression only as a tawdry self-centredness, and it, too, contributes to his death.

II

Among these rootless people Carraway comes to live: implicated to a certain extent in the action which he records, and controlling the tone of the narrative. His implication is impersonal, in that his own emotions and destiny are not centrally involved; personal, in that his humanity forces him, even against his will, to understand and pity Gatsby, and that this amounts to a not uncostly selflessness which turns out to be the most important moral positive the novel has to offer.

Carraway is the one middle-class character in the novel—vaguely at home in the worlds both of Daisy and of Myrtle, but belonging to neither, and so able to see and judge both very clearly. He is conscious of "advantages" of moral education that enables him to see through false romanticisms to their underlying insincerity, and savour their bitter ironies. Yet he, too, has his restlessness, as uprooted as everyone else in truth, though more determined than the rest to preserve some "decencies," to cling to some principle of order and sanity in the wreckage.

His family comes from the Middle West. It is proud of having a Duke somewhere in the family tree, but relies in practice for its safety and self-respect on big-business—the "wholesale hardware business" which Carraway never wholly loses sight of as his birthright. He has been made restless by the war, and is now looking for some sort of armour against life in detachment and moral alertness. The "intimate revelations of young men" bore him. He is tolerant of other people, but would escape from the sloughs of emotional despond into some simple pattern of control and acceptance.

> Conduct may be founded on the hard rock or the wet marshes, but after a certain point I don't care what it is founded on. When I came back from the East last autumn I felt that I wanted the world to be in uniform and at a sort of moral attention for ever; I wanted no more riotous excursions, with privileged glimpses into the human heart.

Cast into the situation which is the subject of the novel, his attitude is from the first ambivalent. "I was within and without, simultaneously enchanted and repelled by the inexhaustible variety of life." He sees the sordidness, the unreality of the New York "rich," and his ironic observation upon it is habitually devastating. But he is able to hope, even while seeing as clearly as he does, that the vitality, the variety, the promise of excitement, may not be wholly false. Infected with the restlessness that he records in others, he is half convinced that some rewarding experience might lie behind the world of throbbing taxis, rich perfumes, gay parties, if one could only find a way through to it. "I began to like New York, the racy, adventurous feel of it at night, and the satisfaction that the constant flicker of men and women and machines gives to the restless eye." He responds almost equally to the haunting loneliness of it, and the unceasing promise. His imagination is willing to entertain what his intellect and experience of life rejects: "Imagining that I, too, was hurrying towards gaiety and sharing their intimate excitement, I wished them well."

Carraway's attitude towards Gatsby is, from the first, typical. He recognises in Gatsby the epitome of his society, and is accordingly enchanted and repelled by him in the highest degree. His conscious moral instinct is to disapprove: but his imagination is fascinated since perhaps here, in this extraordinary man, the romantic promise is at last fulfilled. He wavers, therefore, between almost complete contempt for Gatsby, and almost complete faith in him; and this ambivalent attitude persists until Gatsby's collapse, after which it gives way to a deeper, and costlier, attitude of pity, towards which the whole novel moves. The eventual shattering of Gatsby's high romantic hopes against an inexorably unromantic reality turns him, for Carraway, into a tragic figure. The quality of the ironic observation reflects this change, and Carraway's closing meditation, rising above the particular events, finds a universal, and tragic, significance in Gatsby's fate.

III

Carraway's first mention of the hero, some time before he actually appears, is a clear statement of his own judgment upon him: "Gatsby, who represented everything for which I have an unaffected scorn." But it is an acknowledgment also of the fascination which Gatsby exerts over him. "If personality is an unbroken series of successful gestures, then there was something gorgeous about him, some heightened sensitivity to the promise of life."

In one sense Gatsby is the apotheosis of his rootless society. His background is cosmopolitan, his past a mystery, his temperament that of an opportunist entirely oblivious to the claims of people or the world outside. His threadbare self-dramatisation, unremitting selfishness, and attempts to make something out of nothing are the same in kind as those of the wasteland society, and different only in intensity. Yet this intensity springs from a quality which he alone has: and this we might call "faith." He really believes in himself and his illusions: and this quality of faith, however grotesque it must seem with such an object, sets him apart from the cynically armoured midgets whom he epitomizes. It makes him bigger than they are, and more vulnerable. It is, also, a quality which commands respect from Carraway: since at the very least, "faith" protects Gatsby from the evasiveness, the conscious hypocrisy of the Toms and Daisies of the world, conferring something of the heroic on what he does; and at the best it might still turn out to be the "way in" to some kind of reality beyond the romantic facade, the romantic alchemy which, despite his cynicism, Carraway still half hopes one day to find.

Gatsby's first appearance is in his garden at night looking out at the single green light which is the symbol of his dreams. He is content to "be alone": and isolation is an essential part of his make-up, a necessary part of his god-like self-sufficiency. He is next heard of as a mystery: the man whom nobody knows, but whose hospitality everybody accepts.

> There was music from my neighbour's house through the summer night. In his blue gardens men and girls came and went like moths among the whisperings and the champagne and the stars.

When Carraway meets him as a host, and first hears that "old sport" which becomes so moving at the end, he does not even know that it *is* Gatsby. This social gaffe is an occasion for the sublime courtesy and forgiveness that Gatsby has to dispense, the "charm" which is too deeply a part of his act for any accusation of insincerity to be even remotely appropriate.

> He smiled understandingly—much more than understandingly. It was one of those rare smiles with a quality of eternal reassurance in it, that you may come across four or five times in life. It faced—or seemed to face—the whole eternal world for an instant, and then concentrated on *you* with an irresistible prejudice in your favour. It understood you just so far as you wanted to be understood, believed in you as you would like to believe in yourself, and assured you that it had precisely the impression of you that, at your best, you hoped to convey. Precisely at that point it vanished....

As Gatsby's guests become more hilarious, his own "correctness" grows. He is apart from the chaos which his money has mysteriously called into being, presiding over it with benevolent detachment: considerate to his fellows when they are careless, decorous when they are disorderly. As the party finishes, he remains alone on the steps of his mansion—his formality and his solitude an intriguing enigma, that has still to be explored.

> A sudden emptiness seemed to flow now from the windows and the great doors, endowing with complete isolation the figure of the host, who stood on the porch, his hand up in a formal gesture of farewell.

IV

This, then, is the setting. The novel is concerned with Gatsby's reasons for appearing out of the blue and becoming host to half the rich "moths" of New York. He is, it turns out, in love with Daisy. The whole elaborate decor has been constructed for the sole purpose of staging a dramatic reunion with her: a reunion which will impress her with Gatsby's "greatness," and eradicate, at a stroke, the five years of married life which she has drifted through since seeing him last.

As we soon learn, his affair with Daisy had been a youthful romance, one among many, and nurtured in an atmosphere of cynicism, deceit, purposelessness. But it had, unlike Gatsby's other affairs, been complicated first by Daisy's casualness, and then by their unavoidable separation: and somehow, during the muddle, Gatsby had fallen in love, and the affair had become the "greatest thing in his life." The romantic promise which in Daisy herself was the merest facade became, for him, an ideal, an absolute reality. He built around her the dreams and fervours of his youth: adolescent, self-centred, fantastic, yet also untroubled by doubt, and therefore strong; attracting to themselves the best as well as the worst of his qualities, and eventually becoming an obsession of the most intractable kind.

As Carraway comes to know Gatsby, he wavers between scepticism and faith. He sees, clearly, in Gatsby the faults which he scorns in others—"charm" that is simply a technique for success, self-centredness masquerading as heroic vision, romantic pretensions based on economic corruption and a total disregard for humanity—yet he is impressed, despite himself, by the faith which transmutes all this into another pattern. Gatsby is different from the others in that he means every word he says, really believes in the uniqueness of his destiny. His romantic clichés, unlike those of Tom or Daisy, are used with simple belief that they are his own discovery, his own prerogative, his own guarantee of Olympian apartness and election. He is "trying to forget something very sad that happened ... long ago." He has "tried very hard to die but seemed to bear an enchanted life." To listen to him is like "skimming hastily through a dozen magazines"—and yet is not like that at all, since Gatsby's faith really has brought the dead clichés back to life again, or at any rate to some semblance of life. So much in his account that might have been empty boasting turns out to be true. He has been to Oxford—after a fashion. His credentials from the commissioner of police for whom he was "able to do ... a favour once" are genuine—they prevent him from being arrested for breaking a traffic law. His love for Daisy, too, is real, up to a point: there is a moment when it seems that he has achieved the impossible, and actually realized his fantastic programme for returning to the past.

The tragedy—for it is a tragic novel, though of an unorthodox kind—lies in the fact that Gatsby can go only so far and no further. Faith can still remove sizeable molehills, but is absolutely powerless when it comes to mountains. The ultimate romantic affirmation, "I'll always love you alone" cannot be brought to life: certainly not in the waste land; not when people like Daisy, and Gatsby himself, are involved. Gatsby's faith has to break, in the end, against a reality radically incompatible with it. But in so breaking,, it makes him a tragic figure: and unites him symbolically with many men more worthy than himself—with, indeed, the general lot of mankind.

V

Gatsby's whole project is characterized by that mingling of the fantastic and the scrupulously correct which is his settled attitude to life (the phrase "old sport" is itself a masterly fusion of the two extremes). He approaches Carraway with his all-important request not directly, but by way of Jordan Baker. And why? Because "Miss Baker's a great sportswoman, you know, and she'd never do anything that wasn't right." His "correctness," like most of his other qualities, is peculiarly inverted, but not wholly a sham. He uses it exclusively to get his own way, and yet he is so wholly taken-in himself that he cannot be accused, as anyone else might be, of hypocrisy.

And what *does* Gatsby want of Carraway? "'He wants to know,' continued Jordan, "if you'll invite Daisy to your house some afternoon and then let him come over.'"

He wants Carraway, to put this bluntly, to help him capture a friend's wife—and this simply because Carraway happens to be the man living next door, from which a spectacular view of the Gatsby mansion is to be enjoyed. "The modesty of the demand shook me," Carraway comments: and it is part of the greatness of the novel that though Carraway sees the whole situation very clearly, and has no bias in favour either of emotional extravagance or of Gatsby himself, his comment is not wholly ironical. It is not even primarily ironical, since Carraway is already beginning to see also, in all its tawdry splendour, the nature of Gatsby's vision: and given that, the demand really *is* modest.

> He had waited five years and bought a mansion where he dispensed starlight to casual moths—so· that he could 'come over' some afternoon to a stranger's garden.

Carraway's comment to Jordan ("'Did I have to know all this before he could ask such a little thing?'") is again only marginally ironic. The situation is too unanchored for simple moral judgments—partly because, given Gatsby's faith among the ashes, it is difficult to find norms against which to judge; partly because Gatsby is, after all, "big," so that nothing he does can be simply contemptible; and partly because Carraway himself is not given to conventional attitudes towards human relationships, so that his judgment rises out of a growing awareness of a complex situation and is in no sense imported from outside. He readily agrees, in any event, to Gatsby's request, his "unaffected scorn" of the man wholly overcome, now, by fascinated interest in the unfolding events.

The actual meeting of Gatsby and Daisy is the central episode of the novel. Everything leads up to it, and what follows is a working out of implications which are in the meeting itself. There is the tension as Gatsby waits, and the embarrassing absurdity of the first few minutes together—the irony here highly comic, and very much at Gatsby's expense. Then comes the moment of happiness, when the ideal seems to have been actualised. Daisy herself is carried away by the elation of the moment. " 'I'm so glad Jay.' Her throat 'full of' ... aching, grieving beauty, told only of her unexpected joy." And Gatsby is transfigured: he "literally glowed; without a word or a gesture of exultation a new well-being radiated from him and filled the small room"

This is followed by the slow hint, in the next hour or so, that the dream has already started to shatter against reality. Now, the irony becomes tragic rather than comic in tone, as Carraway's sympathy veers round towards Gatsby, and starts to become engaged. No reality, however great or vital, could have stood up to an illusion on the scale that Gatsby has constructed.

> Almost five years! There must have been moments even that afternoon when Daisy tumbled short of his dreams—not through her own fault, but because of the colossal vitality of his illusion. It had gone beyond her, beyond everything.... No amount of fire and freshness can challenge what a man can store up in his ghostly heart.

And Daisy, far from having "fire and freshness," has only her pale imitation of it. She has grown up in her world of money and carelessness, where "all night the saxophones wailed the hopeless comment of the Beale Street Blues," and dawn was always an hour of disenchantment. What Gatsby demands of her is that she should go to Tom and say, in all sincerity, "I never loved you." This is the unadmirable impossibility upon which his faith is staked: and Carraway's warning to him, as soon as the full extent of the "rather harrowing" intention becomes clear, is a striking example of the way in which the most elementary commonsense can sometimes knock a man's private world to pieces.

> "I wouldn't ask too much of her," I ventured. "You can't repeat the past."
> "Can't repeat the past?" he cried incredulously. "Why, of course you can."

Gatsby has ignored, and disbelieved in, such depressing commonplaces as Carraway's—the depressing commonplaces which are at the heart of Daisy's cynicism, and of the greyness of the ash-grey men. In his own private world past and future can be held captive in the present. His faith allows almost boundless possibilities to be contemplated: and if the "universe" which has "spun itself out in his brain" does happen to be one of "ineffable gaudiness," this does not alter the fact that it is more remarkable, and colourful, than the realities against which it breaks. Like Tamburlaine, Gatsby has made a "Platonic conception of himself" out of the extravagant emotions and aspirations of an adolescent. Like Tamburlaine, too, he has made himself vulnerable by acknowledging the power of a Zenocrate. It is only poetic justice, perhaps, that his own Zenocrate should turn out to be Daisy. But whoever it had been, the result would have been the same.

The battle between Gatsby and Tom is at one level the battle between illusion and reality. Tom has the nature of things on his side, and it is part of the nature of things that he and Daisy belong together. Daisy has to say to Gatsby not "I loved you alone," but "I loved you too." This "too" is Tom's victory, and he can follow it up by equating Gatsby's romance with his own hole-in-the-corner affair with Myrtle—calling it a "presumptuous little flirtation" and announcing that it is now at an end. After this Gatsby has no weapons left for the fight. He goes on watching over Daisy to the end, but half aware himself, now, of the annihilating fact that he is watching over nothing. "So I walked away and left him there standing in the moonlight—watching over nothing."

He has "broken up like glass against Tom's hard malice": and for this reason he can now be pitied, since Tom's attitude, though conclusively realistic, is also hard, and inhuman, and smaller than Gatsby's own. The reality turns out to be less admirable, less human than the fantasy. The events leading to Gatsby's death symbolize, very powerfully, that his downfall, though inevitable, is by no means an unambiguous triumph of moral powers. His death is brought about by Daisy, who first lets him shield her and then deserts him: by Tom, who directs the demented Wilson to the place where he is to be found; and by Wilson himself—a representative of the ash-grey men who comes to Gatsby, in his disillusionment, as a terrible embodiment of the realities which have killed his dream.

> Gatsby must have looked up at an unfamiliar sky through frightening leaves and shivered as he found what a grotesque thing a rose is and how raw the sunlight was upon the scarcely created grass. A new world, material without being real, where poor ghosts, breathing dreams like air, drifted fortuitously about ... like that ashen, fantastic figure gliding towards him through the amorphous trees.

A nightmare of this kind demands some sympathy: and if Dr. Eckleburg is unable to provide it, as he looks down unseeingly upon the drama, then there is all the more call for humanity to supply the need. But Gatsby's "friends" fade away in the hour of death: and Gatsby, whose contributions to his own death has been loyalty to Daisy (the one real and valuable emotion bound up with his fantasy), is left alone at the end.

VI

But not completely alone. His father turns up, with pathetic evidences of Gatsby's youthful aspirations and his generosity as a son; one of the guests who has attended Gatsby's parties attends the funeral; and Carraway himself remains, determined to act in a decently human way. "... it grew upon me that I was responsible, because no-one else was interested—interested, I mean, with that intense personal interest to which everyone has some vague right in the end."

Carraway is also, by now, converted to Gatsby: "I found myself on Gatsby's side, and alone." His final compliment to Gatsby, "They're a rotten crowd.... You're worth the whole damn bunch put together" may not add up to much, but it is at least true, and a statement to which everything has been moving. At the very least, it is recognition that being right about the nature of things is no excuse for being inhuman. In its broader implications, it is part of the larger meaning of the novel: which is that in a tragic and imperfect world scorn and condemnation can often come too easily as attitudes. Human warmth and pity may not be able to set everything to rights: but they are costlier and more decent attitudes than mere judgment; and in the waste land, perhaps juster than judgment itself.

Carraway's befriending of Gatsby is certainly not easy for himself. The cost is symbolized in the ending of his short affair with Jordan Baker. He had been attracted to Jordan in the first place by her self-sufficiency ("Almost any exhibition of complete self-sufficiency draws a stunned tribute from me"), partly by her appearance of "moral attention." ("She was a slender, small-breasted girl, with an erect carriage, which was accentuated by throwing her body backward to the shoulders like a young cadet.") and partly by the needs of his own loneliness. But Jordan turns out, in the end, to be as worthless as the rest: "moral attention" may be necessary at times in self-defense, but as a total attitude to life it has its limits. Carraway's desire for emotional detachment had, from the start, a certain pessimism underlying it—an acceptance of disenchantment which finds expression in some of the most characteristic of his reflections.

> I was thirty. Before me stretched the portentous, menacing road of a new decade.... Thirty—the promise of a decade of loneliness, a thinning list of single men to know, a thinning brief-case of enthusiasm, thinning hair.

He cannot make reality more acceptable than it is, or find a way out of the waste land, or suggest a cure for the cynicism which is eating out the heart of society. He can, however, prize the highest human values that he sees, and respond to the misfortunes of others with a pity which has in it a feeling for human suffering as a whole. It is characteristic that in the closing sentences he should find in Gatsby's tragic awakening a symbol of the disenchantment of mankind as a whole—and end on a note which, transcending both

Gatsby's personal fate, and the *folie-de-grandeur* of the America which he also represents, achieves a universal tragic vision as haunting as any I can think of in a novel.

> As I sat there brooding on the old, unknown world, I thought of Gatsby's wonder when he first picked out the green light at the end of Daisy's dock. He had come a long way to this blue dawn, and his dream must have seemed so close that he could hardly fail to grasp it. He did not know that it was already behind him, somewhere back in that vast obscurity beyond the city, where the dark fields of the republic rolled on under the night.
>
> Gatsby believed in the green light, the orgastic future that year by year recedes before us. It eluded us then, but that's no matter—tomorrow we will run faster, stretch out our arms further ... And one fine morning—
>
> So we beat on, boats against the current, borne back ceaselessly into the past.

90
Plato's Stepchildren, Gatsby and Cohn

◆

PAUL LAUTER

A standard gambit of courses in modern writing—to show how Hemingway's opening sentences and paragraphs epitomize his stories—has strangely not been applied to the beginning of *The Sun Also Rises:* "Robert Cohn was once middleweight boxing champion of Princeton" (p. 3).[1] The classroom approach to this first sentence suggests that the novel's subject (like the sentence's) is Robert Cohn; that its concern is his relationship to whatever Princeton stands for; and that his attempt to relate himself to Princeton is violently and grotesquely at odds with the very nature of his goal. A similar analysis of the rest of the paragraph suggests the ambiguous relationship of the narrator to Cohn, the inevitable failure of Cohn's attempt to be more than a "Jew at Princeton," and the supercilious quality of "Princeton" society.

Such results are particularly startling in light of the usual views of Cohn as morally vacuous and "unmanly" (Carlos Baker), sentimental (Theodore Bardacke) or "damned" (Delmore Schwartz)—in short, as a representative of Gertrude Stein's "Lost Generation." But these views, accepted by critics from the not altogether unbiased opinions of the other characters in the novel (and based on the notion that everyone must "adjust" to his environment, however corrupt), characteristically limit interpretations of *The Sun Also Rises* to contrasting the decadence of international society with the idyllic purity of manly companionship in the mountains and manly enterprise in the *corrida*. We might then well prefer to examine the apparently odd results of classroom empiricism, considering Cohn's nature and function in the novel in a perspective suggested by Arthur L. Scott.[2] From this angle another, perhaps equally important, theme emerges: the search of an innocent outsider to achieve his ideal in an alien social world.

This rings familiarly enough in American literature, especially since James. Indeed, it was the key of the Jazz Age's other most successful novel,

SOURCE *Modern Fiction Studies*, IX, Winter 1963, pp. 338–346.

published the year before *The Sun Also Rises*, Fitzgerald's *The Great Gatsby*. And while there is probably now no way to prove that Hemingway wrote his book partly as a commentary on Fitzgerald's, can the parallels in hero (if we may apply that term to Cohn), narrative technique, and subject be altogether accidental? However deliberate such analogies may be, they provide a little-tested lens for our review.

Gatsby and Cohn, to begin with the obvious, maintain healthy, athletic, outwardly All-American fitness with Franklin-like regularity of exercise. Their avoidance of drink becomes matter for comment among people whose very ambiance is alcoholic. Socially awkward, they speak with stiff formality and in approaching women are encumbered with constraints and delusions. These suggestive details help to picture both as outsiders—we are always on a last-name basis with them—and romantic idealists. Cohn remains, more or less, in the situation of a Jew at Princeton, asleep in Jake's outer office, asleep in the car climbing through the Pyrenees, asleep in the wineshop's rear—an alien among the everyday norms of job, companionship, society. Unassimilable in the liquorish set, he remains too devoted to his vision of the Promised Land—life everlasting with Brett—to retreat, until the end, into virile heroics or Life On The Irati. Nor do French bobs recline on Gatsby's shoulder; we see him, rather, hand raised in a formal gesture of farewell, alone in the doorway of his dreams (p. 56). Theirs are, indeed, dream worlds, in which bliss past can be recaptured happily forever, in which their almost maniacal devotion can reclaim their ladyloves from the clutches of despoiling rivals. Theirs are, in a twisted modern fashion, the lives of the Emersonian American: each tries to impose on a sick and wasting world his individual order, an order founded, as Nick comments of Gatsby, on "his Platonic conception of himself" (p. 99). Cohn and Gatsby thus represent the last stand of the Romantic ideal—in America the Ahab, the Newman, affronting his destiny along the margins of disaster.

Their destinies are irrevocably implicated with their women, the spirits of their green light, their Promised Land. To possess the woman is to attain the felicity of dreams fulfilled. Such incarnated ideals must ultimately fall short of what imagination makes them, but in the modern world of these novels they are corrupt from the very beginning. The girl who might once have been at least the healthy sprite Daisy Miller now is Daisy *Fay*—a fairy, a witch—and Brett is a Circe about whom Pagan revellers dance (p. 155). The societies of the White South and the British Peerage have imposed their decay on their supposedly empedestaled females, translating the Golden Girl into the Girl of Gold. The outsider, seeking entry to the supposed values of chic, moneyed civilization, finds his goals themselves corrupted in the persons of these depraved "heiresses of all the ages," fairy princesses no longer, but Liliths. Hemingway, however, could not be satisfied with Fitzgerald's rather too simple portrait of white innocence betrayed into effete carelessness. Daisy never becomes more than an irresolute Louisville debutante; but Brett, her needs not unlike Daisy's, is capable of passion, of concern, even of moral action—of being, in other words, a woman. One wonders whether Daisy's class is not altogether of Gatsby's invention; certainly, her failure makes moral judgment too easy for Nick, and for Fitzgerald.

Nor could Hemingway accept Fitzgerald's pat reduplication of a Daisy, in the person of Jordan Baker, for Nick to be concerned over. Jordan in dress, manner, and morals, is Daisy's facsimile, but her presence eliminates the possibility of conflict between Gatsby and Nick; each has his own girl, even if she is really the same girl, and thus Fitzgerald need find no conflict between his narrator and hero. But it is optimistic, probably in Hemingway's view unrealistic, to imagine that the idealist's aspirations do not run afoul of others' normal attitudes and desires, especially those of his intimates. And in both the novels at hand, the narrators, attached as they are to social norms, are most often subject to the gaff of the passionate and uncompromising aspirations of the heroes toward whom they are, somewhat despite themselves, attracted.

Nick and Jake do share to some extent the outsider's position: Jake is a sometimes serious Catholic among heathen, and Nick an uncomfortable westerner at East Egg. They participate in the outsiders' primary desire: possession of the idealized girl. But both Jake and Nick are incapable of fulfilling their aspirations, Jake because of his physical impotence, Nick because of a kind of emotional sterility (vide his "affair," his "interior rules"— e.g., pp. 57–59), both because of the ironic, all-but-cynical view of experience that their knowledge of "reality" enforces. They know, or have heard, too much about women to precipitate themselves along the hopelessly idealistic tacks of Gatsby and Cohn; yet they cannot deny altogether the lure of those limitless courses. If Gatsby and Cohn are versions of the active, idealistic American hero, Nick and Jake represent the contemplative, disabused counterpart, the Ishmael whose artist's function it is to tell idealist Ahab's story to the world.

Thus are reporter and participant sundered and Emerson's romantic vision of the Poet as simultaneously Doer and Sayer disintegrates before the tragic limitations of man's real condition. For the ironic perspective that permits Nick and Jake the distance necessary for relating their tales also restrains their fully committing themselves and thus their fully experiencing. On the other hand, the innocent outsider, capable of pursuing his ideal and thus of achieving tragic experience, cannot, as Emerson had hoped, "tell us how it was with him."

Despite this dichotomy of Doer and Sayer, actor and observer, Nick presents Gatsby's life in terms not remote from those Gatsby himself might, after the Plaza catastrophe, have chosen. In the course of the book Nick is so far absorbed by Gatsby that his own responses, however selfish and deceitful at the beginning, end no longer separable from the hero's. In effect, Nick functions less as an artist "absorbing and translating" (in Whitman's terms) Gatsby's life than as a surrogate for the reader himself, suggesting by his attitudes what the reader's ought to become. Hemingway's narrator, on the other hand, does not simply provide a clear glass through which we view distinctly the people of the book; rather, we must always take into consideration Jake's distortions, born of conflict with the others, if we are to locate realities in *The Sun Also Rises*.

The genesis of this antagonism can better be understood if we conceive this artist-actor dichotomy as a way of expressing conflict between outer and inner selves, between the social being involved in the everyday game and what Whitman called the "Me myself," the "essential being" of theological jargon. Both "selves" seek fulfillment, but where the social being, if he sees a final goal at all, sees it in terms of necessary adjustments to and compromises with phenomenal reality—never really having what he desires, but never altogether chancing its loss—the inner self wills risking annihilation in his plunge toward union with the depths of life, possession of his ideal in a here and now. The outer self is implicated in, largely formed by, social norms; his responses are therefore likely to be limited by the stereotypes of everyday reality. To him, a passionate quest to "strike through the mask" (as Ahab puts it) must appear eccentric, if not altogether mad and abhorrent. For the inner self denies the validity of appearances like the passage of time and the standard estimates of what man is "out for", thus placing himself apart from and at odds with normal society. Conflict arises between that of man which would adjust as comfortably as possible to things as they are and that which would force him to contemplate and move together things as they ought to be. These inner convulsions, as has often been pointed out, can symbolically be rendered as a struggle between an observer holding more or less normal standards and an actor bearing his ideal vision.

Allan R. Brick has shown how many novels of the past century in dramatizing this conflict follow the pattern of "The Rime of the Ancient Mariner": the observer (the "Wedding Guest") is induced imaginatively to follow an outré actor into a world of extraordinary experiences; here, the world's stock responses discarded as irrelevant, the actor reveals to him a vision of true reality; in light of this revelation, the observer can return to normalcy sadder, perhaps, but wiser in being freed from the tyranny heretofore imposed by the normal world's stereotypes.[3] Revelation does not come easily—the observer must painfully lay aside his comfortable, traditional points of view if he is to achieve the enlightenment offered. Can he? And are the insights offered by the idealist actor valid?

To these questions Fitzgerald joins with English Romantics and American Transcendentalists in answering an optimistic "Yes." Thus Gatsby *is* "worth the whole damn bunch put together" (p. 154) and Nick can feel solidly with him against the world (p. 166); Gatsby's experience with Daisy *can* produce in Nick a knowledge sufficient to turn him—albeit regretfully—

from his false Jordan and to save him from the phony East (pp. 178–179). Nick can even, in the end, embrace beyond his ironies Gatsby's American dream: "It eluded us then, but that's no matter—tomorrow we will run faster, stretch out our arms farther.... And one fine morning—" (p. 182). But to produce what is both in its optimism and its nonchalance toward ambiguity an anachronistically Emersonian book, Fitzgerald must make us accept an American hoodlum as incurably romantic and naive as James' frontier millionaire, Newman; a narrator amazing at once in his ultimate moral corrigibility and initial insensibility; and the artifice of the two Daisies. Remarkably, he does so (and therein lies the great art of *The Great Gatsby*), mostly, I think, by maintaining through the voice of Nick that peculiarly naive quality which manages to reside even in the most jaded Americans. We might ask how Nick can fail to see the tedious conventionality of the West he boasts and to which he retreats or to be appalled by Gatsby's meretricious livelihood. Simply, Nick's image of the West remains that of adolescent vacations (and so we like it) and his picture of Gatsby the Robber never loses its Schilleresque nimbus (and thus we would see him). In both cases Nick demonstrates and Fitzgerald cashes in on that desire so strong in the United States (in reading, moviegoing, or foreign policy) to maintain outdated or absurd, but comforting or captivating, delusions.

But Hemingway plays the ironic, doubting Melville to Fitzgerald's Transcendentalist. His actor and artist are in the most excruciating of conflicts, for Jake's *modus operandi* is "don't think about it" (p. 31), and it is Cohn's peculiar quality to bring out the worst in others by forcing them to think. Critics have often complained that Heminway fails to show in dialogue and action why people take to hating Cohn. It seems clear, though, that he keeps before their eyes a nasty reality—Brett and Mike never arrive on time, Jake does pimp—which their lives normally are devoted to evading. And even more painfully, he affronts them with an implicit ideal of what existence—even theirs—might be if it were honestly and fully wooed rather than dodged. But if his insistence that life—even a week at San Sebastian—ought to have purpose and meaning exposes the shabby tedium of the "good time" the rest are out for, what alternate set of values does he offer? What can one make of his romantic dream of flying off with Brett when his proposed destination is a "Purple Land" (p. 9)? Can Cohn's passive "niceness" be the way of salvation, the way, to borrow Emerson's phrase, of "advancing on Chaos and the Dark"?

Admittedly, idealist aspirations invariably contain absurdities and elements of adolescent Me-against-the-world bravado; it takes something of the child and something of the madman to play Ancient Mariner at Walden or Heathcliff at Pamplona. But Cohn's attitudes and actions are qualified by the heaviest of ironies, probably because Hemingway was always suspicious of ultimates ("I do not know what Man [with a capital M] means," he said apropos of Nobel Prizes). Mundane life involves a competition of values, all of which can have their claims. Though, for example, women in Hemingway stories often bring the infection of society into a man's pure world, the girl of "Cat in the Rain" and Catherine Barkley carry our sympathy. And while adventures among Alpine ski-slopes or The Green Hills of Africa seem sometimes the ultimate apprehension of the good life, they can also be seen as primitive escapes—however refreshing—from the existence among men that we must carry on. For Hemingway, that is, no way offers pure, final gain: to climb here is to slip there, to have this is to have not that. The inner voice must lead man away from one sort of fulfillment even while it may lead him toward another of, perhaps—and perhaps not—paramount concern. So Cohn's is not the sole value center of the novel. In Fitzgerald, Gatsby's attempt to assert the unique validity of a particular concern remains sufficiently creditable, indeed "Great," for its failure to be tragic—and thus to work the purgation of Nick; in Hemingway, such absolute claims become absurdly cramping and the claimant an object of pathos in his blundering enthusiasm:

"Say something pitiful."
"Robert Cohn."
"Not so bad That's better. Now why is Cohn pitiful? Be ironic" (p. 114).

And so Jake must be.

For Jake can accept Cohn when their conflict is discharged in the trivial competition of the tennis court; but when Cohn forces himself on Jake as a rival for their truelove, Jake acts against him. Bad enough that he cannot have fulfillment with Brett, and, as he emphasizes in the book's last line, could not have had were he well; but now Cohn proposes to remove her altogether from the real, however corrupt, social world in which Jake, like all men, must live. In desperate defense Jake tries to draw Brett into that primitive male world in which he can function at least by proxy of Romero's pure sexual performance. In the *corrida* or the mountains the pale cast of Cohn does not intrude its reflections on the harmony of physical action. But insofar as Jake panders to Brett's lust in bringing Romero to her (and hadn't he led Brett on toward the bull-fighter before he actually unites them at the cafe table?—pp. 174–176), he betrays his *aficion* and his simple Spanish paradise. He knows that Brett's hedonism can only unhinge the fine symmetry that makes Romero the image of man's physical perfection. Women like Brett or Margot Macomber intrude upon and shatter the life of pure masculine action. To be delivered of Cohn, Jake chooses what appears the lesser hurt: selling out his own values for Brett's needs.

Is Jake really so altruistic, however, or is he using her nymphomania to rationalize a further betrayal: of what, strangely, he shares with Cohn? For defining Brett as a woman ruled by her lust, however accurate that description, destroys her as an *ideal*, as someone Jake, as much as Cohn, can love with a committed frenzy. Unlike Mike's, their interest in her amounts to more than the fact that she is a "lovely piece"; both must see her as a dream girl worth their tears, their peace, their normal joys. One might argue then, with Mr. Brick, that what Jake finally betrays is the Cohn in him, destroys his idealizing drive. In this respect, too, Jake is forced by the need to continue existing in a fragmentary, sterile world to extinguish the capacity for fashioning and aspiring toward the ideals which give meaning to existence.

The bull-fight people's stares (p. 187) and Cohn's fists bring home to Jake the full torment of his betrayals. Crossing the square to his hotel after being knocked out, Jake sees a different world, perhaps not unlike the raw, grim, fallen domain revealed both to Gatsby and to Cohn. From this "new and changed" perspective, associated with the painful experiences of adolescence (Jake's football game—p. 192), he wishes to retreat into a warm bath (and does so before the book ends). But, impelled by Bill—who through the last stages of the fiesta demonstrates a peculiar solicitude, as a kind of voice of Jake's conscience, for Cohn—he must once more face this nemesis of his peace:

> I opened the door and went in, and set down my suitcase. There was no light in the room. Cohn was lying, face down, on the bed in the dark.
> "Hello, Jake."
> "Don't call me Jake."
> I stood by the door. It was just like this that I had come home. Now it was a hot bath that I needed. A deep, hot bath, to lie back in.
> "Where's the bathroom?" I asked.
> Cohn was crying. There he was, face down on the bed, crying. He had on a white polo shirt, the kind he'd worn at Princeton.
> "I'm sorry, Jake. Please forgive me." (pp. 193–194).

This confrontation has its analogue in Nick's final conversation with Gatsby outside the Buchanans' (pp. 152–154). The results are quite different, seeing clearly what Buchanan society is, Nick altogether allies himself with Gatsby; but Jake, after his essentially childish responses to Cohn, leaves to seek his tub (the taps of which will not run). For while Cohn has told Jake "how it was with him," Emerson's prediction that "all men will be the richer in his fortune" is borne out only in the most ironic way. If the outsider, the actor, the inner self, as I have variously called him, has an ultimate vision to communicate to the world which ejects him, it is submerged in his sobs and drowned in their jeers. Nonetheless, a lesson is here learned by Jake, and by all men who read the story he is compelled to write—that of the book's title: the earth abides but man and his works go down to sorrow and the dark. Just as Jake's painful experience repeats adolescent traumas, so Cohn's returns him, white polo shirt and all, to his time of Princeton trouble. If *The Sun Also Rises* does not chronicle a single "Great" life or great tragedy, it does engrave the tragic bereavements which life repeatedly exacts of those—Jake and Brett no less than Cohn or Lieutenant Henry or the Major of "In Another Country"—capable of any passionate commitment to it. It records the only-to-be-remembered glory of joys and hopes by whose immolation man purchases his days of labor and vanity under the sun.

And if it gets at a moral, it is not Transcendental scorn for the victims of their own weakness, not even ever-renewed aspiration for a green light. Nor, I think, is it merely the value of a tight-lipped code with which to face, and an absinthe fog in which to forget, the depredations of reality. Rather, it has to do with the universal need for sympathy and succor in a disintegrating world of vanity. Speaking his conscientious judgment of Cohn's life, Bill expresses no panegyric but a kind of epitaph for all the people in Hemingway's book: "I feel sorry about Cohn," Bill said, "He had an awful time" (p. 222).[4]

Notes

1. All page references to *The Sun also Rises* and *The Great Gatsby* are to the Scribner's Student's editions.

2. "In Defense of Robert Cohn," *College English*, XVIII (1957), 309–314.

3. Allan R. Brick, "*Wuthering Heights*: Narrators, Audience, and Message," *College English*, XXI (November, 1959), 80–86. He points out that "For Coleridge, the self consisted of the subject and object egos, the I and Me—the portion of the self which perceives and that which is perceived. Ultimate knowledge could be sought only by a penetration into the consciousness, by which means the subject self would become an object, and I as a Me to be perceived and explored into; such perception of the I as a Me would necessitate the emergence of a more essential and profound subject-perceiver, which would itself become a perceived Me at the next stage.... At the final stage of the inward journey, all object-self dropped away: 'We begin with the I KNOW MYSELF, in order to end with the absolute I AM. We proceed from the SELF, in order to lose and find all self in God' [Coleridge, *Biographia Literia*, I, 186]," pp. 83–84. Analogous patterns can be traced in *Walden* and *Song of Myself*.

4. After this paper was in final form, Professor R. W. Stallman's comparison of *The Sun Also Rises* with *The Great Gatsby*—in his *The Houses That James Built* (Michigan State University Press, 1961)—came to my attention. Our essays are, I think, complementary and provide mutual support. He has shown in great detail how Cohn, rather than Jake, is at the moral center of *The Sun Also Rises*. I think, however, that despite his rich exegesis he has not shown how a shift in critical focus and the necessary review of the Cohn-Jake relationship lead to the novel's inner theme.

91
The Craft of Revision: *The Great Gatsby*

◆

KENNETH E. EBLE

"With the aid you've given me," Fitzgerald wrote Maxwell Perkins in December, 1924, "I can make *Gatsby* perfect."[1] Fitzgerald had sent the manuscript of the novel to Scribner's in late October, but the novel achieved its final form only after extensive revisions Fitzgerald made in the next four months. The pencil draft and the much revised galley proofs now in the Fitzgerald collection at Princeton library show how thoroughly and expertly Fitzgerald practiced the craft of revision.[2]

I

The pencil draft both reveals and masks Fitzgerald's struggles. The manuscript affords a complete first version, but the pages are not numbered serially from beginning to end, nor are the chapters and sections of chapters all tied together. There are three segments (one a copy of a previous draft) designated "Chapter III," two marked "Chapter VI." The amount of revising varies widely from page to page and chapter to chapter; the beginning and end are comparatively clean, the middle most cluttered. Fitzgerald's clear, regular hand, however, imposes its own sense of order throughout the text. For all the revisions, the script goes about its business with a straightness of line, a regularity of letter that approaches formal elegance. When he is striking out for the first time, the writing tends to be large, seldom exceeding eight words per line or twenty-five lines per page. When he is copying or reworking from a previous draft, the writing becomes compressed—but never crabbed—and gets half again as much on a page.

An admirer of Fitzgerald—of good writing, for that matter—reads the draft with a constant sense of personal involvement, a sensation of small

SOURCE *American Literature* XXXVI, November 1964, pp. 315–326. Reprinted in *F. Scott Fitzgerald: A Collection of Criticism*, ed. Kenneth E. Eble, New York, 1973, pp. 81–92.

satisfied longings as the right word gets fixed in place, a feeling of strain when the draft version hasn't yet found its perfection of phrase, and a nagging sense throughout of how precariously the writer dangles between the almost and the attained. "All good writing," Fitzgerald wrote his daughter, "is *swimming under water* and holding your breath."[3]

At the beginning of the draft, there appears to have been little gasping for air. There at the outset, virtually as published, is that fine set piece which establishes the tone of the novel with the creation of Nick Carraway and his heightened sense of the fundamental decencies. As one reads the first chapter, however, the satisfaction of seeing the right beginning firmly established soon changes to surprise. The last page of the novel—"gradually I became aware of the old island here that flowered once for Dutch sailors' eyes—a fresh, green breast of the new world."[4]—was originally written as the conclusion of Chapter I. Some time before the draft went into the submission copy, Fitzgerald recognized that the passage was too good for a mere chapter ending, too definitive of the larger purposes of the book, to remain there. By the time the pencil draft was finished, that memorable paragraph had been put into its permanent place, had fixed the image of man holding his breath in the presence of the continent, "face to face for the last time in history with something commensurate to his capacity for wonder."

The three paragraphs which come immediately after, the last paragraphs of the novel, grew out of one long fluid sentence which was originally the final sentence of Chapter I in the draft: "And as I sat there brooding on the old unknown world I too held my breath and waited, until I could feel the motion of America as it turned through the hours—my own blue lawn and the tall incandescent city on the water and beyond that, the dark fields of the republic rolling on under the night." Fitzgerald expanded this suggestion into a full paragraph, crossed out the first attempt, and then rewrote it into three paragraphs on the final page of the draft. There, almost as it appears in the novel, is the green light on Daisy's dock ("green glimmer" in the draft), the orgiastic future (written "orgastic"),[5] and that ultimate sentence, "So we beat on, a boat [changed to "boats"] against the current, borne back ceaselessly into the past." So the draft ends, the last lines written in a "bold, swooping hand," as Fitzgerald described Gatsby's signature, a kind of autograph for the completed work.

The green light (there were originally two) came into the novel at the time of Daisy's meeting with Gatsby. "If it wasn't for the mist," he tells her, "we could see your house across the bay. You always have two green lights that burn all night at the end of your dock." Fitzgerald not only made the green light a central image of the final paragraph, but he went back to the end of the first chapter and added it there: "Involuntarily I glanced seaward—and distinguished nothing except a single green light, minute and far away, that might have been the end of a dock" (pp. 21–22).

II

Throughout the pencil draft, Fitzgerald made numerous revisions which bring out his chief traits as a reviser: he seldom threw anything good away, and he fussed endlessly at getting right things in the right places. The two parties at Gatsby's house, interesting as illustrations of Fitzgerald's mastery of the "scenic method," are equally interesting as examples of how he worked.

The purpose of the first party as it appears in the draft (Chapter III in the book) was chiefly that of creating the proper atmosphere. Though Gatsby makes his first appearance in this section, it is Gatsby's world that most glitters before our eyes. The eight servants (there were only seven in the draft), the five crates (only three in the draft) of oranges and lemons, the caterers spreading the canvas, the musicians gathering, the Rolls-Royce carrying party-goers from the city, are the kind of atmospherics Fitzgerald could always do well. The party itself as it unfolds in the draft reveals a number of intentions that Fitzgerald abandoned as he saw the possibilities of making the party vital to the grander design of the novel.

Originally, whether from strong feelings or in response to his readers' expectations, he took pains to bring out the wild and shocking lives being lived by many of Gatsby's guests. Drug addiction was apparently commonplace, and even more sinister vices were hinted at. A good deal of undergraduate party chatter was also cut from the draft. What a reader of the novel now remembers is what Fitzgerald brought into sharp relief by cutting out the distracting embellishments. "The Jazz History of the World" by Vladimir Tostoff (it was "Leo Epstien" [*sic*] originally; Fitzgerald deleted a number of "Jewish" remarks from the draft) was described in full. When Fitzgerald saw the galleys he called the whole episode "rotten" and reduced the page-and-a-half description to a single clause: "The nature of Mr. Tostoff's composition eluded me...." (p. 50). By the time the party scene had been cut and reworked, almost all that remained was the introduction of Gatsby's physical presence into the novel and the splendid scene of Owl-Eyes in Gatsby's high Gothic library.

Among the many excisions in this party scene, one seemed far too good to throw away. In the draft, it began when Jordan Baker exchanges a barbed remark with another girl:

> "You've dyed your hair since then," remarked Miss Baker and I started but the girls had moved casually on and were talking to an elaborate orchid of a woman who sat in state under a white plum tree.
> "Do you see who that is?" demanded Jordan Baker interestly. [I use Fitzgerald's spelling here and elsewhere in quoting from the draft.]
> Suddenly I did see, with the peculiar unreal feeling which accompanies the recognition of a hitherto ghostly celebrity of the movies.
> "The man with her is her director," she continued. "He's just been married."
> "To her?"

> "No."
> She laughed. The director was bending over his pupil so eagerly that his chin and her mettalic black hair were almost in juxtaposition.
> "I hope he doesn't slip," she added. "And spoil her hair."
> It was still twilight but there was already a moon, produced no doubt like the turkey and the salad out of a caterer's basket. With her hard, slender golden arm drawn through mine we descended the steps....

It is a fine scene, and the girl with the dyed hair, the moon, and the caterer's basket can be found on page 43 of the novel, so smoothly joined together that no one could suspect, much less mourn, the disappearance of that "elaborate orchid" of a woman. But, of course, she did not disappear. The scene was merely transported to the second party where the actress defined the second party as Owl-Eyes defined the first:

> "Perhaps you know that lady," Gatsby indicated a gorgeous, scarely human orchid of a woman who sat in state under a white-plum tree. Tom and Daisy stared, with the particularly unreal feeling that accompanies the recognition of a hitherto ghostly celebrity of the movies.
> "She's lovely,' said Daisy.
> "The man bending over her is her director." (p. 106).

Two pages later, at the end of the second party, we see her again:

> It was like that. Almost the last thing I remember was standing with Daisy and watching the moving-picture director and his Star. They were still under the white-plum tree and their faces were touching except for a pale, thin ray of moonlight between. It occurred to me that he had been very slowly bending toward her all evening to attain this proximity, and even while I watched I saw him stoop one ultimate degree and kiss at her cheek.
> "I like her," said Daisy. "I think she's lovely."
> But the rest offended her.... (p. 108).

One can almost see the writer's mind in action here. The scene was first created, almost certainly, from the rightness of having a "ghostly celebrity of the movies" at the party. It first served merely as scenery and as a way of hinting at the moral laxity of Gatsby's guests. The need to compress and focus probably brought Fitzgerald to consider cutting it out entirely though it was obviously too good to throw away. By that time, perhaps, the second party scene had been written, another possibility had been opened up. Maybe at once, maybe slowly, Fitzgerald recognized that the scene could be used to capture Daisy's essential aloofness which was to defy even Gatsby's ardor. It may well be that this developed and practiced ability to use everything for its maximum effect, to strike no note, so to speak, without anticipating all its vibrations, is what separates Fitzgerald's work in *The Great Gatsby* from his earlier writing, what makes it seem such a leap from his first novels.

Among the many lessons Fitzgerald applied between the rough draft and the finished novel was that of cutting and setting his diamonds so that they caught up and cast back a multitude of lights. In so doing, he found it unnecessary to have an authorial voice gloss a scene. The brilliance floods in upon the reader; there is no necessity for Nick Carraway to say, as he did at one point in the pencil draft: "I told myself that I was studying it all like a philosopher, a sociologist, that there was a unity here that I could grasp after or would be able to grasp in a minute, a new facet, elemental and profound." The distance Fitzgerald traveled from *This Side of Paradise* and *The Beautiful and Damned* to *The Great Gatsby* is in the rewriting of the novel. There the sociologist and philosopher were at last controlled and the writer assumed full command.

III

Rewriting was important to Fitzgerald because, like many other good writers, he had to see his material assume its form—not in the *idea* of a character or a situation—but in the way character and situation and all the rest got down on paper. Once set down, they began to shape everything else in the novel, began to raise the endless questions of emphasis, balance, direction, unity, impact.

The whole of Chapter II in the finished novel (Chapter III in the draft) is an illustration of how the material took on its final form. That chapter begins with Dr. T.J. Eckleburg's eyes brooding over the ash heaps and culminates in the quarrel in Myrtle's apartment where "making a short deft movement, Tom Buchanan broke her nose with his open hand." Arthur Mizener first pointed out that the powerful symbol introduced in this chapter—Dr. Eckleburg's eyes—was the result of Fitzgerald's seeing a dust jacket portraying Daisy's eyes brooding over an amusement park world. "For Christ's sake," he wrote to Perkins, "don't give anyone that jacket you're saving for me. I've written it into the book."[6] The pencil draft indicates that the chapter—marked Chapter III in the manuscript—was written at a different period of time from that of the earlier chapters. The consecutive numbering of the first sixty-two pages of the novel (the first two chapters) shows that for a long time Fitzgerald intended Chapter II as it now stands in the novel to be the third chapter.

In substance, the chapter remained much the same in the finished novel as it was in the draft. But, in addition to moving the chapter forward, Fitzgerald transposed to the next chapter a four-page section at the end describing Nick's activities later in the summer. Summing up Nick's character at the end of the third chapter gave more point to his concluding remark: "I am one of the few honest ["decent" in the draft] people that I have ever known" (p. 60). Bringing the Eckleburg chapter forward meant that the reader could never travel to or from Gatsby's house without traversing the valley of ashes. And ending the second chapter where it now ends meant that the reader could never get to Gatsby's blue gardens where "men and girls came and went like moths among the whisperings and the champagne and the stars" without waking up waiting for a four o'clock train in Penn Station.

But putting a brilliant chapter in place was only part of the task Fitzgerald could see needed to be done once the material was down on paper. Within that chapter, Fitzgerald's pencil was busily doing its vital work. The substance was all there: Tom and Myrtle and Nick going up to New York, the buying of the dog, the drinking in the apartment, the vapid conversations between the McKees and sister Catherine and Myrtle, the final violence. But some little things were not. The gray old man with the basket of dogs did not look like John D. Rockefeller until Fitzgerald penciled it in between lines; the mongrel "undoubtedly had Airedale blood" until Fitzgerald made it "an Airedale concerned in it somewhere"; and finally, the pastoral image of Fifth Avenue on a summer Sunday—"I wouldn't have been surprised to see a flock of white sheep turn the corner"—this didn't arrive until the galleys.

The appearances of Gatsby, as might be expected, are among the most worked-over sections in the draft. Even when the manuscript was submitted, the characterization was not quite satisfactory, either to Fitzgerald or to Maxwell Perkins. The "old sport" phrase which fixes Gatsby as precisely as his gorgeous pink rag of a suit is to be found in only one section of the pencil draft, though it must have been incorporated fully into his speech before Fitzgerald sent off the manuscript. "Couldn't you add one or two characteristics like the use of that phrase 'old sport'—not verbal, but physical ones, perhaps," Perkins suggested.[7] Fitzgerald chose the most elusive of physical characteristics—Gatsby's smile. How he worked it up into a powerfully suggestive bit of characterization can be seen by comparing the pencil draft and the final copy. Gatsby is telling Nick about his experiences during the war:

Rough Draft

"I was promoted to be a major/ and every Allied government gave me a decoration—/even ~~Bul~~ Montenegro little Montenegro down on the Adriatic/Sea!"

~~He lifted up the w~~ Little Montenegro! He lifted up the them words/and nodded at ~~it~~ with a faint smile. My incredulity had/ had turned to fascination now; ~~Gatsby was no longer a~~ it was/ ~~person he was a magazine I had picked up on the casually train~~

Final Version

"I was promoted to be a major, and every Allied government gave me a decoration—even Montenegro, little Montenegro down on the Adriatic Sea!"

Little Montenegro! He lifted up the words and nodded at them— with his smile. The smile comprehended Montenegro's troubled history and sympathized with the brave struggles of the Montenegrin people. It appreciated fully the chain of national circumstances which had elicited this tribute from

like ~~and I was~~ reading the climaxes of only all the stories/~~it contained~~ in a magazine.	Montenegro's warm little heart. My incredulity was submerged in fascination now; it was like skimming hastily through a dozen magazines. (pp. 66–67)

The smile is described in even fuller detail in a substantial addition to galley 15 (page 48 of the novel). One can virtually see Fitzgerald striking upon the smile as a characteristic which could give Gatsby substance without destroying his necessary insubstantiality.

Gatsby is revised, not so much into a real person as into a mythical one; what he *is* not allowed is to distract the reader from what he stands for. Without emphasizing the particulars of Gatsby's past, Fitzgerald wanted to place him more squarely before the reader.[8] Many of the further changes made in the galley proofs were directed toward that end. In the first five chapters of the galleys, the changes are the expected ones: routine corrections, happy changes in wording or phrasing, a few deletions, some additions. But at Chapter VI the galley proofs become fat with whole paragraphs and pages pasted in. Whole galleys are crossed out as the easiest way to make the extensive changes Fitzgerald felt were necessary. Throughout this section, he cut passages, tightened dialogue, reduced explicit statements in order to heighten the evocative power of his prose.

The major structural change brought the true story of Gatsby's past out of Chapter VIII and placed it at the beginning of Chapter VI. Chapter V, the meeting between Gatsby and Daisy, was already at the precise center of the novel.[9] That scene is the most static in the book. For a moment, after the confusion of the meeting, the rain, and his own doubts, Gatsby holds past and present together. The revision of Chapter VI, as if to prolong this scene in the reader's mind, leaves the narrative, shifts the scene to the reporter inquiring about Gatsby, and fills in Gatsby's real past. "I take advantage of this short halt," Nick Carraway says, "while Gatsby, so to speak, caught his breath" (p. 102). The deliberate pause illustrates the care with which the novel is constructed. The Gatsby of his self-created present is contrasted with the Gatsby of his real past, and the moment prolonged before the narrative moves on. The rest of Chapter VI focuses on the first moment of disillusion, Gatsby's peculiar establishment seen through Daisy's eyes.

The rewriting so extensive in this chapter is as important as the shifting of material. The draft at this point has five different sets of numbers, and these pieces are fitted only loosely together. The Gatsby who finally emerges from the rewritten galleys answers the criticisms made by Maxwell Perkins and, more important, satisfies Fitzgerald's own critical sense. "ACTION IS CHARACTER," Fitzgerald wrote in his notes for *The Last Tycoon*. His revisions of dialogue, through which the novel often makes its vital disclosures and confrontations, shows his adherence to that precept. The truth of Gatsby's connection with Oxford was originally revealed to Nick Carraway in a somewhat flat, overly detailed conversation in which Gatsby tries to define his feeling for Daisy. Most of that conversation was cut out and the Oxford material worked into the taut dialogue between Tom Buchanan and Gatsby in the Plaza Hotel which prefaces the sweep of the story to its final action.[10]

In the draft, Gatsby reveals his sentimentality directly; he even sings a poor song he had composed as a boy. In the novel, a long passage of this sort is swept away, a good deal of the dialogue is put into expositon, and the effect is preserved by Nick's comment at the end: "Through all he said, even through his appalling sentimentality...." (p. 112). In the draft, Gatsby carefully explains to Nick why he cannot run away. "'I've got to,' he announced with conviction, 'that's what I've got to do—live the past over again.'" Substance and dialogue are cleared away here, but the key idea is kept, held for a better place, and then shaped supremely right, as a climactic statement in a later talk with Nick: "Can't repeat the past?" he cried incredulously. 'Why of course you can!'" (p. 111). In the draft, much of Gatsby's story is told in dialogue as he talks to Nick. It permits him to talk too much, to say, for example: "'Jay Gatsby!' he cried suddenly in a ringing voice. 'There goes the great Jay Gatsby! That's what people are going to say—wait and see.'" In the novel even the allusion to the title is excised. Gatsby's past is compressed into three pages of swift exposition punctuated by the images of his Platonic self, of his serving "a vast, vulgar, and meretricious beauty," and of Dan Cody and "the savage violence of the frontier brothel and saloon" from which he had come. Finally, in the draft, the undercurrent of passion and heat and boredom which sweeps all of them to the showdown in the Plaza is almost lost. Instead of going directly to the Plaza that fierce afternoon, they all went out to the Polo Grounds and sat through a ball game.

Of the changes in susbtance in this section—and in the novel—the most interesting is the dropping of a passage in which Gatsby reveals to Nick that Daisy wants them to run away. Daisy, elsewhere in the draft, reveals the same intentions. Perhaps Fitzgerald felt this shifted too much responsibility upon Daisy and made Gatsby more passive than he already was. Or perhaps his cutting here was part of a general intention of making Daisy less guilty of any chargeable wrong. Earlier in the draft, Fitzgerald removed a number of references to a previous romance between Daisy and Nick, and at other points he excised uncomplimentary remarks. The result may be contrary to expectation—that a writer ordinarily reworks to more sharply delineate a character—but it was not contrary to Fitzgerald's extraordinary intention. Daisy moves away from actuality into an idea existing in Gatsby's mind and ultimately to a kind of abstract beauty corrupted and corrupting in taking on material form.

V

After Chapter VI and the first part of Chapter VII, to judge both from the draft and the galleys, the writing seems to go easier. The description of the accident with its tense climax—"her left breast was swinging loose like a flap"—is in the novel almost exactly as in the pencil draft. "I *want* Myrtle Wilson's breast ripped off"—he wrote to Perkins, "it's exactly the thing, I think, and I don't want to chop up the good scenes by too much tinkering."[11] Wilson and his vengeance needed little reworking, and though the funeral scene is improved in small ways, as is the conversation with Gatsby's father, no great changes occur here. The last ten pages, the epilogue in which Nick decides to go back West, are much the same, too.

In these last pages, as in the rest of the manuscript, one can only guess at how much writing preceded the version Fitzgerald kept as the pencil draft. "What I cut out of it both physically and emotionally," he wrote later, "would make another novel!"[12] The differences in hand, in numbering of pages, in the paper and pencils used, suggest that much had preceded that draft. Few of the pages have the look of Fitzgerald's hand putting first thoughts to paper, and fewer still—except those obviously recopied—are free of the revision in word and line which shows the craftsman at work.

These marks of Fitzgerald at work, the revelation they give of his ear and his eye and his mind forcing language to do more than it will willingly do, run all through the manuscript.

The best way of summarizing what Fitzgerald did in shaping *The Great Gatsby* from pencil draft to galley to book is to take him at his word in the introduction he wrote in 1934 for the Modern Library edition of the novel. "I had just re-read Conrad's preface to *The Nigger*, and I had recently been kidded half haywire by critics who felt that my material was such as to preclude all dealing with mature persons in a mature world. But, my God! it was my material, and it was all I had to deal with." What he did with it was what Conrad called for in his Preface, fashioned a work which carried "its justification in every line," and which "through an unremitting, never-discouraged care for the shape and ring of sentences" aspired to "the magic suggestiveness of music."

Notes

1. *The Letters of F. Scott Fitzgerald*, ed. Andrew Turnbull (New York, 1963), p. 172.
2. This study is based on an examination of the original pencil draft and the galley proofs in the Fitzgerald collection in the Princeton Library and subsequent work with a microfilm copy of this material. I am indebted to the University of Utah Research Fund for a grant which enabled me to study the materials at Princeton, to Alexander P. Clark, curator of manuscripts, for his indispensable help in making this material available, and to Mr. Ivan Von Auw and the Fitzgerald estate for permission to use this material.

3. *The Crack-Up*, p. 304.

4. All citations hereafter are from the Scribner Library edition of *The Great Gatsby*.

5. Arthur Mizener points out that Fitzgerald corrected the spelling from "orgastic" to "orgiastic" in his own copy of the book (*The Far Side of Paradise*, Boston, 1951, p. 336, n. 22). Yet Fitzgerald's letter to Maxwell Perkins, January 24, 1925, defends the original term: "'Orgastic' is the adjective for 'orgasm' and it expresses exactly the intended ecstasy. It's not a bit dirty" (*Letters*, p. 175). The word appears as "orgiastic" in most editions of the novel, including the current Scribner's printings.

6. *The Far Side of Paradise*, p. 170. The entire letter is to be found in *Letters*, pp. 165–167.

7. *Editor to Author: The Letters of Maxwell E. Perkins*, ed. John Hall Wheelock (New York, 1950), p. 39.

8. Fitzgerald wrote in response to Perkins's criticism: "His [Gatsby's] vagueness I can repair by *making more pointed*—this doesn't sound good but wait and see. It'll make him clear." In a subsequent letter, he wrote: "... Gatsby sticks in my heart. I had him for awhile, then lost him, and now I know I have him again" (*Letters*, pp. 170, 173).

9. Fitzgerald called this chapter his "favorite of all" ("To Maxwell Perkins," *circa* Dec. 1, 1924, *Letters*, p. 170).

10. Mizener points out that Fitzgerald was revising almost up to the day of publication. The revision of this section came some time around February 18, 1925, when Fitzgerald cabled Maxwell Perkins: "Hold Up Galley Forty For Big Change" (*The Far Side of Paradise*, p. 164; p. 335, n. 63). Fitzgerald returned the proofs about February 18th. In a letter to Perkins, he listed what he had done: "1) I've brought Gatsby to life. 2) I've accounted for his money. 3) I've fixed up the two weak chapters (VI and VII). 4) I've improved his first party. 5) I've broken up his long narrative in Chapter VII" (*Letters*, p. 177).

11. *Letters*, p. 175.

12. Introduction to Modern Library edition of *The Great Gatsby* (New York, 1934), p. x.

92
From *The Machine in the Garden: Technology and the Pastoral Ideal in America*

LEO MARX

> In various quiet nooks and corners I had the beginnings of all sorts of industries under way—nuclei of future vast factories, the iron and steel missionaries of my future civilization. In these were gathered together the brightest young minds I could find, and I kept agents out raking the country for more, all the time. I was training a crowd of ignorant folk into experts—experts in every sort of handiwork and scientific calling. These nurseries of mine went smoothly and privately along undisturbed in their obscure country retreats.
>
> . . . .
>
> My works showed what a despot could do with the resources of a kingdom at his command. Unsuspected by this dark land, I had the civilization of the nineteenth century booming under its very nose! It was fenced away from the public view, but there it was, a gigantic and unassailable fact—and to be heard from, yet, if I lived and had luck. There it was, as sure a fact and as substantial a fact as any serene volcano, standing innocent with its smokeless summit in the blue sky and giving no sign of the rising hell in its bowels.
>
> Mark Twain, *A Connecticut Yankee in King Arthur's Court,* 1889

"So," say the parable-makers, "is your pastoral life whirled past and away." We cannot deny the fact without denying our history. When the Republic was founded, nine out of ten Americans were husbandmen; today not one in ten lives on a farm. Ours is an intricately organized, urban, industrial, nuclear-armed society. For more than a century our most gifted writers have dwelt upon the contradiction between rural myth and technological fact. In the machinery of our collective existence, Thoreau says, we have "constructed a fate, an *Atropos*" that never will turn aside. And until we confront the unalterable, he would add, there can be no redemption from a system that makes men the tools of their tools. A similar insight informs *Moby-Dick*.

SOURCE *The Machine in the Garden: Technology and the Pastoral Ideal in America*, New York, 1964, pp. 354–365.

But in the penchant for illusion Melville saw more dire implications. It is suicidal, Ishmael learns, to live "as in a musky meadow" when in truth one is aboard a vessel plunging into darkness. What was a grim possibility for Melville became a certainty for Mark Twain and Henry Adams; neither was able to imagine a satisfactory resolution of the conflict figured by the machine's incursion into the garden. By the turn of the century they both envisaged the outcome as a vast explosion of new power. Power, Adams said, now leaped from every atom. The closing chapters of *The Education of Henry Adams* are filled with images of mankind in the grip of uncontrollable forces. He pictured the forces grasping the wrists of man and flinging him about "as though he had hold of ... a runaway automobile...." Adams was haunted by the notion that bombs were about to explode. "So long as the rates of progress held good," he observed, "these bombs would double in force and number every ten years."[1]

But the ancient ideal still seizes the native imagination. Even those Americans who acknowledge the facts and understand the fables seem to cling, after their fashion, to the pastoral hope. This curious state of mind is pictured by Charles Sheeler in his "American Landscape" (1930). Here at first sight is an almost photographic image of our world as it is, or, rather, as we imagine it will be if we proceed without a change of direction. No trace of untouched nature remains. Not a tree or a blade of grass is in view. The water is enclosed by man-made banks, and the sky is filling with smoke. Like the reflection upon the water, every natural object represents some aspect of the collective economic enterprise. Technological power overwhelms the solitary man; the landscape convention calls for his presence to provide scale, but here the traditional figure acquires new meaning: in this mechanized environment he seems forlorn and powerless. And yet, somehow, this bleak vista conveys a strangely soft, tender feeling. On closer inspection, we observe that Sheeler has eliminated all evidence of the frenzied movement and clamor we associate with the industrial scene. The silence is awesome. The function of the ladder (an archaic implement) is not revealed; it points nowhere. Only the minuscule human figure, the smoke, and the slight ripples on the water suggest motion. And the very faintness of these signs of life intensifies the eerie, static, surrealist quality of the painting. This "American Landscape" is the industrial landscape pastoralized. By superimposing order, peace, and harmony upon our modern chaos, Sheeler represents the anomalous blend of illusion and reality in the American consciousness.

In F. Scott Fitzgerald's *The Great Gatsby* (1925), another image of landscape provides the indispensable clue to the baffling career of an archetypal American. Like the other major characters, James Gatz is a Westerner who has come East to make his fortune. (In this version of the fable, as in the "international" novels of Henry James, the direction of the journey is reversed: Gatsby moves from simplicity to sophistication.) In the end,

Fitzgerald's narrator, Nick Carraway, realizes that Gatsby can be understood only in relation to the "last and greatest of all human dreams": The original European vision of the "fresh, green breast of the new world." It is Nick who must decide, finally, upon the value of that dream. His problem is akin to the one Shakespeare's Prospero had faced three centuries before; to make sense of his experience Nick must define the relative validity of the "garden" and the "hideous wilderness" images of the New World; he must discriminate between Gatsby's image of felicity, represented by Daisy Buchanan and the "green light," and the industrial landscape of twentieth-century America.

From the beginning Nick is aware of something odd about the elegant green lawns of suburban Long Island. They are green enough, but somehow synthetic and delusive. "The lawn," says Nick, describing his first impression of the Buchanans' home, "started at the beach and ran toward the front door for a quarter of a mile, jumping over sun-dials and brick walks and burning gardens—finally when it reached the house drifting up the side in bright vines as though from the momentum of its run." And then, in the next sentence, he introduces Tom Buchanan: hard, supercilious, arrogant. "Not even the effeminate swank of his riding clothes," says Nick, "could hide the enormous power of that body...." Nick soon discovers that suburban greenness, like Tom's clothing, is misleading. It too is a mask of power, and on the way to Manhattan he sees a more truly representative landscape of this rich and powerful society:

> About half way between West Egg and New York the motor road hastily joins the railroad and runs beside it for a quarter of a mile, so as to shrink away from a certain desolate area of land. This is a valley of ashes—a fantastic farm where ashes grow like wheat into ridges and hills and grotesque gardens; where ashes take the forms of houses and chimneys and rising smoke and, finally, with a transcendent effort, of men who move dimly and already crumbling through the powdery air. Occasionally a line of gray cars crawls along an invisible track, gives out a ghastly creak, and comes to rest, and immediately the ash-gray men swarm up with leaden spades and stir up an impenetrable cloud, which screens their obscure operations from your sight.[2]

This hideous, man-made wilderness is a product of the technological power that also makes possible Gatsby's wealth, his parties, his car. None of his possessions sums up the quality of life to which he aspires as well as the car. "It was a rich cream color, bright with nickel, swollen here and there in its monstrous length with triumphant hat-boxes and supper-boxes and tool-boxes, and terraced with a labyrinth of wind-shields that mirrored a dozen suns." Sitting behind these many layers of glass, says Nick, was like being "in a sort of green leather conservatory." As it happens, the car proves to be a murder weapon and the instrument of Gatsby's undoing. The car and the garden of ashes belong to a world, like Ahab's, where natural objects are of no value in themselves. Here all of visible nature is as expendable as a pasteboard mask:

> Every Friday five crates of oranges and lemons arrived from a fruiterer in New York—every Monday these same oranges and lemons left his back door in a pyramid of pulpless halves. There was a machine in the kitchen which could extract the juice of two hundred oranges in half an hour if a little button was pressed two hundred times by a butler's thumb.

In *The Great Gatsby,* as in *Walden, Moby-Dick,* and *Huckleberry Finn,* the machine represents the forces working against the dream of pastoral fulfillment.[3]

But in Fitzgerald's book, as in many American fables, there is another turn to the story. Somehow, in spite of the counterforce, the old dream retains its power to stir the imagination. From the first moment Nick sees Gatsby, standing alone in the moonlight gazing across the water at "nothing except a single green light," he is aware of a mysterious, indefinable, transcendent quality in the man. At the outset he describes this appealing trait in deliberately vague language: "... there was, " he says, "something gorgeous about him, some heightened sensitivity to the promises of life ... an extraordinary gift for hope, a romantic readiness such as I have never found in any other person and which it is not likely I shall ever find again." Nick's job, as narrator, is to specify the exact nature of the "something"—to find out what it is and where it arises. But the more he learns about Gatsby the more difficult the job becomes. He can find no way to reconcile the man's engaging qualities with the facts: the interminable, senseless parties in Gatsby's "blue gardens," his vulgar show of wealth, his bogus Norman mansion, his monstrous car, and, above all, his bland complicity in crime. What mystifies Nick is the incongruity of the sordid facts, combined as they are with Gatsby's unswerving devotion to Daisy and the ideal of the green light. Only at the very end, when Nick returns to Long Island for the last time, does he find a wholly plausible explanation. And it is here, in the closing paragraphs, that Fitzgerald enlarges the meaning of his fable, extending it to an entire culture that is peculiarly susceptible, like Jay Gatsby, to pastoral illusions. One night, after Gatsby's death, Nick comes back to Long Island. The summer is over. What he now sees, as he sprawls on the beach looking across the water, enables him to place the events he has witnessed in the context of history:

> Most of the big shore places were closed now and there were hardly any lights except the shadowy, moving glow of a ferryboat across the Sound. And as the moon rose higher the inessential houses began to melt away until gradually I became aware of the old island here that flowered once for Dutch sailors' eyes—a fresh, green breast of the new world. Its vanished trees, the trees that had made way for Gatsby's house, had once pandered in whispers to the last and greatest of all human dreams; for a transitory enchanted moment man must have held his breath in the presence of this continent, compelled into an aesthetic contemplation he neither understood nor desired, face to face for the last time in history with something commensurate to his capacity for wonder.

Here, for the first time, Nick locates the origin of that strange compound of sentiment and criminal aggressiveness in Gatsby. Although this vision of the American landscape reverses the temporal scheme of Sheeler's painting (instead of imposing the abstract residuum of the pastoral dream upon the industrial world, Nick's vision discloses the past by melting away the inessential present)—it serves much the same purpose. It also represents the curious state of the modern American consciousness. It reveals that Gatsby's uncommon "gift for hope" was born in that transitory, enchanted moment when Europeans first came into the presence of the "fresh, green breast of the new world." We are reminded of Shakespeare's Gonzalo and Miranda, of Robert Beverley and Crèvecœur and Jefferson: in America hopefulness had been incorporated in a style of life, a culture, a national character. Hence Gatsby's simple-minded notion that everything can be made right again. Daisy is for him what the green island once had been for Dutch sailors; like them he mistakes a temporary feeling for a lasting possibility.

As Fitzgerald's narrator pieces it together, accordingly, Gatsby's tragic career exemplifies the attenuation of the pastoral ideal in America. In the beginning Nick compares Gatsby's "heightened sensitivity to the promises of life" to a seismograph—a delicate instrument peculiarly responsive to invisible signals emanating from the land. Gatsby's entire existence—not only the "romantic readiness" of his spirit, but also his Horatio Alger rise to affluence—had been shaped by the special conditions of which the bountiful, green landscape is the token. Young James Gatz got his start by using his intimate knowledge of the Midwestern terrain to save a rich man's yacht. It was at that moment that Jay Gatsby sprang, like a son of God, from his Platonic conception of himself. The incident, a turning point in his life, marks the enlistment of native energies in the service of wealth, status, power, and, as Nick puts it, of "a vast, vulgar and meretricious beauty." Nick, the real hero of *The Great Gatsby*, is the only one, finally, to understand, but it takes him a long while to grasp the subtle interplay between Gatsby's dream and his underworld life.[4]

In part Nick's difficulty arises from the fact that he is so much like Gatsby. He too is a Westerner, a simple man in a complex society, and when he pays his first visit to the Buchanans, he admits, their acquired Eastern manners make him uncomfortable. He feels like a rustic. "'You make me feel uncivilized, Daisy,'" he said. "'Can't you talk about crops or something?'" And then, just before describing the sordid, drunken brawl in Mrs. Wilson's apartment, Nick makes explicit his own propensity to Virgilian fantasies:

> We drove over to Fifth Avenue, so warm and soft, almost pastoral, on the summer Sunday afternoon that I wouldn't have been surprised to see a great flock of white sheep turn the corner.

The party, as Nick describes it, is a debased bucolic festival: the pathetic little dog at the center, the furniture tapestried with "scenes of ladies swinging in the gardens of Versailles," the brutal outburst of Buchanan's hate, and Nick's yearning, through it all, to get away: "I wanted to get out," he says, "and walk eastward toward the Park through the soft twilight...." Because he, too, is drawn to images of pastoral felicity, Nick is prepared to recognize the connection between Gatsby's sentimentality and the sight that had greeted Dutch sailors three centuries before.

> And as I sat there brooding on the old, unknown world, I thought of Gatsby's wonder when he first picked out the green light at the end of Daisy's dock. He had come a long way to this blue lawn, and his dream must have seemed so close that he could hardly fail to grasp it.

And here, at last, Nick pulls back, separating himself from his dead friend's dead dream.

> He [Gatsby] did not know that it was already behind him, somewhere back in that vast obscurity beyond the city, where the dark fields of the republic rolled on under the night.[5]

The difference between Gatsby's point of view and Nick's illustrates the distinction, with which I began, between sentimental and complex pastoralism. Fitzgerald, through Nick, expresses a point of view typical of a great many twentieth-century American writers. The work of Faulkner, Frost, Hemingway and West comes to mind. Again and again they invoke the image of a green landscape—a terrain either wild or, if cultivated, rural—as a symbolic repository of meaning and value. But at the same time they acknowledge the power of a counterforce, a machine or some other symbol of the forces which have stripped the old ideal of most, if not all, of its meaning. Complex pastoralism, to put it another way, acknowledges the reality of history. One of Nick Carraway's great moments of illumination occurs when he realizes that Gatsby wants nothing less of Daisy than that she should go to Tom, and say, "'I never loved you.'" And when Nick objects, observing that one cannot undo the past, Gatsby is incredulous. Of course he can. "'I'm going to fix everything,'" he says, "'just the way it was before....'" Like Melville's Starbuck, Gatsby would let faith oust fact. He is another example of the modern primitive described by Ortega, the industrial *Naturmensch* who is blind to the complexity of modern civilization; he wants his automobile, enjoys it, yet regards it as "the spontaneous fruit of an Edenic tree." Nick also is drawn to images of pastoral felicity, but he learns how destructive they are when cherished in lieu of reality. He realizes that Gatsby is destroyed by his inability to distinguish between dreams and facts. In the characteristic pattern of complex pastoralism, the fantasy of pleasure is checked by the facts of history.[6]

But what, then, do our fabulists offer in place of the ideal landscape? Nick Carraway's most significant response to Gatsby's death is his decision, announced in the opening pages of the book, to return to the West. (Like Thoreau, Melville and Mark Twain, Fitzgerald tells his tale from the viewpoint of a traveler returned from a voyage of initiation.) In the closing pages

Nick again explains that the East was haunted for him after the murder; and so, he says, "when the blue smoke of brittle leaves was in the air ... I decided to come back home." Nick's repudiation of the East is a belated, ritualistic withdrawal in the direction of "nature." It is ironically set against the fact, which the entire novel makes plain, that the old distinction between East and West has all but disappeared. Nick's final gesture is a mere salute to the memory of a vanished America; and the book ends on a sadly enervated note of romantic irony: "So," Nick says, "we beat on, boats against the current, borne back ceaselessly into the past."

The ending of *The Great Gatsby* reminds us that American writers seldom, if ever, have designed satisfactory resolutions for their pastoral fables. The power of these fables to move us derives from the magnitude of the protean conflict figured by the machine's increasing domination of the visible world. This recurrent metaphor of contradiction makes vivid, as no other figure does, the bearing of public events upon private lives. It discloses that our inherited symbols of order and beauty have been divested of meaning. It compels us to recognize that the aspirations once represented by the symbol of an ideal landscape have not, and probably cannot, be embodied in our traditional institutions. It means that an inspiriting vision of a humane community has been reduced to a token of individual survival. The outcome of *Walden, Moby-Dick,* and *Huckleberry Finn* is repeated in the typical modern version of the fable; in the end the American hero is either dead or totally alienated from society, alone and powerless, like the evicted shepherd of Virgil's eclogue. And if, at the same time, he pays a tribute to the image of a green landscape, it is likely to be ironic and bitter. The resolutions of our pastoral fables are unsatisfactory because the old symbol of reconciliation is obsolete, but the inability of our writers to create a surrogate for the ideal of the middle landscape can hardly be accounted artistic failure. By incorporating in their work the root conflict of our culture, they have clarified our situation. They have served us well. To change the situation we require new symbols of possibility, and although the creation of those symbols is in some measure the responsibility of artists, it is in greater measure the responsibility of society. The machine's sudden entrance into the garden presents a problem that ultimately belongs not to art but to politics.

Notes

1. Adams, *the Education of Henry Adams*, ch. 34. Quoted by permission of the Houghton Mifflin Company.
2. The Buchanans' lawn, ch. 1; the valley of ashes, ch. 2. The quotations from *The Great Gatsby* are by permission of Charles Scribner's Sons.
3. Ch. 4; ch. 3.
4. Ch. 6.
5. Ch. 1; ch. 2; ch. 9.
6. Ch. 6.

93
The Triple Vision of Nick Carraway

E. FRED CARLISLE

Although Jay Gatsby gives his name to the title of Fitzgerald's novel, the book really tells the story of two men, both of whom are searchers who begin their quests in the Middle West. Their stories, however, end differently. For Nick Carraway ultimately succeeds (although not in his original quest) because he achieves awareness; whereas, Jay Gatsby fails because his colossal illusion prevents awareness. As a matter of fact, Nick's experience and growth provide the main continuity in the novel, and in this sense, Nick does not narrate Gatsby's story so much as he tells his own story in which Gatsby becomes an important agent in Nick's movement from innocence to awareness. Nick begins in the innocent West of his youth (a West that had become, however, the ragged edge of the universe for him); he moves through the corrupt East (the Valley of Ashes); and he returns, finally, to the Middle West—a disillusioned, changed, but very moral young man, who can evaluate his experience in the East.

These are obvious points of interpretation, but basic, of course, to any comment on the novel. Beyond these critical *données*, however (and in spite of excellent critical discussions of *Gatsby*)[1] Nick's position, function, and points of view have not been fully defined, and such lack of explanation, it seems, leaves unanswered important questions about the unity or the defects in the novel, about Nick's involvement with or detachment from Gatsby, as well as about Nick's honesty and awareness regarding his whole experience. A careful analysis of Nick's perspectives (of his points of view as narrator) should illustrate *how* Nick provides a unifying center in the novel. Such analysis should confirm, as well, Nick's ability to know Gatsby as a cynical hoodlum and, at the same time, to tell him that he's "worth the whole damn bunch put together."[2] The discussion should also confirm that Nick *is* finally honest and that his ambivalence about Gatsby (if it is ambivalence) does not prevent Nick from clearly evaluating his experience in the East. Besides

SOURCE *Modern Fiction Studies* XI, Winter 1965, pp. 351–360.

defining his moral position and his points of view, his three perspectives each dramatize an important aspect of his experience; for without Nick's attraction to the glamour of the East, or without his detachment, or without his maturity, the action of the novel would be obviously incomplete.

Nick's perspective may be multipled, but it is not confused or blurred. Even though the three points of view are not always separable or distinguishable, nevertheless, they can be identified and frequently isolated. The first—$Nick_1$ for the sake of identification—is Nick the historian: the man who is looking back on an experience that he finally understands. This Nick still retains his double view of Gatsby: he admires the hope, the romantic naiveté, and the colossal vitality of Gatsby's illusion; yet he knows Gatsby is a hoodlum, perhaps a killer, and Nick knows, too, that the fraudulent value system of the East—and of America—made Gatsby what he was and almost corrupted Nick himself. $Nick_1$, then, takes the point of view of the detached moralist—the man who *was* there but who escaped. He is a reliable narrator-observer whose point of view is somewhat distant (in time *and* moral perspective) from the characters in the novel and quite close to the reader's point of view, if that reader accepts the norms of the novels.[3]

The other two Nicks—$Nick_2$ and $Nick_3$—become parts of the action in New York; there the detached narrator disappears, and the other two "Nicks" participate in the action as it *happens* to them. Although the second Nick is an agent in the action (he is there in time) he also maintains a limited perspective as an observer whose distance from the other characters and the reader is midway between $Nick_1$ and $Nick_3$. This $Nick_3$—who has the most limited perspective—becomes an agent who maintains *no* perspective as an observer and no distance from the other characters. He participates fully in the action, as the East attracts him, draws him in, and almost captures him permanently. This Nick fools himself, as he lives an illusion. These last two perspectives on the action, then, reveal Nick as he was both enchanted and repelled during his experience. His existence both in and out of the game becomes quite clear during the unpleasant first scene at Tom's New York apartment:

> I wanted to get out and walk eastward toward the park through the soft twilight, but each time I tried to go I became entangled in some wild, strident argument which pulled me back, as if with ropes, into my chair. Yet high over the city our line of yellow windows must have contributed their share of human secrecy to the casual watcher in the darkening streets, and I was him too, looking up and wondering. I was within and without, simultaneously enchanted and repelled by the inexhaustible variety of life. (p. 36)

Fitzgerald all but merges the two perspectives in the scene, but each narrative view remains separate from the other. The same sort of enchantment strikes Nick when he first visits Tom and Daisy, but Nick also acts as an observer then, for he senses Daisy's insincerity in her apparent confession, "'Sophisticated—God, I'm sophisticated!'" (p. 18). And he feels "confused and a little disgusted" (p. 20) as he drives away from this first visit.

Nick's ability to maintain some detachment while he is in the middle of an experience seems especially evident in his great comic sense. As narrator (either Nick$_1$, or Nick$_2$), he frequently reveals a sense of irony as well as an ability to bring off a series of subtle jokes. His occasional asides show one way his comic sense runs through the novel. Two of these occur in the scene at the Buchanans'. Nick's description of Jordan's "Absolutely" reveals a real comic touch: "At this point Miss Baker said: 'Absolutely!' with such suddenness that I started—it was the first word she had uttered since I came into the room" (p. 11). And his comment about Daisy's description of him as a rose shows his comic detachment, too:

> "I love to see you at my table, Nick. You remind me of a—of a rose, an absolute rose. Doesn't he?" ... "An absolute rose?"
> This was untrue. I am not even faintly like a rose. (p. 15)

This remark comes in the middle of a serious scene, for Nick follows it with a serious remark about Jordan's attractiveness. The jokes, then, function as a kind of counterpoint; they maintain the distinction between Nick$_2$ and Nick$_3$.

These three perspectives seem clear enough generally. Nevertheless, additional explanation and discussion of certain important scenes seems necessary to define specifically the triple vision of Nick Carraway. In the first apartment scene Nick initially maintains a double perspective—enchantment and repulsion. In spite of his awareness of unpleasantness, however, the action slowly draws him in and temporarily absorbs him as he becomes just one more of the participating drunks. The actions, the style, and the point of view reflect his general confusion and vagueness:

> It was nine o'clock—almost immediately afterward I looked at my watch and found it was ten. Mr. McKee was asleep on a chair with his fists clenched in his lap, like a photograph of a man of action. Taking out my handkerchief I wiped from his cheek the remains of the spot of dried lather that had worried me all the afternoon.
> The little dog was sitting on the table looking with blind eyes through the smoke, and from time to time groaning faintly. People disappeared, reappeared, made plans to go somewhere, and then lost each other, searched for each other, found each other a few feet away. Some time toward midnight Tom Buchanan and Mrs. Wilson stood face to face, discussing in impassioned voices whether Mrs. Wilson had any right to mention Daisy's name.
> "Daisy! Daisy! Daisy!" shouted Mrs. Wilson. "I'll say it whenever I want to! Daisy! Dai—"
> Making a short deft movement, Tom Buchanan broke her nose with his open hand.
> Then there were bloody towels upon the bathroom floor, and women's voices scolding, and high over the confusion a long broken wail of pain.
> * * *
> Then Mr. McKee turned and continued on out the door. Taking my hat from the chandelier, I followed.

> "Come to lunch some day," he suggested, as we groaned down in the elevator.
>
> "Where?"
>
> "Anywhere."
>
> "Keep your hands off the lever," snapped the elevator boy.
>
> "I beg your pardon," said Mr. McKee with dignity, "I didn't know I was touching it."
>
> "All right," I agreed, "I'll be glad to."
>
> ... I was standing beside his bed and he was sitting up between the sheets, clad in his underwear, with a great portfolio in his hands.
>
> "Beauty and the Beast ... Loneliness ... Old Grocery Horse ... Brook'n Bridge...."
>
> Then I was lying half asleep in the cold lower level of the Pennsylvania Station, staring at the morning *Tribune*, and waiting for the four o'clock train. (pp. 37–38)

The observer who a few hours before so confidently asserted his detachment, has become Nick$_3$, a confused drunk who has participated in the enchantment *and* the unpleasant violence of the apartment scene.

The scene in which Nick describes the first party he attends at Gatsby's also illustrates important aspects of his perspective. First, Fitzgerald's subtle use of a change in tense shows that the point of view in the scene actually shifts from a narrator-observer who is detached and looking back on his experience to one who *is* participating—a narrator-agent:

> At least once a fortnight a corps of caterers came down with several hundred feet of canvas and enough colored lights to make a Chirstmas tree of Gatsby's enormous garden. On buffet tables, garnished with glistening hors d'oeuvre, spiced baked hams crowded against salads of harlequin designs.... In the main hall a bar with a real brass rail was set up....
>
> By seven o'clock the orchestra *has* arrived.... The last swimmers *have* come in from the beach *now* and *are* dressing up-stairs. The bar *is* in full swing....
>
> The lights *grow* brighter as the earth lurches away form the sun, and *now* the orchestra *is* playing yellow cocktail music.... (pp. 39–40; my italics)

The actual present tense does not continue through the scene; rather Fitzgerald reverts to the past tense. Nevertheless, the shift lasts long enough to suggest that a change in perspective (or point of view) actually occurs.

At the beginning of the scene, after "the party has begun," Nick seems to be an observer (he *is* there, however, and therefore is not the historian Nick): he goes to the party alone; he feels out of place; and he does not become immediately involved until he meets Jordan and, later, Gatsby. For a short time, then, Nick$_2$ seems to go to the party—Nick the limited observer, the one who if not repelled stays outside of the action. Later in the evening Nick becomes more and more a participant, and by the time he meets Gatsby Nick seems to be completely involved:

> At a lull in the entertainment the man looked at me and smiled.
>
> "Your face is familiar," he said, politely. "Weren't you in the Third Division during the war?"

> * * *
>
> We talked for a moment ... Evidently he lived in this vicinity, for he told me that he had just bought a hydroplane, and was going to try it out in the morning.
> "Want to go with me, old sport?" ...
>
> * * *
>
> "This is an unusual party for me. I haven't even seen the host...."
> For a moment he looked at me as if he failed to understand.
> "I'm Gatsby,' he said suddenly.
> "What!' I exclaimed. "Oh, I beg your pardon." (pp. 47–48)

Nick's complete ignorance of the man's identity indicates his complete involvement. Although one cannot always distinguish $Nick_2$ from $Nick_3$ in this scene—occasionally the double perspective merges—the two points of view are present.

At this point in the novel, $Nick_1$, the historian, explicitly resumes the narrative ("Reading over what I have written so far" [p. 56]), so that he might move the action along more quickly and narrate some of the personal affairs that absorbed him through the summer. His asides and ironic comments continue: "I took dinner usually at the Yale Club—for some reason it was the gloomiest event of my day" (p. 57). And with this same sense of irony and honestly he ends the chapter with this extraordinary remark: "Every one suspects himself of at least one of the cardinal virtues, and this is mine: I am one of the few honest people that I have ever known" (p. 60). He means it because it is true, finally, but it must be another dead-pan joke, too. Likewise, the catalogue of names does its honest work by providing a foreshortened glimpse of the social set that attended Gatsby's parties. But that list also performs its ironic and comic function and thus keeps Nick's whole perspective ($Nick_1$ for the moment) quite clear.

The tryst scene in which Gatsby meets Daisy at Nick's house provides examples of Nick's ($Nick_2$) detachment at the time and also of his serio-comic point of view. Previously, Nick arranges the tryst (he panders, in effect); his action indicates the complete involvement of $Nick_3$, for it violates Nick's usual standard of morality. Nevertheless, he does not become involved at any time in the scene, as he does on other occasions; his ironic perspective keeps him on the outside looking in even though he is present. As a matter of fact, he actually stands outside in the rain—a kind of symbolic act which reveals how much of an outsider he actually is. The whole scene, as Nick renders it and comments on it, is remarkably funny. Nick's asides, Gatsby's boyish awkwardness, and Nick's outlandish observations (he visualizes himself, for example, as Kant looking at a church steeple) make the scene one of masterful comedy. Before the tryst Nick drives into West Egg to "buy some cups and lemons and flowers." But

> The flowers were unnecessary, for at two o'clock a greenhouse arrived from Gatsby's, with innumerable receptacles to contain it. An hour later the front

> door opened nervously, and Gatsby, in a white flannel suit, silver shirt, and gold-colored tie, hurried in. He was pale, and there were dark signs of sleeplessness beneath his eyes. (pp. 84–85)

Nick meets Daisy outside; when they come into the house, Gatsby is gone:

> We went in. To my overwhelming surprise the living room was deserted.
> "Well, that's funny," I exclaimed.
> "What's funny?"
> She turned her head as there was a light dignified knocking at the front door. I went out and opened it. Gatsby, pale as death, with his hands plunged like weights in his coat pockets, was standing in a puddle of water glaring tragically into my eyes. (p. 86).

Apparently Gatsby, the embarrassed boy, wanted the meeting to seem wholly accidental. Shortly after his entrance, Gatsby almost knocks a clock from the mantle, and this stimulates more comically awkward dialogue:

> "I'm sorry about the clock," he said.
> My own face had now assumed a deep tropical burn. I couldn't muster up a single commonplace out of the thousand in my head.
> "It's an old clock," I told them idiotically. (p. 87).

Nick's own embarrassment makes him seem both in *and* out of the game simultaneously. Two of the perspectives merge, at least for the moment. Nick caps the scene with his absurd comparison of himself to Kant and with some utterly irrelevant information about Gatsby's house:

> There was nothing to look at from under the tree except Gatsby's enormous house, so I stared at it, like Kant at his church steeple, for half an hour. A brewer had built it early in the "period" craze. (p. 89)

The paragraph serves its purpose of emphasizing Nick's detachment and his irony; as all the comic remarks do, this one also provides a counterpoint to the really serious nature and implications of the meeting which Nick arranges and approves.

At Nick's the seriousness of the situation remains in the background as $Nick_2$ clowns, but shortly, when they move to Gatsby's the mood changes. Significantly, they move *from* Nick's house—suggesting the detachment and comic sense of $Nick_2$—*to* Gatsby's house where his horrid taste and awkwardness are pathetic, not comic, where the scene turns serious, even painful, and where Nick moves "inside" Gatsby's world again as a participant. (Throughout the novel, Nick's house acts as a constant symbol of his detachment and of his difference from Gatsby and the Buchanans. At home he remains $Nick_2$ as he is Nick, the historian, when he returns to the Middle West, to the outside. But he can be drawn from his house, from his detachment, into Gatsby's or Tom and Daisy's house or even into Tom's apartment—into the enchanting world of the rich East.)

The series of events connected with the second trip to New York offers a final example of Nick's perspectives. Of course, he writes the story, finally, from his "experienced" perspective, and, therefore, that point of view dominates the novel even when $Nick_1$ narrates indirectly or presents dramatically. But within the dramatic situation the other two perspectives, Nick the detached participant and Nick the involved participant, become part of the action. In this second New York scene Nick allows himself to be drawn in again as he becomes as drunk, hot, and irritable as the others; his description of their arrival at the hotel indicates how absorbed in the action he is:

> The prolonged and tumultuous argument that ended by herding us into that room eludes me, though I have a sharp physical memory that, in the course of it, my underwear kept climbing like a damp snake around my legs.... (p. 126)

Occasionally, the perspective shifts as the narrator places the scene in a broader perspective: Nick can still evaluate Tom and his "impassioned gibberish"; and he can realize also that Gatsby's life of racketeering and violence remains masked behind his good nature. But through much of the scene Nick participates fully—so much so that he almost disappears as an identity; he becomes almost completely absorbed into the situation as it is. The incident in the city ends, for example, with the Nick of the moment accepting an illusion and Jordan:

> Thirty—the promise of a decade of loneliness, a thinning list of single men to know, a thinning briefcase of enthusiasm, thinning hair. But there was Jordan beside me.... As we passed over the dark bridge her wan face fell lazily against my coat's shoulder and the formidable stroke of thirty died away with the reassuring pressure of her hand. (p. 136)

Only later, when his perspective broadens again, does he reject Jordan and her dishonesty, and accept his age.

At the end of the novel $Nick_1$, the historian, resumes the apparent narrative point of view and relates the final action largely in retrospect. Although he presents the funeral, his break with Jordan, and his final meeting with Tom Buchanan dramatically, the perspective includes constant evaluation that only $Nick_1$ or $Nick_2$ could offer. Thus, in this last chapter only $Nick_2$ participates in the action, for the third perspective ceases to exist as Nick's awareness increases and as his perspective broadens. Finally, the three perspectives come together near the end of the last chapter in the mature, informed vision of Nick, the man who *was* there but who returns to tell his readers of his experience. This Nick understands the social, moral, and mythic implications of his experience. $Nick_3$ was enchanted, irritated, excited, drunk, or attracted, as the situation demanded; $Nick_2$ cracked ironic jokes and found the East repulsive as well as enchanting, but he did not really evaluate his experience as the mature narrator does. The three perspectives of Nick Carraway, then, almost trace his development from a state of hope, innocence, and naive enchantment through a kind of middle state of mind to the clear moral perspective of the thirty year old *man* who goes home again.

But if Nick has changed—if he is sadder and wiser—certainly he does not actually go home *again*, as the phrase might suggest; he does not return to the past as the same Nick who left because his new perspective forbids that. The past of his youth no longer exists; he has stopped thinking of the Middle West as the ragged edge of the universe; he has gone, in a sense, beyond enchantment and simple irony or satire. He returns, then, *to* what, *as* what? If nothing else, Nick gains a perspective on himself. He realizes his own fundamental decency and honesty (his Midwestern values that somehow made him fail in the East), but his sense of irony about himself (for example, "I am one of the few honest people that I have ever known" [pp. 60] and his serio-comic remark that "when I came back from the East last autumn I felt that I wanted the world to be in uniform and at a sort of moral attention forever" [p. 2]) prevents any self-righteousness or any real despair. His satire of himself in the beginning of the book also suggests the self-awareness he has achieved. He talks about himself escaping from that ragged edge of the universe to learn the bond business in the East—just like that. He sardonically refers to himself as "a guide, a pathfinder, an original settler" for whom "life was beginning over again with the summer" (p. 4). His rebirth, however, turns out to be abortive—at least if success and money represent the new life envisioned. Instead, he experiences the same disillusioning "rebirth" that many American heroes discover when the fraudulent nature of their dreams and illusions becomes clear to them.

Besides understanding himself Nick can also evaluate Gatsby. Although Nick's perspective is complex, it is not confused or ambiguous. Of course, he admires Gatsby's hope, his romantic readiness to dream, his good-will and his spirit. He realizes, however, that Gatsby is a fraud, a hoodlum, whose values and assumptions are empty and morally wrong. At the same time, he sees Gatsby more as a victim than an agent—a victim of the fraudulent value system that has been perpetuated ever since the American Dream became confused with money, position, and power—ever since it came into being.

Such knowledge belongs to the Nick who tells the story, not to the ones who went East in search of enchantment and success in the bond business. Nick therefore returns with experience—he has fallen. He has no program, however, no grand solution for the problems of society, but he has escaped from lies and illusions and from moral corruption. Thus his return is just that; it is not a retreat or a flight to safety and comfort—to immaturity. His new perspective prevents that. He returns, instead, fully aware of the confusion of a society in which people try to be free (and irresponsible), to be rich and successful (and immoral), but who all live really in a Valley of Ashes. He goes home knowing that the values implicit in their quests are superficial, selfish, and materialistic—thus decadent and destructive. He returns with a memory of a hero—a mythic hero, really—whose great faith in life has been misdirected and betrayed, who has in effect been sacrificed by the society (corrupted and sacrificed itself long ago) he believed in. Nick admires the faith, but his knowledge of the fraud and failure causes permanent disillusion, for he discovers that the present (reality) repeatedly belies the hopes and dreams, even the memories, of that past golden age or the one that is surely just around the corner or there at tomorrow morning:

> So we beat on, boats against the current, borne back ceaselessly into the past. (p. 182)

Notes

1. Many of these discussions have been collected by Arthur Mizener in *F. Scott Fitzgerald: A Collection of Critical Essays* (Englewood Cliffs, N.J., 1963).

2. F. Scott Fitzgerald, *The Great Gatsby* (New York: Scribner's, 1953), p. 154. All subsequent quotations from the novel will be identified by page number.

3. The terms Wayne Booth uses in *The Rhetoric of Fiction* (Chicago, 1961) to describe variations in narrative distance help here: see especially Chapter VI.

94
Patterns in *The Great Gatsby*

♦

VICTOR A. DOYNO

When Fitzgerald was revising a scene at the end of the second chapter of *The Great Gatsby*, he added some phrases which have no apparent relevance to the novel. The scene involves a photographer showing an album to the narrator, Nick Carraway. Fitzgerald inserted four picture tiles: "Beauty and the Beast ... Loneliness ... Old Grocery Horse ... Brook'n Bridge...." Why did he, when preparing the novel for the printer, wish to insert these titles? What function does this seemingly irrelevant list have? A clue to the answer lies, I think, in two letters from Fitzgerald to his editor, Maxwell Perkins. In 1922, after he began planning his third novel, Fitzgerald wrote that he wanted "to write something *new*—something extraordinary and beautiful and simple & intricately patterned." And in 1924, speaking about his difficulties in composition, Fitzgerald said:

> So in my new novel I'm thrown directly on purely creative work—not trashy imaginings as in my stories but the sustained imagination of a sincere yet radiant world. So I tread slowly and carefully & at times in considerable distress. This book will be a consciously artistic achievement & must depend on that as the 1st books did not.[1]

These statements suggest that a careful study of the text might reveal *The Great Gatsby* to be indeed "a consciously artistic achievement" that is "intricately patterned."

Fortunately, this close study of the patterning can draw upon a wealth of material: the holograph pencil version, the galley proofs, and the extensive galley revisions. Portions of the holograph text include several stages of composition: some parts of this version, usually those written in a large hand, are extensively revised early drafts; those parts written in a small, precise hand with fewer revisions seem to be transcriptions of earlier drafts. The holograph text was revised, presumably in a lost typescript; the revised readings can be found in the galley proofs. This material, with the galley revisions, allows us to see that the patterns which appear in the final text are often the result of laborious revisions.[2]

SOURCE *Modern Fiction Studies* XII, Winter 1966, pp. 415–426.

Several patterns in the novel are obvious. The first three chapters present the different settings and social groupings of three evenings: dinner and strained conversation at Tom Buchanan's house, drinks and a violent argument at Myrtle's apartment, a party and loutish behavior at Gatsby's mansion. Fitzgerald calls attention to this pattern when he has Nick say, "Reading over what I have written so far, I see I have given the impression that the events of three nights several weeks apart were all that absorbed me" (p. 68, *56*). Similarly, through Nick, Fitzgerald emphasizes the patterning of situation which presents two very different characters, George Wilson and Tom Buchanan, as cuckolded husbands: "I stared at him and then at Tom, who had made a parallel discovery less than an hour before" (p. 148, *124*). Clearly Fitzgerald is aware of these patterns and wishes the reader to share this awareness.

There are, moreover, numerous less obvious patterns in the novel which have the important functions of deepening characterization, shaping the reader's attitudes toward events and major themes, and creating and controlling unity and emphasis. Those patternings which affect characterization include the repetition of dialogue, gesture, and detail. For example, Daisy's speech is used to characterize her in two comparable scenes which are far apart. Fitzgerald indicates the relation between the scenes by presenting the same tableau as Nick enters: Daisy and Jordan Baker, both in white, wind-blown dresses, lounge on a couch on a wine or crimson rug. The first scene (in Chapter I) occurs as Nick renews his acquaintance with Daisy; the second (in Chapter VII) when Gatsby intends to reclaim Daisy. In the latter scene Jordan and Daisy say together, "We can't move," and the speech is perfectly appropriate to the hot weather. In the first scene Daisy says, as her first direct statement in the novel, "I'm p-paralyzed with happiness." This statement, however, was inserted after the second scene was written, since it first occurs in the galley proof. This inserted statement, besides presenting an apt characterization of Daisy, likens her feeling at the beginning to those which she has shortly before the argument about leaving Tom. Through this repetition Fitzgerald emphasizes Daisy's lack of growth within the novel.

Fitzgerald also deepens characterization by the repetition of gesture. Nick says that when he first saw Gatsby, "he gave a sudden intimation that he was content to be alone—he stretched out his arms toward the dark water in a curious way, and, far as I was from him, I could have sworn he was trembling" (p. 26, *21*). This picture of Gatsby in the coda of Chapter I presents him with an air of mystery, and in the reader's memory he stands etched reaching for the green light. Gatsby's mysteriousness is transformed later in the novel when he tells Nick that as he was leaving Louisville he went to the open vestibule of the coach and "stretched out his hand desperately as if to snatch only a wisp of air, to save a fragment of the spot that she had made lovely for him" (p. 183, *153*). This repetition of the reaching gesture explains the first picture of Gatsby, establishes the durability of his devotion, and thereby evokes sympathy for one who loves so fervently.

The characterization of Gatsby's rival, Tom Buchanan, is influenced by the repetition of details. Arthur Mizener has noted that Fitzgerald can "sum up all he wants to say about Tom" in his last meeting with Nick.[3] An examination of the composition of the passage leads to a fuller explanation of Mizener's insight and an increased respect for Fitzerald's craftsmanship. The manuscript version reads: "Then he went into the jewellry store *for a* to buy a *pair of c* pearl necklace *and* or pair of cuff buttons," (MS. VIII, 42).[4] The evidence indicates that Fitzgerald probably planned for a moment simply to mention the cuff links, then decided to begin with the necklace. What is gained by the inclusion of a pearl necklace? Tom's wife, Daisy, already has the pearl necklace which was her wedding gift; the necklace is probably not for Daisy; perhaps Tom has found a replacement for his dead mistress. This meeting, which also associates Tom with cuff buttons, occurs directly after Nick's condemnation of the Buchanans for their callous inhumanity: "they smashed up things and creatures and then retreated back into their money or their vast carelessness . . ." (p. 216, *180*). Fitzgerald may have realized that the inhumanity of their attitude could be subtly reinforced by an unfavorable association with the cuff buttons. At any rate he decided to introduce an anterior reference to cuff buttons. Accordingly the galley proofs contain a passage not in the manuscript version in which Meyer Wolfsheim mentions his cuff buttons and calls them "Finest specimens of human molars." The attitude of gross inhumanity latent in this remark carries over to Tom. With the insertion of this unfavorable association for cuff buttons, Fitzgerald decided to alter the syntax of the later reference. The galley proof version is: "Then he went into the jewelry store to buy a pearl necklace, or perhaps only a pair of cuff buttons,". This version, which created a deceptively casual tone while subordinating the cuff links, was modified when Fitzgerald, in revising the galleys, changed the commas to dashes and raised the importance of the alternative (Galley sheet 57). The final elaborated version conveys, in a devastatingly casual tone, oblique references of approximately equal emphasis to Tom's lust and to his inhumanity.

And this passage is not the only implicit character assassination of Tom brought about by a patterning of details. While leaving Gatsby's first party, Nick observes the aftermath of a car accident in which the vehicle is "violently shorn of one wheel." The confusion and discordant noise of the scene create an unfavorable impression which is intensified when Nick tells of the driver's stupid, irresponsible drunkenness. With this scene in mind we can easily visualize an accident which Jordan Baker describes only briefly in the next chapter:

> A week after I left Santa Barbara Tom ran into a wagon on the Ventura road one night, and ripped a front wheel off his car. The girl who was with him got

into the papers, too, because her arm was broken—she was one of the chambermaids in the Santa Barbara Hotel. (p. 93, *78*)

The accident is primarily another indictment of Tom's lust, but the repetition of detail—the loss of a wheel in a night accident—associates Tom with the irresponsible drunken driver.

Besides adding depth to characterization, patterning also shapes the reader's attitudes toward events and themes in the novel. As it happens, this kind of repetition also includes a case of poor driving. Surprisingly few commentators have criticized Fitzgerald for the highly improbable plot manipulation whereby Daisy runs down her husband's mistress. The reader's uncritical acceptance of the accident is influenced, I suggest, by something Nick says in the coda of Chapter III about his relationship with Jordan Baker: "It was on that same house party that we had a curious conversation about driving a car. It started because she passed so close to some workmen that our fender flicked a button on one man's coat" (p. 71, *59*). This near-accident subliminally prepares the reader to think of Daisy's hitting Myrtle not as an unbelievable wrenching of probability but as a possible event. After all, Jordan nearly did a similar thing. Nick's ensuing conversation with Jordan reveals his attitude toward carelessness. This dialogue seems to be relevant only to Nick and Jordan's friendship, but the casual banter presents the same diction and attitude found in Nick's final condemnation of Daisy and Tom for their carelessness. In this case patterning leads the reader to accept both an improbable event and the narrator's final judgment of it.

The reader's attitude is more frequently shaped by an ironic juxtaposition of such themes as romantic idealization and realistic disillusionment.[5] For example, Nick learns from Myrtle of her first meeting with Tom Buchanan on the train to New York, and as she relates the story her limited word choice, additive syntax, and rushing narration establish both her character and her attitude toward the pickup:

> "It was on the two little seats facing each other that are always the last ones left on the train. I was going up to New York to see my sister and spend the night. He had on a dress suit and patent leather shoes, and I couldn't keep my eyes off him, but every time he looked at me I had to pretend to be looking at the advertisement over his head. When we came into the station he was next to me, and his white shirt-front pressed against my arm, and so I told him I'd have to call a policeman, but he knew I lied. I was so excited that when I got into a taxi with him I didn't hardly know I wasn't getting into a subway train. All I kept thinking about, over and over, was 'You can't live forever; you can't live forever.'" (p. 43, *36*)

The style and growing desperation of tone suggest that Myrtle is a socially and morally limited character who acted in an understandable way because of her romantic expectation. But her romantic opinion of her meeting with Tom contrasts with another version of the same situation which is told in a realistic style from a masculine and definitely unromantic point of view when Nick tells this tale of the commuter train:

> The next day was broiling, almost the last, certainly the warmest, of the summer. As my train emerged from the tunnel into sunlight, only the hot whistles of the National Biscuit Company broke the simmering hush at noon. The straw seats of the car hovered on the edge of combustion; the woman next to me perspired delicately for a while into her white shirtwaist, and then, as her newspaper dampened under her fingers, lapsed despairingly into deep heat with a desolate cry. Her pocket-book slapped to the floor.
> "Oh, my!" she gasped.
> I picked it up with a weary bend and handed it back to her, holding it at arm's length and by the extreme tip of the corners to indicate that I had no designs upon it—but every one near by, including the woman, suspected me just the same.
> "Hot!" said the conductor to familiar faces. "Some weather! ... Hot! ... Hot! ... Hot! ... Is it hot enough for you? Is it hot? Is it ...?"
> My commutation ticket came back to me with a dark stain from his hand. That any one should care in this heat whose flushed lips he kissed, whose head made damp the pajama pocket over his heart" (pp. 136–137, *114–115*)

Nick's scornful attitude toward romance refers, in context, primarily to the love of Gatsby for Daisy, but the situation parallels Myrtle's first meeting with Tom and reflects a disillusioned view of such an event. Fitzgerald has controlled his material to make each of the attitudes—Myrtle's desperate romanticism and Nick's uncomfortable realism—valid in its own moment of presentation; but in the context of the novel each thematic attitude toward love is juxtaposed to and qualifies the other.

A similar attempt to influence the reader's attitude occurs with the use of analogous scenes in the codas of Chapters V and VII. And, as shall later become clear, the positioning of the scenes lends them importance. In each case Nick sees a tableau of Daisy sitting and talking with a man who is holding her hand. In Chapter V, of course, the man is Gatsby, who has just re-won Daisy and is experiencing sublime happiness. Nick says:

> As I watched him he adjusted himself a little, visibly. His hand took hold of hers, and as she said something low in his ear he turned toward her with a rush of emotion. I think that voice held him most, with its fluctuating, feverish warmth, because it couldn't be over-dreamed—that voice was a deathless song.
> They had forgotten me, but Daisy glanced up and held out her hand; Gatsby didn't know me now at all. I looked once more at them and they looked back at me, remotely, possessed by intense life. Then I went out of the room and down the marble steps into the rain, leaving them there together. (P. 116, *97*)

However, Fitgerald balances this moment of romantic bliss with a parallel but decidedly realistic description of Daisy after the auto accident:

> Daisy and Tom were sitting opposite each other at the kitchen table, with a plate of cold fried chicken between them, and two bottles of ale. He was talking intently across the table at her, and in his earnestness his hand had fallen upon

and covered her own. Once in a while she looked up at him and nodded in agreement.

They weren't happy, and neither of them had touched the chicken or the ale—and yet they weren't unhappy either. There was an unmistakable air of natural intimacy about the picture, and anybody would have said that they were conspiring together. (pp. 174–175, *146*)

This second scene signals, of course, Gatsby's loss of Daisy. In addition, the repetition destroys the uniqueness of Gatsby's moment of happiness and thereby makes the reader question the validity of his romantic idealization.

The reader's attitude toward romantic idealization and realistic disillusionment is also shaped by the elaborate patterning of a natural enough event—a man and woman kissing. In Chapter VI Nick tells of the movie director bending over his star, who had been described as "a scarcely human orchid of a woman": "They were still under the white-plum tree and their faces were touching except for a pale, thin ray of moonlight between. It occurred to me that he had been very slowly bending toward her all evening to attain this proximity, and even while I watched I saw him stoop one ultimate degree and kiss at her cheek" (p. 129, *108*). Although the setting is described romantically, the event itself is narrated with touches of sarcasm in the involved syntax, elevated diction ("attain this proximity"), and precision of word choice ("kiss *at* her cheek"). The presentation of this kiss, which does not involve any of the major characters, prepares the reader to adopt a complex attitude toward the other kisses. In the coda of the same chapter, Nick relates Gatsby's description of kissing Daisy. Once more Nick's incongruous word choice, e.g., "romp," helps give the passage a peculiar texture.[6] The dominant tone of the passage is, however, certainly one of romantic idealization, culminating in the flower simile:

> His heart beat faster and faster as Daisy's white face came up to his own. He knew that when he kissed this girl, and forever wed his unutterable visions to her perishable breath, his mind would never romp again like the mind of God. So he waited, listening for a moment longer to the tuning-fork that had been struck upon a star. Then he kissed her. At his lips' touch she blossomed for him like a flower and the incarnation was complete. (p. 134, *112*)

The idealization of Gatsby's description is touching, but Nick's sarcastic insertions are not the only means of qualifying the romantic point of view. The reader's attitude toward the kiss has already been influenced by the movie star's kiss and, more importantly, by a similar incident described from a less romantic point of view. In the coda of Chapter IV Nick says:

> We passed a barrier of dark trees, and then the façade of Fifty-ninth Street, a block of delicate pale light, beamed down into the park. Unlike Gatsby and Tom Buchanan, I had no girl whose disembodied face floated along the dark cornices and blinding signs, and so I drew up the girl beside me, tightening my arms. Her wan, scornful mouth smiled, and so I drew her up again closer, this time to my face. (p. 97, *81*)

Throughout this sardonic description Nick has certainly reserved his emotional commitment; neither his motivation nor his choice of words like "scornful" conveys idealistic enthusiasm. As in the other passages the setting is described, and Nick even calls attention to the relation between the kisses by saying "Unlike Gatsby...." Furthermore, the relationship between the kisses in the codas of Chapter IV and VI is subtly emphasized early in Chapter VII, when Tom goes out to make drinks and leaves Daisy alone with Gatsby in front of Nick and Jordan:

> ... she got up and went over to Gatsby and pulled his face down, kissing him on the mouth.
> "You know I love you," she muttered.
> "You forget there's a lady present," said Jordan.
> Daisy looked around doubtfully.
> "You kiss Nick too."
> "What a low, vulgar girl!" (p. 139, *116*)

In this patterning Fitzgerald has presented in order Nick's disenchanted personal account, his sarcastic third-person narration, and Gatsby's romantic, personal version of a kiss; in addition, Fitzgerald includes a scene which draws a parallel between the kisses involving major characters. The sheer idealization of Gatsby's love is qualified by this elaborate repetition, and the reader develops a complex attitude toward a major theme.

With all this evidence of patterning in mind, we may establish still a third function by returning to our original question. Beyond combining the romantic and the mundane, what possible relevance have the picture titles, "Beauty and the Beast ... Loneliness ... Old Grocery Horse ... Brook'n Bridge..."? The first title, of course, refers to the well-known fairy tale or folk tale in which a lowly creature regains his former princely condition by the transforming power of a beautiful girl's kiss.[7] Gatsby's background is analogous to this tale, since was "a son of God" (p. 118, *99*) whose imagination had never accepted his mother and father as his real parents. The transformation of James Gatz to Jay Gatsby was, of course, gradual, but when Gatsby kissed Daisy "the incarnation was complete" (p. 134, *112*): she embodied his dreams, and his princely status was confirmed by the love of "the king's daughter" (p. 144, *120*). And Gatsby's casual remark that in Europe he "lived like a young rajah" (p. 79, *66*) seems quite appropriate to the prince motif.

The next title, "Loneliness," calls to mind Nick's first sight of Gatsby, when "he gave a sudden intimation that he was content to be alone." Several references to Gatsby's loneliness follow: he is "standing alone on the marble steps" (p. 60, *50*) during his party, and Nick mentions the "complete isolation" of the host (p. 68, *56*). The scenes of Gatsby's vigil outside the Buchanans' and of his body's floating in the pool also reinforce the motif of loneliness. Gatsby, when alive, seems quite content with his isolation, but Nick, in a contrapuntal fashion, frequently refers to his own loneliness in terms of discomfort or unhappiness. Nick's dissatisfaction with loneliness makes Gatsby's satisfaction in isolation more striking, more mystic.

Since these motifs sufficiently account for the insertion, admittedly very tenuous suggestions about the last two titles may be offered. The word *grocery* occurs twice in connection with financial necessity. Nick, when he is preparing to leave for the Midwest, sells his car to the grocer. And Tom Buchanan scoffs at Gatsby's financial and social inferiority when he first knew Daisy by saying, "and I'll be damned if I see how you got within a mile of her unless you brought the groceries to the back door" (pp. 157–158, *132*). The other two words of the title also possess some relevance to Gatsby's inferiority. Tom's wealth, of course, is old and established, while Gatsby's richness is quite *nouveau*. Tom's wealth and aristocratic background are indicated by his transportation of his string of polo ponies, and Gatsby's social ineptitude appears in Chapter VI when Tom and the haughty Mr. Sloane dispose of a dinner invitation Gatsby should have refused by riding away without him. There is, then, some evidence that the third title may be a complex and subtle reference to the financial and social differences between Tom and Gatsby.

The last of the titles, "Brook'n Bridge," is even less obvious and has no relevance—unless we consider Fitzgerald's aural imagination and the context of the title within the novel. The brilliance of the catalogue of guests' names at the beginning of Chapter IV is a critical commonplace, but the person who reads these names silently misses a good bit. One must read aloud to appreciate names such as "the Dancies," "Gus Waize," "young Brewer," "Miss Haag," and "Miss Claudia Hip." That Fitzgerald's imagination upon occasion worked aurally is beyond question. The title "Brook'n Bridge" occurs just after Tom has broken Myrtle's nose and may be a punning reference to this incident and thus to the leitmotif of violence in the novel. Each chapter from the first, with Daisy's bruised finger, to the last, with Tom's story of Wilson's forced entry, includes some sort of violence. The only exception to this, of course, is the more or less idyllic Chapter V, in which Daisy and Gatsby are reunited.

Fitzgerald's decision to insert these picture titles in the version used for type setting is quite significant. The titles serve as an index of leitmotifs within the novel. By picking these motifs from the many others in the book, Fitzgerald has singled them out for emphasis, and the presentation in one group subtly helps create unity in the novel.

In addition, the placing of this index in the coda of Chapter II contributes to the structural patterning for unity and emphasis. The conclusion of Chapter III, we remember, is also of particular importance, since by presenting Jordan's near-accident with the discussion of carelessness it prepares for what is to follow. Fitzgerald consciously uses this emphatic position at each chapter's end to call attention to major elements of the novel and frequently creates relations between the structural units.

For example, the codas of Chapters IV and VI present Nick's and Gatsby's versions of a kiss. Fitzgerald's awareness of this patterning is implied in the extensive revisions which brought Gatsby's story to its present parallel position. The story appears in manuscript in the beginning of an early version of Chapter VI and in galley proof at the beginning of Chapter VII (MS. VI. 3; Galley 35). In the galley version Fitzgerald has added a paragraph about a forgotten phrase in Nick's mind. This paragraph dealing with the forgotten phrase was originally written to follow Gatsby's singing of a song he composed in his youth, and Fitzgerald shifted the paragraph, with only a minor change, to its present position after Gatsby's kiss. This shift serves two purposes: it comments upon Gatsby's story, and it creates another analogy to Nick's narration of a kiss, because Nick also had a phrase in mind when he kissed Jordan. The similarities of the events and the phrases were then put into an unmistakable relationship when, in revising the galleys, Fitzgerald shifted Gatsby's narration and the paragraph about the forgotten phrase to a position parallel to Nick's. Thus the codas of IV and VI help unify the book by treating two similar events, and control thematic emphasis by presenting contrasting points of view toward romance. And, of course, the codas of V and VII, which picture first Gatsby and then Tom holding Daisy's hand, also function in this way.

The patterning of alternate codas is tightened to one of direct connection in the last three chapters. In VII and VIII, Gatsby is pictured as alone, first on his vigil and then in his pool. In the one chapter Gatsby is the faithful, devoted, vigilant protector of his lady. In the next he is dead. This contrast, a commentary on romantic idealization, works within the leitmotif of "Loneliness." A similar commentary also links the eighth with the ninth and final coda. At the novel's conclusion Nick likens the human struggle to "boats against the current." And the previous coda presents the image of Gatsby, his struggle over, on a boat going against the current, as the faint wind and a cluster of leaves disturb the course of his mattress in the current of the pool.

The last coda must be discussed in conjunction with the first, since their composition is related. The conclusion of the first chapter was once very different. For example, the manuscript version does not mention that Gatsby was "content to be alone," nor does it include the symbolic green light. Both these insertions were made, however, by the time the novel was ready for typesetting. The insertion of the green light picks up other uses of green as a symbol of romance which occur later in the novel, such as the "green card" which Daisy jokes about as entitling Nick to a kiss, the "long green tickets" which carried young Nick to Midwestern parties, and the "fresh, green breast of the new world" of the conclusion. The description of Gatsby reaching out was not, however, the original end of the chapter. The manuscript first chapter ends with a passage we now find at the novel's conclusion. Only by cutting away this material did Fitzgerald raise the importance of the picture of Gatsby on his lawn, reaching toward Daisy.

It is crucial to a complete understanding of the novel that we realize that this portion of the conclusion was composed early in the writing process:

> And as the moon rose higher the inessential houses began to melt away until gradually I became aware of the old island here that flowered once for Dutch sailors' eyes—a fresh, green breast of the new world. Its vanished trees, the trees that had made way for Gatsby's house, had once pandered in whispers to the last and greatest of all human dreams; for a transitory enchanted moment man must have held his breath in the presence of this continent, compelled into an aesthetic contemplation he neither understood nor desired, face to face for the last time in history with something commensurate to his capacity for wonder. (pp. 217–218, *182*)

The references to the past in this section and in the remainder of the conclusion raise the thematic importance of Gatsby's "can't repeat the past? ... Why of course you can!" (pp. 133, *111*) and of Tom's conversion of a garage into a stable. Both Gatsby and Tom are, each in his own way, borne back into the past. From the early composition of this section we can also surmise that several of the leitmotifs mentioned in the conclusion, such as the notion of pandering and the Edenic conception of America, may have been in Fitzgerald's mind from the beginning.

Similarly, the "new world" seen by the Dutch sailors was already in Fitzgerald's mind when he wrote of the "new world" which Gatsby had seen shortly before being killed by Wilson in the coda of Chapter VIII:

> He must have looked up at an unfamiliar sky through frightening leaves and shivered as he found what a grotesque thing a rose is and how raw the sunlight was upon the scarcely created grass. A new world, material without being real, where poor ghosts, breathing dreams like air, drifted fortuitously about ... like that ashen, fantastic figure gliding toward him through the amorphous trees. (p. 194, *162*)

Fitzgerald's decision to present these radically different "new worlds"—Nick's imputation of Gatsby's realistic disillusionment and the Dutch sailors' romantic idealization—in the codas to the last two chapters reveals once more his consummate use of patterning.

It is clear, I think, that Fitzgerald fulfilled his intention to write a "consciously artistic achievement." And a knowledge of the ways in which the novel is "intricately patterned," from minor details up to large structural units, partially explains how Fitzgerald created a novel that is "something extraordinary and beautiful and simple."

Notes

1. Both letters are quoted by Andrew Turnbull, *Scott Fitzgerald* (New York, 1962), pp. 146–147.
2. I am very grateful to the Firestone Library of Princeton University and to Mr. Alexander

P. Clark, curator of manuscripts, for aiding my study, and to Mrs. Samuel J. Lanahan and Mr. Ivan Von Auw, her agent, for permitting manuscript and galley proof quotation. Similarly, I am indebted to Charles Scribner's Sons, publishers of *The Great Gatsby* (New York, 1925), for permission to quote the text of the first edition. As a convenience I shall also cite in italics the page number of the corresponding section of the widely available Scribner's paperback edition. All references will be included parenthetically.

   3. *The Far Side of Paradise* (Boston, 1949), p. 174.

   4. The cancelled *c* is followed by what appears to be the first vertical curve of a *u*.

   5. For a discussion of the importance of these themes throughout Fitzgerald's career see the unpubl. diss. (Columbia, 1958) by John R. Kuehl, "Scott Fitzgerald: Romance and Realist" (L. C. card no. Mic. 59–747).

   6. The complete passage, which begins with the setting and is too long to quote, has several complicating aspects; it also includes allusions to such religious matters as Jacob's ladder and the incarnation.

   7. For another example of the use of folklore in the novel see Tristram P. Coffin, "Gatsby's Fairy Lover," *Midwest Folklore X* (Summer 1960), 79–85.

95
The Life of Gatsby

◆

JOHN W. ALDRIDGE

It is probably about time we stopped writing essays on *The Great Gatsby*, just at the moment, this is to say, when a really proper criticism seems threatening to begin. Certainly, it has been a saving paradox of criticism up to now that it has taken very little precise note of *Gatsby* while appearing to take vast general note of it. If we are not going to disturb that happy state of affairs, we had perhaps better call a halt before we yield up the book altogether to the dignifying but always transforming fire of criticism, and risk finding, after we have done so, that we are left not with the cleansed bones of the novel itself but with the ashes of one or more of its several meanings. I ask simply that we hold onto the living object in hand: the well-wrought urn on the mantelpiece can remain empty a while longer. Posterity, if it is to get at *Gatsby* at all, will most assuredly have to breathe back into it the life we take out, and we should take care to see that posterity does not waste its breath on a corpse. For *Gatsby* is above all a novel to be directly experienced and responded to; it is a fragile novel, to be sure, in some ways imperfect, in some ways deeply unsatisfactory, but is is clearly alive because produced by a directly experiencing, living imagination, one that habitually and with great innocence so perfectly confused its own longings, fears, defeats, and chimeras with those of a certain portion of American society, that a certain portion of American society ever since has confused its own image with it and made its plans for itself on the vision of an accessible future which, as a skeptical imagination, it tooks pains to condemn. *Gatsby*, therefore, is a work of art particularly prone to being confused with its meanings, just as its meanings, if we are not careful, can be made to substitute for its life as a work of art.

Such a cautionary approach to *Gatsby* should count for something with us, although it probably counts for less than it would have at one time. We are accustomed now to having our experience of life abstracted for us by fiction, and our experience of fiction abstracted for us by criticism, both life and literature projected into a construct twice removed from the original and signed, sealed, and delivered over to our captive imaginations. We no longer

SOURCE *Time to Murder and Create*, New York, 1966, pp. 192–218.

want to do the imaginative job ourselves: we cannot quite afford the time; the code governing the division of imaginative labor would not permit it, nor do we really believe it can or need be done. Undoubtedly one of the reasons *Gatsby* continues to seem alive to us is that it represents one of the last attempts made by an American writer to come directly at the reality of the modern American experience while its outlines were still visible and before the social sciences convinced us that they could do the job and do it better. I assume that those outlines have not since been so visible and that we no longer have the sense of a distinctive American experience or even much of a certainty that there is one. After Fitzgerald, one feels, the door onto the native scene banged shut for American writers; the process of creation ceased to be a matter of opening the eyes and letting the sensibility take moral readings; the forms of social conduct, the traditional modes of action in which the drama of the will in crisis had formerly been displayed, no longer seemed directly accessible to the novel; suddenly no one appeared to know how anyone else behaved. Among the newer writers, certainly, who aspire to something more than journalism, there has been a sort of retreat of consciousness from the nearly insupportable task of dealing creatively with the fluid social situation and with the immense complication of status values and drives that the sociologists have discovered to be typical of the present age, and in comparison with which Fitzgerald's reality seems almost banally primitive. But Fitzgerald came to the novel at a time when the patterns of our present society were just being laid down; he had the inestimable advantage of the primal view, and so we return to him, particularly in *Gatsby*, with the feeling that we are seeing ourselves as we were in the light of an intensity that we are unable to direct upon ourselves as we are. If *Gatsby* is one of the very few books left from the twenties that we are still able to read with any kind of enduring pleasure and without always having to suffer a reminder of emotions we no longer care to feel, I suspect it is so because it dramatizes for us those basic assumptions and modes of assumption about the nature of American experience that belong to the antique furniture of our minds but that our experience of the present age and its literature has not been able to renew or replace. In this sense, *Gatsby* constitutes not only a primal view but, at least to date, a final view; it crystallizes an image of life beyond which neither our books nor our own perceptions seem able to take us; for two generations in fact, in that turgid area of consciousness where life and literature seem interchangeable, it has pretty largely done our perceiving for us. It therefore has about it some of that particular poignancy that we reserve for the lost moments of the past when we felt the emotions we would like still to feel, if we were able to and had again those exactly right opportunities. In this sense too *Gatsby* is mythopoeic: it has created our legend of the twenties, which at the present time is our common legend, and like *Moby-Dick* and *Huckleberry Finn* it has helped to create, by endowing with significant form, a national unconscious; its materials are those of the collective American mind at its closest approach to the primary source of native frontier symbols. As a result, we must all feel on reading it a little as Nick Carraway felt on hearing Gatsby's words—"reminded of something—an elusive rhythm, a fragment of lost words, that I had heard somewhere a long time ago." I do not mean that I much hold to the more obvious and popular mythological view of *Gatsby*: carried too far, as it usually is, it threatens always to smother the novel within the strictures of meaning. But I can understand its attraction and its relevance: Fitzgerald's technique of pictorial generalization, along with what Lionel Trilling has called his "ideographic" method of character portrayal, insists on far more than the novel primarily signifies. Yet at this late stage in Fitzgerald criticism one can hope to escape cliché only by refusing to rest content with meaning and by inducing some contemplation of *Gatsby*'s life as fiction.

A prime feature of that life is of course the marvelous style that shows it forth, and while it is now commonplace to say that in *Gatsby* Fitzgerald found, certainly for the first time and probably for the last, his proper form, it is less so to say that he could not have found the form had he not experienced an immense deepening as well as a marked shift of his relation both to himself and to language. The essentially expressive form of the earlier novels had indulged Fitzgerald in all his younger, easier, and more sentimental mannerisms; it encouraged him to describe emotion rather than to embody it, and whenever he could not find emotion, to fake it; it put up no resistance whatever to his habit of seeking, and then descending to, the lowest level of feeling his characters could sustain, or of making use, whenever he thought he could get away with it, of the cheapest rhetorical devices cribbed from Compton Mackenzie and the gothic novel. It is also evident, particularly now, that the subjects of his first novels were not suitable vehicles for his real emotions, and if they were bad, it is partly because they never allowed him to discover what his real emotions were. Fitzgerald never believed with anything like his full heart in the life he was describing; his deeper sensibilities were not only not engaged but offended, and the necessity to appear to believe, to try to pass off childish infatuation as adult devotion, only served to make him seem frivolous and girlishly Beardsleyan. In this sense, of course, Fitzgerald's first subjects kept him young: they arrested him for the time at a level of emotional development precisely adequate to their capacity for receiving emotion, and they asked nothing more of him than that he disguise the deficiency behind effusion and rhetoric.

It is not clear from his biography exactly what happened in the time between *The Beautiful and Damned* and *Gatsby* to mature Fitzgerald, nor is it very likely that his biography knows. Obviously he found a way of untangling his moral imagination from the gothic bric-a-brac of ghosts, mysterious medieval gentlemen, and wispy lurking presences, among which it had searched for an object through the earlier novels, and under the sponsorship of that imagination he was able to achieve a sufficient penetration of his subject to engage for the first time his real emotions and his best talents. In *This Side of Paradise* "the problem of evil had solidifed" for Amory Blaine "into the problem of sex," and one felt that this had behind it some affront to Fitzgerald's romanticism stemming from the discovery that a physical act could be imagined for nice girls beyond the kiss. By the time he wrote *The Beautiful and Damned* the problem appeared to have risen on the anatomical scale and lodged somewhere near the heart, although one could never be certain whether it really belonged there or in Wall Street. But with *Gatsby* there was no longer any doubt: the problem of evil had by then solidified into a problem of responsibility and spiritual condition in those rich enough to be able to choose their morals; Fitzgerald's opposing selves, the giddy, bibulous boy and the morose, hung-over tallier of emotional chits, had struck a bargain and a balance.

This deepened understanding of his subject inevitably brought Fitzgerald to an awareness of the need for a narrative form far stricter and at the same time far subtler than that demanded by his earlier novels. It is doubtful if up to *Gatsby* he had given any serious thought at all to matters of form, and considering the limited conception he had of his subject at the time, he probably felt little necessity to. By Jamesean standards *This Side of Paradise* was abominably constructed, and *The Beautiful and Damned* was only slightly less so. But the loosely episodic, rather spongy form of the juvenile *bildungsroman* borrowed from Mackenzie and Wells was not hopelessly unsuited to the situation of the young man only faintly disenchanted with the life of glamor, particularly so long as in Fitzgerald's mind the difference between the rich and you and me could still be equated with the possession of more money, better looks, looser morals, and greater daring. All that was required was an involved, naïve consciousness capable of moving more or less horizontally through a series of episodes, the function of which was slow instruction in a kind of eager irony, and for this the one-dimensional mock-heroes, Amory Blaine and Anthony Patch, were perfectly competent pupils. But with *Gatsby* Fitzgerald's talent took a dramatic turn; his sense of his subject and his involvement with it became too complex and ambivalent to be portrayed through the limited single consciousness; he needed a narrative form at once firm enough to correct his tendency toward emotional bloat and supple enough to allow full range for the development of a set of individual characters who would display his theme and at the same time serve as suitable dramatic equivalents for his contradictory feelings toward it. He had suddenly and without quite knowing it arrived at a point where he was ready to put to use his mature understanding of his material within the framework of his advanced knowledge of the formal art of fiction.

The pictorial method of Conrad, James, and Wharton, combining the "single window" technique of the engaged narrator with that of the scenic tableau, made it possible for Fitzgerald to overcome in *Gatsby* the severe limitations of the merely expressive form and to achieve the kind of distance between himself and his subject that must be achieved before the job of true fictional creation can properly begin. In Nick Carraway he found the protagonist of his own most central ambivalence, a median consciousness and conscience vacillating between admiration and judgment, a "first-rate intelligence" able "to hold two opposed ideas in the mind at the same time, and still retain the ability to function." The foil-figures of Gatsby and Tom Buchanan serve him as devices for breaking down into contrasting parts and recombining in even more ambiguous relation his twin senses of the physical glamor of the rich and their spiritual corruption, their force of character and their moral weakness, the ideal nature of romantic vision and the baseness of the methods employed in its service, the essential shabbiness of romantic vision in a society that can measure vision only in money. Daisy Buchanan and Jordan Baker function on a somewhat simpler level to complete the symbolism of identity and contrast—Daisy standing initially as an embodiment of the purity of the vision, finally of the corruption and the baseness of method; Jordan holding up to the world a mask of sophisticated, though precarious, self-composure, but concealing behind it, like Nicole Diver, an awful secret of interior derangement. George and Myrtle Wilson alone remain almost untouched by the process of imaginative revision through which Fitzgerald transformed, by immensely complicating, his typical thematic effects in the novel: Wilson carries forward and for the first time fully characterizes Fitzgerald's earlier horror of poverty and illness, while Myrtle dramatizes his formerly incoherent, at moments hysterical, aversion to direct sexuality when unaccompanied by beauty and wealth.

Lionel Trilling is undoubtedly right in calling this method of characterization "ideographic" and in applying the term as well to the method of the novel as a whole. Nothing and no one in the course of the narrative is really developed; everything is seen in tableau, in a state of permanent pictorial rest. The characters are little more than a collection of struck attitudes, frieze figures carved on the entablature of a moral abstraction, a greatly generalized intuitive view of the nature of American experience. Their individual identities are subordinated to the central idea they are meant to signify, perfectly embodying the "platonic conception" behind the remark made by Gatsby when he admits the possibility that Daisy may perhaps have once loved her husband: "In any case it was just personal." The secret of the entire technique of the novel may in a sense be said to lie hidden in this remark, for its effect is to divert attention from the personal and particular to the abstract conception, the allegorized whole.

In achieving this effect Fitzgerald carried the pictorial method considerably beyond James; in fact, the closest parallel to its use in *Gatsby* is the Joycean "signature" or "epiphany" technique where character is broken down into its separate parts, and one or two of the parts are made to stand for the whole. The result for Joyce, in both *A Portrait of the Artist* and *Ulysses*, was the establishment of a virtual iconography of character, a system of extravagantly distilled symbolic essences, usually suggested by a gesture or an article of clothing, through which the soul of being was shown forth. The result for Fitzgerald is not nearly so elaborate, but it is very similar in kind. Nick Carraway is revealed to us through his signature of honesty; Gatsby is identified by his pink suits, Tom Buchanan by his rippling pack of muscle, Daisy by her voice, Jordan by her balancing act, Myrtle by her fleshy vitality, Wilson by his hollow-eyed stare, Wolfsheim by his hairy nostrils, the butler by his nose. In the case of each of the major characters these attributes take on metaphorical significance in the thematic design of the novel. Nick's honesty is called into ironic question by Jordan in an effort to shift the blame for her own dishonesty; Gatsby's pink suits suggest the meretriciousness of his role, Tom's muscle the brutal strength of his; Jordan's balancing act is indicative of her precarious control over herself and her need for stabilizing moral convention, while Daisy's voice serves as the gauge of her "basic insincerity," which it is the principal business of the novel to penetrate. Initially full of warm excitement and promise, it is finally shown to be "full of money," and in the long interval between the two observations the pathetic futility of Gatsby's dream is gradually made clear.

To create an effect of involvement and movement while retaining the advantage of the pictorial method, Fitzgerald made constant use of ironic parallelisms of both character and event, still very much in the manner of Joyce. Both Gatsby and Daisy are "insincere," Gatsby about his past, Daisy about her present feelings; Tom's unfaithfulness to Daisy is balanced by Gatsby's faithfulness to her; yet Tom and Daisy belong to a "secret society" of ultimately deeper faithfulness. Nick keeps faith with Gatsby to the end, but not with Jordan. Jordan's dishonesty is revealed in time with the Buchanans' and Gatsby's; Jordan like Daisy is a "careless driver," and the episode in which this fact is first made clear to Nick prefigures the moment when Daisy's carelessness results in Myrtle's death; both, furthermore, are anticipated by the comic accident scene in Gatsby's driveway and are finally commented upon during Nick's last meeting with Jordan when, to conceal her own dishonesty, she insists that she met in Nick another bad driver. Just before the showdown scene with Gatsby in the Plaza Hotel Tom feels that he has lost in one afternoon both his wife and his mistress; during the scene he wins back his wife, and Gatsby loses his mistress and is symbolically murdered by Tom—all to the accompaniment of Mendelssohn's Wedding March being played in the ballroom below. As Gatsby the dreamer dies, Nick remembers that it is his own thirtieth birthday, the time of life when, in his and Fitzgerald's romantically limited chronology, all dreams must end. On the way back to East Egg Daisy kills Tom's mistress, Wilson loses a wife, and a while later Tom arranges through Wilson to murder Gatsby in fact, Wilson believing that Gatsby has been Myrtle's lover as well as her murderer. All the principal male characters lose the women they love, and in each case through some act of faithlessness on the part of one or more of the women.

This system of carefully plotted interior parallels and cross-references serves greatly to enhance the thematic "size" of the novel and to give back to it some of the quality of dramatic specification that the method of static character portrayal takes away. The same can be said for the reflexive relationship of the parts in the narrative design as a whole. Each of the nine chapters is composed of one, or very occasionally more than one, dramatic scene presented pictorially and surrounded by skillfully foreshortened panoramic material, and each achieves significance not through the standard depth-wise plumbing of character, but through its contribution of fresh facts to the linearly developing sequence of facts that gradually illuminate Gatsby's central dilemma and mystery. Each functions, furthermore, in reciprocal relation to every other, at times ironically, at times by simple contrast, so that an effect of counterpointed motifs comes ultimately to stand, very much as it does in *The Waste Land*, in place of the more conventional and predictable effect of events arranged chronologically and naturalistically.

The opening and closing pages of the novel frame Gatsby's story within the parentheses of an elegiacally retrospective vision of time, history, and moral conduct. The first two pages state the terms of the ambivalent attitude that Nick is to take toward the subsequent action and which it is to be the task of that action to resolve. Presented initially as a young man taught by his father to "reserve all judgments" in the knowledge that "all the people in this world haven't had the advantages that you've had," Nick describes himself immediately afterward as one who has since been taught better by first-hand contact with some of the people who have had even more of the advantages than he, and who have left him with the feeling of wanting "the world to be in uniform and at a sort of moral attention forever." He then goes on to substitute a new and much more complex ambivalence for the one that, on looking back over his experience, he feels has now been resolved: he has been educated in the power of condemnatory judgment, but he is still unable to condemn Gatsby—"Only Gatsby ... was exempt from my reaction—Gatsby who represented everything for which I have an unaffected scorn." It is to be Nick's fate in the course of the novel, as unquestionably it was Fitzgerald's, that while he is to learn intolerance and finally moral indignation, he is never to come to terms with his contradictory feelings toward Gatsby: his moral indignation remains to the end the slave of his moral idealism. After Gatsby's death it is simple enough for Nick to recognize the Buchanans as "careless people," for he has accumulated more than sufficient evidence of their irresponsibility to cancel out his earlier admiration of them. But of Gatsby the poseur, racketeer, and liar he can only speak in the name of Gatsby the dreamer, and eulogize him only in the name of the founding of America itself, for Gatsby is one who escapes the monitory conscience of the "spoiled priest" by being himself priestlike, with a priest's passionate and self-sacrificing dedication to an ideal, a religion, of romantic transcendence. Nick's point of view, which we see in the process of gradually becoming re-educated with regard to the Buchanans, is incapable of reeducation with regard to Gatsby, for Gatsby is both a suitable object for the fascination that Nick earlier felt for the Buchanans and an embodiment of the ideal against which he measures and condemns them. It is an inadequate ideal, and Nick—or at least Fitzgerald—is entirely aware of the fact, but within the limits of his given experience it is the only one he has to set against the world of Buchanan values, the only one he has, therefore, to exalt into triumph over those values at the end.

But the image of Nick that dominates the opening chapters is of another, as yet uneducated idealism, the kind indigenous to his Middle West, a rural frontier fascination with the appearance of culture and worldly manners. In fact, the first chapter centered in the scene depicting the dinner party at the Buchanan estate is clearly intended to dramatize Nick in his primal condition of reserved judgment juxtaposed with the gradually emerging facts of spiritual corruption and deceit that finally cause him to arrive at condemnatory judgment and become morally initiated. Firmly established amid the grandeur of his physical setting, Tom Buchanan first appears to Nick as an heroic figure, but almost at once Nick is struck by the change in him since their New Haven years.

> Now he was a sturdy straw-haired man of thirty with a rather hard mouth and a supercilious manner. Two shining arrogant eyes had established dominance over his face and gave him the appearance of always leaning aggressively forward. Not even the effeminate swank of his riding clothes could hide the enormous power of that body.... It was a body capable of enormous leverage—a cruel body. His speaking voice, a gruff husky tenor, added to the impression of fractiousness he conveyed. There was a touch of paternal contempt in it, even toward people he liked—and there were men at New Haven who had hated his guts.

This swift appraisal of Tom establishes him in the role he is later to play and constitutes the first element in the developing contrast between appearance and reality on which the chapter turns.

A moment later Nick is taken in to see Daisy and Jordan, and the picture of glamorous buoyancy and charm that they present temporarily restores his powers of admiration. In fact, the quality of physical inflation, suggested entirely in tableau, that pervades the scene stands as an exact equivalent for the emotion the sight of the women arouses in him.

> The only completed stationary object in the room was an enormous couch on which two young women were buoyed up as though upon an anchored balloon. They were both in white, and their dresses were rippling and fluttering as if they has just been blown back in after a short flight around the house.... Then there was a boom as Tom Buchanan shut the rear windows and the caught wind died out about the room, and the curtains and the rugs and the two young women ballooned slowly to the floor.

But the effect is only temporarily. As the scene deflates itself, so subsequent events deflate Nick's illusion and impel him toward condemnatory judgment. At the dinner table he learns that "Tom's got some woman in New York." Gatsby's name is brought into the conversation and hastily dropped. Nick dimly remembers, having seen Jordan, or a picture of her, somewhere before. Sitting on the porch with Daisy after dinner and listening to her tell about the birth of her child and her feelings about life in general, he is suddenly struck by "the basic insincerity of what she had to say" and begins to feel "the whole evening had been a trick of some sort to extract a contributory emotion" from him. A moment later Daisy smirks "as if she had asserted her membership in a rather distinguished secret society to which she and Tom belonged." Nick leaves East Egg that night sufficiently disturbed to want Daisy to "rush out of the house, child in arms," and upon returning home he catches sight of Gatsby standing in the darkness of his lawn and looking across the water to the green light at the end of the Buchanans' dock: Thus, by the end of the first chapter the basic dramatic situation has been established; all the principal characters have been introduced or alluded to; and the destructive element in the Buchanans has been brought into fatal juxtaposition with both Nick's naïve admiration and Gatsby's naïve aspiration. The contest now will be between the force of the secret society, epitomized by Daisy's insincerity and Tom's cruel selfishness, and the persuasive power of Gatsby's illusion. But we already know the outcome: it has been ordained by the quality and content of the action itself.

The second chapter develops the destructive statement of the first in two ways: through the contextual symbolism of the "valley of ashes" image dominated by the gigantic eyes of the oculist Dr. T.J. Eckleburg, and through the pictorial scene of the drunken party at Tom's New York apartment. The valley of ashes establishes the situation of evil that is conventionally, and in Fitzgerald habitually, associated with hopeless poverty, and it projects that evil into literal contrast with the kind that wealth and privilege induce in the Buchanans. Theirs is at once a more serious and reprehensible kind because it involves the possibility of moral choice and an identical kind because it has behind it an equivalent impoverishment of soul. The eyes of Dr. Eckleburg can be variously and, if one is not careful to preserve a sense of humor, fatuously interpreted. They are reminiscent of some of Fitzgerald's earlier gothic figures of evil—The ghostly apparitions and "somber palls" of *This Side of Paradise* and *The Beautiful and Damned*—but they have the virtue of thematic relevance that these lacked, as well as the dramatic advantage of association with a developed physical milieu. They are, of course, suggestive of Nick's monitory conscience and are related to the image of "the casual watcher in the darkening streets" that is evoked during the party scene by his sense of being "within and without, simultaneously enchanted and repelled by the inexhaustible variety of life." They are also specifically associated by George Wilson in the eighth chapter with the eyes of God and, since Gatsby is represented as a son of God, we are probably justified in associating them in turn with the holiness of his romantic aspiration. More generally, they operate as an open symbol of transcendence and judgment set down in an opposing environment of defeat and subhuman amorality, or, to put it differently, they serve as a terminal point for the two principal thematic lines of the novel: the evil of the human condition overseen and modified by conscience.

The party episode pictorializes in scenic form the evil implicit in the valley of ashes, and since it stands in ironic contrast with the earlier scene at the Buchanans', it shows up that evil to be merely the nether side of theirs: the moral debasement of the party is the Buchanans' moral hypocrisy with its clothes off, the ugly truth beneath the veneer of social elegance that first charmed Nick, the corruption behind Daisy's enchanting voice and Jordan's delicate balancing act—in effect, the vulgar barroom scene in *The Waste Land* in comparison with the sterile "game of chess" episode.

The third through the sixth chapters perform for Gatsby the same service that the first two chapters performed for the Buchanans: they present him in the alternating conditions of illusion and reality, mystery and fact, successively as genial host, shady character, and romantic visionary. In the third chapter he is dramatized in his public role of host, but like Conrad's Heyst he is seen by various observers in the roles created for him by his legend, and this has the effect of endowing him with the mythic generality and largeness that his thematic role requires. It also gives concrete endorsement to the premise that he is the product of his "Platonic conception of himself." Nick is himself momentarily taken in by the "Oggsford man" role, but quickly recognizes its absurdity, especially after the luncheon with Wolfsheim when he becomes acquainted with the underworld role. He shortly discovers, however, that the truth about Gatsby, as it is gradually revealed to him, first by Jordan, then by Gatsby himself, is far more remarkable than any of the stories circulated about him, and ultimately far more compelling. By the end of the sixth chapter he has become convinced of the high quality of Gatsby's aspiration, but he has also gathered fresh evidence in the form of the Buchanans' high-handed behavior at one of the parties that that aspiration will eventually be defeated. Daisy has initially been hypnotized by Gatsby's display of wealth and ardor and for the moment is attracted by the prospect of an affair, but during the party she reveals her snobbish inability to participate wholly in any form of life outside herself.

> She was appalled by West Egg, this unprecedented 'place' that Broadway had begotten upon a Long Island fishing village—appalled by its raw vigor that chafed under the old euphemisms and by the too obtrusive fate that herded its inhabitants along a short-cut from nothing to nothing. She saw something awful in the very simplicity she failed to understand.

Like Daisy's first show of "basic insincerity," this reaction is proof that she will never finally join Gatsby in his efforts to "repeat the past."

It is interesting to see how these chapters devoted to Gatsby exactly reverse the revelatory processes of those devoted to the Buchanans. The illusion of sophisticated elegance was penetrated in their case to reveal a basic sickness and poverty of spirit. Gatsby, on the other hand, is seen initially against a veneer of fraudulent finery, is then revealed as actually fraudulent as well as lawless, and finally as morally innocent in the midst of the lawless. Superficially, he is as bad as the Buchanans, but only superficially. Theirs is a fundamental lawlessness of the heart: they are "careless people" in the worst and deepest sense. His is the lawlessness of the merely illegal and is excusable on the ground of the service it renders in enforcing the highest laws of the heart.

The seventh and climactic chapter brings into dramatic conflict the opposing elements of destruction and aspiration, the morally lawless and the morally innocent within the illegal, which have been separately developed in the chapters alternately devoted to the Buchanans and Gatsby. The occasion is a gathering at the Buchanan estate, precisely like that of the first chapter, but the tonal differences between the two are obviously intended to unite them in ironic contrast. Again Daisy and Jordan are seen in tableau, but where formerly they had about them a quality of inflation and buoyancy suggestive of the emotion they first aroused in Nick, they now appear in a state of fatigued deflation, as if the intervening events had drained away their vitality along with their charm. "The room, shadowed well with awnings, was dark and cool. Daisy and Jordan lay upon an enormous couch, like silver idols weighing down their own white dresses against the singing breeze of the fans." The whole situation, furthermore, seems to Nick to be touched with nightmare. He imagines he overhears the butler replying to a telephone request for "the master's body." Daisy impulsively kisses Gatsby the moment Tom leaves the room. Daisy's child is led in by a nurse and introduced to Gatsby who, Nick is certain, had never "really believed in its existence before." Finally, as the party prepares to leave for New York, Gatsby has his first insight into the quality of Daisy's that is to prevent him from winning her.

> "Her voice is full of money," he said suddenly.... That was it. I'd never understood before. It was full of money—that was the inexhaustible charm that rose and fell on it, the jingle of it, the cymbal's song of it.... High in a white palace the king's daughter, the golden girl....

This is the quality that indemnifies Daisy's commitment to Tom's world, but it finally involves much more than just money: it is a whole philosophy and tradition of life belonging to those who have always had money and marking them as a separate breed superior to those who have not. And in the chapter's closing scene, following on Gatsby's defeat and Myrtle's death, the difference is epiphanized:

> Daisy and Tom were sitting opposite each other at the kitchen table, with a plate of cold fried chicken between them, and two bottles of ale.... They weren't happy, and neither of them had touched the chicken or the ale—and yet they weren't unhappy either. There was an unmistakable air of natural

> intimacy about the picture, and anybody would have said that they were conspiring together.

The "secret society" has at last won out over romantic illusion, and Gatsby, standing outside in the dark just as he was at the end of Chapter I, is now "watching over nothing."

The movement of the novel, then, is from illusion to reality, innocence to knowledge, aspiration to defeat, and of course suffusing them all, tolerance to judgment. It is Gatsby who pays the price for the learning, who functions by turns as the hapless Mme. de Vionnet and the finally unteachable Chad, but it is Nick who does his learning for him and through whose experience—as through Strether's in the case of Chad—it is made dramatically concrete. Gatsby's dream is dramatically unspecific because it is unspecific to him. That is, symbolically, its limitation and meaning: it is based not on things as they are, but on things as they might become. It is real only to the extent that one can imagine for it some successful embodiment in action, and this the logic of the novel never permits. Nick's sensibility, therefore, serves as a surrogate for Gatsby's, making external all that the dream, because it lacks concrete basis in fact and action, cannot make external by itself. In doing this, Nick's sensibility fleshes Gatsby out to very nearly epic size, endowing him with the character of heroism seen against a broadly generalized conception of national life and history.

This is accomplished in the novel in two ways: through Nick's direct participation in the life of the Buchanans, which educates him in the folly of innocence, and through the larger symbolism of place against which Nick measures the meaning of both his own and Gatsby's experience. In practice, however, the two function as one: Nick records the experience as well as the meaning lost entirely in terms of place. Place affords him his basis of vision and evaluation, and the change that occurs in his vision and evalation results in a change in his evaluation of place.

At the beginning of the novel the East appears to Nick—as by implication it does to Gatsby—as a land of wealth and future glittering with the promise of "shining secrets." But as the action proceeds, the "shining secrets" tarnish, and it becomes clear that the wealth and quality of purposeful movement into the future are illusory virtues imposed upon the East by the innocence of the beholder. Like Gatsby's isolated dream, the wealth feeds on itself; the Easterners are imprisoned by it to the point of spiritual stagnation; the "flow of life" moves in a purposeless circle. "The rich grow richer" because they have no other way to grow; "the poor get—children" as well as poorer and end ultimately in a "valley of ashes." But the Middle West too is stagnant. There "dwellings are still called through decades by a family's name"; one is oppressed by the "interminable inquisitions" and by a moral code that demands that life survive as a tradition rather than flow dynamically into the future. It follows, therefore, that West Egg, the Eastern analogue of the Middle West, should also end in a "valley of ashes," and that *both* East and

West Egg should be imperfect ovals "crushed flat at the contact end," equally defective in their reception to life.

Fundamentally *Gatsby* is, as Nick says, "a story of the West, after all." It begins in the Middle West, makes a "riotous excursion" into the heart of Eastern promise, and returns to the Middle West in what at first appears to be disillusionment. Actually, of course, it is an affirmation of the true values following on disillusionment: the initial image of Middle Western stolidity resolves itself into a closing image of Middle Western solidity. Upon Nick's return from war the Middle West, "instead of being the warm centre of the world ... seemed like the ragged edge of the universe." Coming East to learn the bond business he settles down in West Egg in a "small eyesore" of a house to enjoy "the consoling proximity of millionaires" and to plumb if he can "the shining secrets that only Midas and Morgan and Maecenas knew." Having just left the restrictive environment of the Middle West, he is at first especially aware of the free flow of life in the East, although he is also aware that it is intimately associated with the free flow of wealth. He speaks of Tom and Daisy as drifting "here and there ... wherever people were rich together." But they "drift unrestfully," and he sees that Tom "would drift on forever seeking, a little wistfully, for the dramatic turbulence of some irrecoverable football game." Like Gatsby's dream, the Buchanans' drifting is an effort to recover in the present some of the lost sensations of the past as well as the sensibilities of youth that, in Americans, alone seem capable of deep response.

But Nick's first impression of the East is one of exciting, restless movement, and throughout the scene of his visit with the Buchanans his enchantment with their kinetic radiance alternates with moments of insight into their superficiality. Their lawn "started at the beach and ran toward the front door for a quarter of a mile, jumping over sundials and brick walls and burning gardens—finally when it reached the house drifting up the side in bright vines as though from the momentum of its run." Tom appears to be "leaning aggressively forward," filling his "glistening boots until he strained the top lacing, and you could see a great pack of muscle shifting when his shoulder moved under his thin coat." Inside the house as well everything seems to be flowing, but only because of a momentary breeze. "A breeze blew through the room, blew curtains in at one end and out the other like pale flags, twisting them up toward the frosted wedding-cake of the ceiling, and then rippled over the wine-colored rug, making a shadow on it as wind does on the sea." On the "only completely stationary object in the room" Daisy and Jordan appear to be "buoyed up as though upon an anchored balloon." But as soon as Tom shuts the window, the wind dies, and the floating effect proves to have been only an appearance. Nick is charmed and enchanted by the appearances, but soon begins to recognize them for they are. Tom and Daisy make only a "polite, pleasant effort to entertain and be entertained. They knew that presently dinner would be over and casually put away."

There is little meaning or sincerity in what is going on. Daisy suddenly declares that Nick is an "absolute rose," but he realizes that she is only "extemporizing." Daisy and Jordan converse in language that "was as cool as their white dresses and their impersonal eyes in the absence of all desire." Inevitably Nick compares the scene with similar occasions in the West "where an evening was hurried from phase to phase toward its close, in a continually disappointed anticipation, or else in sheer nervous dread of the moment itself." But here in the East among expatriated Middle Westerners even anticipation has been lost; all desire is dead; the Buchanans are the spent shadows of action. "You make me feel uncivilized, Daisy," Nick says. "Can't you talk about crops or something," and the "or something substantial" is implied.

In the second chapter culminating in the party at Tom's New York apartment the contrast of place motifs is reinforced by an implicit symbolism relating place to dream and ultimately to Gatsby. The natives of West Egg are depicted as a race of the living dead, "ash grey men ... who move dimly and already crumbling through the powdery air." Only Myrtle Wilson is alive: "There was an immediately perceptible vitality about her as if the nerves of her body were continually smouldering." She alone is free of the "white ashen dust" that veiled her husband's "dark suit and pale hair as it veiled everything in the vicinity," and we learn later that she has remained alive and uncontaminated because she is nourished by her dream of an eventually legal life with Tom in the West.

During the party a change occurs in Myrtle that pictorializes a crucial fact about the nature of her own dream and, by implication, Gatsby's. Although the dream has kept her alive, now that she is surrounded by circumstances approaching those of its fulfillment she undergoes an ugly transformation: "The intense vitality that had been so remarkable in the garage was converted into impressive hauteur." She now presents a pathetic, ridiculous figure dressed in expensive clothes that contrast sharply with her commonness and her "violent and obscene language." Apparently the dream, by the very fact of its existence, can be lifegiving, but as it approaches realization it invests life with inconsistency and vulgarity: it is doomed to remain a "Platonic conception," an ideal incapable of embodiment in fact, particularly when the fact can only be material. But Myrtle's dream is a long way from realization. It is confined, as it turns out permanently, to illegality and the East.

For Nick the party represents a vulgarization of what he previously experienced at the Buchanans. The "flow" of the East has become confusion. "People disappeared, reappeared, made plans to go somewhere and then lost each other, searched for each other, found each other a few feet away." There is a photograph on the wall apparently of "a hen sitting on a blurred rock. Looked at from a distance, however, the hen resolved itself into a bonnet, and the countenance of a stout old lady beamed down into the room." It seems to him that there is a "blurred air" to the faces in the room, and in a fatuous effort to restore order he wipes from McKee's cheek "the spot of dried lather that had worried [him] all afternoon." But he is still "simultaneously within and without, simultaneously enchanted and repelled by the inexhaustible variety of life." Tom has told Myrtle that he cannot get a divorce because his wife is a Catholic, and although Nick "is a little shocked at the elaborateness of the lie," he has not yet learned to relate the lie, in all is elaborateness, to the false promise of the East or to the larger lie on which his whole experience rests.

But we cannot help but see the relation, just as we cannot help but see Nick, Myrtle, and the Buchanans as actors in a dumb show caricaturing Gatsby's tragedy. Like Nick, Gatsby is enchanted by the "shining secrets" of the East and mistakes the purposeless movement for the free flow of life into the future; like Myrtle he is given vitality by a dream that is far larger than any possibility of fulfillment; and like the Buchanans he is thwarted in his efforts to "repeat the past." He shares with them all the deficiency that makes them "subtly unadaptable to Eastern life," but he also shares their fate of inhabiting a culture in which dreams along with most demands of the spirit have no place. He aspires to the good life as though it were a thing of the spirit, while the culture can afford him the means only for a life of material achievement—a material woman or a woman corrupted by materialism. In his aloofness from his own material possessions he dramatizes his uncompromising faith that life can and will yield more, if only he can manipulate circumstances properly. And it is no more than the justice of irony that he should finally be thwarted by an utterly faithless but infinitely more powerful materialism than his own. For the Buchanans, wealth is not a means to the fulfillment of any dream: it is the hard fact of life against which the hard fact of Gatsby's manipulations can have no effect. It is also ironic that the illusions of Gatsby's party guests are seen in conjunction with his cold and aloof factualness, and that this factualness is the product of an illusion far more romantic than theirs. The guests come to his parties in pursuit of some final ecstasy, some ultimate good time that the American Dream has always promised them. Gatsby is the self-appointed agent of that dream, but they can never get close to him or discover his true identity, just as neither he nor they can hope to discover an identity for the dream.

It is dramatically just, therefore, that at the close of the novel Nick should relate Gatsby's aspiration to the feelings aroused in the early Dutch voyagers to America by their first glimpse of the "fresh, green breast of the new world."

> For a transitory enchanted moment man must have held his breath in the presence of this continent, compelled into an aesthetic contemplation he neither understood nor desired, face to face for the last time in history with something commensurate to his capacity for wonder.... And as I sat there brooding on the old, unknown world, I thought of Gatsby's wonder when he

first picked out the green light at the end of Daisy's dock. He had come a long way to this blue lawn, and his dream must have seemed so close that he could hardly fail to grasp it. He did not know that it was already behind him, somewhere back in that vast obscurity beyond the city, where the dark fields of the republic rolled on under the night.

But it is also logically just that he should go on to say that those voyagers were face to face "for the last time in history with something commensurate to" their capacity for wonder. For it may well be that the moment when America was first settled was the last moment when America was able to embody the dream that the settlers brought to its shores, and that ever since the wonder and the dream have lacked a suitable object, or have had to languish and die in pursuit of an unworthy object—mere money or mere surface display—just as Gatsby's dream had to die in part because Daisy was, and could not help but be, unworthy of it.

It is perhaps too much to say, as at least one critic has, that Gatsby is a symbol of America itself. But he is a major figure in the legend created by the complex fate of being American, and he is the hero of the tragic limitations of that fate in a world that, as the eclipsing myth of the twenties recedes, seems more contemporary than we knew.

96
Dream, Design, and Interpretation in *The Great Gatsby*

◆

DAVID L. MINTER

If thou didst ever hold me in thy heart,
Absent thee from felicity awhile,
And in this harsh world draw thy breath in pain,
To tell my story.
       William Shakespeare, *Hamlet*

There is, as Kenneth Burke once noted, "a radical difference ... between building a house and writing a poem about building a house."[1] Like Hawthorne's *The Blithedale Romance* and Faulkner's *Absalom, Absalom!*, Fitzgerald's *The Great Gatsby* is structured by the juxtaposition of men engaged in these radically different pursuits. On one side there is Jay Gatsby, who is a builder as well as a dreamer; on the other, there is Nick Carraway, who is a narrator as well as a spectator. Whereas Gatsby deliberately dedicates himself to realizing his "incorruptible dream," to building according to "the beautiful circuit and subterfuge" of his thought and his desire, Carraway deliberately dedicates himself not only to observing Gatsby's action but to telling Gatsby's story.[2]

The Great Gatsby is permeated with corruption and contains, in the valley of ashes, Fitzgerald's starkest image of the new world as waste land, yet it is not in the end simply a grim story. Jay Gatsby's "incorruptible" version of the "last and greatest of all human dreams"—the dream of building a new and perfect life in a new and perfect world—serves, as several critics have noted, to relieve the novel's grimness, to recast its bleakness.[3] Gatsby's action—his building, both as activity and as artifact—ends, however, in "huge incoherent failure," not in success (181). It serves accordingly rather to

SOURCE: *Twentieth Century Interpretations of "The Great Gatsby": A Collection of Critical Essays*, ed. Ernest Lockridge, Englewood Cliffs, NJ, 1968, pp. 82–89.

make relief possible than in itself to represent relief. The whole of Gatsby's story, including both his dream and his absurd plan for realizing it—his plan for procuring a fortune, a mansion, and a bride—is redeemed from corruption and waste, from failure and absurdity only through Nick Carraway's effort imaginatively to interpret and render it. The first four paragraphs of the novel prepare us for the form the novel's unfolding is to take. In the first three paragraphs, the narrator, Nick Carraway, introduces himself; in the fourth he introduces the subject of his narrative, Jay Gatsby. Carraway's small cottage on the edge of Gatsby's spacious estate suggests the role he is to play within the novel: the role of observer and spectator, critic and interpreter of a scene and an action dominated by Gatsby.

Gatsby represents, Carraway tell us, "everything for which I have an unaffected scorn." Yet, because he has found in Gatsby "some heightened sensitivity to the promises of life"—"a romantic readiness"—and because of the curious way in which Gatsby "turned out ... at the end," Carraway has not been able not to do Gatsby. Having watched Gatsby pursue "his dream" with "unwavering devotion," Carraway knows that Gatsby has lived in faith that man can shape his life at will, compelling it to yield the beauty he seeks and the meaning he needs (2, 110). Carraway accordingly knows that Gatsby has become what he has become through "his extraordinary gift for hope"—his extraordinary faith that through devoted action he not only can shape the future but can "fix" the "terrible mistake" that mars the past (2, 111, 131). Moved as he is by faith in observing closely and "reserving judgments," Carraway is drawn to seek purpose in the "purposeless splendor" and meaning in the problematic fate that define Gatsby's life (1, 79). Unlike Gatsby's faith, which leaves him vulnerable to destruction (see 137), Carraway's faith renders him vulnerable to despair: to loss of "interest in the abortive sorrows and short-winded elations of men" and loss of faith in the effort "to save ... fragment[s]" of "dead dream[s]" (2, 153, 135). If, in Gatsby, Fitzgerald dramatizes the peculiar beauty and vulnerability of one dedicated to actualizing dreams, in Carraway he dramatizes the peculiar beauty and vulnerability of one dedicated to finding meaning in the "undefined consequence" of an action (64).

Behind Gatsby there is a history of dislocation and alienation, the attendants, as it were, of the experience of immigration, and thus of the very process of Americanization.[4] But behind him there also is an imagined history. On one side, he is James Gatz, the son of "shiftless and unsuccessful farm people." On the other, he is Jay Gatsby, the child of "his Platonic conception of himself," the heir to a history almost wholly "invented." Unable in the presence of abundance, of mansions in the town and yachts upon the lake, to accept dislocation and deprivation, his imagination has created an identity, a "conception," to which he remains "faithful to the end" (98–99).

James Gatz's attempt to become Jay Gatsby, his attempt to live out of his invented history, entails an attempt to realize his "unutterable" dream (112). Given his world, his dream, despite its "gaudiness," is necessary. At times its vitality almost overwhelms him, almost reduces him to a mere embodiment of its impulse; and at times he almost fatally betrays it by making devotion to it take the form of service to a beauty that is "vast, vulgar, and meretricious" (98–99). From outset to end, he just misses "being absurd."[5] Yet both his conception of himself and his dream survive everything. To its curiously actual yet unreal world, Gatsby's dream comes as "a deathless song"; in its own way it is so "absolutely real" that it changes everything it touches "into something significant, elemental, and profound" (97, 46–47). Though altogether unactual, it is its world's primary source of positive good, its primary hope of overcoming the "foul dust" and the "valley of ashes" (2, 23).

Before it is finally rendered "incorruptible," however, Gatsby's particular version of "the last and greatest of all human dreams" becomes a "dead dream" and leads to "grotesque" "nightmare" (155, 182, 135, 164). And it does so because, in the design through which Gatsby attempts to actualize it, it is wed to "perishable breath" and mortal mansion. In entering the round world of time-space, it falls victim to the "accidental" and ends in "holocaust" (112, 162–163).

In its earliest recorded form, Gatsby's effort to express "his unutterable visions" takes the form of a "schedule" (a direct descendant of Benjamin Franklin's) copied on a flyleaf of "a ragged old copy of a book called *Hopalong Cassidy*." The schedule itself is intended to enforce industry and frugality, to foster physical, mental, and moral growth, and to encourage development of social graces and personal cleanliness—"No wasting time" / "No more smoking or chewing" / "Bath every other day" / "Practice elocution, poise and how to attain it" (112, 174). Later, goaded by loss of Daisy—to whom he has "felt himself married"—and by knowledge that the "terrible mistake" of her marriage with the wealthy Tom Buchanan is a result of his own poverty, Gatsby turns his dream into a design that dictates a precise course of action. On one side, he will pursue "his phantom millions"—he will accumulate a prodigious fortune and procure a colossal mansion. On the other, he will pursue Daisy, to whom, as an embodiment of ideal beauty, he commits himself as "to the following of a grail" (131, 149).

Although it culminates in his own death, Gatsby's effort to turn dream to design and design to actuality provides the key to understanding his story. When Carraway first realizes that Gatsby's mansion is situated across the bay from Daisy's home, not by "strange coincidence", but by design, the whole of Gatsby's life begins to take form and to demand interpretation anew. "He came alive to me," Carraway says, "delivered suddenly from the womb of his purposeless splendor" (79).

The "romantic speculation" and "bizarre accusations" that Gatsby evokes from all sides represent responses to the rich mystery, the problematic ambience, in which he moves (44, 65). Gatsby takes "satisfaction" in these "legends" and "inventions"—reports, for instance, that he is a murderer, a German spy, a gangster, a nephew of Von Hindenburg, and a nephew or cousin of Kaiser Wilhelm—(44, 61, 33)—not simply because he prizes notoriety, but because he longs to be interpreted (98; cf. 67). What seems to Nick Carraway, who doesn't "like mysteries,"[6] most to demand interpretation, however, is that Gatsby's design itself ends in ironic failure: that Gatsby's effort to right the moment of affront at the door of Daisy's "beautiful house" leads to more humiliating defeat at the more vulgar hands of Tom Buchanan; that Gatsby's effort to establish a grand mansion ends with an "empty" house that speaks only of "huge incoherent failure"; and that Gatsby's effort to have Daisy in order that she may reign as queen in his mansion ends not merely in unsuccess but in his death at the hands of a confused and outraged stranger (148, 181).

Nick Carraway's interpretation of Gatsby's fate involves more, however, than an inquiry into what went wrong in Gatsby's plan. In all Gatsby says and does, despite "his appalling sentimentality," there is an echo of "an elusive rhythm, a fragment of lost words" heard long ago. What accordingly is required of Carraway is that he define what lies behind Gatsby's design; and it is with this, as we shall see, that Carraway ends. Gatsby's sentimentality and silence together represent the residue of a dream for which his design is not an adequate correlative. Although it becomes "his ancestral home," although it corresponds to his invented history and is itself the work of a failed "plan to Found a Family," Gatsby's colossal mansion is not in itself commensurate with his needs. Similarly, despite the vitality of Gatsby's vision of her, Daisy remains, or at least again becomes, a curiously beautiful fraud of a hopelessly corrupt world. Only in Carraway's interpretation is the fullness of Gatsby's dream recovered (112, 154, 89).

Carraway's effort to interpret Gatsby is for the most part rather simple. In some moments he simply discredits what is false: he explodes "wild rumors" and clears away "misconceptions," just as, before leaving the mansion for the last time, he erases "an obscene word" that some unknown boy has scrawled on its white steps (102, 181). In other moments he records what he has directly observed or reports, either directly or indirectly, what he has heard or been told. In his most characteristic moments, however, he redeems failed action by endowing it with narrative order. The first party Gatsby gives on the "blue gardens" and grounds of his glowing mansion is rich in sound and color: while the orchestra plays "yellow cocktail music," the air comes "alive with chatter and laughter" that strain to become an "opera" (39–40; cf. 82). The "few [invited] guests" mingle with strangers who simply come, and together they become a "sea-change of faces" in search of the host no one knows (40–41; cf. 45). For a moment, when Gatsby first appears, the scene becomes what it is all along striving to be: it becomes "something significant, elemental, and profound." But the moment is fleeting. Order promptly gives way to "dissension" and ends in the "violent confusion" of "harsh, discordant din" (47, 52, 54). Only when Carraway glances "back" does Gatsby's failed party become something more than a weird collection of strangers and curiosity-seekers. Indeed, Gatsby himself survives the confused "sound of his still glowing garden" and overcomes the "sudden emptiness" of his mansion only because Carraway sees and renders him standing under a "wafer of a moon." Only in Carraway's narrative is Gatsby able paradoxically to stand at once in "complete isolation" and as a perfect "figure of the host" (56).

Finally, however, especially in recounting Gatsby's past and in reconstructing Gatsby's death, Carraway is forced, before he can give narrative form to Gatsby's story, to become, first, a detective, and then, an imaginative interpreter. The only adequate image of the "unquiet darkness" of Gatsby's world, the only adequate measure of the deep desolation that moves Carraway to assume his final interpretive stance, is the "desolate" "valley of ashes"—the "fantastic farm where ashes grow like wheat into ridges and hills and grotesque gardens; where ashes take the forms of houses and chimneys and rising smoke and, finally, with a transcendent effort, of men who move dimly and already crumbling through the powdery air" (22–23). Above this radically mortal world, in which the mixed motion of time carelessly changes all that men do and all that they are, there brood the grotesque, faded eyes of Doctor T. J. Eckleburg, just as, above the "waste land" of Gatsby's world there brood the eyes of Nick Carraway (23–24).[7] Unlike that of its synecdoche, however, the juxtaposition that defines the structure of the novel is neither specious nor sterile. In contrast to the soiled words and corrupted motives of the advertisement, Carraway's vision participates in the same "creative passion" we see in Gatsby's action. In the interim—"In the meantime," the "In between time"—world of *The Great Gatsby*, Carraway's interpreting vision is all we have (97). It is not to be confused, as George Wilson confuses Eckleburg's "persistent stare" (see 24, 160), with divine vision, but it does arrange and deepen, recapture and relate.

It is in his most fully interpretive moments—when he accepts the burden of imaginative reconstruction, when, in short, he plays the role Fitzgerald planned for Cecilia in his unfinished novel, *The Last Tycoon*—that Carraway most clearly functions as a deputy of the artist.[8] Only in such a moment, moreover—that is, only when he is presenting the events of the day following Tom Buchanan's effectual defeat of Gatsby and Daisy's accidental killing, with Gatsby's car, of Tom's mistress, in picturing Gatsby waiting for a call from Daisy, a call that could revive hope for his miscarried design—is Carraway able to attribute to Gatsby something approaching tragic illumination.

> No telephone message arrived.... I have an idea that Gatsby himself didn't believe it would come, and perhaps he no longer cared. If that was true he must have felt that he had lost the old warm world, paid a high price for living too long with a single dream. He must have looked up at an unfamiliar sky through frightening leaves and shivered as he found what a grotesque thing a rose is and

> how raw the sunlight was upon the scarcely created grass. A new world, material without being real, where poor ghosts, breathing dreams like air, drifted fortuitously about ... [*sic*] like that ashen, fantastic figure gliding toward him through the amorphous trees (162).

When the ashen figure has come and killed the drifting ghost, when the holocaust is complete, all that remains is for Carraway to show why, despite all that is maudlin about him and despite the end with which he meets, Gatsby is worth more than the whole of the "rotten" world that destroys him (154).

The "creative passion" lying behind Carraway's effort to clear up each "tremendous detail" of Gatsby's life and fate enables him finally to render Gatsby's dream "incorruptible" (97, 129, 155). Carraway delivers Gatsby from mere "notoriety" and "wild rumors"; he completes him and makes him great. In themselves Gatsby's bizarre parties, his failed efforts to establish community, remain spectacular yet incoherent anthologies of celebrities and outcasts. In themselves the characteristically hidden scenes in which Gatsby approaches Daisy and seems to near realization of his design know no consummation (98, 102). In Carraway's narration, however, through imaginative translation, the man who in life has been left in "complete isolation" becomes the perfect figure of the host, and the mansion that through action has become a splendid mausoleum becomes again a mansion, its temporary inhabitant's true "ancestral home" (56, 154).

Carraway's triumph derives from his ability to stand both "within and without" the action he narrates—his ability to be a participant yet a "watcher in the darkening streets"—his ability to give himself, like James's wondering dawdlers, to always "looking up and wondering ... simultaneously enchanted and repelled by the inexhaustible variety of life" (36), his ability, in fine, not only in observing to wonder but, through narrating, to cause another to wonder.[9] By suffering within, by understanding and relating the whole of what he sees not simply to his own life, nor merely to his country's history, but to all human endeavor, Carraway brings rich order to Gatsby's story. Having enabled Gatsby to stand under a "wafer of a moon" on the white steps of his mansion, overlooking "blue" grounds and "glowing garden," as a veritable icon "of the host" (56, 182; cf. 154), Carraway moves on to become a lyric poet. The "valley of ashes" and the "the inessential houses" of the Sound together "melt away" until the valley of ashes and the green breast of the new world are coherently related and Gatsby's story (to borrow and reverse the phrase Gatsby himself has used in dismissing any possible love between Tom and Daisy) becomes not in the least "just personal" (23, 182, 152). We accordingly see behind Gatsby's dream an old vision and hear behind his voice "a fragment of lost words" heard long ago; we become aware that "the old island" once had been the "fresh, green breast of the new world," and that the "vanished trees, the trees that had made way for Gatsby's house, had once pandered in whispers to the last and greatest of all human dreams." In response to "something commensurate to his capacity for wonder," poised on the edge of a vast, empty continent of an open and new world, confident in all innocence, believing "in the green light, the orgiastic future" of perfection, man then had dared to respond, as Gatsby later was to respond, with wonder at the distance he had come and with faith that he now would live his dream (112, 182). Thus near to success, thus invited and enticed with pandered whispers by his world, he had dared to move beyond dreaming his dream to an attempt to live it. Because of the beauty of his dream and the heroism of his effort to move beyond it, Gatsby can be made great. Yet, because he has so dared only to see the vanishing trees give way, not to a city of man, but to a valley of ashes, not to the marriage and mansion envisaged, but to "huge incoherent failure" (181), he can be made great only through reconstituting interpretation, reordering art.

Notes

1. Quoted in Stanley Edgar Hyman, *The Armed Vision* (rev. ed., New York, 1959), p. 333.
2. *The Great Gatsby* (New York, 1925), p. 155. All page references in the text are to this edition. Henry James, *The Art of the Novel: Critical Prefaces*, ed. R. P. Blackmur (New York, 1946), pp. 31–32.
3. See pp. 155, 182. See Marius Bewley, "Scott Fitzgerald's Criticism of America," Sewanee Review, LXII (1954), 223–246; and Edwin Fussell, "Fitzgerald's Brave New World," *English Literary History*, XIX (1952), 291–306.
4. See Oscar Handlin, *The Uprooted* (New York, 1951), pp. 4–5 and *passim*.
5. See p. 48. Note that the quoted phrase refers specifically to Gatsby's voice, and cf. p. 174, where we learn that Gatsby's preparation for translating his dream into design includes practicing "elocution."
6. See p. 72. Note that Carraway is extremely fastidious; he likes "to leave things in order" (p. 178).
7. See Milton Hindus, "The Eyes of Dr. T. J. Eckleburg," *Boston University Studies in English*, III (1957), 22–31.
8. See Thomas Hanzo, "The Theme and the Narrator of *The Great Gatsby*," *Modern Fiction Studies*, III (1956–1957), 183–190.
9. See James, p. 254.

97
The Great Gatsby and the American Past

◆

BRIAN M. BARBOUR

"If he'd of lived, he'd of been a great man. A man like James J. Hill. He'd of helped build up the country."

—Mr. Gatz to Nick Carraway

I

The Great Gatsby is a brilliant but sometimes brittle book. The social observation and notation are exact, yet the novel lacks the density of the accomplished novel of manners. Its method is that of poetic suggestion rather than accumulation. A careful symbolism is used to suggest a depth that sometimes isn't there. It is admired as a critique of the American Dream, yet the way its admirers see it making that critique seems to me to be wrong. To set Gatsby off against the Buchanans threatens to seriously upset the novel's balance because the Buchanans can't hold down their side of the scale. Fitzgerald hated the Buchanans and what he saw them as standing for, but there are moments when one might wonder if the hatred was sufficiently controlled by understanding:

> Slenderly, languidly, their hands set lightly on their hips, the two young women preceded us out onto a rosy-colored porch, open toward the sunset, where four candles flickered on the table in the diminished wind.
> "Why *candles*?" objected Daisy, frowning. She snapped them out with her fingers. "In two weeks it'll be the longest day in the year." She looked at us all radiantly. "Do you always watch for the longest day of the year and then miss it? I always watch for the longest day in the year and then miss it."
> "We ought to plan something," yawned Miss Baker, sitting down at the table as if she were getting into bed.
> "All right," said Daisy. 'What'll we plan?' She turned to me helplessly: "What do people plan?"

SOURCE *Southern Review* IX, Winter 1973, pp. 288–299.

> Before I could answer her eyes fastened with an awed expression on her little finger.
> "Look!" she complained; "I hurt it."
> We all looked—the knuckle was black and blue.
> "You did it, Tom," she said accusingly. "I know you didn't mean to, but you *did* do it. That's what I get for marrying a brute of a man, a great, big, hulking physical specimen of a—"
> "I hate that work hulking," objected Tom crossly, "even in kidding."
> "Hulking," insisted Daisy.[1]

He has captured here with impressive exactness the feeling of the Buchanan life in all its sterility, emptiness, and confusion. The egotism behind the thought and feelings is clear. But the tone is too simplistic, too filled with spite. The only possible response—and it is too easily arrived at—is scorn.

Fitzgerald knew the danger here and his method of attacking it is significant. That method is to force our attention not on the scene itself but on the moral consequences of the debased feelings that sustain the dialogue. Thus:

> "You make me feel uncivilized, Daisy," I confessed on my second glass of corky but rather impressive claret. "Can't you talk about crops or something?"
> I meant nothing in particular by this remark, but it was taken up in an unexpected way.
> "Civilization's going to pieces," broke out Tom violently. "I've gotten to be a terrible pessimist about things. Have you read 'The Rise of the Colored Empires' by this man Goddard?"
> "Why, no," I answered, rather surprised by his tone.
> "Well, it's a fine book, and everybody ought to read it. The idea is if we don't look out the white race will be —will be utterly submerged. It's all scientific stuff; it's been proved."
> "Tom's getting very profound," said Daisy, with an expression of unthoughtful sadness. "He reads deep books with long words in them. What was that word we—"
> "Well, these books are all scientific," insisted Tom glancing at her impatiently. "This fellow has worked out the whole thing. It's up to us, who are the dominant race, to watch out or these other races will have control of things." (p. 13)

The tone here is more ironic, but the significance of the passage lies in its moral reordering of what has preceded it. Tom's confused racism throws the whole long dinner scene into a new and darker perspective and we are forced to reevaluate the simple scorn of our response. The Buchanans may be despicable, but they are also dangerous. The racism dialogue acts as a kind of frame for the scene, the upshot of which is that our attention turns from what the Buchanans *are* to what they represent.

Fitzgerald repeats this technique Chapter II. The long party scene in Tom's and Myrtle Wilson's hideaway hardly rises above the level of bathos until the end:

> Some time toward midnight Tom Buchanan and Mrs. Wilson stood face to face, discussing in impassioned voices whether Mrs. Wilson had any right to mention Daisy's name.

"Daisy! Daisy! Daisy!" shouted Mrs. Wilson. "I'll say it whenever I want to! Daisy! Dai—"

Making a short deft movement, Tom Buchanan broke her nose with his open hand. (p. 37)

The method and significance are here the same as they were before. The moral consequences of the bathos, not the bathos itself, are what is being insisted on. He uses the frame technique for a third time in Chapter III, though this time with reverse effect. After the bathos of the drunks and the wrecked car has been established, the frame technique throws the scene into perspective, but by dissociating Gatsby from the life he watches over.

It may seem that I am labouring over the obvious or even perversely refuting my own earlier remarks, but what I am trying to establish is the kind of representative quality the Buchanans have. For they are no meant to be taken as adequate representatives of the American leisure class ("the rich"); rather they represent a deep and permanent tendency in American life, one that surfaces most spectacularly in the leisure class but which is by not means confined to it. The quality they represent, the tendency they embody, is a moral complacency that finds material wealth both self-validating and its own end. The truth about the Buchanans is that they are blind to any values or standards beyond the ones they enact. It is not that they repudiate any deeper wisdom about life and its ends; it is that they are unaware of any such wisdom. "The curse of ignorance," according to Socrates in the *Symposium*, "is that a man without being good or wise is nevertheless satisfied with himself: he has no desire for that of which he feels no want." It is this curse of ignorance that they embody and moral complacency is the quality they represent. Their debased feelings—their infantilism—have the most serious consequences for human life; but the material wealth which validates the moral complacency also makes thinking about ends and consequences unnecessary. The novel lacks the necessary density and roundedness for the Buchanans to be accepted as anything like adequate representatives of the American leisure class. Read like that the novel is not just brittle but absurd. But they represent a quality, a permanent tendency that runs all through American life and which finds its source in Benjamin Franklin.

II

The Great Gatsby is about the American dream—so the truism goes. But the truism in this case is too clumsy, for there are actually two American dreams and *The Great Gatsby* is about them both and the way they interact. It is convenient to employ metonymy and identify these two dreams with the two figures who first articulated them and thereby brought them to consciousness: Franklin and Ralph Waldo Emerson.

Franklin's dream is the dream of *freedom-from* that D. H. Lawrence complained about so bitterly in *Studies in Classic American Literature*. *The Autobiography* is a book shaped by fear, the fear of arbitrary power—tyranny—that prevents a man from becoming himself. The form this fear takes is economic. What does Franklin teach us? That a man has to acquire a certain amount of necessary wealth so that his destiny will be in his own hands and not those of his creditors. Without wealth no man is free—that is the book's secret motto. It is no use being superior about this motto. Franklin was articulating something deep in human consciousness and something given power by the intellectual and political currents of the time. America can be the land of the free because in America every man can acquire the minimum wealth necessary to be his own man. It's a dream not far different from Jefferson's, and it was certainly never intended to license the Robber Barons. But what we must pay attention to is its focus and direction. It is a view that looks exclusively to the past and defines itself in relation to that past. In a way it is transfixed by that past to the extent that it never turns its face forward and asks itself where it is going and what its consequences are. It is so exclusively concerned with *getting free* that it has no energy left for exploring the meaning of its freedom. The wealth that bestows freedom validates itself. Vulgarized, what this means is that wealth is not just means but end; because it means freedom it need not be questioned by any standard beyond itself. (That the emergence of this idea happened to coincide with the vulgarization of certain aspects of Calvinist theology—the Puritan Ethic argument—was doubly unfortunate, for not only was a possible higher standard for judgment lost, but the new tendency received a firm moral—sometimes religious—endorsement.) Having become free, Franklinian man is spared the necessity of having to ask himself, What for? What is my freedom for?

Franklin himself did not entirely escape this vulgarization. It is present in *The Autobiography* in two distinct ways. The first and most famous of these is the schedule of virtues that is attached to the plan for moral perfection. All that needs to be said about them was said long ago by Lawrence. They are hopelessly trivial and the sense of life they betray is likewise trivial. The second is to be found in the basic structure of the book itself. The principle of organization is the anecdotal moral lesson. He retails little events from his past and then points out the lesson to be learned. Franklin was a skilled comic writer and his life gave him a fund of rich material, but because there is no deeper sense of life working through and organizing the material it becomes hopelessly repetitious and finally boring. One reads up to the famous plan and perhaps a little beyond, but the book is unreadable straight through and no one is likely to mind that it went unfinished.

The Autobiography, nevertheless, is the most influential book ever written by an American. It organized, expressed, and made eminently respectable a concept of human life that is seriously deficient but which does not know itself to be so. The view it expresses is the bourgeois outlook of Main Street, and its American dream has been casually and complacently erected into the implicit goal of American life. What makes it pernicious is that the value-words on which it depends, especially freedom, are invoked but not defined. In the nature of the case they cannot easily be, but there is present no reason for feeling that they *should* be. The Franklinian dream, then, is one of the self-validating materialism that is ignorant about the inner, positive meaning of the freedom it posits as its end, and is in fact complacently blind with respect to any positive moral values or genuinely spiritual sense of human life. The Buchanans embody it in its least attractive form.

Emerson's role as an antipode to Franklin has never been adequately stressed, yet it is possible to say that his whole career was a quarrel with the Franklinian spirit and the Franklinian dream. "Quarrel" is perhaps inadequate to suggest that in every line he indited Emerson, was warring against the Franklinian outlook. The main thrust of his career was an attempt to take the American dream away from the Franklinians ("the Party of Memory," he called them) and to redefine it in moral and spiritual terms. For Emerson, too, the meaning of America was associated with freedom, but he set out to explore the nature and consequence of that freedom and to determine its effect on human life. He too articulated an American dream, but one moral and spiritual and always in the state of becoming. It is not a little significant that when—as in *The American Scholar* and *Self-Reliance*—Emerson goes on the attack he writes against an attitude that he posits in unmistakable Franklinian imagery: the "iron lids" of the "sluggard intellect" that never rises above "mechanical skill" and so results in a spirit that is "timid, imitative, tame"; or "the reliance on Property" no matter if it comes through "gift, inheritance, or crime" that marks "the want of self-reliance."

Self-reliance is the foremost Franklinian virtue; it is also the title of Emerson's most powerful essay, and the fundamental differences between the two American dreams can be seen by comparing the inner meanings the concept had for the two men. For Franklin it is a reliance on one's self as an accumulator of wealth; that is, it is a means for becoming free from the power of another. It is indivisible from the credit-enhancing self-discipline which is the highest mark of character. Because this self-reliance *works*—i.e., because it does lead to wealth—the inevitable tendency is to over-value this self of the marketplace, to feel secure in its power and certain of its capacity. And this in turn leads to the moral complacency that abandons any rigorous scrutiny of means and ends and which does not feel itself to be called on to answer any of the deeper questions about life. Its self is a satisfied self. This is most easily seen in the pitch-note of optimism (or, at its most vulgar, back-slapping, flank-rubbing geniality) which has always keyed the Franklinian dream and which is not an optimism that has taken the measure of things, but is only a lack of contact with or concern for any adequate concept of Evil or with the tragic sense. Franklin rose above this through his ideal of public service. But often no such ideal exists, and after the status of leisure has been attained, there is no sense of what to do with it. Life flattens out into a string of "Tomorrow and tomorrow and tomorrow...." "'What'll we do with ourselves this afternoon?' cried Daisy, 'and the day after that, and the next thirty years?'" (p. 118).

For Emerson self-reliance was based on trust, but it was decidedly not a trust in the ordinary self of the marketplace. That self had to be redeemed. Self-reliance begins with a reliance on God and it moves through a purgation of the ordinary self. That movement is from the ordinary self existing at the level of Franklinian materialism to the new self that has left materialism behind in order to live in the spirit. "The one thing in the world, of value, is the active soul." The whole of Emerson's thought is contained in that one sentence with its startling reassessment of the concept of *value*. Where Franklin is concerned with being and having, Emerson is concerned with being and becoming. Where Franklin is concerned with accumulating energy, Emerson is concerned with releasing it. Where Franklin looks to the past to secure his definition and meaning, Emerson looks to the future. Freedom is the condition for man's exploration of the new, higher self. "This one fact the world hates: that the soul *becomes*; for that forever degrades the past, turns all riches to poverty, all respect to shame."

It is difficult to translate the Emersonian vision, with its strong overlaying of mysticism, into the language of ordinary discourse. At his greatest moments Emerson was operating at the frontiers of language, and he knew what obstacles that raised to communication. But it is enough to note the positive, idealist structure of the Emersonian dream, and to note too the stern standard of *character* which Emerson assumed. He had nothing to offer triflers. The real secret of the Emersonian self is that, in contradistinction to the Franklinian self based on wealth, it depends on the moral ground of its own bedrock puritanism. Much of its power lies in its promise to free the ordinary self from the materialism, stagnancy, and moral complacency of the enacted Franklinian dream. Its promise is in the future; it lies in becoming and poses the deepest of moral challenges. In attempting to articulate it, Emerson threw Franklin's dream into a new perspective. Once both are brought to consciousness, the moral deficiency and adolescent cast of Franklin's become glaring. One has to leave it behind and pursue the higher truth. Emerson was a true moral teacher: he called on men to change their lives. His vision involved nothing less than a fundamental revaluation of the meaning of the American experience. The new self is to be a moral self whose duty is to be always becoming, always extending and newly articulating the possibilities of life. "The truth was that Jay Gatsby ... sprang from his Platonic conception of himself. He was a son of God ..." (p. 99).

III

Information about Gatsby is scattered piecemeal throughout the novel and accumulates slowly for the very good reason that Nick Carraway has to realize the significance of Gatsby's career and this realization does not come easily. The last piece of the puzzle is provided by the novel's oddest character, Gatsby's father, who does not enter until the last chapter. What he provides pushes the novel to the full limits of its depth and significance. He takes from his pocket a tattered copy of *Hopalong Cassidy* and shows Carraway Gatsby's boyhood schedule scribbled inside the back cover. This schedule associates quite explicitly Gatsby's youthful dreams with the Franklinian version of the American Dream. But Gatsby is not associated with that dream; his is of a different order altogether.

When Gatsby dismisses his servants at the start of Chapter VII he is registering his attitude toward wealth. He cares nothing for it in itself; its only value is as a means to something beyond itself, some fuller, more graceful sense of life of which Daisy is the symbol. Gatsby's is a version of the Emersonian dream: in a great imaginative act he has created himself and set out to explore the possibilities of life. The Franklinian dream was the dream of his youth, but he repudiated that youth and the dream associated with it. Part of his "greatness" lies in his having transcended the limits of the Franklinian world, but it is his fate that this Emersonian greatness will go largely unnoticed in a world whose fundamental postulates are Franklinian. Gatsby's dream matured, but America's did not. It is again Mr. Gatz who drives this point home. Throughout the novel Gatsby is consistently misunderstood by those who speculate about him, but none hits wider of the mark than his own father:

> "He had a big future before him, you know. He was only a young man, but he had a lot of brain power here."
> He touched his head impressively, and I nodded.
> "If he'd of lived, he'd of been a great man. A man like James J. Hill. He'd of helped build up the country." (p. 169)

The concept of greatness is perfectly representative, the representation underlined by the standard invoked. Greatness for Mr. Gatz lies within the Franklinian vision of America. His desire for his son is that he become another Tom Buchanan. The real nature of Gatsby's greatness takes shape against this concept.

The Franklinian dream leads only to the dead end of money, and the characteristic animus held against the leisure class throughout the novel is associated with their lack of any enlarging vision. The Buchanans possess wealth and its concomitant freedom but they have no idea of living. They just drift "here and there unrestfully wherever people played polo and were rich together" (p. 6). Their concept of life never extends beyond a game. What the novel dramatizes, then, is the conflict between the two American dreams, one whose idea is material wealth and leisure (a restless leisure), the other whose ideal is less restricted and finally spiritual. But the novel argues its point even more closely. The Emersonian dream of the self depends to a certain extent on wealth also, although on wealth as means not as end. The freedom this wealth produces is *freedom-to*, a positive value, one that looks forward to becoming. One way of seeing the conflict is to say that there has been a fundamental confusion of material and spiritual values and that the novel dramatizes this confusion which is deep in American life. The confusion can account for Gatsby's failure—i.e., his unwise location of the meaning of his dream in Daisy.

But Carraway offers another choice. In his final meditation he notes that Gatsby's dream of the future really lies in the past, "somewhere back in that vast obscurity beyond the city, where the dark fields of the republic [roll] on under the night" (p. 182). The transcendental vision collapsed under the weight of the Civil War: that is a primary datum of American intellectual history. Another is that in the vast accumulation of wealth that followed, few noticed that it was gone. Where it endured (John Jay Chapman) or resurges (Martin Luther King) it is a quirk: the American dream is a Franklinian dream. The Emersonian dream is in the possession of the scholars. The older vision was temporarily challenged by Emerson but his dream, which in part was not of this world, ended and the older vision reemerged and changed with the new conditions. It was Horatio Alger, not Emerson, who articulated the sense of the postwar world.

Gatsby's failure is an index of the inability of the Emersonian dream to be focused adequately in this world, which is another way of saying that he fails because he is too innocent. It is a very telling fact that Emerson did not like, and could see no reason to read, fiction. He had no sense that works of art act their moral judgments. His mind, which had a curious eighteenth-century cast to it, wanted just the moral values, stated pure and simple. He truly was once-born. But we must draw back here from the gates of allegory and focus on Gatsby. Gatsby embodies the Emersonian dream, perhaps the most attractive quality in American life, and its weakness is his failure. His dream is so beautiful that he assumes that whatever triggers it must also have its haloed quality. The dazzle of the dream leaves his eyes too weak to gaze on ordinary life. Daisy's value for him is purely symbolic; like his shirts or his servants she means nothing in herself. His vision implicitly evaluates American civilization even as it gives dignity and purpose to his life. But while the Franklinian dream is complacently ignorant about the ends of life, the Emersonian dream runs the danger that the dreamer may be transfixed by his end. He may lose his contact with ordinary living.

IV

The Great Gatsby dramatizes the conflict between the two American dreams. It does this because its characters represent fundamental tendencies in American life, and the novel acts its meaning on this representative level. It reveals a profound insight into the American past and the meaning of that past in the present. Fitzgerald dramatizes with a sure touch the moral consequences of the conflict and the moral differences between the two dreams. Moreover, he lays his finger on what is tragically missing in American life: an articulated awareness of moral evil. Both the Franklinian and Emersonian dreams lean too heavily on the thin reed of optimism. What is wanted is the "wise and tragic sense of life" Fitzgerald found in President Lincoln. The novel, on the literal level, like Gatsby's clothes, always just misses being absurd. But on a different level it reveals, on the part of its author, a rare inwardness with something that one can only call the meaning of American history.

Notes

1. F. Scott Fitzgerald, *The Great Gatsby* (New York, n.d.), p. 12. This and all subsequent page numbers refer to the Scribner Library Edition.

Gatsby and the Failure of the Omniscient 'I'

♦

RON NEUHAUS

Fitzgerald himself was keenly aware that *Gatsby* was a flawed work but the nature and origin of its major flaws escaped him. In a frank letter to Edmund Wilson in 1925, he explained what he takes to be the novel's "BIG FAULT."

> I gave no account of (and had no feeling about or knowledge of) the emotional relationship between Gatsby and Daisy from the time of their reunion to the catastrophe.

But his inability to handle relations between Gatsby and Daisy is merely symptomatic of more crucial faults in the novel: that of a breakdown in narrative technique, and an inability to create fully fleshed characters beneath the "blankets of excellent prose" Fitzgerald refers to later in the letter. *Gatsby* begins with first person narration, but Fitzgerald will not accept the limitation of this self-imposed restriction and constantly strains toward an "omniscient *I*" through diction, flashback, and reconstructed events. Despite his ingenuity, he fails to create a responsible fiction. He finds the first person perspective inadequate for the credibility of his moral stance, yet he will not take the responsibility involved with an omniscient perspective. The first person limitation enables him to avoid the scenes (as he notes in his letter) that his insights could not handle. Nick literally chaperones what could be scenes of revealing intimacy between Gatsby and Daisy.

Another factor, not stylistic but of strong influence, was the cultural climate of the post-war decade. The problems of character and style reflect a mood in which a desire for moral security remained ("the world to be in uniform and at a sort of moral attention," as Nick says), but found itself in a world which could not provide that fulfillment. The moral authority of first person narrative was not adequate for such a context, and Fitzgerald tried to create esthetically what could not be discovered naturally. To this end, he experimented with multiple perspective. The efforts at extending perspective

SOURCE *Denver Quarterly* XII, Spring 1977, pp. 303–312.

are admirable enough: the later movement into Gatsby's and Daisy's minds, into Michaelis' account of the car accident, as well as the intimate details of Gatsby's past—but through the early extended use of first person Fitzgerald has painted himself into a corner. As point of view makes some blatant shifts late in the novel, there is no sense of multiple perspective or modulation, but rather of an attempt to maintain, however thinly, the moral perspective of the first person narration, while at the same time trying to bring in third person credibility. The reader has a collection of fragments, conceivably from different perspectives, but what differentiates Fitzgerald from Pound, Eliot, Joyce, or Faulkner in his later work is that they did not structure their respective works around a solitary informing consciousness.

Conrad's *Heart of Darkness* furnished a good model for the type of problem in *Gatsby* as does Ford's *The Good Soldier*. But Marlow doesn't come across as an obtrusive sensibility, while Nick does. By the same token, Dowell's moral tone does not pretend to accurately assess the situation, but rather to characterize *him*. The genitive fault of *Gatsby* is not in the omission of certain scenes, but in Nick as a narrative voice. He lacks Marlow's effective transparency, and when the third person passages late in the book use the same rhetoric as Nick has used in his own voice, the congruity of tone makes us realize that there is in fact no ironic tone.

Were it not for this later under-cutting of irony, the opening paragraphs would provide a revealing anatomy of Nick through his commentary on the supposed moral climate in which he finds himself. In the full run of the book they provide an introduction to the sensibility of what will become the omniscient *I*. The first sentence sets the mood. "In my younger and more vulnerable years, my father gave me some advice that I've been turning over in my mind ever since." The crucial phrase here is "more vulnerable." It indicates that, in the scheme of things as perceived by the narrator, he occupies a position of some emotional and moral security, almost to the point of smugness. Fitzgerald does not dwell on this note, but shifts the focus to the nature of the advice, advice which predicates the existence of hereditary moral decency and, naturally, moral aristocracy. The tone is set for the third paragraph, in which Nick demonstrates a short-sightedness which his later explanations cannot offset. He points out that he is inclined to reserve all judgments, yet pontificates on psychology in the next sentence. "The abnormal mind is quick to detect and attach itself to this quality when it appears in a normal person ..." As the sentence continues it reveals a sensibility that increasingly distances itself from literal reality by inflated rhetoric.

> ... and so it came about that in college I was unjustly accused of being a politician, because I was privy to the secret griefs of wild, unknown men.

This is virtually unintelligible. The diction evades understanding: "secret griefs," "wild unknown men." The attention falls of necessity on the man using such diction to communicate his experience, such as it may be. The smugness becomes an almost leaden irony. Nick is not simply told things; on the contrary, he is "privy" to them. Later, in speaking of his war years, the diction shows his irony at its most arch. He does not just go into the army or off to war; rather he "... participated in that delayed Teutonic migration known as the Great War."

An inescapable problem with such a distancing tone is credibility. If, as a matter of course, the informing sensibility transforms reality into the adornments the mind projects, how can its evaluation be seen as authentic? Its reconstruction of past events credible? Its judgments appropriate? Fitzgerald's treatment of Nick establishes him as a character who cannot deal with the literal, and who must always construct an elaborate and moralistic rhetoric to insulate him from confrontation. Almost immediately, his smugness and complacency become too fulsome.

> The intimate revelations of young men, or at least, the terms in which they express them, are usually plagiaristic and marred by obvious suppressions.

Plagiaristic terms could well apply to the way in which Nick sees Gatsby later in the novel, yet he will not apply this observation to himself when he sees Gatsby in the borrowed phrase a "son of God," nor will he apply it to the plagiarized romanticizings of Gatsby.

Nick's limitations as an objective commentator are definitely established through the impressive architecture of one sequence in particular. Note the degree of smugness (or the injection of the author's rhetorical flourishes): "... as my father snobbishly suggested, and I snobbishly repeat, a sense of the fundamental decencies is parcelled out unequally at birth." The sentence is relentless in its assumption of a moral determinism as absolute as that of Calvin. It indicates a universe in which the snobbish Nick finds himself not only well placed, but one of the elect, possessed of congenital moral wealth. When he exercises his moral faculty, the prose approaches the gothic.

> It is what preyed on Gatsby, what foul dust floated in the wake of his dreams that temporarily closed out my interest in the abortive sorrows and short-winded elations of men.

Even if justified as a characterization of the narrator, this is extreme. It no longer reveals, but cloys. However, a certain pattern of interpretation has been established in which the narrator infuses events with a diction that basically ignores their literal significance ("wild, unknown men" instead of "college freshmen"). As the novel progresses this pattern becomes embodied in images, events, and actions. Any banal event, any simple action will have embellishments heaped on it to create magnitude and significance.

As one check on this, whatever Nick or the omniscient voice in the later part of the book tells us about Gatsby, we must keep in mind the literal man (such aspects as are given) and his goal. Gatsby is a man trying to break up a marriage in order that he may resume a relationship with a woman who is bland at her most appealing. Concerning the man himself, although we are told that "Gatsby turned out all right," we must remember that he was a passenger witness to a hit-and-run homicide, and was not fluffed in the least by it. His criminal contacts do not bother him, and he has an almost total insensitivity to human nature.

Yet, given the assumptions of Nick's rhetoric (and ultimately, Fitzgerald's), anything can be transformed into anything else, including its literal opposite. Given this, whatever is most characterless, banal, or undefined can be more easily assigned qualities, since it has no strong features of its own, and can so allow the projecting consciousness fuller play. It may even follow that this type of sensibility will seek out the vague and shallow elements of life in order to exercise this faculty. An early metaphor for just this process occurs in the "valley of ashes" trope which introduces chapter 2. The literal image is that of a dumping ground with drifting dust clouds. But under the transformative vision of Nick (in a third person tone), the literal scene functions as a blank screen on which forms are first projected, and then assumed to be innate.

> This is a valley of ashes—a fantastic farm where ashes grow like wheat ... where ashes take on the form of houses and chimneys ... of ash-gray men who move dimly and already crumbling through the powdery air.

The literal aspect is clear: here is a locale of shifting dust where ashes and clouds of dust can be imagined to take on forms. But the prose quickly abandons the metaphorical origin of the forms, and the illusion receives treatment as though it were a literal event.

> Occasionally a line of gray cars crawls along an invisible track, gives out a ghastly creak, and comes to rest, and immediately the ash-gray men swarm up with leaden spades and stir up an impenetrable cloud, which screens their obscure operations from your sight.

The description is very deft, and must be reread for assurance that this is in fact an evolved illusion, not a real scene. The illusion grows out of a literal vagueness, presents itself as a definite scene, and then dissolves into a vagueness generated by that scene. It reveals the informing sensibility of the novel (which is not Nick Carraway's) at work on a landscape. The same technique of disguising reality obtains in Gatsby's idealization of Daisy and his romance with her, of Tom's attraction to racism (especially his observation that it was all "scientific stuff"), and of Nick's creation of Gatsby's identity.

The "valley of ashes" trope parallels in method the rhetoric at the beginning of chapter 1. There, too, Fitzgerald used an inflated rhetoric, the "abortive sorrows," the "riotous excursions ... into the human heart." Here, the process develops into a series of images imposed upon the formless. It moves from the literal "desolate area" to the figurative "valley of ashes" to the metaphorical "ashes grow like wheat" to the mimetic "ashes take the form of houses ... of ash-gray men" to the actual, the "gray cars" passage above. In the final stage, the transformative process has been forgotten, and the illusion becomes the reality.

Following this, we see the enormous eyes of Dr. T. J. Eckleburg, an image of sterile vision, vision that has no connection with any past, or any particular origin. The oculist's sign could be seen as a symbol of an omniscient God, but not in this novel. The context of images, as well as the narrative voice, deals with the human problem of perception and interpretation, and of the subsequent verbal units used to evade the literal world by the "westerners," and to a much lesser degree by the party goers who playfully ascribe mysterious and shady histories to Gatsby. Has the narrative voice remained within focus, the novel could have been a superb exploration of the ironies in attempting to discover values and grand identities in a world which does not contain them. In such a world, in order to find gold one must seed the mine, and then forget the deception.

This ironic technique can work well as a structuring device, an informing metaphor, and also provide a core around which to build a character, all of which effects occur in the first half of *Gatsby*. But when Fitzgerald tries to use it as a means to move into a third person point of view, and have this baroque subjectivity function with the authority of an omniscient voice, the narrative structure of the book begins to crumble. One excellent example of this comes immediately before Gatsby is shot, at the end of chapter 8. As far as Nick knows, Gatsby has merely been waiting for a call from Daisy. But Nick moves from this to an amplification and speculation on the event, and then, as in the ashes trope, reaches a certainty. In his initiating speculation, he begins conservatively, with a straightforward qualification. "I have an idea that Gatsby himself didn't believe it would come, and perhaps he no longer cared." This pretends to be nothing more than honest speculation. Yet he immediately jumps from this to an elaborate hypothesis which assumes the tone of verity. "If that was true he must have felt that he had lost the old warm world, paid a high price for living too long with a single dream." At this point, we have definitely lost touch with Gatsby's consciousness. Losing the "old warm world" is not in his diction. Fitzgerald labors it even further, as the narrative voice fully enters the world of its own speculations, and responds to them with its own sensibility.

> He must have looked up at an unfamiliar sky through frightening leaves and shivered as he found what a grotesque thing a rose is and how raw the sunlight was upon the scarcely created grass.

This is impossible to read as an insight into Gatsby's character; it becomes a blanket, not a window. Yet if we read it only adding to Nick's character, it repeats what we already know. But Fitzgerald is trying awkwardly to reach toward an "omniscient *I*" and we lose both Gatsby and Nick in the process. The tone also gives an intimation that Nick has never been ours at all; we have had only a mask and a device to conceal a lack of character development. The passage concludes with an ooze of saccharine rhetoric addressed to no one, from no one, and about no one whose identity has been established in the fiction.

> A new world, material without being real, where poor ghosts, breathing dreams like air, drifted fortuitously about ... like that ashen, fantastic figure gliding toward him through the amorphous trees.

We are asked to see the judgements of a narrative voice, not as that of a particular character who forces his interpretation onto a reality incompatible with them, but that of a trustworthy narrator, almost an omniscient voice presenting us with legitimate insights into the world of the fiction.

Still, we may be, by some stretch of perspective, within Nick's consciousness. But earlier, at the end of chapter 6, we have a passage whose details would be totally inaccessible to Nick, yet the diction and tone belong to what we expect to be his voice. At this point we can no longer withhold the observation that the stylistic aberrations which could have been seen as character development of the narrator must now be laid to the author as flaws in the narrative structure. In the following passage, through the third person perspective, we are totally in Gatsby's mind; Nick is nowhere near as a justified mediator, and we have no idea where this information comes from.

> Out of the corner of his eye Gatsby saw that the blocks of the sidewalks really formed a ladder and mounted to a secret place above the trees—he could climb to it, if he climbed alone, and once there he could suck on the pap of life, gulp down the incomparable milk of wonder.

At the end of the chapter the prose goes even further afield, and confirms that much of what had earlier passed for ironic language was, in actuality, maudlin sincerity. The irony of the novel has been totally undercut. For Nick to take his own romanticizing insights seriously might reveal his character; for Fitzgerald to present the diction of these insights as informative comment indicates a great flaw in his creation.

> He knew that when he kissed this girl, and forever wed his unutterable visions to her perishable breath, his mind would never romp again like the mind of God.... At his lips' touch she blossomed for him like a flower and the incarnation was complete.

Fitzgerald wants to deal with superhuman characters, people whose thoughts might plausibly romp like God's, but he can't create them; he can only raise the type of prose associated with them. Nineteen twenty-five was too late for such characters to be treated sincerely, and yet Fitzgerald doesn't want to maintain the mask of irony. He wants us to somehow take the story of Gatsby seriously—otherwise we would always have the buffer of Nick as an ironist. To this end, the passage above employs the tactics of smooth propaganda: the glittering phrase, the slick allusion, the "deep" thought. The technique can be pleasing, well-cadenced, and with great surface attraction. But it can not be responsible fiction, no matter how adept its rhetoric. We have too many Gatsbys, and not only are they unrelated but they are not rooted in the text. If, as Nick speculates at the beginning of the novel, "personality is an unbroken series of successful gestures," Gatsby as a character has no personality. His development is, at best, a broken series of unsuccessful gestures. There is nothing to connect the implied heroism of "unutterable visions" or "son of God" with the Gatsby we see; nothing to connect the "old sport" Gatsby with the romantic figure of Nick's narration. Even so, Fitzgerald makes the most extreme attributions to Gatsby in the omniscient voice, and these ignore the literal man as he has been portrayed in the same manner that Nick ignores the basic quality of the reality around him. What is haunting about Gatsby, if anything, is not his "extraordinary gift for hope," but that he is actually so banal.

The failure in voice leads to other weaknesses in the narration. Not only does Fitzgerald have difficulty in rendering his evaluations of Gatsby, he has great difficulty in setting up the machinery to bring in particular material about him to occasion the romanticizing prose. One notable case is in the sequence after the auto accident, when Nick says that Gatsby tells him the story of his youth. Up to this point Gatsby has not been particularly open with Nick, nor has he indicated a desire to be. But Fitzgerald wants to play around with Gatsby's past, and tries to account for his motivation by using a poetic metaphor to distract the reader from the improbability of the confession. According to Nick, Gatsby "... told it to me because 'Jay Gatsby' had broken up like glass against Tom's hard malice...." The metaphor is interesting, but it doesn't cover the fact that Fitzgerald has failed to provide a fictive motivation for the confession. He could have solved the problem by using third person, but he has to maintain the limited point of view as a vehicle for value judgments and highly extravagant diction. Also, he has failed to create a character with sufficient substance to supply an omniscient perspective with material. The mask of first person narration protects him to a degree, but ultimately it fails to conceal the fact that the "BIG FAULT" was not that he had no notion of the "relations" between Gatsby and Daisy, but that he had developed no characters of sufficient depth to have relations.

Chapter 8, more than any other, dodges from one perspective to another in an effort to substitute expanse for depth. We are in Nick's mind, Gatsby's mind, even Daisy's mind. One interesting passage gives an excerpt from Gatsby's talk with Nick and thus provides a measure for what is attributed to him earlier and later. His own diction is direct, unembellished, and with a functional banality that allows Nick (Fitzgerald's omniscient voice at this point) to project on to it whatever he chooses.

> "I can't describe to you how surprised I was to find out I loved her, old sport.... Well, there I was, 'way off my ambitions, getting deeper in love every minute, and all of a sudden I didn't care. What was the use of doing great things if I could have a better time telling her what I was going to do?"

Compare this with the supposed reconstruction of a past event that follows. Is it likely that Gatsby would recount to Nick the details of his intimacy with Daisy? And with such attention to particulars?

> It was a cold fall day, with a fire in the room and her cheeks flushed. Now and then she moved and he changed his arm a little, and once he kissed her dark shining hair ... They had never been closer in their month of love, nor communicated more profoundly one with another ...

Only if we could imagine Gatsby saying to Nick, "Once I kissed her dark shining hair, old sport, and we never communicated more profoundly with one another than then," would the passage be acceptable. But at this point clearly there are two novels being written here: one from Nick's ironic perspective, and one from third person. Yet they share the same voice. One paragraph later, when we see things from Daisy's perspective, any pretense of this being a narrative from Nick's point of view has vanished—with absolutely no fictive modulation. The material is simply unloaded onto the page.

> Through this twilight universe Daisy began to move again with the season; suddenly she was again keeping half a dozen dates with half a dozen men, and drowsing asleep at dawn with the beads and chiffon of an evening dress tangled among dying orchids on the floor beside her bed. And all the time something within her was crying for a decision.

The nature of the difficulty here can be brought out by a question: if Fitzgerald can move into omniscient author here, why can't he use it in the crucial scenes between Gatsby and Daisy? When Gatsby takes Daisy through his house, Nick comes along as a chaperone at their request. Gatsby particularly wants him there, and when Nick tries to go Fitzgerald attempts a weak justification for keeping him there. "I tried to go then, but they wouldn't hear of it; perhaps my presence made them feel more satisfactorily alone." Conceivably, the lovers might feel reluctant to enter into an intimacy which being alone might force, but the problem here is that of style and character, not of thought. Fitzgerald has created such literally vapid and unfilled-out lovers that the love story can only be maintained by keeping them out of the reader's sight, and by attributive rhetoric to supply what characterization does not. Given what he has created (or failed to create), he can't bring them together, because they lack sufficient depth to work in a love scene. His switches in perspective attempt to draw the reader's attention away from this, much as a series of clever camera shots can distract a viewer from the superficiality of a movie love scene. Fitzgerald predicates an ideal, but his prose cannot work up to it. He is unable at this point in his career to provide characters as suitable vehicles for insight. Having created mere outlines, he can only adorn, not reveal.

Had Fitzgerald not used third person as a platform for his romanticizing, his efforts to work toward a type of omniscient quality would have made a more substantial novel. Some of the approaches to a third person perspective are quite ingenious, as when Nick describes a typical Gatsby party. The information in the description is far beyond what he would have access to, but the passage is smoothly done. We begin with emblematic detail and end up with the flushed jaundice of expressionistic rhetoric.

> By seven o'clock the orchestra has arrived, no thin five-piece affair, but a whole pitful of oboes and trombones ...
> The lights grow brighter as the earth lurches away from the sun, and now the orchestra is playing yellow cocktail music ...

Fitzgerald handles it differently when he uses the ploy of a timetable dated July 5 on which Nick writes down the "names of those who came to Gatsby's house that summer." The mention of the day following Independence Day is intriguing, as is the image of society being numbered on a timetable. But it is unlikely that Nick, as a character, would gather such information as "All these people," and the parties themselves do not maintain a custom of name giving. The catalogue is an early effort at an "omniscient *I*," but does not obtrude as much as the later shifts in perspective. However, the smoothest attempt comes with the diary brought by Gatsby's father. The incident has some credibility, and provides a different perspective within the limits of the first person narrative.

But on the whole the shifts in perspective destroy any integrity in the fiction. Yet Fitzgerald's failure of narrative voice in *Gatsby* comes in part because he is trying to make first person narrative do something which, by 1925, could no longer be done. He wants us to look at a highly romanticized (not merely romantic) figure and grant it serious consideration, to trust the teller and not the tale. The ideal and the characters he postulates do not fit the reality in which he wants them to exist, a reality roughly parallel to his own social and historical context, and his evasions take the form of switches and dodges in point of view in order to conceal the basic shallowness of his vision. He can handle only the plot of the romance, he cannot create the people necessary to animate it. For all that Gatsby tells Nick, never does he refer to any recent contact with Daisy—a void in the narration which corresponds to that of figures seen in shadow profile. Ironically, the firmest character in the book is the distinctly unromantic Meyer Wolfsheim.

In *Lord Jim* and *Heart of Darkness* Conrad handled the problem of the "omniscient *I*" much better than did Fitzgerald, perhaps because he was not as anxious about getting credence for an unrealistic romanticization and its corresponding philosophy. But Fitzgerald has an afflicting ambivalence; he sensed that the somber moralizing of Nick could not be anything but ironic in modern fiction, yet he yearned for a modern context to validate a romanticizing moral sensibility. His problems with style and point of view begin as soon as he tries to present an unrealized character in sympathetic and favorable light. Fitzgerald refuses to be confined within first person, yet he will not accept the responsibility of omniscient author, because he cannot develop characters adequate to his vision of what those characters should be. Gatsby is a figment of the imagination of the novel that bears his name. For this reason, there are no "emotional relations" accounted for between him and Daisy.

The failings in *The Great Gatsby* are fascinating and it survives as a novel quite possibly because of the intriguing nature of its weaknesses. We reject Carraway's pompous moralizing after the first few paragraphs, and his reliability as a witness by the end of the second chapter; yet when his voice occurs later under the aegis of third person, trying to construct insights and gain sympathy for Gatsby, we cannot help but reject it there as well. Yet the later use calls upon us to reject, not the credibility of a narrator, but that of the author.

99
Fiction as Greatness: The Case of *Gatsby*

◆

ARNOLD WEINSTEIN

More than half a century after its publication, *The Great Gatsby* is still a vexed case, seen variously as a portrait of the 20s, a picture of the American Dream that is at once lyrical and critical, an example of point-of-view narrative that draws shrewdly on James and Conrad.[1] All these things Fitzgerald does, no one would deny; what is vexing is what to make of them? Is the novel, ultimately, a critique of either Gatsby or his dream? What, ultimately, does Nick Carraway or the reader learn? Finally, what does the greatness of Gatsby and Fitzgerald's novel consist of?[2]

In looking at Fitzgerald criticism, one frequently discerns a certain petulancy: Gatsby's dream is itself so meretricious and vulgar, why all the ado? Nick himself is too smug on the one hand ("I am one of the few honest people that I have ever known") and too conniving on the other (Jordan Baker's not-so-broad hint at the book's close). Or else, Fitzgerald the author comes up short: unable to see through his tinsel materials, unable to sort out his ironies, unable to curb his rhetoric. The book seems to be imbued with excess: the tawdry excesses of the Flapper Age, the wild parties, the flashy and not-so-flashy materialism of Gatsby, the excesses of capitalism, the sentimental and blinding excesses of the rags-to-riches story itself, the American Dream. It is in this light that *Gatsby* criticism often seems to dig its heels in, roll up its sleeves, and perform *analysis*, i.e., reveal these puffed-up Appearances and Myths for what they truly are: spurious, specious and inflated. The critical act itself—practiced in all our disciplines—seems imaged here: to see through, to become undeceived, to deflate, to deconstruct. Fitzgerald criticism, even more than most, is marked by the moral fervor of exposure and judgment.[3]

On the face of it, indeed, *The Great Gatsby* falls into the 19th-century tradition of "great expectations" and "lost illusions," as two of its greatest exemplars termed it. Such a fiction chronicles the lure of worldly success and

SOURCE *Novel*, 19, Fall 1985, pp. 22–38.

the gradual education of the hero as he comes to measure the moral cost involved in secular achievement. The focus of such texts is quintessentially critical, as Pip and Rastignac and their followers encounter and expose the rottenness of social systems and, hence, the *illusory* nature of any triumph within that context. Nick Carraway begins the narration of *Gatsby* in a posture much like that of Pip as he finishes his narrative: he has seen—and seen through—the parade and pretensions of high society, and he returns to the Midwest where principles might still be found: "Conduct may be founded on the hard rock or the wet marshes, but after a certain point I don't care what it's founded on. When I came back from the East last autumn I felt that I wanted the world to be in uniform and at a sort of moral attention forever."[4] The figurative gesture behind or beneath appearances, zeroing in on the "foundation" can in fact be recognized as the fundamental realist act.

It is worth passing a minute with this critical metaphor of examining foundations. One thinks of Mrs. Eberhardt whom Myrtle Wilson mentions at her party, Mrs. Eberhardt who "goes around looking at people's feet in their own homes" (37). Nick Carraway is, at the outset, appropriately *dis*enchanted, *dis*illusioned, for the grand pageantry has been exposed for a very small and mean operation. Dickens calls Pip's expectations "great," just as Renoir titles the illusion of his film, "grande"; we see a recurring feature of realism in this movement from *large* appearances to *small* explanations. As I have suggested, a good deal of Gatsby criticism works along these lines: the critic begins work, if you will, on July 5th, just as Nick listed the names of those who came to Gatsby's parties on an old timetable of July 5, 1922, and he metaphorically sizes up the damage done the night before.[5] Things always look smaller, less glamorous, on July 5th, because the magic, the *Rausch*, is over, the grand and ecstatic moments of the party are now, in the harsh light of day, embarrassments. Criticism deflates, exposes, shows the ugly underpinnings which support the show. Nick expresses the sobering effect of such an education in graphic terms: his stint with Gatsby and Co. is akin to his carefree 20s, indeed the entire nation's 20s; but now he is 30—and one can hardly avoid thinking of the American '30s here: "Thirty—the promise of a decade of loneliness, a thinning list of single men to know, a thinning briefcase of enthusiasm, thinning hair" (142). "Thinning" betokens the same shrinkage that July 5th brings, and the question that must be posed here is, "Is Gatsby still great, once the novel is over?"

There can be little doubt that he appears dreadfully exposed in his own underpinnings. Surely, the thinnest, barest document in the novel is the pathetic SCHEDULE on the flyleaf of *Hopalong Cassidy* which graphically spells out the young Gatz's program for success, including such exhortations as "Practice elocution, pose and how to attain it" and "Read one improving book or magazine per week." Here is the meanest prop of all, a July 5th document if ever one existed, the vulgar, irreducible blueprint underlying Gatsby's fabulous career, a humble and humbling Fitzgeraldian *Ding an sich* which emerges at the novel's close. In its factual, evidential status, as ultimate as an X-ray, this SCHEDULE wrings the neck of fiction and glamour, showing it all to be no more than a con game. One imagines Tom Buchanan's glee in the face of such a document, the final demystification of Gatsby, brought back at last to his lowly origins. Let Gatsby be pegged as no more than the outgrowth of his SCHEDULE, and immediately an edifying congruence is revealed between first stages and last stages, origins and destiny, illuminating the kind of causality achieved by centripetal thinking, homing in on the hidden center, moving mercilessly from the grand circumference back to the pitiful center: Jay Gatsby and his mansion exposed as Jimmie Gatz and his SCHEDULE.

But, of course, that is not *The Great Gatsby*, or more precisely, it is *Gatsby* in reverse. The living truth of the novel is centrifugal rather than centripetal, projected outwards rather than homing in, generating reality rather than proving it, invested in a "fattening" rather than a "thinning" enterprise, dedicated to the heroic cause of making July 5th rival with July 4th, the chronicle of the Dream thereby capturing its enduring beauty and magic, its "elusive rhythm" as well as displaying the "foul dust [that] floated in the wake" (8). I share Hugh Kenner's conviction that Nick Carraway's role is not so much to critique Gatsby as to preserve him, that, in Kenner's words, "a man hard to convince shall have been convinced of his worth," because, as Kenner concludes, "it is important, in short, that Gatsby shall be Great. It is important because the central myth of the Book has to do with Appearance made Real by sheer will: the oldest American theme of all" (37–38).[6]

It is doubtful whether Americans have a monopoly on that particular theme, but Fitzgerald's book is peculiarly modern in its focus on belief rather than truth. Ford Maddox Ford, in a different book entirely devoted to the dismantling of illusions, expressed the nostalgic hope that beauty is not destructible, even though destruction is real, that the dream continues strangely to live even if it has been wholly discredited:

> You can't kill a minuet de la coeur. You may shut up the music-book, close the harpsichord; in the cupboard and presses the rats may destroy the white satin favors. The mob may sack Versailles; the Trianon may fall, but surely the minuet—the minuet itself is dancing itself away into the furthest stars....[7]

Fitzgerald's interest, I think, is in that minuet that can't be killed. His book stands, then, on the far side of the divide marked by Balzac and Dickens; exposure and education are their central purposes, whereas *Gatsby* is about the power of belief. In that light, the death of Goriot is radically different from that of Gatsby: Balzac's figure dies so that all can witness the collapse of an ethos, but Gatsby's death is, in words he himself applied to Daisy's love for her husband, "just personal," in no way affecting his potency as a figure, a legend, an image.

Images, more than minuets, may be said to have a life of their own. They certainly appear to do so in *The Great Gatsby*. It is no accident that Henry

Gatz so treasures the *photograph* of his son's house that it seems "more real to him now than the house itself" (179).⁸ The so-called "real thing" can hardly compete with constructs of desire; hence, a green light on a dock can embody and figure forth all of Gatsby's longing, but such magic can have no truck with real people. Reunited with Daisy, Gatsby realizes that "it was again a green light on a dock. His count of enchanted objects had diminished by one" (100). Gatsby himself senses that the flesh-and-blood Daisy can not measure up to the image he has made of her:

> There must have been moments even that afternoon when Daisy tumbled short of his dreams—not through her own fault, but because of the colossal vitality of his illusion. It had gone beyond her, beyond everything. He had thrown himself into it with a creative passion, adding to it all the time, decking it out with every bright feather that drifted his way. No amount of fire or freshness can challenge what a man can store up in his ghostly heart. (102–3)

In responding to such a passage, we are at a very real critical crossroads. To be sure, Fitzgerald is not shying away from the theme of disappointment, but his ultimate game, I think, is the bigger game of belief and illusion. Gatsby, even knowing that Daisy is incommensurate with the Dream, goes on, and much of the novel's pathos hinges on his efforts to remake the world, the past, to fashion a reality of his own that would correspond to the dream. Whereas a writer like Flaubert is corrosive when it comes to dreams and hyperbole, Fitzgerald's subject is more truly that of creation rather than deflation. Note the sense of magnitude expressed in that passage: "colossal," "beyond her, beyond everything" and finally, we are told that the "ghostly heart" outrivals matter, that it generates and stores up visions to which flesh and blood and things cannot measure up.

The mean, phenomenal world of flesh, blood and things is of interest only to the extent that it can be transformed into "enchanted objects." Even the most debunking literature gets an unavowable mileage out of enchantment. The scalpel-like probing and lucidity of Flaubert and Joyce depend, parasitically, on the prior energies of belief: Emma and Frédéric and Félicité; Stephen in the *Portrait* and all the huffers and puffers of *Ulysses* are so many entryways through which the indispensable "stuff of dreams" can be freighted into the work. Indispensable because the "after" critique feeds on a "before" illusion, just as getting thin hardly makes sense if you haven't been fat; but indispensable also because literature has always known itself to have common cause with illusion, has always taken con men like Gatsby to its bosom because they have been its truest apostles. Whereas the realist mission is "to show things as they are," Fitzgerald seems altogether more committed to the project of making things from nothing. Daisy does not measure up, because Gatsby's dream cannot be outfitted with checks and balances, or any kind of external referent; it is, instead, supremely autonomous, auto-generative, fed from within.

The larger thesis which I would now like to develop is that the notion of making something from nothing, or, in Kenner's words, "appearance made real," is not only an American theme but also a paradigmatic formula for literature itself. *The Great Gatsby* depicts things being made from nothing, and objects becoming enchanted objects. Both these operations depend, quite simply, on belief. Nothing in the novel is more endowed with this magic power than Daisy's voice. Everyone remembers Gatsby's own definition of that voice: "Her voice is full of money" (126), and money has long been seen as the central magic in Fitzgerald's scheme; but Daisy's voice is still more crucially defined in other ways: in it Fitzgerald finds a miraculous equivalent to the Dream, something beyond disenchantment: "I think that voice held him most, with its fluctuating feverish warmth, because it couldn't be overdreamed—that voice was a deathless song" (103). Daisy's voice is a veritable siren song, enchanting all men who come her way, Tom and Nick as well as Gatsby, and we would do well to attend to it, indeed, as voice, as language:

> Daisy began to sing with the music in a husky, rhythmic whisper, bringing out a meaning in each word that it had never had before and would never have again. When the melody rose her voice broke up sweetly, following it, in a way contralto voices have, and each change tipped out a little of her warm human magic upon the air. (115)

This voice which "men who had cared for her found difficult to forget" (15) transforms the world in a remarkable way: its magic is equated with new meanings, meanings never before seen and never to be seen again. Daisy's voice has the promise of genesis, of making things anew. Daisy's voice points us to a world of dazzling freshness and mobility, a world responsive to our will, unbound by old definitions and dispensations. This is to be Fitzgerald's New World, and it is also his book. Thus, the characters and setting in *The Great Gatsby* are oddly maneuverable, alterable. In this realm the World Series is quite naturally "fixable" and alterable, rather than given. The dog bought by Tom for Myrtle Wilson is significantly both a boy and a bitch, and at Myrtle's party everything seems to be strangely fluid: people's names seem especially up for grabs, as Nick tries to read a chapter of *Simon Called Peter*: Myrtle's sister Catherine is "said to be very beautiful by people who ought to know," much as they "say [Gatsby's] a nephew or a cousin of Kaiser Wilhelm's" (34, 38). The entire party has a theatrical, improvisational dimension to it; characters seem to be posing, as if Mr. McKee, who is in the "artistic game," were going to photograph them. Things are strangely malleable here, so that the tapestried furniture, with its "scenes of ladies swinging in the gardens of Versailles," seems to spawn a new Myrtle Wilson, one whose "personality had also undergone a change," and whose vitality "was converted into impressive *hauteur*" (36). Anything can happen in these precincts, just as Nick claimed of Fifth Avenue that he "wouldn't have been surprised to see a great flock of white sheep turn the corner" (34). There is a "musical chairs" element to *The Great Gatsby*, and at critical junctures Myrtle

Wilson will mistake Jordan for Daisy, and Gatsby will be fatally mistaken for the driver of the car, just as the party will predictably go to and from New York in swapped cars. One might argue, feebly I think, that the plot requires some of these confusions, but we will be on firmer ground if we acknowledge that *The Great Gatsby* has a bizarre ludic quality, that its materials refuse to stay put, that Fitzgerald, in pirouetting his materials, is doing pretty much the same kind of thing that he ascribed to Daisy's voice: "bringing out a meaning in each word that it had never had before and would never have again." The mean phenomenal world can be altered. As the song intones "I'm the sheik of Araby," we sense a yearning for metamorphosis as well as romance. Innocent prose reveals odd linkage and twinning; "We backed up to a grey old man who bore an absurd resemblance to John D. Rockefeller" (33).[9] Just as some chemicals, when brought to a certain temperature, decompose and change form, so does Daisy become catalyzed by the New York heat: "We'll meet you on some corner. I'll be the man smoking two cigarettes" (131). None of these passages has any literal truth, nor do they further the plot; but they are indices of the novel's figurative activity, of the play of metaphor and masquerade, of self-projection and self-creation, which are at the heart of the book. To be free from the constraints of proof or evidence, to alter one's identity, to be multiple rather than single, to overcome the laws of time and space and background: such are precisely the virtues of fiction, of the American Dream, and of Jay Gatsby.

All the items just named involve the creation of belief, the making of something from nothing, the sovereign power of language and imagination over against the paltriness of evidence. Gatsby is the consummate hero of belief: his belief in Daisy, in the green light, is of such a magnitude as to move worlds; no less important is others' belief in him. It is possible to regard Fitzgerald's novel as an experiment in semiosis, the ways in which meaning is produced and belief established. This text is especially illuminating here, because it spews forth signifiers, sometimes as metaphors, sometimes as lies, sometimes just as an exercise in dissemination; but its secret truth is that there is no truth, no reliable referent, no fixed center to which the signifiers point. Fitzgerald has discovered that the secret to the self-made man is hardly a secret for the novelist, for such a man is pre-eminently made of words rather than flesh, and thus heir to a peculiar freedom which flouts all constraints. And what is the American Dream if not a limitless freedom of the sign?[10] The American Dream, like Daisy's voice, may be confused with money, but it is ultimately an exhilarating kind of liberty which deifies the individual will and erases all its impediments. The American, more than most, dreams of being freed from his origin, so as to make his or her self and world in an endless process of generative activity. Thus, that "green breast of the new world" which the Dutch sailors saw, like the "pap of life" and the "incomparable milk of wonder" which Gatsby sucked and gulped, are Edenic in their promise that desire and reality shall be one, that "fiction" and "fact" shall be coerced into a new etymological unity as *made* things, subservient to human will. In this dream, as perhaps in all dreams, the world produces the deed, the desire forges the object, the imagination makes the world. Desire and will are entirely potent here, capable of producing their own artifacts and setting up their own regime. Not only is the traditional bugbear of social origin transcended, but, in the process, all impediments to self-enactment are removed. This New World is a sorcerer's apprentice world in which naming something brings it into existence, in which the signifier is endlessly potent. Granting some exaggerations, such is the ontology of the American Dream; it is also the *modus operandi* of the con man and the writer, specialists as well in passing off the world for the thing itself, dependent on belief for whatever success they are to enjoy.

We have come at last, although obliquely, to Gatsby, and this is as it should be, since no single path leads to him, no single past has produced him. Like the ancient gods for whose birth multiple legends can be found, so Gatsby is at once "a nephew or a cousin of Kaiser Wilhelm's," "a German spy during the war," "an Oxford man," "a bootlegger," "a person who killed a man." Mysterious, elusive, multiple, "Mr. Nobody from Nowhere," Gatsby has no single referent. He is not there when you look for him, and mysteriously present when least expected, such as in Nick's first encounter, or when Nick arranges his meeting with Daisy. He seems endlessly replicated and mirrored in the text, and there is something apt in Daisy's admiring claim: "'You resemble the advertisement of the man,' she went on innocently. 'You know the advertisement of the man—'" (125). Likewise, when Tom Buchanan announced that he has "made a small investigation of this fellow," Jordan's humorous reaction seems closer to the poetic truth: "'Do you mean you've been to a medium?'" (128). Jordan, as we shall see, is close to the mark in pointing us to the spirit world if we want to find Gatsby's origins.[11]

It is in this light that the delayed disclosure of Jimmie Gatz and his SCHEDULE must be seen as essentially a foil, the mockery of an origin. To be sure, the "young roughneck" that Nick sees derived biologically from Mr. and Mrs. Henry Gatz, just as James Gatz was "really, or at least legally, his name" (104). The search for origins, which is a hallmark of realist fiction, is not absent from this novel, but it is rendered peripheral; it is quite simply backstaged by the dazzling appearances, the performance of Gatsby as persona, and the impact he has on others. The book itself is a testimonial to his enduring reality, and Nick invariably identifies Gatbsy with the future: his "heightened sensitivity to the promises of life," his "extraordinary gift for hope," his "romantic readiness." Even in the most literal sense, Gatsby cannot be pinned down: "He was never quite still; there was always a tapping foot somewhere or the impatient opening and closing of a hand" (70). And there is the matter of his smile. Like Daisy's voice, Gatsby's smile is infinitely seductive, for it projects the archetypal magic fable to which we never fail to respond: our own life. Here too, Gatsby's business is with the future, a future for us, one that we liked. Gatsby's smile is truly generative, "constituting" not so much himself as you:

> It was one of those rare smiles with a quality of eternal reassurance in it, that you may come across four or five times in life.... It understood you just so far as you wanted to be understood, believed in you as you would like to believe in yourself, and assured you that it had precisely the impression of you that, at your best, you hoped to convey. (54)

Gatsby embodies the power of belief. He extends it to others, and he exists only insofar as they extend it to him. Belief, as I have repeatedly said, does not require evidence or proof or referent or origin. The believer makes his own world, and that is what Gatsby has done:

> His parents were shiftless and unsuccessful farm people—his imagination had never really accepted them as his parents at all. The truth was that Jay Gatsby of West Egg, Long Island, sprang from his Platonic conception of himself. (105)

There is doubtless no more perfect piece of Americana in all of literature. Horatio Alger, rags-to-riches, the American Dream, upward mobility: it is all there. Fitzgerald has grasped the enormity of the American cliché, the self-made man, and he has properly understood it to be a spiritual, even an artisanal phenomenon, every bit as much as an economic statement. Yet we know that self-made men are cluttering the offices of analysts and doctors all over the United States, looking backward, often painfully, to determine where in fact they came from. Gatsby, as we know, finishes up supine as well, lying afloat in a pool, abandoned by all except Nick Carraway. We know too that Gatsby's exploits are even a bit darker than those of con men, that his shady dealings and obsession for power mirror some of the most diseased aspects of the American psyche. Ultimately, one must also ask just how far fiction can take you, at what point the world of fact and referent finally catches up to the high-flying gold-hatted imagination that longs to make its own world.

The Great Gatsby is great, I think, because it is willing to hint, more than once, that fiction just might take you all the way. This book is, from beginning to end, despite its revelations and weary narrator, committed to the power of the dream. Or more precisely and more to the point, the power of fiction. It is now time to substantiate this claim by looking at some central passages that depict the complex war between fact and fiction. Let us begin with Gatsby's own impassioned statement of origin to Nick:

> "I'll tell you God's truth." His right hand suddenly ordered divine retribution to stand by. "I am the son of some wealthy people in the Middle West—all dead now. I was brought up in America but educated at Oxford, because all my ancestors have been educated there for many years. It is a family tradition." (71)

This sequence begins right at the top, as God, the final guarantor of all utterances, the one who separates the true from the false, is invoked as authority. God's truth would be pure referent, and Gatsby's speech act would be totally at one with its meaning, so much so that divine retribution is standing by to punish any and all discrepancies between language and truth. This assurance of verbal legitimacy has, as its social cohorts, "all my ancestors," "family tradition" and Oxford itself, all venerable displays of origin, all respected emissaries of the Old World. Now my argument all along has been that Fitzgerald is depicting a New World, one that dispenses with those fixed entities, and either invents or projects its own data; Nick indeed suspects that Gatsby's claim is spurious:

> "What part of the Middle West?" I enquired casually.
> "San Francisco."
> "I see."
> "My family all died and I came into a good deal of money."
> His voice was solemn, as if the memory of that sudden extinction of a clan still haunted him. (71)

One hardly knows what to admire most here: Gatsby's answer of San Francisco or Nick's assent, "I see." Where is God's truth here? For there is a choice. Either this is outright balderdash, part of Gatsby's flimflam, the sort of thing you'd expect from a bootlegger; or this just may be, on some level, real if not true. Nick's "I see" opens just the tiniest bit of space for squeezing San Francisco into the Midwest, but a very special map will be needed for this. The more Gatsby talks—and he talks very little in this book—the more extravagant he becomes:

> "After that I lived like a young rajah in all the capitals of Europe—Paris, Venice, Rome—collecting jewels, chiefly rubies, hunting big game, painting a little, things for myself only, and trying to forget something very sad that had happened to me long ago." (71–72)

The hackneyed character of these clichés is so pronounced, the phrases themselves, as Nick realizes, are "so threadbare," that the whole performance seems patently theatrical, literary, evoking "no image except that of a turbanned 'character' leaking sawdust at every pore as he pursued a tiger through the Bois de Boulogne" (72). But now the fun begins, because in Fitzgerald fraud can be the beginning rather than the end of things. Gatsby quite simply authenticates his performance: he produces signs of legitimacy, such as the military decoration from Montenegro and the Oxford photograph, and in the face of such evidence, Nick is "converted."

> Then it was all true. I saw the skins of tigers flaming in his palace on the Grand Canal; I saw him opening a chest of rubies to ease, with their crimson-lighted depths, the gnawings of his broken heart. (73)

Nick's musings are deliciously tongue-in-cheek, but they are hardly an indictment; on the contrary, they are an homage to Gatsby's version of things, and they express Nick's willingness to play Gatsby's game, to add furnishings of his own to Gatsby's place. We see Nick moving into Gatsby's sphere in this passage, and it is worth noting that the whole transition from hoax to belief has a distinct *literary* coloration. The Romantic clichés are found to have some life left in them, so that even the jaded and condescending Nick Carraway can come under their spell.

Breathing life back into melodrama is just one of Fitzgerald's tricks. At privileged moments in this narrative, we may see objects become enchanted and characters spawn new identities, as Fitzgerald gently reminds us that literature has a pulse and a heartbeat of its own. Consider, for example, the fine passage when Nick and Gatsby cross the Queensboro Bridge and encounter the City. Fitzgerald ushers in this scene with language that pointedly foreshadows his famous concluding image of Dutch sailors and the New World: "The city seen from the Queensboro Bridge is always the city seen for the first time, in its first wild promise of all the mystery and the beauty in the world" (74–75). As we shall see, this New World is very much, to use Tony Tanner's significant phrase, a "city of words," a place whose verbal freedom turns it into a "lexical playfield."[12] Here is what Nick sees:

> A dead man passed us in a hearse heaped with blooms, followed by two carriages with drawn blinds, and by more cheerful carriages for friends. The friends looked out at us with the tragic eyes and short upper lips of southeastern Europe, and I was glad that the sight of Gatsby's splendid car was included in their sombre holiday. As we crossed Blackwell's Island, a limousine passed us, driven by a white chauffeur, in which sat three modish negroes, two bucks and a girl. I laughed aloud as the yolks of their eyeballs rolled toward us in haughty rivalry. (75)

On the face of it, we have here an innocent slice of American life; if pushed, one might claim that this scene has a mildly symbolic dimension, a discreet evocation of the American Dream *in petto*.[13] In this light we see America the melting pot, with its southeastern Europeans and its Negroes, and the possibility of limousines and wealth for all; looking still more closely, we note the death or decline of the Europeans and the rise or dawning of the Blacks, this too an apt figure for American freedom and mobility. But, the more one scrutinizes this passage, the more playful and sibylline it becomes. There is an uncanny fixation with eyes, as each segment concludes by an ocular close-up, and one begins to wonder if there is not something pathological in this book about perception, perspective, Owl-Eyes, T. J. Eckleburg and the like.[14] One is also entitled to question whether southeastern Europe is as fixed a proposition as is the location of San Francisco in the Middle West. Certainly the Negroes appear to have come verbally from "Blackwell's Island," indeed to have emerged from the "sombre holiday" every bit as much as to make a social statement. The passage starts to appear far more pictorial than social, with its arrangement of black and white, its flower-heaped hearse and splendid cars. It is a portrait of life and gaiety, and the lead-off item that begins the procession, the man with the four-letter adjective "dead," is not more without life than "black" and "white" are sociological. "A dead man passed us...," and he is merely, grandly, part of the parade, filled with verbal life, here in Fitzgerald's New World where language actualizes "the wild promise of all the mystery and the beauty in the world." And tucked in the middle of this mystery and beauty is one of the most shimmering sights of all, that of Gatsby's car, which can demonstrably bring to life as well as put to death.[15] Nick himself sums it up: " 'Anything can happen now that we've slid over this bridge,' I thought; 'anything at all....' " (75). To "slide" over that magic bridge is seductively easy in Fitzgerald, for the glamor of that other world, its "haughty rivalry," beckon to us at every turn. That bridge turns out to span realms more distant than Queensboro and the City, and the final scene I want now to analyze illustrates the freedom which Fitzgerald found on its far side.

On that far side we encounter what is arguably the most fascinating sequence in *The Great Gatsby*, and the most ignored: namely, the saga of "Blocks" Biloxi.[16] This is the centerpiece of my interpretation, and therefore I need to quote it in full:

> "Imagine marrying anybody in this heat!" cried Jordan dismally.
> "Still—I was married in the middle of June," Daisy remembered, "Louisville in June! Somebody fainted. Who was it fainted, Tom?"
> "Biloxi," he answered shortly.
> "A man named Biloxi. 'Blocks' Biloxi, and he made boxes—that's a fact—and he was from Biloxi, Tennessee."
> "They carried him into my house," appended Jordan, "because we lived just two doors from the church. And he stayed three weeks, until Daddy told him he had to get out. The day after he left Daddy died." After a moment she added, "There wasn't any connection."
> "I used to know a Bill Biloxi from Memphis," I remarked.
> "That was his cousin. I knew his whole family history before he left. He gave me an aluminum putter that I use to-day." The music had died down as the ceremony began and now a long cheer floated in at the window, followed by intermittent cries of "Yea-ea-ea!" and finally by a burst of jazz as the dancing began.
> "We're getting old,' said Daisy. "If we were young we'd rise and dance."
> "Remember Biloxi," Jordan warned her. "Where'd you know him, Tom?"
> "Biloxi?" He concentrated with an effort. "I didn't know him. He was a friend of Daisy's."
> "He was not," she denied. "I'd never seen him before. He came down in the private car."
> "Well, he said he knew you. He said he was raised in Louisville. Asa Bird brought him around at the last minute and asked if we had room for him."
> Jordan smiled.
> "He was probably bumming his way home. He told me he was president of your class at Yale."
> Tom and I looked at each other blankly.
> "Biloxi?"
> "First place, we didn't have any president—"
> Gatsby's foot beat a short, restless tattoo and Tom eyed him suddenly.
> "By the way, Mr. Gatsby, I understand you're an Oxford man."
> "Not exactly."
> "Oh, yes, I understand you went to Oxford."

"Yes—I went there."

A pause, then Tom's voice, incredulous and insulting: "You must have gone there about the time Biloxi went to New Haven." (133–35)

Perhaps it is best to start with the truism that *The Great Gatsby* is never regarded as an experimental novel, nor is Fitzgerald generally appreciated as the creator of narrative high jinks, say, in the manner of Joyce or Faulkner. Moreover, this particular scene is positively crucial, from a realist point of view: it is, in effect, Fitzgerald's showdown scene, his "high noon" moment of truth in a sweltering New York hotel room where the two males finally fight it out for the golden girl. Tom has done his sleuthing, and Gatsby has finished his courting; who will carry the day? Here, if ever, Fitzgerald needs tame, univalent prose, needs to etch this battle with clarity and force.

But what do we have? Coming out of nowhere—and this, from any perspective in which you care to examine it—is "Blocks" Biloxi. He enters this story very like an unbidden but irrepressible ghost, like tidings that must be proclaimed. Almost like an epiphany, he is a radiant image of what Gatsby has only been striving to be: the complete self-made man.

More even than other fictional characters, Biloxi is a construct of words: "A man named Biloxi. 'Blocks' Biloxi, and he made boxes—that's a fact—and he was from Biloxi, Tennessee."

Like a child's game, "Blocks" are put together to make Biloxi; he is a fabrication, and he makes such objects for others: "he made boxes," boxes which contain whatever fictive meaning we insert in them. To emphasize the pure artifice of this gambit, Fitzgerald makes name and place exactly the same, much like a child who had only one kind of block for two separate purposes: "and he was from Biloxi, Tennessee." We are indeed in a New World, a writerly wonderland, where the artist's blocks and letters and boxes can deliver up a geography and a history all of their own making, claiming as truth—"that's a fact"—all his magic, including the location of Biloxi in Tennessee, which can only have "left" Mississippi in the same way San Francisco "moved" to the Middle West: by verbal fiat.[17]

Outfitted with a dazzlingly specious origin, the Biloxi-character can now begin to perform with the fiction. Jordan first contributes to his career by "appending" the story of Biloxi's momentous stay at her house. He enters her house supine (from drink, supposedly), and his exit three weeks later triggers the supine departure of Daddy (from death, this time). Jordan hastens to explain, "There wasn't any connection," but the reader who has any experience with blocks is bound to suspect a pattern here, at least a metaphorical linking, a Wolfsheim-type "gonnegtion" forged by the text's generative activity. coming into Jordan's house "just two doors from the church," Biloxi is perhaps even more a ghost than we thought, a somehow holy figure whose presence is life and whose leaving is death.

Nick joins in the collective fabulation and spreads Biloxi a little further, adding a block in Memphis: "'I used to know a Bill Biloxi from Memphis.'"

Jordan provides the missing referent ("cousin"), and returns to the mystery of origin: "'I knew his whole family history before he left,'" This is, of course, oral history, "Blocks'" own tale of his past, forcing any "constructive" reader to think of that other inventor of his past, Jay Gatsby. The "gonnegtion" between Biloxi and Gatsby is only beginning.

As the noises of the marriage ceremony and the subsequent jazz music filter into the hotel room, Daisy muses, "'We're getting old.... If we were young we'd rise and dance.'" She is cautioned by Jordan, "'Remember Biloxi,'" causing the reader once again to ponder the connections here. Daisy is obviously recalling her own marriage to Tom, but beyond that she is encountering time itself. "'We're getting old'" is a recognition that one's romance and youth are going (if not gone), and her wistful statement, "'If we were young we'd rise and dance,'" connotes a "rising and dancing" of special poignancy, a retrieval of youth, a hint even of resurrection.[18] Jordan warns her by referring to Biloxi, yet Biloxi's presence maintains life; only when he leaves, do we die. How can we not recall Gatsby's own imperious desire to stop time, his spirited answer to Nick's earlier warning:

> "I wouldn't ask too much of her," I ventured. "You can't repeat the past."
> "Can't repeat the past?" he cried incredulously. "Why of course you can!"
> (117)

I do not for a moment suggest that the ghost imagery I have used has a genuine religious significance. But it is clear that the issue of lost youth and irretrievable past is at the heart of the book, as it is at the heart of the dream. And the radiant answer, the splendidly American response, is to recreate what has been lost, to invent one's past and to harness desire as the very reality principle itself. Nothing need be over for the self-made man. The "gift of hope" may be illusory, but it is life-sustaining, and once it is gone, once "Blocks" Biloxi leaves your house, life is not worth living. The "realist" exposure of illusion, the sleuthwork of Tom Buchanan and his ilk, is not so much an education as a loss of something magic and indispensable; this, Fitzgerald took to be the burden of his novel: "the loss of those illusions that give such color to the world so that you don't care whether things are true or false so long as they partake of the magical glory."[19]

But the dreamer has to awake, and no fiction can ignore the inescapable constraints of Reality. Moreover, the object of the dream cannot be protected against time, nor can *its* beauty ever match that of the dream. Finally, the achievements furthered by the dream may be tawdry and corrupt, although the dream never can be.

Fitzgerald had no choice but to expose his quester for a fraud, the quester's materials for vulgar and meretricious. But the deeper challenge he faced, and the one he met so perfectly that *The Great Gatsby* continues to perplex its readers today, is the dilemma of conveying the beauty and power of the dream, while discrediting its object, its "occupant" and its effects. The power of belief is Fitzgerald's true subject, and he brilliantly saw that it is allied to semiosis, to the production of meaning. He intuitively grasped that the virtues of the dream are synonymous with the virtues of language. Time cannot kill it, nor can origin or fixed referent determine or immobilize it. Language "rises and dances" in *The Great Gatsby*, and it offers its most perfect performance in the figure of "Blocks" Biloxi. Biloxi, the put-together amalgam of person and place, spewing cousins, putters and death in his wake, commences to look more and more like Gatsby. No one knew him, but he was allegedly "a friend of Daisy's." She claims that he was not, that he had come down in "the private car," which points at both Gatsby and the railway coach. Biloxi made his own story, claiming that he knew Daisy, was raised in Louisville, had done more yet. His most extraordinary achievement, the novel's very finest transposition of fiction to fact, dream to reality, and language to deed, is the rank he acquired: "'He told me he was president of your class at Yale.'" No longer "out there" in Tennessee or even Louisville, Biloxi has finally come home, home to the Fitzgerald citadel where he takes his rightful place on the throne. Here is the "high noon" showdown at last, in a different key, reminiscent more of the Quixote's encounters than those of gunfighters. If "Blocks" Biloxi can be president of your class at Yale, then America is not only a genuine "rags-to-riches" virgin land, but literature has finally outtrumped life by getting its own man elected.[20]

The forces of order man their defenses at once:

> Tom and I looked at each other blankly.
> "Biloxi?"
> "First place, we didn't have any president—"

But it is manifestly too late in the game for such reneging, and Tom Buchanan rises oddly to the occasion, dropping Biloxi and moving on to Gatsby, with a sure sense that the story of one is the life of the other, and vice versa. Closing in on Gatsby's Oxford stint, approaching ever more closely the so-called boundary between fact and fiction, Tom finally makes the ultimate connection and delivers one of the most perfect lines of the book: "'You [Gatsby] must have been there [Oxford] about the time Biloxi went to New Haven.'" At this point Gatsby produces a compromise answer, and the interlude with Biloxi comes to a close. In some sense, the remainder of the book is something of a come-down, a return to Reality and its unavoidable assortment of evidence and corpses and cold fried chicken.

But the issues raised in the Biloxi episode and the ringing identification of Biloxi and Gatsby as one, their careers as intertwined, these concerns illuminate the larger purposes of the novel, and to shed light on them has been the object of this study. "Blocks" Biloxi is not only a "made" person, a construct; he is also positioned in a homemade world of the group's devising, the kind of place where Biloxi can be in Tennessee and San Francisco in the Middle

West. This flim-flam man who manufactures his past, crashes the wedding, does in Jordan's father, and is president of your class at Yale, is a potent figure, free of all prior conditioning and constraints (since he is shaped and constructed in front of our eyes) and strangely memorable (he is only "there" in the narrative because he is memorable). Pure artifice, yet he intrudes into the Real World, leaving Jordan a putter and leaving her father to die. His meteoric career is a bold parable of Jay Gatsby's life, a shorthand version of the same magic and creation of belief which constitute Gatsby's particular greatness. "Blocks" Biloxi is the liberated signifier, the unit or "block" of language that can be molded and connected in countless ways, to yield countless boxes, each with countless possible contents or signifieds.

The novel does not close with Biloxi, nor shall I. Jay Gatsby is also a hero of self-creation, but unlike the enigmatic Biloxi, he is a passionate, tragic character, one who brought to the potential of signs the energy of his life. His smile, his parties, his love are profoundly creative, constitutive gestures, enabling others to take form and life. He is the prime mover in Fitzgerald's scheme, the "Son of God" who is a consummate fiction-maker, acting through the shape he gave to himself and to others. There is a remarkable kind of freedom in this act of shaping, and I have argued that it can be understood as a peculiarly American freedom, an imperious desire to make reality rather than to undergo it. But, this freedom can only be exercised by dint of energy and will. The con man, like the artist, replaces the given world by a construct of his own, but it can rival with reality only if he invests it with life, with his life. Those splendid parties of Gatsby's and the aura which surrounds the scattered details of his life, these are the properties of legend, and they bear witness to a strange kind of public belief, a kind of reciprocity whereby Gatsby is himself brought to life by those who surround him. Such reciprocity also defines the basic aesthetic miracle that brings art to life, that makes the page seem real, that makes it endure. Hero of dreams, Gatsby is dreamed by others. Only in such a way can the artist then act on his public, appeal to or coerce their belief, and ultimately withdraw from the scene, confident that his creation is alive, kept alive by the belief of his public.

Fitzgerald achieved that final transfer in *The Great Gatsby*, and the book is endowed with an indigenous energy and power that mocks both closure and exposure. This brings me back, even if circuitously, to the question with which I began: what is Gatsby's greatness? My answer is in my title: fiction as greatness. There can be no fixed, measurable index of greatness, no specifiable amount of dollars or military victories or literary prizes which must be earned before greatness is bestowed. I am not suggesting that it therefore does not exist. Greatness has common cause with fiction because it hinges on belief, because it can only be achieved if it is conferred. To be great requires a crucial measure of *public* endorsement; indeed, it requires being "ratified," much as one must be "elected" president of your class at Yale. Biloxi achieved his ghostly triumph in these precincts, yet his more flesh-and-blood cousin Gatsby remains ultimately the more compelling candidate. The fiction-making for which he stands is a passionate act of transformation not unlike Rimbaud's *alchimie du verbe*, but it can make its magic and enchanted objects only through the gift of self and the response of others. To phrase it that way is to run the risk of Gatsby's own "appalling sentimentality," but it is also to underscore the humane value of belief, even fictional belief, as the goal of language and literature.

Notes

1. Fitzgerald's debt to Conrad is a commonplace in the secondary literature. The Jamesian influence (center of consciousness, *ficelle*, etc.) is equally pervasive but more diffuse. James E. Miller, Jr. offers a fine discussion of Fitzgerald's borrowings, and he has also highlighted the possible connection with Willa Cather in his *F. Scott Fitzgerald: His Art and his Technique* (New York: New York University Press, 1964), pp. 87–92; Lawrence Thornton has made the case for Ford's influence in *Fitzgerald/Hemingway Annual 1975* (pp. 57–74). As for the treatment and nature of the American Dream in *Gatsby*, I would single out Edwin Fussell's well-known "Fitzgerald's Brave New World" and Marius Bewley's "Scott Fitzgerald's Criticism of America," both reprinted in *F. Scott Fitzgerald: A Collection of Critical Essays*, ed. Arthur Mizener (Englewood Cliffs, N.J.: Prentice-Hall, 1963). One may also consult the essays by Floyd C. Watkins, Irvin G. Wylie and David F. Trask, listed under the heading "The American Dream," in *Fitzgerald's The Great Gatsby: The Novel, The Critics, The Background*, ed. Henry Dan Piper (New York: Scribner's, 1970).

2. Here, too, everyone has had his say, but the essay of Charles Samuels, "The Greatness of *Gatsby*," reprinted in Piper's critical edition, remains a pithy and strong tribute to the artistic and moral beauty of Fitzgerald's book.

3. This posture in Fitzgerald criticism seems to set in, right at the outset, with H. L. Mencken's review of *Gatsby* in the Baltimore *Evening Sun* (May 2, 1925), also reprinted in Piper. The latest variant of it can be seen in the jaundiced but brilliant Fitzgerald commentary offered by Hugh Kenner in *A Homemade World: The American Modernist Writer* (New York: Morrow, 1975), pp. 20–49; Kenner is petulant not only about the spurious glamor that is Fitzgerald's subject, but also the mellifluous, overdone cadences of the author's "high style."

4. *The Great Gatsby* (1925; Harmondsworth, Middlesex: Penguin, 1982), pp. 7–8. All subsequent citations in parentheses in the text are to this edition.

5. The list of Gatsby's guests has been the frequent subject of Fitzgerald criticism, although Kenner takes the honors here as well:

> (Real names *are* extraordinary; Gus Mozart sells Volkswagens a morning's drive from where this page you are reading was drafted.) And G. Earl Muldoon, further down, is "brother to that Muldoon who afterward strangled his wife." We have heard of him, surely? We seem to have. Dickens is behind this characterization by naming, and so is J. Alfred Prufrock, whose surname came from a St. Louis furniture house. ("You bring the girl," said the sign on a window full of bridal suites; "Prufrock does the rest." T. S. Eliot and the mother of William S. Burroughs, the eminent junkie, used to walk past that sign en route home from dancing class. Whoever can believe that—and it is true—understands how to go about according Fitzgerald the order of belief he is soliciting.) (*A Homemade World*, pp. 40–41)

July 5th itself has frequently been noted as the "day after," but no critic, to my knowledge, has invested this day with the kind of artistic challenge that I am interested in.

6. I want to acknowledge my indebtedness to Kenner's reading of Fitzgerald in particular, and of American literature in general. His notion of the "homemade world" and his frequently zany illustrations of such American tinkering strike me as a perfect framework for considering *Gatsby*.

7. *The Good Soldier: A Tale of Passion* (New York: Knopf, 1927), p. 6.

8. This cult of the image is an inverted view of the "aura" that Walter Benjamin ascribed to the original, in his fine discussion of photography. "The Work of Art in the Age of Mechanical Reproduction," *Illuminations* (Frankfurt: Suhrkamp Verlag, 1955). Fitzgerald seems closer to the kind of image-worship that one finds in Genet, as strange as that association may appear.

9. It turns out that most of these delightful, surrealist touches were added when Fitzgerald was revising *Gatsby*; see Kenneth Eble, "The Craft of Revision: *The Great Gatsby*," reprinted in Piper.

10. I realize that a semiotic interpretation of the American Dream will seem harebrained to those who regard this topic as a strictly "substantive" history-of-ideas proposition, dating at least from the legacy of Benjamin Franklin. Yet, the dynamic of the dream is what fascinates Fitzgerald, and it clearly fuels his narrative; there is a crucial volitional element in both language and desire, and I think there is considerable evidence (see the Biloxi section later) that Fitzgerald was aware of their common virtues.

11. One wishes that more Fitzgerald critics heeded Jordan's warning. All too numerous are the claims made for "discovering" who Gatsby "really" is. A case has been made for worthies such as Max Fleischman, Edward Fuller, Robert Kerr and Max Gerlach; the author of one of these attribution studies was introduced to Kerr's daughter as "the daughter of The Great Gatsby" (Joseph Corso, "One Not-Forgotten Summer Night: Sources for Fictional Symbols of American Character in *The Great Gatsby*," *Fitzgerald/Hemingway Annual 1976*, p. 13). This effort to pin down Gatsby can be ludicrous, but it is not surprising, and it points to the central enigma of the novel, an enigma that made the author himself uneasy. It is well known that Edith Wharton emphasized Gatsby's "fuzziness" as a flaw in the novel, and Maxwell Perkins urged Fitzgerald to make Gatsby more distinct, more fleshed-out, less mysterious. Fitzgerald's own comments on this issue are fascinating: "I myself didn't know what Gatsby looked like or was engaged in," he wrote to Perkins, and to John Peale Bishop he added the clincher: "Also you are right about Gatsby being blurred and patchy. I never at any one time saw him clear myself—for he started as one man I knew and then changed into myself—the amalgam was never complete in my mind" (this material is cited in Piper, pp. 106–107). There can be no question that the novel would be utterly different, not only in tone, but in meaning, if Gatsby were "clearer," less enigmatic. Gatsby's mystery, the aura he has, the appeal and power he exerts over others, these are the central constituents of the novel, not the incidental aftereffects of Fitzgerald's presentation.

12. Tanner's general view of American letters in terms of a search for freedoms that are verbal as well as moral is one that has greatly influenced my view of Fitzgerald (*City of Words: American Fiction, 1950–1970* [NY: Harper and Row, 1971]) He and Kenner strike me as the two most congenial interpreters of American literature, because they brilliantly fuse the social and the aesthetic at every turn.

13. The Queensboro Bridge episode has been mentioned by several critics, usually in cautionary terms. Richard Lehan (*F. Scott Fitzgerald and the Craft of Fiction* [Carbondale: Southern Illinois University Press, 1967]. p. 119) stresses the death motif in the passage, and Joan Korenman devotes an entire article to the moral implications of this vignette ("A View from the [Queensboro] Bridge," in *Fitzgerald/Hemingway Annual 1975*, pp. 93–96). To be sure, this sequence does its share of foreshadowing, but its sheer verbal inventiveness, its strange lexical autonomy, have not been noticed.

14. The emphasis on perception is a stock item in most *Gatsby* criticism. The fun begins, however, when Fitzgerald's prose starts to look "decentered", i.e., the various motifs of this novel, such as "seeing," or the automobile, begin to acquire a life of their own, a demonic kind of authority, so that one feels that events take place because the language and the metaphors "will" them. Once T. J. Eckleburg is on the scene, Owl-Eyes cannot be far behind. Perhaps all art has its subtle teleology, but when the form-imperative becomes truly noticeable, when it seems more urgent than any meanings that limp afterward, then we are in the presence of a playful text that is asserting the kind of peculiar freedom I am investigating. My argument, obviously, is that we associate such verbal behavior with the Surrealists or Joyce, but rarely with Fitzgerald.

15. The automobile has claimed the lion's share in a goodly amount of *Gatsby* criticism. The imagery and rhythm of this modern form of locomotion have been assessed in various ways, ranging from a celebration of technology to a foreboding sense of the demonic. Kenner's designation of Gatsby riding in a majestic vehicle "bright with nickel, swollen here and there in its monstrous length with triumphant hat-boxes and supper-boxes and tool-boxes, and terraced

with a labyrinth of windshields that mirrored a dozen suns!" (70) as a "Renaissance Magnifico" seems closer to the mark than any kind of futurist nightmare scenario, like, say, Stephen King's horror movie *Christine*. Above all, Gatsby's fabled car with its dozen suns, outrivals poor life by a score of 12 to 1, once again flaunting the supremacy of art over reality.

16. Amazingly enough, Biloxi has escaped the attention of Fitzgerald criticism. People have, of course, known that he was there, but it was never thought necessary (or worthwhile) to attend to him. Lehan is one of the few critics who mentions him (p. 102), but he has nothing to say about the spectacular performance which Biloxi carries off.

17. There will doubtless be some readers who think I'm insane on this Biloxi, Tennessee issue since their text reads "Biloxi, Mississippi." But textual reality here is as slippery as the World Series. The more recent editions of *Gatsby* including Scribner's latest paperback, the current Penguin edition, and the Scribner's text used by Henry Dan Piper, op. cit., in 1972, all print "Biloxi, Tennessee." The older Scribner's editions carry "Biloxi, Mississippi." Scribner's has not responded to my inquiry as to *why* the "Mississippi" was changed to the more interesting (to me) "Tennessee." Whatever Fitzgerald's original wording was, the book exists as public domain, and the more modern version, one is tempted to say, "the more modernist version," does read "Tennessee." The very confusion itself gives evidence that Biloxi is alive and well, at least in the newer reprints.

18. The American Dream, as Edwin Fussell and others have emphasized, is never far from the cult of youth. Ponce de León is a true American hero in this light, and, of course, the career of F. Scott Fitzgerald is shot through with this mythic yearning.

19. Quoted by Mizener in his Introduction, *F. Scott Fitzgerald*, p. 10.

20. All parallels with the current American political scene are unintended.

100
Literary Pragmatics: A New Discipline. The Example of Fitzgerald's *The Great Gatsby*

◆

GEOF COX

Discussions of the production of meaning in language nowadays usually adopt, in one guise or another, a distinction between *semantics*, a potential reference produced by the combination of purely linguistic elements, and *pragmatics*, a reference potential produced by a combination of linguistic and other constraints on the communicative situation, such as social expectations and norms.[1] The meaning of an utterance like 'Waiter, there's a fly in my soup' may be used to illustrate this distinction. Any number of joke responses—'Don't worry Sir, the spider in your roll will catch it'—achieve some of their humour precisely because they are responses to the semantics of the utterance, but not to its pragmatics: the joke-waiter has ignored the meaning-effects of the normal social relations of diners to waiters on what, on the semantic face of it, might indeed have been an innocent proposition on the whereabouts of an insect. It should be noted, incidentally, that the social relationship involved in the joke is a relation of dominance. The humour in fact arises partly from the shocking subversion of a typical power relation; a relation normally disguised by, precisely, the semantic form of the original utterance. By stating what is actually a complaint/instruction in the form of an innocent proposition the diner simultaneously *realises* and *disguises* this power relation. Considerations of 'conspicuous leisure' apart, I would guess that 'manners' have come to occupy the priority they often have among ruling classes precisely because they incorporate this form of language. It is typical, in fact, of those *ideological* forms of language in which semantics appear as universal, common to all language and all people, purely propo-

SOURCE *Literature and History* 12, Spring 1986, pp. 79-96.

sitional, but which from a pragmatic point of view simultaneously realise and disguise social differences and conflicts.

I will explore this aspect of ideology in more detail below. It will be seen that the general thrust of my approach is to draw attention away from the textuality of the world which has recently so preoccupied academic studies, even those concerned with the 'text' of history itself, and instead to focus on those aspects of our lives which still seem to me to fall outside such preoccupations. Within this, I mean to intervene in the current debate on ideology, to bring to bear what will seem to many a surprising implication of Althusser's theory, which would place the systematic distortion of ideology not specifically in signifying practices but rather in any social practice. In my view recent writers on ideology have tended to retreat from Althusser's position, sometimes even while claiming to relate the question of ideology more closely to that of domination, so that in some cases ideology has become hardly distinguishable from the more specifically linguistic distortions usually thought of simply as lies, rhetoric or propaganda.[2] I hope that by working through the example of a particular novel I can shed rather more light on the relationship between language and ideology. For the moment, let me just state what I take to be the genuinely Althusserian view that the representations symptomatic of ideology may be perfectly faithful and rational, in fact 'true', even though what is fundamentally represented is our imaginary relationship to the world. Which is to say that the distortion involved is of ourselves, before it is in our signifying practices.

In any case, I think it is clear enough that the production of particular meanings depends partly on the language used and partly on the situation and the way in which it is used. I want first to consider the implications for this state of affairs for the kind of meanings produced when a novel is read—for instance *The Great Gatsby*.

How are we to think of the *context of reading* a novel? This question involves notorious difficulties, and might on the face of it invite discussion of a whole host of strange 'readers' that have recently wandered through literary-theory: implicit textual readers (as in German Reception Theory), particular empirical readers (American Reader Theory), abstract literary super-readers (French Semiotics), and so on. From the perspective I hope to develop here, all such readers will appear rather as red-herrings, and ideological red-herrings at that! In the meantime, however, perhaps I can dodge these difficulties by focussing on just two aspects of most reading contexts.

1. If, whenever we talk about literature, we are to avoid introducing, at least implicitly, the abstraction 'the reader'—equally an abstraction whether it refers to one particular empirical reader or to some kind of generalised reader—then we must introduce some idea of the forms taken by individuals' relations with the world, reading being such a relation. The point here is that to conceive of readers as all equally different or all equally the

same is in either case to ignore any structural inequality; indeed, it is to assume the absence of any kind of real social structure whatever. I will not belabour here the political implications of such a conception; but I should at least say that I believe all attempts by literary critics, whatever their personal political views, to interpret texts, rely in some way on such a conception of the reader. If, on the other hand, we are to take the idea of social structure seriously, then individuals' relations with the world are not merely particular but also, indeed primarily, formal. Furthermore, there is good reason to assume here that at least two forms of such relations can be distinguished: ownership and non-ownership. I am therefore led to consider social class as an important constraint within reading contexts. This is not to imply any simplistic reduction of social structure to 'ruling class' versus 'working class'—but I do think this distinction has been well enough established historically to be used as a starting point from which literature can be hermeneutically related to the general structure of society precisely as a means of interpreting the latter's real complexity.

2. What most literary critics nowadays think of as a *text* is usually only to be found in a book: an object made mainly out of paper; indeed a commodity (in the marxist sense) like any other, with its specific plot of manufacture, marketing and consumption. I wonder if the overwhelming concern of literary theory—precisely during the development of mass book production—to define such an object of enquiry as 'the text', is not also a way of *not* drawing attention to this more obvious object: the book-commodity. And my wonder here again extends to many theorists of explicitly marxist views, who attempt to reintroduce the text to some kind of social context only at the point of its literary production—the historical context of its writing—rather than looking at the commercial processes of book production. My point, on the contrary, is that readers usually follow the plot of the commodity rather than or before that of the text. Unlike most critics, therefore, I will consider the different constraints within reading contexts introduced by a number of different books; all of which, however, have the title *The Great Gatsby*.

I want to argue that a 'pragmatics of literature' must begin by exploding the twin ideological supports of much current literary criticism: 'the reader' and 'the text'. My strategy of forcing these twin notions towards *classes of readers* on the one hand and *book-commodities* on the other may well appear merely impressionistic at this point; however, my argument is, as will be seen, necessarily hermeneutic rather than propositional, and can only be established via consideration of real reading experiences.

The main text in a book entitled *The Great Gatsby*[3] begins with the following paragraph.

> My name is Nick Carraway. I was born in a big city in the Middle West. My family has been well-known there for seventy years. My father's university was

Yale and I went there too. I graduated in 1915 and then went to fight in the Great War.

This seems to raise a number of questions, probably the most central of which is that of to what extent this text *is* Fitzgerald's *Great Gatsby*. Given my comments on the whole idea of 'the text', however, it will come as no surprise that I view such questions as beside the point; indeed, just as purposefully, ideologically off the point as the parallel conception of 'the (ideal Fitzgerald) reader'. Let me briefly put forward here three clarificatory arguments for this view of literary texts.

1. Any text is merely an abstraction, except as on the one hand a literally meaningless collection of ink marks, or on the other, a site for the production of meaning. But in the latter case meanings must be produced not only within the semantic constraints of the text but also within the pragmatic constraints of the reading context, such as social class and the book-commodity. Although it might be argued that these pragmatic factors do not affect the text 'as such'—indeed that some virtual tendential unity of *Gatsby* is assured by the very fact that it can be 'retold', as in the above quotation— such a text cannot be read, but only theorised after the fact. Furthermore, such a theorisation would be inadequate unless it could deal methodologically with the fact of its departure from actual reading(s). This has been the problem with those forms of structuralism that have perhaps come closest to realising what a text's semantics might look like apart from pragmatic factors. In general, therefore, pragmatic factors are included in what we mean by *The Great Gatsby*.

2. Most recent literary criticism would find the foregoing statement thoroughly shocking: one of its implications, for instance, is that the design on the dust-jacket of a book is effectively a part of the meaning(s) of that book. Yet this should come as no surprise to Fitzgerald scholars, since Fitzgerald has himself stated that he incorporated one of his publisher's dust-jacket designs for *Gatsby* into the novel. Fitzgerald was not only influenced by his publisher's views and requirements, and in fact happy for certain changes to be made which he would not even see before publication; but also at the same time he was deeply concerned about details of the actual book-commodities to be produced—their price, size, binding, and so on—and their advertisement.[4] In fact, I think it's fair to say that Fitzgerald was himself more concerned with marketing his books than he was with the kind of textual details that often preoccupy literary critics. Now this interest of Fitzgerald in the book-commodity may seem incidental to my point, which is indeed that the process of meaning production in reading *necessarily* involves such social forces as class and commodity. Yet the fact that Fitzgerald could apparently move so freely between the supposedly distinct worlds of literacy and commercial production, surely helps to explode the rigidity of this distinction in general. If a dust-jacket can find its way into the writing of a

novel, why shouldn't it find its way into its reading?

3. One last thing about texts: even as a collection of ink marks the 'same' text is different in different books. There are large numbers of differences between texts printed in different editions of *Gatsby*, even excluding retold or edited versions. One famous variation is between 'orgastic' and 'orgiastic' in the penultimate paragraph of the novel; a variation which goes back to a pencil mark inserted in the word 'orgastic' in Fitzgerald's own copy of the first edition of *Gatsby*—although this mark cannot be certainly identified as an 'i', let alone as in Fitzgerald's hand. We might ask where the idea of an 'authoritative text' is left if rewriting goes on after printing. What if a completely 'retold' version of *Gatsby* were now to be found among some lost Fitzgerald papers—would this new version become the 'authoritative' *Gatsby*? I am not trying to make a case for the first edition of a novel being regarded as the authoritative text. I have no interest in the orgastic/orgiastic debate, for instance, except in so far as it is symptomatic of such ideological notions as 'the text', and can be used to reveal this ideology's contrived ignorance of book-commodities. Rather, I merely re-pose the problems of establishing an authoritative text—or we might use the phrase 'authorised version' to more clearly indicate the kind of ideology we are dealing with, as will be seen—as evidence of the inadequacy of such notions to the real processes of literary and commercial production.

The first of the foregoing arguments should offer some support and clarification for my view that a text is only meaningful within a reading context, and the other arguments are for the importance of the book-commodity in this context. They form a negative characterisation of my view of the production of meanings in novels like *Gatsby*. A more positive formulation of this view—and turning now to the importance of social class in reading contexts—can depart from recent work by Renée Balibar on the opposition between 'national French' and 'fictional varieties of French'. English readers will probably be most familiar with Balibar's essay on George Sand's 'The Devil's Pool': an analysis of different versions of the same text (if I may risk such a phrase) designed for different educational levels and purposes.[5] Balibar's point is that the different versions have identifiable ideological functions which are in turn related to definite class positions. These ideas offer difficulties for translation: Balibar's analysis seems to depend to some extent on peculiar features of the French education system. Nevertheless, I will assume that this analysis is broadly applicable to the roles of text-books within the admittedly variable educational subject area of 'English'. This is to assume that in primary education texts are used mainly as a basis for work on language aimed at generating a certain level of access to the national language equally for everybody, and that this level is adjusted to the requirements of a rationalised industrial base for a unified, easily penetrated home market and a linguistically uniform labour market; but that in secondary, and more particularly in higher education, the unified language structure that has thus been produced—and which may be conceptualised as 'la langue'—becomes the basis for work on texts aimed at generating a differentiated access to certain forms of language, and that this difference is adjusted to the requirements of specifically capitalist industrial formations for the cultural legitimation of class difference. This would explain, for instance, why 'English Literature', as opposed to just 'English', has tended to appear as a separate subject only at 'higher' levels in the education system: in Grammar Schools but not Secondary Moderns, at 'O' Level but not C.S.E., and especially in higher education. In this direction, Balibar's work extends towards the sociology of education; and indeed could provide a useful hypothetical framework for empirical investigation of the teaching of English.

In a similar direction, work has already been done on the historical emergence of English Literature as an educational subject—indeed as a new concept—in the second half of the last century.[6] This view points to the change in this period in the actual meaning of the word 'literature': from 'writing in general' towards 'writing which has claim to consideration on the ground of beauty of form or emotional effect' (I will hereafter indicate the latter meaning with a capital 'L'). It is easy to see how English Literature fulfilled the ideological requirements of the new capitalist class, in much the same way as a Classical education had fulfilled the slightly different requirements of aristocracy; and again, historical studies of the decline of classics in higher education in favour of Literature have centred on this very point. This kind of historical and sociological analysis is now well established. My argument here does not seek to go beyond such socio-historical approaches, but rather to lay their foundations, or perhaps more accurately to relocate them. They have in general continued to operate within the terms of ideological notions of 'the reader' and 'the text' because they have sought the social relations of abstract readings, rather than starting from real—I do not mean empirically given—books and readers. This problem is manifested in the extent to which such analysis tends to miss the point that has often preoccupied conventional Literary criticism: that Literature, in general, represents experience, and the study of Literature is one of the few subject areas that can deal in detail with actual experience of everyday life; that it can pose the question 'How should I live?' in such a way that it finally eludes even the social and historical dimensions of the ideology associated with Literature. Confronted with a study of Literature that seeks mainly to identify the complex historical formations which determined the writing of a text, or the 'reading formations' which have shaped its history, I think many more conventional critics would be left with the feeling that such a study, although interesting in itself, has failed to grasp the centre of their reading experience. More importantly, I think it fails to grasp the experience of most people. What is actually required here is an account of how particular Literary books in the context of reading reproduce an ideology which their writers—certainly Fitzgerald—their readers, and even their very semantics would want to or seem to reject. This is why I said earlier that my argument is necessarily hermeneutic, rather than socio-historical; it must deal with reading contexts at a level as it were 'below' such conceptualisations as 'texts' or 'reading formations'. I will argue, in fact, that Literary books are rendered ideological by the pragmatic constraints on the production of meanings in reading contexts: specifically by class and commodity. My argument here will be focussed on moments in reading contexts in which low semantic density requires pragmatic intervention for the production of meaning. 'Semantic density' is a new term for a familiar enough idea. It may be imagined as a scale from empty (literally nonsense) to full (logical propositions, although perhaps finally only in symbolic form); the low areas being occupied by such linguistic phenomena as deictics and figurative language. More specifically, the focus will be on the identifications which can take place in reading contexts between readers and fictional persons, especially, as in *Gatsby*, a first-person narrator—that is, I will consider the deictic function of proper names and pronouns in fiction—and also on the ways in which readers can construe semantic deviance in fiction by calling on pragmatic factors. This will lead finally to consideration of the secondary ideological content—although this part of ideology is often mistaken for the whole—of a scholarly edition of *Gatsby*.

One aspect of reading fiction remarked by theorists as diverse as Paul Ricoeur and Michel Pêcheux is its potential production of a particular subjectivity via a reader's appropriation of a fictional person as a possible way of being in the world.[7] So powerful is this identification reckoned to be that Pêcheux is able to claim that fiction is the linguistic modality in which coincidence is established between the subject and himself, through which he learns his place in the world, or is *subjected*. This can be viewed as a development of Hegelian conceptions of self recognition in recognition of the other; except that in Pêcheux's Althusserian terms such a meeting of pure consciousness is inconceivable, and instead the identification takes place through a language whose meanings, as we have seen, are produced via social relations, including power relations, and the consequent subjectivity is thus always already subjected to those established relations: the subject of a particular society. Perhaps these Hegelian and Althusserian processes are not mutually exclusive, but different stages or forms of socialisation. In any case, Pêcheux traces in some detail the historical development of grammatical persons, especially the first-person, from pre-capitalist discourses in which such persons were interchangeable roles—predicates, we might even say, of actions and processes, and more especially of language itself—to the post-capitalist convergence of persons with 'subjects' in Althusser's sense: precisely the ideological sources of various predications, and of language. In part, as with 'literature', this development was a change in the meaning of the word 'person': the older semantic form surviving precisely in grammatical terminology. Pêcheux's point, which he makes by linking this linguistic development with the emergence of new philosophical ideas, is that the changes apparently taking place in language were actually also changes in the experience of subjectivity itself: changes in what forms of subjection were available. That individuals experience themselves and express themselves as determined by the whole social structure of which they are in turn, as subjects, the crucial support, the primary ideological effect, is the circular foundation of social stability which also at the same time opens up the possibility of revolutionary change. It would be interesting to bring to bear Pêcheux's perspective on the Literary development from 'Everyman' to the most clearly post-capitalist Literary form, the novel. The very specific content of the first person in *Gatsby* must in any case be admitted:

> My father's university was Yale and I went there too. I graduated in 1915 ...

Clearly, the appropriation of an 'I' like this as a possible way of being in the world is a different matter for readers of different classes. This is an aspect of the old—although still valid—complaint about the strangeness to working-class children of the social roles most frequently represented in school textbooks—indeed, I would add, in virtually *all* books. I must say I take it for granted—from my own experience if nothing else—that most working-class children experience almost everything about the education system as monstrously alien, and that this is closely related to their educational 'failure' in comparison to children from middle-class homes.[8] It is a result of the earlier remarked ideological universality of bourgeois culture that this monstrous mistreatment of most children can be seen as the children's own failure. But the point that must be kept in mind here is that the specific role of Literature legitimating class difference depends on this 'failure' of most working-class children to reach 'higher' levels of education, where, precisely, Literature takes on its privileged role. This is why I earlier referred to the ideological content of a scholarly edition of *Gatsby* as 'secondary', despite the fact that such ideological forms are often misunderstood to be the only form of ideology. The mistake is that mentioned earlier of seeing ideology only at the level of representation, whereas in fact ideological representations are of distortions which take place at the level of lived experience: ideology is a function not merely of signifying practices but of all social activity. In this case, as will be seen, it is certainly possible to analyse scholarly essays on *Gatsby* to reveal the systematic distortion characteristic of ideology; but there remains a sense in which this is secondary to the ideological position of Literature as a whole, which is based on just such material arrangements as educational curricula. This means, for instance, that the difference in experience between the fictional first-person and most readers in the retold version of *Gatsby* so far quoted becomes in most versions of *Gatsby* a class difference that has found its way into language itself. But this is not just a question of the language becoming more complex—compare:

I graduated from New Haven in 1915, just a quarter of a century after my father

—rather, the point is that the particular forms of language involved have become ideologically functional; in much the same way as the statement 'There's a fly in my soup', despite its own semantics, realises relations of dominance.[9] Let me give a clearer example of what I mean. If most people were asked to read and summarise the two pages or so that precede the sentence just quoted in most versions of *Gatsby*, then I think they would say something very similar to the first paragraph of the retold *Gatsby* quoted earlier. This is not surprising: the retold version is, precisely, a kind of summary.[10] But having said this most Literary critics would want immediately to point to semantic and cultural values in most versions of *Gatsby* that for various reasons escape summary: what, they would for example ask, about Fitzgerald's *style?* I, however, want to point instead to the way in which such 'values' are in fact the inverse of a wider lack of value, because within most reading contexts the forms of language involved are loaded with pragmatic reference to the socially differentiated access to these very forms of language. Interestingly enough, this pragmatic reference takes place most clearly with unfamiliar vocabulary, which should of course be literally (semantically) meaningless—the fact that we might be able to derive some meaning from context, etc., does not affect the point I am making. Most people are a little unwilling to admit they don't know the meaning of a word, there is a certain shame attached to this, for what we do know, at least in most broadly educational situations, is that somebody does know the meaning, and perhaps we ought to know it too. Thus the very meaninglessness, for us, refers to educational or cultural inequality, and hence to class difference. It should be clear by now, furthermore, that all Literary books—this is overwhelmingly what defines them *as* Literature—carry with them their own educational and cultural context, of which a reader is usually reminded by words such as 'Penguin Modern Classics', or the reproduction of a painting by Kees Van Dongen on the cover.

I have here reached the very centre of my argument. The reading of Literature is an activity almost everywhere saturated with the absence of all those who do not read it. Literary value is one side of an exclusive coin: a currency of class difference. Nor can it be made less exclusive without prejudice to Literature itself; for let me emphasise here again my view of Literature not as a matter of theoretical taxonomy, or any kind of analysis of intrinsic differences between texts, but rather as a material category, as an educational subject or bookshop section, as defined by practical relations which again precede, even while they depend on, signifying practices. It may be objected that even given such a social definition there are differences between texts on which their categorisation must at some point depend; but I would argue that to focus on such differences is always to play into ideological hands. The publishing industry is acutely aware of how the smallest details of a book's format can place it in Literary or, say, 'Popular Fiction' markets—I hope elsewhere to show how *Gatsby* has at times, and sometimes at the same time, appeared in both of these—yet, to repeat, most Literary critics remain wilfully ignorant of the ways in which these details of the book-commodity affect the 'text' they are so fond of.

I believe unfamiliar vocabulary is one of the clearest examples of pragmatic reference because it features one of the lowest possible semantic densities. This demands a historical-materialistic approach because at such points of disappearance the systematicity of language, its wider social determinants assert themselves most clearly. Pêcheux acknowledges this by theorising such language phenomena as 'definite non-communication' whose function is to 'impose class barriers inside language'. He goes on to relate the low semantic density associated with figurative language to the general requirements of capitalism: the requirement of mechanisation and standardisation for 'unambiguous *communication*—"logical" clarity of instructions and directives, aptness of terms used, etc.,'; which is also at the same time a requirement for '*non-communication* separating the workers from the organisation of production and making them subject to the "rhetoric" of authority.'[11] The low semantic density of such rhetoric leads to non-communication that nevertheless has a pragmatic function, and this may be viewed as an aspect of a general tendency for capitalism to remove social distinctions from the linguistic system into more pragmatic aspects of communicative situations.[12]

Pêcheux's specific point is that the classical distinction between logic and rhetoric becomes functional, in response to the emergent contradiction between mode and relations of production, in the form of the communication/non-communication pair. Now the most important consequence within language of this fundamental contradiction between mode and relations of production is of course the simultaneous appearance of both a common language and a socially differentiated language. The importance of the development of Literature for the imposition of class barriers within the apparently common language has already been emphasised. In addition, Pêcheux's comments on rhetoric remind us that attempts to define specifically Literary language have often focussed on the supposedly high figurative content of Literary discourse. Indeed, it is figurative language that is most obviously absent from the retold *Gatsby*; while analysis of the Literary-critical essays included in a scholarly edition—I refer here to the Scribner Research Anthology *Gatsby*—reveals an overwhelming focus on passages with a high figurative content.[13] We are here talking about a Literature at the heart of which is the contradiction of a language which must both tell the truth and simultaneously conceal it—that is, we are talking about the ideological subject area of Literature—and a glance through the Literary-critical material included in the Scribner Research Anthology *Gatsby*—and therefore included in the reading context of this edition of the novel—quickly reveals that what we call 'interpretation' under capitalism is rather the attempt by a handful of academics, under the aegis of the publishing industry, to fill out the sparse semantic structure of a few chosen passages with the comparatively dense content of Literary ideology.

I will use as an example here what is probably the most celebrated of such Literary passages in *Gatsby:* the first two paragraphs of Chapter Two, about the valley of ashes and the eyes of Doctor Eckleburg. Given my previous remarks, something of the 'Literariness' of this passage seems to be indicated by the fact that it can be summarised, in the retold *Gatsby*, in the single sentence: 'It was an ugly place'. Eckleburg's eyes themselves are thus completely absent from this version. In other versions, furthermore, the passage is marked by its use of the second-person form:

> But above the gray land and the spasms of bleak dust which drift endlessly over it, you perceive, after a moment, the eyes of Doctor T.J. Eckleburg.

This is one of only two uses—that is, outside direct speech—in *Gatsby;* the other being in the opening passage of Chapter Four—the list of those who attended Gatsby's parties—which has also been the subject of much debate by Literary critics and, I suspect, much skimming by most readers. A better understanding of the specific links between the figurative and deictic language and its Literary significance can be gained by the application here of Paul Ricoeur's theorisation of metaphor, etc.[14] Ricoeur rejects the Aristotelian (and post-structuralist) view of metaphor as epiphora of the name. Instead, he describes metaphor phenomenologically as a series of moments, the first of which is a semantic clash in which 'meaning abolishes itself'. This is the moment of low semantic density that I believe is similar to unfamiliar vocabulary and the appearance of deictics in fiction. However, according to Ricoeur this semantic ebb in metaphor is merely the negative condition for a productive process of semantic construal, via which the reader 'makes sense' of the metaphorical phrase. It is no accident that 'the reader' should enter at this point in my account. Ricoeur's main concern is with what happens to *reference* during these semantic changes: he believes that because at each moment we try to refer meaning to our experience of the world, when we construe metaphors etc. we also produce new ways of seeing the world. This will immediately be seen as a most important point for those who still want to find some specific 'value' in figurative discourse or in Literature. But what must not be overlooked here is that Ricoeur's theory is basically 'epistemological': in practice, not all readers in all situations can deal equally with low semantic density, and this inequality is, again, structural—built into capitalist educational and cultural formations. Even for students of Literature the low semantic density is experienced as difficult, and—this will come as no surprise to teachers in higher education—is often dealt with only with the help of Literary criticism. At this point we must reject a model of education which even Balibar and Pêcheux, but perhaps more particularly Basil Bernstein, have been guilty of perpetuating.[15] It is not a question of leaving the majority 'inside' ideologically motivated language while educating an elite to manipulate such language from the outside. On the contrary, 'educated people' are nowadays mainly middle-class—professional or managerial—rather than the kind of ruling class Marx had in mind, which really did privately own social wealth, and thus had an overwhelming material interest in its own elitism. Higher education in these conditions cannot be expected to encourage 'free' thinking beyond certain 'disciplines'. In fact, the study of Literature ends largely by enabling students to introduce Literary-critical constraints into all reading contexts—an activity lately enshrined in post-structuralism. Such practice has the double ideological structure of middle-class experience: it is exclusive in itself, but it tends to operate with meanings that would support a much more material privilege. Nor is it open to us here to locate the inequality within capitalism but not within Literature, thus leaving intact the pure positivity of whatever insights Literature has to offer. For the point is that these very insights—even when they shed light on injustice itself—have been made constitutive of privilege. The attempt to preserve Literature as a positive value in the face of capitalism has been typical of Literary critics of all political persuasions. I think this depends on the divorce of 'the text' and 'the reader' from real books and readers, that is on a contrived ignorance of literary pragmatics the extent of which indicates the pervasiveness of a Literary ideology which, by this very contrivance, subsumes such politics. Thus although it may be possible to construct a context in which the Eckleburg figure might fulfill its Ricoeurian potential, and disrupt ideology, such a context is decidedly not provided within the material category of Literature—and indeed is only to be provided via changes that are in part material themselves: in the education system and more especially, as will be seen, in the publishing industry. Without such social change, what Ricoeur posits as a pure 'epoche' of figurative discourse, a utopian moment awaiting the freely productive process of semantic construal, becomes instead a moment filled in advance by Literary ideology; the freedom to produce becomes precisely the 'freedom' of the capitalist labour contract.[16]

We should look here at the way in which the Literary-critical essays in the Scribner Anthology do in fact deal with the Eckleburg passage. Daniel Schneider's view is typical:

> Fitzgerald wants us to view T.J. Eckleburg as a symbol of the corruption of spirit in the Waste Land—as if even God has been violated by materialism and hucksterism—reduced to an advertisement.

Literature as a spiritual preserve, critically detached from commercial processes like advertising—the Literary ideology I am describing could not be clearer than here.[17] First, Schneider relies on ideas of capitalism most comfortable for the middle class, which would connect exploitation with consumption rather than production. This goes back to economic ideas around in Marx's time, which saw profit as the result of clever or underhand salesmanship. In fact, however, the sharp end of capitalism points not so much at consumers, but at workers. But moreover, Schneider can see Eckleburg as a criticism of capitalist marketing and consumerism only via the connection of Literature with 'spirit', or its disconnection from its own equally capitalist production, marketing and consumption. This opens up a superb irony at the heart of Schneider's view: as mentioned earlier, Fitzgerald has said that the idea for Eckelburg came not from an actual billboard, but from his book's own dust-jacket. This is just too much for Arthur Mizener:

> The dust-jacket was not, of course, the real source of that symbol, but it was the only source Fitzgerald consciously understood, and he was hardly more aware of his literary sources. Gilbert Seldes said that the book was written in 'a series of scenes, a method which Fitzgerald had learnt from Henry James through Mrs. Wharton'; and Seldes had talked to Fitzgerald about the book.[18]

The focus on 'sources' here reflects an aspect of Literary ideology that is fully represented in the Scribner Anthology. Its Preface, Introduction, Part One—and 'authoritative' text of *Gatsby*—Part Two—'Intention and Genesis: The Author's View'—and its guides to research at the back, all deal substantially with the idea of sources. The first page of the book not given over to titles, etc., is in fact a facsimile of a manuscript page of *Gatsby*. This ought to raise the question of the relationship of a commercially produced book to the author's activity of composition, a particularly interesting relationship in Fitzgerald's case, given his own active interest in the book-commodity. But the Scribner Anthology glosses over this potentially uncomfortable area by attaching the origin of the text to an actually transcendent idea of 'Fitzgerald', whose hand-writing (artisanal) work is naturally prior to and untouched by its marketing, and who is in any case protected by an established mythology of the-poet-in-his-garret. The very first paragraph of the 'Introduction' of the Scribner Anthology is instructive here:

> Shortly before his death, in 1940, F. Scott Fitzgerald had the humiliating experience of walking into a large city bookstore and finding that none of his books were carried in stock and his name had been forgotten. But since then things have changed. The emergence of *The Great Gatsby* from a position of comparative obscurity a generation ago to its present position as a modern classic is one of the most remarkable events in recent American literary history. According to a recent *New York Times* report on paperback sales, more people are buying *The Great Gatsby* today than any novel by any writer of Fitzgerald's generation, including Faulkner and Hemingway.

This at least has the honesty to explicitly connect the Literary text with the workaday world of bookselling; but the full implications of this connection are glossed by a number of ideological elements: (1) the construction of 'Fitzgerald' as the familiar garret figure—genius misunderstood and ignored in its own time; (2) the application of value-free and motive-free vocabulary—'things have changed', 'one of the most remarkable events'—to historical processes that were actually largely controlled by the publishing industry, as will be seen; and (3) the presentation of a familiar model of marketing in which the consumer is in sole control, in which Scribner's own advertising, for instance, is merely the provision of innocent information. Fitzgerald, the unacknowledged (and thus moreover unmarketed) genius of those bad old days has become, as is the right and natural way of things, just what the public wants! Such an ideological fiction should be viewed alongside the actually much stranger facts.

The Fitzgerald revival of the late 1940s and early '50s did not merely appear remarkable in the retrospect of the 1970 Scribner Anthology—it was the subject of contemporary Literary-critical debate. Martin Shockley (*Arizona Quarterly*, Summer 1954) saw it as

> a calculated campaign ... which not only successfully revived an almost forgotten minor novelist but approached the proportions of a literary hoax.[19]

Such judgements, by no means uncommon at the time, now seem farfetched. The position of *Gatsby* in the Literary canon now seems perfectly natural: the social processes that continually produce such Literature have achieved the naturalness of ideology. In fact, however, a periodic revival of interest in back-list authors is of key economic importance to many publishers, who might well view the frequently posited ability of true Literature to transcend its own time as an ideal means of long-term market development, complementary to the more immediate market penetration of 'best-sellers'; and it is easy to trace during the 1940s a commercial exchange between media interest and new publications which largely determined the Fitzgerald revival. Now the central events of this revival are usually regarded as the publication of 1945 of *The Crack-up* and *The Portable F. Scott Fitzgerald*—a piece of back-list refurbishment typical of its time. I would add here the New Directions edition of *Gatsby*—also published in 1945—with its influential introduction by Lionel Trilling, a version of which later appeared in his aptly titled *Liberal Imagination*. However, Jackson Bryer's bibliographical work can be read to reveal that these books in turn owed their publication to the media interest already aroused by Fitzgerald's death—or I should rather say on the occasion of his death, because I think the media response was not so much to the death itself as to a mythologised version of it.[20] Bryer points out that between 1934—the publication of *Tender is the Night* and the Modern Library *Gatsby*—and his death in December 1940, Fitzgerald was 'generally ignored'; but in the first three months of 1941 some 30 newspaper editorials and 13 articles on him appeared. Why did the death of such an 'almost forgotten minor novelist' become a media event in this way? Precisely, I would argue, because by dying in relative obscurity at the age of 44 Fitzgerald seemed to fulfill the already outlined mythology of thepoet-in-his-garret. Fitzgerald had of course been something of a media figure in the 1920s, and a marketable nostalgia for the excesses of that period was possible now given the very different conditions of the planned economy of the New Deal and Second World War. The tone of Trilling's 1945 'Introduction' is elegaic; but the lament seems not so much over Fitzgerald, but things much more suggestive to a liberal's imagination:

> Fitzgerald was perhaps the last notable writer to affirm the Romantic fantasy, descended from the Renaissance, of personal ambition and heroism, of life committed to, or thrown away for, some ideal of self. To us it will no doubt come more and more to seem a merely boyish dream; the nature of our society requires the young man to find distinction through co-operation, subordination, and an expressed piety of social usefulness.[21]

In these conditions, remembering perhaps Fitzgerald's own invocation of the consumptive Romantic poet Keats—for instance in *Tender is the Night*—and also perhaps the now inescapably autobiographical elements of the 'Crack-up' stories—already published in *Esquire*—Fitzgerald's life and death must have seemed to newspapermen too good a 'human interest' story to be missed. Never mind if it was also too good to be true. And Scribners were not slow off the same mark, as they rushed publication in 1941 of the suggestively unfinished *Last Tycoon*.

It should not be surprising, by now, that a significant role must be assigned to the publishing industry in the establishment of Fitzgerald as a Literary figure—a phrase which might, in view of the ideas of 'Fitzgerald' we are dealing with, be understood in its rhetorical sense. But this is a far cry from the view of the Fitzgerald revival as some kind of natural process, which was implied by the Scribner Anthology 'Introduction'. Nor is there much evidence that Literary critics, or valuation by any specifically Literary criteria, played a part in this revival. *The Last Tycoon* attracted some favourable reviews, but before 1945 really very few Literary-critical essays on Fitzgerald appeared, and most of those that did were fairly dismissive.[22] Even the influence of Trilling's 1945 'Introduction' depended largely on the fact that it was, precisely, an introduction to an important new edition of *Gatsby*—the publication of which had therefore been previously determined. The first book on Fitzgerald was Mizener's biography in 1951, by which time *Gatsby* was in any case popular enough to justify a Penguin paperback edition. I am not arguing that Literary criticism has no significance, but that Literature is a category finally controlled by the publishing industry, and Literary criticism has an ideological role within this control. Particular commercial practices in publishing businesses form probably the most important mediation of the general relationship between culture and economy.

Thus when Mizener employs the transcendent idea of 'Fitzgerald' mentioned earlier, he does so within the context of a wider Fitzgerald myth developed over the previous ten years: a myth propagated by the publishing industry precisely, we might be forgiven for concluding, in order to disguise that industry's economic interest in Literature. Similarly, Mizener will not accept commercial art work—he revealingly judges the dust-jacket design in question 'a very bad picture'—as inspiration for Eckleburg. No doubt he would have preferred Kees Van Dongen. The whole force of Mizener's previously quoted remarks on Eckleburg is to place the source of the symbol outside even Fitzgerald's consciousness; indeed, as nothing at all positive is said about this mysterious source, we seem to be left with the impression that it lies in some hardly to be grasped region, outside both of discourse and the rest of the world. This Fitzgerald is, in fact, a kind of 'transcendental signified'! How delighted Derrida would be to discover that Mizener, having denied Fitzgerald's own *written* account of this inspiration for Eckleburg, ends up with evidence from Seldes who, it is assumed, must be right because 'he had *talked* to Fitzgerald about the book' (my emphasis). But this is not really a question of the logocentrism of Western philosophy: this validation of speech over writing, of hand-writing over printing, and—to refer to the Scribner Anthology's research guides—of 'primary' over 'secondary' sources, has much more to do with such similar ideological constructions as the 'authoritative text' and the 'Fitzgerald myth'. Now although I have perhaps used the idea of Literary ideology loosely—and anyone abreast of the current debate on ideology will recognise the difficulty of achieving any precision here—my approach has been broadly Althusserian; and within this— although again it is a point that Althusser himself does not develop—the general idea of the Literary Source may be seen as a version of the Althusserian Subject, which via the representative structure of Literature conditions the particular subjectivity of the (abstract) reader.[23] In this way, the twin notions of 'the reader' and 'the text', which I began by pushing towards classes of readers on the one hand and book-commodities on the other, become rather interdependent effects of the whole structure of Literary ideology—just as, in fact, the realities of class and commodity are different manifestations of the single form of value which dominates capitalist production.

These broad relations are again mediated by specific social practices. The idea of the Source is connected with labour and commodity markets via the practice of Literary criticism in higher education. With its research guides and biographical introductions to each essay, which always give first mention to academic posts held by critics, the Scribner Anthology is clearly aimed at the production of *Gatsby* as—so it says in the 'Introduction'—'a modern classic'—deserving of a place on higher educational curricula. The continual return to the Source helps divorce the book-commodity from the object of Literary-critical enquiry, both of which—the enquiry and its object—appear as prior to and outside of the market; and this purity of criticism is parallel to the professional purity of the academic critic. The whole idea of 'professionalism' disguises capitalist relations of production: it thus comes as quite a shock to teachers forced to protect their living standards by taking industrial action, or to those facing redundancy, that they don't seem to have a vocation at all—just a job. And of course, Literary ideology here affects not only the academic labour market, but the commodity market as well, both because the object of critical enquiry ends up on educational curricula, which are seen as key vehicles of market penetration and development in bookselling, and also because a text whose source is completely outside of the world, forever mysterious, itself becomes endlessly reproducible; itself an endless source of new books. In this light, the attitude of a friend of mine to buying books—'No thanks, I've already got one'—takes on a less comic significance. From the point of view of production a book is an ideal commodity, and a glance at current production figures quickly reveals the scale of the industry involved.[24] Guy Dubord creates the correct perspective:

> Culture turned completely into commodity must also turn into the star commodity of the spectacular society ... The complex process of production, distribution and consumption of *knowledge* already gets 29% of the yearly national product of the United States ... In the second half of this century culture will hold the key role in the development of the economy, a role played by the automobile in the first half.[25]

The social superstructure is transforming itself into the industrial base. And I think Literature has a kind of advanced standing as commodified culture and knowledge—a standing indicated, perhaps, by the post-structuralist tendency to apply basically Literary-critical standards to other disciplines. The study of literary pragmatics, on the contrary, must dissolve these very standards, must focus not on the textuality of the world, or on the universality of reading, but precisely on the inadequacy of such notions as the text and the reader to the world as it is.

In this study I have glanced briefly in a number of directions: towards education, and its reproduction of class differences within culture; to the effects of books as commodities; the secondary ideological effects of Literary-criticism; and towards the central importance of the publishing industry in all of this. But the most important point is the old marxist stand-by: we cannot know the world without changing it. I believe it is a central implication of literary pragmatics that ideology is at present built into all actual experience of Literature. If we seriously want to tell the truth about novels like *Gatsby*, we have to begin by changing the real social conditions that make distortion inevitable.

I am reminded of Gatsby's library, where the pages of the books were left un-cut. As early as 1899 Thorstein Veblen could point out that long after cheaper books were produced with chopped pages, certain elite publications retained the hand-cut look.[26] By the 1920s, therefore, the fact that Gatsby had not cut the pages must have seemed secondary to the fact that he had invested in books 'exclusive' enough to need such cutting. An advertisement for a book-club edition of *Gatsby* asks

Just think how beautiful these books will look on your shelves with their rich burgundy red bindings and golden blocking.

These, too, are literary pragmatics. Typically, most Literary critics fix on the point that Gatsby could not have read his books—that his culture was an empty, if successful, gesture—and miss entirely the more important point that even if he had read them they would still reflect elitism, still reproduce class difference. Indeed, they would have filled this difference with ideological certainty.

Notes

1. See, for instance, Leech, Geoffrey, *Semantics*, Penguin, Harmondsworth, 1981, passim.

2. See Thompson, J.B., *Studies in the Theory of Ideology*, Polity Press, Oxford, 1984, especially Chapter Three. Althusser's main work on ideology has been collected in Althusser, Louis, *Essays on Ideology*, Verso, London, 1984.

3. Fitzgerald, F. Scott *The Great Gatsby*, retold by Margaret Tarner, illustrated by Kay Mary Wilson, Heinemann Guided Readers, London, 1979.

4. Most of the basic evidence can be found in the following: Bruccoli, Matthew, *Apparatus for The Great Gatsby*, University of South Carolina Press, Columbia, 1974, pp. 118–119; Mizener, Arthur, *The Far Side of Paradise*, Vintage Books, New York, 1959, p. 186; Turnbull, Andrew, (ed.) *The Letters of F. Scott Fitzgerald*, Penguin, Harmondsworth, 1968. Perhaps the following lengthy quotation is justified here.

> I should suggest the following contract.
> 15% up to 50,000
> 20% after 50,000
> The book is only a little over fifty thousand words long but I believe, as you know, that Whitney Darrow has the wrong psychology about prices (and about what class constitute the book-buying public now that the lowbrows go to the movies) and I'm anxious to charge two dollars for it and have it a *full-size* book.
> Of course I want the binding to be absolutely uniform with my other books—the stamping too—and the jacket we discussed before. This time I don't want any signed blurbs on the jacket—not Mencken's or Lewis' or Howard's or anyone's. I'm tired of being the author of *This Side of Paradise* and I want to start over.
> About serialization ...
> (Letter to Max Perkins of Scribners, October 27th 1924).

5. Balibar, Renée, 'An Example of Literary Work in France,' in Barker et al, *1848: The Sociology of Literature*, University of Essex, 1978.

6. See, for instance, Davies, Tony, 'Education, Ideology and Literature', in *Red Letters*, 7, 1978, pp. 4–13. Work in this field is also discussed in Bennett, Tony, *Formalism and Marxism*, Metheun, London, 1979.

7. Ricoeur, Paul, *Interpretation Theory*, Texas Christian University Press, Fort Worth, 1976; Pêcheux, Michel, *Language, Semantics and Ideology*, Macmillan, London, 1982.

8. See, for instance, Keddie, Nell, (ed.) *Tinker, Tailor*, Penguin, Harmondsworth, 1973. In my view the recent trend towards 'non-sexist' and 'non-racist' children's books has often made this situation worse because such social concerns can be, and usually are, pursued only within certain class interests.

9. It is useful to bear in mind the work of William Labov when thinking about the varying 'complexity' of language. For instance Labov, William, 'The Logic of Nonstandard English', in Keddie (1973) op. cit., pp. 21–66; also in Giglioli, P.P., (ed.) *Language and Social Context*, Penguin, Harmondsworth, 1982, pp. 179–215.

10. Such summary will usually pick out elements important to the *narrative*—which Literary criticism has tended to ignore. This point deserves to be investigated further, but I would not

expect it to affect my conclusions here.

11. Pêcheux (1982) op cit., p. 10.

12. This tendency has been remarked by linguists. See for instance Brown, R. and Gilman, A., 'The Pronouns of Power and Solidarity', in Giglioli (1982) op. cit., pp. 252–282.

13. Piper, Henry Dan, (ed.) *Fitzgerald's 'The Great Gatsby': The Novel, The Critics, The Background*, Scribner Research Anthology, New York, 1970. My research indicates that in this book the three most frequent discussed passages in *Gatsby* are: (1) the opening paragraphs of Chapter Two; (2) the last three of four paragraphs of the novel; and (3) the short passage in Chapter Seven centred on Gatsby's remark that Daisy's voice is full of money.

14. See especially Ricoeur, Paul, *The Rule of Metaphor*, R.K.P., London, 1978.

15. I am sensitive to the widespread misrepresentation of Bernstein's work over the last decade or so, but I stand by my statement here as an implication of, for instance, the following.

> Where codes are elaborated, the socialized has more access to the grounds of his own socialization, and so can enter into a reflexive relationship to the social order he has taken over. Where codes are restricted, the socialized has less access to the grounds of his socialization, and thus reflexiveness may be limited in range. One of the effects of the class system is to limit access to elaborated codes. Bernstein, Basil, 'Social Class, Language and Socialization', in Giglioli (1982) op. cit., p. 164.

16. For some this will raise the question of whether prosaic statement, for instance of political arguments, is preferable to figurative content in literature. I must say I believe it is, although I have no great hopes either for its acceptance as 'Literature', or for its social efficacy: Literature as it appears today, as it is materially determined in advanced capitalist societies, is far too removed from such consequences.

17. Schneider, Daniel, 'Colour-Symbolism in *The Great Gatsby*', in Piper (1970) op. cit., p. 147.

18. Mizener, Arthur, '*The Great Gatsby*', in Piper (1970) op. cit., p. 128.

19. Quoted in Bryer, Jackson, *Sixteen Modern American Authors*, Norton, New York, 1973, p. 229.

20. On this see especially Bryer, Jackson, *The Critical Reputation of F. Scott Fitzgerald*, Archon Books, 1967.

21. Trilling, Lionel, *The Liberal Imagination*, Penguin, Harmondsworth, 1970, p. 249.

22. See again Bryer, op. cit., Notes 27 and 28.

23. For the idea of the Subject/subject of ideology see Althusser (1984) op. cit., pp. 52–56.

24. In 1970 for instance over 33,000 new titles were published in Britain alone, and over £150 million spent internationally on British publications. See Laing, Stuart, 'The Production of Literature', in Sinfield, A., (ed.) *The Context of English Literature*, Methuen, London, 1983. Laing also points out that most publishing is now controlled by multinational companies with diverse interests. The British publishers of *Gatsby* I have mentioned here, for instance, are Heinemann, owned by the transport company Tillings, and Penguin, owned by Longman Pearson, whose main interests lie in banking and the media.

25. Debord, Guy, *Society of the Spectacle*, Black and Red, Detroit, 1973, paragraph 193.

26. Veblen, Thorstein, *The Theory of the Leisure Class*, Unwin, London, 1970, pp. 116, 117.

101
'The Self-Same Song that Found a Path': Keats and *The Great Gatsby*

◆

DAN McCALL

F. Scott Fitzgerald's favorite author was John Keats. Of the "Ode on a Grecian Urn" Fitzgerald wrote, "I suppose I've read it a hundred times. About the tenth time I began to know what it was about, and caught the chime in it and the exquisite inner mechanics. Likewise with the 'Nightingale' which I can never read without tears in my eyes." And "The Eve of St. Agnes" has "the richest, most sensuous imagery in English, nor excepting Shakespeare."[1]

Even without such an explicit statement from Fitzgerald, we might assume Keats meant something like that to him. In *This Side of Paradise* (II, ii), Amory Blaine declaims "the 'Ode to a Nightingale' to the bushes" and then talks about poetry, distinguishing between Keats and himself on what each finds "primarily beautiful." In the opening chapter of *The Great Gatsby* there is a nightingale singing in the Buchanan yard, the "very romantic outdoors." Several scenes in *Gatsby* take place in starlit nights; it is there that we so often see the title figure in his most characteristic pose, and it is the pose of the speaker in the Keats lyric: the man under the wandering stars who wants to comprehend and join his life to a precious being of eternal beauty. Fitzgerald quite consciously draws upon Keats's language; near the end of the fifth chapter, "there was no light save what the gleaming floor bounced in from the hall" is clearly an echo of Keats's phrase in the "Nightingale": "there is no light, / Save what from heaven is with the breezes blown...." And another line from that poem will provide the title for Fitzgerald's most ambitious work, *Tender Is the Night*.

Keats's influence on *The Great Gatsby* should not be understood exclusively in the terms of "literary imitation."[2] The distinguishing and compli-

SOURCE *American Literature* XLIV, November 1970, pp. 521–530.

cated similarity is in a realization of the ambivalence of beauty. Lionel Trilling has suggested in his essay on "The Fate of Pleasure" that Keats is our greatest poet of pleasure, that Keats understood pleasure with a greater intensity than any other figure in our literature.[3] There is a preoccupation in both Keats and Fitzgerald with the saturation of sense in beakers of wine, "the purple-stainéd mouth." Yet the traditional intoxicant to make us forget the world's pain is not heady enough; the effort is to confront a kind of total beauty in an exalted moment, where all the senses are throbbingly alive and "thou art pouring forth thy soul abroad / In such an ecstasy!" Fitzgerald wrote of the happiest moment of his life that he was "riding in a taxi one afternoon between very tall buildings under a mauve and rosy sky; I began to bawl because I had everything I wanted and knew I would never be so happy again."[4] The surrounding force of a real world will not allow the moment to be sustained. The "real" world—real by virtue of its oppressiveness—denies the existence in time of the ecstatic exaltation. When Nick Carraway says you can't repeat the past, Gatsby cries out "incredulously," "Can't repeat the past? Why of course you can!" And he looks "around him wildly, as if the past were lurking here in the shadow of his house, just out of reach of his hand." What he must touch, what all his money is intended to buy back, is the moment of joy on an autumn night five years previously when he had kissed Daisy and "wed his unutterable visions to her perishable breath." Gatsby is trying to escape time and "return to a certain starting place." Keats surrounds his joy of the nightingale's song with the bitter temporal world which renders the dream powerless because "Beauty cannot keep her lustrous eyes." Both Keats and Fitzgerald posit an idea of the beautiful moment, testing it and understanding it against the forces of time.

But there is finally a drastic contradiction in the beautiful moment itself. In the poetry of Keats and in *The Great Gatsby*, the greatest threat of all may come not from the outside, that cold rude world, but from an overabundance of the beautiful. In *Lamia* Keats writes that "Love in a palace is perhaps at last / More grievous torment than a hermit's fast." And in the "Ode on Melancholy,"

> *Pleasure nigh,*
> *Turning to poison while the bee-mouth sips:*
> *Ay, in the very temple of Delight*
> *Veiled Melancholy has her sovran shrine....*

From the impulse to beauty, the visionary figure passes from dream to dream, finds himself "too happy in thine happiness," and becomes "half in love with easeful death." In the work of Keats the love of beauty becomes so intense, wrought to such a pitch, that it becomes almost indistinguishable from pain. Complete fulfillment is death. At the beginning of Fitzgerald's career he wrote that Amory Blaine's romantic commitment to beauty was an "overwhelming desire ... to sink safely and sensuously out of sight" into "that long chute of indulgence which led, after all, only to the artificial lake of death."[5]

When Nick Carraway recounts the story of Gatsby's kissing Daisy he is "reminded of something—an elusive rhythm, a fragment of lost words, that I heard somewhere a long time ago." Perhaps on the Eve of St. Agnes. Both Keats's poem and Fitzgerald's novel are drenched in a spirit of ancient revelry. Keats's palace is the ancestral home of Gatsby's mansion where "The silver, snarling trumpets 'gan to chide: / The level chambers, ready with their pride, ... glowing to receive a thousand guests...." Keat's hero partakes of the "magical glory" that Gatsby will; on the Eve of St. Agnes young Porphyro stands the way Gatsby later will stand, "with heart on fire ... beside the portal doors, / Buttressed from moonlight" imploring "all saints to give him sight of" his beloved. Porphyro's fondest wish will become Gatsby's: "that he might gaze and worship all unseen; / Perchance speak, kneel, touch, and kiss ..." We get the lush exotic feel of gorgeous gifts from foreign places that the lover brings to his lady. In chapter five of *Gatsby*, after the tea party at Carraway's house in West Egg, the trio of Jay and Daisy and Nick wander over to Gatsby's mansion. In his "own apartment" Gatsby

> took out a pile of shirts and began throwing them, one by one, before us, shirts of sheer linen and thick silk and fine flannel, which lost their folds as they fell and covered the table in many-colored disarray. While we admired he brought more and the soft rich heap mounted higher—shirts with stripes and scrolls and plaids in coral and apple-green and lavender and faint orange, with monograms of Indian blue. Suddenly, with a strained sound, Daisy bent her head into the shirts and began to cry stormily.
> "They're such beautiful shirts," she sobbed, her voice muffled in the thick folds. "It makes me sad because I've never seen such—beautiful shirts before."

In "The Eve of St. Agnes" Madeline dreams in an "azure-lidded sleep, / In blanchéd linen, smooth and lavendered" when her suitor "from forth the closet brought a heap" of

> *Candied apple, quince, and plum, and gourd;*
> *With jellies soother than the creamy curd,*
> *And lucent syrops, tinct with cinnamon;*
> *Manna and dates, in argosy transferred*
> *From Fez; and spicéd dainties, every one,*
> *From silken Samarcand to cedared Lebanon.*

When all "these delicates he heaped with glowing hand" on bright baskets and golden dishes he plays upon "her hollow lute" and— as Daisy wept into Gatsby's shirts—so, in the Keats poem, "fair Madeline began to weep" at the tune proclaimed "every sweetest vow."

Henry Dan Piper, in *F. Scott Fitzgerald: A Critical Portrait*, has suggested that the Keats stanza is echoed in the third chapter of *Gatsby*, the presentation of the refreshments at Gatsby's first party.[6] It is true that there we can see Fitzgerald consciously imitating the poet's description of sweetmeats; Fitzgerald's adjectives have a richness ("garnished," "glistening," "spiced") that Keats's do ("candied," lucent," "silken," and, again, "spiced."). But the more resonant echo is perhaps the less consciously imitative one, the scene with the shirts and Daisy. There Fitzgerald is not just drawing up a menu which indicates that he had a copy of his Keats open beside him; he modulates the whole emotional importance of the moment, the meaning of the foreign treasures to the young man and woman, and the intense feeling that the objects stand for an occasion in their minds. The pervasive influence of Keats upon Fitzgerald will not be adequately understood if we confine ourselves to the abundant technical similarities and ironic imitations that Fitzgerald made of any particular Keats passage; these surface similarities are expressions of the fact that Keats's work touched Fitzgerald at the deepest reaches of his ideas and emotions.

The lovers, Porphyro and Gatsby, are both "famished pilgrims" who seek to be "saved by miracle." There is a religious quality to their service: just as Porphyro proclaims "Thou art my heaven, and I thine eremite" so Gatsby seeks through Daisy to go "to a secret place above the trees" and by kissing her "forever wed his unutterable visions to her perishable breath." At the very moment of the kiss she might blossom for him "like a flower and the incarnation" could be "complete." Porphyro and Gatsby come from afar to the inaccessible saintly girl—"high in a white palace the king's daughter, the golden girl"—and seek by strategy, by gifts, and by devotion to take her away forever into a land of sensuous delight and eternal, abiding love.

In the "Ode to a Nightingale" the speaker is alone with his desire, listening to the haunting music of the lovely presence; the devotion to the ideal beauty is so intense that the young man is blinded to the lesser things around him:

> *I cannot see what flowers are at my feet,*
> *Nor what soft incense hangs upon the boughs,*
> *But, in embalmèd darkness, guess each sweet. . . .*

The same emotion and echoes of that language persist in *Gatsby*. Both Keats and Fitzgerald are able to impart an opulent sensuous surface to their writings, and they are at their very best when the imagery is chiefly visual, though other senses are often called upon to deepen and enrich the appeal. One of Keats's finest technical accomplishments was his rich and subtle presentation of one sensory experience in terms of another: wine tastes of color and sound. Similarly in *The Great Gatsby* Fitzgerald writes of "yellow cocktail music."

Fitzgerald's use of technique in *The Great Gatsby* reflects a general cultural urge which his visionary bootlegger represents. One of the most difficult things to account for in the novel is the content of Gatsby's vision—to account, that is, for its imaginative power, the sheer thrill of it and the dangerous dark attraction it has for us. We know that the actual mechanics of a moneyed empire did not engage Fitzgerald. Max Perkins was terrifically enthusiastic about the manuscript that Fitzgerald had sent him from St. Raphael in the fall of 1924, but Perkins had some objections mainly to the figure of Gatsby himself and to the nature of his wealth. Perkins wrote back,

> Now almost all readers numerically are going to be puzzled by his having all this wealth, and are going to feel entitled to an explanation. To give a distinct and definite one would be, of course, utterly absurd. It did occur to me, though, that you might here and there interpolate some phrases, and possibly incidents, little touches of various kinds, that might suggest that he was in some active way mysteriously engaged....

Fitzgerald replied in December, from Italy; he thought he had located the real basis of the objection:

> *I myself didn't know what Gatsby looked like or was engaged in* and you felt it. If I'd known it and kept it from you you'd have been *too impressed with my knowledge to protest.* This is a complicated idea but I'm sure you'll understand.
> Anyhow after careful searching of the files (of a man's mind) for the Fuller McGee [sic] case....[7]

The point is that the actual sources of Gatsby's wealth, and the nature of his manipulations of it, were not an essential part of the vision Fitzgerald had. What did engage him was the presence and elaboration of signs of wealth as a signal of power exercised in the service of beauty. Gatsby's massive heaps of imported shirts are expressions of his devotion to a woman who had money in the sound of her voice. He presents such magnificent piles of luxury—in the sight and touch of his clothes, the joyous rhythms of his parties—to overwhelm her with beauty, an appeal to all her senses. He must get her to forget her husband and child and situation; to do that he must re-create the past by stocking and opening vast closets of sensory pleasure for a fairy princess. The commercial enterprise, in this way, becomes a function of amorous energy and a visible expression of it. The Chivalric Hero does not stand in armor, the Knight who slays the dragon for the love of the lady; he is, instead, a man "in a white flannel suit, silver shirt, and gold-colored tie" (Gatsby's incredible costume for the Carraway tea party) whose very splendor is nothing armed, all his aggression having been spent in the acquiring of "gorgeous rags."

When Fitzgerald would count up the five good things he had done in his revisions he would include "I've accounted for his money." But that accounting comes to us only in hints and nods that Fitzgerald gleaned from the newspaper accounts of Edward M. Fuller. Nick hears Gatsby say into the phone: "Well, he's no use to us if Detroit is his idea of a small town." Gatsby is quite right, the man is of no "use" to him, for Gatsby's perception of the sizes of American things is part of "the colossal vitality of his illusion." His sense of American geography is so vastly inaccurate that he is of the same breed as the unnamed business connection; on the ride in his fabulous open car, Gatsby does place San Francisco in the Middle West.

The essence of Gatsby's vision is willful ignorance, a refusal to recognize the unalterable distances of the world. Keats expresses again and again in the "Ode to a Nightingale" the desire to "Fade far away"; as the contrast between his imagined participation in beauty and his sad circumstance becomes unbearable, he cries out "Away! away! for I will fly to thee...." To be an inhabitant of this world, to see oneself in it, is agony. There are "sleeping dragons all around," and true lovers must fly "o'er the Southern moors" to home. All around Gatsby's pleasure dome there are dragons sleeping in the valley of ashes. "The waste land" is presided over by Dr. T.J. Eckleburg, and "ashes grow like wheat into ridges and hills and grotesque gardens." Gatsby must get away from that corroding presence, refuse to inhabit the mundane world as anything other than "an ecstatic patron of recurrent light."

When Nick tries to find out what the source of Gatsby's money is, his neighbor admits that he was "in the drug business" and he was "in the oil business" and then says, "But I'm not in either one now." Fitzgerald's point is that Gatsby is in the pleasure business itself—his teeth set "at an inconceivable pitch of intensity." Where Gatsby gets all his wealth is where Porphyro in "The Eve of St. Agnes" gets all his treasures, from the immensity of devotion. The lover is true only if he creates "a world complete in itself." Wealth, in *The Great Gatsby*, is not the familiar notion of American money as the expression of a raw and ruddy frontier power; it is wealth chastened by a notion of romance, possibilities of great life beyond the rim of the actual. Wealth is beauty; it has been brought from all over the world, as Keats's treasures were "in argosy transferred from Fez" and "silken Samarcand" and "cedared Lebanon."

There is also the sense in *Gatsby* that to obtain beauty is to lose it. No present pleasure, realized and consummated, can fulfill the yearning for "the orgiastic future." In his autobiographical first novel Fitzgerald wrote of his hero, "It was always the becoming he dreamed of, never the being." And in *Gatsby*, after she cries in his shirts, Gatsby takes Daisy out to survey his grounds; he says, "You always have a green light that burns all night at the end of your dock." And Nick Carraway observes, "Daisy put her arm through his abruptly, but he seemed absorbed in what he had just said. Possibly it has occurred to him that the colossal significance of that light had now vanished forever." At the moment that was supposed to be the greatest triumph, the ecstasy, Gatsby loses sight of the "golden girl." Daisy accessible is not Daisy. At last when they can touch, when she does what he thinks is exactly the distinguished thing that all his effort will finally make her do—"put her arm through his"—Gatsby is lost. His vision had provided "a satisfactory hint of the unreality of reality" and promised him that the solid earth was finally malleable, if only his dream could be sufficiently large and intense. Gatsby knows that he must create a privileged community and abundant wealth; to live in that community is supposed to provide a heightened perception of the world, to extend one's awareness into a realm where the moment of splendor puts the dreamer in touch with the truth of a "Platonic conception." Fitzgerald conceives of truth in this novel much as Keats does in his poem on the Grecian Urn: those semi-tragic, semi-historical poses of immaculate desire where love is "forever warm and still to be enjoyed."

> *Bold Lover, never, never canst thou kiss,*
> *Though winning near the goal—yet, do not grieve;*
> *She cannot fade, though thou hast not thy bliss,*
> *Forever wilt thou love, and she be fair!*

Winning too near the goal results in grieving. Daisy can only exist for Gatsby so long as he cannot have her, so long as she is "as close as a star to the moon." And when he finally does have her again, "his count of enchanted objects" must necessarily be "diminished by one."

The ecstasy of longing is thwarted by possession. *The Great Gatsby* properly ends with images of running after, beating backward against the tide, a hopeless commitment of the self to the unobtainable. When Jordan Baker tells Nick that "Gatsby bought that house so that Daisy would be just across the bay" the overt implication is that some evening, sooner or later, she would be able to come over to him, wander into the blue ken of his yard; but the real power of Jordan's line, as the book displays Gatsby to us, lies in the covert meaning that the distance set up is exactly the right one. It is far enough to need the green light shining into the mist, far enough to establish the appropriate distance for the preservation of the dream as dream.

Critics have noted that there is a good deal of death imagery in *The Great Gatsby*. Henry Dan Piper writes that "the entire novel seems to have been conceived by Fitzgerald as the expression of a death wish."[8] In the first chapter, in a passage which Fitzgerald later revised, Nick Carraway said, "I suppose the urge to adventure is one and the same with the obscure craving of our bodies for a certain death." And in another draft of the book when Nick first sees Gatsby's car he is immediately reminded of a hearse.[9] On the ride into New York Gatsby and Nick pass a funeral procession, another of the several symbols in the book which connect the automobile and death.

But we should not understand these images of death merely as the counterpart to a dream of youth. When Nick says he is giving us "a story of the west after all" he is connecting Gatsby with the voyagers to the New World, linking Gatsby's dream to the dream of Columbus. Here the modern explorer sets out to find his New World. But to reach it he must go back, from West to East, just as he must go back in time, attempting to regain his youthful love affair. Spatially and temporally, *The Great Gatsby* is a voyage into the past, and the passion is in the voyage itself. Gatsby is a man of infinite will attempting to free himself of the known world's boundaries; he reaches blindly back to a moment of beauty, attempting to give it permanent status. To overpower the valley of ashes, massive creative devotion must recapture a lost state of amorous beatitude.

Death is at the center of the dream. For Fitzgerald as for Keats "the dreamer venoms all his days." In the "Ode to a Nightingale" the longing at the moment of greatest happiness is not for life:

> *Now more than ever seems it rich to die,*
> *To cease upon the midnight with no pain....*

"Rich to die." And the ultimate meaning of the nightingale's song goes back into the world of the dead to become a historical recapitulation of lost dreams. The vision of ecstasy, pitched at death, reaches to "emperor and clown" in "ancient days" and the "self-same song that found a path / Through the sad heart of Ruth, when, sick for home, / She stood in tears amid the alien corn...." Nowhere do we see the influence of Keats on Fitzgerald more strongly than in this notion of the ultimate extension of the yearning for ecstasy as visionary encapsulments of mortality. Keats hears the nightingale's "high requiem" fading away from him into the neighboring countryside. Gatsby on his blue lawn finds his dream "already behind him ... where the dark fields of the republic rolled on under the night." The nightingale's song and the green light flow into richly storied scenery; for Keats beauty is "buried deep in the next valley Glades" and for Gatsby the dream "vanished" into "the old island." The self describes the scene into which the personification of desire recedes, a lyric epiphany of loss. The romantic desire for mystical union with the beautiful drives both Keats and Fitzgerald back into legends of "vast obscurity," visionary dreams and loves surrendered to time.

Notes

1. From a letter to his daughter, August 3, 1940. Included in *The Crack-Up*, ed. Edmund Wilson (New York, 1959), p. 298.

2. See R.L. Schoenwald, "F. Scott Fitzgerald as John Keats," *Boston University Studies in English*, III (Spring, 1957), 12–21, and also John Grube, "*Tender Is the Night*: Keats and Scott Fitzgerald," *Dalhousie Review*, XLIV (1964), 433–441. Schoenwald mentions Keats's influence on *The Great Gatsby* very briefly (pp. 16–17), and Grube not at all.

3. Trilling includes the essay in *Beyond Culture: Essays on Literature and Learning* (New York, 1965), pp. 57–87. He maintains that Keats "may be thought of as the poet who made the boldest affirmation of the principle of pleasure and also as the poet who brought the principle of pleasure into the greatest and *sincerest* doubt" (p. 67).

4. *The Crack-Up*, pp. 28–29. There is a recurring concentration throughout his work on the moment of beauty *as moment*. "After all," he wrote, "any given moment has its value; it can be questioned in the light of after-events, but the moment remains. The young prince in velvet gathered in lovely domesticity around the queen amid the hush of rich draperies may presently grow up to be Pedro the Cruel or Charles the Mad, but the moment of beauty was there." Quoted by Malcolm Cowley in his introduction to *The Stories of F. Scott Fitzgerald* (New York, 1951), p. xiv.

5. *This Side of Paradise* (II, v).

6. New York, 1965, p. 313, no 16.
7. Piper presents the letters, pp. 112–113.
8. P. 107
9. See Piper's discussion of the Princeton manuscripts, p. 109.

102
Versions of Form in Fiction—*Great Expectations* and *The Great Gatsby*

◆

NORMAN FRIEDMAN

'Tis a very old strife between those who elect to see identity, and those who elect to see discrepancies.

—Emerson

I

What are the factors governing the author's *choice* and *organization* of his materials? This, I take it, is the basic question to which statements about the particular form of any given literary work are answers. When we have discovered, that is, the principle or principles which account for these two things—selection and arrangement—we have defined the form of that work. The trouble is, however, with all the critical furor besetting us today, that no single version of the kinds of causes which may be seen to govern such artistic choices has received uncontested currency, nor does the dust of battle show signs of settling.

We are told by the symbologists, for example, of the existence of universal patterns in myths, rituals, dreams, and folk-tales which, when their presence is detected in literary works, explains their organization and their moving power. The structure of these patterns, which derives from the felt parallels between the curve of human life and the natural cycle of the seasons, is largely subconscious and compulsive, being common to mankind at large; works which are archetypally organized, therefore, touch the deepest springs of human emotion and raise thereby the artist's vision into the sphere of the universal.[1] Thus one may account for the form and force of *Moby-Dick* by

SOURCE *Accent* XIV, Autumn 1954, pp. 246–264.

finding analogues in such various works as *Pinocchio* and the Book of Jonah, where the theme of death and rebirth seeks its image in the sea journey involving incarceration in a whale's belly and the subsequent escape therefrom. The reason why Melville's novel took the shape it did (Ishmael's initial melancholy, the journey-hunt, the evolution in his attitudes, and the death of all but Ishmael, who survives by using a coffin as a lifebuoy) is explained by reference to the hypothesis that such a theme frequently finds its embodiment in such an image because of a primordial necessity of the human mind to search for psychic equilibrium through a ritualistic projection of its basic conflicts through natural symbols.

It may be objected, however, that such an approach in itself, while extremely useful in its own way, tends to reduce literary works to a common denominator, with the result that any number of poems, plays, and novels are seen as having the same form. If we want, then, a sounder view of the unique particularity of any work, we will be well advised to narrow down the range of determining factors a bit further; for, if the archetype is by definition ubiquitous, it will also by definition be found everywhere.

That kind of inquiry which traces the rise and fall of literary modes and themes in relation to the surrounding cultural and intellectual milieu offers another kind of answer. An author, we are told here, writes in such and such a way and uses such and such materials because these are the subjects, techniques, and forms made available to him by his age. Thus Shakespeare wrote sonnets and verse plays because these were the dominant forms used by his contemporaries; the theme of revenge in *Hamlet* is seen in relation to the other revenge plays of the period; the development of dramatic blank verse is studied as a phase of the growth of the English language during the sixteenth century; and the ideas and attitudes embodied in Elizabethan drama are analyzed in relation to the religious, military, economic, and intellectual commonplaces of the period.[2]

But this endeavour is open to a similar objection, in that its notion of literary form is only a little less reductive than that of the archetypalists. Assuredly Elizabethan can be distinguished from Restoration Drama by such a procedure, but how are we to distinguish *Hamlet* from *The Spanish Tragedie, The Way of the World* from *Love's Last Shift?*

A third step in limiting the range is found in those efforts to locate the causes of a writer's productions in himself. Here we may be merely biographical and look for as much evidence relative to our author's life and habits as we can assemble—his letters, the testimonies of his friends, his reading, his travels, and so on—or we may be psychological and look for evidence relative to his temperament, his attitudes toward his parents, the quantity and quality of his sexual experiences, his repressions, anxieties, fantasies, traumatic experiences, and so on.[3] Thus we will explain the imagery of *Kubla Khan* by reference to Coleridge's reading, the ambivalent structure of *Sons and Lovers* by reference to Lawrence's unresolved attempts to free himself from his emotional bondage to his mother, the prudery and orthodoxy of Wordsworth's later poetry by reference to the guilt which haunted him as a result of the Annette Vallon affair, the complexity of the attitude toward woman revealed in *Paradise Lost* by reference to Milton's many wives and his treatment of his daughters.

We frequently find ourselves here, however, in the same kind of trouble: many writers turn out to have read *Don Quixote*, *The Divine Comedy*, the Bible, to have had mother-fixations and/or father-hatreds; indeed, many non-writers have read the same books and have suffered from similar emotional tensions. We are forced to look further still if we are interested in discovering the distinctive *artistic* causes which are able to shape out of all these things— the archetypes, the traditions of an age, and a personality—a poem, a play, or a novel. The final step, therefore, is to concentrate on the work as an independent whole by locating its formal causes within the work itself.

The answer provided by one variety of "formalist" is that the organization of a particular work is governed by the author's attempt to balance opposites, harmonize conflicts, fuse tensions. The assumptions here are that imaginative writing is sharply distinct from scientific writing, that the former has ends (the creation of meanings through the reconciliation of contraries) and means (irony, ambiguity, puns, metaphor, paradox, and so on) of its own (as opposed to the communication of information through prose statement), and that each literary work is a self-sustaining organism to be read on its own terms rather than by reference to external and ancillary causes. The difficulty here is that, while some breathtaking analyses have resulted from the reading of novels and plays as poems,[4] and while poetry is seen as different from prose, the form of all of literature is viewed as having its generic cause in the attempt to establish ironic attitudes and ambiguous contrasts.[5]

There is another kind of internal analysis which views each literary work as indeed a unique particular, yet puts its emphasis upon literary forms rather than the Form of Literature. Here the causes of the selection and arrangement of materials in a given work are sought in a determination of what ends it in itself is apparently trying to achieve. The assumption here is that one cannot tell what a given poem, play, or novel is trying to do by deciding in advance that literature in general has as its purpose the balancing of opposites. Thus, for example, a lyric poem may be seen as a verbal action in which the structure of the utterance implies a dramatic situation in which the speaker is trying to solve a problem, persuade a mistress, curse an enemy, and so on, and it is the effort to effect these kinds of ends which is seen as governing the organization of that work. Or a play or novel may be seen as having as its end the achievement of some sort of change in the protagonist's fortune, his state of mind, or his moral character, involving a certain kind of person with a greater or less degree of responsibility for his actions. Here the selection, rendition, and arrangement of parts are seen in relation to one of these sorts of ends.[6]

If one novel—to concentrate henceforth on fiction—is indeed a unique and organic whole unlike any other, it will appear so only from the perspective offered by this last notion of its form. And what I wish to urge here is that the perception of differences is just as important as the perception of similarities for a complete definition of the form of a novel, and that such a definition may be obtained by following in sequence all four of the steps outlined above. In this way we will avoid partial truths and partisan feuds at one and the same time.

Since, as we have seen, an analysis of the specific end which a novel is attempting to effect is the only way in which we can account for the causes which are sufficient to make it the novel it is and not another novel or poem or myth or cultural document or case history in abnormal psychology, it is a consideration of that end with which we must begin if we want a sense of that novel's particularity. The temperament of an author, which stamps all his works, and the quality of an age, which marks all its productions, and the archetypal necessities of the human mind, which characterize all of literature, are indeed causes, but they are merely necessary rather than sufficient in themselves to create a novel. It is the choice of the immediate organizing principle of a novel which determines the channels through which these other causes may operate, it is the crucial choice which limits the range of all the others—which phase of the author's experience will be relevant to that special end, which aspect of the age will pertain to that specific problem, which of the archetypes will serve appropriately to maximize that particular plot. Although these latter may indeed *suggest* to the author his principle of organization—as, for example, in naturalistic fiction where a change in fortune without a corresponding change in the protagonist's state of mind seems to be dictated by the artistic premises of that particular school—once such a choice is made, it is that principle which takes over and by which we must check any other hypothesis we might frame about its form. By thus discussing the range of factors governing the selection and arrangement of materials, from the most specific to the most general, we will arrive at a more complete definition of the form of a novel than any one of the approaches outlined above in itself will allow.

Great Expectations and *The Great Gatsby* offer a challenging case by which these notions may be tested because they are so alike—both involve a young man spurred on to immoral ambitions by a woman—and yet so different—the hero of the one survives his catastrophe while that of the other does not.[7]

II

In attempting to define the specific organizing principle which shapes the development of these novels, we notice in the first place that Pip's career involves essentially the *pursuit* of illusory values, which he never manages to believe in, provoked by his desire to be the social equal of Estella ("The beautiful young lady at Miss Havisham's [is] more beautiful than anybody ever was, and I admire her dreadfully, and I want to be a gentleman on her account" [p. 130]); while Gatsby's career, although quite similar at certain points (for example, his desire to be worthy of Daisy: "He hadn't once ceased looking at Daisy, and I think he revalued everything in his house according to the measure of response it drew from her well-loved eyes" [p. 99]), involves essentially not the pursuit of but the *dedication* to the illusion of the ostensible value of its object. Pip, that is to say, is never quite at home in his role as gentleman, never puts his heart into it ("I lived in a chronic state of uneasiness.... My conscience was not by any means comfortable...." [p. 275]); whereas Gatsby entertains what amounts to a passionate conviction in the absolute truth of his dream ("Can't repeat the past?" he cried incredulously. "Why, of course you can!" [p. 118]).

The specific change, therefore, which the climax of *Great Expectations* is designed to effect is a reestablishment of a true sense of values in Pip's outlook and hence in his behavior—a change in his moral character. The needs dictated by this end are: to provide a motive for Pip's desire to be a gentleman at the cost of his self-respect and moral feelings (his resentment of Estella's scorn coupled with his love for her), to present the means whereby that desire can be fulfilled (his mysterious inheritance), and then to develop a shock strong enough to make him realize the falsity of his values and change his ways (the successive discoveries that his benefactor is a convict, that this man is Estella's father, and that Magwitch has been treated unjustly all along).[8]

The change effected by the climax of *The Great Gatsby*, however, is the disillusionment of Gatsby's faith in his ideal—a change in his state of mind. And the needs dictated by this end are correspondingly different: to present Gatsby as possessed by his dream (his mysterious mansion), to reveal the causes of its growth and how it came to be identified with Daisy (Dan Cody and Officer's Training School), and then to confront him with a betrayal (Daisy's hit-and-run killing of Myrtle, which forces her to choose in favor of Tom and immunity from the consequences, is the means whereby Gatsby is forced at last to realize the true inadequacy of the star he hitched his wagon to).

It is true that Pip also becomes disillusioned, but it is this disillusionment as to the source of his fortune which is material to his moral regeneration; although it was his love for Estella which originally prompted his desire to raise his social status ("I had never thought of being ashamed of my hands before.... I wished Joe had been rather more genteelly brought up, and then I should have been so too" [pp. 60–62]), he never becomes disillusioned in that love for her, even when he discovers the secret of her parentage, and, particularly in the revised "happy" ending, he is still eager for union with her ("Estella, to the last hour of my life, you cannot choose but remain a part of my character, part of the little good in me, part of the evil. But, in this separation I associate you only with the good, and I will faithfully hold you to that always, for you must have done me far more good than harm...." [p. 368]). Through his discoveries he is forced to acknowledge the essential worthlessness of the values he had come to associate with his love for her; what survives at the end of his love minus his snobbery—a reaffirmation of the true and homely virtues associated with Joe and the forge ("If you can't get to be oncommon through going straight, you'll never get to do it through going crooked. So don't tell no more [lies], Pip, and live well and die happy" [p. 71]).

With Gatsby, on the other hand, the reverse is true: he had already become addicted to his rosy ambitions before he met Daisy, and it was with some hesitation that he succeeded in identifying their attainment with the winning of her hand ("He knew that when he kissed this girl, and forever wed his unutterable visions to her perishable breath, his mind would never romp again like the mind of God. So he waited, listening for a moment longer to the tuning-fork that had been struck upon a star. Then he kissed her. At his lips' touch she blossomed for him like a flower and the incarnation was complete" [p. 119]); but when his faith in her was destroyed, everything else went along with it—the world was stripped bare of value altogether—and no subsequent reintegration of values and habits ensued.

Coming now more specifically to the ways in which these two changes—in moral character, and in state of mind—served as the principle of selection in choosing the kinds of incidents and characters to be utilized in bringing such changes about, we notice the great care which Dickens took to establish at the outset the positive quality of the relationship between the young Pip and Joe, for it is the values which inhere in such a relationship that Pip must reject in favor of the false ones of social status, and it is these values to which he must return in order that his moral change be made manifest (Joe "was a mild, good-natured, sweet-tempered, easy-going, foolish, dear fellow—a sort of Hercules in strength, and also in weakness" [p. 6]). We notice further, however, that the presence of his nasty sister serves to make probable and believable his desire to leave the forge ("My sister's bringing up had made me sensitive.... Within myself, I had sustained, from my babyhood, a perpetual conflict with injustice" [p. 62]). Since, on the other hand, Fitzgerald's problem was to effect a final recognition of the utter valuelessness of his ideal in the mind of Gatsby, he took no such pains to establish any affirmative elements in his childhood to which he could return. Indeed, the picture we get of his father at the close of the book only serves to promote our sympathy for the young Jimmy's rejection of him.

We notice, in the second place, the different kinds of personality, developed from out of these backgrounds, required of the protagonists to bring about the different kinds of changes. Gatsby was a solitary youth with a great capacity for believing in himself. ("His parents were shiftless and unsuccessful farm people—his imagination had never really accepted them as his parents at all. The truth was that Jay Gatsby of West Egg, Long Island, sprang from his Platonic conception of himself. He was a son of God.... So he invented just the sort of Jay Gatsby that a seventeen-year-old boy would be likely to invent, and to this conception he was faithful to the end" [p. 106]), and a correspondingly great capcity for deluding himself. There is consequently a pathetic naiveté in his character, an anachronistically eager boyishness which survives in spite of his rather sinister under-world dealings and which finds its chief dramatic manifestation in his compulsive repetition of the "old sport" form of address. Pip, although he is, to be sure, equally ambitious, has that within him which constantly opposes his ambition; he has, in effect, a much more critical temperament ("Conscience is a dreadful thing when it accuses man or boy; but when, in the case of a boy, that secret burden cooperates with another secret burden down the leg of his trousers, it is (as I can testify) a great punishment. The guilty knowledge that I was going to rob Mrs. Joe ... almost drove me out of my mind" [p. 11]). These differences are the natural result of their different childhoods: Jimmy's essential rootlessness as opposed to Pip's early and close involvement with a true and humble Christian man.

Thus, thirdly, the nature of the responsibility involved for their respective misdeeds is radically different. Both become entangled in immoral acts—Pips boyhood theft of file and food for the convict, his rejection of Joe, his idleness, his involvement with law-office and prison, his snobbery, his initial revulsion from Magwitch when the latter returns to reveal himself as Pip's benefactor; Gatsby's lies, his complicity in crime, his irresponsible parties, his maintenance of a magnificent establishment without visible means of support—but Pip is constantly hounded by a sense of guilt whereas Gatsby has never a qualm. Pip practically *allows* himself to be deluded into thinking Miss Havisham is his benefactor because it suits his plans so well (the fact that she encourages him in this delusion works to preserve our sympathy for him—he would be something of a monster otherwise), but Jimmy never knew any better. "I had believed in the forge as the glowing road to manhood and independence," Pip says. "Within a single year all this was changed. Now it was all course and common, and I would not have had Miss Havisham and Estella see it on any account. How much of my ungracious condition of mind may have been my own fault, how much Miss Havisham's, how much my sister's, is now of no moment to me or to any one. The change was made in me; the thing was done. Well or ill done, excusably or inexcusably, it was done" (p. 107). It is clear that Fitzgerald was interested in something else—an indictment of a culture which had nothing to offer an ambitious young man but the hollow shell of an ideal and the ambiguous means for its achievement—and that we are meant to feel the pathos of such a man cheated in such a way; his responsibility, therefore, is kept to a minimum. "Gatsby turned out all right at the end," says Nick, after speaking of his hero's "heightened sensitivity to the promises of life" and "extraordinary gift for hope"; "it is what preyed on Gatsby, what foul dust floated in the wake of his dreams that temporarily closed out my interest in the abortive sorrows and short-winded elations of men" (p. 10). Dickens, on the other hand, wants us to reject Pip in his snobbery (as Pip comes to reject himself) and to feel the justice of his return to Joe and the old values; his personal responsibility is thus made more palpable.

Finally, the rendition and arrangement of incidents in these two novels are accordingly of a different nature. *Great Expectations* is narrated by its hero in the first person, and we are thus allowed to follow the rise and fall of his snobbish attitudes, with their accompanying sense of guilt, and to be present as he makes his discoveries and changes his attitudes; *The Great Gatsby* is narrated by a witness in the first person, and we are thereby allowed to trace a sympathetic observer's feelings and reflections about Gatsby, the people he is involved with, the quality of his dream, and the nature of his death. The point here is that the demands of the plot are such in each case that a critical narrator is required, and Gatsby, even if he had lived, could never have qualified for the job and have retained at the same time his unsullied capacity for hope; Gatsby himself is unaware of the cultural implications which are supplied by Nick. Further, the chronology of *Great Expectations* is largely that of an extended and straightforward autobiographical account, although there are of course elements of mystery which cannot be introduced in their due order without spoiling the force and point of Pip's discoveries; but since we are meant to follow Pip's rejection of moral values and his subsequent return to them, we must be shown his career in its large outlines from childhood to maturity. *The Great Gatsby*, however, covers only the last few months of its hero's life, although knowledge of his background which is essential to the plot is introduced at key intervals (indeed, one of the chief devices for arousing and sustaining suspense which Fitzgerald uses is to raise the question early as to "Where is he from, I mean? And what does he do?" [cf. pp. 19, 40, 51–52, 57–58, 69, 73–77, 105, 116]). What must be done here if we are to see Gatsby's final disillusionment is to present him, with all his meretricious glory and mystery, in the state of illusion from which he must fall, then gradually to introduce his background and motivations so that we may understand and sympathize with his dream (while at the same time being prepared for its collapse), and finally to set in motion the accumulation of incidents which will bring about the climactic situation where he is forced to see through Daisy at last.

If the problem, in sum, is a change in moral character, there must be provided a source of value upon which the protagonist may ultimately draw, and the choice Dickens made in starting at the beginning of Pip's career can be seen as dictated by that end; if the problem is a change in knowledge, we must be shown the state from which the protagonist will change, the reasons why he was in that state, and the factors which bring about that change, and

Fitzgerald's choice of a limited time-frame can be seen as governed by these necessities. The one novel, in short, involves two changes, while the other involves only one. We may notice finally that the series of delayed revelations which work their way through both plots are different in that those in Dickens come as discoveries to the hero whereas those in Fitzgerald come as discoveries to the observer.

III

Once all these crucial and sufficient choices have been made, the direction which the other necessary choices—regarding the temperament of the author, his cultural milieu, and universal symbols—may take is delimited and their relevance indicated (the order we are following is analytic rather than genetic: we shall not be concerned here with the reasons why an author chose such and such a plot in the first place, nor shall we speculate as to the probable order in which these problems presented themselves to him as his novel grew in his imagination and through its successive stages of composition and revision).[9] We may now ask—what elements of selection and arrangement are accounted for, not by the specific necessities of the shape of the plots in these novels, but rather by the psychological necessities of the individual authors which all their works reveal?

The central situation in *Great Expectations*—an underprivileged boy receiving an inheritance from a mysterious benefactor—must have come to the young Charles Dickens many a time in the form of a wish-fulfilment fantasy. We are told by his biographers of his acutely sensitive reaction to the shameful conditions which his father's improvidence reduced the family to, of the necessity for working in a factory which the boy was forced into, of his agonizingly early experience of the need for money and security. His novels are full of orphans who have been the victims of a monstrous betrayal, alienated children cast adrift in the big, unfriendly, adult world. There is no special reason why, for the requirements of the plot, Pip need have been an orphan; that fact of course plays its part—he is all the more ready for some fairy god-father or -mother—and the opening scene at the grave of his parents where he first meats Magwitch is practically indispensable. Yet there is nothing to prevent a sensitive child with two perfectly healthy parents from imagining a benefactor, nor need the graveyard scene have included the tombstones of his parents—any beloved but deceased relative would have served to bring Pip there at that time. The ubiquity of orphans in Dickens's other novels argues against the supposition that the presence of an orphaned protagonist in this one was dictated by its peculiar formal problems alone. Do we have here, then, a symbolic reflection of the anxieties Dickens faced as a boy, a psychological projection of the desire to get rid of one set of parents in favor of another, a relic of the loneliness and humiliation felt by the author when he was a child? Does this also account for the special poignancy of the sense of guilt which haunts Pip throughout his career?[10]

By the same token we may hazard some guesses as to the personal factors controlling the qualities of Fitzgerald's protagonist. I believe it is commonly agreed that Gatsby is a symbolic projection of certain aspects of the personality of Fitzgerald, who was, as his other works reveal as well, haunted by the problems of wealth and social status. Perhaps Gatsby as the man with a consuming dream which is betrayed by its false associations with wealth, crime, and privilege, may be viewed as a paradigm of his creator's deep-seated disillusionment and frustration regarding his own plight as an artist in a commercial society (the tension between integrity and financial-social success) which Fitzgerald, along with Vachel Lindsay, Sherwood Anderson, and Thomas Wolfe, among others, felt so keenly. Gatsby's ambivalent idealization of the rich resembles his creator's, Gatsby's pathetic desire for recognition is a reflection of Fitzgerald's early college days when he tried unsuccessfully to become a big man on the Princeton campus.

But if this were all, if Dickens and Fitzgerald were merely letting off symbolic steam, their novels would be of interest merely as case histories. The fact, however, that they also managed to *judge* their fantasies through the medium of art makes them of special interest to the student of literature. This is what is missing from their biographies—their superior power as artists for self-criticism. When we come away from reading about Fitzgerald's rather chaotic life we feel that he was a weak-willed but ambitious alcoholic. How, we ask ourselves, did he come to write at all? But if Gatsby's dream was Fitzgerald's, we must also remember that Nick Carraway, who passes judgement on that dream, was also created by Fitzgerald. If Pip's dream of a mysterious benefactor was Dickens's, we must recall that Dickens brought Pip to the mature position of rejecting it as false. Perhaps this is what D. H. Lawrence meant when he said an author sheds his sicknesses in his books, projects and dramatizes them in order to master and be rid of them.[11]

IV

The peculiar temperament of a writer, then—the pattern of his intellectual and moral qualities—plays its part as a selecting principle in the form of his works. We have now to consider the general cultural causes which can account for the similarities found among the novels of two different writers. Of course, since Dickens and Fitzgerald are separated by a hundred years and three thousand miles, the surface differences regarding mores and locale between their two novels are quite marked, but in so far as they are both written within what may be called, for lack of a better term, the post-Renaissance tradition, these differences are more apparent than real. Surely the world of Barnard's Inn is not the world of East Egg nor are sexual relations therein treated in a similar spirit; but consider, as the most obvious example of similarity within difference which comes to mind, the attitude shared by Pip and Gatsby toward fine clothes: for both of them the proper clothing was a symbol of acceptance in the eyes of their respective ladies—Pip and his gentleman's suit purchased to offset the scorn Estella expressed at his course laborer's boots, Gatsby and his excited display of imported shirts to convince Daisy that he was what she wanted. The fact that Pip wears knee-breeches and Gatsby pink silk slacks does not obscure this basic resemblance.

Probing a bit deeper now, consider the problem of moral values. Notice the degraded position occupied by the Bible in Pip's education (p. 73) and the whimsical progress of his schooling; the barbarity with which convicts are treated, and the unjust preference given to a "gentleman" in court (pp. 353–354); the purposelessness of his idle life in London; the dehumanized atmosphere of the law office (pp. 199–200). Are not these factors paralleled by the pathetic code of Franklin scribbled on a fly-leaf of "a ragged old copy of a book called *Hopalong Cassidy*" (p. 183) upon which Gatsby schools himself; the comfort and ease enjoyed by his early mentor, Dan Cody, the debased heir of the pioneer tradition; the ambiguous means to success offered by American gangsterdom; the superficiality of Gatsby's human attachments and the flashy vacuity of the lavish parties at which he entertained them (p. 64)? The world of London in the 1820's is only a little less disinherited than that of Long Island in the 1920's; all we are left with there is the natural goodness of the individual which shines from Joe like a halo in the midst of the chiaroscuro of greed, jealousy, envy, spite, hatred, snobbery, and cruelty with which Pip becomes surrounded (see, for example, p. 267). And Nick, in rejecting the dislocated Midwesterners who make messes for other people to clean up, can find no better course than to reject the East altogether and go back home where he belongs.

In each case, institutions—home, church, school—are found wanting; we have a hero with no proper object for his heroism. In one of the most frightening passages in *Gatsby* the grief-crazed Wilson looks out at the eyes of Dr. T. J. Eckleburg: " 'God sees everything', repeated Wilson. 'That's an advertisement,' Michaelis assured him" (p. 170). Here, in both novels, is a world in which values are either lost or are non-existent; and, if they are found, they are found only tenuously and at a tremendous cost of human waste and suffering. The time is out of joint, and the attempt to set it right involves either an act of personal redemption on the part of the hero-victim or his being destroyed in the attempt. The individual vs. society, and the problem of appearance and reality, the two great complementary themes of "modern" literature, are tensions which contribute one order of structure to these novels, tensions which they share in common with such otherwise various works as *Don Quixote*, *The Red and the Black*, and *A Farewell to Arms*.

V

Thus the cultural factors governing the form of these novels. We come now finally to an examination of those factors which account for the selection and arrangement of symbolic devices in a novel that serve to maximize its plot—causes which are the least differentiated of all. Among the many heroes whom Lionel Trilling mentions, in his essay on James's *The Princess Casamassima*,[12] as following what he calls the Young Man from the Provinces formula, are to be found Pip and Jimmy Gatz. The provincial hero "starts with a great demand upon life and a great wonder about its complexity and promises"; he is poor, prideful, and intelligent, standing on the outside of life seeking a way in. Mr. Trilling goes on to stress the source of this motif "in the very heart of the modern actuality" (as we have just outlined it) as well as its roots in folklore (the youngest son of the woodcutter, Parsifal at the castle of the Fisher King), for "through the massed social fact there runs the thread of legendary romance, even of downright magic." Similarly, Edwin S. Fussell offers an interpretation, in "Fitzgerald's Brave New World,"[13] of *The Great Gatsby* which sees the object of the Young Man's quest as embodied in the fabric of American experience as well as in the ambiguous archetype of Paradise: on the one hand an image of release from limitation and the consequent fulfilment of capacity for wonder, and on the other of blasphemous denial of mortality and the consequent search for an earthly Eden (Hubris). And was there indeed not something "mythic" in the Renaissance journey west to the American Hesperides, El Dorado, the land of the Fountain of Youth?

It remains to explore in greater detail this legendary or archetypal formula, as it appears in both these novels, which these remarks suggest. In the first place, the most obvious symbolic element which these two share in common is the youth of vaulting ambition. The problem of adolescence, of the search for something in the adult world—now to be entered—commensurate to the capacity for wonder inherent in the child's world—now to be abandoned—is surely one of the most dramatic loci in human experience. Thus, in both Pip and Jimmy we note the characteric pattern: the dissatisfaction with home-life (the first step toward heroic status and consequently toward hubris is the rejection or loss of substitution of parents, a symbolic denial of mortality), the inexplicable feeling of restlessness, and the frequent and vivid wish-fulfilment fantasies. Along with this are to be found the naive attempts at self-improvement: Gatsby's self-imposed schedule and moral maxims, Pip's persistent attempts to educate himself; Gatsby's efforts to improve his father's eating habits, Pip's vain gestures to teach Joe how to write. And all the while each is waiting for his vague but impetuous Destiny to materialize.

We note further that the dream is in each case ironically realized through substitute fathers who are outside the law. The wavering scale of values, teetering now to one side and now to the other, is finally weighted in favor of what seems to be fulfilment, and the protagonist makes the immoral choice for which he will have to pay dearly before his fate plays itself out. Thus Gatsby gets his start through Dan Cody, "the pioneer debauchee, who during one phase of American life brought back to the Eastern seaboard the savage violence of the frontier brothel and saloon" (p. 108), and is launched finally by Wolfsheim, the gambler who fixed the 1919 World Series:

> "Did you start him in business?" I inquired.
> "Start him! I made him."
> "Oh."
> "I raised him up out of nothing, right out of the gutter."
>
> (p. 181)

So, too Magwitch exclaims, "Yes, Pip, dear boy, I've made a gentleman on you! It's me wot has done it! ... Look'ee here, Pip, I'm your second father. You're my son—more to me nor any son. I've put money away, only for you to spend" (p. 324). We see in both instances that the capacity for wonder is accompanied by an equally strong capacity for self-deception.

In the third place, the dream of both our heroes becomes identified with a woman. Just as Gatsby's dream finds its focus in the remote and mysterious green light at the end of Daisy's dock (cf. pp. 29, 101), so Pip's dream centers upon Estella, the remote and mysterious "star": "Whenever I watched the vessels standing out to sea with their white sails spread, I somehow thought of Miss Havisham and Estella; and whenever the light struck aslant, afar off, upon a cloud or sail or green hill-side or waterline, it was just the same.—Miss Havisham and the strange house and the strange life appeared to have something to do with everything that was picturesque" (p. 110). Similarly, the image of woman as the embodiment of desire, grace, and beauty becomes confused with the leisure class in both cases: "Gatsby was overwhelmingly aware of the youth and mystery that wealth imprisons and preserves, of the freshness of many clothes, and of Daisy, gleaming like silver, safe and proud above the hot struggles of the poor" (pp. 158–160). Compare this from Dickens: "Truly it was impossible to dissociate her presence from all those wretched hankerings after money and gentility that had disturbed my boyhood—from all those ill-regulated aspirations that had first made me ashamed of home and Joe" (p. 238).

In both cases the dream becomes objectified in a house. Although Dickens is not content to allow us merely to infer the inner corruption of Satis House and Barnard's Inn (pp. 173–174, *e.g.*), but rather presents them as literally decayed, there is a palpable similarity in the fact that both Pip's and Gatsby's dreams find symbolic tenancy in mansions. Miss Havisham's and Gatsby's homes are the external emblems of the paradisal vision, which is ironic in both cases since the latter is an imitation old-world castle (pp. 13, 96) and the former is a kind of witch's den into which the abandoned Hansel and Gretel of the novel wander to be destroyed by the child-devouring crone (pp. 84, 307).

On the other side are the corresponding images of hell. The polarizing symbols, counterbalancing Satis House and the Star, Gatsby's castle and the Green Light, are to be found in Pip's marshes (the repeated references to which throughout the novel, on both the literal and figurative levels, form an infernal cluster: pp. 84, 108, 253, cf. 161–162, 218, 439, 445, 477) and Nick's valley of ashes (p. 31). From these wastelands emerge Gatsby's nemesis (Wilson) and Pip's (Orlick), demanding vengeance from the hero for his hubris.

As a consequence of reaching too high, each hero becomes involved in a penitential or redemptive journey. Gatsby's tragic self-discovery—"he must have felt that he had lost the old warm world, paid a high price for living too long with a single dream" (p. 172)—results in no personal purgation: he is simply shot down by Wilson. But, in so far as there is a moral choice made as a result of his fall from high place, it is made by Nick "Carry Away." In his rejection of Gatsby, Jordan, Tom, and Daisy, and in his decision to return to "my Middle West ... where dwellings are still called through the decades by a family's name," Nick is symbolically bringing the purged Gatsby back to where he started and where he belongs (pp. 164, 186). This is a redemptive choice, a return to the moral values and the stable life of childhood; a purification, as far as it goes, of hubris. So, too, does Pip experience his inevitable self-revelation—"All the truth of my position came flashing on me; and its disappointments, dangers, disgraces, consequences of all kinds, rushed in in such a multitude that I was borne down by them and had to struggle for every breath I drew" (pp. 323–324)—and, at first revolted by the returned convict, he makes the crucial moral choice to devote himself to Magwitch's safety (pp. 453–454). Although he is not killed, he does suffer physically for his hubris: he is burned (pp. 407–408), tortured by Orlick (pp. 429–436), and falls deathly ill. During the period of his sickness and recuperation he is nursed by the ever-loyal Joe, and regresses to the state of childhood ("I fancied I was little Pip again" [p. 474]) when he and Joe were "ever the best of friends." Soon after his recovery, we note, he makes a pilgrimage to the forge in order to cleanse his conscience completely: "My heart was softened by my return, and such a change had come to pass, that I felt like one who was toiling home barefoot from distant travel, and whose wanderings had lasted many years" (p. 485).

Finally, in both novels the narrator enacts the choral role of moral commentator. Although, as we have seen, *Great Expectations* is told by the "I" as Protagonist and *The Great Gatsby* by the "I" as Witness, we have in both cases a double perspective. In the former, the mature Pip recounts the story of the immature Pip living through a crucial initiatory experience, thus allowing for the narration of immoral deeds in a moral context—somewhat after the fashion of Greek tragedy wherein the chorus provides a backdrop of normalcy for the abnormal central action. Thus Pip the narrator can say of Pip the protagonist: "I was too cowardly to do what I knew to be right, as I had been too cowardly to avoid doing what I knew to be wrong" (p. 40); or, "So, throughout life, our worst weaknesses and meannesses are usually committed for the sake of people whom we most despise" (p. 220); or, "All the other swindlers upon Earth are nothing to the self-swindlers, and with such pretences did I cheat myself" (p. 227). Similarly, Nick comments, "They're a rotten crowd.... You're worth the whole damn bunch put together"; but then continues, "I've always been glad I said that. It was the only compliment I ever gave him, because I disapproved of him from beginning to end" (p. 164). Or again: "They were careless people, Tom and Daisy—they smashed up things and creatures and then retreated back into their money or their vast carelessness, or whatever it was that kept them together, and let other people clean up the mess they had made..." (p. 189).

VI

In progressing, then, from the most central to the most peripheral of selective principles governing the choice and organization of materials in these two novels, we have outlined briefly the ways in which they are unlike as well as the ways in which they are alike. We have regarded the kind of change involved in the plot, the personality of the hero, and the degree of his responsibility involved, as comprising the specific and sufficient formal cause; and here we discovered that *Great Expectations* turned upon a change in moral character while *The Great Gatsby* turned upon a change in state of mind, and we noted the difference among the kinds of incidents and patterns of sequence chosen to effect those ends. The next most specific cause we found in the personalities of Dickens and Fitzgerald, where the temperamental problems of the individual authors were seen as projected in their novels: the prevalence of orphaned children, substitute parents, and a mysterious guilt in Dickens; the naive fascination with wealth, success, and social position in Fitzgerald.

If the first level of analysis distinguishes one novel from another, and the second finds all the novels of a given author similar to one another but different from those of another author, the third examines the ways in which most serious novels of the past few hundred years are alike—in that the cultural and spiritual dislocation of the age serves as a governing principle in their organization: the inadequacy of institutions for providing a proper set of values, the necessity for the hero-victim to make up his own as he goes along, the enormous cost involved in the recovery of traditional values, and the tenuous conclusions thereto. And finally, when we traced the archetypal patterns which exist in both novels we recognized the ways in which they developed a symbolic resonance which brings them into contact, not only with all the literature, but also with man's immemorial store of legends, myths, dreams, and rituals—that dramatic repository which has its source in the primordial necessities of the human mind. And we noted here that one of the most basic of these necessities involves the symbolic quest for immorality (innocence, irresponsibility, freedom, and security, which finds its image in Paradise), coming-of-age (initiation into adulthood), death (the punitive loss of the dream of Paradise), and rebirth (the redemptive acceptance of mortality, of the past and of moral values).

And it is only through some such multiple perspective, I submit, some such consideration of different versions of form with a view to their relationships, apart from all partisan debate and vested interest, that the full life of any given novel as an artistic whole will come home to us in its entirety. If we are interested in truth rather than literary politics, in seeing justice done to the facts rather than establishing a favored hypothesis, we have no other way.

Notes

1. See C.G. Jung, "On the Relation of Analytical Psychology to Poetic Art," *Contributions to Analytical Psychology*, Translated by H.G. and Cary F. Baynes (London and New York, 1928), pp. 225–249: A poet using archetypes speaks in a voice stronger than his own, "he raises the idea he is trying to express above the occasional and the transitory into the sphere of the ever-existing. He transmutes personal destiny into the destiny of mankind.... That is the secret of effective art." Jung also warns against reducing the work of art to its creator's neurosis: "The plant is not a mere product of the soil; but a living creative process centered in itself, the essence of which has nothing to do with the character of the soil. In the same way the art-work must be regarded as a creative formation, freely making use of every precondition. Its meaning and its own individual particularity rests in itself, and not in its preconditions." Cf. Maud Bodkin, *Archetypal Patterns in Poetry* (London, Toronto, and New York, 1948 [1934]); Northrop Frye, "Yeats and the Language of Symbolism," *University of Toronto Quarterly*, XVII (1947), 1–17, and "The Archetypes of Literature," *Kenyon Review*, XIII (1951), 92–110; W.H. Auden, *The Enchafèd Flood; or, The Romantic Iconography of the Sea* (New York, 1950).

2. As, for example, in L.C. Knights' *Drama and Society in the Age of Jonson* (London, 1937); Hardin Craig, *The Enchanted Glass; The Elizabethan Mind in Literature* (New York 1936); Theodore Spencer, *Shakespeare and the Nature of Man* (New York, 1942); and the well-known studies in the 17th, 18th, and 19th centuries of Basil Willey (London and New York, 1934, 1940, 1949).

3. For the biographical approach, see J.L. Lowes, *The Road to Xanadu* (Boston and New York, 1927), which traces back certain of Coleridge's poetic images to the poet's reading; for the psychological approach, see Kenneth Burke on Coleridge, *The Philosophy of Literary Form* (Louisiana, 1941), pp. 21 ff., *et passim*, and on Arnold, *A Rhetoric of Motives* (New York, 1950), pp. 10–13, *et passim*. Burke may be said to combine the archetypal and the psychological methods. Cf. also Edmund Wilson, *The Wound and the Bow* (Cambridge, Mass., 1941), which purports to examine the way in which an author's psychological "wound" becomes transformed into art.

4. As, for example, in F.R. Leavis, "The Novel as Dramatic Poem (series)," *Scrutiny*, Autumn 1940, March 1951, June 1951, etc.; William Troy, "Virginia Woolf: The Novel of Sensibility," *The Symposium*, III (1932), 53–63, 153–166; G. Wilson Knight, *The Wheel of Fire* (London, 1930), pp. 1–18, *The Imperial Theme* (London 1931), pp. 19–22, *The Shakespearian Tempest* (London, 1932), pp. 1–19, *The Christian Renaissance* (Toronto, 1933), p. 4.

5. It will suffice to mention here, in addition to those listed above, the familiar works of such critics as Empson, Brooks, Warren, etc.

6. R.S. Crane, "The Plot of *Tom Jones*," and Elder Olson, "An Outline of Poetic Theory," *Critics and Criticism*, R.S. Crane, ed. (Chicago, 1952), pp. 616–647, 546–566.

7. The page numbers throughout refer to the Bantam Edition of *The Great Gatsby* (#7) and the Rinehart Edition of *Great Expectations* (#20).

8. Cf. John H. Hagan, Jr., "Structural Patterns in Dickens's *Great Expectations*," *English History*, XXI (1954), 54–66, where the "rhythm" of the novel (in E.K. Brown's sense of the repetition and variation of a pattern of incidents) is examined.

9. The account of the ensuing causes must, because of the magnitude of the problems raised, perforce be merely suggestive. The most that can be accomplished in an outline such as this is to indicate briefly what directions such questions may take.

10. Cf. Dorothy Van Ghent, *The English Novel: form and function* (New York, 1953), pp. 125–138. Although I arrived at my conclusions independently, I find myself in agreement with Miss Van Ghent regarding the significance of the parent-child relationships in this novel as well as on the related matter of the symbolism of the redemptive act required of Dickens's children (see below). See also G. Robert Strange, "Expectation Well Lost," *College English*, XVI (1954), 9–17, which appeared after my own article had been completed.

11. Cited by Diana Trilling in *The Viking Portable D.H. Lawrence* (New York, 1946), p. 19.

12. *The Liberal Imagination* (New York, 1950), pp. 61–64.

13. *English Literary History*, XIX (1952), 291–299.

103
Great Expectations and *The Great Gatsby*

◆

EDWARD VASTA

Great Expectations is, indeed, as G.R. Stange has labelled it, a fable for its time.[1] Recent studies emphasising the novel's moral and psychological aspects as well as the sociological, have revealed the depths of Dickens's response in this work to the Victorian age. Little attention has been given, however, to the novel's fundamental Romanticism. In a central way, I wish now to suggest, *Great Expectations* deals with the fostering and then quelling of the Romantic temperament by the Victorian culture.

Dickens's central story can be approached as concerning a "visionary boy—or man," as Estella pointedly characterises Pip,[2] living in a world which evokes and nourishes dreams yet is ultimately inimical to them. Pip's basic idealism is the root from which springs the complex traits of his character: his imaginativeness, aesthetic sensibility, compassion, courage, ambition, strong sense of guilt, and the rest. Essentially, his struggle is to define concretely and possess in fact a life commensurate with his visionary nature. But the age itself, although stimulating such a quest, prevents the possibility of fulfilment. The financial and social conditions it demands for dream-fulfilment make success impossible, and its hard-headed materialism is incompatible with the visionary temperament itself. Pip's dreams can only turn out to be "poor dreams." So Jaggers calls them near the end of the novel (Bk. III, ch. XII, p. 189), and the epithet "poor" signifies more than merely material disappointment.

In order to bring Pip's story into focus, and simultaneously to expose its Romantic character, I shall set it beside the story of Jay Gatsby. Despite inevitable differences, *The Great Gatsby* is very nearly a severely trimmed re-telling of *Great Expectations*. Even Fitzgerald's handling of his tale is in several ways a variation of Dickens's management.

So fundamental, in fact, are the points of similarity here that besides inviting consideration of Pip as a Romantic hero, I wish also in this paper to

SOURCE *The Dickensian* LX, September 1964, pp. 167–172.

invite consideration of the achievements of these two novels relative to each other. Richard Chase has suggested that "the story of Jay Gatsby is in origin an archetype of European legend." Recalling Lionel Trilling's list of novels which develop the legend of "the Young Man from the Provinces," Chase names *Great Expectations* among those which give this legend expression.[3] It may be, however, that *Great Expectations* is more than merely an archetypal predecessor of *The Great Gatsby*.

Both Philip Pirrip and Jay Gatsby—or rather James Gatz of North Dakota—begin life in a small country town far from the Great Metropolis. Pip's parents are dead, and James Gatz's parents are "shiftless and unsuccessful farm people."[4] Neither heritage nor inheritance, consequently, serves the future of either boy. Both have sensibilities and inclinations superior to their breeding and to the material and social possibilities their circumstances provide. Pip has no chance for an education commensurate with his talent, and after two weeks at St. Olaf's in southern Minnesota, Gatz finds his educational possibilities incompatible with his sense of destiny. They are poor boys, in short, whose spark and energy are in danger of being forever smothered by dismal circumstances.

But Pip is called to the home of Miss Havisham, and James Gatz, already turning into Jay Gatsby, rows out to the yacht of Dan Cody. Here each boy has his first glimpse of the life of money and power, the great life as defined by the age. Their past and present lives become unbearable when their future hopes are visibly expressed to each in concrete and practical terms. Bedazzled by wealth and status, neither boy gives due consideration to the lovelessness and physical degeneracy which Miss Havisham and Dan Cody have in common, nor to the way in which their respective masters are but objects of financial exploitation by persons closest to them. The boys take account of only what their awakened and concretised aspirations wish to notice. Although the ruin of dreams is evident in the very models which evoke them, both forget the evident ugliness, betrayal, and decay; instead, they carry with them only illusions of beauty, command, and life.

Their everyday lives hereafter become one long preoccupation with self-improving attempts to meet the requirements imposed by the shape of their dreams. Pip gleans every fragment of education he can from Biddy and Wopsle's great aunt, reads whatever comes to hand, is embarrassed by the manners and dress of Joe Gargery and is studious about his own. Gatsby, similarly, lives by his schedule of exercises, study, work, play, and the practice of "elocution, poise and how to attain it" (p. 174). He also has his resolve about idleness, smoking, personal hygiene, treatment of parents, and the reading of "one improving book or magazine per week" (*Ibid.*). Gatsby never becomes more than "an elegant young roughneck" (p. 48), but Pip, more patient and domesticated than Gatsby, ultimately achieves the learning and grace of a gentleman.

Crucial to the attainment of the required financial means is Pip's and

Gatsby's acquaintance with criminals: Pip helps Magwitch, and later the deported criminal stores up a fortune to pay for Pip's tutelage in London and to offer him the promise of becoming a man of property. Gatsby, on the other hand, a hard-up major newly discharged from the army, meets Meyer Wolfsheim in New York and is tutored into becoming the head of a mysterious and vast underworld racket yielding a seemingly endless supply of money. Although Gatsby, unlike Pip, actually becomes a criminal, nevertheless both men are sustained by money tainted with criminality. And while Gatsby does not ultimately reject this tainted lucre, as Pip does, both seek to conceal its true character. Dream fulfilment in this financial age requires money, but the social values of this same age require that the money be clean. Indeed, the best money is the kind that Drummle has in *Great Expectations* and that Tom and Daisy have in *The Great Gatsby*: leisure money, unearned, requiring no labour but the labour of spending it. Pip almost has this kind of money, and Gatsby pretends to have it.

Just as one's finances must ideally be that of a gentleman, so one's background in this age must ideally be of a gentlemanly strain. History is also part of the means of success. Neither Pip nor Gatsby has any more choice about his background than about his money, and both are as embarrassed by the one as they are by the other. Pip tries to conceal by silence his having been a blacksmith's apprentice. Gatsby, on the other hand, with less moral hesitation, conceals his humble origins under the image of a war hero and Oxford man pieced together from scraps of truth. Both men try to keep embarrassing friends and relations out of sight. Pip strives to keep Joe Gargery's world and its people away from the world and important people of London. The country folk must await his visitations and the time when he may grandly bestow on them some of the fruits of his wealth and station. Similarly, Gatsby seldom visits his father and nervously strives to keep his underworld colleagues away from the world of the Buchanans. Two years before his death, Gatsby manages to do what Pip cannot—he builds his parents a new house.

Both Pip and Gatsby degenerate morally by these attempts. The age takes this kind of toll. With his acutely developed conscience, the retrospective Pip is remorseful for his treatment of Joe and Biddy. The conscientious and sensitive Nick Carraway, who is the counterpart in Fitzgerald's novel of the adult Pip in Dickens, can admire Gatsby's capacity to dream but still is repulsed by what Gatsby has made of himself. The nearer Pip and Gatsby come to acquiring the means of making their dreams come true, the further they diminish in moral stature.

In the end both visionaries are doomed to failure because both make the same fatal mistake. They pin their dreams on the most beautiful and desirable girl they know. Estella becomes for Pip what Daisy becomes for Gatsby; and just as Estella's name suggests the star Pip dreams of possessing, so the green light on Daisy's dock becomes the emblem of what she means for

Gatsby. Pip meets and falls in love with Estella during his first visit to Miss Havisham, but he makes her the focal point of his aspirations after she has grown up, learned the ways of a lady, and achieved a final polish in France. The exact moment of Pip's focusing his dreams irrevocably on Estella takes place at Miss Havisham's:

> We sat in the dreamy room among the old strange influences which had so wrought upon me, and I learnt that she had but just come home from France, and that she was going to London. Proud and wilful as of old, she had brought those qualities into such subjection to her beauty that it was impossible and out of nature—or I thought so—to separate them from her beauty. Truly it was impossible to dissociate her presence from all those wretched hankerings after money and gentility that had disturbed my boyhood—from all those ill-regulated aspirations that had first made me ashamed of home and Joe—from all those visions that had raised her face in the glowing fire, struck it out of the iron on the anvil, extracted it from the darkness of night to look in at the wooden window of the forge and flit away. In a word, it was impossible for me to separate her, in the past or in the present, from the innermost life of my life.
> (Bk. II, ch. X, p. 161.)

Gatsby's acquaintance with Daisy is similar to Pip's acquaintance with Estella: meetings and partings, intimacy with distance. The exact moment in which Daisy becomes the incarnation of Gatsby's dream takes place five years before Gatsby's death:

> ... One Autumn night, five years before, they had been walking down the street when the leaves were falling, and they came to a place where there were no trees and the sidewalk was white with moonlight. They stopped there and turned toward each other. Now it was a cool night with mysterious excitement in it which comes at the two changes of the year. The quiet lights in the houses were humming out into the darkness and there was a stir and bustle among the stars. Out of the corner of his eye Gatsby saw that the blocks of the sidewalks really formed a ladder and mounted to a secret place above the trees— he could climb to it, if he climbed alone, and once there he could suck on the pap of life, gulp down the incomparable milk of wonder.
>
> His heart beat faster and faster as Daisy's white face came up to his own. He knew that when he kissed this girl, and forever wed his unutterable visions to her perishable breath, his mind would never romp again like the mind of God. So he waited, listening for a moment longer to the tuning-fork that had been struck upon a star. Then he kissed her. At his lips' touch she blossomed for him like a flower and the incarnation was complete.
> (p. 112).

Although Estella and Daisy differ in many ways, both girls bear the same relationship to their respective visionaries. On the one hand, they are beautiful ladies of the highest and best circumstances life has to offer. For their men, their appeal is aesthetic, symbolic, Romantic. On the other hand, they are totally unsuited to their respective visionaries; the proud, wilful, practical-minded Estella is as unworthy of Pip as the egoistic, shallow, and affected Daisy is unworthy of Gatsby. The two dreamers are half aware of these forbidding facts, but impelled by their own aspirations, they ignore the unfavourable qualities in their ladies as deliberately as they ignored the sordid circumstances surrounding Dan Cody and Miss Havisham.

The marriage of Estella and Daisy also bear important similarities. First, each marries the same kind of husband: Estella marries the crude, offensive, even cruel Drummle while Daisy marries Drummle's counterpart, the equally cruel and obnoxious Tom. Second, in each case the decision to marry is an agonising one: marriage to Drummle is a kind of self-punishment for Estella while marriage to Tom is a kind of drunken self-surrender for Daisy. Third, the effect of the marriage is the collapse of dreams. Whatever happens to the money Pip expected, and the gentleman's status which the money could bring about, the loss of Estella constitutes the real collapse of his dream. The same is true, of course, for Gatsby. In both cases, desire for material and social gains had been stimulated by the more fundamental desire to win the dream-lady. For the heroes of both novels, money and status become the required means rather than the goal. Finally, the marriage of both girls involves partly a yielding to the pressure of the age. By marrying men presently established in their own levels of wealth and social status rather than men of strong aspirations but mere future promises, Estella and Daisy accept with finality the safety of the times. They thus become half-willing agents, as it were, of the culture itself, which "uses" the dream-ladies first to inspire the dreamers, then to abandon them by retreating among the age's gifts. Daisy abandons Gatsby twice: first when she marries Tom, then after the accident when she in effect reconfirms her marriage. If Dickens had not changed his first ending, an alteration which amounts to serious disregard for his theme, Estella would also have abandoned Pip twice: first when she marries Drummle, then as the wife of a Shropshire doctor exchanging a few words with Pip from her carriage.

The material, progressivistic, socially self-conscious culture with which both novels deal not only abandons the Romantic aspirants but also seeks to retaliate for their having dared to take up the dream it inspired. In Pip's case retaliation comes within a hair's breadth of success; in Gatsby's case retaliation is complete. Pip is nearly slain by Orlick, who is jealous of Pip's having come between him and Biddy. After Gatsby is sickeningly abandoned, he actually is slain, immediately and tragically, by Orlick's counterpart, George Wilson. In both cases, vengeance is misdirected and founded on ignorance.[5] In both cases, also, vengeance comes from the Wasteland: the marshes to which Orlick is relegated in *Great Expectations*; the ash heaps to which Wilson is confined in *The Great Gatsby*.[6] These parallel regions in the two novels have parallel symbolic significances as the hell for those barred from the cultural heaven—and as the region from which punishment may come for the Pips and Gatsbys who have refused to be consigned there.

The differing fates of Pip and Gatsby point up the differing perspectives Dickens and Fitzgerald give their similar themes. Dickens's concern is primarily sociological, his aim primarily journalistic. His characters, consequently, are fully developed, even minor ones, and his novel is populated with lives of such diversity as to evoke the business and complexity of the times. Fitzgerald's concern is primarily philosophical, his aim primarily poetic. He is interested in the principle itself, the idea of the death of dreams. He makes his characters serve the idea rather than themselves, consequently, and roots his theme in the myth of America as the El Dorado. Thus while the journalistic Dickens spares Pip's life and grants him a modest success, the poetic Fitzgerald brings about a tragic close, the injustice of which is emphasised by the details of Gatsby's burial.

Despite the differing approaches, mentalities, and styles of these two writers, finally, their novels are similar in the handling as well as the theme. As Dickens does, Fitzgerald doles out information a bit at a time and renders events mysterious by inviting us to speculate. He, too, milks his story for suspense, enhancing this effect by breaking up and mixing the chronology of past events, the knowledge of which is necessary to make sense out of the present. Both novelists also use a point of view which creates a double vision. In *Great Expectations* the central intelligence is Pip himself; but the adult Pip recounts his story after the fact and judges his actions at every stage from an adult point of view. Thus we are the immediate observers of Pip's entire development, yet also the transcendent sharers of the adult Pip's retrospective view of himself. The same is true in *The Great Gatsby*, except that the retrospective, evaluative mind is separated from the hero and placed in Nick. But Nick, as well as Gatsby, is very like Pip. Nick undergoes a kind of variation of the main story, as well as providing the dominating point of view. He also has the girl back in Minnesota whom he leaves behind, a kind of counterpart to Biddy in Dickens's novel. Nick's story concludes in a way similar to Pip's: he re-evaluates the provincial Midwest against his newfound understanding of the Great Metropolis and the East. Giving up his ambitions, he returns to the Midwest reconciled.

Some seventy-five years before Fitzgerald, then, Dickens saw fundamentally the same characteristics and consequences of the commercial, hard-headed age that Fitzgerald saw. While the differences between the two novels cannot be ignored, the similarities between them require notice. Only basic correspondences have been noted here, but they are sufficient, I feel, to warrant reconsideration and re-evaluation of these two novels in light of each other.

Notes

1. "Expectations Well Lost: Dickens's Fable for His Time," *College English*, XVI (1954), 9–17.
2. Charles Dickens, *Great Expectations*, 1861.
3. *The American Novel and Its Tradition* (Garden City, New York: Doubleday and Co., 1957), pp. 162–3.

4. F. Scott Fitzgerald, *The Great Gatsby* (New York: Charles Scribner's Sons, 1953), p. 99. All references are to this edition.

5. But see Julian Moynahan, "The Hero's Guilt: The Case of *Great Expectations*," *Essays in Criticism*, X (1960), 60–79, who argues that Orlick is Pip's *alter ego*, and that the guilty Pip provokes his own punishment.

6. I am indebted to Prof. Francis E. Moran of the University of Notre Dame for pointing out to me the similar functions of the marshes and the ash heaps. He also suggested, rightly, I believe that the neighbourhood around Old Bailey is also parallel to the ash heaps. That neighbourhood certainly is a kind of extension of the marshes.

104
Traces of *Tono-Bungay* in *The Great Gatsby*

ROBERT ROULSTON

Scholarship on F. Scott Fitzgerald might lead us to believe that when he began work on *The Great Gatsby* in 1924 he was under the spell of just about every major late nineteenth and early twentieth century English and American novelist except the one who half a decade before had been his idol—H. G. Wells. Thus, whereas this character or that structural device in *The Great Gatsby* supposedly evinces an indebtedness to Joseph Conrad, Henry James, Edith Wharton, Willa Cather, James Joyce, George Eliot, Theodore Dreiser, or Mark Twain, the impact of Wells upon Fitzgerald presumably vanished along with his infatuation with Compton Mackenzie and Rupert Brooke.[1] Indeed, some critics have seen Fitzgerald's development as a literary morality play in which the fledgling author had to discard the artistic vices he had acquired from Wells—discursiveness, authorial intrusions, and an over-emphasis upon ideas and character at the expense of unity and control in order to achieve the Jamesian compactness, allusiveness, stylistic polish and moral perspicacity of *The Great Gatsby*.[2]

Although Fitzgerald undoubtedly learned much from other writers between 1920 and 1924 (and learned even more from life and from the diligent practice of his craft), a comparison of *The Great Gatsby* with what not long before had been his favorite novel, *Tono-Bungay*,[3] reveals that by the middle of the decade he had far from exorcised the influence of Wells. Actually, the conventional view of Fitzgerald's evolution as an artist obscures an important quality about him—that growth for this past-haunted man was often less a process of rejection and displacement than one of accretion. Not only are there important similarities between the plots, characters and themes of *Tono-Bungay* and *The Great Gatsby*: the very first page of Fitzgerald's novel indicates a linkage between the two works in an area where anyone heeding most Fitzgerald scholarship would be least inclined to seek one—the use of point of view.

SOURCE: *Journal of Narrative Technique* 10, Winter 1980, pp. 68–76.

According to that scholarship Fitzgerald, after falling under Conrad's spell, abandoned not just the sprawling form but the omniscient narration frequently favored by Wells.[4] Thus Nick Carraway is held to serve the same function in *The Great Gatsby* that Marlow serves in *Lord Jim*, *Chance*, and *The Heart of Darkness* by operating as a controlling center through which action external to himself is perceived. Willa Cather's use of a similar technique in *My Antonia*, where the heroine's story is told by a younger male friend, Jim Burden, is also often cited as a model for *The Great Gatsby*.

Yet, in truth, Carraway's function resembles that of George Ponderevo in *Tono-Bungay* as much as it resembles Marlow's and Burden's. Wells does not in this novel employ the omniscient point of view which Henry James regarded as characteristic of the sort of "saturation novel" that was Wells' specialty during this phase of his career. George narrates the entire work. To be sure, he philosophizes to a degree inconsonant with James's and Conrad's aesthetic of selectivity. And, when George occupies the center of action, *Tono-Bungay* becomes a first-person *Bildungsroman*. But, whenever the focus shifts to George's uncle, Edward Ponderevo, the inventor of the patent medicine that gives the book its title, George becomes a critical yet sympathetic observer: a man who likes the entrepreneurial swindler but who disapproves of his methods and of the economic system which permits him to flourish. In short, George is to his uncle much what Nick is to Gatsby. George could truthfully apply to Edward Nick's words about his West Egg neighbor: "Gatsby ... represented everything for which I have an unaffected scorn."[5] Despite such disapproval, though, both narrators get drawn ever closer to these figures who fascinate them far more than they repel them. And in both cases the attraction leads to moral complicity. Nick abets Gatsby's attempt to lure Daisy Buchanan away from her husband. George, after branding Edward's patent medicine scheme a fraud, proceeds to participate in the enterprise—a betrayal of principle which elicits from him the following remark: "I parted with much of my personal pride when I gave up science for Tono-Bungay."[6] And, like Nick, who stands by Gatsby when everyone else has spurned him, George remains loyal to his uncle to the very end, helping him escape to France to elude the law and maintaining there a vigil by his deathbed.

Even on the structural level, despite obvious dissimilarities, there are significant parallels between the two works. First of all, they begin in an analogous manner. Both start with the narrator trying to establish his credibility. Nick's comment that he has gained insight into "many curious natures" (p. 1) has an almost exact counterpart in George's announcement that he has seen "a curious variety of people and ways of living together" (p. 4). Furthermore, just as Nick dangles Gatsby tantalizingly before us even though he will not give us a close view of him until the third chapter, George builds up Edward Ponderevo in the opening pages then defers bringing him into the action until—yes—Chapter Three.

The novels are also alike in their endings. They both conclude not merely with their narrators rejecting the milieus which they have been describing but with panoramic pictures of their respective countries. Nick lyrically equates Gatsby's "wonder when he first picked out the green light at the end of Daisy's dock" with the awe Dutch sailors felt when they first glimpsed the "fresh green breast of the new world" (p. 218). But Gatsby's dream, Nick contends, was "already behind him where the dark fields of the republic rolled on in the night" (p. 218). George, more expansively but for the same reason, gives an Olympian view of Britain starting in Craven Reach "in the heart of old England" (p. 453) and moving along the Thames past "Kew and Hampton Court with their memories of Kings and Cardinals" (p. 453) and then concluding in London where he sees evidence of "England as a feudal scheme overtaken by fatty degeneration and stupendous accidents of hypertrophy" (p. 455). Thus both writers in their final chapters contrast past with present to the latter's disadvantage.

In between the first and last chapters the two books, it is true, do follow divergent courses. Wells's novel offers a detailed Chronological account of George Ponderevo's boyhood and early manhood. *The Great Gatsby*, on the other hand, concentrates on a single summer in the New York area but uses Conradian flashbacks to enlarge the scope of the story. But as *The Great Gatsby* unfolds, its characters often behave like comparable characters in *Tono-Bungay* and exhibit strikingly similar motivations. The two plots, consequently, frequently have similar configurations.

The most patent parallel is the one between Gatsby's affair with Daisy Buchanan and George Ponderevo's liaison with Beatrice Normandy. In both instances the woman is socially superior to her lover. Gatsby, "a penniless young man without a past," meets Daisy only because "a colossal accident," the war, provides him with the officer's uniform that gets him invited to the home of Daisy's parents in Louisville (p. 178). George first encounters the high-born Beatrice when she is a guest at the great country house, Bladesover, where his mother is housekeeper. Although Beatrice and George are children when they meet, they are no chaste babes in the woods for their sylvan idylls are given over to kisses and embraces. But, just as Gatsby's romance is interrupted when Daisy marries the wealthy, socially prominent Tom Buchanan, George's pre-pubescent dalliance is shattered when he gets into a fight with Beatrice's snobbish half-brother and is banished from Bladesover.

True, George does not pine for Beatrice for half a decade as Gatsby pines for Daisy. But when George and Beatrice meet again years afterward at the estate of George's now wealthy uncle, a full-fledged amour soon develops. But, anticipating the way Daisy, despite her love for Gatsby, rejects him in favor of her brute of a husband because she knows Tom's world is the only one where she can live comfortably, Beatrice refuses to marry George whom she adores and weds instead the odious Lord Carnaby because he belongs to her own class. Thereafter George does not die as Gatsby does after Daisy rejects him. But, embittered by what he has seen of the rich, he becomes a designer of naval destroyers, indifferent to how they are used or by whom because, as he says: "I have come to see myself from the outside, my country from the outside without illusions" (p. 460).

George's decision to become a weapon maker is obviously closer to Nick Carraway's flight from Long Island to his native Midwest than it seems to Gatsby's final actions because both Nick and George eventually reject the milieu of the wealthy in a way Gatsby is unable to do. If we seek an analogue to Gatsby's yearning for wealth, social status, and a life of extravagant splendor we must turn not to George but to George's uncle, Edward Ponderevo. When we first encounter Edward, the small-town chemist (pharmacist) seems an almost clownish figure as, amid the squalid realities of his lower middle-class existence, he dreams of becoming a millionaire. But the fantasy becomes actuality after a nostrum he concocts catches on with the public. To his nephew's observation that Tono-Bungay is a "damned swindle," Edward replies with a flourish of gaudy rhetoric and a feat of moral judo worthy of Fitzgerald's noble crook and impostor and fellow drugstore owner, Jay Gatsby: "I grant you Tono-Bungay *may* not be—not *quite* so good a find for the world as Peruvian bark, but ... it *makes* trade! And the world lives on trade. Commerce! A romantic exchange of commodities and property. Romance. 'Magination. See?" (p. 155).

Like Gatsby, whom we are supposed to admire despite his involvement with a wide range of criminal actitivies including bootlegging, selling stolen bonds, bribery, and gambling—Edward Ponderevo remains an appealing figure even though his rise is due to activities seldom less than morally dubious and eventually sufficiently illegal for his enemy, Lord Boom, a press magnate, to turn him into a fugitive who dies in the Pyrenees after a dramatic airplane flight to the continent with George.[7] Before his downfall, however, Edward is absorbed with constructing Crest Hill, a grandiose mansion that would have delighted Gatsby with his imitation "of some Hotel de Ville in Normandy" (p. 6). (It should be recalled that the last name of George's patrician enamorata, Beatrice, is Normandy.) Much as Gatsby's mind has been filled from youth with "a Platonic conception of himself" that impels him into the service "of a vast, vulgar, and meretricious beauty" (p. 118), Edward Ponderevo fancies himself as a Napoleonic hero. In fact, George's assertion that his uncle would "have made a far less egregious splash if there had been no Napoleonic legend to misguide him" (p. 309) indicates that Edward is no less a product of Europe's obsession with the Man of Destiny than Gatsby is a victim of America's Alger myth. And George's contention that his uncle is "in many ways better and infinitely kinder than his career" (p. 309) is surely akin to Nick Carraway's perception of Gatsby.

Far more significant than the plot affinities between the two novels are certain thematic ones. The basic view of life that pervades Fitzgerald's book, in fact, is quite close to the one that we find in *Tono-Bungay*. We need not turn to Oswald Spengler as some have done to account for the sense of civilization on the wane that *The Great Gatsby* exudes.[8] Not merely does Wells depict a society rife with injustice and tainted with corruption: he gives vent to an apocalyptic pessimism that makes Spengler's *The Decline of the West* seem by comparison downright cheerful. For Spengler, after all, history is a cyclical process whereby decay is succeeded by renewal. But at one point in *Tono-Bungay*, George Ponderevo self-evidently speaking for his creator, says: "To my mind radio-activity is a real disease of matter ... It is in matter exactly what the decay of our old culture is in society, a loss of traditions and distinctions and assured reactions ... Suppose, indeed that is to be the end of our planet; no splendid climax and finale, no towering achievements, but just atomic decay" (pp. 386–87). One of the glories of *The Great Gatsby* is that it makes its points with few such bald expository intrusions. And one of Fitzgerald's most felicitous inspirations was to have the obtuse Tom Buchanan from time to time blurt out gargled accounts of purportedly scientific books which predict the demise of the social order and the destruction of the world. However ludicrous Tom's pronouncements sound, the story that Fitzgerald tells us through Nick Carraway sustains Tom's fears that "civilization is going to pieces" even if it does not indicate whether Tom's alarms about the earth's falling into the sun are warranted (pp. 19, 141).

The world depicted in *Tono-Bungay*, like the one in *The Great Gatsby*, is a topsy-turvy place where distinctions are crumbling and moral values are awry. In Wells's novel the great country estate of Bladesover, which represents "the Gentry, the Quality, by and through and for whom the rest of the world ... breathed and lived," is taken over by Sir Reuben Lichtenstein, a Jewish entrepreneur, and nearby Redgrave falls into "the hands of brewers" (pp. 9–10). Wells's dislike of the class system, however, did not make him behold such economic and social pole-vaulting with delight. On the contrary, he once has George Ponderevo remark: "One felt that a smaller but more enterprising and intensely undignified variety and stupidity had replaced the large dullness of the old gentry" (p. 71). Furthermore, George learns that in England dishonesty has become so pervasive and mere success so admired that, rather than being imprisoned for large-scale fiscal impropriety, "anyone who could really bring it off would much more likely go into the House of Lords" (p. 77). Fitzgerald depicts a similar breakdown of social and moral norms. At Gatsby's parties patricians mingle with entertainers and gangsters, and debutantes debauch themselves. Nick once passes a limousine "driven by a white chauffeur" containing "three modish negroes" (p. 83). The Buchanans' upper-class friend, Walter Chase, becomes a colleague of the racketeer, Meyer Wolfsheim. And in and out of the book flit people whose very names suggest social confusion—Stonewall Jackson

Abrams, Fontana O'Brien, Willie Voltaire, Ardita Fitzpeters, and so on.

But where Fitzgerald stands closer in *The Great Gatsby* to Wells than he stands to Conrad, James, Cather, or the other authors under whose thrall he was supposed to be in 1924 and 1925 is in his hostility to the rich. Back in 1920 in his semi-autobiographical first novel he had made the hero, Amory Blaine, declare himself to be a socialist. Since at Princeton Fitzgerald evidently gave little more thought to politics than Amory gives to the subject throughout *This Side of Paradise*, the declaration is sometimes seen as evidence that the youthful author was merely echoing the ideas of his literary idols, Shaw and Wells. But, in truth, Fitzgerald, for all his supposed apoliticality, at every stage of his career disliked unmerited privilege however much he may have envied the possessors of such privilege. If that animosity toward the "leisure class" to which he would later confess had about it "not the conviction of a revolutionist, but the smouldering hatred of a peasant,"[9] it also had more than a little in common with Wells's attitudes as they are expressed in *Tono-Bungay*—attitudes, as we have seen, that their pessimistic undercurrent ran counter to the drift of thought of Karl Marx and perhaps even of Wells's former associates in the Fabian Society.[10] This is not to say that in *The Great Gatsby* Fitzgerald fails to exhibit the "romantic awe" Hemingway accused him of having toward the wealthy.[11] Daisy's voice is irresistible because it is "full of money" (p. 144). And certainly Nick, the bond dealer who sees a resemblance between a street peddler and John D. Rockefeller and who finds the proximity of millionaires "consoling" (pp. 6, 32), shares Gatsby's tendency to glamorize great wealth in a way that George Ponderevo does not share the similar tendency on the part of his Uncle Edward.

Nick's eventual rejection of the Buchanans and their class, however, could not be more emphatic. For him they have become "a rotten crowd" of sybarites, and his final assessment of them reeks with scorn: "They were careless people ...—they smashed up things and creatures and retreated back into their money or their vast carelessness, or whatever it was that kept them together, and let other people clean up the mess they had made" (p. 216). Nick's perception of them in many respects echoes Beatrice Normandy's bitter outburst in *Tono-Bungay* against their British equivalents: "I'm spoilt! I'm spoilt by this rich, idle way of living, until every habit is wrong, every taste wrong ... People can be ruined by wealth just as much as by poverty" (p. 446). Beatrice's remark about poverty and wealth both being agents of corruption, moreover, is also reflected in *The Great Gatsby*: the impoverished George Wilson is quite as unpleasant as the millionaire, Tom Buchanan. And, if the world of the rich destroys Gatsby, the tawdry life of poverty he has led as a boy on the prairies seems as dismal as the existence endured by George Ponderevo at the home of his poor and pietistic cousin, Nicodemus Frapp.

But the brunt of the moral indignation in both novels falls upon the rich.

The high-living author of *The Great Gatsby* was no less ready than the philandering creator of *Tono-Bungay* to mount the pulpit and denounce sin, especially sin committed by the wealthy. Both writers declared through their narrators a solidarity, if not with the angels, then with certain old-fashioned virtues that they found sadly in abeyance in their own fallen times. Appalled by the profligacy he sees about him, George asserts: "I've never been in love with self-indulgence. That philosophy of the loose lip and the lax paunch is one for which I have always had an instinctive distrust" (p. 325). Although a bit less the scoutmaster, Nick too assures us he is no wastrel. Unlike the debauchees around him (but not unlike Gatsby), he shuns excessive drinking, having been intoxicated, he insists, just twice in his life. Dishonesty in sports, whether by Jordan Baker when she moves a ball in a golf tournament or by Wolfsheim when he rigs the World Series, repels him. At one point he assures us with devastating modesty: "I am one of the few honest people I know" (p. 72).

This similarity between Nick Carraway and George Ponderevo does not mean that, in fashioning his narrator, Fitzgerald was in no way affected by Conrad's Marlow or by Willa Cather's Jim Burden. Neither do the numerous parallels cited throughout this essay between their themes, characterizations, plot elements, and the beginnings and endings by *Tono-Bungay* and *The Great Gatsby* indicate that in 1924 and 1925 Fitzgerald was writing the same sort of novel, albeit with infinitely greater skill, he had written five years earlier when the influence of Wells upon him was strongest. But the techniques Fitzgerald had absorbed from Conrad and Cather—and perhaps from Joyce, Wharton, and James—did not supplant, as critics have been too inclined to declare, the lessons he had learned from Wells. With the chemistry of his newly matured art, he compounded the crude but solid metal of *Tono-Bungay* with the finer minerals he had extracted from more recent models to produce that stunning alloy, *The Great Gatsby*.

Notes

1. The impact of Conrad upon *The Great Gatsby* is at least touched upon in nearly all extended discussions of the writing of Fitzgerald's novel. Among the most detailed of these examinations are those by James E. Miller, Jr. in *The Fictional Techniques of Scott Fitzgerald* (The Hague: Martinus Nijhoff, 1957), pp. 129–33; Henry Dan Piper in *F. Scott Fitzgerald: A Critical Portrait* (New York: Holt, 1965), pp. 129–33; and Robert Sklar in *F. Scott Fitzgerald: The Last Laocoon* (New York: Oxford University Press, 1967), pp. 151–52. All three mention the influence of Cather as does Sergio Perosa in *The Art of F. Scott Fitzgerald*, tr. Charles Matz and the author (Ann Arbor: University of Michigan Press, 1965), pp. 76–78. Although no evidence exists that Fitzgerald had read much of Henry James before writing *The Great Gatsby*, Piper notes parallels between the novel and *Daisy Miller* and *The American* (pp. 128–29). He also comments upon similarities between *The Great Gatsby* and Edith Wharton's *Ethan Frome* (p. 127). Sklar (pp. 154–55) discusses Joyce's influence on Fitzgerald. Horst H. Kruse in "'Gatsby' and 'Gadsby'" *Modern Fiction Studies*, 15 (Winter, 1969–70), 539–41 contends that Fitzgerald used Mark Twain's *A Tramp Abroad* as a source for *The Great Gatsby*, Paul A. Makurath, Jr. in "Another Source for

'Gatsby,'" *Fitzgerald/Hemingway Annual*, 1975, pp. 115–16 proposes that Fitzgerald borrowed elements in *The Great Gatsby* from George Eliot's *The Mill on the Floss*. The Dreiser influence was suggested by Maxwell Geismar in "Theodore Dreiser," *Rebels and Ancestors: The American Novel, 1890–1915: Frank Norris, Stephen Crane, Jack London, Ellen Glasgow, Theodore Dreiser* (Boston: Houghton, 1953), p. 342 and reinforced by Eric Solomon in "A Source for Fitzgerald's *The Great Gatsby*," *Modern Language Notes*, 73 (1958), 186–88.

2. Miller devotes most of his book to arguing that Fitzgerald's career was a progression from writing what Henry James, who cited Wells as an example, called the novel of "saturation" to producing the sort of novel of "selection" that was the forte of James and Conrad. Perosa writes of Fitzgerald's conversation from "the dominant influence of H.G. Wells and Theodore Dreiser ... to James through Conrad in *The Great Gatsby*" (p. 185). Other critics, evidently assuming that Wells's influence vanished in the early 1920s, do not even mention Wells when they discuss *The Great Gatsby*.

3. John Kuehl, "Scott Fitzgerald's Reading," *The Princeton University Library Chronicle*, 22 (Winter, 1961), 87–88.

4. See, for example, Piper, pp. 129–33; Miller, pp. 90–92; and Perosa, pp. 78–79.

5. *The Great Gatsby* (New York: Scribner's, 1925), p. 178. All subsequent references will be to this edition and will be cited in parentheses in the text.

6. *Tono-Bungay* (New York: Duffield, 1909), p. 460. All subsequent references will be to this edition and will be cited in parentheses in the text.

7. *Tono-Bungay* was published the year before Louis Blériot made the first actual flight across the English Channel.

8. In a letter to Maxwell Perkins, 6 June 1940, Fitzgerald claimed that he had read Spengler the summer he was writing *The Great Gatsby*—*The Letters of F. Scott Fitzgerald*, ed. Andrew Turnbull (New York: Scribner's, 1963), pp. 289–90. Sklar (p. 24) notes that Fitzgerald must have been in error because *The Decline of the West* did not appear in English translation until the year after the publication of *The Great Gatsby*. However, Dalton Gross in "F. Scott Fitzgerald's *The Great Gatsby* and Oswald Spengler's *The Decline of the West*," *Notes and Queries*, 17 (1970), 476 suggests that Fitzgerald could have been familiar with Spengler's arguments in 1924 because in July of that year an article on Spengler was printed in *Yale Review* which, Gross contends, "was precisely the type of magazine Fitzgerald read to keep abreast of current literary developments."

9. *The Crack-Up*, ed. Edmund Wilson (New York: New Directions, 1956, p. 77.

10. Wells joined the Society in 1903 but left it three years later.

11. "The Snows of Kilimanjaro," *The Short Stories of Ernest Hemingway* (Scribner's, 1938), p. 72.

105

Conrad and
The Great Gatsby

◆

R.W. STALLMAN

Deep memories yield no epitaphs.

—*Moby-Dick*, XXIII

Fitzgerald's literary sources include the conjectured influence of Thackeray ("so far as I am concerned," he wrote an inquirer, "you guessed right"). Another conjectured influence is that of Edith Wharton (through Henry James), which Gilbert Seldes pronounced in a *Dial* review in 1925. Seldes discussed the Wharton relationship with Fitzgerald, and so if we accept the author's own word for it he derives from Thackeray and Edith Wharton inasmuch as he himself admits the influence of these authors. These authorized influences strike me as peripheral because the central one, as I see it, is the obsessive hold of Conrad in shaping Fitzgerald's greatest novel. His biographer reports that Fitzgerald "was never very conscious of his literary debts," but so numerous are his debts to Conrad that it is (I think) misleading to swallow this false notion in good faith. In Mr. Arthur Mizener's version of him, Fitzgerald is an Original Genius—almost nobody at all influenced this Very Bright Boy. He tells us that Fitzgerald had an "intuitive way of working," and that the source of one of his symbols in *The Great Gatsby* was a dust-jacket picturing two enormous eyes which suggested "Daisy brooding over an amusement-park version of New York." This dust-jacket, as Mr. Mizener admits, "was not, of course, the real source of that symbol," but he insists that "it was the only source Fitzgerald consciously understood, and he was hardly more aware of his literary sources."[1]

Shortly after writing *The Beautiful and Damned* Fitzgerald listed for *The Chicago Tribune* the ten most important novels, and Conrad's *Nostromo* was the one he singled out as "the greatest novel since *Vanity Fair* (possibly excluding *Madame Bovary*)."[2] He does not say what Conrad works he read other than the admitted *Nostromo*, but these must have included *Heart of*

SOURCE *Twentieth Century Literature* I, April 1955, pp. 5–12. Reprinted in *The Houses That James Built*, East Lansing, 1961, pp. 150–158.

Darkness and *Lord Jim*. What he learned from Conrad includes not only the device of the perplexed narrator and turns of phrasing, but also themes and plot-situations, ambivalence of symbolism, etc.—in fact, the craft of the novel, including a theory of its construction. Fitzgerald, as he wrote in his notebooks, examined "Conrad's secret theory" and discovered the secret, that Conrad wrote the truth—"adding confusion however to his structure." How closely he studies Conrad is indicated also by what he says in this same note: "Nevertheless, there is in his scheme a desire to imitate life which is in all the big shots. Have I such an idea in the composition of this book?" And how much of Conrad he must have read is indicated by the very next note: "Conrad influenced by *Man Without a Country*." (In *The Crack-Up* by F. Scott Fitzgerald, 1945, p. 179.) The claim of his biographer that the extent of Conrad's influence on Fitzgerald is limited to his use of the Conradian narrator and "the constant and not always fortunate echoes of Conrad's phrasing" collapses, I think, in the face of the present analysis.

While writing *The Great Gatsby*, Fitzgerald read that same summer[3] Oswald Spengler's *The Decline of the West*, and the influence of Spengler's mixed perspectives of history is manifested in Fitzgerald's conception of a hero who confuses the past with the present and whose confused time-world embraces all history. "Spengler prophesied gang rule, "young people hungry for spoil," and more particularly 'the world as spoil' as an idea, a dominant, supersessive idea." (Fitzgerald to Maxwell Perkins, quoted in FSP, 336.) Gatsby as gangster represents this idea of the world as spoil. Now this idea of spiritual cannibalism which Fitzgerald met in Spengler he had already found in Conrad. The world as spoil is the dominant idea in *Heart of Darkness* and also in *Nostromo*. *The Great Gatsby* transposes Conrad's world-as-spoil idea into the contemporary idiom. Transported from the gang-ruled wilderness of Conrad's *Heart of Darkness*, Fitzgerald's reformed cannibals, reoriented in the gang-ruled wasteland of *The Great Gatsby*, prosper now in the "Swastika Holding Company." Kurtz's enslaved blacks have escaped the wilderness to become now a threat to white supremacy. "Civilization's going to pieces. ... Have you read 'The Rise of the Colored Empires' by this man Goddard?" (GG, 16). Kurtz's so-called humanitarianism—"Exterminate all the brutes"—is faintly echoed by Daisy Buchanan's mocking plea: "We've got to beat them down." Kurtz's wilderness rings with the voice of ivory, and Daisy's voice rings "full of money." Meyer Wolfsheim's barbaric cuff-buttons—"Finest specimens of human molars"—substitute for Kurtz's hoarded ivory.

Like Kurtz, Gatsby is unscrupulous and without restraint (as Marlow says of Kurtz), except for the restraint of keeping up appearances. Like Gatsby, Kurtz lacks "restraint in the gratification of his various lusts ... there was something wanting in him...." (HD, 573). Gatsby violates Daisy, taking "what he could get, ravenously and unscrupulously," and then at the end when time overtakes him Gatsby still has his future in front of him; and

Kurtz at the end similarly stands "on the threshold of great things" when his life begins "ebbing out of his heart into the sea of inexorable time" (HD, 589). Both Gatsby and Kurtz violate time; they corrupt the point-present Now. Kurtz's name contradicts him, and Gatsby's name is false. "Mr. Nobody from Nowhere" (as Tom Buchanan calls him) is beguiled by a dream, and likewise Kurtz. Kurtz's "unlawful soul" is "beguiled ... beyond the bounds of permitted aspirations" (HD, 586). What Marlow says of that "universal genius" defines also Gatsby's unlawful soul: "I had to deal with a being to whom I could not appeal in the name of anything high or low" (HD, 586). Born from "his Platonic conception of himself," "a Son of God," Gatsby is like Kurtz, a "universal genius"—"he was liable at the whim of an impersonal government to be blown anywhere about the world" (GG, 179). The godlike Gatsby has a metaphysical smile "of *eternal* reassurance in it.... It faced—or seemed to face—the whole eternal world for an instant, and then concentrated on *you* with an irresistible prejudice in your favor" (GG, 58). Kurtz does not smile, but his stare has the same metaphysical attribute— "wide enough to embrace the whole universe ..." (HD, 592).

Both Kurtz and Gatsby are conceived in the mode of a deity, with the difference that Kurtz is idolized and Gatsby is not. No more than a voice he seems to Marlow: an anonymous, disembodied voice, "an eloquent phantom," a Shade unrooted in reality, an "initiated wraith from the back of Nowhere" honoring Marlow with "its amazing confidences before it vanished altogether" (HD, 560). "Mr Nobody from Nowhere" unidentifiable and mysterious, unpredictable, inexplicable, anonymous, has his counterpart in Kurtz, for whom the parallel in Conrad's story is the fabulous Russian: "His very existence was improbable, inexplicable, and although bewildering. He was an insoluble problem" (HD, 568). Gatsby shares the same attributes, and he posseses also Kurtz's phenomenal capacity for vanishing from sight.

Kurtz's final cry—"The horror! the horror!"—testifies to the appalling truth that there is a hollowness inside all of us, a moral depravity from which no man is exempt, and also it is a testimony of Kurtz's personal greatness in facing up to that dark selfhood he has dared to probe. It is reckoned by Marlow as "an affirmation, a moral victory," and that is why Marlow remains loyal to Kurtz to the last. He remains loyal to Kurtz because he feels that Kurtz—"All Europe contributed to the making of Kurtz"—redeems mankind by his triumph over "victorious corruption," the powers of darkness that once claimed him for their own, and he triumphs because of the magnitude of his vision and because of his unflinching faith in that vision. The corrupted Kurtz and the corrupted Gatsby are, after all, incorruptible.

Though Gatsby trades on time and bargains with the clock, he never trades on the dream that possesses him. He remains loyal to his transcendent vision, and that is why Nick is moved to write the book which bears Gatsby's name. In *Heart of Darkness* Marlow saves Kurtz "out of an impulse of unconscious loyalty" (HD, 596). As Marlow remains loyal to Kurtz, so Nick remains loyal to Gatsby—in spite of his scorn for everything that Gatsby represents. Nick intuitively recognizes Gatsby's unique and heroic stature (Gatsby's greatness is, after all, impersonal), and he ends exempting Gatsby from his bitter—and Conradian—indictment of "the abortive sorrows and short-winded elations of men."

What redeems Gatsby is his fidelity to an idea, his faith in the power of dream, and what redeems Nick Carraway is his fidelity to Gatsby.

Fidelity is for Conrad the all-redeeming virtue; and Conrad's works are in the main variations on this theme. Betrayals condition Conrad's plots, and they shape Fitzgerald's plot in *The Great Gatsby*. Daisy is disloyal to her husband, and twice she is deceived by him; Jay Gatsby is tricked by two women, both having names that rime on his—Daisy Fay and Ella Kaye.[4] Nick cheats in his affairs with Jordan Baker and the unnamed girl out West; and Myrtle Wilson deceives her husband, Tom Buchanan cheating on George B. Wilson.

Nostromo is riddled with betrayals. Both Gatsby and Nostromo are self-deluded heroes, and both are doomed by the past. The theme of time in *Nostromo* is uttered by Mrs. Gould: "It had come into her mind that for life to be large and full, it must contain the care of the past and of the future in every passing moment of the present." (Modern Library edition, p. 582.) Conrad's time-theme is inverted in *The Great Gatsby*: the corrupted present violated by the corrupted past. As Mrs. Gould meditates on time, "a great wave of loneliness . . . swept over her head." Gatsby's loneliness is proverbial, and Nick shares it in admitting "a haunting loneliness" that he feels in himself and at times in others. Though he disapproves of him from beginning to end, Nick Carraway allies himself finally with Gatsby. The loneliness of Lord Jim adds somehow to his stature, and it moves Marlow to observe: "It is as if loneliness were a hard and absolute condition of existence . . ." (LJ, 180). The isolated hero is typical of Conrad's plots: Kurtz as Chief of the Inner Station, but off from the outer world; Haldin (in *Under Western Eyes*) isolated by his betrayal of Razumov; the lonely Leggatt and the untried captain in *The Secret Sharer*; and in *Victory* Heyst on his island.

Nick knows his Conrad. As the final image of Conrad's *Heart of Darkness* returns us to the opening scene on board the *Nellie*, where the story about Kurtz began, so *The Great Gatsby* is shaped in the same circular form, ending so as to circle us back to the beginning. The story about Kurtz begins and ends with Marlow sitting on board the *Nellie* "in the pose of a meditating Buddha." And Nick at the conclusion of his story about Gatsby imitates—and not by chance!—Marlow's Buddha pose: "I sat there brooding on the old, unknown world . . ." Nick in beginning his story portrays himself on the first page of the book as a sort of college father-confessor to the "privy secret griefs of wild, unknown men." Nick is bored by their intimate revelations, and he resents his unsought role as priest. The Marlow of *Lord Jim* begs off the same assignment out of his sense of humility: "I am not particularly fit to be a receptacle of confessions." Marlow is unfit for this priestlike role because of his own dark sins, though what he feels guilty of we do not know. It makes him feel like an impostor—"as though—God help me!—I didn't have enough confidential information about myself to harrow my own soul till the end of my appointed time" (LJ, 34). Nick lacks Marlow's warm humanity, his compassion and humility. Nick's "morality" camouflages his hypocrisy. He masks his duplicity. Nobody wrings from him a confession, but everybody confesses to Nick: Gatsby lays bare his soul to Nick; Myrtle discloses to Nick her affair with Tom Buchanan; Jordan tells him of Daisy's past; and Catherine confides in him Myrtle's past as well as her own. Nick hears Gatsby's confession—"the strange story of my youth"—on the night before he is murdered. In *Lord Jim*, similarly, Jim tells his past to Marlow in darkness. (There is a distinction between what Gatsby reveals about himself in darkness and what he tells Nick in sunlight. What he tells Nick in sunlight is chiefly falsehood; the occasion—Chapter IV—is a Sunday in late July. In sunlight Gatsby fabricates.)

The Marlow of *Heart of Darkness* is burdened by his own dark past, and he declares himself on Kurtz's side out of sympathetic kinship with Kurtz for that reason. "It is strange how I accepted this unforeseen partnership, this choice of nightmares forced upon me in the tenebrous land invaded by these mean and greedy phantoms" (HD, 589). Nick's ambiguous honesty—"I am one of the few honest people that I have ever known"—suggests comparison with Marlow's pride in the same cardinal virtue: "You know I hate, detest, and can't bear a lie, not because I am straighter than the rest of us, but simply because it appals me. There is a taint of death, a flavor of mortality in lies...." (HD, 526). Yet at the end, in masking the truth from Kurtz's intended so as to save Kurtz by a lie, Marlow perjures himself in ironic contradiction of his adamant scruple not to lie. As Marlow lies to save Kurtz, so in *Nostromo* Mrs. Gould lies to save Nostromo.

The Great Gatsby refashions in contemporary idiom what was for Conrad "the moral problem of conduct,"[5] the problem which Conrad explored notably in *The Nigger of the "Narcissus"* and in *Lord Jim*. Jim is admonished by his dad *not* to "judge men harshly or hastily," and Nick gets the same advice from his dad: "Reserving judgments is a matter of infinite hope." Gatsby and his neglected dad (Gatsby denies his parents) have their parallel in Jim and his neglected dad (Jim without a clean slate cannot go home). Fitzgerald's conception of the cosmic Gatsby—"a son of God" going about "his Father's business"—returns us to Jim and his Heavenly Father—Jim's dad. Conrad defines Jim's dad with cosmic wit: "the finest man that ever had been worried by the cares of a large family since the beginning of the world" (LJ, 79).

When the rajah asks Jim to repair his clock ("a nickel clock of New England make"), Jim refuses to tinker with it and drops the thing "like a hot potato." His refusal to tamper with time is what Jim later on regrets; he longs to be back there in prison, "back there again, mending the clock. Mending the clock—that was the idea" (LJ, 254). Mending the clock—that is the idea not only of *Lord Jim* but also of *The Great Gatsby*. To reinstate the past, that is Gatsby's illusion; to obliterate the past, that is Jim's illusion. Jim's faith is that life can be begun anew, with the past wiped off the slate. "A clean slate, did he say? As if the initial word of each our destiny were not graven in imperishable characters upon the face of a rock" (LJ, 186). Gatsby's faith is that life can be begun anew, with the past reinstated; his way of wiping the slate clean is "to fix everything just the way it was before." Time, that is what Gatsby cannot repair nor Jim Escape. Jim turns his back on the past, and the past catches up with him. What he escapes from overtakes and destroys him, his past which confronts him in the person of Brown. Marlow describes Jim as standing "on the brink of a vast obscurity, like a lonely figure by the shore of a sombre and hopeless ocean" (LJ, 173). Jim's "hopeless ocean" transposes into the "courtesy bay" that separates Gatsby from Daisy, that distance of dark water with the green light burning on the Buchanan dock before which Gatsby—with arms outstretched as though in prayer—appears in Nick's first glimpse of him and again in Nick's final recollection. Gatsby seeks his destiny across that stretch of water, and Lord Jim faces his destiny across the creek at Patusan—Jim confronting Brown at the hour of high tide. Jim cannot escape the past, and Gatsby cannot repeat it.

Jim, says Marlow, "appeared to me symbolic." What Jim symbolizes is the same as for Gatsby: the power of dream and illusion. Fitzgerald's romantic idealism *and* satiric detachment are patterned upon the characteristic Conradian ironic combination employed in the creation of Jim, Nostromo, and Kurtz. Deluded idealists! "The mind of man," as Marlow reports it in *Heart of Darkness*, "is capable of anything—because everything is in it, all the past as well as all the future" HD, 540). Conrad's dictum fits Gatsby, and Fitzgerald's romantic dogma fits equally Gatsby and Lord Jim: "No amount of fire or freshness can challenge what a man can store up in his ghostly heart" (GG, 116). At the core of *The Great Gatsby* is Conrad's paradox: the reality of dream. Stein's famous metaphor in *Lord Jim* poses the enigma of life: to be or to become. To be is to submit to the destructive element, the sea of struggling mankind. It is "the sea with its labouring waves for ever rising, sinking, and vanishing to rise again—the very image of struggling mankind ... soaring towards the sunshine ... like life itself" (LJ, 243). That is Marlow's metaphor, and it serves as the corollary to Stein's: "The way is to the destructive element submit yourself, and with the exertions of your hands and feet in the water make the deep, deep sea keep you up. So if you ask me—how to be?" But man cannot exist without his illusions, those aspirations by which he soars into the unknown, and that way too is destructive. "A man that is born falls into a dream like a man who falls into the sea. If he tries to climb into the air ... he drowns." Stein's butterfly finds a heap of dirt and sits on it; "but man he will never on his heap of mud keep still" (LJ, 214, 215). That heap of mud is the destructive element, life as it is—the colorless routine existence of our submission to the established order of things, undisturbed by any flights or quests. Now that way of life is what Jim's dad advocates in the last letter Jim gets from the old man back home. Back home is a place of peace and of faith in the conventions by which the world is conveniently regulated. Stein advocates the same thing: submit!

Like Jim, Gatsby does not submit. Like Jim, Gatsby transcends reality and time. Gatsby shares the myth attributes of Jim as Icarus, Jim going about "in sunshine hugging his secret," gazing "hungrily into the unattainable," and tumbling "from a height he could never scale again" (LJ, 198, 19, 112). On his journey into Patusan Jim singes his "wings." He gets his back blistered by the sun and he experiences "fits of giddiness." He has an uncommon habit of leaping and of taking falls; and in *The Great Gatsby*, Everyone hovers on the edge of an abyss ready for a fall. In *Lord Jim* Jim leaps over the stockade "like a bird," and the earth as he races from his prison "seemed fairly to fly backwards under his feet." Perched on the heights, he appears in one of Marlow's characteristic visions of him with "the incandescent ball of the sun above his head; the empty sky and the empty ocean all a-quiver; simmering together in the heat as far as the eye could reach" (LJ, 253, 167). To the natives at Patusan Lord Jim "appeared like a creature not only of another kind but of another essence." Had the natives not seen him coming up by canoe "they might have thought he had descended upon them from the clouds" (LJ, 229). At Gatsby's July party Owl Eyes has a wreck, and after a ghostly pause an apparition of a man ("a pale, dangling individual") steps out of the wrecked coupé to stare at the "amputated wheel—he stared at it for a moment, and then looked upward as though he suspected that it had dropped from the sky" (GG, 67). Brown accuses Lord Jim of having wings so as not to touch the dirty earth; Marlow accuses Lord Jim of being a romantic and repeats Stein's words: "In the destructive element immerse! ... to follow the dream, and again to follow the dream—and so—always...." That was the way (LJ, 334, 214). (We are as perplexed as Marlow as to what Stein means, for Stein fails to unriddle the enigma of his metaphor.) Conrad concludes his novel with the image of Stein gesturing vaguely at his butterflies in regret for dreams unpursued. As Fitzgerald puts it, there are the winged and the wingless.

In Gatsby's "incorruptible dream" and "unutterable visions"—the very epithets are Conrad's—Fitzgerald's hero wears the look of Nostromo and Lord Jim. All three are dream-deluded romantics. Inconceivable is Marlow's word for Jim, and Gatsby is in the same sense "inconceivable." Isolated and lonely, both Jim and Gatsby suffer bad names and are pursued by calumny; both are betrayed, and both are crucified—"Jim was to be murdered mainly on religious grounds, I believe" (LJ, 310). Gatsby's life divides into two parts, and Jim's life similarly divides into two parts: first his leap from the pilgrim ship, and secondly his leap into Patusan. Marlow defines not only Jim's plight but Gatsby's: Jim "was overwhelmed by the inexplicable; he was overwhelmed by his own personality—the gift of that destiny which he had done the best to master" (LJ, 341). The Conradian attributes of the legendary Gatsby—namely the night-day, moon-sun attributes of his divided selfhood—bear striking resemblances to Jim's duality: "He appealed to all sides at once—to the side turned perpetually to the light of day, and to that side of us which, like the other hemisphere of the moon, exists stealthily in perpetual darkness, with only a fearful ashy light falling at times on the edge. He swayed me. I own to it, I own up" (LJ, 93). In comparison with Marlow's devotion to Jim, Nick is noncommittal; his admission of Gatsby's greatness is an enforced admission. Too sophisticated to show any emotion, Nick exhibits no such spontaneity as Marlow shows in his fascination for the enigmatic Jim. Nick's inherited "provincial squeamishness" sets him off from Marlow; and Nick's mind, though quite as perplexed as Marlow's, lacks Marlow's range and points of curiosity. In his inveterate curiosity Marlow reminds us of the village gossip, and in his habitual indecision he suggests an old woman sitting metaphorically on the fence. But he penetrates the mask of Kurtz and the soul of Jim, whereas Nick Carraway presents Gatsby only from the outside.

Notes

1. *The Far Side of Paradise* (Boston, 1951), p. 170. In taking the line that Fitzgerald was hardly aware of his literary sources Mrs. Mizener conveniently forgets to make any mention of Petronius Arbiter's *The Satyricon*. It is difficult to believe that Fitzgerald was not consciously aware of his sources inasmuch as Gatsby is patterned upon Trimalchio. (See the opening sentence of Chapter VII of *The Great Gatsby* where Gatsby is identified as Trimalchio.) For points of parallelisms see Paul MacKendrick's "*The Great Gatsby* and Trimalchio," *Classical Journal*, 45 (April 1950), pp. 307–314.

2. Quoted by Mizener in *The Far Side of Paradise*, in the notes to Chapter IX, p. 336. This book is hereafter coded as FSP. Page references to *The Great Gatsby* are to the first edition: Scribner's, 1925. (The reprint edition by Grosset & Dunlap, n.d., has the same pagination.) For Conrad's *Heart of Darkness* I have used *The Portable Conrad*, edited by M.D. Zabel (New York, 1947). For *Lord Jim* I have used the Dent edition, first published in 1900. (Pagination is the same in the Modern Library edition of *Lord Jim*, 1931.) For *The Great Gatsby* I have used the abbreviation GG; for *Heart of Darkness*—HD; for *Lord Jim*—LJ.

3. Fitzgerald told Maxwell Perkins in 1940 that he read Spengler "the same summer I was writing 'The Great Gatsby,' and I don't think I ever quite recovered from him." (FSP, p. 336.) Perkins wrote Fitzgerald in 1926: "I'm almost afraid to tell you about a book that I think incredibly interesting—Spengler's 'Decline of the West'—for you'll tell me it's 'old stuff' and that you read it two years ago—for it was published eight years ago in Germany, and probably six, in France, and has been a long time translating into English." *Editor to Author: The Letters of Maxwell Perkins*, edited by John Hall Wheelock (New York, 1950), p. 47.

In "The Waste Land of F. Scott Fitzgerald," Mr. John W. Bicknell comments briefly on some points of parallelism between Gatsby and Lord Jim and Kurtz, and he notes an analogy between Conrad's Marlow and Fitzgerald's Nick Carraway, in *Virginia Quarterly Review*, 30 (Autumn 1954), 562.

Professor Dan Piper, whose book-length study of Scott Fitzgerald will appear in 1960, wrote me (September 4, 1956) that my "Conrad and *The Great Gatsby*" eliminated the need for his writing on the same topic. "I have paid particular attention to Fitzgerald's many references to Conrad among his manuscript papers. And while, from them, a more elaborate study could be put together concerning Conrad's influence, I doubt very much if the results of all that work would modify appreciably the fair and penetrating conclusions you reached in your independent study."

4. Everything in *The Great Gatsby* is reported ambiguously; the facts resist reduction to simple certitude. They lend themselves readily therefore to misreadings. The evidence for my reading of the Ella Kaye affair is based on what Nick reports, namely that James Gatz inherited from Dan Cody a legacy of twenty-five thousand dollars. "He didn't get it. He never understood the legal device that was used against him, but what remained of the millions went intact to Ella Kaye. He was left with his singularly appropriate education...." (GG, 121.)

5. Conrad in his preface to Thomas Beer's *Stephen Crane*, 1923, p. 3.

106
The Great Gatsby and the Tradition of Joseph Conrad: Part I

◆

ROBERT EMMET LONG

One of the most difficult problems in Fitzgerald scholarship in the nineteen-fifties and sixties has been the attempt to explain the sudden maturing of Fitzgerald in 1925, with the publication of *The Great Gatsby*. Nothing in Fitzgerald's earlier writing prepares for the authority and the aesthetic control over material that is so impressive in his third novel. For some time *The Great Gatsby* was considered merely as a "phenomenon," as an unaccountable and nearly miraculous occurrence in Fitzgerald's development; this attitude was supported by the popular conception of Fitzgerald as an author who was not well read and who wrote by inspiration. But more recent studies, which have included examinations of Fitzgerald's manuscripts and papers at the Princeton University library, have indicated that he was better read than anyone had supposed and that *The Great Gatsby* was the result of a very conscious, deliberated craftsmanship. A major step in the recent attempt to explain how *The Great Gatsby* was formulated, one which relates the novel to formative influences outside of America, was taken by James E. Miller in *The Fictional Technique of F. Scott Fitzgerald* (1957).[1] The clue for Miller's study came not only from Fitzgerald's fiction, but also from his letters and book reviews which indicate his developing attitude toward fictional form; the clue, Mr. Miller believed, led inescapably to Joseph Conrad.

There is no doubt whatever, judging by his letters, that Fitzgerald was familiar with Conrad's writing and that he had begun at an early stage of his own career to look to Conrad as a standard of excellence in art. In the five-year period before *The Great Gatsby*, Conrad's name appears in the letters probably more often than that of any other author. In 1920, on the request of

SOURCE *Texas Studies in Literature and Language* VIII, Summer 1966, pp. 257–276.

the *Chicago Tribune*, Fitzgerald compiled a list of the ten most important novels ever written and included *Nostromo* as "the greatest novel since *Vanity Fair* (possibly excluding *Madame Bovary*)."[2] Later, while he was staying in England, Fitzgerald was invited to meet John Galsworthy; at dinner, he told Galsworthy that he was one of the three living authors he admired most—the others being Joseph Conrad and Anatole France. Asked what Galsworthy had replied, Fitzgerald said, "I don't think he liked it much. He knew he wasn't that good."[3]

References to Conrad continue and are particularly frequent during the period in which *The Great Gatsby* was written. In his introduction to a later edition of the novel, Fitzgerald explained that before beginning to write *The Great Gatsby* he reread Conrad's preface to *The Nigger of the "Narcissus,"* which sets forth the terms to be fulfilled by "a work which aspires to the condition of art." In the same paragraph and obviously with Conrad in mind, he says that he intended his third book to be "an attempt at form."[4] Writing to H. L. Mencken in 1925, Fitzgerald defended *The Great Gatsby* by comparing it with Conrad's writing: "Despite your admiration for Conrad you have lately ... become used to the formless. It is in protest against my own formless two novels ... that this was written."[5] During the same summer he wrote to Mencken once again, citing Conrad in reference to himself even more dramatically:

> By the way, you mention in your review ... that Conrad has only two imitators. How about
> O'Neill in *Emperor Jones*   (*Heart of Darkness*)
> Me in *Gatsby*   (God! I've learned a lot from him)[6]

By considering Fitzgerald's fiction together with the views expressed in letters and reviews of the same period, Miller is able to document in a convincing way his argument that the craftsmanship and the surprising degree of control in *The Great Gatsby* were related to Fitzgerald's rapidly developing adherence to the aesthetic ideals of Conrad. Miller's discussion, briefly stated, places Fitzgerald's growth as a novelist within the framework of the Henry James-H. G. Wells controversy, still current in the 1920's, over the most satisfactory form for the novel. In *The New Novel* James had made the distinction between two genres of fiction: the novel of "saturation," which he associated with discursiveness and "the affirmation of energy, however directed or undirected" and the novel of "selection," which he associated with a controlling idea and a clear center of interest. Using illustrations from Fitzgerald's writing, Miller maintains that Fitzgerald's career forms an almost perfect arc from the time of *This Side of Paradise* (written under the spell of Compton MacKenzie, whom James cited as a "saturation" novelist) to the time of *The Great Gatsby* (indebted to Conrad, whom James cited as a "selective" novelist). In his conclusion, Miller discusses specific evidence in *The Great Gatsby* of Conrad's narrative method: the Conradian narrator, allowing both involvement and detachment; the use of irony and indirection;

the fragmented chronology. Since the publication of *The Fictional Technique of F. Scott Fitzgerald*, critics have generally accepted Miller's thesis. Kenneth Eble, for example, in his recent study *F. Scott Fitzgerald*, endorses Miller's position emphatically, although he does not expand upon it.[7]

But if Miller's study is the first to establish the importance of Conrad to *The Great Gatsby*, it is nevertheless not definitive. It seems to me, for example, that he confines his examination of Conrad and Fitzgerald to "form," or to what he calls "fictional technique." A more organic criticism would consider not only form but also content, structure, and treatment of subject. Since Miller's book there have been a few brief articles which have, in fact, taken this direction; one of these is Robert W. Stallman's seven-page note, which discusses parallel treatment of subject in Conrad and in *The Great Gatsby*.[8] Stallman reviews similarities in plot and characterization between Fitzgerald's novel and three Conrad novels: *Nostromo, Lord Jim,* and *Heart of Darkness*. He makes a number of valid comparisons: the loyalties of the Fitzgerald and Conrad narrators to their heroes in *Heart of Darkness* and *The Great Gatsby*, and the pride they both take in their personal honesty; the time motif in *Lord Jim* and *The Great Gatsby*; the common subjects of isolation and illusion. There does not seem, however, to be a single idea unifying his observations, and the note suffers, in addition, from a forcing of doubtful similarities. Stallman speaks, for example, of Jim and Gatsby as figures who are "pursued by calumny ... betrayed ... and crucified," and of Gatsby as having the "moon-sun attributes of Jim's duality.... In sunlight, Gatsby fabricates."[9] Nevertheless, the Stallman article is a beginning in a comparative examination of structure which I would like to undertake in the following pages, in order to see what a detailed and careful consideration of their fiction may bring to light about *The Great Gatsby*. If substantial correspondence exists between *The Great Gatsby* and Conrad's early fiction (before 1900) in structure and theme, it should be possible to find in Fitzgerald's novel a new dimension.

Almayer's Folly and *The Great Gatsby* have never, as far as I know, been compared; yet their affinity in plot and theme is striking. The epigraph of *Almayer's Folly* (from Amiel) expresses the situation to be explored in both novels: "Qui de nous/ n'a enterre promise,/ son jour d'extase/ et sa fin en exile?" Thus both Almayer and Gatsby have an exalted dream which is to be realized in the future, and whose realization seems very near; their obsessive, futuristic dreams are even described with the same vocabulary. Almayer's future is repeatedly imagined to be "splendid;" Conrad insists upon his "dream of a splendid future" (p. 3) and his "gorgeous future" (p. 10) to be realized in Europe with his daughter Nina.[10] These characterizing phrases are used so often that they have, as it were, the function of a recurring motif. The vocabulary occurs again in *The Great Gatsby*. Carraway says of Gatsby, for instance, that "there was something gorgeous about him" (p. 2),[11] and the quality of his life is suggested in capsule form in his "gorgeous car" (p. 76) and the "gorgeous pink rag of a suit" (p. 185) which he wears. Gatsby's house, closely identified with Gatsby himself, is described with sunlight playing across the whole front of it in a dazzling brilliance, and Carraway has to agree with Gatsby that "the sight is splendid" (p. 108). There is a difference, naturally, between the heroes themselves; Gatsby comes to share in the nature of his life something of the wondrousness of the epithets with which he is described, while Almayer never does. Yet they are strikingly alike in their fate: both envision a splendid destiny, about which they are deceived by their naïveté. The naïveté of Almayar is fabulous, and is captured in a moment when the Dutch naval officers visit his house and he tells them of his ambitious plans: "They listened and assented—amazed by the wonderful simplicity and foolish hopefulness of the man" (p. 36). The phrase echoes ominously in Gatsby's "extraordinary gift for hope" (p. 2).

It should be noted that in both *Almayar's Folly* and *The Great Gatsby* the heroes' illusions are embodied in their houses. Almayer's house becomes synonymous with his dream as early as the opening page of *Almayer's Folly*, where he meditates on the future, on the verandah of "his new but already decaying house—that last failure of his life" (p. 4). On the occasion of the naval officers' visit, the half-finished house built for the reception of Englishmen and in the short-lived expectation of the renewing of his fortunes, becomes the joke of the seamen as they leave their host. The house "received on that joyous night the name of 'Almayer's Folly' by the unanimous vote of the lighthearted seamen" (p. 37). Almayar's folly is both his house and his dream: the one is the outward symbol of the other.

Similarly in *The Great Gatsby*, the history of Gatsby's house at West Egg is a prophecy of Gatsby's own life. It had originally been built by a brewer with the quixotic notion of establishing a feudal estate; his children had sold the house while the funeral wreath was still on the door. The "feudal silhouette" of the house is an ironic commentary on Gatsby's impractical dream, just as its windows, in a dazzling burst of sunlight, evoke the wondrous quality of Gatsby's imagination. The evening before the reunion of Gatsby and Daisy the house is lit up from top to bottom, and wind in the trees—blowing the electric wires—causes the lights to flicker on an off, creating impressionistically the effect of spectacular fantasy. After Gatsby's death Gatsby's father produces for Carraway some papers which had belonged to his son, among them a crumpled photograph of Gatsby's house: a mirage of success. Appropriately, summing up Gatsby's strange life, Nick Carraway goes over to look "at that huge incoherent failure of a house once more" (p. 217).

The two houses, moreover, are located near water, across which may be seen, or glimpsed, the house of the heroes' more securely established opponents. The establishment of Abdulla, the native Rajah of Sambir, is part of the monolithic opposition to Almayer:

> From the low point of land where he stood he could see both branches of the river. The main stream of the Pantai was lot in complete darkness ... but up the Sambir reach his eye could follow the long line of Malay houses ... with here and there a dim light twinkling through bamboo walls, or a smoky torch burning on the platforms built out over the river. Further away ... founded solidly on a firm ground with plenty of space, starred by many lights burning strong and white ... stood the house and the godowns of Abdulla bin Selim, the great trader of Sambir.... The buildings in their evident prosperity looked to him cold and insolent and contemptuous of his own fallen fortunes. (p. 15)

Almayer, who dreams of becoming a self-made millionaire in the manner of Captain Lingard, and who had come to the tropics to "woo fortune ... ready to conquer the world, never doubting that he would" (p. 5), finds that very harsh and intractable realities (such as those represented by Abdulla) lie in his way.

In *The Great Gatsby*, the Buchanan house is located across the bay from Gatsby's, and is visible at night only by its dock light; the two houses are in a position of confronting one another, though distantly. The estates are not as closely situated as the houses in *Almayer's Folly*, nor could Gatsby's fortunes at this point be said to be fallen. Yet even the Georgian Colonial architecture of the Buchanan house suggests its solidity and permanence and its essential difference from Gatsby's, with its evocations of fantasy. The confrontation of the houses dramatizes the conflict between the actuality represented by one, and the quixotism of the solitary outsider, represented by the other; in their isolation and inevitable exclusion, Almayer and Gatsby share a similar fate. As the lone white man in that part of the East where he has come to settle, Almayer will be frustrated in his ambitions by the material realities of Sambir; Gatsby also is an outsider, and his bizarre estate at West Egg is as close as he will ever come to the established society of the Buchanans.

In the backgrounds of Almayer and Gatsby—in the progression of events bringing them to Sambir and West Egg, with their beliefs in a "splendid future"—there is a remarkable parallel. Almayer is "adopted" by Lingard, "the old adventurer" (p. 11) who takes him as a young man aboard his yacht, the *Flash*, on a cruise in which every island of the archipelago is visited. Vinck had first spoken of Lingard to Almayer, and his words, "He has lots of money.... You know, he has discovered a river" (p. 7), give Lingard a fabulous background. The cruise aboard the *Flash* is Almayer's initiation into life and into his dream. In *The Great Gatsby*, the role of Lingard is played by Dan Cody, who brings young James Gatz aboard his yacht, the *Tuolomee*, for a voyage which takes them three times around the continent. Dan Cody, whose name suggests the American frontier, is like Lingard, "an old adventurer" of a former age who has made his fortune from slender beginnings, and he poses for Gatsby the same possibility. In each of the novels the figure of the older man stands in the background of his protégé's dreams. Cody's yacht, the *Tuolomee*, is named after the gold fields in northern California, and underlies the idea of grandiose promise betrayed by brutalized reality;

Lingard's yacht, the *Flash*, is symbolic of brief and illusory grandeur.

These initiations, similar as they are, are followed by events even more strikingly similar, for both Almayer and Gatsby come to fix their conception of the future upon the idealization of a girl. For Almayer it is his daughter Nina, towards whom he appears to feel more nearly the emotions of a lover than a father. "His faith in Nina had been the foundation of his hopes, the motive of his courage" (p. 192). He has fantasies of a life in his mother's native Amsterdam, with Nina accepted and admired by all, and vindicating his life. "I myself have not been to Europe," he tells her, "but I have heard my mother talk so often that I seem to know all about it. We shall live a—a glorious life, You shall see" (p. 18). Without Nina, Almayer's dream may never be realized. In this respect it is similar to Gatsby's, which is centered upon Daisy Fay. Like Nina, Daisy is the incarnation of the hero's dream. Gatsby "knew that when he kissed this girl, and forever wed his unutterable visions to her perishable breath, his mind would never romp again like the mind of God" (p. 134). Nina and Daisy both, however, repudiate at the end the promise they seemed to assure. They had seemed to belong with the heroes, as if by some unquestioned right sanctioned by their vision; yet they reveal, finally, prior and stronger commitments to the forces which oppose and overcome the heroes.[12]

In *Almayer's Folly*, Almayer is opposed by a difference in race between himself and the entire community of Sambir. Nature, too, seems massed menacingly against Almayer's dreams, and ironically he is frequently seen laying plans against a background of Nature's capricious violence. In the opening scene, he is shown standing on his verandah at night, meditating on his grandiose future, while in the darkness a storm rages and the river is swollen ominously by rain: "The tree swung slowly round, amid the hiss and foam of the water, and soon getting free of the obstruction began to move down the stream again, rolling slowly over, raising upwards a long, denuded branch, like a hand lifted in mute appeal to heaven against the river's brutal and unnecessary violence" (p. 4).

As the only "civilized" man in Sambir, Almayer is most alien to Nature, while Mrs. Almayer and Dain are more closely associated with the "triumphant savagery of the river" (p. 28). Nina is Almayer's own child, but she is also the daughter of his native wife, who reverts to her native character not long after their marriage. The child Nina is sent to live with the Vincks in the capital of Singapore for several years, but becomes unwelcome in the "white nest" of the Vincks when she deflects the attention of suitors from their own daughters. Captain Ford, who returns Nina to Sambir, offers Almayer good advice: "You can't make her white. It's no use swearing at me. You can't" (p. 31). In the course of time, Nina is won over to her mother. "She had little belief and no sympathy for her father's dreams; but the savage ravings of her mother chanced to strike a responsive chord" (p. 151). The suit of the young nephew of Abdulla is refused by Almayer with barely concealed fury, but

Nina is obviously moved by the possibility of love with one of her own race; and it is not long after that Dain Maroola appears. At their first meeting Dain feels "the subtle breath of mutual understanding passing between their two savage natures" (p. 63). At the end Nina chooses Dain, destroying her father's dreams. "I am not of your race," Nina tells Almayer, "between your people and me there is a barrier that nothing can remove" (p. 179).

Like Almayer, who sees Nina not as she is but as she appears to him in felicity of his vision, Gatsby understands little of Daisy or of the social realities she represents. Although of a different kind, the opposition to Gatsby is nearly as great as that which overwhelms Almayer. While Gatsby, as a young officer during the First World War, is stationed at Camp Taylor in Louisville, he is brought into contact with Daisy's circle; it is possible for him momentarily, in the social mobility which the war brings about, to pass as one of Daisy's own class. "In various unrevealed capacities he had come into contact with such people, but always with indiscernible barbed wire between" (p. 177). Daisy's large home, its corridors redolent of gaiety and excitement, opens before Gatsby exalted romantic dreams, centering upon Daisy herself; the real rather than romantic intimations of wealth Gatsby never perceives. Fitzgerald's insight into the nature of wealth in *The Great Gatsby* is that while wealth ought to heighten romantic possibilities of life, it more often restricts and brutalizes the sensibilities of those whose possess it. The wealth of the Buchanans has not been recently acquired, like Gatsby's; they have grown up with wealth, and their sense of superiority, moulded by it, places them beyond the reach of a genuine relationship with other people. The insincerity of Daisy is figured in the coy use she makes of her voice; at Gatsby's parties she admires only the actress whose studied pose under a white-plum tree is a vacant gesture. In the end her affair with Gatsby is revealed also as coy and insincere. In Tom Buchanan physical prowess combines with the petulant wilfulness of a spoiled adolescent to focus the destructive effect of wealth. Daisy and Tom are members of a "distinguished secret society," membership in which is not extended to Gatsby. Boundary lines have already been firmly drawn between the classes, and when Gatsby attempts to cross them he finds only callous and merciless exclusion. In this respect, that of the heroes' deception about the realities they face, Almayer and Gatsby are not greatly different. Both are outsiders, "isolates," separated from the worlds they envision by barriers of race and social class.

The *symbolic moment of defeat* for Almayer and for Gatsby occurs in a confrontation scene near the conclusion of each of the novels. In *Almayer's Folly* the scene takes place at an island beyond Sambir. Nina, Dain, and Almayer are brought face to face in a critical moment of decision, and Nina—forced to choose between the two men—chooses Dain. It is here that she announces to Almayer that barriers of race divide them; it is Almayer's great moment of recognition and awakening, the defeat of a lifetime's hopes. The defeat of Almayer occurs at the moment of Nina's repudiation. A parallel confrontation scene in *The Great Gatsby* occurs at a rented suite at the Plaza Hotel. Compelled to choose, in effect, between Gatsby and Tom, Daisy makes it clear that her loyalties are, after all, with Tom's world. Gatsby's illusion that nothing could violate the ideality of their romance is shattered in Daisy's admission that since her affair with Gatsby, she has loved Tom. Tom drives a final wedge between Gatsby and Daisy when he reminds the group that Gatsby's suspect wealth is hardly the same as theirs. As in *Almayer's Folly*, it is in this confrontation scene that Gatsby's dream is actually destroyed. "Only the dead dream fought on as the afternoon slipped away, trying to touch what was no longer tangible, struggling unhappily, undespairingly, toward the lost voice across the room" (p. 162). These scenes mark a sudden reversal in the novels, for just before them the hopes of the heroes had been at their highest; Almayer cries of Nina (and it could be said also of Daisy) that her betrayal comes "cruelly, treacherously, in the dark; in the very moment of success" (p. 192). Dain and Tom Buchanan usurp the dream of the heroes as they go off with Nina and Daisy.

The houses in *Almayer's Folly* and *The Great Gatsby*, which had been identified earlier with the heroes' dreams, are reintroduced at the end to heighten the shattering of their illusions. Almayer goes to live in the half-finished house known along the river as "Almayer's Folly," where he attempts vainly to find peace amid the confusion and disorder of decaying planks and half-sawn beams. Assuming the total isolation which had always been his destiny, he is like "an immense man-doll broken and flung there out of the way" (p. 204). He dies unmourned, hardly an object of curiosity. At the end of *The Great Gatsby* Gatsby's house has a similar quality of disorder and incoherence; it is described as "ghostly" when Nick and Gatsby roam through its empty rooms looking for cigarettes, and with Gatsby relating the last fragments of his late-summer romance with Daisy Fay. An autumnal motif rises up through the narrative, and the color evocations of Gatsby's dream return and become autumnal too. The yellow cocktail music of Gatsby's parties dissolves into "yellowing trees" and the blue associated with Daisy becomes the "blue smoke of brittle leaves" (p. 213), and "ghostly birds singing among the blue leaves" (p. 182). Gatsby's body as it drifts aimlessly in his swimming pool suggests a ritual of death and oblivion: fall leaves cluster around the rudderless drift of the air mattress, with its trail of blood. Only Nick and Gatsby's father trudge through the rain to attend Gatsby's funeral, joined later by the man whose enormous spectacles had given him the "unusual quality of wonder." Owl Eyes, as he is called, pronounces a final requiem: "'The poor son-of-a-bitch', he said." The careers of Almayer and Gatsby thus come full cycle from their early visions of a transcendent future, to the isolation, death and oblivion, which their actual futures hold.

That the similarities in these two novels have never been noted is perhaps due to the fact that Almayer and Gatsby are quite different in *one* respect. Almayer never confronts his destiny with a heroic will; almost the opposite of a hero, in its original sense, he seems feckless and defeated from the beginning—as wooden as the broken man-doll he is said to resemble at the end. Gatsby, on the other hand, does achieve heroic stature by the intense life of his imagination. The conception of Jay Gatsby, whose collision with reality grows out of his uncompromisingly romantic conception of himself, is so unique that I know of only one other parallel to Gatsby in modern fiction—that of Jim in *Lord Jim*.

Between *Almayer's Folly* (1895) and *Lord Jim* (1900) a new type of hero begins to appear in Conrad's fiction in the short story *Youth*—a hero different from the straw figures of Almayer and Willems, and more nearly suggesting the type of Jim. He is the young naval officer (in *Youth* it is the young Marlow himself) who is tested in his first command at sea, and his story celebrates youthful illusion, the promise that grows dim with every year of experience: "But for me all the East is contained in that vision of my youth. It is all in that moment when I opened my young eyes on it. I came upon it from a tussle with the sea—and I was young—and I saw it looking at me. And this is all that is left of it! Only a moment; a moment of strength, of romance, of glamour—of youth!" (p. 42).[13] Marlow's discovery in *Youth* informs the theme of both *Lord Jim* and *The Great Gatsby*: it is that the "glow in the heart" belongs not as it seems with the future, but with the past—with the unattainable dreams of youth.

According to James E. Miller, Fitzgerald had prefaced a 1923 book review of Thomas Boyd's war novel *Through the Wheat* with a quotation from *Youth*. Miller gives the quotation which Fitzgerald had used:

> I did not know how good a man I was till then.... I remember my youth and the feeling that will never come back any more—the feeling that I could last forever, outlast the sea, the earth, and all men ... the triumphant conviction of strength, the beat of life in a handful of dust, the glow in the heart that with every year grows dim, grow cold, grows small, and expires too soon—before life itself.[14]

"So, in part," Fitzgerald began his review, "runs one of the most remarkable passages of English prose written these thirty years... Since that story I have found in nothing else even the echo of that life and ring."

Fitzgerald obviously admired more in this passage than its lyric cadences, for a number of his own best stories during the 1922–1925 period take the thematic direction of Conrad's *Youth*. "The Sensible Thing" (1924) and "Winter Dreams" (1922) have to do with the loss of the ability to feel with the romantic intensity of youth. Dexter Green, the hero of "Winter Dreams," in losing the heroine also loses his dreams, and thus his youth:

> Even the grief he could have borne was left behind in the country of illusion, of youth, of the richness of life, where his winter dreams had flourished.
> "Long ago," he said, "long ago, there was something in me, but now that

thing is gone.... I cannot cry. I cannot care. That thing will come back no more."[15]

In "The Diamond as Big as the Ritz" (1922), Fitzgerald remarks that youth can never live in the present, "but must always be measuring up the day against its own radiantly imagined future ... prophecies of that incomparable, unattainable young dream."[16] At the end, Kismine speaks of the diamond mountain as seeming like a dream, even though it had been where she had spent all her youth; and the young hero, John Unger, tells her that it *was* a dream: "Everybody's youth is a dream."

But not until *Lord Jim* for Conrad, and *The Great Gatsby* for Fitzgerald does there occur the conception of a hero who is the prophet and incarnation of youthful imagination. Unlike the heroes of the short stories which immediately precede *The Great Gatsby*, and unlike Marlow in *Youth*, Jim and Gatsby know nothing of the disenchantment experience brings; with colossal naïveté they will not allow that the dream of youth *is* unattainable. Their conceptions of themselves and of their destinies have indeed, a godlike character. Marlow says of Jim that he "must have led a most exalted existence" (p. 95), and later he comments that "the point about him was that of all mankind Jim had no dealings but with himself" (p. 339).[17] He is so alone in the elusive grandeur of his conception that Marlow finds nothing whatever with which he can compare him. When Gatsby says that Daisy's love for Tom was "just personal," Carraway can only wonder at "some intensity in his conception of the affair that couldn't be measured" (p. 182). Gatsby seems to have "sprung from his Platonic conception of himself" (p. 118).

The careers of Jim and Gatsby begin alike, with boyhood dreams. Jim is sent from the country home of his clergyman father at an early age, and from the foretop of a training ship, he looks out over the scene of departing ships; the sea, shining with a hazy splendor, seems to stir with intimations of romantic achievement: "He loved these dreams and the success of his imaginary achievements. They were the best parts of life, its secret truth, its hidden reality. They had a gorgeous virility, the charm of vagueness.... They carried his soul away with them and made it drunk with the philtre of an unbounded confidence in itself" (p. 20).

Young Gatsby also lives in his dreams; the son of unsuccessful farm people in North Dakota whom his imagination cannot accept as his parents, he lies in bed at night imagining all manner of future glory. The boy is so immersed in dreams that he comes to regard them as (Marlow's phrase) the greater part of reality. Gatsby's early reveries were "a satisfactory hint of the unreality of reality, a promise that the rock of the world was founded securely on a fairy's wing" (p. 119). As Jim and Gatsby grow older, they do not leave their boyhood dreams behind as most people do, but attempt to live them out in their full measure in the years of their young manhood.

As young men they have certain similarities even in their appearance and manners. They are described as immaculate and as having chivalrous manners, and there is a strong hint of boyish restlessness about each of them. Gatsby is an "elegant young roughneck" (p. 59), and Marlow speaks of Jim's boyishness repeatedly, particularly of his boyish eyes that looked straight into his, "his artless smile, his youthful seriousness" (p. 78). Gatsby's smile, as he focuses his entire attention upon Nick Carraway and looks straight into his eyes, is one of the many fine gestures with which Gatsby's character has been suggested. Carraway says that Gatsby's was "one of those rare smiles with a quality of eternal reassurance in it, that you may come across four or five times in your life" (p. 58). The last time Nick sees Gatsby alive, he tells him that he is worth the whole crowd at East Egg, and Gatsby again breaks into a smile that is at first merely polite and then suddenly radiant. While Jim is talking about his plans, Marlow notices that a "strange look of beatitude overspread his features.... He positively smiled! ... It was an ecstatic smile that your face—or mine either—will never wear, my dear boys" (p. 84). Their smiles and other details of their appearance are perhaps expressions of a single quality; Fitzgerald uses the phrase "romantic readiness" to describe Gatsby, and the same idea is conveyed in Marlow's saying of Jim that "he had the faculty of beholding at a hint the face of his desire and the shape of his dream" (p. 175). "It was extraordinary," says Marlow, "how he could cast upon you the spirit of his illusion" (p. 109).

The naïveté of Jim and Gatsby, furthermore, has the same vast scale as their visions. Musing over Jim's situation, the scholarly Stein sighs "Yes; he is young," and Marlow replies: "The youngest human being now in existence" (p. 219). Marlow calls Jim "fabulously innocent" (p. 94), and the insidious Cornelius, intriguing with "Gentleman Brown" against Jim, cries that Jim is, after all, vulnerable: "He's no more than a little child ... like a little child" (p. 327). One of Jim's employers, a friend of Marlow's, gathering from what has been said that Jim may have been guilty of some offense, writes to Marlow that he is "unable to imagine him guilty of anything much worse than robbing an orchard" (p. 188). Gatsby's entire conception of Daisy, his mansion and elaborate lawn parties which exist merely as a ploy for meeting Daisy, are staggeringly innocent. In the scene in which Gatsby shows Daisy his collection of colored shirts, Daisy can only remark that she would like to put him in one of the pink clouds overhead and wheel him about.

But as young men both Jim and Gatsby meet with a stunning defeat which threatens their dreams and their ideal conceptions of themselves; the crucial incident in which the defeat occurs has the form in each novel of a *central symbolic scene.*[18] In *Lord Jim* it is Jim's jump from the *Patna*; in *The Great Gatsby* it is Daisy's marriage to Tom Buchanan. Jim's jump from the *Patna* is the focal point of the novel, for it is here that his destiny is revealed, that the discord between his imagination and his performance is forever fixed. In *The Great Gatsby* the wedding of Tom and Daisy permanently decides Gatsby's fate. Yet neither Jim nor Gatsby can accept the finality of these occurrences; their conceptions of themselves threatened, they still believe that the past can be reclaimed. Carraway says that Gatsby had "talked a lot about the past, and I gathered that he wanted to recover something, some idea of himself, perhaps, that had gone into loving Daisy" (p. 133).

Following these critical incidents, the careers of Jim and Gatsby proceed from the illusion of a "second chance," or as Jim puts it, the possibilities of beginning with a "clean slate." "A clean slate, did he say?" cries Marlow. "As if the initial word of each [sic] our destiny were not graven in imperishable characters upon the face of a rock" (p. 186).[19] Carraway advises Gatsby that "you can't repeat the past." "Can't repeat the past?" he cried incredulously. "Why of course you can! I'm going to fix everything just the way it was before" (p. 133). Jim believes that "some day one's bound to come upon some sort of chance to get it all back" (p. 179). It would be for Jim, as it would for Gatsby, as if the past had never existed. "Never existed—that's it, by Jove!" Jim murmured to himself" (p. 232).[20]

In their attempts to relive the past Jim and Gatsby begin a second career which bring them to a pinnacle of fame and success. Patusan, according to Marlow, is a land without a past, and in Patusan, with his past disguised or apparently effaced, Jim achieves heroic stature. The time comes when Marlow sees Jim "loved, trusted, admired, with a legend of strength and prowess round his name as though he had been the stuff of a hero" (p. 175). Jim seems to lead a charmed life, and tells Marlow that he feels nothing can touch him now. Everything redounds to his fame and splendor, which are considerable, for Jim becomes a myth in Patusan, where he is known as Tuan Jim, or Lord Jim. When Marlow comes to Patusan, he meets a native on the coast who speaks of Jim. "He called him Tuan Jim," says Marlow, "and the tone of his references was made remarkable by a strange mixture of familiarity and awe" (p. 242). Fabulous stories circulate about him, one about a priceless emerald supposed to be concealed on the person of Jewel, the native girl who loves and is protected by Jim. Jewel, too, Marlow comments, "was part of this amazing Jim-myth" (p. 280).

Jim's second career has its parallel in the second career of Gatsby which leads him to a mansion in West Egg, and the kind of glamor and success he may have dreamed about as a boy. The parties he gives are on an epic scale: his garden glows with colored lights, and movie stars and financiers arrive from New York to add to the variety and gaiety of life. Even nature—the moon being produced from a caterer's basket—seems part of the gaudy splendor Gatsby has created. In the midst of this brilliance Gatsby stands alone, dominating the entire scene. Like Jim, Gatsby appears to have come out of nowhere, to have no past; and also like Jim, he is the subject of rumor and aprocryphal legends. Even the speculations that he is the nephew of the Kaiser, or that he once killed a man, or that he was a German spy during the War, merely add to Gatsby's mystery and stature; people who have never gossiped about anything in their lives have confidently held theories about Gatsby.

In Patusan and West Egg, where their pasts are unknown, Jim and Gatsby live out a dream life of their own making; their identities, like their names, are assumed. Conrad uses the word "incognito" in connection with Jim; Jim's last name is never specified in *Lord Jim*, and after the *Patna* incident, when Jim drifts from one obscure job to another, not wishing to be recognized, he goes only by his first name. "His incognito," Conrad remarks, "which had as many holes as a sieve, was not meant to hide a personality but a fact. When the fact broke through the incognito he would leave suddenly the seaport where he happened to be at the time and go to another—generally farther east" (p. 4). When he works for the ship chandlers, Egstrom and Blake, he is called Mr. James; the title Tuan Jim, or Lord Jim, is the last of his assumed identities, and it is never clear whether this identity is a disguise for a vulnerable Jim, or a fantasy self which becomes the genuine selfhood he achieves. In a similar way Jay Gatsby is the creation of James Gatz, a fictional identity or incognito which is at all times threatened by reality; yet in the end James Gatz come to seem less real than Jay Gatsby.

Involved in the problem of identity relating to Jim and Gatsby are two mutually exclusive selves, and a pattern of behavior which a psychologist would surely call schizophrenic. Neither is able to accept that part of reality which contradicts his imaginative identity. Jim cannot believe, despite his intense awareness of lost honor, in the reality of his desertion of the *Patna*; it is to him as if only his *physical self* had jumped, his "imaginative" self remaining uncompromised. Gatsby's wealth is derived from his association with "Wolfsheim's crowd," and from various kinds of illegal traffic, yet he does not regard this as having anything to do with himself; the same impulse which causes him to reject his own childhood, and parents, and even his name, also causes him to see in the superficial Daisy Fay ideal qualities commensurate with his vision.

This problem of identity and the romantic will is diagnosed authoritatively by the scholarly Stein in Chapter Twenty of *Lord Jim*, a chapter forming one of the most brilliant scenes in the novel. Stein's butterflies are a masterwork of nature. "So fragile!" says Stein, "and so strong! And so exact! This is Nature—the balance of colossal forces. Every star is so—and every blade of grass stands *so*—and the might Kosmos in perfect equilibrium produces—this ... this masterpiece of Nature" (p. 208). Man, however, is an imperfect creature; and it seems to Stein that man has come where he is not wanted, where there is no place for him: "We want in so many different ways to be.... This magnificent butterfly finds a little heap of dirt and sits still on it; but man he will never on his heap of mud keep still. He want [sic] to be so, and again he want to be so.... He wants to be a saint, and he wants to be a devil—and every time he shuts his eyes he sees himself as a very fine fellow—so fine as he can never be ... in a dream" (p. 213).

The romantic will resolves itself, for Stein, into the question of "how to be, or become." Because of the nature of human limitations, Jim's case is hopeless, and it might be better for him if he were buried and underground; the next best thing is to submit himself to the "destructive element," or to find in action as near an approximation of one's dream as possible. "To follow the dream, and again to follow the dream—and so—*ewig—usque ad finem*" (p. 214). Jim in Patusan, and Gatsby at West Egg, take the course Stein prescribes, enter into the destructive element, attempting to become "so fine" as they can never be.

In this attempt, in the second careers of Jim and Gatsby—despite the fame and success they achieve—the limitations which they cannot accept reassert themselves. The past breaks in upon them in the form of *recurrences of central symbolic scenes*, and this time dooms them irrecoverably. The implication of re-enactment is apparent even in the name of Patusan, an approximate anagram of *Patna*; Jim has the entire community in his trust, as before he had been entrusted with the lives of the eight hundred passengers aboard the *Patna*, bound toward Mecca on a "mission of faith." In the incident, at the height of Jim's apparent success, in which Jim is confronted by the renegade Brown, the central scene is re-enacted. Brown at once searches out Jim's weak spot and fastens upon it. "And there ran through the rough talk a vein of subtle reference to their common blood, an assumption of common experience; a sickening suggestion of common guilt, of secret knowledge that was like a bond of their minds and of their hearts" (p. 387). Jim is again immobilized in the moment of crisis and decision, this time by a psychic identification with Brown. He releases Brown, with the result that Brown slaughters a party of natives, including Dain Waris, the faithful friend of Jim and the idol of his father, the old chief, Doramin. Jim's facing death at the hands of Doramin is his last attempt to recover the broken remains of his dream. His death, however, is perhaps his final defeat, for he does not surrender his life in the name of fidelity to others, but in defiant assertion of his egoistic vision. In *The Great Gatsby* the wedding of Tom and Daisy is re-enacted in the scene at the Plaza. The stifling heat of New York introduces the wedding motif, calling to mind the heat of June in Louisville when Daisy had married Tom; the music of Mendelssohn's Wedding March is heard from the apartment below as Daisy tells Gatsby she cannot say she has never loved Tom. It is the crush of reality against the fragile fantasy of James Gatz, and it is at this moment that Gatsby's dream is shattered.

But in addition to these parallels in the conception of the heroes and the sequence of events, there is also the parallel in the narrative frame in which both heroes appear. The first-person narrators, Marlow and Carraway, are themselves characters in the novels; they find themselves reluctantly but unavoidably drawn into the lives of the heroes, and they observe them with a sense of their having perhaps a moral reference to themselves. The result is a double sense of immediate involvement, and of detachment and objectivity.

There are even similarities in the two narrators' introductions of themselves. They both complain, for example, that they have always been singled out as (in Marlow's words) "the recipient of confidences" (p. 324). Carraway protests that "most of the confidences were unsought" (p. 1) and had come about as the result of his reserving of judgment, "a habit that has opened up many curious natures to me" (p. 1). Something about Marlow makes the same appeal to men with "hidden plague spots ... and loosens their tongues at the sight of me for their infernal confidences" (p. 34).[21]

The ambivalence of Marlow and Carraway toward the heroes creates much of the play of tension and irony in the novels. Carraway says in the opening pages of *The Great Gatsby* that Gatsby represented everything for which he had an unaffected scorn, and his account of Gatsby's career reveals a sympathy that is always qualified by his awareness of Gatsby's gaucherie and illusion. Marlow's sympathy for Jim is repeatedly undercut by his referring of Jim's intentions back to his evasion of moral responsibility. He speaks of Jim's "high-minded absurdity of intention" (p. 197), and when Jim tells Marlow of his boyhood dreams, Marlow remarks that "with every word my heart, searched by the light of his absurdity, was growing heavier in my breast" (p. 95). This ambivalence, of course, works in an opposite way, complicating the judgement of the heroes which the narrators attempt to make. Marlow speaks of the "subtle unsoundness" of Jim; yet he affirms that Jim had achieved genuine greatness!

The heroic stature of Jim and Gatsby is called up in the great tableaux which occur in the two works. In the most memorable tableau scene in *Lord Jim* Marlow sees Jim as a solitary, enigmatic figure against the sombre and darkening sea:

> He was white from head to foot, and remained persistently visible with the stronghold of the night at his back, the sea at his feet.... For me that white figure in the stillness of coast and sea seemed to stand at the heart of a vast enigma. The twilight was ebbing fast from the sky above his head, the strip of sand had sunk already under his feet, he himself appeared no bigger than a child—then only a speck, a tiny white speck, that seemed to catch all the light left in a darkened world.... And, suddenly, I lost him. (p. 336)

In the tableau of Gatsby calling forth the promise of the green light, Gatsby is a solitary figure observed in the darkness by Nick, and he vanishes from sight as suddenly and strangely as does Jim. In a second tableau Gatsby is contrasted with the chaos of a procession of stalled cars on his drive. "A sudden emptiness seemed to flow now from the windows and the great doors, endowing with compete isolation the figure of the host who stood on the porch, his hand up in a formal gesture of farewell" (p. 68). The tableaux serve to heighten the sense of Jim and Gatsby as mythic heroes, their greatness involving a total isolation from the lives of ordinary men. The quality of mystery and wonder surrounding them has been evoked mythopoeically, with a fusion achieved between the felt presence of the heroes and the mood conjured up in the physical world.[22]

But their greatness is precarious, menaced by the darkness against which they are seen in representative tableaux, and by the material world from which their Platonic imaginations divorce them. The "destructive element" in *Lord Jim* includes an extraordinary number of vicious and warped characters, among the first in Conrad's gallery of grotesques. There is, for example, the strange pair of Chester and Robinson, who have no use for idealism or for men who take things to heart; old Robinson, who has shrugged off the notoriety of an incident in which he had been guilty of cannibalism, conforms to Chester's idea of what a man ought to be like. Robinson "sees things as they are" (p. 162). They form a company to exploit a guano deposit and would like to engage Jim as an overseer for impressed coolie workers. Jim's remorse over lost honor makes him, in their view, "not much good ... too much in the clouds" (p. 168), and consequently suitable for such a gruesome assignment. The German captain who had been the chief officer aboard the *Patna*, and the first to desert, flees a court inquiry, his conscience untroubled. And in Patusan, Jim is confronted by the malevolence of "Gentleman Brown" and Cornelius. Cornelius is so abject and immoral that he seems scarcely human; Conrad says that his abjectness was so complete that even his loathsomeness was abject, "so that a simply disgusting person would have appeared noble by his side" (p. 286). Jim's idealism is challenged by a world peopled by such depraved characters, who heap upon him the full measure of their imprecation. Cornelius passes judgment upon Jim in the name of all of his kind. "He throws dust into everybody's eyes; he throws dust into your eyes, honourable sir, but he can't throw dust into my eyes" (p. 327). Tom Buchanan, speaking for the subordinate characters of *The Great Gatsby* who are alike in the meanness and confusion of their lives, makes a similar indictment of Gatsby: "he threw dust into your eyes just like he did in Daisy's, but he was a tough one" (p. 215).

At the end of *Lord Jim* and at the end of *The Great Gatsby* the brutal and callous characters triumph, and the heroes are defeated in worlds far from ideal. The pattern of their careers is Icarian (Conrad uses the word to describe Jim, as well as Icarian imagery); their flight toward the ideal had been foredoomed by the human limitations their imaginations could not accept. But they are redemptive figures too, alone of all the characters possessing vision. "The sheer truthfulness of [Jim's] last three years of life," Conrad says, "carries the day against the ignorance, the fear, and the anger of men" (p. 393). Taking up the romantic position at one point, Conrad remarks that it is only through imagination that anything exists, that Jim exists. It is the final irony of the two novels, and the distinguishing feature of their correspondence, that although Jim and Gatsby pursue illusion and are defeated, their "exuberant imagination" (*LJ*, p. 176) gives them both heroic stature and exemplary truthfulness.

Notes

1. James E. Miller, Jr., *The Fictional Technique of F. Scott Fitzgerald* (The Hague, 1957).
2. Arthur Mizener, *The Far Side of Paradise* (Boston, 1949), p. 336, n. 6.
3. *Ibid.*, p. 132.
4. F. Scott Fitzgerald, "An Introduction to *The Great Gatsby*," Modern Library Edition of *The Great Gatsby* (New York, 1934). Reprinted in *The Great Gatsby: A Study*, ed. Frederick J. Hoffman (New York, 1962), pp. 166–167.
5. F. Scott Fitzgerald, *The Letters of F. Scott Fitzgerald*, ed. Andrew Turnbull (New York, 1963), p. 480. Letter to H.L. Mencken, May 4, 1925.
6. *Ibid.*, p. 482. Letter to H.L. Mencken, May or June, 1925.
7. Kenneth Eble, *F. Scott Fitzgerald* (New York, 1963), pp. 85–105.
8. Robert Wooster Stallman, "Conrad and *The Great Gatsby*," *Twentieth Century Fiction*, I (April, 1955), 5–12. Reprinted in R.W. Stallman. *The Houses That James Built* (Ann Arbor, 1961), pp. 150–157.
9. Stallman, *The Houses That James Built*, p. 157, n. 3.
10. All page references to *Almayer's Folly* are from *The Complete Works of Joseph Conrad*, Canterbury Edition (New York, 1924).
11. All page references to *The Great Gatsby* are from the original edition (New York, 1925).
12. The roles of Nina and Daisy as simultaneously objectifying and denying the heroes' dreams are suggested in the detail of the white dresses they both conspicuously wear. Nina's white dress is alluded to so often that it becomes a defining feature. Dreaming of her, Dain closes his eyes "trying to evoke the gracious and charming image of the white figure ... that vision of supreme delight" (p. 166). In the climactic scene in which Nina goes away with Dain, Almayer has a final view of his daughter: "He followed their figures moving in the crude blaze of a vertical sun, in that light vibrating, like a triumphal flourish of brazen trumpets. He looked at ... the tall, slender, dazzling white figure" (p. 194). White in *Almayer's Folly*, as well as in other Conrad novels, is associated generally with illusion. The idea of illusion is implied in the scene in which the young lovers drift in their canoe under the white mist of the river, oblivious of the world and dreaming of an ideal life that will be unattainable. It is present when Almayer's imagination soars far above the treetops "into the great white clouds away to the westward ... to the paradise of Europe" (p. 63). Remembered always by her white dress, Nina stands for an enchanting, deceptive vision.

Daisy, in *The Great Gatsby*, is presented in a somewhat similar way. In the opening scene, Carraway enters the Buchanan living room and sees Daisy for the first time in the East; in this important opening impression she wears a white dress, and appears in what is actually a symbolic tableau. Seated on a cloudlike couch in a "bright rosy-colored space, fragilely bound into the house" (p. 9), Daisy's white dress ripples in an unnatural breeze blowing through the room; the ethereality of the view creates a sense of Daisy as a goddess figure. Later, when Nick enters the room a second time, Daisy and Jordan Baker are seated on the same couch, seeming "like silver idols weighing down their own white dresses against the singing breezes of the fans" (p. 138). The detail of the white dress is brought into play again as Jordan describes Daisy when Gatsby first met and fell in love with her: she always dressed in white, even drove a white roadster. A pattern of color imagery develops through the novel ("the milk of wonder;" the "white palaces" of East Egg; the illusion from the Queensboro bridge of New York as a "white city" made with a wish out of nonolfactory money) culminating in the reversal of the white dress as the wedding gown worn by Daisy when she married Tom Buchanan. Like the "white city," the white figure of Daisy comes to represent the wondrous as illusion.

19. All page references to *Youth* are from *Youth & Two Other Stories*, in *The Complete Works of Joseph Conrad* (New York, 1924).
14. Quoted in Miller, *The Fictional Technique of Fitzgerald*, pp. 69, 104–105.
15. F. Scott Fitzgerald, "Winter Dreams," in *The Stories of F. Scott Fitzgerald*, ed. Malcolm Cowley (New York, 1951), p. 145.
16. "The Diamond as Big as the Ritz," in *The Stories of F. Scott Fitzgerald*, p. 18.
17. All page references to *Lord Jim* are from *The Complete Works of Joseph Conrad*, Vol. 21 (New York, 1924).
18. The use of a central symbolic scene, as Frederic Karl points out, is a convention of the Conradian novel. It appears not only in *Lord Jim*, but also in many of Conrad's other works. See

Frederick R. Karl, *A Reader's Guide to Joseph Conrad* (New York, 1960), pp. 16–17; passim.

19. Dorothy Van Ghent's well-known essay on *Lord Jim* examines the relationship between "the conscious will and the fatality of our acts." She cites Marlow's comment about one's destiny being already determined (the quotation marked by this footnote) to support her contention that Conrad's world view is a closed and static system "incapable of origination though intensely dramatic in its revelations." She compared Conrad, in this respect, with Henry James, whose system is open and fluid, and whose characters are self-creating. Fitzgerald's "system" in *The Great Gatsby* is like Conrad's: closed and predetermined. See Dorothy Van Ghent, *The English Novel* (New York, 1953), pp. 229–244.

20. The heroes' preoccupation with time is underscored in the novels, in part, by the use of a clock imagery. In his confinement as he first reaches Patusan, Jim is given an old clock to repair, and later with an irony of which he is unaware, his thoughts keep recurring to the idea of "mending the clock." *The Great Gatsby* is filled with schedules, timetables, and clocks. When Gatsby was a young boy, "a universe of ineffable gaudiness spun itself out in his brain while the clock ticked on the washstand" (p. 119). When he meets Daisy again at West Egg, he seems, in his reaction, to be "running down like an overwound clock" (p. 111). In the same scene Gatsby brushes against a mantelpiece clock and for a moment it seems almost as if the clock had fallen and smashed; as if in his reunion with Daisy, the clock had stopped and the past had been recovered.

21. Carraway's habit of reserving judgment is the result of his father's advice not to judge men too hastily. Jim's father also advises his son not to "judge men harshly or hastily" (p. 341).

22. Morton Zabel refers to Conrad's romanticism as endowing appearances with an "internal glow;" the effect of this, he feels, is a heightened sense of moral implication involved in occurrences. The "realism" of Conrad, and of certain other modern writers including F. Scott Fitzgerald, he continues, was "always conditioned by an abstracting tendency and mythopoeic habit" (Morton Dauwen Zabel, Introduction to Joseph Conrad, *Youth & Two Other Stories* [New York, 1959], pp. 9–10).

107
The Great Gatsby and the Tradition of Joseph Conrad; Part II

◆

ROBERT EMMET LONG

Part II

In 1898 Conrad interrupted his work on *Lord Jim* to write the much briefer *Heart of Darkness*, completed that year and published in the *Youth* volume in 1902. The two works may seem, but are not actually, very different; it is possible, in fact, to see them as "companion" novels. Marlow appears again as the narrator in *Heart of Darkness*, and there is again a reluctant identification on the part of Marlow with the central character, a division of sympathy, a conflict between the claims of imagination and the ethics of conduct. Both Jim and Kurtz are "isolates"—illusionist heroes whose imaginations set them apart from the other characters. Jim is isolated from other men by his Platonic ego, while Kurtz is isolated by his knowledge of "unexplored regions" and by his vision of the horrendous in the remote interior of the Congo. The great difference between *Lord Jim* and *Heart of Darkness* in this respect is that in *Heart of Darkness* the hero's experience is directed back much more specifically to the failure of contemporary society. It is the juxtaposing of the imagination of an "isolate" hero and the ethos of a particular society that gives *Heart of Darkness* its special relevance to *The Great Gatsby*.

The themes of *Heart of Darkness* and *The Great Gatsby* are worked out on two distinct levels: one, the drama of spiritually alienated hero; another, the gradual exposure of a society with which his life places him in opposition. The two levels impinge upon one another. Though different in kind, the societies in *Heart of Darkness* and *The Great Gatsby* are both described impressionistically, the use of distortion giving them something of the atmosphere

SOURCE *Texas Studies in Literature and Language* VIII, Fall 1966, pp. 407–422.

of waking dreams. In *Heart of Darkness*, the "mournful and senseless delusion" (p. 61) which the Company's enterprise represents takes the form of weird incongruity in the series of images presented at each step of Marlow's journey overland and up the river.[1] The ship which takes Marlow into the interior discharges custom-house clerks to levy toll in the middle of a forsaken wilderness. Soldiers are landed too, and some of them drown in the surf; yet no one seems particularly to notice or to care. One day a man-of-war is sighted shelling the bush, with no object in sight: "There she was, incomprehensible, firing into a continent" (p. 62). At the Outer station Marlow comes upon a ravine where blasting can be heard and where a railway is apparently being built; the odd thing, however, is that the cliff is not in the way of anything; this pointless blasting is the only work going on. Walking into the shade of the ravine (for relief from what he has seen), Marlow has the sudden sensation that he has wandered into "the gloomy grove of some Inferno" (p. 66). It is the Grove of Death, where natives, dehumanized by the forces of "progress," are dumped like damaged cargo and left to die. They have the appearance of unearthly apparitions, "black shadows of disease and starvation lying confusedly in the greenish gloom" (p. 66).

While the world of *The Great Gatsby* is not as radically irrational as the Congo milieu of *Heart of Darkness*, it nevertheless shares with Conrad's novel a certain similarity in atmosphere—an incongruity and grotesqueness. Carraway says that "even when the East excited me most ... even then it had always for me a quality of distortion" (p. 212).[2] Fitzgerald's valley of ashes is both real and fantastic: "Ashes take the form of houses and chimneys and rising smoke and, finally, with a transcendent effort, of men, who move dimly and already crumbling through the powdery air" (p. 27). The latter part of Chapter Two, which begins with the valley of ashes, is devoted to the apartment scene in New York, which is prepared for and grows out of the earlier scene, and which communicates a similar sense of waste. The distortions in the apartment scene are predominantely optical, and begin almost unnoticeably. An overenlarged photograph on the wall seems to have the blurred indistinctness of an ectoplasm, at first appearing to be a picture of a hen sitting on a large rock, and at a distance focussing into a view of a stout old woman wearing a bonnet. Myrtle's sister Catherine has eyebrows that have been plucked, with the eyebrow line redrawn at an acute angle, so that her face seems blurred like the photograph. Later Carraway has an impression of Myrtle that is like a hallucination: "Her laughter, her gestures, her assertions became more violently affected moment by moment and as she expanded, the room grew smaller around her, until she seemed to be revolving on a noisy, creaking pivot through the smoky air" (p. 36). He picks up a copy of a novel about the Christ story, only to find in this atmosphere that it makes no sense. By the end of the scene (Myrtle moaning from time to time, the room as smoky as the valley of ashes, people stumbling about confusedly) Fitzgerald has presented a world that is morally unintelligible.[3] In the progression of effect in *Heart of Darkness* and *The Great Gatsby*, Conrad uses broad, bold images, while Fitzgerald employs images (also frequently visual) which are less obtrusive. But the progression of effect in either case works toward the same end: the creation of a lingering sense of the "actual" as hallucinatory.

The heroes too, Kurtz and Gatsby, are presented in atmospheres of the bizarre and fabulous. The approach to Kurtz is a "weary pilgrimage amongst hints for nightmares" (p. 62), but when he is actually found the final nightmare takes shape. Marlow's party first encounters a young Russian, who prepares him for the sensation of being "captured by the incredible" (p. 82). The Russian youth—the "harlequin," as he is called—is characterized by his uncritical wonder and awe, continually expended in the direction of Mr. Kurtz. "I tell you," he proclaims enthusiastically of Kurtz, "this man has enlarged my mind!" (p. 125). At this point Marlow comments: "He opened his arms wide, staring at me with his little blue eyes that were perfectly round" (p. 125). The harlequin, who prepares for the meeting with the fabulous Kurtz, anticipates Owl Eyes in *The Great Gatsby*, who appears just before Nick's first meeting with Gatsby, introducing the incredible reality of the hero. The enormous spectacles worn by Owl Eyes gives him, like the young Russian, a quality of ceaseless wonder; it is in this attitude that he is discovered marveling at the real books in Gatsby's library. "This fella's a regular Belasco," he cries; "It's a triumph! What thoroughness! What realism!" (p. 55).

The dreamlike meeting with the "harlequin" in *Heart of Darkness* is merely a prelude to the actual meeting with Kurtz. The view of Kurtz borne on a stretcher is conveyed by a phantasmagoric optical effect. "The stretcher shook as the bearers staggered forward again, and almost at the same time I noticed that the crowd of savages was vanishing without any perceptible movement of retreat, as if the forest that had ejected these beings so suddenly had drawn them in again as the breath is drawn in a long aspiration" (p. 134). Kurtz is seen at this point in an El Greco-like distortion: "He looked at least seven feet long. His covering had fallen off, and his body emerged from it pitiful and appalling as from a winding sheet. I could see the cage of his ribs all astir, the bones of his arm waving.... I saw him open his mouth wide—it gave him a weirdly voracious aspect, as though he wanted to swallow all the air, all the earth, all the men before him" (p. 134).

Obviously, the horrific character of Kurtz in the farthest reaches of the Congo is not suggested in *Gatsby*; nevertheless, there is a "dream sensation" about Gatsby's life at West Egg. Gatsby's mansion and his spectacular parties are described with a grotesque foreshortened effect which some critics have called "almost surrealistic," an effect which underscores the quality of fantasy surrounding Gatsby. Even his automobile is described as if it were an optical illusion, with windshields reflecting a dozen suns. Crossing the bridge into Manhattan, the automobile is chimerical: "with fenders spread like wings, we scattered light through half Victoria" (p. 82). In the hotel Plaza scene, when Tom is triumphant, Gatsby vanishes (not for the first time) like a phantom: "They were gone, without a word, snapped out, made accidental, like ghosts" (p. 162).

Part of the structural similarity then between *Heart of Darkness* and *The Great Gatsby* consists of the confrontation of two "nightmares," one of the hero and the other of society, and of the choice finally made by the narrator in favor of the hero. "It was strange," comments Marlow, "how I accepted this unforeseen partnerhip, this choice of nightmares forced upon me in the tenebrous land invaded by these mean and greedy phantoms" (p. 147). Gatsby's gaucherie and illusion is preferred at last by Carraway to the confusion and callousness of the inhabitants of the valley of ashes and of the Buchanans. If the aberrations of Kurtz and Gatsby are described with the quality of a strange dream, the "normal" world also, seen from a higher perspective, is hallucinatory, almost insane. In this way, the case for Kurtz and Gatsby is stronger than it might at first seem.

But putting aside for a moment the question of the treatment of society by Conrad and Fitzgerald, another avenue to the correspondence of the two works is worth noticing—the relationship between the narrators and the heroes. As in *Lord Jim*, the relationship in *Heart of Darkness* is one of ambivalence. Kurtz is a "hollow sham", and the heads drying on the stakes before his hut seem to Marlow symbolic. "They only showed that Kurtz lacked restraint in the gratification of his various lusts, that there was something lacking in him—some small matter which, when the pressing need arose, could not be found under his magnificent eloquence" (p. 131). Yet Marlow also finds Kurtz "remarkable" and his defeat a kind of triumph. "He had summed up—he had judged.... After all, this was the expression of some sort of belief" (p. 151). Carraway says of Gatsby late in the novel that he "disapproved of him from beginning to end" (p. 185), yet he is also loyal to Gatsby at the end, as Marlow is to Kurtz.

In addition to the similarity in the narrators' loyalties, likeness appears also in the narrators' personal honesty in their introductions of themselves. "Everyone," Carraway says, "suspects himself of at least one of the cardinal virtues, and this is mine; I am one of the few honest people that I have ever known" (p. 72). Marlow, too, prides himself on his honesty. "You know I hate, detest, and can't bear a lie.... There is a taint of death, a flavour of mortality in lies" (p. 82). Both, however, in the course of the novels, compromise themselves. Carraway drifts into an affair with Jordan Baker, thinking apparently that he can accept her while disregarding her values. His honesty—that is, his personal honesty with himself—is not as invulnerable as he had thought, though he reaffirms it at the end in his break both with Jordan Baker and the East. Marlow finds himself involved in a lie to Kurtz's Intended; to tell her the truth would have been "too dark—too dark altogether" (p. 162). The complications which challenge the narrators' honesty are merely part of larger questions of value illuminated by their meetings with Kurtz and Gatsby.

The meetings themselves do not take place immediately; Marlow and Carraway approach the heroes very gradually, hearing of them first by rumor. Marlow hears of Kurtz even on the coast, and at points thereafter asks information about him, receiving peculiar answers. On his asking who "this Kurtz" was, the bookkeeper at the Outer station replies factually that Kurtz was a first-class agent, and then, seeing that this answer was not satisfactory, adds that Kurtz was a "very remarkable person" (p. 69). Marlow, at the Central station, again asks about Kurtz, and the Brickmaker tells him sarcastically that Kurtz "is an emissary of pity, and science, and progress" (p. 79). Kurtz is whispered about and conspired against by the Manager and his uncle, who are displeased to learn that he is spoken of even on the coast. Gatsby's name is also mentioned well before he appears. He is "this man Gatsby," as Kurtz is "this Kurtz;" Nick, asking for information, says to Jordan Baker, "this Gatsby you spoke of ..." (p. 18), but is cut short by a gesture from Jordan, who is attempting to hear what is being said in the next room. At the first party Nick attends people whisper about Gatsby's corruption, and Gatsby like Kurtz (whose "corruption" is real) is kept fascinatingly vague. Kurtz is encountered only near the end of *Heart of Darkness*, while Gatsby appears in the early part of *The Great Gatsby*, but in either case the actual meetings are delayed and come as the climax of mounting suspense. Once they appear, they dominate the scene as compellingly as they had previously in the rumor and speculation about them.

The extravaganzas which Kurtz and Gatsby act out end with their deaths, but by this time the narrators have become seriously involved in their lives, and by the end of both novels the narrators finally make some sort of affirmation about the heroes. After the death of Kurtz, Marlow and the Manager of the Central station talk together, and the Manager is barely able to conceal his satisfaction, his "peculiar smile sealing the unexpressed depths of his meanness" (p. 150). He speaks of Kurtz's "unsound method" and of his unfortunate duty of having to report it in the proper quarters. Marlow agrees that Kurtz had no method, but adds: "Nevertheless, I think Mr. Kurtz is a remarkable man," I said with emphasis. He started, dropped on me a cold heavy glance, said very quietly, "He *was*," and turned his back on me. My hour of favour was over; I found myself lumped with Kurtz as a partisan of methods for which the time was not ripe. I was unsound!" (p. 138). At the crucial moment in *The Great Gatsby*, when Gatsby's dream is fast crumbling and his great house practically deserted, Nick Carraway makes a dramatic, because long-suspended judgment: "They're a rotten crowd," I shouted across the lawn. "You're worth the whole damned bunch put together" (p. 185).

Marlow stays with Kurtz to hear his last words and to receive from him some personal papers and his report ironically entitled "The Suppression of Savage Customs." Kurtz dies alone in the cabin of the ship, scorned by the Manager and Company "pilgrims"; and Marlow buries him along the bank of the river. "I remained to dream the nightmare out to the end," Marlow remarks, "and to show my loyalty to Kurtz once more" (p. 150). He says that it was preordained he should never betray Kurtz: "... it was written I should be loyal to the nightmare of my choice" (p. 141). Like Marlow, Carraway shows his loyalty to Gatsby, gathers up the broken fragments of his life, and attends to the arrangements for the funeral which no one bothers to attend. Carraway at the conclusion of *The Great Gatsby* becomes the spokesman for Gatsby, as Marlow had for Kurtz. After Gatsby's death "every surmise about him, and every practical question was referred to me" (p. 197).

It is in this "dying fall" with which both *Heart of Darkness* and *The Great Gatsby* conclude that many of the parallels in their plots are concentrated. One of the most noticeable of these concerns the packet of papers and photographs which Kurtz, just before his death, gives to Marlow. An official-looking man with gold-rimmed spectacles calls on Marlow after Marlow's return to the city, and asks that the papers and photographs which Kurtz, just before his death, gives to Marlow. An official-looking man with gold-rimmed spectacles calls on Marlow after Marlow's return to the city, and asks that the papers by given to him. They would no doubt be of great value to the Company, because of Mr. Kurtz's "knowledge of unexplored regions." The phrase gives rise to Marlow's ironic reply that Kurtz's "knowledge of unexplored regions, however extensive, did not bear upon the problems of commerce or administration" (p. 153). To another man, calling himself Kurtz's cousin, Marlow gives the chief document among the papers: Kurtz's pathetic and unfinished report on the "Suppression of Savage Customs." The final scene with Kurtz's Intended contains the most pointed ironies of all; it reintroduces the illusion of the original Kurtz, who was to have been an emissary of light but who dies in darkness, with the words "the horror!" on his lips. Kurtz's Intended assures Marlow that it was she who "knew him best," and finally Marlow is unable to tell her Kurtz's actual last words; he says, instead, that Kurtz had died speaking her name, sheltering her from stark reality by a story of a death scene worthy of a sentimental romance. She cries exultantly that she "knew it—was sure" as the room seems to darken around them. "They," Marlow had said, "the women, I mean—are out of it—should be out of it. We must help them stay in that beautiful world of their own, lest ours gets worse" (p. 115).

In the "dying fall" in *The Great Gatsby* Carraway has an experience similar to Marlow's. Gatsby's father arrives from North Dakota for the funeral and produces for Carraway some papers which had belonged to his son. As with the packet of Kurtz's papers, there is a photograph (in this case, a crumpled picture of Gatsby's mansion), together with an old schedule and list of resolutions for self-improvement. The schedule and list of boyhood resolves have the same ironic function as the packet of papers which had belonged to Kurtz; they introduce again the illusions of the young Gatsby after the sombre outcome of Gatsby's life is known. Henry C. Gatz—Gatsby's father—is like Kurtz's Intended too, in his being so entirely in the dark at the end:

> "If he'd of lived, he'd of been a great man. A man like James J. Hill. He'd of helped build up the country."
> "That's true," I said, uncomfortably.
>
> (p. 202)

Gatz's naïve view of the industrialists of our "gilded age" is equalled only by his misunderstanding of his son; in missing the overwhelming implications of what has taken place he emphasizes them all the more.

In the final summing up in *Heart of Darkness* and *The Great Gatsby* the narrators have "visions" which, with great economy, bring the experience they have lived through into perspective. The visions are similar not only in being "fantastic dreams," but also in concrete details, such as their mournful city settings. Marlow's vision brings together in one scene the two phases of the story which he wishes to contrast: Kurtz's spiritual crisis and death in the Congo, and the life of the "sepulchral city":

> Between the tall houses of a street as still and decorous as a well-kept alley in a cemetery, I had a vision of him on the stretcher, opening his mouth voraciously, as if to devour all the earth with all its mankind. He lived then before me; he lived as much as he had ever lived.... The vision seemed to enter the house with me—the stretcher, the phantom-bearers ... the beat of the drum, regular and muffled like the beating of a heart—the heart of a conquering darkness.
>
> (p. 155)

Nick's "vision" also incorporates both the idea of the hero's fate and the life of the city; like Marlow's vision, too, it reintroduces an earlier scene (in this case, a version of Daisy's marriage to Tom) and projects it against a sinister city background:

> West Egg, especially, still figures in my more fantastic dreams. I see it as a night scene by El Greco: a hundred houses, at once conventional and grotesque, crouching under a sullen, overhanging sky and a lustreless moon. In the foreground four solemn men in dress suits are walking along the sidewalk with a stretcher on which lies a drunken woman in a white evening dress. Her hand, which dangles over the side, sparkles cold with jewels. Gravely the men turn in at a house—the wrong house. But no one knows the woman's name, and no one cares.
>
> (pp. 212–213)

Emphasized in these "visions" are the societies that have been presented in the novels: Conrad's "monstrous town" and Fitzgerald's "East." The narrative structure of *Heart of Darkness* and *The Great Gatsby* is circular, the endings leading back to the beginning of the narratives. Both end in the city where Marlow and Carraway, after the death of the heroes, feel a numbing lack of interest in the affairs of ordinary men. Carraway says that the fate of Gatsby "had temporarily closed out my interest in the abortive sorrows and shortwinded elations of men" (p. 3). Marlow's reaction, following the death of Kurtz, is even more extreme: "I found myself back in the sepulchral city resenting the sight of people.... They trespassed upon my thoughts. They were intruders whose knowledge of life was to me an irritating pretense" (p. 152).

At the ends of the two works the city has become the point toward which all that has happened is made to refer. In *Heart of Darkness* an image of the city, overclouded by an unnatural darkness, is presented portentously in the opening pages; the scene is returned to at the conclusion and given greater emphasis, the darkness of the Congo now directed back to the moral life of the city. There are actually two cities in *Heart of Darkness*: London, and another not named but obviously Brussels, the point of departure for the Congo adventure, which Marlow says has always made him think of a "whited sepulchre." He refers to it as the "sepulchral city," and the house in Brussels where he finds the Company offices is "as still as a house in the city of the dead" (p. 57). In either case, the city becomes a focus, a culture symbol of modern Europe.[4] "All Europe contributed to the making of Kurtz" (p. 117).

Marlow's return from the last agony and death of Kurtz could not provide a greater contrast with the meanness and materialism of the city. He sees its inhabitants "hurrying through the streets to filch a little money from each other, to devour their infamous cookery ... to dream their insignificant and silly dreams" (p. 152). Marlow tells his listeners aboard the yacht in the Thames estuary that they could not even understand Kurtz. "How could you? ... surrounded by kind neighbors ready to cheer you or to fall on you, stepping delicately between the butcher and the policeman.... How can you imagine ... that utter solitude, where no warning voice of a kind neighbor can be heard whispering of public opinion" (p. 116). The bourgeois life of the town is "monstrous" in its absence of any inner life or spiritual vitality. Carraway's repudiation of the East (symbolized by the New York metropolis and its outlying communities on Long Island) is a rejection of its culture, which like that of the society in *Heart of Darkness* is characterized by sterility and spiritual depletion.

In their unusual careers Kurtz and Gatsby become critics of their times; for if their imaginations take them "out of bounds," and they are defeated, they nevertheless reveal the greater failure of their societies, failing in the opposite and greater way in having no vision at all. Kurtz's final anguished cry seems to Marlow a moral victory: "It had candour, it had conviction, it had a vibrating note of revolt in its whisper, it had the appalling face of a glimpsed truth" (p. 151). Like Kurtz, who has "stepped over the edge of the invisible," Gatsby dwarfs the other characters, whose lives are enlarged by nothing. As the result of their meetings with the heroes, the narrators arrive at new understandings of their societies. The interest of the two novels has centered steadily upon the heroes until the end, and then it suddenly shifts to the reality underlying contemporary life which the heroes' careers have illuminated. And this revelation becomes the theme of the novels.

Perhaps the revelations at the end also explain the hallucinatory atmospheres investing both hero and milieu in the two works. Marlow had spoken of "the dream sensation that pervaded all my days at that time" (p. 105) and the billboard-sized spectacles of Dr. T.J. Eckleburg in *The Great Gatsby* brood not only over the immediate scene of ashes and dumping grounds, but also over the action of the novel. The spectacles hint at optical illusion (ultimately a metaphor for the displacement of values), and a reality that is stranger than the wildest dream. It is as if the narrators, who face a "choice of nightmares," have entered into an enchanted wood, where life is transformed, where the familiar is perceived as strange and wondrous. The novels seem in this way to have the quality and the form of fables. Like fables (*Heart of Darkness* and *The Great Gatsby* have also been called "modern moralities"), they conclude with parables. Their parables are indictments of modern culture, their concluding "illuminations" singularly dark. Darkly pessimistic in their revelations, *Heart of Darkness* and *The Great Gatsby* conclude literally in darkness. The final scene in *Heart of Darkness* shows the city shrouded by a menacing darkness, and *The Great Gatsby* closes with the image of a benighted continent. Gatsby's dream, Carraway says, "was already behind him, somewhere back in that vast obscurity beyond the city, where the dark fields of the republic rolled on under the night" (p. 218).

The parallels in structure in *The Great Gatsby* and the early fiction of Joseph Conrad which have been documented in the previous pages raise questions, the answers to which may help to explain the composition of *The Great Gatsby*. The questions which are brought to mind cannot be answered with complete certainty in every case, but certain tentative conclusions do seem possible. A first question might be why the parallels occur in the early rather than in the middle or later Conrad, and if Fitzgerald had actually read the works from which the parallels have been drawn. References in the letters and manuscripts indicate that Fitzgerald had apparently read *Almayer's Folly, Youth, The Nigger of the "Narcissus"* (including its Preface), *Lord Jim, Heart of Darkness,* and *Nostromo* by 1925;[5] other Conrad novels were in Fitzgerald's personal library, but there is no specific reference to them in his papers. *Nostromo* was published in 1904 and is a transitional work, carrying to a conclusion some of the themes of the early fiction and preparing for Conrad's great middle period, which includes *Under Western Eyes* (1911), *Chance* (1912), and *Victory* (1915). It is this middle period that F.R. Leavis argues for as the most socially interested point of Conrad's career, allying him with what he terms "the great tradition" in the English novel.[6] Leavis objects to the "romanticism" of Conrad's early period, to his preoccupation with illusionist heroes considered in isolation from complex social values;

and it is true that Conrad's early period is dominated by studies in romantic illusion. But for this very reason one may see why this particular period should have appealed to Fitzgerald. Fitzgerald's first two novels, *This Side of Paradise* and *The Beautiful and Damned*, describe young idealists and their engagement with romantic illusion, their collision with reality, their disenchantment. The subject matter of the early Conrad was Fitzgerald's also.

The inevitable question then is whether Fitzgerald's sudden maturity in treating the subject of illusion in *The Great Gatsby* was not materially influenced by his reading of Joseph Conrad, who had treated the subject authoritatively a generation earlier. Direct influence is naturally always difficult to verify, short of a statement on the author's part that such influences existed, which is not to be expected. Even Fitzgerald's own statement that in writing *The Great Gatsby* he acted as a "Conrad imitator," is not specific enough. Yet evidence, both circumstantial (Fitzgerald's reading) and textual, argues that such influences did exist. The biographies of Fitzgerald by Arthur Mizener and Andrew Turnbull indicate how surprisingly impressionable Fitzgerald was to the writing of the most gifted of his contemporaries, his near adulation of Conrad, T. S. Eliot, and Joyce. Critics also agree that Fitzgerald's first novel was written under the spell of Compton Mackenzie, one critic even pointing out nearly a hundred points of similarity between *This Side of Paradise* and Mackenzie's *Sinister Street*.[7] It is a matter of agreement too that *The Beautiful and Damned* reflects the social attitudes and literary prejudices of H. L. Mencken. On the basis of this background it would not be surprising to find evidence of additional influence in *The Great Gatsby*. James E. Miller has already established a convincing case for Conrad's influence upon *The Great Gatsby* in Fitzgerald's adherence to the principle of control and "selectivity," and in his use of impressionistic form. The correspondences detailed here, however, in the structuring of theme and plot and in the conception of character argue for the even more important point of Conrad's influence upon Fitzgerald's treatment of his material, the ordering of his fictional world.

The internal, textual evidence formed by these parallels is quite substantial, leading to the likely conclusion that Fitzgerald made conscious adaptations from Conrad in structuring *The Great Gatsby*. It is not necessarily a contradiction in considering three of Conrad's works at once, for each emphasizes some feature of *The Great Gatsby*, and taken together they form a *composite* background. *Almayer's Folly* sets up a framework for the illusionist hero, whose "future" is in conflict with the realities of the present, and whose dream is destroyed symbolically by a "betraying heroine." With this as scaffolding, *Lord Jim* adds the dimension of the attempt to recover the past, and thus to reinstate a Platonic identity. Finally, *Heart of Darkness* adds a cultural reference and theme, contrasting the "exuberant imagination" of a defeated hero with a visionless society.

These correspondences are all the more compelling in their being both great and small, a combination illustrated, for example, in *Heart of Darkness*. The Marlow role played by Nick Carraway; the circular form of *Heart of Darkness* and *The Great Gatsby*, in which the action has already ended at the beginning; the quality of both works as fables or moralities—these fundamental features of the two novels are supplemented by many similarities in detail. Many of these details are conspicuous; Marlow and Carraway as the "recipient of confidences"; their loyalty to the heroes at the end; the "dying fall," in which they act as executors of the dead heroes' estates; the packet of papers reintroducing the early illusions of Kurtz and Gatsby; the figures of Kurtz's Intended and Gatsby's father, who even at the end are unaware of the hero's illusion; the brief sinister dreams of the narrators which summarize the theme of the stories near their close. When correspondences both great and small combine in this way the evidence seems all the greater that Fitzgerald was indebted to Conrad in the craftsmanship of *The Great Gatsby*.

But most of all the relation of Conrad to *The Great Gatsby* can be seen in the total moral vision of Fitzgerald's novel; its authority stands in contrast to Fitzgerald's earlier attempts to understand his heroes' involvement with illusion. His too-complete identification with his heroes had resulted in a vivid foreground of incident and impression, but the background—where theme and total meaning should coalesce—was lost to view in nostalgic vagueness. The authority of *The Great Gatsby* on the other hand is the result of perfect knowledge, knowledge of the clear relation of parts—of the relation of author to hero, and hero to theme. As in Conrad, there is an ordering of character and scene, so that everything relates in a kind of symbolic structure to the whole and to the theme. The fundamental insight in *The Great Gatsby* into the nature of illusion ("So we beat on, boats against the current, borne back ceaselessly into the past") appears to derive from Conrad's *Youth*. Given this understanding of romantic imagination, Fitzgerald could at last separate himself from his hero, could—using a Conradian narrator—hold in balance both Gatsby's greatness and his folly; the conservative, moral position of Marlow informs the vision of *The Great Gatsby*. This is not to say that *The Great Gatsby* is weakly derivative, for it carries conviction in every line, Fitzgerald's own voice and sensibility. There are indeed places where Fitzgerald might be said to improve on the material he uses; Gatsby's father is more human and believable than Kurtz's Intended, to whom Dr. Leavis objects as a contrived device for ironic effect, and Gatsby's boyhood program of resolves is more memorable and touching than Kurtz's unfinished report on the suppression of savage customs. That Fitzgerald may have used Conrad as a model of method does not "explain" the maturity of *The Great Gatsby*—it does not explain how Fitzgerald was capable of assimilating and transforming the material from which he drew—but it does explain more coherently the process of composition of the novel, and is an answer to the early view that Fitzgerald's sudden maturity was merely "miraculous."

The correspondences with Conrad (apart from the probability of influence) are useful in yet another way in indicating the place of *The Great Gatsby* within a particular historical perspective. In order to see this relationship it is necessary to move back into the nineteenth century, where may be observed the formation of a tradition which comes to include both Conrad and Fitzgerald in *The Great Gatsby*. The exploration of illusion is anticipated authoritatively in the nineteenth century in Flaubert, whose most famous novel, *Madame Bovary* (1856), created a classic and ironic genre in fiction which has influenced much of the writing of our own century. Illusion is at the heart of *Madame Bovary* and of Flaubert's aesthetics. "Reality," Flaubert once remarked, "is no more than an illusion to be described." In *Madame Bovary*, Emma Bovary's romantic longings end inevitably in a series of disappointments; her expectations are mere illusions in a world entirely indifferent to them. The failure of Emma's expectations is not due to the boorishness of Charles, or to the inconstancy of Rodolphe or Leon; her attempts to find the "reality of poetry" in life are projections of transient emotions which can never be satisfied in actual life. Even as her longings are described most suggestively, they are undercut by Flaubert's style, the impersonality of which emphasizes Flaubert's denial of value or significance in human experience. There is in *The Great Gatsby* a trace of Flaubert's treatment of illusion (what French critics have called Bovaryism), as well as something of Flaubert's meticulous craftsmanship; but there is no direct line of descent. Intervening between the two, however, and giving a new interpretation to Flaubert's analysis of illusion is Joseph Conrad, among the most eminent of the post-Flaubertian realists.

Conrad's first two novels, *Almayer's Folly* and *An Outcast of the Islands*, explore the subject of illusion and continue the theme of Bovaryism in Far Eastern settings. The dreams of the ineffectual Almayer and Willems have their eventual denial in the harsh and hopeless realities of the tropical outposts, where they are the solitary white men. Almayer's longings, like Emma Bovary's, end in frustration as he is forced to confront a world inimical to his quixotic dreams. Despite the surface coloring and exotic setting of *Almayer's Folly*, Conrad's method has the impersonality and proliferating irony of Flaubert, and the novel is written in the Flaubertian tradition. But in the brief period between *Almayer's Folly* and *Lord Jim*, Conrad went beyond Flaubert to create a style and an attitude towards illusion that were distinctively his own.

In his well-known Preface to *The Nigger of the "Narcissus,"* Conrad set forth a statement of the aesthetics which underlie his newly forming impressionism. The distinction he makes between the scientist, or thinker, and the artist is remarkably similar to Coleridge's in *Biographia Literaria* between the separate faculties of intuition and intellection:

> It is otherwise with the artist.
> Confronted with the same enigmatical spectacle the artist descends within

> himself, and in that lonely region of stress and strife, if he be deserving and fortunate, he finds the terms of his appeal. His appeal is made to our less obvious capacities: to that part of our nature which, because of the warlike condition of existence, is necessarily kept out of sight within the more resisting and hard qualities.... His appeal is less loud, more profound, less distinct, more stirring—and sooner forgotten. Yet its effect endures forever. The changing wisdom of successive generations discards ideas, questions facts, demolishes theories. But the artist appeals to that part of our being which is not dependent on wisdom: to that in us which is a gift and not an acquisition—and, therefore, more permanently enduring. He speaks to our capacity for delight and wonder, to the sense of mystery surrounding our lives; to our sense of pity, and beauty, and pain; to the latent feeling of fellowship with all creation.[8]

Through the "magic suggestiveness of prose" the artist rescues a "fragment of truth" from the onrush of time by penetrating to the "stress and passion within the core of each convincing moment"; in so doing he presents a vision that "awakens in its beholder that feeling of unavoidable solidarity ... which binds men to each other and all mankind to the visible world." Conrad's conception of the artist who seeks inward for his vision is certainly romantic, and further, in his conviction of the "unavoidable" solidarity of mankind, it is also moral; in both respects Conrad's aesthetic is a departure from Flaubertian realism. In *Lord Jim*, Conrad's impressionism comes fully into being, fusing the opposite sides of his imagination: the aloof, analytical mind of the literary naturalist; and the subjective, intuitive temperament of the romantic. The tension of the two in *Lord Jim* produces a richer and more complex work than any which had preceded it in Conrad's career.

Lord Jim began as a short story which was to have ended with the *Patna* episode, and it was apparently to have been a variation on the theme of Bovaryism. It developed, however, into a full-length novel with the expanding conception of Jim as an embodiment of youthful romantic imagination; and the novel became an exploration of romantic imagination and reality. The moral problem raised by Jim is really the same issue which had been created by nineteenth-century romanticism: the moral conflict between personal or social duty, and the perhaps higher duty of self-realization. The moral problem posed by the romantic ego, which is argued in the novel to a final ambiguity, came to engage the two opposing sides of Conrad's temperament, and the result was a new kind of illusionist hero. Nineteenth-century French naturalism provides many striking instances of victims of illusion; and Conrad, whose reading was largely in French literature and whose adoption of the French language preceded his learning of English, has many affinities with this tradition. But in *Lord Jim* Conrad's interpretation of illusion is a radical departure from the spare, ironic studies of the illusionist in Flaubert, and later in Maupassant, and Anatole France. Conrad's "romantic realism" and newly evolving conception of the illusionist hero in *Lord Jim* prepare inevitably for Fitzgerald's conception of Gatsby.

For Gatsby is not merely a victim of illusion, observed with merciless irony; he is evoked through the "magic suggestiveness of prose" and with a kind of mythopoeia. The ambivalence of Conrad's temperament, resulting in romantic involvement and yet a sense of aesthetic distance, in his creation of Jim, is repeated in Fitzgerald's treatment of Gatsby. This new mode of hero in Conrad, and later in Fitzgerald, is unique in that even though he is deceived by illusion he is yet extraordinary in his "truthfulness." This paradox in Gatsby can be traced back to Conrad's impressionism, which denies validity to any absolute system of value or philosophic position, and which stresses instead the intensity and sincerity of imagination in its approach to truth.

The doubleness of Conrad's mind also makes necessary a new mode of narrator, even as it creates a new mode of hero. Conrad's ambiguity, as between imagination and analysis, requires a Marlovian narrator who expresses this ambiguity at one remove from the author himself; later, Carraway has the same function. And both Marlow and Carraway reveal the moral vision of the novels they narrate, which are distinctly conservative and moral. Carraway is aware, like Marlow before him, of the illusion involved in the romantic imagination, yet he also sees the meanness of life without imagination. It is this ability to see the limitations of both sides of the question of imagination, as well as the conservative, middle position taken by the narrator (the unsatisfactoriness of which leaves the narrator darkly pessimistic about human fate) which reveals *The Great Gatsby* as distinctly in the Conrad tradition.

The mode of illusionist hero, the ambivalence of the narrator, and the moral imagination of *The Great Gatsby* relate the novel back to a tradition in the treatment of illusion which reaches to Flaubert, and is reinterpreted in the romantic realism of Joseph Conrad; and it is out of Conrad's romantic interpretation of French realism that *The Great Gatsby*, putting aside the question of direct influence, may be seen logically to evolve. The American and local character of *The Great Gatsby* has often been discussed, yet criticism has not yet taken adequately into account that *The Great Gatsby* represents an extension in American literature of a European tradition—a tradition which has been concerned above all with the subject of romantic illusion and with the problem of aesthetic form in the novel. Against the background of the Conrad tradition *The Great Gatsby* takes on its distinctive character as a work of art, while at the same time it becomes coherent in the continuity of culture.

Notes

1. All page references to *Heart of Darkness* are from *The Complete Works of Joseph Conrad*, Doubleday Canterbury Edition (New York, 1924), XVI, 45–162.
2. F. Scott Fitzgerald, *The Great Gatsby* (1st ed., New York, 1925).
3. The correspondence between the apartment scene in *The Great Gatsby* and T.S. Eliot's "Sweeney Agonistes" has often been noted by critics. "Sweeney Agonistes" appeared first, but

was not completed in its final form until after the publication of *The Great Gatsby*. Eliot himself called attention to the correspondence.

4. The use of a great modern city as a culture symbol relates *Heart of Darkness* and *The Great Gatsby* to a tradition of social criticism developing from the nineteenth century. The city of Paris in Baudelaire's *Les Fleurs du mal* has already been one of the great culture symbols of the nineteenth century, and its influence upon *Heart of Darkness* is very probable. Baudelaire was among Conrad's favorite poets, and he had used a passage from one of Baudelaire's poems, "Le Voyage" (which contains the phrase "the horror!") as an epigraph to one of his own works. Baudelaire had written that evil, though destructive, is more *human* than passive nonentity; and this vision of evil forms a criticism of the spiritual inertia of modern culture. The same criticism applies in *Heart of Darkness*, where the infinite potentialities of the human soul are evoked by Kurtz, contrasted with the complacency of the "monstrous town." The theme of the dehumanization of contemporary society appears later in the century in T.S. Eliot's "The Waste Land" (1922), which is again focussed by a great modern city, in this case London. As in Conrad's "city of the dead," the inhabitants of Eliot's London lead an existence that is a form of death-in-life. Eliot had *Heart of Darkness* in mind when he wrote "The Waste Land," and had even intended to use a passage from the novel as the poem's epigraph. Fitzgerald had read and admired "The Waste Land," and its influence had been attributed to him in *The Great Gatsby* in his social attitude and in the wasteland idea of the valley of ashes. His use of a large city as a symbol of a culture, however, is closer to its use in *Heart of Darkness* than to that in "The Waste Land."

5. A detailed study of Fitzgerald's reading is contained in John Richard Kuehl's *Scott Fitzgerald: Romantic and Realist*, an unpublished doctoral dissertation (Columbia University, 1958). Also see Fitzgerald's letters in *The Crack-Up*, ed. Edmund Wilson (New York, 1945), and particularly the more complete and more nearly accurate *The Letters of F. Scott Fitzgerald*, ed. Andrew Turnbull (New York, 1963).

6. F.R. Leavis, *The Great Tradition* (New York, 1954).

7. Fitzgerald admitted the influence himself: "I sent the novel to Mencken with the confession that it derives from Mackenzie (and) Wells" (Mizener, *The Far Side of Paradise*, p. 97).

8. Joseph Conrad, Preface, *The Nigger of the "Narcissus,"* in the Canterbury Edition, *The Complete Works of Joseph Conrad* (New York, 1924), pp. xi, xii.

108
Against *The Great Gatsby*

♦

GARY SCRIMGEOUR

Since the Fitzgerald revival took shape, we have all tended to regard *The Great Gatsby* as the redemption for the manifest sins of Fitzgerald's other works. It is just good enough, just lyrical enough, just teachable-to-freshmen enough (and more than "American" enough) for unwary souls to call it a classic. Its superiority is seen in its craftsmanship, especially in a tighter structure that gives much greater depth and integrity to its content. It is usually difficult to evaluate the truth of claims that an author is both a fine technician and an intelligent moralist, but in this case Joseph Conrad's *Heart of Darkness* offers an appropriate measuring-stick. Conrad, as is well known, stood persistently firm in Fitzgerald's disorderly pantheon. There is evidence especially in *The Great Gatsby* that Fitzgerald's admiration extended as far as imitation, and the similarity between these two works enables us to challenge claims for Fitzgerald's intellectual and artistic merit by showing how much better Conrad could think and write.*

The most important of the similarities between the two novels is the use of the first-person narrator as a character in his own story. In both novels a thoughtful man (Carraway, Marlow) recounts his moralized tale of the fate of an exceptional man (Gatsby, Kurtz). Their tales are essentially adventure stories. Both narrators are stirred by restlesssness to seek exotic experience, encounter their "hero" by chance, become unwillingly intrigued by him, and are caught up in an intimacy which ends with the hero's death. Both are forced to pay tribute to their dead in the form of resounding lies (Marlow to Kurtz's finacée; Carraway at the inquest), and then they retire for wound-licking and the later creation of their understated moralizations. Marlow and Carraway are alike in nature as well as function. Neither story would be about men possessed of absurd but enormous romantic dreams unless both narrators were of the kind of sensitivity that enabled them to see *la condition humaine* in the fates of irritating and egocentric individuals. Both feel a simultaneous repulsion and attraction for their heroes, dislike for their personality countered by admiration for their magnitude. Both men pretend to open-

SOURCE *Criticism* VIII, Winter 1966. pp. 75–86.

mindedness, modesty, and honesty. It is certain Marlow learns something from Kurtz's fate; it is claimed that Carraway learns from Gatsby's failure.

I give special emphasis to the use of the first-person narrator in the two novels for a particular reason. One forgets how recently we have come to see that Marlow is a character in the story he tells, rather than a translucent medium for transmitting a tale. In some novels the first-person narrator is merely a convenience in achieving selectivity, and in others at the opposite extreme the narrator himself is the object of our study. In *Heart of Darkness* both purposes are served; Marlow is both a technical device and part of the subject-matter. In *The Great Gatsby* the situation of Carraway is the same as that of Marlow, but I believe that Fitzgerald, never a great critical theorist, did not realize the dual nature of his narrator and therefore handled him very clumsily—and very revealingly.

When a narrator is also a character, with all that this implies of personality, individuality, and responsibility, we readers are forced to be more alert. We must question the accuracy of the narrator's account. When he makes judgments, we have to decide whether his special interests betray the truth and whether the meaning of each particular event and of the whole fable differs from the interpretation he offers. In *Heart of Darkness* Conrad is highly conscious of these problems and takes steps to solve them. Not all of the novel is in Marlow's words. He is presented and characterized by another narrator. He is given a setting, and he tells his story for an audience. He interrupts his own narrative several times, once to comment that "Of course in this you fellows see more than I could then. You see me, whom you know...." By thus drawing attention to his existence as a character in the story he tells, he refuses to allow us to ignore his subjectivity, so that it becomes difficult to read *Heart of Darkness* without realizing that it is not just a fable about universals but also an interpreted personal experience.

Things are otherwise with *The Great Gatsby*. The entire novel is the narrator's written word, and with peril do we underestimate the significance of the change in manner from Marlow's oral delivery, full of hesitations, temporizings, and polished lack of polish, to the smooth veneer of Carraway's public, written narrative. It is quite legitimate to ask why Fitzgerald should follow Conrad closely in narrative technique except for those elements which warn us that the narrator may be giving us a truth which is anything but unvarnished. Why remove Conrad's surrogate audience and inset narrative? Why exchange the honest hesitancy of Marlow's manner for Carraway's literary imitation of charming spontaneity? Carraway is a disarmingly frank chap, and, as with most such fellows, his self-revelations are highly contrived. Is his opening characterization of himself as accurate as it is influential? During the narrative he tells us what to think of his actions, but should we judge by what he says or what he does? It is an obvious enough point, but it is exactly here that readers go astray and that Fitzgerald's artistic and ethical inferiority lie. Conrad knew that problems would arise and provided material to alert the reader. Fitzgerald promptly abandoned that material and led readers to follow Carraway's interpretation of events without realizing that there should be a difference, a gap, a huge gulf, between Carraway's and their conceptions of the affair.

Let us examine the relationship between the two novels more deeply. In *Heart of Darkness* the point of the use of a first-person narrator is that what has happened to the central figure is explained by what we see happen to the narrator; and, reciprocally, the weakness evident in the central figure reveals a similar but unsuspected flaw in the character of the narrator. Kurtz is presented to us at the moment when failure overwhelms him, and it is in the development of Marlow that we see the causes of Kurtz's defeat. Marlow feels and explains to us his awareness of the same decay that overcame Kurtz. The melodrama accompanying Kurtz's magnificence prevents its direct presentation, but it can be comprehended through the more life-size abilities and weaknesses of Marlow. In return, the fate of Kurtz reveals the peril of weaknesses which Marlow shares, and we thus realize that the same destruction could overcome the balanced, "normal" Marlow, and by corollary, any human being.

A very similar relationship exists between narrator and central figure in *The Great Gatsby*, but unless Fitzgerald was much subtler than anyone has yet suggested, I do not think he realized it. While he tried to create a Marlovian narrator by asserting that Carraway has all of Marlow's desirable characteristics, his abandonment of the material which would allow an objective evaluation of his narrator's character shows that he understood neither the full purpose of Conrad's technique nor that Carraway's character is in fact very different from what Carraway claims it to be. Indeed Fitzgerald reveals a fault frequent in romantic writers, the inability to understand the true natures of the characters he created.

Take, for example, Gatsby himself, a character who usually and despite Carraway's warnings wins grudging admiration from readers. Like all romantic ideals, he is what personally we would not be so foolish as to imitate but nonetheless admire for its grandeur. It is refreshing to see, without Carraway's intervening intelligence, exactly to what sort of person we are giving our sympathy. Gatsby is boor, a roughneck, a fraud, a criminal. His taste is vulgar, his behavior ostentatious, his love adolescent, his business dealings ruthless and dishonest. He is interested in people— most notably in Carraway himself—only when he wants to use them. His nice gestures stem from the fact that, as one character comments, "he doesn't want any trouble with *any*body." Like other paranoaics, he lives in a childish tissue of lies and is unaware of the existence of an independent reality in which other people have separate existences. What lifts him above ordinary viciousness is the magnitude of his ambition and the glamor of his illusion. "Can't repeat the past?" he says to Carraway. "Why of course you can...." To Gatsby, to repeat the past is to suppress unwanted elements of it and to select only nice things from which to make an uncontaminated present. Grand this defiance of reality may seem; silly it nonetheless is. Indeed it is no more than "a promise that the rock of the world was founded securely on a fairy's wing," and it crumbles as soon as it encounters reality in the form of Daisy. As long as his life is controlled by his own unattained desires, Gatsby's vision remains safe; he continually recreates the present in the light of his own needs. But as soon as Daisy's independent will enters the dream, Gatsby is forced to attach himself to the real world, to lose his freedom of action, and to pay the penalty for denying the past in having that past destroy the romantic present.

Gatsby's moral error is at least as clear as Kurtz's, and yet we give him our sympathy. Sneakingly we like Gatsby, while I defy anybody to *like* Kurtz. Partly this is because of Gatsby's adherence to the official American sexual code, the only moral code he does obey (whereas Kurtz has his native wife and indulges in "unspeakable rites"), but the major reason for the difference in our attitudes to the two men is the different reactions of Carraway and Marlow to their heroes' moral weaknesses. Where Marlow ends up loathing Kurtz, Carraway specifically tells us that he is not disgusted by Gatsby but by the mysterious "foul dust that floated in the wake of his dreams." Fitzgerald provides many obscure but pretty metaphors to evoke Carraway's ambiguous attitude to Gatsby's faults, and I think he is forced into metaphor because only metaphor will conceal the fact that the story as Carraway tells it is a paean to schizophrenia. Carraway is not deceived, of course, into admiring the superficialities of Gatsby's character and behavior; he represents everything for which Carraway professes an "unaffected scorn." And yet at the same time something makes Gatsby "exempt" from Carraway's reaction to the rest of the world. Carraway tells us that Gatsby's great redeeming quality is his "heightened sensitivity to the promises of life." Whether we criticize or praise Carraway for being sufficiently young to believe that life makes promises, we should notice at once that it is the promises—not the realities—of life to which Gatsby is sensitive, and that Carraway is in fact praising that very attempt to deny the past and reality whose failure he is recounting.

This flaw in Carraway's moral vision is illuminating because it shows that Gatsby stands in relationship to Carraway as Daisy stands to Gatsby. Gatsby represents the promises of life with which the rootless, twenty-nine year old, hazy-minded Carraway is as obsessed as is Gatsby himself. It is important in this respect to notice how closely Carraway's development is tied to Gatsby's and that, just as Kurtz's career is paralleled up to a point by that of Marlow, so does Carraway's reflect Gatsby's. It is not simply that Carraway becomes emotionally involved in Gatsby's affairs but that his attitude towards his own life is entirely dependent on his feelings about Gatsby. As one small example from many, his most lyrical expression of the rapture he feels for the East comes immediately after he has been convinced of the genuineness of

Gatsby's romantic history. More important, his love affair with Jordan Baker is a second-hand impulse stirred by her revelations of Gatsby's love for Daisy. These are Carraway's words:

> Unlike Gatsby and Tom Buchanan, I had no girl whose disembodied face floated along the dark cornices and blinding signs, and so I drew up the girl beside me, tightening my arms. Her wan, scornful mouth smiled, and so I drew her up again closer, this time to my face.

As though they were shadows of Gatsby's emotions, Carraway's feelings for the city and his love for Jordan both instantly collapse as soon as Daisy's infidelity to Gatsby is apparent, and he returns to the Mid-West, to what had previously seemed the "ragged edge of the universe" but has now become a haven. Gatsby's defeat brings down Carraway's dream as well.

In fact Gatsby himself is Carraway's romantic dream. The only difference between the world that Carraway despises and the man he admires is that Gatsby does things more spectacularly. In not seeing this, Carraway reveals that just like Gatsby he is willing to accept only those parts of reality which please him. He wants Gatsby to be different from the rest of the world; therefore Gatsby *is* different from the rest of the world. If we look at Carraway's behavior more closely, we may see that he shares others of Gatsby's failings, and that if Gatsby is no romantic hero, Carraway is even less the pleasant, anonymous, and highly principled character that he seems to be.

Were Carraway to characterize himself in a traditional phrase rather than metaphor, that phrase would be "man of principle." And yet his principles are challenged by the person who is presumably closest to him: Jordan Baker. Early in their relationship, Carraway and Jordan have a conversation which ends with Jordan saying, "I hate careless people. That's why I like you." After the sudden collapse of their affair, Jordan returns to this conversation in their last interview, when she accuses him of having thrown her over:

> "Oh, and do you remember"—she added—"a conversation we had once about driving a car?"
> "Why—not exactly."
> "You said a bad driver was only safe until she met another bad driver? Well, I met another bad driver, didn't I? I mean it was careless of me to make such a bad guess. I thought you were rather an honest, straightforward person. I thought it was your secret pride."
> "I'm thirty," I said. "I'm five years too old to lie to myself and call it honor."

Jordan is right about Carraway's character. The crisis of their affair reveals to her what she must have suspected before, that Carraway is neither as honest nor as high-principled as he might like to seem. It is interesting to note that she accuses him of the same "carelessness" that is the refrain in Carraway's attack on the Buchanans and the rest of the world. Her accusation suggests that at least in his dealings with her he has been as shabby as anyone else in East Egg.

And certainly his behavior with Jordan is no worse than the rest of his personal relationships, from the girl back home to Gatsby himself. Involved as he is with Daisy, Tom, Gatsby, and the Wilsons, he never acts well, just weakly. He fails to sense any obligation to avoid the flagrant dishonesty of his position and—far from feeling any qualms about playing either God or pander—he actually helps the others to continue activities which he later claims to regard as unworthy. His main principle is to say nothing. Most important is the final falsehood into which his loyalty to the dead Gatsby forces him. There is no intimation at all that at the inquest he feels his position of concealing the true facts to be in any way anomalous. Where we might reasonably expect some explanation of his attitude, he dismisses the event with the comment that "all this part of it seemed remote and unessential." He simply prefers to conceal the truth rather than have the story "served up in racy pasquinade" and praises Mrs. Wilson's sister for "character" when she, "who might have said anything, didn't say a word." Is his behavior here, or even his attitude, superior to that of Tom, Daisy, Gatsby, or any other of the inhabitants of the ashland? Let us not be deceived by his condescension towards Wolfsheim's "gonnegtions" or his smugness about people who cheat at golf.

Another significant episode occurs near the end of the novel, when he encounters Tom for the last time. At first he avoids him because he is convinced that Tom was the cause of Gatsby's death. He says that he could neither forgive nor like Tom and Daisy because of their talent for "smashing up things" and retreating into "their vast carelessness," a firm moral judgment in words which we might expect from a principled man. But let us look at the act that follows:

> I shook hands with him; it seemed silly not to, for I felt suddenly as though I were talking to a child. Then he went into the jewelry store to buy a pearl necklace—or perhaps only a pair of cuff-buttons—rid of my provincial squeamishness forever.

While shaking hands with Tom may be an urbane gesture to avoid embarrassment, it is certainly not honest either to Tom or to Carraway's principles, and to turn from recognition of the villainy of Tom's behavior to dismissal of it as the behavior of a child is not a sign of moral profundity or consistency. Carraway's honesty is a matter not of principle, but of convenience. (Whether the reader likes or dislikes men of principle is irrelevant—we are concerned only with Carraway's claims to be one.)

One could attack Carraway's nature further; to one who dislikes him, the opening and closing pages of the novel are a lexicon of vanity. But the key issue is undoubtedly his honesty, because that provides the basis of the reader's reaction to the novel. It is here that he contrasts most strongly with Conrad's Marlow. For example, both Marlow and Carraway are reticent about many important matters, but when Marlow refuses to linger on a subject (such as the rites in which Kurtz participates) it is because enough has already been said; more would be too much. Carraway's reticences, however, verge on falsehood. Instead of stopping short with just the right impression, they often succeed in giving the wrong impression. The lie that Carraway acquiesces in at the inquest and the complaisance he reveals in finally shaking hands with Tom have as their motive no nobler desire than to let sleeping dogs lie, whereas Marlow, who finds himself pushed at the end of *Heart of Darkness* into an agonizing untruth, lies because the truth would be infinitely more damaging and useless. The truth about Mrs. Wilson's death could be damaging, but it is more likely to be simply incommoding. We have, in any case, no sign from Carraway that he even considered the problem.

Honesty can in the end be based only on some kind of powerful drive, and this is something that Carraway does not possess. The real nature of his principles appears if we contrast his own estimate of his integrity with a similar statement by Marlow. Long after the events which wrapped him inextricably in falsehood, Carraway writes, "Everyone suspects himself of at least one of the cardinal virtues, and this is mine: I am one of the few honest people that I have ever known." Marlow, on the occasion not of a falsehood but of a minor false impression, says:

> You know I hate, detest and can't bear a lie, not because I am straighter than the rest of us, but simply because it appalls me. There is a taint of death, a flavor of mortality in lies—which is exactly what I hate and detest in the world—what I want to forget. It makes me miserable and sick, like biting something rotten would do. Temperament, I suppose.

The difference between Marlow's and Carraway's words is the difference between a man who cannot deny reality and a man who cannot face it. Both men feel deeply, but Marlow, at the cost of real pain, has to push forward until he understands the meaning of what he feels, until he is honest with himself, whereas Carraway stops short with whatever feeling he can conveniently bear, dreading what further effort might uncover. Both men record as much as they understand, but Marlow's honesty forces him to a much deeper understanding than Carraway achieves. To Marlow, feeling is part of the process that creates understanding, and honesty is his strongest feeling; to Carraway, feeling is the end product of experience, and honesty a matter for self-congratulation.

If the reader cannot accept Carraway's statements at face value, then the integrity of the technique of the novel is called in question. Rather than accepting what Carraway claims to be the effect of the events on his nature, the reader must stand further off and examine Carraway's development as though he were any other character, in which case a second vital weakness becomes obvious. Again like Gatsby, he never realizes the truth about himself, and despite the lesson of Gatsby's fate he fails to come to self-knowledge. There is a curious use of the conditional in Carraway's introduction to his story. He writes, "If personality is an unbroken series of successful gestures, then there was something gorgeous about [Gatsby], some heightened sensitivity to the promises of life." The reason for Carraway's hesitancy over a matter that should present no problem is that he himself is trying to construct a personality out of a series of gestures such as the "clean break" with Jordan or the final handshake with Tom, behavior which results from his inability to decide what he should be doing or why he should be doing it. He is a moral eunuch, ineffectual in any real human situation that involves more than a reflex action determined by social pattern or the desire to avoid trouble with "*any*body." At one stage Carraway senses that something is wrong and suggests that Tom, Gatsby, Daisy, Jordan, and he all "possessed some deficiency in common," but he fails to see that the deficiency is the hollowness in their moral natures that leaves them prey to self-deception and "carelessness."

Consequently Carraway's distinctivness as a character is that he fails to learn anything from his story, that he can continue to blind himself even after his privileged overview of Gatsby's fate. The defeat evident in his disillusionment is followed not by progress but by retreat. He returns not only to his safe environment in the Mid-West but also to the same attitudes from which he started. One cannot praise him for being disillusioned with the ashland life of the East. For him to be disillusioned with values that are, after all, transparently unworthy, is not as remarkable as the fact that he remains enamored of the person who represents those values in their most brilliant and tempting form. He refuses to admit that his alliance with Gatsby, his admiration for the man, results from their sharing the same weakness. Writing when he has had time to deliberate on Gatsby's fate, he says, "Only Gatsby ... was exempt from my reaction—Gatsby, who represented everything for which I have an unaffected scorn." This is precisely the attitude which he held long before, at the height of his infatuation with Gatsby's dream. He has learned nothing. His failure to come to any self-knowledge makes him like the person who blames the stone for stubbing his toe. It seems inevitable that he will repeat the same mistakes as soon as the feeling that "temporarily closed out my interest in the abortive sorrows and short-winded elations of men" has departed. The world will not, despite his wishes, remain "at a sort of moral attention forever."

Because of the weakness of Carraway's character, the meaning of *The Great Gatsby* is much blacker than that of *Heart of Darkness*. In the latter Marlow progresses through his encounter with Kurtz to a greater self-knowledge; and even if we consider self-knowledge a pitiful reward to snatch from life, we must still admit that it has a positive value and that the gloom of the story is not unrelieved. Such cautious optimism is apparent only if we can see first that the narrator of *Heart of Darkness* is a reliable purveyor of truth, and second that he has come to greater self-knowledge. It is to the end of emphasizing these qualities that Conrad fashions the structure of the novel. The beginning of the work and the interruptions in Marlow's narrative have the purpose of reminding us at key points that the story is being refracted through Marlow's mind and that he is a character whose reactions are as important as his tale. The most emphasized of Marlow's qualities are his self-knowledge (we recall his Buddha-like pose) and the stress of his desire to fight his way through the material of his experience to reveal the truth. We can accept Marlow's recounting of the events only if we believe that, both as narrator and as person, his judgment is to be respected, and Conrad takes some of the novel out of Marlow's hands for exactly this purpose.

But we have seen that it is just here that Fitzgerald makes a major change in the structure of *The Great Gatsby*. There is little doubt that we are intended to see Carraway both as a reliable narrator and as a character learning from experience, but because we see only his version of the events and of his character, an objective evaluation is difficult. When we do attempt to be objective, we find that we have to impugn Carraway's honesty as a narrator and his self-awareness as a person. In this way Fitzgerald's change in technique makes *The Great Gatsby* a much more pessimistic novel than *Heart of Darkness*. If the story means (as Fitzgerald probably intended) that Gatsby's romantic dream is magnificent and Carraway's change a growth, then we have a somber but reasonably constructive view of life. But if our narrator turns out to be corrupt, if our Adam is much less innocent than we suspected, then despair replaces elegy. Had Carraway been defeated by the impersonal forces of an evil world in which he was an ineffectual innocent, his very existence—temporary or not—would lighten the picture. But his defeat is caused by something that lies within himself: his own lack of fibre, his own willingness to deny reality, his own substitution of dreams for knowledge of self and the world, his own sharing in the very vices of which his fellow men stand accused.

The irony produced by a comparison with the superficially gloomier *Heart of Darkness* is the realization that while Marlow sees the events as typical and Carraway as crucial, in effect they are crucial for Marlow and typical for Carraway. Where Marlow gains an expansiveness of outlook from his experiences, we find Carraway saying that "life is much more successfully looked at from a single window, after all," surely a supreme expression of the ethical vacuity which brought about his sufferings in the first place. If the one person who had both the talent and the opportunity to realize his own weaknesses remains unchanged, then we have a world of despair. Perhaps in this light the final image of the novel gains a new felicitousness: "So we beat on, boats against the current, borne back ceaselessly into the past."

It is usually considered that Fitzgerald intended *The Great Gatsby* to warn us against the attempt to deny reality. My interpretation of the novel goes further to suggest that unwittingly, through careless technique and cloudy thinking, Fitzgerald in fact created a novel which says that it is impossible for us to face reality. One would like to think that Fitzgerald knew what he was doing, that in the opening pages he intended Carraway's priggishness and enervation to warn the reader against the narrator. Certainly there is enough evidence in the novel to support such a view, which can no more be completely disproven than can similar readings of *Moll Flanders* and *Gulliver's Travels*, but before we accept it we have to answer two questions: was the young Fitzgerald capable of such ironic perception, which would involve an extraordinarily complex attitude not just to his characters but to his readers and to himself as writer and individual? And if so, why did he choose deliberately not to make the irony clearer to the reader, especially with the example of Conrad in front of him? My own belief is that Fitzgerald achieved something other than he intended. Knowing that he always had difficulty in distinguishing himself from his characters (and admitted to being even Gatsby!), we can legitimately suspect that Carraway's failure is Fitzgerald's failure, and that Fitzgerald himself was chronically unaware of the dangers of romanticism. If Daisy is Gatsby's dream, and Gatsby is Carraway's dream, one suspects that Carraway is Fitzgerald's dream.

Much of *The Great Gatsby* is of course brilliant, and its historical position as one of the earliest American novels to attempt twentieth-century techniques guarantees it a major position in our literary hierarchy. But it is usually praised for the wrong reasons, and we should take care that Fitzgerald does not become our dream, as the recent spate of biographies and articles might suggest. The character of Carraway as Fitzgerald saw it, the innocent Adam in the school of hard knocks, appeals to our liking for sentimental pessimism; critics and teachers can overvalue romanticism as much as authors, and thus damage our literary tradition by mistaking delicate perceptions for sound thinking. Unless we wish to teach what Fitzgerald intended rather than what he wrote, unless we prefer an attractive exterior to an honest interior, unless we cherish a novel because we think it says the things we want to hear, then we should be very precise about the value of what the novel actually says. Ultimately, to withdraw our sympathy from Carraway, even to lower our estimation of Fitzgerald's skill, is not to depreciate but to change the worth of *The Great Gatsby*. It may serve to teach both readers and writers that careful technique is worth more to a novel than verbal brilliance, and that honest, hard thinking is more profitable than the most sensitive evocation of sympathy. We may no longer be able to read it as a description of the fate that awaits American innocence, but we can see it as a record of the worse dangers that confront American sentimentality.

Note

*This essay brings a new point of view and fresh material to a controversy raised by previous critics. Rather than expressing my agreements or disagreements in a series of footnotes, I refer the reader to the following articles: R.W. Stallman, "Gatsby and the Hole in Time," *Modern Fiction Studies*, I (Nov. 1955), 2–16; T. Hanzo, "The Theme and the Narrator of *The Great Gatsby*,"

Modern Fiction Studies, II (Winter, 1956–57), 183–190; J. Thale, "The Narrator as Hero," *Twentieth Century Literature*, III (July 1957). 69–73. On Conrad's influence on Fitzgerald see James E. Miller, *F. Scott Fitzgerald: His Art and His Technique* (New York, 1964), especially pp. 92–95, 106–113; R.W. Stallman, "Conrad and *The Great Gatsby*," *Twentieth Century Literature*, I (April, 1955), 5–12; John Kuehl, "Scott Fitzgerald's Reading," *Princeton University Library Chronicle*, XXII (Winter, 1961), 58–59. Miller writes: "Probably the greatest influence on Fitzgerald during the gestation period of *The Great Gatsby* was Joseph Conrad" (p. 92). The parallels between *Heart of Darkness* and *The Great Gatsby* are sufficiently striking to suggest direct influence, but even if Conrad were not the source of Fitzgerald's technique, the Marlow stories would remain valid as a standard of comparison for the use of first-person narration.